# INDIA
# NEPAL & SRI LANKA

## THE TRAVELLER'S GUIDE

### By BARBARA RAUSCH & PETER MEYER
### Travel Translation By David Crawford

THE RIVERDALE COMPANY, PUBLISHERS
COPUBLISHERS / DISTRIBUTORS
5506 KENILWORTH AVENUE, SUITE 102
RIVERDALE, MARYLAND 20737
(301) 864-2029

## SPRINGFIELD
## BOOKS LIMITED

## &

## DAVID CRAWFORD

INDIA - NEPAL - SRI LANKA
The Traveller's Guide
Translated from the 4th German-Language Edition

ISBN 0 947655 31 X
Springfield Books Limited

ISBN 3-926118-00-8
David Crawford Publications

ISBN 3-922 057-12-8
German 4th Revised Edition
mandala verlag

Publisher: David Crawford Publications

Layout: David Crawford

Photography: The Authors, David Lyczyn, Government of India

Printed and bound in Great Britain by The Guernsey Press Co.
Ltd., Channel Islands.

Comments To:
David Crawford Publications
P.O. Box 110232
D 1000 Berlin 11
Germany

Telex:
933524 geonet g BOX:DWC

First Edition 1987
Reprinted 1987

Copyright of the 4th German Edition 1986
mandala verlag Peter Meyer

Meyer, Peter
  India, Nepal & Sri Lanka:
  the traveller's guide.
  1. South Asia- Description & Travel-Guide Books
  I. Title II. Rausch, Barbara
  III. Indien - Nepal. English
  915.4'04 DS337
  ISBN 0 947655 31 X

# CONTENTS

## Barbara

Libra, Dragon, studied
Education & Psychology.
She has travelled exten-
sively in Europe, re-
siding a while in Tur-
key. Her first trip to
Asia was in 1978 to
1979. Barbara's produc-
tive activities include
book translations, writ-
ing, travel group
leader, small publisher,
therapist with children
and drug addicts.

## Peter

Electrician, studied Eth-
nology, numerous blue-
collar and white-collar
jobs. Today he is a
small publisher. Inter-
ests include alternative,
ecologically sound tech-
nology. He has been
travelling since 1970.
In 1978, he began
globetrotting through
Asia.

# BEFORE YOU GO

## Documents

Your travel documents are your
most important possessions; guard
them accordingly. The simplest
security, which won't fool anyone,
is a breast pouch. Look for a
secure leather case with a sturdy,
slip-proof belt that shuts tight.
Reinforcing with a guitar string
might foil cut and run thieves. If
you use a cloth pouch, pack your
papers in plastic to protect
against dampness and sweat.

A less obvious method: sew
pockets inside your shirts and
pants. Use a plastic bag to prevent dampness.

The third alternative is a mon-
eybelt worn underneath your clothes. Sew a large cloth pouch
with a strap you can tie around your waist. Again protect your
papers in plastic! One variation is the leg pouch big enough for
your passport, secured with elastic below your knee.

No matter which method you use, there will always be situations where you've no good choice, i.e. when swimming. That's
when you need a trusted (and trustworthy) friend to watch. Carry photocopies of all your documents, particularly of traveller's
check sales receipts, and the first pages of your passport. Keep
these separate from the actual documents!

When sleeping outside, beware: prowlers are known to slit
open a sleeping bag and make off with valuables inside. You
might discreetly dig a hole to bury your valuables and sleep on
top of it. But original ideas are best!

**Passport:** Should be valid for at least one year, with a photo
matching your appearance, and enough free pages for visas,
entry and exit stamps, etc. Memorize your passport number, you
have to write it constantly, and it will help if you lose your
passport and photocopies!

**ID Card** or **2nd Passport:** If your home country provides a national ID card or issues 2nd or 3rd passports, be sure to take
advantage. A second passport is particularly helpful if you want
to visit both sides of an international conflict. Some countries

won't issue a visa if you've a stamp from its enemy. And you can apply for visas from several countries at the same time. But it is illegal to use multiple passports to overstay a visa.

**Driving Documents:** To bring a car on a temporary visa, you'll need a Carnet de Passage. This is valid for 6 months. You also need the car registration. An International Driver's Licence is accepted. For more information consult your national automobile club.

**Immunization Certificate:** Few countries require immunizations any more, but a cholera inoculation is recommended. If there's a sudden epidemic, other inoculations can be suddenly required, so carry your Certificate of Immunization just in case, see Health.

**Student ID:** In many countries you get enormous discounts upon presentation of a student ID. Valid for everything from museums to plane tickets, this can be a real boon to your travel budget. Generally accepted is the ISIC (International Student Identification Card) available at student travel agencies around the world for a nominal fee. You'll need a passport photo. The ISIC must be renewed annually with the purchase of a membership stamp. These IDs are also available on the black market, but experts, such as airline ticket clerks, can spot most fakes easily.

**Youth Hostel Card:** This permits you to stay inexpensively in youth hostels. There are no youth hostels in Nepal.

**Passport Pictures:** Carry lots of spares - at least 4 photos for each country you plan to visit. You need them for visa extensions and permits of every variety. If you spend a long time on the road, carry a black and white negative of your passport picture.

**Plane Tickets:** If you're carrying your plane ticket around with you, be careful: there is no replacement of lost or mangled discount tickets. But even tickets for regularly scheduled (expensive) flights are a bother when lost. Keep a record (photocopy) of your ticket and number.

**Visas & Special Permits:** Many countries require a visa from some or all foreign visitors. A stamp is placed in your passport, generally to restrict your length of stay. A visa usually costs money, and is valid only if used within a short period of time. Visas can be issued at a consulate outside the country, or at the border upon entry. More about visas under Country & Culture sections. For Special Permits to visit restricted areas, see Country & Culture, and the local sections.

## REPUBLIC OF INDIA CONSULAR OFFICES

**Australia:** 92 Mugga Way, Red Hill, ACT 2603, tel.(062) 950 045.

**United Kingdom:** India House, Aldwych, London WC2B 4NA, tel.(01) 836 8484.

**United States:** 2107 Massachusetts Ave. NW, Washington D.C. 20008, tel.(202) 265 5050.

**Burma:** 545-547 Merchant St., Rangoon, tel.15933 or 16381.
**Malaysia:** Asian Bank Berhad Building, 19 Malacca St., Kuala Lumpur, tel.21728.
**Nepal:** Lainchaur, Kathmandu, tel.11300.
**Singapore:** 31 Grange Road, tel.7376809.
**Sri Lanka:** 3rd Floor, State Bank of India Building, 18-3/1 Sir Baron Jayatilaka Mawatha, Colombo 1, tel.21604 or 22788.
**Thailand:** 139 Pan Lane, Bangkok, tel.35065.

## ROYAL NEPALESE EMBASSY & CONSULATE OFFICES
**United Kingdom:** 12 A Kensington Palace Gardens, London W8 4QU.
**United States:** 2131 Leroy Place NW, Washington D.C., 20008
   820 2nd Avenue, Room 1200, New York, New York, 10017.

**Bangladesh:** House No. 82 Dhanmondi R.A. Road No. 21, Dacca.
**Burma:** 16 Natmauk Yeiktha (Park Avenue), P.O. 84, Tamwe Rangoon.
**People's Republic of China:** No. 11 San Li Tunxiliujie, Beijing.
   Norbulingka Road 13, Lhasa, Tibet Autonomous Region.
**Egypt:** 9 Tiba Street, Dokki Cairo.
**France:** 7 rue Washington, 75008 Paris.
**West Germany:** im Haag 15, 5300 Bonn, Bad Godesberg 2.
**India:** Barakhamba Road, New Delhi-110001.
   19 Woodlands, Sterndale Road, Alipore, Calcutta 700027.
**Japan:** 1623 Higashi-Gotanda 3-Chome, Shinagawa-Ku, Tokyo (141).
**Pakistan:** No.506, 84th Street, Attaturk Avenue, Ramina-6/4, Islamabad.
**Saudi Arabia:** P.B. No. 7358, Al Hamra Kilo-5, Mecca Road, Jeddah.
**Thailand:** 189 SOI 71, Sukhumvit Road, Bangkok.
**Soviet Union:** 2nd Necpalimovsky Pereulok 14/7, Moscow.
**Hongkong:** C/O H.Q. Brigade of Gurkhas, H.M.S. Tamar, British Forces Post Office No. 1.

## SRI LANKA EMBASSIES
**India:** High Commission, 21 Kautilya Marg, Chanakyapuri, Delhi 110021, tel.371226.
**Maldives:** Embassy, M/Muraka 4/44, Orchid Magu, Male, tel.2845.

# Information Offices

## GOVERNMENT OF INDIA TOURIST OFFICES
**Australia:** Carlton Centre, 55 Elizabeth St., Sydney, NSW 2000, tel.(02) 232 1600.
**United Kingdom:** 7 Cork St., London WIX 2AB, tel.(01) 437 3677.
**United States**
   **New York:** 30 Rockefeller Plaza, Room 15, North Mezzanine, New York, New York, 10020, tel.(212) 586 4901.
   **Chicago:** 201 North Michigan Avenue, Chicago, Illinois 60601, tel.(312) 236 6899.

**Los Angeles:** 3550 Wilshire Blvd., Suite 204, Los Angeles, California 90010, tel.(213) 380 8855.
**Nepal:** Indian Embassy, Lainchaur, Kathmandu, tel.11300
**Singapore:** Podium Black, 4th Floor, Ming Court Hotel, Tanglin Road, Singapore 1024, tel.2355737

**CEYLON TOURIST BOARD - SRI LANKA**
**Australia**
    **New South Wales:** Mr. Geoffrey Holt, M/S F.P. Leonard Marketing Services Ltd., 241 Abercrombie Street, Chippendale, NSW 2008, tel.(02) 698 5266.
    **Western Australia:** Hony. Director, Ceylon Tourist Board, 439 Albany Highway, Victoria Park, Western Australia 6100, tel.(09) 362 4579
**United Kingdom:** Mr. Brian Allen, Ceylon Tourist Board, 52 High Holborn, London WC1V 6RL, tel.(01) 405 1194
**United States:** Mr. W.B.M. Abeysekera, Director, Ceylon Tourist Board, Suite 714, 609 Fifth Avenue, New York, New York 10017, tel.(212) 935 0369

**Japan:** Mr. Yukinori H. Ohta, C/O Amo Inc., 5th Floor, Kono Building, 23-9 Nishi-Shimbashi, 1-Chome, Minato-ku, Tokyo, tel.(03) 595 0127
**Thailand:** Mr. Soji Robert, Hony. Director, Ceylon Tourist Board, P.O. Box 316, 1/7-1/8 Soi 10, Sukhumvit Road, Bangkok, tel.(215) 8062 251

# Travel Budget

First off calculate how much money you will need on your trip; or conversely, how long you can travel with the money you have. Here are a few tips for globetrotting on the cheap.

The overland route from Europe to India takes 2-4 weeks and requires about 150.-US$ for transport. Calculate another 6.-US$ per day for food and accommodations; think 250. - 350.-US$ overland.

If you go by air, the cost will depend greatly on where you originate. Charter flights are often cheaper than regularly scheduled flights, but permit only a brief stay.

On the Indian subcontinent, you can usually get by on 200.-US$ per month, including transport. The frugal might survive on 150.-US$. Think in terms of 60.-US$ to 80.-US$ a week depending on how much you travel, where you stay, or the food you eat. In 1979-80 we spent 2000.-US$ in 9 months including round trip airfare Amsterdam - Kathmandu, and a Colombo-Kathmandu flight. But that didn't include any major purchases. Those were the days.

Today a month-long stay (budgeting 600.-US$ airfare) costs just under 1000.-US$. Think 1200.-US$ for 6 weeks, or 1500.-US$ for 3 months. You can travel all of southern Asia for a year for just 3000.-US$ if you plan a couple of longer stays on the road.

**Money:** Large amounts of cash, the sales receipts of your travel-ler's checks, and photocopies of your travel documents are most secure and easy to carry in a moneybelt. This looks just like a normal belt, but with a zipper along the entire length inside, providing ample hiding space for folded paper. Otherwise, use the same care necessary for all important papers.

**Traveller's Checks:** The safest way to carry large amounts of cash. American Express checks are conveniently denominated in US$, German DM, or Swiss sFr. If you lose your checks, you can get them replaced upon presentation of the sales receipt at the nearest Amexco office. Ask for a list of Amexco offices when you purchase your checks. You can also have your mail sent to Amex-co offices (see Mail). DM and sFr traveller's checks are sold in the following denominations: 50.-, 100.-, 200.-, and 500.-, and US$ checks: 10.-US$, 20.-US$, 50.-US$, 100.-US$, and 500.-US$. Larger checks can be exchanged at any Amexco office for smaller denominations.

**Personal Checks:** Generally not accepted. For **Eurochecks** try at an overseas branch of a major European bank. American Express card holders can cash a personal check for up to 650.-US$ once every three weeks.

**Credit Cards:** Accepted in southern Asia, at least by banks, air-lines, and major hotels. Most accepted are American Express, VISA, and Diner's Club.

**Wire Transfers:** Of money to India, see Country & Culture.

**Cash:** Always comes in handy, particularly for changing money at the border, or if you're low on local currency. A supply of one-dollar bills is helpful if you just have to pay off a taxi, and keep a couple of ten dollar bills. Bring only new looking bills, and starting now, do not accept any tattered money. You'll never get rid of it. Large denominations are hard to change. The ex-change rate for checks is better than for cash. But you have to pay 1 % of the value as insurance.

**Barter:** Objects will be listed in your passport if you have more than one of any item, in which case you should be sure to take it back out with you! Worth the load are calculators, digital watches, cassette recorders, walkmans, etc. Always take the cheapest of cheap. Disposable lighters, pens, magic markers, pictures of home, or personal photos make good small gifts. See Entry Formalities.

**Save Money Exchange Receipts:** Plus the Foreign Exchange Declar-ation you filled out upon entry. These papers are particularly important for people staying longer than three months in India, due to the required Income Tax Declaration!

# Outfit

Two rules of thumb:  take as little as possible,  but everything
absolutely necessary.  And everything is cheaper in Asia,  except
toilet paper!

**Backpack / Travel Bag:**  Those who plan to hike or do a lot of
walking should look for a comfortable but not too large backpack.  Lots of small compartments and outer pockets keep everything handy.  Packs with a metal frame begin at US$30.-. Install
wheels at the bottom to smooth your way through airports and
train stations.

Except on treks,  you'll be using public transport, and rarely
have to tote your bags very far.  Why not find a less bulky travel bag with enough room for a light sleeping bag.

Many people choose the new compact backpacks with a plastic
frame inside.  These are less bulky than metal-framed packs, and
some can be converted to travel bags.

**Sleeping Bag:**  Not necessary.  Better is a comforter case (or two
sheets sewn together to form a sack),  or perhaps just a cloth
sleeping bag liner.  Tropical heat makes a warm bed uncomfortable,  but your own clean sheets can be worth their weight in
gold in a cheap hotel. Sheets are easier to clean than a sleeping
bag. In the mountains, have the clerk give you a couple of extra
blankets. But if you plan trekking in the Himalayas, particularly
in winter, a down sleeping bag is an absolute necessity.

**Clothes:**  Shouldn't weigh you down.  Except for good jeans and
cotton underclothes,  clothes are cheaper and nicer in India. And
you don't wear much in the tropics.  Pants should be wide
enough,  and sturdy. Take lots of plastic bags to keep out dampness and for dirty laundry. Don't forget a bathing suit. Skinny
dipping is rarely possible.

**Toilet Articles:**  Cheap and available everywhere,  except toilet
paper! You might want nail files, tweezers, a mirror, or laundry
soap.  But be sure to bring strong suntan lotion (at least factor 6), and sunglasses! Bring your own tampons.

**Birth Control Pills:**  Lose their effect if you get sick. If you still
want the pill,  bring your own.  Indian birth control pills have
dangerously high dosages.

**Insect Repellent:**  Available in India; try Citronella (rub on insect repellent) or mosquito coils (which you burn in your room).
Coils aren't great for your health, but neither is malaria.

Bring a pocketknife, plus a padlock and chain to lock your hotel
room in cheap hotels,  and lock your baggage to the luggage rack
on the bus or train.  A cable combination bike lock is perfect.
Earplugs are wonderful in noisy hotel rooms and trains. Bring a
sewing kit,  safety pins,  thin but strong string for repairs or a
quick clothes line,  tape,  a calendar notebook,  two sets of eye
glasses;  or buy the second pair in Asia where glasses and con-

tact lenses are cheap! A pen and the addresses and telephone
numbers of friends and relatives back home. Perhaps an art
guide to India.

# Photo Equipment

**Photo permits:** At many places of interest a photo permit is required. They are usually available at the admission ticket stand,
check!

**Camera equipment:** Can weigh you down and stamp you as a tourist. Leave your ten pound gadget bag at home; it's the last
thing you want to carry and the first thing they steal. You
decide if you're satisfied with a simple instamatic, or need to
pack a couple lenses.

A wide angle is great in narrow streets or temples. A light
telescopic lens can pull in distant landscapes. In the bright
tropical sun, almost any picture will be sharp, but in the sha-
dows of the jungle or temple interior, faster lenses and faster
film might just make that super shot possible.

Before you add a gadget to your equipment think about how
often you'll actually use it; could you get those shots, without
the extra weight? A shutter release timer, for example, will give
you the same low-light pictures as a tripod; there is always some
place to brace your camera.

Pack everything in plastic bags. Film should be kept in the
middle of your bag in an aluminium can or a film bag to protect
against airport security x-rays. You could carry a stamped envelope for sending film home to be developed. You might trust a
fellow traveller heading home to drop it in the mail when they
get back.

Take enough film and a UV filter, plus a rubber lens shade.
Film and equipment is expensive on the road unless you pass
through Hongkong. Don't forget spare batteries! Singapore is no
longer a photographer's paradise. A 100 ASA black and white film
will get you through most situations. Black and white negative
film keeps best in heat and humidity. Most sensitive is colour
negative film. Slides are somewhere in the middle. Used film is
more sensitive than unused.

After a tour of the tropics, have your camera equipment
checked out, perhaps even cleaned.

# Health

**Insurance:** Never assume you're insured before you go. Check
with your insurance company! Many companies offer worldwide
coverage, including treatment and an emergency flight home if
necessary. Ask! You will have to pay for treatment on the spot
yourself, however. Later, the insurance company reimburses you:
upon presentation of bills for doctor, hospitalization and pre-

scriptions. Each bill should include the following information: the patient's name, diagnosis, treatment, medication administered, doctor's name, date, and price in local currency (if you pay in dollars or other currency then list this amount too). Don't forget the doctor's stamp and signature!

**Immunizations:** No longer required on the Indian subcontinent. But who wants cholera, typhoid, paratyphoid, malaria, hepatitis, polio, or tetanus. Don't land in a Third-World hospital when all the above can be prevented.

Visit your doctor at least eight weeks before your departure date (or an institute of tropical medicine if one is handy!) and work out a' schedule of immunizations. You need at least 4 weeks between your immunization for polio and those for yellow fever and smallpox. Your insurance company may defray some of the cost; ask.

Don't forget to take your malaria pills! Start one week before you enter a malaria region, and keep taking them for three weeks after leaving (incubation period)! Risk regions include northern India, the Terai in Nepal, almost all Sri Lanka and Bangladesh, the lower regions of Afghanistan, Iran, Pakistan, much of Indonesia, Malaysia, Thailand, and China. The more swamp and stagnant water you see, the more likely that anopheles mosquitoes await you. Malaria pills are cheaper in Asia than in most western countries.

## FIRST AID KIT

The following list has been kept to a minimum because we've found most things are cheaper in Asia. But don't forget any medication you need regularly (i.e. for hypertension).

**Malaria:** Resochin, Daraprim, or Fansidar (only for brief periods); consult your doctor.

**Antibiotics:** Bactrim or Ampillicin (20 tablets each).

**Aspirin, Cough Syrup, Throat Lozenges.**

**Diarrhoea / Irregularity:** Charcoal tablets (50 tablets), Elotrans, Tannacomb, Imodium or Enterocura. As laxatives: Depuran or Ducolax.

**Allergy / Itching:** Tavegil (20 tablets) and something against skin fungus infection (due to persistent dampness).

**Wound** or **Burn Salve:** Betpanthen (50 g).

**Wound Disinfectant:** Leukomycin Salve (25 g).

**Stings / Bites:** Soventol jelly (50 g).

**Eye Drops:** Aristamid.

**Vitamin C:** In short supply in many areas.

**Water Purification Tablets:** Micropur (take enough for the duration of your stay).

**Bandages:** Gauze bandages, tape, large band-aids, an 8 cm wide (2 1/2 inch) wide elastic bandage, burn bandages, iodine.

**Sprains:** Heparin Salve.

**Thermometer.**

**Hypodermic Needles:**  Bring two each of the following sizes: 2 ml, 5 ml, and 10 ml; 10 alcohol swabs (sterile packed!). These are in short supply,  so unless you want to risk sharing with a possible hepatitis carrier, even at a major hospital, be sure to bring your own.

## PLEASE

Before you leave,  turn over any unused medication to a responsible doctor. You'll find addresses listed under Tips.

## STAYING HEALTHY

Hygiene in southern Asia,  like most of the Third World,  is catastrophic;  medical treatment is little better. Here're a few rules of thumb travellers use to guard against infection.

**Bad Water:**  The principle carrier of disease. So don't drink water,  even if it is said to be okay or filtered... unless you know that it has been boiled for at least fifteen minutes! Avoid ice like the plague! Bring water purification tablets from home (Micropur available at your pharmacist.  100 MT tablets for 1 liter water costs 6.-US$. Twenty MT 20 tablets for 20 liters water each (or split for 2 X 10 liters) cost about 10.-US$. This tasteless and odourless silver-based chemical should be allowed one hour to work before drinking.  Then you won't need to boil or filter the water.  Cloudy water, however, won't turn clear. Mica-rich water should be filtered if you drink it for more than a year (i.e.  in Nepal). Iodine (available everywhere) can be used to disinfect water (beware of any allergic reaction),  but it has a distinctive taste.  Water filters are available in shops catering to backpackers.

For your main drink,  we recommend tea,  available fresh and cheap everywhere.  You can fill your water bottle with it. Fresh milk from fresh king coconuts is another tasty but cheap thirst quencher.

**Ice Cubes:** Refuse any drink!

**Milk & Icecream:**  Frequented by incalculable germs,  including tuberculosis bacteria!

**Unskinned Fruit,  Raw Vegetables,  Green Salad:** Say no; who knows whose hands they've passed through.  And vegetables here are fertilized with human sewage; germs are absorbed and passed on.  Not even a thorough cleaning will remove amoeba from green salad,  and amoebic dysentery is torture in the highest degree! Tomatoes are easy to skin if you place them briefly in boiling water.

**Meat:**  Just look in a butcher's;  we recommend abstention for the duration.  There is no veterinary control.  Meat lies around uncooled,  at the mercy of flies and maggots.  You don't have to be a strict Hindu to turn vegetarian.  Raw meat is absolutely taboo!

**Colds:** One of the most common tropical illnesses. Avoid air conditioning if possible, and dress warm enough or you'll sniffle your way through India - Nepal - Sri Lanka.

**Mosquitoes:** Carry more than just malaria (anopheles mosquito); among the other risks is encephalitis (a deadly infection of the brain). Protect yourself with a mosquito net or by burning coils, a biological product that burns like incense, driving mosquitoes crazy. You might rub on some Citronella, available everywhere.

**Vermin:** Fleas, lice, and bedbugs cheer at the sight of fresh blood; there's hardly a way to avoid them. Just bear it and try not to scratch. Many vermin leave of their own accord if you hang your things in a cool place for a couple days. Bedbugs, by nature, stay in one place and prefer not to travel with you. There are numerous ways to jettison lice. The best means of avoiding crabs is abstention. When that is not practical, or just doesn't work, try Jacutin and wash your clothes. Sleep with your own sheet, and wash it frequently!

**Fungus Infections:** Of the skin (dermatophyte) usually disappear in the sun on the beach.

**Sun:** Can be too much without a protective hat, and a strong lotion. If you run out, there's always coconut oil. See Sunstroke below.

**Clothes:** Should be very baggy and light due to the heat. Wear only cotton, no synthetics, particularly as undergarments. Always wear sandals, or you risk getting hookworm, reputedly leading to elephant feet.

**Knee Pain:** A hazard faced by out of shape hikers, especially going downhill. Never brace your knee when descending. Follow through to absorb shock, particularly when weighted down.

**Dehydration:** A threat in the heat and dry air. Always drink one more than your thirst. At the same time eat lots of salt so your body can hold the water. The old saying, "drink less and sweat less" is certainly out of date. Sweating is the means your body has of keeping cool; but lots of salt is lost. Unless you compensate, your body will dry out. One symptom of this problem is too little and too dark urine. Try to drink 3-5 liters (3-5 quarts) of liquids daily.

**Irregularity:** Also a symptom of too little liquid intake. So drink more, eat papaya seeds, and exercise.

**Hepatitis:** An infectious disease found particularly around junkies, and in the pubs and lodges they frequent. Be careful in Kathmandu, Pokhara, Bombay, Goa, Pushkar, etc. Infection can result from sex, dirty water, insects and dust. Another source of infection is unsterile needles at the doctor's or in hospitals. So bring your own disposable needles with you! The first symptoms are lack of energy, loss of appetite, liver pains, jaundice, dark urine.

**Diarrhoea:** Can result from the adjustment to new food. It can also be caused by an infective disease, which the body wants to get rid of quickly. Drink lots of liquids and eat salt. Consult a doctor if it lasts more than a couple days.

**Fever:** A defensive mechanism. So don't take any medication for just a light fever and diarrhoea. It might prolong the pain. Fever is also a sign of...

**Sunstroke:** The brain is overheated, leading to powerful reactions: fever, vomiting, diarrhoea, sometimes days of drowsiness and lack of appetite. Bed rest and fever-breaking measure are an absolute must when the body temperature exceeds 38° C (100° F). Try wrapping the legs in cool, wet rags for periods of five minutes!

**Wounds:** Treat with iodine (or a disinfecting salve) and bandage at once before they have a chance to get infected.

**Psychological Make-up:** Is very important. Anxiety and overcaution not only take the fun out of travelling, but can lead to physical illness. Psychosomatic illnesses should also be taken seriously. When you're down, don't ask as much from yourself. Rest, find yourself again... Look for a stable, happy person to travel with. It's more fun anyway.

# Climate & Travel Seasons

The nicest time to visit is October or November, just after the monsoon season. Everything's dry, green, in bloom. The air is clear. Certainly it is the best time of year in all of India, Nepal, and Sri Lanka except on the southeast coast where the less important (for India) southeast monsoon brings some rain.

The best time to visit southern Asia in general is from October to March. But keep in mind that during December / January, temperatures on the Indian subcontinent are just as varied as places distant. There is snow in the Himalayas; it's ski season in Kashmir; the Leh / Ladakh Pass is snowed shut. Nights are cold on the Ganges plain and in Rajasthan. Further south it's much warmer. South of the Bombay / Calcutta line, all winter it's a nice Mediterranean summer.

Trekking in Nepal is best in October / November, when the view is clearest and good hiking weather predominates. The second best time is after the brunt of the winter in March and April, before it's too hot to walk in the lower lying areas.

From the end of February to early April, you've ideal travel weather everywhere on Sri Lanka.

Temperatures of 45° C (113° F) in the interior and 35° C (95° F) on the coast in April and May make this an ideal time to escape to high altitude Himalayan resorts: Mount Abu and the Nilgiris (Ooty, Periyar) etc. In June the higher passes through the Himalayas open, and the monsoons move from south to north. May / June is the best season for trekking in the northwestern Himalayas. The monsoon barely touches Kashmir and Ladakh, making monsoon season the best time to visit: all the passes are open, and it's warm.

**During Monsoon Season:**  June / July to September / October;   it doesn't rain constantly,  but when it does rain,  it's in buckets. Frequently bridges and dams are washed away.  Flooding on the Ganges and Brahmaputra Plains make travel difficult,  as in the delta region of every major river.
**Rules Of Thumb:**  Visit Nepal in October / November;   the north-western Himalayas from April to July,  The Indian peninsula and Sri Lanka from November to March.

# Alien

To each their own!  Keep this in mind when confronted on the road with new cultures and traditions. As the saying goes, "When in Delhi, do..."!

**Religious Sites:**  Treat all sites with respect.  Many sites should only be visited without shoes,  particularly Buddhist shrines.  In Buddhist temples,  never wear a hat or other head cover.  Some Hindu temples may only be visited if you void yourself of all leather,  including belts,  bags,  and any other animal products. Inside the temples,  please don't touch sacrificial flowers,  prayer flags,  or any other religious object.  Mosques and other Muslim holy sites should only be visited with head covering!  Please, no shorts,  women only with shapeless,  long-arm clothing.  That's good advice for women in any Muslim region.  Respect the posted rules, and your hosts in the temples and mosques.
**Photography:**  Don't be rude.  Try to see each situation from the other point of view.  A Martian hops out of his spaceship and starts taking pictures of you in the most private situations.  How would you feel if that happened every ten minutes?  So respect photography prohibitions,  and the wish of any individual not to be photographed. And in many countries fear of spies can lead to embarrassing situations.  Such innocuous things as train stations, airports,  harbors,  factories,  government buildings might be con-sidered strategic installations in local eyes.  Careful where you point that camera!
**Kissing:**  Cuddling in public is taboo here.  Skinny dipping just isn't understood,  and should be avoided! Occasional police raids can lead to an embarrassing arrest.
**Food:** Never refuse to eat a dish prepared for you. That would be the ultimate insult to someone willing to share what little they have with you!  Never touch food or eat with your left hand! The left hand is used here to clean after the toilet,  and is consid-ered unclean by all levels of society.  More about food in its own chapter.
**Hospitality:**  Remember that hospitality is a two-sided coin.  Re-member to bring a gift.  And don't be surprised if your host doesn't open the gift in your presence.  It would be very impo-lite.  It might offend another guest who couldn't afford to make such a valuable gift.

## TWELVE VIRTUES OF THIRD WORLD TRAVEL

Travel with a will to learn about the country and its people.

Respect the feelings of your hosts. Your behavior can offend even unintentionally. This is particularly true of photography.

Listen and observe rather than look and speak.

Other cultures have different conceptions of time. That doesn't mean that ours are better, only that theirs are different.

Discover how interesting and valuable it is to learn another way of life.

Get acquainted with local habits and traditions. You're sure to find someone who can help.

Don't be the person who has an answer for everything; be the person who asks questions.

You're just one of thousands of tourists visiting India, Nepal, and Sri Lanka; don't expect any special privileges.

If you make a cheap buy, keep in mind that extremely low wages make such purchases possible.

Never make promises which you don't intend to keep.

Take time each day to absorb your experiences, you'll get more from your trip.

If you want to have everything like it is back home, then don't waste money travelling: stay home. (Christian Conference, Singapore)


Never overload your plate so that food gets thrown away. Remember these countries frequently face starvation.

Drunks - particularly singing - are not liked.

Don't shake hands in greeting unless the other offers first. Instead press the flat of your hands together (prayer-like) in front of your breast with your fingers pointing up, nod your head slightly and say "Namastê".

Never pat anyone on the shoulder, stroke their hair, or in any way touch their head: this is home to their spirit or soul.

Never put down any objects in a holy site, not even simple household altars. They would be thereby desecrated.

Never point the soles of your feet toward altars, holy sites, or other people. Learn to sit in the lotus position, cross-legged, or something similar.

Remove your shoes at the door when entering a home.

Give beggars who truly are needy or unable to work a small offering, but never more than 20 paisa. Never give children anything, even if they seem extremely poor. Otherwise they never go to school; teens stop work. Some beggar children earn more than their fathers as craftsmen.

Snake charmers and artists are not beggars, but respected professions. Make a small offering if you watch or photograph.


**Don't Be Confused**: Shaking the head means "yes", confirmation of what you say. Sometimes nodding the head means "no".

**Acha**: Means "Okay", "yes", "understood", "ahah", "certainly" and a few other ideas. Used mostly in northern India.

# INDIA

# भारत

# COUNTRY & CULTURE

## GEOGRAPHY

The Republic of India is situated in southern Asia on the Indian subcontinent between 68° and 89° east longitude and 8° and 36° north latitude; i.e. north and south of the Tropic of Cancer, roughly as far north as the Sahara desert.

The northern border is shaped by the Himalayan mountains and highland region. India's highest mountain, Nanda Devi, rises 7819 m.

To the south-west is the Arabian Sea where India lays claim to the Laccadive Islands. To the southeast is the Bay of Bengal into which all India's major rivers mouth: the Ganges, Brahmaputra, Godavari, Krishna, and Cauvery. Indian sovereignty extends off the southeast coast to the Andaman and Nicobar islands.

India boasts 5600 km of coastline. Running almost parallel to the coast, the West Ghat and the (less tall) East Ghat mountains merge with the Nilgiri Hills. Further south, the Cardamon Hills reach 2694 m at Anaimudi peak.

Most of the western border to Pakistan is formed by the Thar Desert. Adjacent to the south is the Rann of Kutch, a huge salt marsh.

Bangladesh is situated to the east, with the southern reaches of the Himalayas forming the border. Altogether, the land border runs 13,000 km.

India has borders with the following countries: China (Tibet), Nepal, Sikkim (annexed), Bhutan, Burma, Bangladesh, Pakistan, and Afghanistan. However, Kashmir, which was annexed by India, has been half occupied by Pakistan and in part by China. The result leaves India without a de facto border to Afghanistan. Neighboring countries also include the island nation of Sri Lanka, off the southern tip of the Indian subcontinent.

India is the seventh largest country in the world covering 3,287,590 km$^2$ (including Sikkim and the Indian administrated regions of Jammu and Kashmir). Running 3,200 km$^2$ from north to

# THE REPUBLIC OF INDIA

south and 2,800 km² from east to west, India covers just 2.4 % of
the earth's surface, but harbors one-sixth of the world's population (760 million people)!

## CLIMATE

Though the Indian subcontinent is dominated by a maritime tropical climate in the south, and a subtropical continental climate in
the north, high mountains in the north produce regions of moderate or even arctic conditions.

June to September, the Great (or southwest) Monsoon (from the
Arabic "mausim" = season) creates steamhouse conditions over
much of the country. The months of April and May are terribly
hot, 45° C (113° F). An ideal travel season is during winter:
November to March.

The rainy season works its way from south to north, disap-
pearing again from north to south. The result is a much shorter
period of rain in the north. Except on the western slopes of the
West Ghats, precipita-
tion is much less heavy
in the south. The
southwest monsoon
brings the subcontinent
80 % to 90 % of its
yearly precipitation
(except in the south-
east). Kashmir doesn't
experience the monsoons.
Each year during and
after the monsoons,
floods cause great dam-
age and chaotic traffic
conditions in the Jumma,
Ganges, and Brahmapu-
tra valleys.

Precipitation is
heaviest on the wind-
ward slopes of the
mountains, i.e. the
western slopes of the
West Ghat and the
southern slopes of the
Himalayas. During mon-
soon season, travel is
best restricted to the
northeast or southwest.
However, cool highland
resorts are crowded
(and expensive) then.

The Small (or
northeast) Monsoon only
affects the southeast of

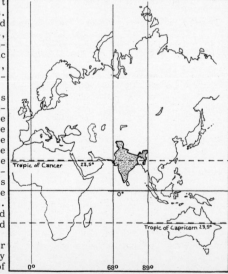

|  | Jan | Feb | Mar | Apr | May | Jun | Jul | Aug | Sep | Oct | Nov | Dec |  |
|---|---|---|---|---|---|---|---|---|---|---|---|---|---|

**Amritsar** 91 m above sea level

| °C | 5 | 6 | 11 | 17 | 21 | 25 | 26 | 25 | 24 | 17 | 9 | 5 | °C |
|---|---|---|---|---|---|---|---|---|---|---|---|---|---|
| °C | 19 | 23 | 28 | 34 | 38 | 40 | 36 | 34 | 34 | 31 | 26 | 21 | °C |
| mm | 29 | 31 | 24 | 14 | 15 | 47 | 161 | 155 | 70 | 9 | 2 | 13 | mm |

**Andaman & Nicobar Islands** Winter Maximum 31° C Minimum 22° C
Precipitation: 3130 mm annually

**Bangalore** 920 m above sea level

| °C | 14 | 15 | 18 | 20 | 20 | 19 | 18 | 18 | 18 | 18 | 16 | 14 | °C |
|---|---|---|---|---|---|---|---|---|---|---|---|---|---|
| °C | 25 | 29 | 32 | 33 | 32 | 29 | 27 | 27 | 27 | 27 | 26 | 25 | °C |
| mm | 6 | 6 | 10 | 40 | 105 | 72 | 99 | 126 | 169 | 149 | 67 | 11 | mm |
| % | 81 | 73 | 67 | 72 | 76 | 83 | 88 | 88 | 87 | 84 | 81 | 81 | % |

**Bombay** 10 m above sea level

| °C | 19 | 19 | 22 | 24 | 26 | 25 | 24 | 24 | 24 | 24 | 22 | 20 | °C |
|---|---|---|---|---|---|---|---|---|---|---|---|---|---|
| °C | 28 | 28 | 30 | 31 | 32 | 31 | 29 | 29 | 29 | 31 | 31 | 30 | °C |
| mm | 3 | 2 | 1 | 1 | 16 | 484 | 616 | 340 | 263 | 64 | 13 | 2 | mm |
| % | 73 | 74 | 76 | 78 | 77 | 82 | 86 | 86 | 88 | 84 | 76 | 73 | % |

**Calcutta** 5 m above sea level

| °C | 12 | 15 | 20 | 24 | 25 | 25 | 25 | 25 | 25 | 23 | 17 | 12 | °C |
|---|---|---|---|---|---|---|---|---|---|---|---|---|---|
| °C | 26 | 28 | 33 | 36 | 35 | 33 | 31 | 31 | 32 | 31 | 29 | 26 | °C |
| mm | 9 | 29 | 34 | 44 | 139 | 296 | 325 | 328 | 252 | 113 | 20 | 4 | mm |
| % | 85 | 82 | 79 | 76 | 77 | 82 | 85 | 88 | 86 | 85 | 73 | 80 | % |

**Chandigarh** 61 m above sea level

| °C | 7 | 8 | 14 | 19 | 23 | 26 | 24 | 23 | 22 | 17 | 10 | 8 | °C |
|---|---|---|---|---|---|---|---|---|---|---|---|---|---|
| °C | 20 | 23 | 29 | 34 | 38 | 39 | 34 | 33 | 32 | 31 | 27 | 22 | °C |
| mm | 52 | 8 | 26 | 9 | 11 | 71 | 269 | 252 | 188 | 51 | 7 | 23 | mm |

**Cochin** 3 m above sea level

| °C | 23 | 24 | 25 | 25 | 25 | 23 | 23 | 23 | 24 | 24 | 24 | 23 | °C |
|---|---|---|---|---|---|---|---|---|---|---|---|---|---|
| °C | 30 | 30 | 31 | 31 | 30 | 29 | 28 | 28 | 28 | 29 | 29 | 30 | °C |
| mm | 22 | 20 | 51 | 125 | 296 | 723 | 592 | 352 | 195 | 339 | 177 | 40 | mm |
| % | 63 | 76 | 78 | 78 | 83 | 89 | 90 | 89 | 87 | 85 | 82 | 76 | % |

**Darjeeling** 2270 m above sea level

| °C | 2 | 2 | 6 | 9 | 11 | 13 | 14 | 14 | 13 | 10 | 6 | 2 | °C |
|---|---|---|---|---|---|---|---|---|---|---|---|---|---|
| °C | 8 | 8 | 13 | 16 | 17 | 18 | 18 | 18 | 18 | 16 | 13 | 10 | °C |
| mm | 13 | 30 | 47 | 105 | 244 | 614 | 836 | 674 | 480 | 137 | 20 | 6 | mm |
| % | 78 | 79 | 72 | 75 | 89 | 96 | 96 | 95 | 93 | 84 | 72 | 69 | % |

**Delhi** 215 m above sea level

| °C | 6 | 9 | 13 | 19 | 26 | 28 | 26 | 25 | 24 | 17 | 11 | 7 | °C |
|---|---|---|---|---|---|---|---|---|---|---|---|---|---|
| °C | 21 | 23 | 29 | 35 | 40 | 39 | 35 | 33 | 34 | 33 | 28 | 23 | °C |
| mm | 25 | 21 | 13 | 8 | 13 | 77 | 178 | 183 | 122 | 10 | 2 | 10 | mm |
| % | 68 | 71 | 55 | 40 | 49 | 56 | 77 | 80 | 74 | 58 | 53 | 57 | % |

|  | Jan | Feb | Mar | Apr | May | Jun | Jul | Aug | Sep | Oct | Nov | Dec |
|---|---|---|---|---|---|---|---|---|---|---|---|---|

|        | Jan | Feb | Mar | Apr | May | Jun | Jul | Aug | Sep | Oct | Nov | Dec |        |
|--------|-----|-----|-----|-----|-----|-----|-----|-----|-----|-----|-----|-----|--------|
| **Goa** 0 - 1022 m above sea level |||||||||||||
| ° C    | 19  | 20  | 22  | 26  | 26  | 24  | 23  | 23  | 23  | 23  | 21  | 20  | ° C    |
| ° C    | 32  | 31  | 32  | 33  | 33  | 30  | 28  | 29  | 29  | 31  | 32  | 32  | ° C    |

Precipitation: 304 mm to 381 mm, mostly June to September

|        | Jan | Feb | Mar | Apr | May | Jun | Jul | Aug | Sep | Oct | Nov | Dec |        |
|--------|-----|-----|-----|-----|-----|-----|-----|-----|-----|-----|-----|-----|--------|
| **Hyderabad** 545 m above sea level |||||||||||||
| ° C    | 14  | 16  | 20  | 23  | 26  | 24  | 22  | 22  | 21  | 19  | 16  | 13  | ° C    |
| ° C    | 29  | 31  | 35  | 31  | 39  | 34  | 30  | 29  | 30  | 31  | 29  | 28  | ° C    |
| mm     | 7   | 9   | 11  | 29  | 27  | 112 | 152 | 134 | 163 | 62  | 29  | 7   | mm     |
| %      | 78  | 68  | 59  | 57  | 55  | 74  | 83  | 83  | 83  | 75  | 72  | 74  | %      |

|        | Jan | Feb | Mar | Apr | May | Jun | Jul | Aug | Sep | Oct | Nov | Dec |        |
|--------|-----|-----|-----|-----|-----|-----|-----|-----|-----|-----|-----|-----|--------|
| **Jaipur** 390 m above sea level |||||||||||||
| ° C    | 8   | 10  | 13  | 20  | 24  | 26  | 25  | 24  | 22  | 17  | 12  | 8   | ° C    |
| ° C    | 22  | 25  | 31  | 36  | 40  | 39  | 34  | 32  | 33  | 34  | 29  | 24  | ° C    |
| mm     | 11  | 8   | 8   | 4   | 14  | 56  | 196 | 204 | 81  | 12  | 3   | 7   | mm     |

|        | Jan | Feb | Mar | Apr | May | Jun | Jul | Aug | Sep | Oct | Nov | Dec |        |
|--------|-----|-----|-----|-----|-----|-----|-----|-----|-----|-----|-----|-----|--------|
| **Leh / Ladakh** 3500 m above sea level |||||||||||||
| ° C    | -13 | -12 | -6  | -1  | 1   | 6   | 10  | 10  | 5   | -1  | -6  | -10 | ° C    |
| ° C    | -1  | 1   | 7   | 13  | 16  | 20  | 25  | 23  | 21  | 15  | 8   | 2   | ° C    |
| mm     | 10  | 7   | 7   | 5   | 5   | 5   | 12  | 15  | 7   | 2   | 2   | 5   | mm     |

|        | Jan | Feb | Mar | Apr | May | Jun | Jul | Aug | Sep | Oct | Nov | Dec |        |
|--------|-----|-----|-----|-----|-----|-----|-----|-----|-----|-----|-----|-----|--------|
| **Madras** 10 m above sea level |||||||||||||
| ° C    | 19  | 20  | 22  | 25  | 27  | 27  | 26  | 25  | 25  | 23  | 22  | 20  | ° C    |
| ° C    | 29  | 31  | 33  | 35  | 38  | 37  | 35  | 34  | 34  | 32  | 29  | 28  | ° C    |
| mm     | 35  | 10  | 7   | 15  | 26  | 47  | 91  | 116 | 118 | 267 | 308 | 138 | mm     |
| %      | 87  | 83  | 80  | 74  | 63  | 59  | 65  | 71  | 75  | 83  | 86  | 87  | %      |

|        | Jan | Feb | Mar | Apr | May | Jun | Jul | Aug | Sep | Oct | Nov | Dec |        |
|--------|-----|-----|-----|-----|-----|-----|-----|-----|-----|-----|-----|-----|--------|
| **Madurai** 101 m above sea level |||||||||||||
| ° C    | 20  | 21  | 22  | 25  | 26  | 26  | 25  | 25  | 24  | 24  | 23  | 21  | ° C    |
| ° C    | 30  | 32  | 35  | 37  | 37  | 36  | 35  | 35  | 34  | 32  | 30  | 29  | ° C    |
| mm     | 19  | 13  | 17  | 54  | 69  | 39  | 49  | 103 | 119 | 188 | 145 | 51  | mm     |

|        | Jan | Feb | Mar | Apr | May | Jun | Jul | Aug | Sep | Oct | Nov | Dec |        |
|--------|-----|-----|-----|-----|-----|-----|-----|-----|-----|-----|-----|-----|--------|
| **Mount Abu** 1203 m above sea level |||||||||||||
| ° C    | 10  | 11  | 15  | 19  | 21  | 20  | 18  | 17  | 18  | 17  | 14  | 11  | ° C    |
| ° C    | 18  | 19  | 24  | 28  | 30  | 28  | 23  | 22  | 23  | 25  | 22  | 18  | ° C    |
| mm     | 5   | 6   | 2   | 2   | 10  | 90  | 633 | 665 | 248 | 13  | 8   | 2   | mm     |

|        | Jan | Feb | Mar | Apr | May | Jun | Jul | Aug | Sep | Oct | Nov | Dec |        |
|--------|-----|-----|-----|-----|-----|-----|-----|-----|-----|-----|-----|-----|--------|
| **Mysore** 767 m above sea level |||||||||||||
| ° C    | 16  | 18  | 20  | 21  | 21  | 20  | 19  | 19  | 19  | 19  | 18  | 16  | ° C    |
| ° C    | 28  | 31  | 33  | 34  | 32  | 28  | 27  | 27  | 28  | 28  | 27  | 27  | ° C    |
| mm     | 2   | 5   | 12  | 67  | 159 | 60  | 71  | 80  | 116 | 179 | 66  | 14  | mm     |

|        | Jan | Feb | Mar | Apr | May | Jun | Jul | Aug | Sep | Oct | Nov | Dec |        |
|--------|-----|-----|-----|-----|-----|-----|-----|-----|-----|-----|-----|-----|--------|
| **Ooty** 2268 m above sea level |||||||||||||
| ° C    | 5   | 6   | 8   | 10  | 11  | 11  | 10  | 10  | 10  | 10  | 8   | 6   | ° C    |
| ° C    | 19  | 20  | 21  | 22  | 21  | 18  | 16  | 17  | 18  | 18  | 18  | 19  | ° C    |
| mm     | 25  | 12  | 29  | 108 | 172 | 139 | 176 | 128 | 109 | 213 | 126 | 59  | mm     |
|        | Jan | Feb | Mar | Apr | May | Jun | Jul | Aug | Sep | Oct | Nov | Dec |        |

|        | Jan | Feb | Mar | Apr | May | Jun | Jul | Aug | Sep | Oct | Nov | Dec |      |
|--------|-----|-----|-----|-----|-----|-----|-----|-----|-----|-----|-----|-----|------|
| **Puri** 600 m above sea level | | | | | | | | | | | | | |
| ° C    | 17  | 20  | 24  | 26  | 27  | 27  | 26  | 26  | 26  | 25  | 20  | 17  | ° C  |
| ° C    | 26  | 28  | 30  | 30  | 31  | 31  | 30  | 31  | 31  | 31  | 29  | 27  | ° C  |
| mm     | 9   | 19  | 13  | 12  | 62  | 186 | 296 | 256 | 257 | 242 | 7   | 7   | mm   |
| **Srinagar** 1586 m above sea level | | | | | | | | | | | | | |
| ° C    | -2  | -1  | 2   | 7   | 10  | 14  | 17  | 17  | 11  | 4   | 0   | -2  | ° C  |
| ° C    | 5   | 6   | 13  | 19  | 25  | 29  | 31  | 30  | 28  | 23  | 16  | 9   | ° C  |
| mm     | 73  | 72  | 91  | 92  | 63  | 35  | 59  | 61  | 38  | 29  | 11  | 33  | mm   |
| **Trichy** 78 m above sea level | | | | | | | | | | | | | |
| ° C    | 20  | 21  | 33  | 26  | 26  | 26  | 26  | 25  | 25  | 24  | 23  | 21  | ° C  |
| ° C    | 31  | 33  | 36  | 38  | 38  | 37  | 36  | 36  | 35  | 33  | 31  | 30  | ° C  |
| mm     | 25  | 12  | 9   | 45  | 84  | 41  | 34  | 97  | 119 | 183 | 148 | 71  | mm   |
| **Trivandrum** 60 m above sea level | | | | | | | | | | | | | |
| ° C    | 23  | 23  | 25  | 26  | 26  | 24  | 24  | 24  | 24  | 24  | 23  | 23  | ° C  |
| ° C    | 30  | 30  | 31  | 31  | 30  | 29  | 28  | 28  | 29  | 29  | 29  | 30  | ° C  |
| mm     | 20  | 19  | 39  | 115 | 223 | 334 | 197 | 120 | 114 | 272 | 177 | 62  | mm   |
| **Udaipur** 577 m above sea level | | | | | | | | | | | | | |
| ° C    | 8   | 10  | 15  | 21  | 26  | 26  | 24  | 23  | 21  | 17  | 12  | 9   | ° C  |
| ° C    | 24  | 26  | 31  | 36  | 39  | 36  | 31  | 29  | 30  | 33  | 29  | 25  | ° C  |
| mm     | 5   | 3   | 2   | 2   | 18  | 77  | 217 | 178 | 87  | 14  | 2   | 2   | mm   |
| **Varanasi (Benares)** 76 m above sea level | | | | | | | | | | | | | |
| ° C    | 8   | 11  | 16  | 22  | 26  | 27  | 26  | 25  | 25  | 20  | 13  | 9   | ° C  |
| ° C    | 23  | 26  | 33  | 38  | 40  | 38  | 33  | 32  | 32  | 32  | 28  | 24  | ° C  |
| mm     | 18  | 18  | 9   | 5   | 13  | 115 | 300 | 305 | 183 | 55  | 9   | 6   | mm   |
| %      | 81  | 72  | 51  | 42  | 48  | 64  | 83  | 87  | 83  | 72  | 71  | 79  | %    |
|        | Jan | Feb | Mar | Apr | May | Jun | Jul | Aug | Sep | Oct | Nov | Dec |      |

India, because its winds originate on the central-Asian land
mass. The dry air can't pick up moisture until it crosses the
Bay of Bengal. This occurs between December and February. India's lowest annual temperatures are charted during this period.
In the south, temperatures range from 20 - 25° C (68 - 77° F),
to 15° C (59° F) in the Punjab, and 10° C (50° F) in the north-
west. Up here, you'll even find occasional evening frost.

# Flora & Fauna

**VEGETATION**
India's fauna typify its tropical location. Heavy precipitation on
the windward western slopes of the West Ghat in the south, and
the eastern bend of the Himalayas gives rise to evergreen
tropical rain forest. Varied levels of moisture on wind-shadowed
slopes of the West Ghat, in the central mountains, and on the

northern and eastern Deccan Plateau, provide ideal conditions for
deciduous (leafy) monsoon forest, and dry monsoon forest in parts
of the south.

Cotton and millet crops on the great plains of the Decca give
way to grass and shrub-covered steppe in the arid windshadow of
neighboring mountains.

In the lowlands of northern India, local culture has voided
the natural vegetation in favor of a wheat crop in the west, rice
and sugar cane in the central regions, jute in the east, interspersed with intensive planting of banana and other fruit trees.
Parts of the Ganges and Brahmaputra Deltas are covered with
mangrove swamp (sundarbans).

A small strip of coast at the foot of the West Ghats and a
large section of the east coast river delta host wet rice and
several species of palm. In highland regions of surrounding
mountains and the southern Himalayas, tea is harvested (Assam,
Darjeeling), along with fruit and vegetables.

Since the primary source of rain (the southwest monsoon) is
pushed to the north-west by the Himalaya mountains, precipitation
ranges along the slopes from east to west. Accordingly the jungle
is most dense in the east, slowly thinning to the west, ranging
from intermittent damp, to dry deciduous, forest. Further on in
Kashmir and Ladakh you'll find desert and steppe-like valley
floors. This is the transition zone between steppe and desert on
the Indus plains, to the alpine tundra of central Asia (Tibet).
On the other hand, jungle in the Sack of Assam grows all the
way up Brahmaputra Pass into Tibet. In other spots, the central
(and highest) section of the Himalayas forms a distinct barrier
between the subcontinent's maritime climate featuring tropical and
subtropical vegetation, and the continental climate marked by
central Asia's highland desert. Correspondingly, the Himalayas
boast a tremendous variety of vegetation, providing yet another
enticement for visitors.

## THE ANIMAL KINGDOM

The Indian subcontinent is reputed to have the greatest variety
of fauna outside of Brazil. But tourists shouldn't expect spectacular collections of animals as in African national parks. Even in
India's nature reserves, only small numbers of mammals have
survived the pressure of human overpopulation. For too many
years, large cats, elephant, and rhinoceros have fallen prey to
passionate hunting by maharajas, their guests, and even common-
ers. Low wages on the Indian subcontinent certainly make
poaching an attractive source of income. Advancing civilization
has diminished natural habitats. placing many species on the
brink of extinction.

A number of important mammal species are found only in India, or are best known here (e.g. the tiger). Other animals
achieve their highest state of development here, although they
may also find habitats elsewhere, e.g. the elephant, gaur (bovine), and sambar (deer), or local species of ape.

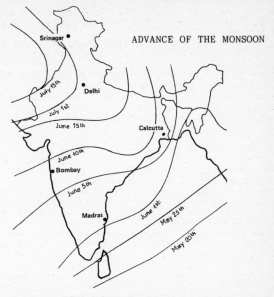

ADVANCE OF THE MONSOON

The only species of monkey found throughout India is the common langur. The rhesus monkey, while best known, finds its habitat only in the north. The toque macaque (monkey) is found only in India, south of the Godavari River. The Nilgiri langur and the lion-tail monkey in the south are animals of the deep jungle, found only in India.

The Indian lion makes its habitat in Gujarat. Indian wild buffalo and the Indian one-horned rhinoceros (which were threatened with extinction just a few years ago) have been preserved there. The Himalayan black bear is India's (and the Nilgiri-Thar's) national bear. The chinkara, deergoat, and the four--horned antelope, along with the marsh deer and the axis deer are all found only in India. India boasts a great variety of wild animal species, including a wide spectrum of cat species, ranging from domestic cats to heavyweights. Few wildlife reserves in the world combine exceptional collections of wildlife with scenery as unique as in the Manas Nature Preserve, or Kaziranga in Assam. These sanctuaries, famous for their efforts to preserve the Indian rhinoceros and wild buffalo, also provide habitats for their own characteristic bird populations. (M.Krishnan)

India's winged population is enriched by thousands of migratory birds from the north: siberian cranes, geese, ducks, teals, storks. Dancing peacocks (an insatiable flycatcher), pheasants, jays, parrots, magpies, kingfishers, woodpeckers, golden orioles, and nightingales fill the country with color and music. Almost everywhere in India, but particularly in the forests of the east and south, the cobra and king cobra find their habitat. Python snakes and crocodiles make homes in the swamps. The gavial (a reptile similar to a crocodile) and the dolphin are only found in the Ganges. A variety of lizards live in the rocky regions of Rajasthan.

# National Parks

Of India's five national parks and 126 nature reserves, eight spots are particularly recommended:

**Corbett Park:** Near Naini Valley, provides sheltered habitats to tigers, leopards, deer, sambars, hyaenas, jackals, and elephants. The best season to visit is February to April.

**Bharatpur:** In northeastern Rajasthan is a major water bird sanctuary. Migratory birds such as geese and ducks visit from November to February. During July to October, the greatest numbers of water birds can be found: Indian openbills, white ibis, wood ibis, three species of heron, cariama, and night heron. On dry land you'll find herds of black antelope, axis deer (chital), and other wildlife.

**Sariska:** Rajasthan is blessed with a wealth of wildlife, picturesque landscapes, and a good road system. Finding habitats are sambar, Nilgiri antelope, four-horned deer, chinkara gazelle and wild boar, and a few leopards and tigers feast here. For bird lovers, Sariska offers: partridge, quail, peacock, flying gurnard (flying robin), and green pigeon.

**Gir Forest National Park:** This is the region where the last 300 Indian lions have survived. The species once ranged all the way to the Mediterranean and was the lion known to ancient Greece. Around the turn of the century, the species was in greatest danger of extinction. The best time to visit this park in Gujarat (in the south) is January to March.

**Kaziranga:** Situated in the less visited eastern state of Assam. The 400 km$^2$ park harbors several one-horned Indian rhinoceros (otherwise found only at Chitwan National Park in Terai, Nepal), along with wild buffalo, elephants, marsh deer and sambar. The best season is November to April.

**Kanha National Park:** This 250 km$^2$ of seasonally wet monsoon forest, in the state of Madhya Pradesh, is an important sanctuary for both plant and animal wildlife. 180 km south-east of Jabalpur, well off the beaten trail, unblemished sal and bamboo forest is interspersed with maidans (= meadows). The large animals include leopards, tigers, sloths, hyaenas, jackals, gaur, a variety of deer, antelope, monkeys, and snakes. Plus there is a wealth of birds. Best time to visit is from March to May. Come by rail on a side trip between Delhi and Madras, or between Bombay and Calcutta.

**Mudumalai** & **Bandipur**:  The two are separated by a river (and
the border between Karnataka and Tamil Nadu) in the central,
high–altitude regions of the Nilgiri Hills. Both are rich in birds,
buffalo,  and deer.  A road system connects the various observa-
tions points (hides).  Easiest to reach from Mysore;  come between
March and June.
**Periyar Sanctuary**:   One of the prettiest spots in southern India!
Motorboats ferry visitors across an artificial lake to several observation points.  Excursions out to the elephants are fun.  The
park is worth visiting year round,  but most interesting between
November and March.
   More info on the National Parks in the regional sections.

# PEOPLE

After the People's Republic of China, India is the second most populous country in the world. 760 million Indians (1986 estimate) make up 15 % of the world's inhabitants, but occupy just 2.4 % of the earth's land surface. That works out to a density of 231 people per km$^2$. Most of the population lives on the fertile Ganges plain, or concentrated in the cities, and major portions of the country are inhospitable, as desert or high mountains. Population density achieves 1000 per km$^2$ in some areas.

Average life expectancy is 52 years. 40 % of the population are under 18. Three-fourths of the population are agricultural. The population has doubled since independence, with enough Indians being born each month to populate the city of Goa (one million). If growth continues at a rate of 2.1 % until the year 2000, India's population will pass one billion.

A 1952 family planning program set the following goals:
  Reduce children per family from 4.2 to 2.3.
  A birth rate of 21 per 1000 inhabitants.
  A death rate of 9 per 1000 annually, child mortality at 60 or less.
  60 % of the families should use family planning (26 % in 1984).

This requires improvements in health care. Campaigns have been launched against early marriage and child mortality. Camps are set up for mothers, babies, sterilization, use of contraceptives. Indira Gandhi once said, "Family planning must become a people's movement - of the people, by the people and for the people." But first a new idea must take hold: a small family is a happy family. Economics work against this premise. Care of elders is largely dependent on the number of children. The campaign of forced sterilization has fallen into disrepute. Another hurdle is India's two-thirds illiteracy rate.

About one-fourth of the population lives in the cities: Calcutta (10 million), Bombay (8.5 million), Delhi (5.8 million), Madras (4.5 million), Bangalore (3 million), Hyderabad (2.8 million), Ahmedabad (2.6 million), Kanpur (1.8 million), Poona (1.7 million), Nagpur (1.5 million), Jaipur (1 million), Lucknow (1 million). Altogether, we count 145 cities of more than 100,000. Numbers vary considerably according to the type and timing of the census, particularly whether suburbs are included.

## Language

About 72 % of the population speak an Indo-European language, particularly: Hindi (30 %), Bengali, Bihari, Marathi, Oriya, Punjabi, Gujarati, Assami, Kashmiri, Nepali, and Urdu. In the south, Dravidic languages (25 % by population) are spoken, including Tamil, Tenlugu, Malajalam, and Kannada. Mongolian languages are spoken by 3 % of India's people, including 350,000 Nagalands in the north-west.

The national language is Hindi, but 14 regional languages are protected constitutionally. All of the above (except Nepalese) are included, along with Sanskrit. Without counting dialects, about 220 different languages are spoken, though most are used only by small groups or isolated tribes.

Ethnic minorities in India include Tibetans, Chinese, and scattered groups of Europeans.

Those interested in low caste people and tribal culture should check with a Tribal Research Institute in Ahmedabad, Udaipur, or Calcutta. 7 % of India's population belong to tribes, mostly in the north-east, in Orissa, Rajastan and Gujarat.

The bureaucratic language is Hindi, written in Devanagari script. English is frequently used as an intertribal and commercial language. In the north, Hindi is understood everywhere, in the south it's English. Regional languages have equal standing. You can get around just about everywhere with English.

# A few Words of Hindi & Tamil

Normally you'll have no problem being understood in English, but in rural areas of the north, a few words of broken Hindi are a help. People respect you for trying to learn their language. Generally Hindi has simply assumed the English words dealing with technology and commerce: steamer, luggage-office, ticket, sleeper, bus, telephone, platform.... But train = gari! Plus a couple of words of the major regional languages, such as Tamil (in Tamil Nadu), can be useful.

| ENGLISH | HINDI | ENGLISH | HINDI |
|---|---|---|---|
| greeting | namasté | tea | chai |
| please | mehrabani se | coffee | coffee |
| thank you | dhanyabad | milk | dudh |
| yes | han | sugar | chini |
| no | nahin | thirsty | pyasa |
| pardon | maaf karije | fresh | taza |
| hotel | hotel | enough | kafi |
| room | kamra | healthy | tandurust |
| bed | charpoi | sick | rogi |
| palace | tala | big | bara |
| baggage | saman, asbab | small | chhota |
| lamp (light) | chiagh | tired | thaka |
| friend | mitra | clean | saf |
| medicine | dawa | when? | kab? |
| paper | kaghaz | now | ab |
| street | rasta | evening | scham |
| temple | mandir | day | din |
| cheap | sasta | hour | ghanta |
| food | khana | Monday | somwar |
| rice | chawal | Tuesday | magalwar |
| potato | alu | Wednesday | budhwar |
| vegetable | sabzi | Thursday | guruwar |
| bread | chapati,roti,nan | Friday | schukrawar |
| butter | makkhan | Saturday | schaniwar |
| salt | namak | Sunday | rawiwar |
| (drinking) water | (pine ka) pani | holiday | tschutti ka din |
| today | adsch | yesterday | kal |
| this evening | adsch scham | tomorrow | kal |
| (next) week | (agale) saptaa | | |

| ENGLISH | HINDI |
|---|---|
| What is your name? | apka schubh nam? |
| How much (money)? | kitne (paise)? |
| The bill please (eating out) | bill lao |
| That is too expensive | jeh bahut mehnga hä |
| What's this called in Hindi? | isse hindi mä kja kahte hä? |
| I can't speak Hindi! | mä hindi nahi dschanta |
| Do you speak English? | kja aap inglisch bolte hä? |
| Understand | adscha |
| I don't understand! | mudscha samadsch nahi ata! |

| ENGLISH | HINDI | ENGLISH | HINDI |
|---|---|---|---|
| 0 | sifar | 8 | aath |
| 1 | ek | 9 | no |
| 2 | do | 10 | das |
| 3 | tin | 11 | gjaara |
| 4 | tschaar | 12 | baara |
| 5 | pansch | 13 | tera |
| 6 | tsche | 14 | tschoda |
| 7 | saat | 15 | pandra |

| ENGLISH | HINDI | ENGLISH | HINDI |
|---------|-------|---------|-------|
| 16 | sola | 80 | assih |
| 17 | satra | 90 | nabbhe |
| 18 | ataara | 100 | so |
| 19 | unis | 200 | do so |
| 20 | bis | 1000 | hasaar |
| 30 | tis | 2000 | do hasaar |
| 40 | tschaalis | 10,000 | das hasaar |
| 50 | patschas | 100,000 | lakh |
| 60 | saath | 1,000,000 | das lakh |
| 70 | satar | 10,000,000 | crore |

| ENGLISH | TAMIL | ENGLISH | TAMIL |
|---------|-------|---------|-------|
| good day | vanakkam | tea | chai |
| goodbye | poi varukiren | small | sirijathu |
| yes | ahm | big | perithu |
| no | illai | good | nallathu |
| please | tajavu sai du | bad | kettathu |
| thank you | nandri | today | indru |
| pardon! | mannijungal | day | pahal neram |
| how much? | vilai enna? | night | iravu neram |
| too expensive | athika vilai | week | vaaram |
| food | sappidu | month | maatham |
| drink | kudi | year | varudam |

| | | | |
|---|---|---|---|
| 1 | on dru (onru) | 7 | eilu |
| 2 | irandu | 8 | ettu |
| 3 | mondru | 9 | onbadu |
| 4 | naangu | 10 | pattu |
| 5 | ejendu | 100 | nooru |
| 6 | aaru | 1000 | aajiram |

# Women In India

In keeping with the contradictions seen in every facet of Indian life, the position of Indian women ranges from absolute authority to total submission, from supreme self-confidence to sad self denial, from constitutionally entrenched equality to the real world where each right must be fought for (Rambi Chhabra).

**Matriarchy:** Practised in Dravidic India, during the pre-Vedian era. A female deity was worshipped, and women held in great respect. The patriarchal Aryans pushed back and repressed this culture without ever completely eradicating it.

**Patriarchy:** Holds firm grasp in most of India today. As under Christianity and Islam, religion provides a major tool for the repression of women. In **MANUS**, the Hindu book of law, it's written that the woman must submit to a man all her life: first her father, then her husband, later her son.

**Dowry System**: A price paid by the bride's family to the husband upon marriage. A daughter is a major financial burden. Many families are forced hopelessly into debt. Money lenders profit. For much of India, a daughter means bad luck: she costs money, but after marriage she works for her husband's family. And if her marriage goes sour, a daughter can never return home. She would be one more mouth to feed, and the neighbors would never cease gossiping. A son, conversely, brings an additional worker into the family, along with her dowry.

If the marriage goes completely awry, or the promised dowry can't be raised, the solution often lies in suicide, sometimes with in-law support. In one year there were 350 cases in Delhi of young women burned to death in their homes.

**Sati** (= honorable woman): Still practised, though banned in the early 19th century. According to age-old tradition, a widow follows her husband in death, usually by burning herself alive on his pyre, and by no means voluntarily. Spectators flock to a sati because the witnesses are blessed.

**The Indian Women's Movement**: Yes, there is one, primarily concerned with outlawing the dowry system. Women are the most undernourished people in India: first the family patriarch is fed, then the children, and anything left goes to the women. Women have a shorter life expectancy than men. Heavy physical labor, 14 - 16 hours a day, combines in deadly union with too many children. The woman's standing in her new family is dependent on her ability to provide sons. The women's movement has set its sights on ending discrimination, demanding equal wages for men and women, and equal opportunity in the universities and job training. Conferences are held annually to coordinate strategy.

**Equality**: Under Indian law, men and women are equal. Discrimination in job training and wage scales is forbidden. Legislation outlawed dowry obligations in 1961. In 1971 new legislation instituted paid vacation during pregnancy, legalized abortion, and forbade child marriages. But word of law alone won't make good ideas a reality. Education and mobilization of the women's movement are a must.

**Mahatma Gandhi**: A strong supporter of women's rights. He considered men and women equal, both in talent and social value. Gandhi rejected patriarchal domination out of hand. Gandhi was conscious of the scars born by women after 2000 years of repression, and that recovery (led by a change in attitude) would take time. Gandhi looked back on Indian historical tradition, which found no difficulty in accepting Indira Gandhi as Prime Minister. Indian women can be found in trusted positions ranging from government minister to judges, doctors (40,000), teachers (600,000), and highly-trained scientists (15,000). Between the polar phenomenon of qualified career women and the destructive burden seen in a daughter, the female destiny takes all shapes and hues. Speak to your Indian sisters, you'll be amazed. Only then can you discover what it's like to be a woman in India.

# RELIGION

Though sources vary in their estimates, India is about 82 % Hindu, 11 % Muslim, 2.5 % Christian, 2 % Sikh, 1 % Buddhist, 0.5 % Jain, with about 200,000 Parsi, and 12,000 Jews.

How well do these diverse faiths get along? Relatively peacefully, with some major exceptions. The world's greatest flood of refugees (12 million people) was set in motion following the division of India and Pakistan. Tremendous massacres, particularly between Sikhs and Muslims, have not been forgotten today. And Hindus on the border to Bangladesh are touchy about being swamped by Islamic refugees. Relatively peaceful too, compared to religious wars seen in Europe, between Catholic and Protestant, Christian and Jew, or the Inquisition!

India's major religion, Hinduism, isn't missionary by nature. Only a few fanatic orthodox worry about possible conversion of lower caste or casteless Hindus to caste-free religions such as Buddhism, Islam, or Christianity. In recent years, southern India has seen conversions to Islam, while Buddhism has gained popularity in northern India. Radical Hindus felt the need to protest against a Papal visit to India in February 1986.

Hinduism, itself, has innumerable subgroups, with contradictory practices, ranging from asceticism to tantrism, all striving toward a common goal. But these ideals aren't restricted to Hinduism. Any visitor to India hears that "all the great prophets and teachers, whether Hindu sadhu, Muslim sufi, Sikh guru, Christian mystic, or Buddhist, have taught that the essence of all religion is worship of the same God, addressed by each religion with a different name." It's also said that there is the outer religion with a cult structure (priests, temple life), and an inner religion which can be expressed through outer cult features, but which frequently remains hidden. This inner teaching has to be discovered and worked out by each individual for his or her self. But one can be helped by the spiritually advanced. In India such wise men are usually called guru.

## Hinduism

A brief description of Hinduism is a pretty bold idea. Consider this a very subjective attempt, without any pretensions of completeness. The true meaning of Hinduism can't be garnered from books. But you can get some idea by participating in Indian life, visiting a Pooja (prayer meeting), speaking to Hindus, swamis, sadhus, observing a cremation, or staying in an ashram. Hinduism is particularly difficult to fathom because it doesn't have a founder like other religions. There is no fixed, dogmatic teaching. Many people participated in its creation. And Hinduism is still changing with new inspiration and reinterpretation of its writings (see Classical Indian Literature). Thoughts, explanations, and experiences of new generations add to the composite of religious experience. Among the outstanding personalities of the past and present are Ramakrishna, Vivekananda, Yogananda, Ramana Maharishi, and Sathya Sai Baba. They, and their inspirational followers have colored and intensified the mosaic of perception, but at the same time made clear that the inner truth is, and remains, the same.

Early Hinduism (also called Brahmanism) began between 1000 BC and 200 BC as a mixture of local non-Aryan Dravidian beliefs with the ancient Aryan Vedic religion, brought by an invasion of Arya. The Aryans (ancient Indo-Europeans who spoke Indo-Iranian, common Iranian, or common Indic) were able to achieve political control, under which the Brahman, as the upper caste, reserved for themselves the

**PARVATI**

right to perform sacrificial ceremonies (see the caste system). The
deities of the Vedic period were Agni, God of the Sacrificial
Fire; Surya, the Sun God; and Indra, the God of Rain and Storm.
In the 8th century BC, the **UPANISHAD**, ancient Hindu
philosophical writings (perhaps the first ever) took shape,
expounding on the earlier **VEDA** (passed by word of mouth). This
marks the evolution from Brahmanism to Hinduism. See Classical
Indian Literature, and History.

The Hindu reform movement has struggled for centuries against
the rigid caste system. Buddhism, Jainism, and later Islam have
left marks, but Hinduism has managed to integrate new lines of
thought. Buddha is seen to be another incarnation of Vishnu,
allowing Buddha's teaching to be neatly incorporated into
Hinduism. So don't be surprised if a faithful Hindu decorates his
wall with pictures of Vishnu, Shiva, Buddha, and Jesus, all next
to each other! I've found most Hindus to be tolerant in their
religious beliefs. They couldn't even conceive of converting a
Christian to Hinduism. No missionary ideas.

For Hindus, there are many ways to enlightenment (Nirvana,
Moksha and many other names), the highest goal in a seemingly
endless cycle of reincarnations. Each Hindu has the right to
worship the god of his or her choice, whether this be by preference or momentary convenience. Many pray to Ganesh (son of
Shiva and Parvati), the popular god with an elephant head and
thick belly, because he removes all obstacles, and is considered
the God of Wisdom. In case of financial difficulties, there are
other, more specialized, gods. For Hindus the various deities are
manifestations of the different aspects of godliness. The best
known, and most important gods are: Brahma, Vishnu, and Shiva.

**Brahma:** Creator of the universe: his four heads symbolize complete awareness.
Each god has its
individual mount.
Brahma rides Ham-
sa, a wild goose.
With him is his
companion, Saras-
vati, the Goddess
of Art and Know-
ledge. She is de-
picted with the
Vina, a stringed
instrument.

**Vishnu:** The Pre-
server, sits on a
lotus (a sign of
purity), flies
through the air on
Garuda (a bird),

*Vishnu, Shiva and Brahma*

or lies on a snake. In his four
hands he holds a discus, sea
shells, lotus blossoms, and a club.
His companion is Lakshmi, the Goddess of
Beauty, Fortune, and Wealth. Vishnu
reincarnates from age to age to reinstate the
Dharma (law) on earth. His most recent
incarnations are Rama, Krishna, and
Buddha (the latest). Due now is his 10th
incarnation, the Kal-
kinavatar. Rama's life
and deeds with his
companion
Sita are de-
picted in the
**RAMAYANA.**

**Krishna:** The Blue
Shepherd God with
a flute was raised
by            shepherds.
Countless       stories
describe    his   play
with the Gopis (milkmaids). Most pictures of Krishna show him
with the gopi, Radha. Krishna's followers seek enlightenment by
total submission to Krishna (Bhakti). Krishna is depicted in the
**BHAGAVADGITA.** Here he is Arjuna, the coachman. Krishna teaches:
accept dharma and trust God, don't look for success or failure.

**Shiva:**  God of Destruction and Renewal. He can take many forms.
Sometimes he appears as an ascetic, clothed in a tiger skin. Most
Sadhu (wandering holy men) dedicate themselves to him; many
carry the Shiva trident.  It is said that Shiva smokes ganja.
That's why you meet, particularly in Nepal, so many Sadhus with
shilloms. Shiva's mount is the bull, Nandi.
    Shiva is depicted and worshipped in the form of the Shiva-
lingam, a phallus. The shivalingam is always found in the Yoni,
the female symbol.  Together they are the symbol for the joining
which brings new life.

**Parvati:**  Shiva's companion, riding a peacock, mother of Ganesh
and Skanda, the God of War.  She is a beautiful and eccentric
goddess.  Like Shiva, she personifies the double aspects of destruction and renewal.  Parvati takes the form of the life-giving,
life-preserving mother.  In Shaktism (see Religion-Nepal), she
personifies the holy energy (shakti), without which the resting
god, Shiva, wouldn't be able to perform his functions. When she
takes on the aspect of destruction, she is called Kali or Durga.
Kali is black and dances with a necklace of human skulls around
her neck. One of Kali's most passionate followers was Ramakrish-

na (1834 - 1886), who lived near Calcutta, raising a large group
of followers.  If you'd call his mother (Kali) "simply horrid",
he'd just smile knowingly.

**Ganesh:**   Son of Shiva and Parvati,   has an elephant head. Shiva

cut his head off in a fit
of anger,  and had to re-
place it quickly from the
next living thing to pass
by.  Fortunately an ele-
phant was convenient. Ga-
nesh's mount is a rat.
The rat is a symbol for
the power found in even
the   smallest   creature;
enough to carry even an
elephant.

As previously mentioned,
Brahma,   Vishnu,   Shiva,
and their female coun-
terparts,  Sarasvati, Lakshmi,   Parvati (Kali) are
not actually separate de-
ities,  but manifestations
and symbols of the ab-
solute,   the inexplicable,
Brahman or Atman.
Brahman is seen as
the  soul  of  the  world,
while  Atman  personifies
the individual soul.   The
relationship between Atman and Brahman is a major theme of the
Upanishad (see classical Indian poetry).   Hinduism is all
encompassing,  seeing no conflict between belief in one or more
gods,   and the Buddhist belief that there aren't any gods.
Buddhists believe in enlightenment and Nirvana;   Hindus have
Brahman.
That's why there are so many splinter groups,   ranging from
the strict ascetics who suppress every passion,   to the tantra
adherents,   who harness sexual energy to achieve the goal (see
Kharjurao Temple and Religion-Nepal).

**Reincarnation:**  Another important feature of Hinduism.   The principle of reincarnation was borrowed from Hinduism by both Buddhism and Christianity. Every living creature has an eternal soul
(Atman), which is destined upon death to be reborn. According to
karma (i.e.  according to the positive and negative behavior,
thoughts and desires) the soul is reborn to a preordained position in life. Since a rebirth as an animal is always possible, the
killing of any animals is taboo for strict Hindus.   The greatest

wish of any Hindu is to escape from this circle of endless reincarnations, and to achieve Nirvana: to be one with Brahman, the
eternal and absolute. Meditation, yoga, and asceticism are aids
toward this goal, as is working with a guru.

**Dharma**: Defines moral and ethical values, social life, the rules
of caste, and the universal law. Hindus try to live according to
the Dharma (law). The universal dharma also explains to the
Hindu that we live in the age of Kaliyuga, an age when values
are lost and materialism takes hold. Just as the individual is
subject to death and rebirth, so the universe is undergoing constant change. Following an age when humanity turns to materialism, there are spiritual periods when humanity possesses higher
genius, and new high cultures are created.

Once upon a time, the Hindu life was seen as consisting of
four parts: childhood, time of learning, time of founding a family
and acquiring wealth, and a time of abandoning all earthly
wealth and dedicating one's full self to spiritualism.

Belief in reincarnation creates a very particular attitude
toward death. Death is something natural, in which the soul
abandons an old body and seeks reincarnation in a brand new
body. The soul is eternal, being part of the Almighty, but still
separate. For this reason, all living creatures are damned to
Samsara, the eternal cycle of death and rebirth. The soul always
has to return, evolving into more pure and conscious forms,
which eventually will return to the original form of oneness with
Brahman. All life leads toward this goal, and everyone knows
that even Buddha himself needed hundreds of lives before
achieving enlightenment. So why worry about this life? An Indian
adherent to this faith is very confident, and can find happiness
even under the worst possible circumstances. Particularly among
beggars, I've found some strong and loving personalities, offering me thousands of times more in love than I could ever repay
materially. But first I had to learn to look closer, without being
deterred by the abject poverty, to see this inner reality.

# The Caste System

Nothing in India took me longer to understand than the caste
system. Each person, according to his or her karma, is born into
a caste. Karma is determined by good or bad deeds performed in
previous lives. Caste membership is inherited. In the rule, caste
determines eligible marriage partners, and one's whole way of
life (i.e. profession). The caste system was particularly inexplicable to me because Indians generally show great flexibility in
religious matters, whereby all contradictions can be united, and
each individual can go his or her own way. Why then an inhu-
manly rigid caste system, providing the framework for the inhu-
man exploitation of lower caste members by the upper castes?

One explanation, written by Yogananda (a spiritual teacher) is that this caste system is merely a decadent reflection of a long gone spiritual caste system. The original caste system had nothing to do with inheritance or economics, but was an acknowledgement of personal spiritual development.

## SPIRITUAL CASTE SYSTEM

**Brahman**: Wise men were called Brahman after achieving the highest state of enlightenment, during their final lives, before becoming one with Brahman.

**Kshatriya**: Warriors, who still fought for truth, and were on the road to enlightenment.

**Vaishya**: Still enthralled in the chains of materialism.

**Sudra**: At the lowest level of spiritual development.

In keeping with these spiritual groupings, the newly born of the three upper castes are considered Sudra until after the rites of initiation (presentation of the holy string). Until these rites, they are even free to eat any type of food. Only through the rites of initiation (performed by Brahman priests) do they achieve the caste of their parentage.

In time the spiritual order evolved into an economic order. This resulted from a general degradation of values, which occurred when the Aryans (i.e. people of ancient Iranian or ancient Indian ancestry) began to intermarry with non-Aryans. Members of the Brahman caste accepted bribes in exchange for admitting new members to their caste. Brahmans, performing the purification ceremonies for a fee, thus allowed the wealthy into the upper castes.

**Purification Rites**: Originally rites of initiation, a wise man (Brahman) guided a pupil on the road to knowledge (without any materialistic arrangement), with the goal of helping the pupil become a Brahman one day. As Brahmans lost their standing through materialism and bribery, they sought to protect their advantages by making caste membership hereditary with a steady prebend (stipend) as a family priest.

Besides the four main castes, Brahman (priest), Kshatriya (warrior), Vaishya (tradesman and artisan), and Sundra (laborer and farmer), countless sub-castes were created through separation of the professions and intermarriage (i.e. the caste of Dhobi (washers), goldsmiths, etc).

During the age of orthodox Hinduism, also known as Brahmanism, light-skinned Aryans were able to solidify their political domination over the non-Aryans. Religion became a means of maintaining power, overclouding its original meaning. The four main castes were seen as the head, shoulder and arm, guts and feet of the true people, respectable members of God's congregation, created by Brahman.

According to the new decadent Aryan caste system, only the upper three castes could call themselves Aryan. Criticism of the caste system from within the ranks led to the creation of new

religions including Buddhism and Jainism, both of which reject
the caste concept. Buddha himself was born into the warrior
caste, and lived a life in keeping with a warrior in the original
spiritual sense, becoming a wise man. The holy people of India,
the Sannyasin, regard themselves as above and beyond the caste
system, each finding an individual spiritual path.

**Pariah** (Untouchables, Harijan): Casteless, social outcasts. With
the independence of India, the caste system was outlawed. But
discrimination against the Pariah, while illegal, remains a fact
of everyday life. Indian newspapers carry frequent reports of
protest when Pariah students are allocated a specific number of
spots in Indian universities. Sometimes the huts of the untouch-
able castes are burned down by members of the upper castes.
Today the untouchables call themselves Harijans, meaning children of God, a name coined by Mahatma Gandhi, who occasionally
lived and ate with them (see Mahatma Gandhi). The Harijan have
begun to stand together against repression. In the countryside,
farm workers hold meetings to demand higher wages. Harijan
women refuse to do dirty and unpaid(!) work for landowning
families. Resistance by large landowners ranges from importing
new workers (who receive higher wages) to burning down the
homes of those who demand their rights. Such crimes are rarely
prosecuted where the police have a higher opinion of money than
justice. The power structure remains rigid.

# Classical Indian Literature

Anyone interested in experiencing the spirit of India should study
its classical literature. For literature we could just as well substitute philosophy or religion since the thoughts and ideas expressed are those dominating Hindu India today. You'll hardly
meet a Hindu who doesn't know the **VEDA, UPANISHAD, MAHABHARA-
TA, BHAGAVADGITA,** and **RAMAYANA.** These writings depict the
religion and philosophy, in short the Dharma, meaning the values
and goals set forth for Hindu society and individuals. This, of
course, can be only a brief discussion, which shouldn't prevent
anyone from visiting a library for closer examination!

# The Veda

The roots of Hinduism lie in the **VEDA** (= Sacred Knowledge),
which was perceived by The Wise (rishi) and formulated into
words. For centuries the wisdom was passed by word of mouth,
the guardians of this knowledge known as Brahman. According to
Yogananda, Brahman was originally a spiritual title for a wise
man who stood in contact with Brahman (see the Caste System).

Only later were rituals, rites of magic, songs, sacrificial
rites, and hymns written down in ancient Sanskrit. Of primary
importance was the sacrifice, which must be performed under
rigid guidelines, in order to ensure the benevolence of the gods

and universal harmony. The importance of the sacrifice can be
seen in the fact that the Aryans were a nomadic people of herd-
ers and warriors. Ritual temple life as in present-day Hinduism
was impractical. Naturally, in such an age, personifications of
nature's power, such as Agni (God of Fire), Surya (Sun God),
and Indra carried great importance. Sacrificial rites are designed
to please the gods in order to win such earthly rewards as lots
of sons, wealth, etc. Those who lived a life in obedience to the
Dharma, in keeping with caste, profession, social standing, etc.
would after death find the ancestral lands open, something equal
to the Christian paradise.

This joyous religious concept must be contrasted to the later
Upanishad, where emphasis is placed on salvation (moksha). The
most ancient Vedan hymns are said to date from 1500 BC, while
the Upanishad first took shape around 750 BC.

# The Upanishad

The emphasis looks away from sacrificial ritual, toward the relationship between Brahman and Atman, i.e. between the soul of the
world and the soul of the individual. Brahman is depicted as
cosmic energy, the absolute which no words can describe. Atman
is the true self, complete and independent, an unchanging and
intransient being, founded on the individual conscious personal-
ity. The goal of Indian philosophy is to experience unification of
Atman and Brahman, thereby ending the eternal circle of death
and reincarnation (see Hinduism).

The **UPANISHAD** (= Secret Teaching) offers various answers to
the question: How can one recognize Atman and Brahman? The
assumption is that the power of recognition resides in everyone.
The **UPANISHAD** also looks at a question which has been a focus
of modern psychology in recent decades: the states of dreaming,
deep sleep, awareness, death, etc. It is apparent that India
achieved a level of knowledge 2000 years ago which western
science is only slowly and superficially coming to grips with.

Indians recognize the necessity of protecting all forms of life.
The soul, found in all forms of life, is respected, leading to the
principle of non-violence "ahimsa" (see Mahatma Gandhi) and the
tendency toward vegetarianism practised by many Hindus.

# The Mahabharata

This is the greatest Hindu epic. Ideas are conveyed through the
history of Bharatas, an Indian tribe. Historians assume that the
ballade originated about 3000 BC. The **MAHABHARATA** we know
today, however, dates from the 4th or 5th century BC. Bharata
was a ruler, whose wisdom and bravery helped him conquer the
entire Indian subcontinent. Indians still call themselves Sons of
Bharata and India as a whole Bharat or Bharatavarsha. Kuru, a
descendant of Bharata, was the founder of the Kauravas royal
line. A family quarrel led to an 18-day fratricidal war on the

Kurukshetra battle field.  The original tribe was almost exter-
minated. Part of the **MAHABHARATA** is the **BHAGAVAD GITA.**

# The Bhagavad Gita

The **BHAGAVAD GITA** depicts a conversation between Arjuna (a
Pandava) and the god Krishna,  who was fighting on the side of
the Pandavas. Arjuna wants to avoid the fratricidal war, because
he sees no reason to kill his uncle and cousins.  The god, Krishna,  however, urges him to fight, with the admonition: Arjuna as
a Kshatriya (warrior) should conform to the law of his caste,
and besides, nobody really dies, because the Atman (or true self)
is indestructible.  Krishna taught Arjuna submission to God's will
through clear examples.  Krishna dismisses inaction and urges
Arjuna to do his duty without regard to the fruit of his actions.
Selfless sense of duty,  and the loving faith in God of a true
believer, would lead to eventual salvation. Even today, Krishna's
followers,  and many Hindus,  dedicate themselves to the Bhakti
(devotion to God) lifestyle.

# The Ramayana

The second most important epic for Hindus is the **RAMAYANA.** Here
too the Indians receive insight into social and traditional dharma.  **RAMAYANA** depicts the life and deeds of Rama, considered an
incarnation of the god Vishnu, as he remains faithful to dharma.
    Rama is the son of King Ayodhya,  and designated his heir.
One of the King's wives, however, schemes to put her own son on
the throne,  creating a situation where Rama is doomed to spend
14 years in the forest.  He is accompanied upon this journey by
his wife,  Sita,  and brother,  Lakshmana.  One day, while Rama
and Lakshmana are hunting,  Sita is kidnapped by Ravana,  the
ruler of the island Lanka (Sri Lanka). The island is the home of
the Raksha,  fearsome monsters and demons. Rama and Lakshmana
take up the search for Sita,  and meet Hanuman,  an advisor to
the Monkey King, who promises his assistance. Hanuman discovers
Sita in Lanka, and informs Rama. With an army of monkeys, they
build a stone bridge from India to Sri Lanka.  The present-day
Adam's Bridge between India and Sri Lanka is seen as the
remains of this construction (see Rameswaram).  There is a battle
with the Rakshas, and Rama defeats Ravana and frees Sita. There
are several versions dealing with the reunion between Rama and
Sita.  Rama has trouble with his conscience and the dharma: how
can he live with a wife who has lived with another man?  The
best version I've seen was performed at the Kalakshetra Theater
in Madras.  Sita demands that Lakshmana build a fire, which she
enters to demonstrate her innocence.  The God of Fire,  Agni,
himself intervenes by lifting her out of the fire and returning
her to Rama.  Rama,  Sita,  and Lakshmana return to Ayodhya,
where after 14 years they are greeted enthusiastically and Rama
is crowned king with Sita as his queen.

Rukmini Devi, the (female) director of the Kalakshetra Theater offers an excellent explanation for the Sita story, which should also serve notice that this is much more than just a nice story without deeper meaning. Sita is seen as a symbol for humanity, who must withstand the Fire of Suffering in order to achieve the chastity and purity necessary to be one with god (Rama).

Among Indians too, there are differing opinions concerning the Sita story, which has led to great suffering by Indian women. Sita is seen as the example of the ideal wife, which each wife must emulate. Quickly forgotten is the fact that few men do much to emulate Rama.

# Buddhism

Despite its origins in India, Buddhism has a poor following here: just 1 % of the population considers itself Buddhist. Buddhism's golden age was under the rule of King Ashoka (268 - 227 BC), who brought Buddhism to Sri Lanka, where Hinayana Buddhism remains the official national religion today.

Ashoka exemplifies the just and benevolent ruler. He lived according to the principles of ahimsa (revering and protecting all forms of life) and dharma. He ordered stone plaques erected all over the country detailing Buddhist teachings. He built stupas (heaps of rice, or bell-shaped closed structures in which a relic would be guarded), monasteries for monks, artificial caves for pilgrims. Buddhist art, which originally consisted of symbolic depictions of Buddha (i.e. footprints or lotus blossoms), evolved in time to statues.

Remnants of Buddhism can be seen particularly in Maharasthra, Sanchi, Mathura, and Andhra. A Brahman counter offensive in the 8th and 9th centuries succeeded in almost exterminating Indian Buddhism.

The founder of Buddhism was Prince Siddharta Gautama, a member of the Hindu Kshatriya (warrior) caste in northern India. He was born in 560 BC at Lumbini in present-day Nepal. He lived the picture-book life of luxury, married a princess and sired a son with her. Then, at the age of 29, he underwent a change. On a journey, he met four men: an old man; a sick man, a corpse, and an ascetic. He recognized the transitory nature of earthly life, and decided to withdraw from the world as an ascetic. After seven years of self castigation and fasting, he recognized that this wasn't the road to salvation. His followers abandoned him. Then sitting alone under a bo tree in a wood near Bodhgaya, he attained enlightenment, an experience beyond all words. According to legend, it was Brahma at first who pleaded with Buddha (= the Enlightened) to open his knowledge to the world. At the core of Buddha's teaching are:

The Four Holy Truths

| | | |
|---|---|---|
| 1st Truth: | All life is ill (suffering). | |
| 2nd Truth: | The source of this ill (suffering) is subconscious desire. | |
| 3rd Truth: | It is possible to overcome ill (suffering). | |
| 4th Truth: | There is an eight-fold path to this goal: right views, right intentions, right speech, right conduct, right livelihood, right effort, right mindfulness, right concentration. | |

This has become known as the Middle Path, because Buddha re-jects both asceticism and selfish submission to every worldly whim. Buddha offered his teaching to all people without caste consideration: a revolutionary idea in a country founded upon the principles of caste affiliation (see The Caste System). In the Sarnath Deerpark near Varanasi, Buddha inaugurated his teaching with the Speech of Benares. Then his teaching took him through the eastern plains of the Ganges. Followers quickly flocked to him, and he founded an order of monks, the Sangha.

Buddhism recognizes no gods, not even an inner self. The ego is considered only a burden.

**Yana** (= vehicle or ferry): Buddha's teaching. The image of a ferry is said to depict the essence of his teaching. "Board the Buddhist vehicle – the ferry of instruction across the stream of life, i.e. from the bank of practical, unenlightened experience (avidya), desire (kama), and death (mara) to the bank of tran-scendental wisdom (vidya), leading to salvation (moksha) from general servitude" (translated from Heinrich Zimmer: **The Philo-sophy And Religion Of India**, page 424). Buddha offers only the aid for the journey; on the opposite bank, his teaching is mean-ingless.

There are two branches of Buddhism: Hinayana-Buddhism (the small vehicle), and Mahayana-Buddhism (the big vehicle).

After Buddha's death, there was a split at the Council of Vaischali in 360 BC between the monks of two persuasions. The Hinayana faction, called Theravada on Sri Lanka, assumed that

Buddha's teaching and religious order should continue unchanged through the ages. The Mahayana, however, instituted the concept of the Boddhisattva, an enlightened leader, who would be forever reborn, to aid others on the road to enlightenment. More about Mahayana-Buddhism in the Nepal religion section.

**Enlightenment**: Requires countless reincarnations. Buddha was reborn hundreds of times before becoming Buddha. The next incarnation is based on one's karma, i.e. each action in one's life has its effect. Attempting to live according to the eight principles will reduce bad karma. For people who take this seriously, and want to start work in this lifetime, Buddha founded orders for monks and nuns (the sangha). A monk gives up his worldly possessions except for a habit, an alms bowl, and a razor. he live⁻ as ⁻ beggar, travelling from house to house. The monks are completely dependent upon the Buddhist layman for food and clothing. Through donations, lay followers can put themselves in a good position for eventual enlightenment in a later life, if they also choose to follow the eight-fold Path.

Despite Buddhism's poor following in India, you'll see numerous depictions of Buddha. Hinduism again shows its ability to unite contradictions. Hinduism reveres Buddha as an incarnation of Vishnu. Buddha is said to be Vishnu's ninth incarnation. Vishnu's tenth, the Kalkinavatar, is presently awaited.

# Jainism

Jainism too was founded in India during the 6th century BC. It too rejects the caste system and addresses itself equally to people of all origins. The founder, Vardhama Mahavira, was renamed Jaina (= victor) by his followers after achieving enlightenment, thereby giving name to the religion. Mahavira saw himself as the last of 24 Tirthankars (= world teachers), who show the way to salvation. The Jaina are vegetarian, strictly against all killing, tend toward asceticism, and view meditation as an important tool. Like most Asiatic religions, they believe in cycles of death and reincarnation, and the possibility of salvation from this endless wheel. They acknowledge no gods. Gods are just normal beings who've achieved a higher state of consciousness.

Many Jains live in monasteries. Some wear surgical masks so as not to swallow insects by accident, and sweep the ground before them at every step. There are two types of monks: the "Digamaras" (= air clothed) who never wear any clothes, and stay only in monasteries; and the "Schwetamaras" (= white clothed).

The prettiest Jain temples are at Mount Abu and Palitana. We strongly recommend a visit to Mount Abu. About 2.6 million Jains live in India. They are very successful sociologically, and have great influence.

# Sikhism

About half of all Sikhs live in the northwestern state of Punjab. Its capital, Amritsar, location of the Golden Temple, is their religious center. Here too, the sacred book, **GRANTH**, is preserved. In Punjab, Sikhs form an ethnic majority of 52 %.

Sikhs are easy to recognize with their great turbans and long beards. Originally they were a Hindu sect, founded by Guru Nanak (1469 - 1538) to seek understanding between Hindus and Muslims. Muslim persecution persuaded Guru Govind Singh, the last of the 10 Sikh gurus, to alter his pacifist following into a fighting organization. Everyone received the last name 'Singh' (= lion). Like the Hindu, they believe in karma and in cycles of reincarnation. But Sikhs disavow the Hindu caste system.

One sad chapter in Sikh history was the bloody fighting in Punjab between Sikhs and Muslims during the first days after India's independence, and after the division of India and Pakistan in 1948. The Punjab was also divided. For a good description of this period, read **Freedom At Midnight** by Collins / Lapiere.

Otherwise, Sikhs are well known for their hospitality, friendship, tolerance, and gratitude. Their temples are open to visitors, and provide food to all. Religious Sikhs live according to a strict code: they don't smoke or drink alcohol, and cut neither beard nor hair. Sikhs are powerful in India, filling important

administrative and military offices; plus they're good business-
men. Sikhs lean toward learned professions. Sikh wives enjoy
more freedom than under most Indian religions.

After the unrest of 1984 and 1985, there is relative calm in
the Punjab today, despite attempts by radical Sikhs to keep
things hot. Sikhs are becoming polarized.

# Islam

Islam is a strict monotheistic religion founded by the prophet
Mohammed. Born in 570 AD, Mohammed's visionary experiences
called on him to act as prophet for the only God, Allah. He ac-
knowledged both Moses and Jesus as previous prophets, but de-
nied that Jesus was actually the son of God.

"There is only one god, Allah, and Mohammed is his prophet."
Mohammed died in 632 AD in Medina, where he founded his religion in 622 AD after fleeing from his birthplace, Mecca.

By the time of his death, Islam had spread far. Later his
successors, the Caliphs, brought Islam with fire and sword to
India in the 11th and 12th centuries. According to the Koran,
Muslims are obligated to participate in the jihad (= holy war).
The aim of a jihad isn't the conversion of new believers; rather
the expansion of Islamic states, requiring submission by non-
believers, but allowing the free practice of religion. That's why
Islam had poor success in India, only the casteless, and lower
castes were willing to convert.

The basic requirement for followers of Islam is the acknowledgement: "La-illaha-illa-Allah, Mohammed-ar-Rasul-Allah",
"There is no god besides Allah, and Mohammed is his prophet."

## FUNDAMENTAL PRINCIPLES OF ISLAM

**Prayers:** Five times daily, facing toward Mecca.
**Ramadan:** Observance, during daylight hours, of the month-
long fast.
**Giving:** Alms to the poor.
**Taboo:** Against wine or alcohol consumption and eating of
pork. Anthropologists suggest that a desert people (i.e.
Arabs, Jews) would be foolish to eat pork, not because it is
unclean as is frequently suggested, but because pigs eat the
same food as humans, and pigs eat 20 times as much food as
they give on average!
**No Gambling**
**Polygamy:** Is okay, but the Koran suggests just four wives.

There are two main branches of Islam, The Sunni, and the Shiah.
While the great majority of all Muslims (90 %) are Sunni, the
Shiah branch has been getting all the headlines in recent years
(i.e. Islamic fundamentalists in Iran and Lebanon). Most Muslims
in India belong to the Shiah branch, which was founded by Mohammed's son-in-law, Ali, who was murdered by his enemies.

Shiites look to an Iman (religious teacher), who should be a direct descendent of Ali. The Indian festival, Moharram, is in honour of the third Iman, Hussein, one of Ali's sons, who was also murdered.

Sunni Muslims, with 90 % of the following worldwide, don't recognize any special position for Mohammed's descendants. They

look for guidance to the **SUNNA**, a work containing everything known about Mohammed, and his word.

After the division of the British Raj into India and Pakistan, many Muslims abandoned India for Pakistan. This led to tensions between Sikhs and Muslims (see Sikhs and their history), and has cost many lives. About 80 million Muslims still live in India.

Hindus have a hard time understanding Islam: the eating of animals; taboo against depictions of God, people or animals; rejection of reincarnation. There have been attempts to combine Hinduism and Islam. The Sikh religion was founded by Guru Nanak, but its adherents are persecuted by the Muslims.

# Sufism

Equally persecuted was Sufism, a mystical movement arising within Islam in the 8th century. The Sufi, like Indian yogis, seek unification with God. They are little interested in superficialities, or adherence to religious structure. Not until the 11th century was the theologian, Al Ghasali, able to piece togeth-

er the official Sufistic theology. For Sufis, the essences of all
religions are the same, as are the teachings of all great
teachers.

A number of Sufi congregations has sprung up in India, some
of which still thrive. Sufis are respected as miracle-making holy
men in India. It is worth picking up a book on Sufism.

You might have heard some Sufi jokes, though often they
reach us under other genre. Usually the jokes are about Mulla
(= master) Nasrudin, a figure created by the Dervishes "...to
depict momentary situations demonstrating various states of consciousness" (Indries Shah). These stories can be fathomed at
several levels of meaning. That something extra is designed to
help one on the road to self-development. Here's an example:

> Every day Nasrudin took his donkey across the border with
> a basket full of straw. Since he admitted being a smuggler,
> the customs officials searched him every time. They performed
> strip searches, sifted through the straw, even dipping it in
> water and burning it from time to time. But Nasrudin's
> wealth increased steadily over the years.
>
> Finally Nasrudin retired, and moved to a different region.
> Years later he met one of the former customs officers. "Tell
> me now," pleaded the retired official, "What you were smug-
> gling, all those years?"
> "Donkeys."

The Sufis have their own code system. There is a message hidden
in every Sufi name, whether Fariduddin Attar or Al Ghasali. The
message can be decoded through terminological analysis. The
Arabic roots of the words (usually combinations of just two or
three letters) have multifaceted meanings. Some letters symbolize
numbers, whereby the flow of letters to numbers and back to new
letters can create new meanings. Sufis also practise music and
Dervish dance. Aspiring Sufis usually study under a Sheik
(teacher) and belong to a Sufi congregation.

# Parseeism

The Parsee (also Parsi) originally came from Persia (hence their
name). They fled to India to escape persecution by Islam. Parseeism was founded by Zarathustra, after whom the religion was
called Zoroastrianism. Little is known about Zarathustra's life.
Reportedly, he was born in the 6th century BC in present-day
Afghanistan, to a noble family, and trained as a priest. He proclaimed the existence of a single, almighty, unseen benevolent
God. The God's name was Ahura Masda, the God of Light, symbolized by fire. That's why a fire always burns in Parsee temples.
But there's also an evil power: the evil spirit, Angra Manju,
leading to an eternal conflict between good and evil. The individual is called upon to take sides. The triumph of goodness can

be aided through good deeds, good thoughts, and good words. The teaching is contained in the holy book, **AWESTA**; though only a few writings, the **GATHAS**, date back to Zarathustra himself. Over time the original teaching was supplemented with the prophecy: that a saviour would appear at the last judgement. Sauschjants, the saviour, is scheduled to appear 3000 years after Zarathustra.

The elements (fire, water, earth, and air) are considered holy by the Parsee and should not be polluted. For this reason their dead are placed upon grids in the Towers of Silence to be eaten by birds. Most famous are the Towers of Silence in Bombay, home of the largest Parsee congregation in India (80,000 members). The Parsee, like the Sikhs, are wealthy by Indian standards, possess above average economic power, and are well known for their public service activities. Their numbers  are declining because Parsee may only marry Parsee. Children from mixed marriages aren't considered Parsee.

# Christianity

Certainly a religion familiar to Indians; the Apostle Thomas brought Christ's word here in the 1st century AD. About the same time, Christian Orthodox Syrians fled to India to escape persecution. Christianity had roots in India well before most of Europe.

Later, Portuguese missionaries found success converting low caste and casteless Indians. However, Christianity never achieved much importance beyond the coastal strip in the south where it is still alive today. Hinduism was able to incorporate Christianity; many Hindus regard Christ as another incarnation of Vishnu.

Bastions of Roman Catholicism include the former Portuguese colony of Goa, plus the tribal areas of Mizoram and Manipur.

India is home to Catholics, Presbyterians, Syrian Orthodox, Anglicans, Seventh-Day Advocates, Methodists, Baptists, and others.

# Ashrams

For religious Hindus, an important part of their spiritual development is to spend some time in an ashram. The ashram provides
an opportunity to deepen one's spiritual involvement, meditate,
practise yoga, and have Darshan (encounter) with a spiritual
teacher. The encounter with a spiritual master can take place
while the teacher is still alive, or even after he has left his
body.

Westerners often find it difficult to comprehend what it means
to be a guru (spiritual master). The word has taken on negative
connotations, partly from ignorance, partly from bad experiences
with import-export gurus. Chögyam Trungpa therefore suggests the
term "Spiritual Friend", a concept implying a very different relationship: a relationship designed to expand one's consciousness.

A spiritual friend can act as a mirror, reflecting one's true
self back for you to see, including games and deceitfulness. A
real guru doesn't make you dependent upon him, rather helps you
to find your own guru within yourself.

Westerners can live for a time in an ashram, if they are
willing to accept the strict rules usually found. If you aren't
interested in making a commitment, you would be wasting your
time in an ashram, and make yourself a burden to other ashram
members. Ashram life is not a sightseeing tour.

A visit to an ashram is a very personal experience, and each
ashram has its own individual character. Only you can tell if
the ashram you visit is the right spot for you.

The spiritual path leads to increased consciousness and self-
responsibility. Blind adherence, and participation without inner
reflection, can be dangerous for your development. You dare not
turn your own responsibilities over to the guru with the attitude
that he'll do it. He won't do anything. He is only a catalyst
who can speed up the changing processes within yourself. Select
your guru with the same care you use when selecting a doctor.
Don't make decisions based on just one person's opinion, or
common preconceptions, or what you would like to believe. Don't
believe what your teacher says, just out of respect for your
teacher. But no matter what path you choose, after careful
consideration, to the happiness of all creation, follow this path
as the moon follows the path of the stars.

**Rishikesh:** Famous in the west as the ashram where the Beatles
visited Guru Maharishi Mahesh Yogi. In Muni-ki-Reti, you'll
find a large number of ashrams, most catering to Indian pilgrims. Many are wonderfully moulded to Indian taste, and well
worth a visit. Two ashrams offer Hathayoga classes for westerners: Yoga Niketan Ashram, and on the same street, Shivananda Ashram. If you want to stay at Shivananda Ashram, you
have to register four weeks in advance: Divine Light Society,
Shivananda Ashram, Muni-ki-Reti, P.O. Shiya Nanda Nagar,
Rishikesh, tel.40. The yoga class with brief meditation in the

morning and evenings is open to everybody.  Plus there is an
excellent library.  Swami Krishnananda holds daily Darshan,
and answers questions when his health permits.

**Mc Leod Ganj:** Home of the Dalai Lama and many Tibetans. If you
are interested in learning Mahayana and Vajrayana Buddhism,
this is the best place. The Tibetan Library is open to the public,  with an excellent selection of books. Meditation and Tibetan language classes are always in session.  Plus there are the
Tushita Meditation Centre,  above Rishibawan,  and a Hindu
Meditation Centre outside town.

**Calcutta:**  Ramakrishna Mission; Ramakrishna lived near Calcutta.
There are Ramakrishna Missions in several major cities.  For
information and books about Vivekananda (Mission organiser),
visit Gol Park, tel.463431, in the south of town.

**Puri,  Orissa:** Karar Ashram,  Swargadwar, Puri, home of Swami
Harikarananda Giri,  a direct student of Sri Yukteswar and
Paramahamsa Yogananda.  The ashram was founded in 1903 by
Sri Yukteswar Giri. You can study Kriya Yoga Meditation.

**Delhi:** Sufi Centre, Hayat Bowman, 6 Birberl Road, B-Block, Jang-
pur Extension,  New Delhi 14.  Check if the guru,  Pir Vilayat
Inayat Khan, will be at the ashram when you plan to visit.

**Bombay:**  You can learn more about Parseeism from the priests at
the Zoroastrian Temple,  Petit Fasali Alash-Kadeh, 44 New Marine Lines, Bombay. Just a walk from Churchgate Station.

**Ganeshpuri:**  By bus from Bombay,  you can visit the ashram of
Swami Muktananda. One of the prettiest ashrams in India; it is
like staying in a maharaja palace.  Unfortunately,  Swami
Muktananda left his body in 1984.

**Gondia**, Maharasthra: Yogashakti Ashram, Sivananda International
Public School.  The guru is Ma Yogashakti,  called Mataji,
daughter of the well-known yogi from Benares,  Swami Vidyaa-
nanda. Several types of ycga are taught.

**Vrindaban:** 10 km from Mathura, between Delhi and Agra. Krishna
is said to have lived here.  A large festival is held in July or
August to celebrate his birthday.

**Poona:**  Only part of the tremendous Rajneesh Ashram remains,
administered by his Indian Sannyasins.

**Igatpuri:**  Buddhist Centre where classes in Vipassana Meditation
are held.  Be sure to write in advance because only a limited
number of participants can be accepted: Vipassana International Academy, Dhammagiri, Igatpuri 422 403, Dist. Nasik, Maharasthra, India.

**Shirdi:**  This is where Shirdi Sai Baba taught. He is considered a
previous incarnation of Sathya Sai Baba.  Shirdi is between
Bombay and Aurangabad.  Bus tours are organized by the Tourist Office in Bombay.  You can combine a visit to Shirdi with
stops in Aurangabad and the Ellora Caves.

**Bangalore:**  Brindavan is the name of Sai Baba's ashram in
Bangalore.  During the hot summer months he is usually here
instead of in Puttaparthi.

Very well recommended is Mr. Janakiraman, Atma Jyoti, Sara-
sya, 297, 10th Main Road, Jayanagar, Bangalore, tel.605972.
Mr. Janakiraman is a humorous man in his mid sixties, who
once worked as an engineer in the space industry, but now has
turned his attention to healing. His methods of healing include
yoga breathing methods and practice, plus sounds which create
certain oscillations. You can study with him, and he offers a
three-month yoga class.

**Puttaparthi:** The ashram of Sai Baba, Prasanthi Nilayam, is 4 h
north of Bangalore. The ashram is open to everyone. The emphasis is placed upon darshan with Sai Baba and singing.
Everyone may meditate alone in their room. For more information see Puttaparthi, Andhra Pradesh.

**Madras:**

Theosophical Society, see Madras. You must apply in advance
if you want to stay here, generally only members are accepted.

Kalakshetra, Besant Cultural Centre, Thiruvanmiyur, Madras.
In a very spiritual atmosphere, foreigners can study Indian
dance and music.

Sri Satchidananda Yogi, Sri Madras Yogaashram (Institute for
Yoga), 38, Godown Street, First Floor, Madras 1, near the
YMCA Building. Guru: Swami Satchidananda Yogi.

Sri Ramakrishna Math and Mission, 11 Ramakrishna Road,
Mylapore, Madras 4.

**Bukkapatnam:** Swami Nagananda lives just outside Pattaparthi. He
is about 30 years of age, runs a small preschool, and gives
meditation classes. He is in the process of building facilities
for meditation students.

**Pondicherry:** Sri Aurobindo Ashram maintains a number of guesthouses in town where anyone can stay. In the guesthouses you
can purchase meal tickets for good, cheap ashram food. The
ashram and the town project Auroville have little in common
any more. There are also guesthouses in Auroville where you
can stay, see Pondicherry and Auroville.

**Mangalore:** Near Mangalore in Kahnagad, Cannanore District, is
the ashram of Mother Krishnabai. The atmosphere is lovely.
From Kanhangad, get a taxi to Maunngal.

**Tiruvannamalai:** The ashram of Sri Ramana Maharshi and the
mountain, Arunachala, radiate tremendous peace. The influence
of Ramana Maharshi is still felt everywhere. If you wish to
stay here a while, be sure to register in advance.

**Kerala:** The address of two Christian ashrams:

Ashram of Reverend K.K Chandy, Manganam, P.O. Kottayam
686018.

Kurisimala Ashram, Vagamon, P.O. Kottayam District, Kerala.
The teacher is Francis Acharya, a Belgian priest.

**Trivandrum:** The ashram of Vishnudevananda.

# Indian Festivals

Indian festivals are usually of religious origin. In India, Hinduism, Buddhism, Jainism, Parseeism, Islam, Sikhism, and Christianity live peacefully, for the most part, side by side. As each religion enjoys its own festivals, lots of festivals await your participation. Many Hindu holidays are connected with the harvest, in keeping with an agricultural tradition. The change of seasons is celebrated with song and dance. Other holidays are named for specific gods. You can fast and sing in the temple, all night long, in honor of Shivaratri. If you participate, be sure to conduct yourself like an Indian, and not like a tourist.

Festivals are set by full and new moon, falling on different days each year. In 1982, the Indian lunar calendar had 13 months, complicating things further. The Durga Puja, Dussehra, and Diwali Festivals are celebrated with up to a month's difference in time in different locations.

**THE FULL MOONS**
**1987:** January 15, February 14, March 15, April 14, May 13, June 12, July 11, August 9, September 7, October 7, November 5, December 5.
**1988:** January 4, February 3, March 3, April 2, May 1 and 31, June 30, July 29, August 27, September 26, October 25, November 23, December 23.
**1989:** January 22, February 20, March 22, April 21, May 20, June 19, July 18, August 17, September 15, October 15, November 13, December 12.

You can figure the new moon dates yourselves. Here is a list of the most important festivals. Always ask for exact details at the Tourist Office.

**JANUARY**
**New Year:** Throughout India.
**Amber Festival:** Amber, Jaipur.
**Pongal-Sankranti:** A harvest festival always on the 14th in Tamil Nadu, Karnataka, Andhra Pradesh, especially Madurai, Madras, Tiruchirapalli.
**Republic Day:** Parade, folk dance in Delhi, always on the 26th.

**FEBRUARY**
**Desert Festival:** Jaisalmer.
**Vasanta Panchami:** A festival in honor of Saraswati, goddess of scholars, Celebrated primarily in North India, i.e. Punjab, Delhi, West Bengal.
**Floating Festival:** Madurai-Cochin, temple godheads in silken robes and decorated with jewels and flowers are carried in a procession to the lake and accompanied over the lake on a colorful, brightly lit raft, with music and songs.
**Carnival:** Celebrated in Goa.

## MARCH / APRIL

**Holi:** Celebrated throughout India, a rollicking holiday on which people spray each other with red paint to celebrate the start of spring.

**Easter:** Goa, Cochin, South India.

**Mahashivaratri:** Usually the start of March, sometimes in Feb, in honor of the god Shiva, celebrated in all his temples in all of India. Many Indians spend Mahashivaratri in an ashram singing and fasting.

**Gangaur Festival:** Mainly in Rajasthan, Udaipur, Jaipur, and Jodhpur. Celebration in honor of the goddess Parvati, Shiva's spouse. Girls pray to Gauri (Shiva) for good husbands.

**Mewar Festival:** In Udaipur and Rajasthan.

## APRIL / MAY

**Meenakshi Kalyanam:** Manakshi's marriage with Shiva (Madurai). The mythical wedding is the end of a 10-day continuous festival. The gods are carried through the city in a procession.

**Buddha Purnima:** Sarnath, Dharamsala, Bodh Gaya.

**Vaisakhi:** Punjab, Haryana, Delhi, Calcutta.

## MAY

**Labour Day:** Always on the 1st, speeches.

**Tagore's Birthday:** On the 8th, especially in Calcutta and other big cities.

**Pooram:** On the 2nd, celebrated nights at the temple of Vadakkunathan near Trichur.

## JUNE / JULY

**Rath Yathra:** Temple cart procession in Puri, Orissa, in honor of the god Jagannath, Lord of the Universe.

**Summer Festival:** At Mount Abu and Sirohi, usually early in June.

**Id-uh-Fitr:** A Muslim celebration of the end of the fasting month Ramadan.

**Hemis Festival:** In Leh-Ladakh.

## AUGUST

**Janamashtami:** Krishna's birthday, celebrated throughout India, especially at Mathura and pilgrimage sites

**Independence Day:** The 15th, especially in Delhi.

**Teej:** Primarily in Rajasthan and Uttar Pradesh. The monsoon is greeted and the goddess Parvati honored. Women dress in green, and there is a procession with dancers, elephants, and camels.

**Naag Panchami:** Jodhpur, Delhi, Maharasthra, dedicated to the cobra (naag), on which Vishnu rested before creating the world. In Jodhpur, huge cloth snakes are shown.

**Raksha Bandhan:** In north and west India. The god Indra received a rakhi, a silken amulet, from his woman companion, which brought him luck in his campaign against the demons. On this day, each girl seeks a "brother", on whose wrist she puts a rakhi. He is then her protector.

**Amarnath Yatra:** In Kashmir. In the caves of Amarnath, thousands of Hindus gather by full moon to worship Shiva.

## SEPTEMBER / OCTOBER

**Onam Harvest Festival:** Snakeboat races in the lagoons of Kerala.

**Dussehra:** Celebrated throughout India, especially Delhi, Varanasi, Mysore. Scenes from the Ramayana are performed in Delhi, and on the last day, demons made of bamboo and papier mâché and filled with firecrackers are burned. In Mysore, huge processions. In Kulu, there is a huge fair, into which the gods are carried in sedan chairs.

**Ganesh Chaturthi:** In Bombay and Maharasthra. A rollicking festival in honor of Ganesha, the god with the elephant head. Dancing, singing. Huge figures of Ganesha are carried through the city and dipped into the sea.

**Id-ul-Zuha:** Delhi, Lucknow, Calcutta, Ajmer, Kashmir, a Muslim festival in memory of Abraham.

**Mahatma Gandhi's Birthday:** October 2.

## OCTOBER / NOVEMBER

**Diwali:** Celebrated throughout India, especially Delhi, Bombay, Calcutta, Varanasi, Madras. A festival of lights in which all towns are decorated with oil lamps or candles. Also a family holiday with presents and sweets. Sometimes fireworks and games of chance in the evening.

**Muharram:** A Muslim festival in honor of the martyr Imam Hussain, Mohammed's grandson. Processions in Lucknow, Delhi, Bombay, Kashmir.

## NOVEMBER / DECEMBER

**Nanak's Birthday:** The coming of the Sikh Guru is celebrated in Punjab and Delhi, on December 1.

**Pushkar:** Celebrated in Ajmer, with camel races and riding sport.

**Bikaner Festival:** A desert festival usually beginning at the end of November.

**Christmas:** December 24–26.

**Winter Festival:** Mount Abu.

Don't forget to ask for the dates and descriptions of the festivals at the Tourist Office. A new list appears at the beginning of each year.

## WRITE TO US

Which festivals did you enjoy? Why? David Crawford, Peter Meyer, Barbara Rausch - P.O. Box 110232 - 1000 Berlin 11 - Germany.

# CULTURE

## Music

A thorough look at Indian music is beyond the capacity of any travel guide (or even your ability to carry!). Here's a quick picture, so you'll look smart when the talk turns to music.

### HISTORY
India is heir to the world's most ancient musical tradition. Its origins are lost in prehistory, but likely date from the 6th millennium BC. According to ancient Indian mythology and historical works by the Puranas, Shiva taught humanity music around 6000 BC.

In the third millennium BC, the Vedic Aryans settled in northern India. They brought their own religion, language, culture and music which differed greatly from those before them. In this melting pot stirred the origins of Hindu culture with its multitude of depictive deities and symbols. Southern India experienced an autonomous cultural development, adding additional elements.

We can recognize two major schools of music, based in the north and south respectively: the autochthonous Shivaist school and the Aryan Vedic school. They are commonly referred to as north-Indian classic music and south-Indian karnative music (with a folk music character).

Beside the two major schools, there are remnants of other completely unique schools of music. The southern Indian mountain tribes: Santal, Gond, and Toda; along with the Ahir, a north-India caste of breeders and shepherds, each have their own schools of music.

Hindu music was forced underground following Persian and Mongolian invasions of northern India in the early 12th century. But the suggestive and expressive music remained popular despite energetic repression by successive emperors in Delhi. At the turn of the 14th century, the imperial court was purebred Persian. But with time, some Islamic rulers found pleasure in the music, and it spread throughout the Muslim world. It isn't surprising that a Muslim poet and musician named Amir Khusru is credited with inventing the sitar at the court of Sultan-Ala-ud-din-Khilji (1295 - 1315). The sitar was actually based upon the ancient Persian long lute.

India's music springs from two sources:
**Folk Music:** A great Indian tradition. An abundance of lovely music, renowned for its spontaneity and lyric variety, gives note to the changing seasons, times of day, or the toil of peasants, fishermen, boatmen and camel drivers.

**Religious Music:** The recitative singing of ancient Vedic hymns.

## MUSIC THEORY

As discussed above, Indian music traces its roots back to the notes of creation. When the god, Shiva, created the world, he accompanied himself with flute, and danced, as he twirled through the cosmos. That's why music plays such an important role in the Indian religious experience. At its peak, Indian music provides a structure permitting maximum creative freedom. The musician uses free improvisation, to converse with the Creator.

When listening to Indian music, let's forget our western way of listening, and with full concentration immerse ourselves completely in the musical experience. We experience a sensation lost in the western world, as music transcends to a mystical religious experience closely associated to yoga.

## STRUCTURE

Notice the lack of major-minor harmonies. Indian music is modal, centring around one ground note. This ground note, and usually its fifth, are constantly repeated by accompanying instruments, attuning to the desired character of sound, i.e. mode. Indian musicians use 72 different modes, while western music knows only two, major and minor, outside of a few church modes.

There isn't a specified pitch for the ground notes, whereas western music uses 440 oscillations per second. Indian musicians, particularly sitar players, tune their instruments to their own internal ground note. Indian music is soloist oriented. The musician speaks through the instrument, developing a raga (see below) to create a mood or communicate with the audience. Several sitars playing together could only result in musical mumble jumble, with each player taking off on an individual interpretation. This burdens Indian musicians with the challenge of giving their musical language a new birth at each performance.

## THE MUSICAL SCALE

A scale developed over the course of centuries. In recitative Rig-veda hymns (telling the Indian story of creation), we can follow the development as more notes were added to the ladder. First there were three, then five, and finally seven notes today. Adding five sharps and flats to the seven main notes produced a scale with twelve easily identifiable notes.

**Shruti:** 22 micro-intervals, dividing the range of the twelve notes. The micro-interval is less than a half-tone interval in western music. Each shruti has its own recognizable expressive character. Imagine the multitude of aesthetic and mood variations possible. But Indian music requires a good ear by the listener, and repeated hearings.

## RHYTHMIC STRUCTURE

As with every form of art, Indian musicians work within structural guidelines. These include the raga and tala. The raga is the fundamental element of melody; the tala personifies rhythm.
**Raga:** Musical mode, a group of notes, depicting a particular mood which the musician develops thematically within predefined bounds, generally through improvisation. Classical ragas frequently are designed to be performed at specific times of day. Unfortunately, these guidelines are increasingly forgotten.

## CHARACTERISTIC RAGA ELEMENTS

**Musical Scale:** With precise intervals, encircling a fixed and constantly echoed ground note.
**Melodic & Ornamental Elements:** Rules of approach for certain notes, which vary from raga to raga.
**Vadi & Samvadi:** Two characteristic notes, beginning and ending, one of which is the ground note, building the melody.
**Improvised Elements:** Based more or less upon the mode.

According to ancient Sanskrit texts, there are more than 16,000 different ragas. Some musicians today are familiar with about 300, but only about 100 are played.

**The Tala:** A structured rhythmic cycle, which can consist of various measures. No other musical culture has such a shrewdly designed structure of rhythmic subtleties. The rhythmic elements are logically conceived, and capable of detailed denotation. Every means of playing a drum can be depicted with a symbol: with one finger or two, the flat of the hand, on the side, or in the middle... In this way, musicians can learn complicated variations by heart, and even rework them without actually having to play. The improvisation frequently includes artistic rhythmic sculptures, based upon the rhythmic cycle. The ratio between rhythm and time corresponds to the interval between notes in the raga. Certainly the rhythmic aesthetic, and the moods created by the various rhythms, carry just as much meaning as the mode.

## MUSICAL INSTRUMENTS

In keeping with India's ethnic diversity, a wide range of traditional instruments is popular. Important stringed instruments include the vina, sitar, sarod, sarangi, esraj, and dotara.
**The Vina:** Viewed historically, this is India's most ancient fretted, string instrument. It features seven strings and 22 frets stretching along a bamboo. At each end, a large gourd is attached as a resonator. The vina is considered the most noble, and the most difficult, Indian instrument.
**The Sarod:** The most sonorous Indian stringed instrument, built similarly to a banjo or guitar, but without frets. Instead it features a smooth metal plate for fingering notes.
**The Tanpura:** Primarily an accompanying instrument. Lacking frets, the four strings are open picked. Larger than the sitar.

**The Sitar:** Certainly the best known Indian instrument; it has seven playing strings, 18 frets, and 20 smaller resonator strings.

**Sarangi** and **Esraj:** While the above four instruments are plucked, the sarangi and the esraj require a bow. Both are similar to the sitar, but smaller.

**The Dotara:** A small lute with four gut strings. It's the instrument of the wandering minstrels who entertain the villages of East Bengal with erotic songs of a religious nature.

### Flutes

India is home to a variety of flutes played both lengthwise and sideways (cross flutes).

**The Murali:** A six-holed bamboo cross flute.

**The Shahnai:** Or Indian oboe, the best known.

### Drums

Among various percussion instruments, the mridanga and the tabla are most popular.

**The Mridanga:** The classic Indian drum, big-bellied and cylindrical, with a skin spanned at each end.

**The Tabla:** Perhaps the best-known rhythm instrument, in reality it's a two-piece mridanga. A small drum is played with the right hand and a larger drum with a deeper tone for the left hand. Both drums can be tuned precisely. Furthermore, the drum's special skin combined with practised technique allows a good tabla player to play a fast roll ranging over two octaves!

**The Ghatam:** Less familiar to western ears, this is a simple earthen jug, played with the fingers. Very subtle rhythmic patterns can be performed.

**Natural Elements:** A record by **Shakti**. Gongs, cymbals, dulcimers, bells, and other instruments round out the spectrum of Indian folk music.

### BUYING AN INSTRUMENT

Many of you will want to take an instrument home. If you want a good buy, keep the following in mind:

The instruments with the best handwork and sound (particularly sitars and flutes) are made in Bengal. The largest selection can be found in Calcutta, along with Delhi and Bombay. Good tablas are found almost everywhere.

But most important, take your time. Don't buy the first instrument you see. Settle down in a music shop and test a few instruments. I once spent three days visiting a music shop before the owner finally broke out a wonderfully sounding sitar.

It's traditional that you'll be offered a few lessons upon purchase of an instrument. If not, ask! Lessons provide an excellent inside look at Indian music. And, should you chance upon an experienced instructor, the lessons might be your nicest experience in India. My sitar instructor said during the first lesson: "Indian music is like a deep sea. You can dive into it as deep as you like, but you will never find the ground."

# Classical Indian Dance

Indians trace the spirit and technique of their dance back to the god Brahma, who revealed the art to Bharata, a wise man. Over 2000 years ago, Bharata wrote **NATYA SHASTRA**, the bible of Indian dance and drama. Classical Indian dance consists of three basic elements:

**Natya:** The combining of dance and drama.

**Nritta:** Pure dance, demonstrating technique, rhythm, various positions, and foot technique.

**Nrtya:** Creates a mood, and conveys a story or an entire drama. Eyes and eyebrows, fingers and hands, throat and feet, the entire body is used as a vehicle of expression.

Dance, drama, and music are inseparable. Indians believe that dance preceded even creation: Shiva, the cosmic dancer, always existed.

**Nataraja:** Statues of Shiva dancing, found everywhere in India. Shiva symbolizes the energy which creates all, transforms all, and gives life. Dance is a sacred act, always beginning with a call to Shiva. For centuries dances were performed only in the temples to charm the gods.

**Devadasis:** Temple servants who as small girls dedicated their lives to the temple, living an ascetic life, specially trained as dancers. As high religion fell into decadence, they became the toys of wealthy maharajas and colonial masters, and gained a reputation as prostitutes. Dance became secularized.

The revolt against British colonialism in the 1930s led to a revival of temple dance. Personalities, no less than Mahatma Gandhi, Rabindranath Tagore, Jawarharlal Nehru, and dancers such as Ram Gopal, and Rukmeni Devi, looked for strength in Indian tradition, reviving the spirit of Indian dance. Dance was now performed on stage, in a theatre, which through the artistry of a great dancer would become a temple. Thousands were able to see **RAMAYANA,** or the story of Shiva, and Krishna's play with the Gopis in dramatic dance, accompanied by music and song. The ancient faith is revived, as the dancers summon forth a god, by depicting his mudra and movements.

There are several schools of Indian classical dance, developed in different geographical regions.

**Bharat Natyam:** Best known, originating and practised in temples of the south. This is a very stylistic form of dance, telling a story through the language of gesture and mime, accom-

panied by music and song. The costumes and make-up are exactly prescribed. Girls require ten years of intensive training
to master the art of Bharat Natyam dance.

**Kathakali**: An ancient form of dance developed in Kerala, katha
(= story), kali (= play), "kathakali" (= dramatic dance). The
dance is usually performed outdoors for religious festivals at
temples and palaces. The art form is usually performed at
night by the light of oil lamps, creating a lovely atmosphere,
accompanied by music and song. Artistic make-up and extravagant costumes are featured, depicting the characters. Exceptional characters, such as Krishna and Arjuna, wear green
make-up. Red make-up is reserved for enraged, stupid characters, such as demons and evil spirits. See a Kathakali performance while you are in Ernakulum. Unlike Bharat Natyam,
kathakali is danced only by men. The themes are usually taken
from the epics, **RAMAYANA** and **MAHABHARATA.** Artistic gesture
and mime are accompanied by tabla and song.

**Kathak**: Restricted to northern India. Performances matured under
Moghul rule from a traditional form of dance to a highly
developed art form. Characteristic are lightning-fast foot movements and precise rhythms

**Manipuri**: Originated in eastern India, a graceful dance, made
even more lovely by the attractive costumes.

**Orissi**: Developed in Orissa, similar to Bharat Natyam, but more
graceful and sensuous. Since the 12th century AD, the dance
has played an integral role in the ritual of Jaganath Temple
in Puri, where it is still performed today.

# Arts & Crafts

Archaeological finds on the subcontinent show evidence of an artistic tradition dating back at least to 2500 BC – 1500 BC in the
Indus Valley. Ancient scriptures, such as the **RIGVEDA** (2000 BC),
the **RAMAYANA**, and the **MAHABHARATA** speak of jewelry making.
Many art forms, like so much of Indian life, have their roots in
religion. Classical traditions in music, dance, architecture,
sculpture, theater, and literature have been preserved to this
day. In fact, they thrive in universities and such private institutions as Kalakshetra Art Academy in Madras.

Cultural exchange with neighboring races and cultures has
influenced Indian art through assimilation. Muslim influence seen
in palaces, mosques and tombs testifies to an intermixing of
Saracenic style with Hindu style beginning in the 12th century.

Once upon a time, handicrafts were preserved and financed by
the aristocracy. During the industrial era, this support waned.
Many artists became unemployed, seeing no possibility of making
a living with their craft. Before the industrial revolution, 15 %
of India's GDP (gross domestic product) was produced by arts
and crafts.

In 1952 the All India Handicrafts Board was founded with the goal of breathing new life into handicrafts, particularly by creating new markets. Today, every major city has a national handicraft shop, Handicraft Board, or State Emporium. Since 1962, The Handicrafts and Handloom Exports Corporation of India Limited (HHEC) has found markets in 90 countries by opening trade missions around the world and exhibiting at trade fairs.

The All India Handicrafts Board began presenting annual awards in 1956 to India's ten best artists. Each prize is endowed with 2500.-Rs. Some very extravagant, therefore almost extinct, art forms receive support.

India is a paradise for handicrafts featuring stone, wood, bronze, brass, ivory, bone, bamboo, clay, papier mâché, gold, silver, precious and semiprecious stones. You'll see lovely silver filigree, but also massive gold pieces wrought with expensive jewels.

Indian textiles are particularly advanced. Besides colorful everyday cloths (i.e. saris), artistic cloth paintings and hand-knotted rugs featuring century-old traditional patterns are available. Selection of cloth and designs is tremendous. It ranges from hand-printed cotton and silk, fine embroidery, delicately woven cloth to heavier materials. Gold and silver thread are frequently woven into silk or cotton patterns.

Devotional articles made of brass gleam in every bazaar. Household and other consumer goods made are artistically crafted in copper, brass, and bronze, sometimes inlaid with silver.

Besides these highly regarded handicrafts, there is a number of lesser known crafts performed by Indian women. In front of houses and temples, notice the good-luck symbols (mandala) drawn in white chalk, colored on the pavement, drawn in sand, or strewn with colors.

Traditional architecture is an art in itself, as reflected in regional variances of rural homes. Notice how building style and materials fit in with their surroundings: palm-wood buildings in Kerala, sandstone in the Thar Desert, stone buildings in the Himalayas, mud huts (or buildings) on the Deccan. Materials and style express the nature of a culture and its people.

# Omen & Astrology

Life in India is greatly influenced by belief in good and bad omens. Read the **MAHABHARATA**; there are several references to generals, who on the morning of an important battle refused to heed a series of bad omens. In each case the battle was lost.

There are many travel omens: rain upon an arrival morning is a good omen. However, rain at departure is bad. Equally worth heeding are taboos against travel in certain directions on certain days. Monday and Saturday are certainly the wrong day to head east! Never go north on a Tuesday or Wednesday. Thursday is not a day to travel south. On Friday or Sunday, go anywhere, but not west! If you leave a town on Wednesday, expect never to return. And remember, never begin a long journey on a Thursday afternoon.

These omens are particularly important in Nepal. Expect difficulty getting any Nepalese to begin a journey on a Saturday. Saturday and Tuesday are considered very inauspicious. Animal sacrifices are made on Tuesdays and Saturdays in Dakshinkali in the hope that the goddess, Kali, will be pleased and provide protection on these unlucky days.

It's considered good luck to see a dead body. If you meet an elephant in your dreams, you're in store for riches. According to a legend surrounding the Buddha's birth, his mother dreamed of an elephant before he was born, which she considered very auspicious.

Astrology plays a very important role in India.  At childbirth, when picking a marriage partner, before important business decisions, or at the start of a major journey, an astrologist is usually consulted.  By creating a horoscope, lucky and unlucky days are determined.

When India and Pakistan were divided, the astrologers were unanimous in advising against the chosen day, August 15th, 1947, which was obviously inauspicious. The resulting civil war provided ample confirmation. And astrologists predicted, to the year, when East and West Pakistan would be split into Pakistan and Bangladesh.

Parents who want to marry off their sons and daughters do well to consult an astrologist with the exact birthdates of any possible partners.  When two horoscopes fit together properly, then the marriage is considered lucky. It's reasoned that, in keeping with karma, time and place of birth are not coincidental. Two mutually harmonious horoscopes show that in previous lives, the partners made the decision to live together.  An astrologist also calculates an auspicious date and time for the marriage ceremony.  Since the planet venus should always be in the sky, certain days and months are swamped with marriages.

The Indian horoscope is slightly different from the one familiar to us.  Indians also take the planets Kethu and Rahu into consideration.  There is also a slight readjustment of astrological signs.  A scorpio in our astrological calculation is a Libra according to Indian reckoning.

When they have problems, Indians occasionally visit a pandit, learned in ancient scriptures.  Everyone's life is said to be contained in these ancient texts.  Using astrology and palm reading, taking account of time, day, shadow length, etc., a pandit can find the appropriate spot in his books answering questions about the past and future.

There is no future in not knowing your future.  See Tips, in the local sections, for addresses of The Wise along your travel route.

# HISTORY

## The Precolonial Era

What little we know about India's early history is based largely upon legend, or archaeological finds near rivers and caves. It's assumed that the subcontinent's prehistoric inhabitants were dark-skinned Dravidian people, forefathers of today's Tamil population in southern India. Superior swordsmanship by immigrating, light-skinned Aryans (Indo-Iranian nomads) forced sedentary Dravidians south, around 1500 BC. Even today, Indians often point to a common heritage with Germanic Aryans (Arya).

The world's most ancient sacred scriptures, the **VEDA** (=I know, holy knowledge, compare with Latin vidi = I saw), date from 1000 BC, testifying to Aryan philosophy and religion. Orthodox Hinduism, also known as Brahmanism, resulted from the mixing of the Aryan Vedic religion with pre-Aryan Harappa culture, a Dravidian-neolithic high culture, which was at least familiar with the deity, Shiva. After introduction of a Brahman (priest) controlled caste system, white-skinned Aryans were able to solidify and preserve political power.

**Sanskrit:** The sacred language took shape from the Aryan language. The heroic epics **RAMAYANA** and **MAHABHARATA**, along with the mystical **UPANISHAD** scriptures, were written in Sanskrit, from which, thousands of years later, modern Hindi would evolve.

### CASTE SYSTEM

Life was largely determined by caste. Each caste, inherited at birth, was bound by strict obligations. The four major castes stood at the top:

| | |
|---|---|
| **Brahman:** | Priests |
| **Kshatriya:** | Warriors |
| **Vaishia:** | Farmers & Craftsmen |
| **Sudra:** | Lowly Workers |
| | |
| **Paria:** | Casteless, at the lowest level. |

**Brahman:** Brahman priests saw the god, Brahman, as the founder of the caste system.

**Opposition:** Gautama Siddharta, founder of Buddhism, and opponent of the caste system, born 560 BC into the warrior caste. At the same time, the caste system came under attack by Mahavira (= great hero) Vardhamana (born 540 BC), founder of Jainism. Both religions were open without discrimination to converts of every caste. Buddha proclaimed that enlightenment had nothing to do with praying to God; but rather was a consequence of one's perfection, attained through meditation.

The centuries following saw repeated tribal invasions. The north-west was captured by Darius for the Persian Empire in 512 BC. From 327 - 325 BC, Alexander the Great marched through India, defeating the elephant-mounted armies of Poros the Great in the Battle of Hydaspes, before being forced to turn back following a mutiny by his own troops.

Later Indian Mauryas established an empire, which achieved its peak under King Ashoka (272 - 231 BC). After the gruesome Battle of Kalinga, marked by 100,000 dead and 150,000 deported, Ashoka converted to Buddhism, and ruled peacefully with tolerance of other religions, despite his energetic support of Buddhism.

After Ashoka's death, his mighty empire crumbled, as Turkish-Tatar tribes, Greeks, and Sythians, forced their cultures through the Khyber Pass into India. Not until the 4th century AD was there another Indian golden age with the Guptas ruling from their capital, Pataliputra (Patna). This empire fell in 430 AD and was divided after an invasion by white Huns (Hephtalites).

Buddhism lost ground and almost completely died on the subcontinent in the 8th century. The Brahmans, whose powers had been waning, developed a new Hinduism which permitted worship of pre-Aryan deities, but held fast to the caste system. During this period, Hindu architecture reached a peak, witness Khajuraho Temple.

Invading Muslim armies (beginning in 711 AD) found converts among Parias, eager to escape persecution under the caste system. Islam's ideas of one God and equality for all found popular support when Rajput disunity permitted resistance. Still, it was not until the start of the 13th century that the first Sultanate could be established. The period from the 13th to the 16th centuries was marked by fighting between Hindus and Muslims.

An attempted invasion by Ghengis Khan was repulsed at the Khyber Pass (1221 AD), along with later Mongol invasions, but in the 16th century the Afghan Muslims were defeated by the Moghul Babur. The greatest Moghul ruler was Akbar (1555 - 1605), who controlled the entire.north with a professional army, and demonstrated tolerance for many religions. The greatest architectural masterpieces of the Moghul era (16th - 18th centuries) can be seen in Akbar's residential city, Fatehpur Sikri near Agra; and the Taj Mahal in Agra, a mausoleum for Shah Jahan's favorite wife. Also lovely is Go Mandal Temple (built in Rajput style) in Udaipur.

# Colonialism

In 1498, the Portuguese under Vasco da Gama raised the first European flag on the Indian subcontinent since the ancient Romans and Greeks. Trading and missionary stations were established on the west coast.

The 17th century brought new divisions of power and territory: the French occupied Pondicherry in 1672; Calcutta fell to the British in 1690. The Maratha, led by Shivaji, fought the Moghuls and freed all of central India. In the 18th century, the Persians captured Delhi, taking as a prize the peacock throne, dating from the reign of Shah Jahan. Conflicts between the French and British were resolved by a British victory at the Battle of Plassey in 1757. The British Empire was born.

From the beginning, trade interests had priority. The most powerful company in the world, the British East India Company, exploited one-fifth of the world's population. By the middle of the 19th century, the British, through shrewd negotiations and military might, had attained control over most of the subcontinent. The Maharajas were permitted to enjoy their insatiable pleasures, while the British exported such raw materials as spices and cotton.

1857 saw a mutiny against British rule. Parts of the British-Indian Army revolted, and several Indian princes turned against the British. But the uprising was put down with the aid of Nepalese Gurkhas and British troops brought in quickly from abroad. Thereafter political power passed from the East India Company to the British Throne.

In 1858 Queen Victoria was proclaimed Empress of India, which was annexed by the British Empire. European technology and British law took hold. The Indian upper class was admitted to newly founded schools and universities. Below this class of Britain-oriented intellectuals, the masses pressed for freedom from foreign occupation. In 1887 the Indian National Congress was founded with the goals of preserving local tradition and independence from England. These ideas didn't find much support among middle and upper class Indians, who after centuries of political repression had become apathetic. Only under Mahatma Gandhi (1869 - 1948) did the independence movement get rolling.

# Mahatma Gandhi & Independence

Mahatma is a title of honor (= great soul, maha = great, atman = soul). Born in 1869, Mohandas Karamchand Gandhi studied law without controversy in England. Later, as a lawyer in South Africa, Gandhi experienced the insult of being forced from a whites only train compartment. The seeds were laid for Gandhi's fight for Indian equality. After ten years in South Africa, another train ride brought him to an important crossroads in his life. After reading **Unto This Last**, by John Ruskin, Gandhi was motivated to put all materialism behind him; a remarkable step for a successful lawyer with a family and an annual income of 5000 pounds!

Thereafter, Gandhi lived according to Bhagavad Gita ideals: abstention from passion and material goods. He began doing everything for himself, cutting his own hair, cleaning his privy: unworthy jobs for a man of his standing.

**Brahmacharya:** The final step of acceptance for Gandhi came at the age of 37. Brahmacharya involves absolute sexual abstinence, control of thoughts, suppression of emotions such as anger, hate, or rage, plus moderation in speech and eating habits. He shared a bed each night with his niece to demonstrate a lack of sexual desire. Brahmacharya also involves selfless love and giving to others. It was the definitive step on the road to asceticism, intrinsic to Gandhi's goal of self transformation.

Gandhi studied Henry David Thoreau's **On Civil Disobedience**, and consequentially landed in jail for the first time. After his transformation, Gandhi returned to India on January 9, 1915. He founded an ashram in Ahmedabad, which can still be visited today. Gandhi took part in the developing conflict with Britain, calling for non-violent resistance, using civil disobedience, i.e. non-cooperation with the occupying power.

**Be Indian, Buy Indian:** It became a point of honor to risk jail. The British were driven mad by Indians who ignored regulations and orders, or boycotted British products.

**Salt March:** From Ahmedabad to the coast, one of the most spectacular actions. The British enforced a monopoly on all raw materials, including salt. Gandhi led thousands on a march to the coast where each demonstrator let a handful of water evaporate in the sun until only the salt remained.

As a member of the Indian National Congress and its two-time president (1924 – 1937 and 1940 – 1941), Gandhi was received by the King of England. Gandhi arrived for tea at Buckingham Palace dressed as ever in a self-spun sheet. His self-made clothing was for himself and many others a protest against British imperialism, but also part of his religious meditation. The visit to England didn't bring success. After returning with empty hands, Gandhi took his ideas to the people of India, travelling as a Hindu priest on foot or by third-class rail.

In 1942, Britain offered India a dominion constitution for institution after the war, eliciting from Gandhi the remark: "England is leaving India!" The Labour government under Attlee recognized quickly after the war that Britain was going to lose control of India. Attlee sent Lord and Lady Mountbatten (a grandson of Queen Victoria, and direct descendant of Charlemagne) as the last Viceroy to India. He was charged with negotiating a settlement which would at least keep India in the British Commonwealth as a trading partner. Mountbatten demanded and received a number of special powers, and through shrewd negotiation and a personal friendship with Gandhi, managed to arrange independence for India within a period from March to August 1947. Neither Mountbatten nor Gandhi, however, could prevent conflict at meetings of Indian leaders, between members of the

Congress Party, Muslim League, and Sikhs. The age-old conflict between Hindus and Muslims couldn't be resolved, leading to the implementation of the Cunningham Plan dividing the subcontinent into Muslim Pakistan and Hindu India. Until the last, Gandhi spoke out against such a division, calling for peaceful coexistence between the religions and reduction of class differences.

The Independence of India on August 15, 1947 was marred by a state of civil war between Hindus, Muslims, and Sikhs. Millions of Muslims fled Hindu India for refuge in newly created East and West Pakistan. There were attacks on villages and on flocks of refugees. Conditions were particularly harsh in the divided Punjab, where the Sikhs came out on top despite the combined powers of the British and Indian armies.

Mahatma Gandhi risked life and limb to prevent continued fighting in Calcutta, a hot spot second only to Punjab. When, after a long truce, sporadic fighting resumed, Gandhi began a hunger strike (a weapon he often used with success). The holy man refused to eat until the Hindu and Muslim leaders could agree on peace. Within a few days, his plan succeeded, where the border army in the midst of the conflict had failed.

A single man, by risking his life, had proven to be mightier than an entire army. A fascinating story, only probable in India where religion and politics are so intermixed that it was impossible even for Muslim leaders to let a Hindu Mahatma (preacher) die.

For more information about Gandhi read **Freedom At Midnight**, an exciting book by Larry Collins and Dominique Lapiere. Also worth a look is the outstanding film **Gandhi**, by Richard Attenborough, though it confines itself to the most important points in Gandhi's public life.

Independence also marked the end of maharaja rule except in the kingdoms of Junagadh and Hyderabad, which joined India in 1948.

Just a few months after Independence, on January 30, 1948, Mahatma Gandhi was shot to death by the radical Hindu, Nathuram Godse, during a public, evening prayer in front of Birla House in Delhi. His last words were "He Ram" (= Oh God). In earlier conversations with his disciples, he'd commented that he could be a true Mahatma only if he died conscious of God's presence, and not of a natural death!

Mahatma Gandhi was a remarkable man, and a living example of the power of religion in Indian life and politics. He must certainly be admired no matter what one thinks of his ascetic, Brahmacharya lifestyle.

# The Maharajas

A lost world can come to life when you see the maharaja palaces in Jaipur and Udaipur, or visit Fatehpur Sikri. At the Taj Mahal in Agra, I sometimes like to close my eyes and try to imagine... Let's talk about the pomp, power, and insanity of India's royalty.

In 1947, a third of India's land and population were ruled by 565 maharajas (maha = great, raja = king). Their kingdoms varied greatly, from the size of western Europe to as small as a city park. Roughly dependent upon the greatness would be the number of wives, children, elephants, Rolls Royces, and other titles. Under British colonialism, nominal political power remained in maharaja hands in exchange for a treaty granting Britain a monopoly to exploit raw materials.

Before independence in 1947 (when they were dethroned), the maharajas found time for sport, women, cars, the hunt, ownership of pearls and precious jewels, and a life of conspicuous luxury in palaces famous for extravagant festivities and special events. High point of the festival was frequently a splendid elephant procession, since the power of a maharaja could be judged by the number and harness of his elephants. In later years Rolls Royces were deemed acceptable replacements for elephants. From this standpoint, a ninety-Rolls collection is in keeping with great tradition. Mr. Rajneesks had a goal of acquiring 365 Rolls Royces before leaving the United States. Unfortunately he was deported while still pushing the hundred Rolls hurdle.

And with the high taxes a maharaja could press from his realm, even the most eccentric hobbies could be realized. The book **Freedom At Midnight** describes the Maharaja of Gwalior's hobby of model trains. The royal banquet hall was connected by railway tunnel with the kitchen. Electric trains ferried in the food. During meals, the Maharaja sat at the head of a tremendous console boasting thousands of switches, knobs, and control lamps. Between bites he'd steer food to his guests. It's told that at one important affair, the ruler lost control of his trains: chaos! The guests dodged chicken and vegetables. Whether this incident deterred the Maharaja from his hobby is left unanswered.

Maharaja festivals featured elephant fights and dog weddings (where the King's favorite dog would be wed with full ceremony attended by thousands). Tiger hunts were another social event not to be missed even if the crippled Maharaja of Udaipur had to be carried (which he often was!).

Sometimes a royal passion didn't originate in India, but resulted from a visit to Europe's royal houses. After the Maharaja of Kapurthale visited Versaille, he recognized himself as a reincarnation of Louis IV (the Sun King). There was nothing to do but redecorate, and dress his Indian servants and officials in white powdered wigs.

The harem was a favorate royal perk, which if used optimally left a prince with little time for government, and a ready customer for any bizarre aphrodisiac.

Many maharajas trace their ancestry back to a god. Some let themselves be honoured once a year as a reincarnation of the god. Perhaps the most extravagant was the Maharaja of Patiala. He was considered to possess a manifestation of the Shiva Lingam. Once a year, with a magnificently erect penis, he would appear naked, to be worshipped and admired by his people. This ritual gave the Maharaja supernatural powers which he used to drive away evil spirits.

Not every maharaja was of that calibre. Some saw the writing on the wall, and were willing to give up their palaces and some luxuries when independence arrived. By dedicating themselves to politics or big business, they maintained their respect and wealth. Many are still influential today.

# The Indian Republic

Mahatma Gandhi's partner and companion in arms **Jawahal Nehru** served as Prime Minister and Foreign Minister of the Indian Union Republic from 1947 to 1964. A constitution developed by Gandhi according to principles of English law was instituted in 1950.

Administrative reforms reduced the number of states from 27 to 14, all subordinate to the national government.

Despite the Friendship Policy with China, and the mutual proclamation of Five Principle of Coexistence, skirmishes with China took place between 1959 - 1962 in the northeastern provinces and in Ladakh, which for a time was occupied by China. The Chinese thus controlled the strategic Karakorum Pass between Tibet and Sinkiang. In the north-east, differences were resolved mostly in keeping with the original borders.

After revolts by Hindu volunteers and Afghan tribes (in which both India and Pakistan intervened), an armistice agreement negotiated under UN auspices led to the division of autonomy-seeking Kashmir. Following the arrest of Prime Minister Sheik Abdullah, India annexed its part of Kashmir, in disregard of a UN resolution. Today, this region is part of the Union Republic, but enjoys autonomous status.

Conditions in Pakistan have been dominated by unending national crises and conflict between the eastern and western sections of the country. In 1956 Pakistan proclaimed itself an Islamic Republic (and Commonwealth member). A number of border disputes and incidents involving precious Indus water was resolved through negotiations between India and West Pakistan. Nevertheless, actions by Islamic guerrillas in Kashmir in 1965 led to the India - Pakistan war, which was ended at Soviet initiative after UN sponsored negotiations in 1966 at the Tashkent Conference.

The conflict rekindled, however, in 1971 when East Bengal felt patronized by West Pakistan, and with military aid from India was successful in its bid for independence. Today, East Pakistan is known as Bangladesh (sometimes Bangla Desh). This major foreign policy success by Indira Gandhi established India clearly as southern Asia's dominant military and economic power.

Portuguese Goa was forcefully annexed by India in 1961 against much of the population's will. Later the former colonial power declined to seek enforcement of international law.

Sikkim had a similar experience after being declared an Indian protectorate in 1948. It joined the Union of India more or less voluntarily in 1975.

**Indira Gandhi:** Nehru's daughter was elected Prime Minister in 1966, and re-elected in 1970 despite divisions in her Congress Party (which she considered a personal vote of confidence).

In 1977, Indira was voted out of office in reaction against authoritarian policies. Complaints included the arrest of political opponents, frequent resort to presidential rule, increased press censorship, and the ruthless implementation of a family-planning program featuring forced sterilization, led by Indira's son Sanjay. Nevertheless at the lowest ebb of her political influence, Indira garnered 34.5 % of the national vote. Her electoral loss was only possible because, for the first time, almost all opposition parties were able to forget differences and unite behind one candidate in opposition to the Congress Party candidate in each electoral race.

**Morarji Desai:** Elected Prime Minister in 1977 (Janata Party), proved to be a good administrator, but not much of a politician. With Indira Gandhi out of office, Desai never found a uniting factor to keep his political coalition together. In the end, he found himself without a political majority, leading to his resignation in June 1979. Because President Sanjiva Reddy couldn't find any other candidate able to put together a political majority, Charan Singh was given charge of a transition, minority government until new elections were held in January 1980.

Indira Gandhi took full advantage of the political instability. An overwhelming victory by the Congress (I) Party returned her to the office of Prime Minister. At the end of June 1980, Indira's son Sanjay crashed to his death while flying an aerobatic airplane. This laid momentarily to rest the hopes of Mrs. Gandhi (and the middle and upper classes) for a stable family dynasty. Indira Gandhi's opponents, however, couldn't cluck for long. Indira brought her second son, Rajiv (who until then had shown no political ambition) out of political obscurity, and built him into Sanjay's successor.

**Rajiv Gandhi:** Never caught the public eye with the same intensity as his brother Sanjay, until the murder of Indira Gandhi on October 31, 1984. As his mother would have wished, Rajiv was elected Chairman of the Congress (I) Party on November 2, 1984, and assumed the role of Prime Minister. He formed a transition government, and called quick parliamentary elections for late December 1984. Winning 401 of 508 seats, Rajiv achieved a three-fourths majority.

Since then he has maintained an astonishing political profile, quite unlike his mother, and has developed his own liberal style. Fighting corruption, tightening the administration, and propelling his country into the computer age, have been his primary goals. He receives support from India's youth, who are attracted by the honest and youthful appearance of their leader, born in 1944. Rajiv Gandhi (who has an Italian wife) has gained international respect and understanding through his remarkable self-confidence.

You might have noticed that we've avoided an in-depth look at any of India's political parties. Our reasoning is we see little importance in the numerous splits, reunifications, regroupings and coalitions. They happen so frequently that they have little long-term effect on party policy. Except for the Indian Communist Party, no party has a real rank and file membership. Indian politics has always been oriented toward leadership at the top. The family plays a vital role in everyday life, so it's not surprising that a dynasty at the peak of national politics should be considered respectable. A person's origins and standing, power and appearance are important, perhaps to their personal policy, but not their political party.

# Change Of Government

By 1984, Prime Minister Indira Gandhi had lost charisma. As a member of the freedom-fighter generation, she had little in common with the new Indian youth. When persistent religious unrest rekindled after several years' respite, Indira Gandhi herself became a victim. Was it dharma? A quick look at the chronology:

Toward the end of May, fighting erupted between Hindus and Muslims in the state of Madhya Pradesh. In the middle of May, heavy unrest was felt first in Bombay, continuing for some time. About 300 people died here and in other Maharasthra cities. Following the murder of a militant Hindu leader on June 24th, martial law was declared in Bombay.

January 1984 saw an intensification of the year-long conflict in Punjab between a small group of radical Sikhs and a large minority of Hindus 'representing' the central government. Dozens were killed in confrontations, hundreds injured. Akali radicals, under the leadership of Sant (= saint) Jarnail Singh Bhindranwale, barricaded themselves inside the Golden Temple in Amritsar. This holiest of Sikh symbols was turned into an armed fortress. About 100,000 militant Sikhs, over an 18-month period, took an oath vowing to fight to the death.

Faced with mounting violence, in mid-February the central government broke off negotiations for increased political freedom with moderate Sikhs. Heavily-armed police began to return sniper fire from the Golden Temple.

By the beginning of March at least 55 people had died, and many more were injured. Tens of thousands of soldiers were mobilized, a state of emergency declared, and press censorship and curfews instituted. Roads were closed to traffic. Mrs. Gandhi's central government assumed direct control of the state of Punjab, but couldn't get unrest under control. Fighting even spilled over to the neighboring state of Haryana with its Hindu majority.

On June 6, 1984, in an operation code-named "Blue Star", the Indian army stormed the Golden Temple. Bhindranwale was killed. By this time about 300 people had died. During the following week, a large portion of Sikh soldiers in the Indian army mutinied. Loyal government troops put down the uprising after hard fighting. Altogether, about 2,500 people were dead.

In London a Sikh government in exile was formed. On 23rd June, Indira Gandhi visited the Golden Temple and spoke to Sikh leaders; but the state of emergency continued.

On 5th July 1984, more than 10 radical Sikhs skyjacked an airliner en route from Srinagar Delhi to Lahore, Pakistan. They demanded the release of compatriots in India arrested upon the storming of the Golden Temple, and $25 million. The Indian Government refused to meet these demands. The skyjackers surrendered a day later.

Attempts to negotiate just Sikh demands for religious freedom were torpedoed in part by a campaign of political assassination, with radical Sikhs killing moderate Sikhs. Unrest surfaced too in Kashmir, where there's a strong Muslim minority in Hyder-abad. And in Tamil Nadu, Tamil solidarity for freedom fighters in Sri Lanka proved explosive.

On 31 October, Mrs. Gandhi walked to work through her garden, just after 09:00 h, as she did every morning. She offered her bodyguard of ten years, Beant Singh, the namastè greeting. He and his colleague, Satwant, riddled her with bullets.

Indira Gandhi's death was announced at 13:45 h. In Delhi and other cities in the north, her death marked the start of several days of savage Hindu revenge against Sikhs and their property.

By 18:00 h on the day of his mother's death, Rajiv Gandhi, who hurried back from a campaign trip through West Bengal, was named by the Congress Party to succeed his mother, and sworn in by India's President (another Sikh) as Prime Minister. At mid-night, he went on national television to ask his countrymen to stop fighting and "put an end to insanity", without success.

The bloodshed continued as Mrs. Gandhi was cremated on Nov-ember 3rd by the Jamuna River. Not until her ashes were cere-monially received on November 5th, did tensions begin to ease. Rajiv had by then met with a delegation of Sikhs and with Paki-stan President Zia-ul-Huq. The determination shown by India's new Prime Minister impressed all ethnic groups. His nomination was confirmed by India's Parliament.

On 4 November Rajiv Gandhi formed a transition government and called for new lower house (Lok Sabha) elections between 24th and 27th December. He won an overwhelming majority.

On 24 July, 1985 Rajiv Gandhi signed with moderate Sikhs the Punjab Accord, conceding increased freedom for members of the Sikh faith. On 26 November, 1985 the Sikh political party, Akali Dal, won an absolute majority in Punjab elections.

Rajiv Gandhi's cabinet of 31 December, 1884 has remained largely unchanged until today (December 1986). India's future looks bright, even if conflict in the Punjab is not permanently put to rest. The situation has relaxed to the extent that the state of emergency could be lifted, and the region reopened to tourism.

# GOVERNMENT

The Federal Republic of India expanded beyond the borders of British-India to a size never before achieved by an Indian Em-pire. This concluded a long fight for independence under the leadership of the Indian National Congress (whose chairman was Mahatma Gandhi). Another important force, the Muslim League (led by M.A. Jinnah) demanded its own country of Pakistan which achieved independence on August 15, 1948, but remained a British dominion until 1950.

The Indian Constitution took effect on 26 January, 1950. The Congress Party under Jawaharlal Nehru was an easy victor in the first 1951 - 1952 elections.

**Country's Name:** Bharat Juktarashtra

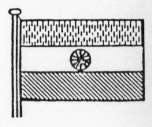

**Capital City:**     New Delhi (a section of Delhi)
**National Holiday:** Republic Day, 26 January
**Flag:**             Three stripes crosswise:  saffron yellow,  white
                      (with blue Ashoka wheel), and green

**Constitutional Structure:**  India is a parliamentary democracy with 22 states and 9 union territories.
**The President:** Head of state, enjoys a five-year term, and is elected by an electoral college composed of members of the national and state parliaments. The President can be re-elected any number of times. The President is Commander in Chief of the military, nominates state governors, high officials, and judges. He possesses emergency powers, has a veto against unwanted legislation, and can dissolve the lower house of parliament. He names the candidate of the most powerful lower house party to the office of Prime Minister.
**The Vice President:** Elected by members of the upper and lower houses of parliament, also serves as chairman of the upper house.
**Prime Minister:** Since November 1984 Rajiv Gandhi of the Congress Party. At the advice of the Prime Minister, the President nominates all members of the cabinet (who must be members of the upper or lower house of parliament).
**Lok Sabha:** The lower house of parliament, most powerful of the two houses, with 544 representatives elected by direct majority vote in electoral districts to terms of five years. 78 seats are reserved for Scheduled Castes (untouchables), and 38 seats for Scheduled Tribes. Three members are named by the President. All citizens over 21 years of age are eligible to vote.

At the moment, the Congress Party, with 401 seats, enjoys a stable two-thirds majority. The Janata Party

(= people's party) has dropped from a high of 298 seats to just 10. Otherwise the Moscow-oriented Communist Party of India has 6 seats, and the formerly Peking-oriented CPI (Marxist) has 22 seats in the Lok Sabha. The All India Dravida Munetra Kazhagam (12 seats) seeks autonomy for Tamil Nadu. Andhra Pradesh's regional party, Telugu Desam, under the leadership of movie star Rama Rao has garnered 28 mandates. All other parties have little national importance.

**Rajya Sabha:** The upper house of parliament. The 236 members are elected in one-third lots by the state parliaments every two years to terms of six years. The President names another eight members. The Congress Party with 153 members holds almost a two-thirds majority.

The central government has charge of foreign policy, foreign trade, taxes, currency, banking, the armed forces, transportation. The states handle education, health, agriculture, and police. State and national governments share responsibility for planning, social services, justice, industry, and trade. National law predominates over state law.

The Federal Republic of India consists of 22 states (including the occupied parts of Kashmir and Sikkim) and 9 union territories, which frequently coincide with principal language regions. State governors are appointed by the central government to a term of 5 years. Each governor nominates a prime minister, state ministers and other officials according to the advice of the state's prime minister.

**President's Rule:** If necessary, the central government can place state administration directly in the hands of the governor. Then new elections must be held within 6 months. These emergency laws were used frequently by Indira Gandhi to discipline state governments at odds with her central administration. They were used any time new elections seemed likely to increase the mandate of the ruling party. Over the long term, this tactic served to maintain a majority in the upper house (Rajya Sabha). Her son Rajiv, however, supports a policy of regional self determination, without putting Indian unity on the line.

This regionalization policy under strong central leadership has a good chance of preserving national unity. This can be seen in relaxation of tensions in Punjab, where radical Sikhs strive for independence or autonomy.

The union territories are administered by the central government. These include Goa, Daman & Diu, Pondicherry, Chandigarh, Delhi, Arunachal Pradesh, Mizoram, and the various islands.

A couple of curiosities deserve mention: Chandigarh serves at the same time as capital of the territory of the same name and as capital of the states of Punjab and Haryana. Jammu and Kashmir have two capitals: in the summer Srinagar, and in the winter Jammu Tawi. The states are divided into districts, with these further divided into towns and villages. In most states, the local Panchayat (village council) or Gram Sabha (village parliament) has control of education, health and building administration.

**The Court System:** Hierarchical with the High Court in Delhi ranking over state high courts, district courts, and at the lowest level magistrate courts, and village small-claims courts. The judicial system is based on English law.

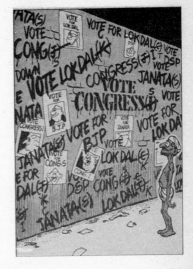

A constitutional amendment passed in 1977 legalized a military draft, but it has never been implemented. The standing army is one million strong, with airforce strength at 115,000, and a navy of 50,000. Additionally, there are about 280,000 paramilitary, including border guards. The military budget runs about 70 billion rupees annually (15.5 % of a national budget of 450 billion rupees).

India is a member of the British Commonwealth, the Colombo Plan, The United Nations (including its subordinate organizations), and a leader of the Bloc-free movement. Rajiv Gandhi has maintained the treaty of friendship with the Soviet Union, though he follows a much more neutral policy than his mother. He has continued relaxation of tensions with Pakistan. A Most Favored Nation trade agreement has been concluded with the European Common Market.

# A New Book Is Coming

Few corners of the earth are changing as fast as the Indian subcontinent. Even as you travel, we are hard at work writing a new edition. Write to us if a hotel we recommend has salted its prices. Let us know if we've missed something important. We take note of your comments, in fact many tips find their way into the next edition. And it is no coincidence that most travel book writers got their start by submitting readers' letters.

Writing is a lonely profession, even in this age of lap-top word processors. Make the dialogue two-way:

David Crawford
Peter Meyer, Barbara Rausch
India - Nepal - Sri Lanka
P.O. Box 110232
1000 Berlin 11
Germany

# ECONOMY

Despite great poverty - 50 % of India's population hungers on less than 2100 calories per day - India is the economic leader of southern Asia. In fact India is one of the world's top ten industrial nations. The gross national product runs at US$200 billion. Economic growth barely exceeds the birth rate. Per capita income is just 270.-US$ a year, and unlikely to rise in face of the population explosion. Still, unlike the Soviet Union or China, India is self-sufficient in agriculture. The primary crops are rice, wheat, millet, chickpeas, and lentils. Tales of catastrophic hunger in India belong largely to the past. But lack of hygiene, disastrous floods, and poor nutrition (white rice, or vegetables cooked too long), combined with inadequate medical service, leaves India a fertile ground for epidemics. Hunger too results from rural migration into the cities far beyond any economy's ability to provide new jobs. No job means no money to buy food. Infrastructural difficulties in food storage and distribution, plus inequities in income and land ownership intensify the suffering.

40 % of GNP is produced by 70 % of the population in agriculture, forestry, and fishery. Industry accounts for 28 % of GNP. Two-thirds of India's industry is state-owned. Half of the last third belongs to ethnic Parsees, including TATA, although Parsees make up just one thousandth of India's total population. Sikhs are also strong industrially. All domestic banks are stateowned.

**Child Labor:** Common, 12 million children torture through ten-hour workdays for just 50.-Rs a month.

**Trade Unions:** No national trade unions. India's 30,000 structurally weak, company-wide unions are loosely affiliated with other organizations of a similar political persuasion. All parliamentary attempts to reform the outdated tradeunion laws of 1926 (unions must ask the employer for recognition) have failed.

## RESOURCES & INDUSTRY

Despite major setbacks caused by the separation of India and Pakistan, whereby planting and processing of cotton and jute were torn apart, the textile industry remains paramount with centers in Ahmedabad, Madras, and Bombay.

Concentrated in Maharasthra are oil, chemical, pharmaceutical, car-making, and precision-manufacturing industries. Jute processing is big in Calcutta. India's high-tech capital is Bangalore.

British, Soviet and German aid have helped build heavy industry in the Singhbum region of Madhya Pradesh, Orissa, Bihar, and West Bengal where some of the world's largest iron reserves (ore exports) and coal are located.

**Mineral Resources:** Rich. India produces 73 % of its oil needs domestically. India possesses major reserves of manganese, bauxite, titanium, copper, lead, zinc, mica, and thorium. Large coal reserves combined with hydropower potential make India's energy outlook bright. Plus India has a number of nuclear power plants. 30 % of India's power (160 billion kW/h) is provided by three hydropower TATA facilities in the West Ghats near Bombay.

**Cooking Fuel Crisis:** Traditionally firewood, pushing India toward ecological catastrophe. India's forests have been reduced by half since 1940!

**High Technology:** Precision manufacturing, chemicals, car-making, atomic energy, and its space program give India the appearance of a threshold nation. But industrialization is pushing India toward ecological disaster. Two-thirds of India's water resources are polluted; half the arable land has been lost to erosion or chemical pollution.

## THE SPACE PROGRAM

India successfully launched a satellite on 18 July, 1980 using Indian-made rockets and electronics. Since then, a rocket has been launched every Wednesday at the Trivandrum rocket production center. The satellites are built in Bangalore, home of India's aircraft and electronics industry. The control center near Madras also performs international services, i.e. satellite monitoring and telecommunications. A control center for India's weather satellites (Insat I and II) has been set up in Hassan, near Bangalore.

India's space priorities are primarily peaceful: high-altitude research, weather studies, climate, water resources, mineral reserves, pest control, etc. The program budget (US$400 million over 20 years) might seem high until we remember that India loses US$200 to 300 million annually to weather damage, which could be partially prevented by good long-term forecasting. Additionally, India earns foreign exchange by marketing its space research abroad. After all, a rocket launch in India costs just a fraction of the investment required in developed countries.

## AGRICULTURE

About 44 % of India is used for agriculture. 37 % of agricultural land is given over to pasture and forest. Crop farming far outweighs livestock production. Grains and legumes predominate. In recent years, India has achieved agricultural self- sufficiency. But this says little about the quality or distribution of food.

The main crops are rice, wheat, millet, and barley; plus legumes such as chickpeas, pigeon peas, and lentils. About 12 million tons of oil-bearing seeds are harvested annually, including: peanuts, rapes, mustard, sesame, castor oil, and linseed. Potatoes are gaining importance. Cotton, jute, Bombay hemp, sugar cane, tobacco, coffee, tea, and spices once made India an important colony. Today these crops are India's primary exports, along with fish and other seafood (overfishing with new trawlers), leather and leather goods.

## FOREIGN TRADE

Agriculture produces two-thirds of India's export earnings. These include: tea (10 %), plant oils, spices, fruit, vegetables, and tobacco. Cotton and jute each provide another 10 % of export earnings. However, processed goods account for just 20 % of total exports!

The primary imports are machinery and electronics (almost 50 %). India faces a dilemma felt by most Third-World countries: its products on the world market bring decreasing income, while import prices increase. Foreign debt is relatively low at just 10 % of GNP.

The main trade partners are the USA (23 %), Japan, USSR, Great Britain, West Germany. The European Community meets 23 % of trade, while East Bloc countries combine for 17 %. The balance of trade remains steady at a slight deficit. Tourism has risen from 300,000 in 1971 to 1.4 million in 1985, bringing US$100 million in needed foreign exchange. You are a major economic factor. However, the increase has slowed in recent years. Inflation (today 10 %) has been declining in recent years.

# The Health System

India's health care is completely inadequate, although an enormous standard has been set in both ayurvedic (naturopath) medicine and in traditional western medicine. Only the rich (you included) can afford a doctor. India's 500,000 hospital beds are far too few, particularly as they're concentrated in urban areas. Patients' families are expected to assist the nurses by bringing food, washing the patient, looking after medication. 3,000 patients overwhelm each doctor; per dentist the figure is 90,000. Pharmacies play an important role in Indian medicine, even offering simple diagnostic advice.

The main goals of India's national health program are expansion of medical facilities, improvement in food and water supplies, better hygiene. Any successes are quickly overrun by increasing environmental pollution and the population explosion, doubled in 40 years since independence. Just one-fourth of all people of child-bearing age use birth control. And no wonder, children remain the only certain support for the aged. Birth-control devices and sterilization are free of charge. One friend of ours had himself sterilized while visiting India.

Malaria is endemic with 2 million new cases in 1982. Three million Indians suffer from leprosy. Cataracts afflict 20 million. India's physically handicapped number 60 million!

Should you need medical attention, ask your consulate for the name of a recommended doctor or dentist. They usually aren't expensive, and most speak English. Sample price: two fillings in New Delhi cost 80.-Rs.

## AYURVEDA

Hindu philosophy rejects the concept of surgical medicine, but has given birth to extremely effective naturopathic treatment. Ayurveda (= knowledge of life) is also frequently translated as the science of long life. This science of healthy living emphasizes keeping people healthy, and use of special remedies to return the sick to good health. Ayurveda is by no means just a science of drugs, herbs or minerals; it goes much further.

Like other forms of alternative medicine (homeopathy, acupuncture, or neural therapy), the doctor under ayurveda is called upon to view the patient as more than the chance victim of bacteria, viruses, chemical pollution, etc.: rather as a complete organism. Such factors as nutrition, age, workload, stress, drugs, and season of the year are taken into account. These factors not only provide (or dissuade) a fertile environment for bacteria, they also influence the psyche, which is seen as equally important in ayurvedic medicine!

India's 300,000 ayurvedic doctors try to recognize disturbances within this complex system of forces. Patient treatment goes beyond treating the symptoms, to bringing the patient back to healthy equilibrium.

## CONTACT ADDRESSES

**Vaidya C.G.Joshi**, 22 New Shukrawar Rd., Poona 2, Attn: Ayurveda and Yoga Courses; include a self-addressed stamped envelope or international postage reply coupons.

**Dr.P.J. Deshpande**, Dean, Faculty of Indian Medicine, Institute of Medical Sciences, B.H.U., Varanasi 221005; internship - only for qualified doctors.


# The Education System

According to the law, all children between the ages of six and fourteen are required to attend school, but limited financial and personal resources prevent compliance. Only 40 % of India's children attend school beyond the age of ten. Girls are hit especially hard: just 30 % of secondary school pupils are female! 500,000 schools employing 1.4 million teachers provide for 80 million pupils between the ages of 6 - 11.

Additionally, India's education system is handicapped by a tremendous social gulf between rich and poor, and a student body with hundreds of different languages. Grade school classes are held in the regional languages. At secondary level, classes are in English. In southern India Hindi is taught. In northern India, a southern Indian language is required. Since independence, literacy has risen only slightly to 35 %.

At colleges and universities, English is only slowly giving way to Hindi. The result is a language barrier preventing the rural population and lower classes from increasing their education. Just one-fourth of India's 3 million university students (composing 5 % of 17-23 year olds) is female.

Adult education concentrates on job training in practical areas, particularly agriculture, through schools and colleges. Correspondence courses via radio and television are being expanded. Over 300 schools offer computer training.

# Mass Media

### THE PRESS

Yes, there's masses of it. Radio and television are nationalized, hence subservient to official whim. This gives increased importance to the printed medium (which celebrated its 200th anniversary in 1980). In 1780, the Englishman Augustine Hicky founded in Calcutta the **Bengal Gazette**, a "weekly newspaper of politics and trade, open to all parties, but influenced by none".

Today the Indian press has an annual circulation of 51 million. Newspapers are published in 85 languages; 19,144 different publications are produced including 1256 daily papers, and 5624 weeklies. The largest readership is Hindi (4,200 publications, circulation 14 million annually), followed closely by English (3,000 publications, 11 million circulation). Most dailies are published in Maharasthra, followed by Uttar Pradesh, Delhi, West Bengal, and Tamil Nadu. 8 % of all publications deal with religious and philosophic matters. Literary and cultural periodicals account for 25 %.

Despite these high statistics, the press reaches only 40 % of the urban and just 7 % of rural population. Daily papers are read by just 2 % of India's population. Certainly India's low literacy rate plays a role: in the cities only 52 % can read, in the country just 25 %. Nationally, literacy is about 35 % (men 39.5 %; women 18.7 %). India's most literate state is Kerala (70 %) followed by Maharasthra (48 %).

The largest press agencies are PTI (Press Trust of India, owned by Reuters) and UNI (United News of India). Since 1978, they operate with satellite communications, exchanging info with multinationals AP, UPI, and AFP.

65 % of all newspapers controlling 30 % of circulation are owned by several influential families. 17.5 % of the publications (39 % of circulation) are owned by corporations. Just 3.4 % of the publications are government owned. Political party newspapers, with a circulation of just 280,000 (0.7 %), have little influence. Newsstand prices are government regulated.

The major English-language newspapers are **India Express** (550,000 circulation in the west and south), and **The Times Of India** (600,000 circulation, mostly in the west). The latter (India's largest press organization) also controls a number of weekly papers, magazines, and trade publications. The **Statesman** predominates in the major cities. **The Hindustan Times** is big in northern India; **The Hindu** does well in the south.

**India Today** is a fortnightly magazine emphasizing domestic news. **Illustrated Weekly Of India** presents a **Life Magazine** style.

**Destination: India** is a tourist-oriented geographical magazine featuring good photography with extensive coverage of India.

In the major cities, the usual foreign magazines, **Asia Week**, **Newsweek**, and **Time**, are available.

Since lifting of the state of emergency imposed under Indira Gandhi (1975-1977), press censorship has ended, but not government influence: through distribution of rationed newsprint and in the purchase of advertisement space.

## TV & RADIO

Private radio clubs in Calcutta, Bombay, and Madras provided India's first programming using tiny transmitters. In 1927, the privately-owned Indian Broadcasting Company Ltd. took to the air, but was forced to close after just three years. With only 7000 radios in all of India, the audience was lacking. Only when the BBC began short-wave service did the number of receivers begin to rise. A former BBC man, Lionel Fieldman, turned a till-then (1936) unimportant ISBS (Indian State Broadcasting Service) into **All India Radio**. During WWII, programming and frequencies were expanded in response to Nazi short-wave propaganda.

Even so, after the war, just 250,000 radio receivers were served by six stations. Today India has 90 AM stations, employing 12,000 people, transmitting in 24 languages and 36 dialects. Indian radio has broadcast overseas since 1939 in eight Indian and 17 foreign languages. Domestic programming covers 78 % of India geographically, reaching 90 % of the population.

Vividh Bharati (an entertainment program) began transmission on medium wave (AM) and short wave in 1959 to compete with commercial Radio Ceylon, with little success. The formula is 60 % show music and 20 % classical or regional folk music. News and reporting remain secondary.

If you'd like to catch Indian short-wave broadcasting at home, consult **World Radio TV Handbook** (revised annually) with times, frequencies, addresses, and languages of all the world's radio and television stations. India's short-wave service, AIR, broadcasts daily in English on the 25 m and 31 m wave bands. It's a great way to get ready for your trip, or keep in touch upon return.

# TRAVEL TIPS

In this chapter you'll find information which everyone needs for
travel in India. Be sure to read
this section long before you reach
the subcontinent, to avoid any un-
pleasant surprises. Note when applications can be filed, and the
processing time required for visa
applications, money transfers, mail,
etc.

## Visa

**Entry & Exit:** People from Commonwealth countries (except Pakistan) and the Irish can visit
India for 90 days without a visa.
Your passport must be valid for at
least six months beyond the planned length of your trip. When
entering without a visa, you receive a landing permit of 30 days
at the airport. But not when coming overland! This landing
permit is issued only once in a six-month period, and only if
you haven't visited India within the last six months!

The landing permit also serves as a temporary visa for Nepal,
for visits to Lumbinis (Terai) via Natanwa or Naugarh, but only
if you leave within 48 hours! The landing permit is free of
charge.

Coming overland from Europe, your last chance to pick up a
visa for India is in Islamabad, Pakistan, if you want to stay
longer than 30 days.

**Immunizations:** There are no immunization requirements any more,
but you would be foolish to do without immunizations for cholera,
polio, typhoid, paratyphoid, tetanus, and malaria pills. See
Health.

**Customs:** You can import any articles for person use. Anything
beyond the everyday, or of value, will be listed in your passport. This applies particularly to small electrical instruments:
all must be listed in the Tourist Baggage Re-Export Form. This
applies to anything beyond a camera with 25 rolls of film and a
watch. Anything else you might want to sell or trade in India
will have to be smuggled in.

You can export that which you brought in, plus any souvenir (even an expensive one), as long as it isn't 100 years old. Antiques require a special export license from the Deputy Director General of the Archaeological Survey of India, Janpath, New Delhi. Or the Director of the Prince of Wales Museum in Bombay-Fort. Gold can only be exported up to a value of 10,000.-Rs.

**Income Tax:** If you stay for more than 90 days, you must fill out an Income Tax Clearance Certificate before departing India. Be sure to save all your money exchange receipts so you can prove that you were spending money you brought with you. Otherwise you must pay tax on any money you earned in India. Particularly save receipts for money transferred,

telexed, or telegraphed from home!
**Visa Extension:** To extend your visa, apply at the Foreigners' Regional Registration Office in your nearest provincial capital. In major cities, officials are generally less friendly than in the smaller towns. An extension for longer than a month is difficult to get. You are best off applying for a 3 or 6 month visa before leaving for India (see above). Should you make an excursion to Nepal or Sri Lanka, you can get (non-Commonwealth citizens: apply for) a new 3 month visa. Sometimes you'll only get a visa for one month. Often the export regulations ordered by the central government are unknown (or misinterpreted) by provincial officials. Be prepared for surprises. Always plan a couple days before expiration of your visa to deal with bureaucratic twists.

# Special Permits

**Special Permits:** Along India's northern border are regions where tourists require a travel permit from an Indian consulate, Ministry of Home Affairs in Delhi, or a Foreign Registration Office. Sometimes, there are special regulations as to what one may or may not do in the region. In some restricted regions, a permit is granted only under exceptional circumstances, after several bureaucratic adventures.

Special permits are required to visit Darjeeling, Sikkim, Andaman Islands, Nicobar Islands, and major sections of the north-east including Assam and Meghalaya. Other restricted areas include regions east of Darjeeling: Manipur, Nagaland, Arunachal Pradesh, and the nominally independent country of Bhutan.

A second closed region is located north and east of a demarcation line running sometimes just 1 km from the Srinagar - Leh Road and the Leh - Manali Road (closed to public transport). Careful!

For exact info on how and where to apply for permits, see local sections. Applications frequently take 6 weeks for processing.

### INDIAN CONSULATES ABROAD
**Australia:** 92 Mugga Way, Red Hill, ACT 2603, tel.295 0045.
**UK:** India House, Aldwych, London, WC2B 4NA, tel.836 8484.
**UN:** 3 East 64th St., New York, NY, 10021.
**USA:** 2107 Massachusetts Ave. NW, Washington DC, tel.265 5050.

**Austria:** Operringhof 17, 1010 Vienna, tel.651 86660.
**Switzerland:** Weltpoststr. 17, 3015 Bern, tel.440193.
**W. Germany:** Adenauerallee 262-4, 5300 Bonn 1, tel.8817067.

**Burma:** 545-7 Merchant St., Rangoon, tel.16381.
**Malaysia:** Asian Bank Building, 19 Malacca St., KL, tel.21728.
**Nepal:** Lainchaur, Kathmandu, tel.11300.
**Singapore:** 31 Grange Rd., tel.737 6809.
**Sri Lanka:** 3rd Floor, State Bank of India Building, 18-3/1 Sir Baron Jayatilaka Mawatha, Colombo 1, tel.21604.
**Thailand:** 139 Pan Lane, Bangkok, tel.35065.

### FOREIGN EMBASSIES IN INDIA
**Australia:** 1/50G Shantipath, Chanakyapuri, New Delhi, tel.690336.
**Canada:** 7/8 Shantipath, Chanakyapuri, New Delhi, tel.619461.
**UK:** Shantipath, Chanakyapuri, New Delhi, tel.690371.
**USA:** Shantipath, Chanakyapuri, New Delhi, tel.690351.

**Austria:** EP 13 Chandragupta Marg, Chanakyapuri, New Delhi 21, tel.601112.
**Denmark:** 2 Golf Links, New Delhi, tel.618354.
**Finland:** 4 Golf Links, New Delhi, tel.611547.
**Ireland:** 13 Jor Bagh, New Delhi, tel.617435.
**The Netherlands:** 6/50F Shantipath, Chanakyapuri, New Delhi, tel.699271.
**Norway:** Kautilya Marg, Chanakyapuri, New Delhi, tel.615982.
**Sweden:** Nyaya Marg, Chanakyapuri, New Delhi, tel.694225.
**USSR:** Shantipath, Chanakyapuri, New Delhi, tel.615708.
**W. Germany:** 6/50 G Shantipath, Chanakyapuri, New Delhi, tel.604861.

**Bangladesh:** 56 Mahatma Gandhi Road, Lajpat Nagar III, New Delhi, tel.615668, open Mon–Fri 10:00–12:00 h, visa 100–200.-Rs (depending on nationality), 2 passport photos, one day wait.
**Bhutan:** Chandra Gupta Marg, Chanakyapuri, New Delhi, tel.699227.
**Burma:** 3/50-F Nyaya Marg, Chanakyapuri, New Delhi, tel.600251.
**People's Republic Of China:** 50D Shantipath, Chanakyapuri, New Delhi, tel.600328.
**Indonesia:** 50A Chanakyapuri, New Delhi, tel.692392.
**Iran:** 65 Golf Links, New Delhi, tel.699521, visa takes 5–6 weeks (faster in Islamabad, Pakistan: only 2 days).
**Japan:** 4/50G Chanakyapuri, New Delhi, tel.694271.
**Nepal:** Barakhamba Road, New Delhi, tel.381484, open Mon–Sat 9:00–13:00 h, (near Connaught Place), Nepal visa costs US$10.-, 2 passport pictures required.
**Pakistan:** Shantipath, Chanakyapuri, New Delhi, tel.699271.
**Singapore:** 48 Golf Links, New Delhi, tel.618139.
**Sri Lanka:** 27 Kautilya Marg, Chanakyapuri, New Delhi, tel.370201, Mon–Fri 09:00–13:00 h, but the three-month visa is only given out in Madras!
**Thailand:** 56 Nyaya Marg, Chanakyapuri, New Delhi, tel.615985.

# Cultural Institutes

Anyone who's been on the road for several months knows about cultural deprivation. In major cities and tourist areas, pancakes, french toast, and scrambled eggs await you. But if you just want to relax, read a western newspaper, browse through an English-language library, or perhaps see a play, then check out the cultural centres. In many cities you'll find a British Council Library, an American Institute, a French Cultural Centre, or a German Max-Mueller-Bhavan. You'll find the addresses in the local chapters of Bangalore, Bombay, Calcutta, Hyderabad, Madras, New Delhi, and Poona.

# Information Offices

In most western countries, information offices have been set up to help tourists plan their trip to India. In India itself, you'll find Tourist Offices run by both the Indian Tourism Development Corporation (ITDC) and the individual states, e.g. the Tamil Nadu Tourism Development Corporation (TNTDC). Unfortunately these offices compete more than they cooperate, often throwing away money on superficial materials and poorly-trained, unmotivated employees. Still, a visit can be advisable when you don't know where else to ask. And if the employees are unable to help you, there is a possibility of meeting another traveller who has resolved your problem for herself. Most competent are the offices in Delhi and Bombay. You'll find the Tourist Office addresses in India, along with other sources of info under TIPS at the end of each local chapter.

# Indian Bureaucracy

If you get annoyed by unnecessary bureaucracy, expect a shock. If you've read our piece on the Indian rail service, you know what's in store. It's the same at the post office, hospital, bank, policestation, when extending a visa, crossing a border - everywhere. Be sure you have lots of patience, and fill out the proper forms. If even that doesn't work, demand to see the next higher official, the boss or the manager. When you get to him, be sure to emphasize your personal difficulties, while at the  same time flattering him with how important this institution is, all the wonderful things it can do, how much faith you have in him - after all, he is certainly the most competent person here. Be patient, even if it takes hours! If he doesn't handle your problem immediately, sit tight and wait. Doing nothing but waiting works wonders in India, much to the surprise of most western visitors. Anyone who flips out, screams, or makes a fool of themselves, is just seen as being sick. Only if demanding the complaint book (which nobody may refuse) fails, the last resort, should you consider making noise. But there is no guarantee that a flipped-out crazy will be considered worthy of aid.

Small gifts can work wonders if they aren't seen to be pushy. Perhaps at the end of the first fruitless negotiation, you could forget your pen or lighter before continuing the conversation half an hour later. Then with the same peaceful demeanour, and no mention of what you forgot, begin the conversation anew. A personal picture can work wonders. Careful, many officials are very sensitive against attempted bribes with money! Ask fellow

travellers for info on the officials before you deal with them.
And when visiting an office bring your passport, several passport
pictures, a pen, and something to read. Forget the time; it'll
pass eventually...

# Calendar & Time Differences

Indian Standard Time is 5 hours and 30 minutes ahead of Greenwich Mean Time (GMT) or 10 hours and 30 minutes ahead of Eastern Standard Time (EST).

India uses the western Gregorian calendar, just as we do, but
some holidays are based on the traditional moon calendar (as is
Easter). For exact dates of these holidays and festivals check
with the Indian tourist offices.

**OPEN - CLOSED**
**Banks:** Generally open Mon-Fri 10:00-14:00 h, Sat 10:00-12:00 h,
no break. You can often exchange small amounts of money in
luxury hotels.
**Offices:** Governmental and private, open Mon-Fri 10:00-16:00 h (or
17:00 h), closed for lunch 13:00-14:00 h, closed Sat & Sun.
**Consulates:** Usually open Mon-Fri just till 12:00 h, sometimes open
Sat, closed on national holidays.
**Shops:** Open Mon-Sat 09:00 h (10:00 h) till 19:00 h (20:00 h). Bazars often stay open till 21:00 h. Sometimes closed for lunch from
13:00-15:00 h (16:00 h). In rural regions only the lunch hour is
fixed.

# Money

India's monetary unit is the Indian rupee, **Rs**; one rupee contains 100 paise, **P**. All prices in the India section are in Indian
rupees unless otherwise specified.

**COINS**
Denominated in 1, 2, 3, 5, 10, 20, 25, and 50 paise. The value
is conveniently displayed in arabic numerals (same as ours!).
Paise coins are rare; so don't be surprised if you receive too
little change, or instead candy or stamps, or ridiculously hear
"No change!".

**PAPER MONEY**
Denominated in 1, 2, 5, 10, 20, 50, 100, and 500 rupees. Be sure
you receive Indian rupees: everything else is worth less. Refuse
any old, torn, or dirty bills; you'll never get rid of them. For
some strange reason they have no value in everyday exchange.
That's why shopkeepers, recognizing you as new, will pawn them
off on you. As a foreigner, all you can do is exchange these
bills at a bank. And that is only possible at the State Bank of

India (but not every branch!). Even there it takes hours. Particularly bad are weekends; it's impossible to change money, and if all you've got are dirty 100.-Rs notes...

## CURRENCY IMPORTS
The import of hard currency in cash or traveller's checks is unrestricted. If you bring more than US$1000.-, you're required to fill out a currency declaration form. The import of Pakistani, Nepalese, or Sri Lankan currency is prohibited. Indian rupees can only be imported in the form of checks, obtainable at major banks and from overseas branches of the State Bank of India.

## BLACK MARKET
On the black market in cities like Bombay, you can receive 2.-Rs more per US$, than that offered officially in banks, hotels, and some shops. But the better the exchange rate for you, the more likely you'll simply be ripped off!

Remember too that changing on the black market does great damage to your host country; you're putting your money in the hands of economic criminals. Ask yourself whether the small gain you make in exchange rate is really worth it. An important development project in a needy region shouldn't be held up because the necessary foreign exchange has been siphoned off for the import of luxury goods.

## EXCHANGE RATES
    1US$ = 14.00 Rs
    AUS$1.- = 10.04 Rs
    UK£1.- = 22.95 Rs
    Nepal 1.-Rs = 0.59 Rs
    SL 1.-Rs = 0.49 Rs

Exchange rates for cash are slightly less than those for checks. The rupee floats against all western currencies: expect fluctuations! When the dollar falls, European currencies are worth more here and vice versa. You might want to take half your travel funds in US$, and the other half in DM or Swiss Francs.

Save your currency exchange receipts. You need them for your income tax clearance should you stay over three months. Every time you change money, you have to present a passport.

The best exchange rates are offered by the State Bank of India, sometimes the Overseas Bank, American Express, Indian Bank, or Bank of Baroda. Exchange rates can vary by up to 10 % between banks; keep your eyes open!

On weekends you can change money at the international airports, and in expensive hotels.

## MONEY TRANSFERS
Fast and reliable are telegraphic transfers to branch offices of Bank of Baroda in the major cities, and other commercial banks.

If you need cash in a hurry, you can get a telegraphic transfer within three days via a Thomas Cook Travel Agency. But it costs between US$20.- and US$70.-, depending on the amount.

It's best to transfer money through one of the major commercial banks with branch offices both in India and your own country. Ask at your bank before you go, just in case!

A telegraphic transfer usually takes less than 14 days. Have your home bank telegraph: Pay to (Mr. Mrs. Ms.) Jolly Traveller, Passport number (GB) Y12345678, the sum of US$1000.-, payable in US$. Sometimes you might still be paid in Indian rupees, or in traveller's checks.

## WAGES & PRICES

Industrial workers earn 600.-Rs to 800.-Rs a month; farm workers bring home just 200.-Rs per month. The maximum wage for government officials seldom reaches 3000.-Rs per month; no wonder corruption abounds.

High unemployment, without unemployment compensation or welfare, forces many to work for 50.-Rs a month plus board, or as a serf or bondsman for just room and board.

Compared to wages, prices are atrocious: 1 kg rice costs 2.-Rs, an egg 1.-Rs, 1 l coconut oil 15.-Rs, 1 kg sugar 6.-Rs, 100 g chillies 1.-Rs, 1 kg tea 20.-Rs. The cheapest sari is 50.-Rs, a cheap lungi 30.-Rs, 1 m shirt or blouse cloth 5.-Rs, 10 km by bus 1.-Rs.

Or look at it this way: the best paid industrial workers in India work one hour to pay for 1 kg rice. In Europe the average worker gets 10 kg rice for an hour's pay. For a kilo of tea, an Indian worker puts in a whole day of sweat; in Europe, less than an hour. Remember the price of your plane ticket (return) is about a year's wage in India. One night in a hotel with dinner costs what your waiter earns in a month! Never forget this when bargaining, giving tips, and donations.

# Mail

## LETTERS HOME

1986 prices: postcards 2.75 Rs, aerogramme 3.75 Rs (it's illegal to put anything inside the forms!), available at the post office. Letters, according to weight cost at least 4.75 Rs. Have them weighed at one counter, then buy stamps at the stamp counter, and have them cancelled at the cancellation counter. Don't just turn in the letters, or throw them in a mailbox. Post office employees often tear off uncancelled stamps for resale; your letter lands in the trash! Registered letters cost 3.25 Rs extra.

## PARCELS & SEAMAIL
Parcels mailed overseas can weigh up to 20 kg and be valued up
to 1000.-Rs.  Costs:  1 kg 61.-Rs,  3 kg 81.-Rs,  5 kg 109.-Rs,
10 kg 154.-Rs,  15 kg 203.-Rs, 20 kg 249.-Rs. Packages are shipped out just twice a month, and take two to three months.

Your parcel can be neatly packed in a fruit or wine case available for just 1.-Rs at any dealer.
A metal box,  costing 15.- to 30.-Rs
is good if you have to carry the
stuff quite a ways,  or if you want
to chain it shut a while (e.g.  on
the train).  Every package has to
be sewn shut in cloth,  otherwise it
won't even be accepted.  A tailor
will do it cheap,  or just sew it
yourself.  Be sure to use as short a
string as possible, then the official
sealing isn't as expensive. A scribe
will charge you 0.20 Rs per seal.
With a waterproof pen you can address the package.  Frequently you
will find parcel sewers sitting in
front of post offices,  or a Parcel
Packing Service nearby.
Only if the package has been officially sealed can it be
insured,  which costs 1.-Rs for every 100.-Rs of insurance.  An
engraver will make you your own personal seal for just 5.- to
10.-Rs!
At the counter,  pick up the three customs declaration forms
and the international parcel card;  fill them out including contents and value.  Always check the spot marked gift (cadeau),
and on the back fill in a second name and address in case the
first addressee isn't found.  Otherwise the package might be sent
back to India,  after you're gone.  A parcel can be up to 1 m
long,  with total length and width together up to 180 cm maximum.
You're best off having your things packed by the shop where
they're purchased.  Anything else you can have packed.  We've
never had any problems,  and it costs 20.- to 40.-Rs depending
upon size.
One package we sent from Bombay took 6 months getting to
Europe,  another sent from Madras took just 2 months.  Pack
everything carefully,  and fill in any empty spaces so that
nothing breaks even should the case be squashed.  One of our
metal cases arrived in Europe in tatters.

## AIRMAIL PARCELS
The first 250 g costs 67.-Rs,  each additional 250 g adds 14.-Rs,
maximum 10 kg; takes about one week.

**BOOKPOST**
A cheap way to send books and maps if no handwritten notes or
messages are added; other printed material including brochures
and postcards is also prohibited: 1 kg 20.-Rs, 2 kg 30.-Rs, each
additional kilogram 10.-Rs, maximum 5 kg, not to be sewn!

**RECEIVING MAIL**
When having mail sent to you on the road **Poste Restante** (general
delivery), mail is usually sorted alphabetically according to the
first letter of your family name. You will have to sort through
the pile yourself. Registered mail is kept separately; they'll give
you a pile of slips to sift through. Emphasize to anyone writing
to you that they should make your family name easily
discernible:

> Mr. Jolly **MAILGETTER**
> POSTE RESTANTE
> GPO
> Name of City (town)
> Name of State
> INDIA

Better than poste restante is the address of some place you'll be
visiting, e.g. Tourist Office (under the address write "will be
collected") or American Express (below the address write "Client's
Mail". For a list of addresses visit any Amexco office. Non-customers have to pay US$1.-. A hotel where you've advance reser-
vations is also a good address.

**TELEPHONE**
For overseas calls, try to register a day or half-day in advance.
Good, immediate connections from the Overseas Communication
Centres in the major cities.
    Domestic calls, long distance, during business hours, are a
real catastrophe: poor connections, wrong numbers, can't get
through, or the conversation breaks off.

**TELEX**
When the phone system is this bad, consider sending a telex.
You'll find telex facilities in large hotels, travel agencies, at
airlines, and other large companies. One advantage: everything
is in writing.

# Electricity & Water

Indian current runs at 220 V and 50 Hz, but expect fluctuations,
and brown outs. In rural areas, there's often no electrical
system, but generators are available.
    Water generally flows, but certainly isn't healthy. Even in
cities, boil water at least 15 minutes before drinking.

# A Night's Rest

In this book we've restricted ourselves to listing low and medium-priced accommodations. Expensive hotels (starting at US$30.- are generally out of the question for globetrotters. Addresses and prices of expensive hotels are listed in information brochures at every tourist office. These brochures also mention "Indian Style Hotels" which do fit into the budget-traveller's range: 30.- to 80.-Rs per night. Also in this range: government-owned tourist bungalows.

From **(S)**10.- to **(D)**1000.-Rs per night, there's a bed for everyone. The cheapest addresses run **(D)**20.- to **(D)**40.-Rs (no breakfast), perhaps adequately clean, sometimes lovely.

If we mention a hotel in the next higher category (up to **(D)**100.-Rs), then it offers something extra: a lake, garden, peace and quiet, sensational service, or there's just nothing cheaper in the area, e.g. Bombay.

If you want to travel cheap, don't expect very much. Hotel descriptions are necessarily subjective, you might have a different opinion, according to mood (or the employees working that day).

**LODGING CODE**

| | |
|---|---|
| **(S)** | Single |
| **(D)** | Double |
| **(Tr)** | Triple |
| **(Dm)** | Dormatory |
| **(Eb)** | Extra Bed |

None of the managers in any of the lodgings mentioned knew who we were, or that we write travel guides. We were treated just like any other traveller; nobody was especially friendly to us.

We rarely mention private lodgings to avoid masses of people storming one or two beds in a small household. A super tip, if mentioned here, would be exactly the opposite within two months of the publication date. And we don't mention individual lodgings where it's simple to find a room: e.g. by the beach at Goa. The situation changes so quickly, you're best off asking one of the hundreds of fellow travellers you stumble over for the latest info.

At private lodgings, your rickshaw driver, taxi driver and other touts get a hefty commission, which you pay for, often without knowing. You're in a much better bargaining position if you arrive alone!

Please don't be angry if things are different when you arrive. Everything changes quickly in India, and we can't be everywhere, even if we're busy revising the next edition. So write and tell us what's changed, where you stayed, what you paid, your likes and dislikes. The next edition will blossom with your thoughts.

**Youth Hostels:** The Indian government has established a number of youth hostels offering a night's rest for **(Dm)**6.- to **(Dm)**8.-Rs.

Each hostel has three 6-bed rooms. Two single rooms are available for group leaders. Common toilets and showers are segregated for men and women.

You can eat in the hostels; shopping is generally convenient. A kitchen equipped with utensils lets you do your own cooking. Most hostels have a dining room, library, and terrace. Sports and cultural events are frequently organized.

## HOSTELS

**Amritsar** Youth Hostel, Mal Mandi, G.T. Road.
**Aurangabad** Youth Hostel, Aurangabad, Maharasthra.
**Bhopal** Youth Hostel, North T.T. Nagar, Bhopal, M.P.
**Dalhousie** Youth Hostel, Dalhousie, Himachal Pradesh.
**Darjeeling** Youth Hostel, 16 Dr. Zakir Hussain Rd., Darjeeling.
**Gandhinagar** Youth Hostel, Sector 16, Gandhinagar, Gujarat.
**Hyderabad** Youth Hostel, Hyderabad, Andhra Pradesh.
**Jaipur** Youth Hostel, S.M.S Stadium, Jaipur, Rajasthan.
**Madras** Youth Hostel, Indira Nagar, Madras, Tamil Nadu.
**Nainital** Youth Hostel, Mallitan, near Ardwell Camp, The Mall, Nainital.
**Panchkula** Youth Hostel, Haryana Tourist Complex, Panchkula, Distt. Ambala, Haryana.
**Patni Top** Youth Hostel, C/O Tourist Office Kud, Jammu & Kashmir.
**Panji** Youth Hostel, Goa-Daman-Diu, Goa.
**Puri** Youth Hostel, Chakratirath Rd., Puri (Orissa).
**Trivandrum** Youth Hostel, Trivandrum (Kerala).
**Wishwa Yubak Kendra**, 5 Nyaya Marg, Chankyapuri, New Delhi-110021; the National Secretary has its office in the Delhi Youth Hostel, where you can pick up an event program.

# Food

During my travels in India, I've become a real fan of Indian food. It's impossible for me to understand stiff-necked individuals who maintain there's no decent food in India.

The basic Indian foods, which you'll find in the most isolated villages, include rice (pullao = boiled rice), dhal (= mashed lentils), vegetables, and chapati. There are countless sorts of rice in India, and each has its own name. Rice is usually cooked with saffron, lending a yellow color.

**Chapati:** A flatbread made of corn, wheat, or other flour, mixed with water. Flat bread is cooked on a round plate over a fire, and must be flipped several times. Similar types of bread are puris, paratha, and nan.
**Puris:** Made of flour, salt and water; unlike chapati, **ghee** (= melted butter) is added; the batter is rolled thin and baked floating in oil, causing the puris to puff out.
**Paratha:** Made of cornmeal, water and ghee, formed into flatbread

and fried; you'll find them with every imaginable filling.

**Nan:** A yeast-batter bread, particularly popular in Muslim regions.

**Curry:** With rice, thousands of recipes! There are vegetable curries, meat, fish, and egg curries. And don't confuse real curry with that powder seen in the west. Curry can contain an infinite variety of spice mixtures, combined in a sauce. Every household has its own recipe for curry, combining up to 300 types of herbs and grains.

## SNACKS

**Pakora:** Try egg pakora (eggs rolled in batter and fried), countless vegetable varieties (our favorite).

**Samosa:** Vegetable, usually potato (in India, potatoes are definitely vegetables), stuffed in batter, and fried in oil.

**Dosas:** Crispy baked rolls, filled with vegetable, sometimes 50 cm long!

**Halwa:** Colorful, small, rectangular sweets, filled with nuts, sometimes covered with a thin film of edible silver.

**Gulabs:** Dark-brown balls, made of curds, sugar, and a touch of flour.

**Berfis:** Made of coconut, almonds, and pistachio.

**BEWARE:** All sweet snacks are super sweet.

And fruit comes in ample variety: bananas, oranges, pineapple, papaya, kiwi, mango, etc. Skinned fruit preferable (more hygienic!).

Every region of India has its own specialities. All the way from north to south India, you'll be delighted by new treats. I can still remember my surprise ordering breakfast in a southern Indian railway station. The waiter brought **Iddlis** (steaming, flat rice cakes) spiced with linseed vegetable and fresh chutney.

And how about the first lunch in a restaurant catering just to Indians: We were presented with a banana leaf, washed in water; then someone brought rice; and another appeared with a bucket full of various types of vegetable curry. With ceremonious flourish, a spoonful of each curry was placed on the banana leaf, with the rice. Everyone could have as many servings as they liked. After the meal the banana leaf lands in a pail for the livestock: ecologically sound disposable plates! There wasn't any silverware.

**Right Hand:** I now understand Indians who say, "Food tastes best when eaten with the fingers!" Of course, they mean the fingers of the right hand. Traditionally, the left hand is used to clean after using the toilet! The left hand is therefore considered unclean. Unless you want to insult people or make a fool of yourself, treat it as such. Never offer anyone your left hand! The art of eating isn't just getting the food into one's mouth (try to do it the Indian way, without swallowing your fingers), it's the

mixing of hot and less spicy curries. Super hot curry can be
toned down a notch with coconut and hot tea. A curry lunch can
cost 2-3.-Rs; sometimes just 1.-Rs.

Indian food is very spicy, keeping stomach acids at full
march, an important defence against food poisoning when sanitary
conditions aren't the greatest. Lots of salt is important, holding
water is vital in a hot, sweaty environment.

**Drink**: At meals you drink water or **chai** (= tea). But be sure
your water is boiled for 15 minutes. Popular drinks are chai
(-.50 Rs to 1.-Rs), coffee (rare), coconut milk (cheapest), **lassi**
(yoghurt thinned with milk or water), cola, and if you came to
India just for a cold one: beer (prohibition has been lifted in
several states in conjunction with price increases). For those into
hard liquor, there's **fenny** and **toddy** (from palm juice), **arrak**
(distilled from rice or palm juice). Soda water is sold in some
regions, a 200 cl bottle runs to 1.-Rs to 2.-Rs.

And one last word. Most people assume Indian food is strictly
vegetarian. But vegetarianism is an individual decision. Actually
there are numerous meat specialities. But each religious community has its own list of meat from which it abstains: Hindus
won't eat beef, Muslims avoid pork, Jains are strict vegetarian.·

If you are into meat, then stick to the better restaurants,
which take hygiene seriously, or you'll quickly lose your carni-
vorous instincts. But note, the meal we remember with horror was
in an expensive, European-style restaurant. Along the coast,
enjoy seafood: squid, crabs, shrimp, and fish.

Bon Appétit! My mouth is watering all over the word processor.

# The Travel Adventure

You can travel by air, rail, bus, or with your own wheels. We
prefer to patronize public transportation. It's a great way to
meet Indians and their bureaucracy.

**Women**: Travelling alone is usually no problem if you maintain a
strong composure. Only in Muslim regions might it seem advisable
(in the first few weeks) to stick with a partner.

**Thieves**: Keep a wary eye on all your things. Take special care
with your money, passport, immunization card, return ticket, etc.
We can't say it enough! A robbery makes any trip a bad trip.
Thieves thrive in trains, buses, anywhere people mass, e.g.
freak hang-outs: beaches, dorms, pubs... northern India (Kashmir and Varanasi) is worst.

**Local Buses**: At bus stands, Indians queue, just like in England.
You'll be amazed how often they manage to form a queue. But
this ordered environment dissolves into chaos the second a
crowded bus comes into view. Anyone new to India is sure to see
their rightful seat disappear without them. But learning from
your neighbors has a great tradition; you'll learn. Rule one:
don't panic, even if the running board of a doorless bus is
packed to the hilt. Running board riding is no shame! Remember,

there's always room for one more!  But you do need presence of
mind,  and an ability to remain calm,  even if you're accidentally
jabbed in the ribs or when someone steps on your foot.  Such are
the joys of bus riding.  With luck,  there might even be a seat.
In southern India,  buses have male and female sides,  sit accordingly.  Tickets are sold on board,  the conductor is usually found
near the door.  Buses swim with pickpockets,  beware!

**Overland Buses**:  Certainly preferable to an Indian train if the
ride isn't too long,  and doesn't last overnight.  Nobody sleeps
well on a bus.  One advantage:  a bus ticket guarantees a seat.
There's tremendous competition among bus companies.  Buses cost
1.-Rs per 10 km,  a touch more than the train.

At large bus stands,  it's difficult to determine the departure
point for your bus.  We once waited three hours at the wrong
spot.  Because it seemed strange,  we checked with Information at
least four times,  always receiving the same answer.  It took a
miracle and a change of personnel to find us the right spot.  At
such times, I trust in karma, and imagine a bus accident.

## TRAINS
Just the thought of procuring a ticket and seat reservation makes
me weak in the knees. So first the basics:

**2nd Class**:  Wood benches seat
four or more, a baggage rack,
and a refreshing fan.  Second-class sleeping cars offer
double-decker and triple-
decker beds.  In the double-
deckers,  lightly padded beds
are fixed above the regular
seating (where someone sits
not sleeping).  In triple-
decker,  somebody sleeps on
the seat.  All three levels are
unpadded.  Doubles and triples
cost the same,  but aren't always found in the same train.
On a few express trains,  e.g.
Pink City Express,  you can
book **2nd class ACCC** (Air Con-
ditioned Chair Car):  airplane-
style seating (or a European
Intercity);  nice,  but rare.
Costs 45.-Rs per 500 km,  plus
the struggle for a seat or
sleeping reservations.  ACCC-
class is twice as expensive.

**1st Class**:  Padded four-seat compartments.  Each seat comes complete with sleeping accommodations.  At night the compartments are
locked.  Sheets are available upon advance request.  AC 1st class
costs eight times the 2nd class rate.  For the same price, fly.

**Indrail Pass:**  Tourists are offered unlimited travel for a period of 7 to 90 days.

| Days | 1st Class | 2nd Class | AC 1st Class |
|------|-----------|-----------|--------------|
| 7    | US$80.-   | US$35.-   | US$160.-     |
| 15   | US$100.-  | US$45.-   | US$200.-     |
| 21   | US$120.-  | US$55.-   | US$240.-     |
| 30   | US$150.-  | US$65.-   | US$300.-     |
| 60   | US$225.-  | US$100.-  | US$450.-     |
| 90   | US$300.-  | US$130.-  | US$600.-     |

Children's discount:  50 %.  Period of validity begins with the first day of use (not day of purchase).

The Indrail Pass is sold only for hard currency (US$, SFr, DM, etc.) in Indian railway offices and large travel agencies. On the pass your name and passport number are printed, officially non-transferable.  The first date of validity is written in the up-per-right corner.  Often they forget at smaller stations so you have unlimited travel until you decide to reserve a seat.  Write the beginning date yourself with a dark pencil...  But calculate in advance whether the pass will actually save you money;  usu-ally it doesn't.  Of course you do save the hassle of buying tick-ets,  but not the struggle to reserve a seat,  even if you receive preferential treatment.  Each seat reservation is processed indivi-dually,  train number and date are printed on the back. Returned tickets are exchanged in Indian rupees.  Sometimes travellers under age 33 are offered the Indrail pass at a 25 % discount, check if the offer is presently in effect!

**Ticket Tribulations:**  There are separate ticket windows for 1st and 2nd class,  and for various types of trains.  First you have to decide which class;  second if you want a Mail, Express,  or just a Passenger (slow) train;  third if it's an **Up** or **Down** (dir-ection) train.  With this info in mind,  you might ask at the info counter which ticket window to use,  e.g.  where to queue. Check repeatedly to be sure you're in the right queue.

**Ladies Only:**  Women can take advantage of the Ladies Only Win-dow,  where you can also make reservations for male travel com-panions.  As a woman you can go to the front of the line if there isn't a Ladies Only window (at least try).

After 30 minutes or so,  when you finally get to the counter, the official will usually say you're in the wrong line. If you are in the right line, don't let yourself be put off; it'll cost another hour.  When you're certain you are at the proper window, ask for the ticket a second time,  perhaps even a third time more force-fully,  but don't lose your cool. If that doesn't work, demand the **Complaint Book.**  That should ensure you a ticket,  if you are truly at the proper window.  But don't forget to count your change, short changing has a long tradition.

**Seat Reservations:**  You don't have to reserve a seat.  But a re-served seat or bed can be a tremendous relief to uninitiated individuals with a European rail-passenger background.  After a

few days on board, you'll master the art of getting a seat without advance reservations. To reserve a bed, pick up a requisi-
tion form (at the info counter) and fill in your name, travel
date, route, train number & description, and your passport number. Your passport number signifies you as a tourist entitled to
preferential treatment under the Tourist Quota, even if everything's booked - ask specifically! If it's impossible to get a reservation aboard a specific train, have yourself placed on the
waiting list (which ostensibly doesn't exist). Be sure your reservation is confirmed on your ticket when you turn in the requisi-
tion form. A 2nd class seat reservation costs 2.-Rs (10.-Rs for a
bed). Seat reservations for Indrail Pass holders are free (even if
some ticket sellers try to make you pay!). Changing a reservation costs 10.-Rs (just forget the old reservation and make a new
one). Indrail Pass holders receive preferential treatment, even
without a reservation. The whole process takes 1-5 hours. You
might be wise to check with the station-master about his VIP
quota, or otherwise ask for aid. They are usually friendly, elderly, English-speaking men.

### MEDITATE!

In Delhi, you can pick up the **Railway Tourist Guide** in Baroda
House, near India Gate. There too, you can sometimes get a re-
servation for the same day (otherwise impossible). The guide is
also available in Bombay (Central Railway, Victoria Terminus or
Western Railway, Churchgate Station), Calcutta (Eastern Railway,
Fairlie Pl. or Central Reservations Office, South Eastern Railway,
Esplanada Mansions), and Madras Central Station.
    Reserve a seat early; foreigners can make reservations a year
in advance!

**All Aboard:** So you've got your ticket and reservation? Now keep
in mind that every town has at least two railway stations, e.g.
Delhi: New Delhi Railway Station, Delhi Junction (Old Delhi),
Hazrat Nizamuddin (south Delhi). Some stations have a name completely different from the town: Howrah for Calcutta, Mughal
Sarai in Varanasi. Ask specifically from which station your train
departs. At the originating station, trains usually depart on
time. Along the way, delays of several hours build up.
    To locate your reserved seat, find the car number on your
ticket. On the car (or on a chart at track side) is a list of
names with seat numbers. You might need a good imagination to
recognize your name (Karm instead of Mark). If it's impossible,
ask the conductor at track side; he has his own list. Here too
you can get on the waiting list if you haven't yet a reservation.
    If you don't have a reservation, a muscle-bound porter will
certainly have no problem finding you a seat, though that has
its price. Most globetrotters avoid such tactics, in favor of other
tricks. Women can find a spot in the **Ladies Only** section, recommended for women travelling alone; reserve a seat in advance, or

## MAP OF NORTHERN INDIA

## MAP OF NORTHEASTERN INDIA

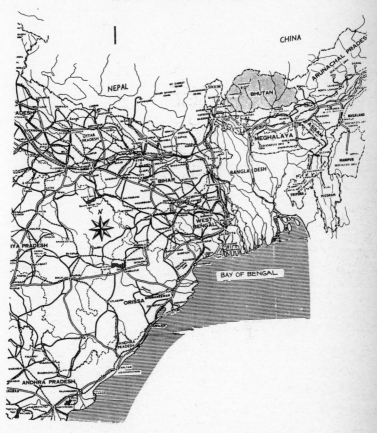

# MAP OF SOUTHERN INDIA

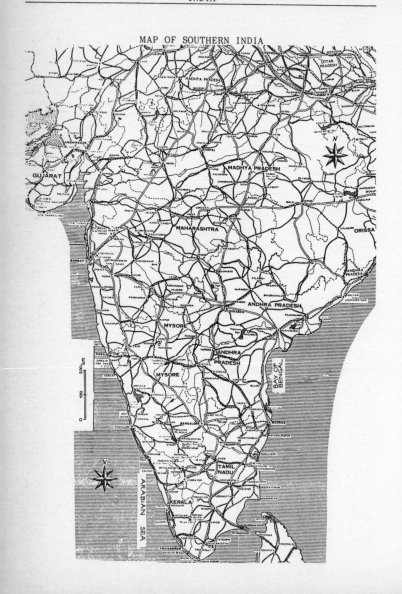

take a seat immediately upon boarding.

If every seat is hopelessly occupied, cast an eye to the baggage rack; nobody up there? Then quick with your luggage and you on its heels. Among the luggage, it's easy to jerryrig a seat. People below are usually willing to stow bothersome bags under their seat. Be friendly, cooperative, but fast.

It's simplest as a duo, one squeezes aboard and locates a place for both, then calls out the window for the luggage. You might even have company in your lofty seat. Our personal record was 24 people in an 8-seat compartment. Next to the fan, up in the luggage, is the most comfortable spot in a crowded train.

And while you're resting on your bags, you don't need to worry as much about thieves. 2nd class is a nightmare (paradise) for thieves. Secure your bags with a chain or wire combination bike lock. Your passport and money should be doubly secured, i.e. in a pocket sewn inside your pants between your thighs. Or secure the band of your breast pouch around your waist and keep it tucked into your pants. With all the heat, thumping, and shaking on board, you hardly notice when someone razors open a thin piece of cloth. We've never been robbed on rails, but we keep watch at night, especially if there are two or three of us.

Even on the longest ride, you'll never hunger. Hawkers constantly come by with all types of edibles. At a station, chai (tea) and other drinks, fruit, or cookies are sold at your window. On longer runs, the train usually stops for 15 minutes at major stations. If you're quick, you can visit the restaurant. But that's only for experts, or you'll surely lose your luggage.

Don't imagine a chapter on Indian railway is this quickly finished. After a few journeys aboard the noble service, you'll have your own stories to tell.

**Baggage Check:** Offered at every railway station. At tiny stations, the station-master is responsible. Bags are only accepted if they are locked; you might want to rig a locking system. Costs 1.-Rs for 24 hours.

**Technology:** The Indian Railway uses four track widths: broad gauge (BG, 1676 mm), metre gauge (MG, 1000 mm), and narrow gauge (NG, 762 mm and 610 mm). 11,000 trains run daily, carrying 10 million passengers over 70,000 km of track. Some of the main routes have been electrified. Lots of steam locomotives are still in service.

In recent years, many lines have been modernized, i.e. replacing metre gauge track with broad gauge, or laying new track alongside. The number of cars has been increased to 400,000.

India is heaven for railway fans, if you don't, thereby, land in Hell: India averages 900 railway accidents yearly.

Two of the longest lines in India are express trains from Jammu Tawi in Kashmir (or Gauhati in Assam) to Kanyakumarin at the southern tip of the subcontinent. The 3913 km (or 3525 km) route takes 4 days and costs US$20.- in 2nd class.

If you plan to do a lot of rail travel, pick up the helpful
schedule, **Trains At A Glance**, at a 1st-class ticket window or
from a Railway Tourist Guide.

# Domestic Flights

For long hops on a short trip, flying is certainly a worthwhile
alternative; after all, Indian Airlines offers one of the world's
cheapest route systems. Airbus service has been inaugurated on
some of the main routes by Air India. Airports in the north-east,
and smaller airstrips, are served by smaller Vayodoot planes.

Many routes are constantly booked out, meaning you get a
seat only at the last second if at all. Only Standby is available.
The worst I've seen was the Trivandrum - Maldives route: booked
out for an entire year...

There is no airport tax on domestic flights; for neighboring
countries it's 50.-Rs, others 100.-Rs.

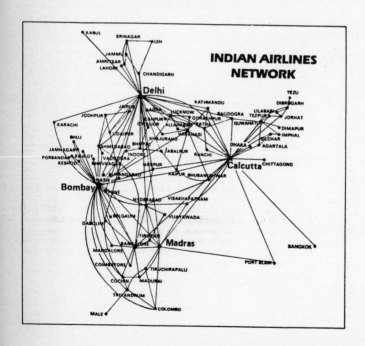

**Youth Discounts:**   Indian Airlines offers passengers under 30 a 25 % discount on domestic flights (and to Nepal!).   But you have to pay in hard western currency, which eats up any advantage.

**Southern India:** Anyone arriving with Indian Airlines from Colombo or Male is entitled to a 30 % discount (for 21 days) on the IA southern India system.

**Discover India Ticket:**   This ticket is available to all foreigners and Indians residing abroad.   It allows unlimited travel within a specified period,   but you can't fly into the same airport twice (except the originating airport);   costs US$375.- for 21 days.   If there isn't a daily flight, the validity of your ticket is extended by the time you are grounded.   It will also be extended if your flight is booked out.   Tickets available through travel agencies and direct from Indian Airlines (Central Space Control),   PTI Buildings,   Parliament St., New Delhi, 110001, or any Indian Airlines office.

Indian   Airlines   also   offers   7 days   of   unlimited   travel (US$200.-) between 19 towns in the west,   12 airports in the south, 17 stops in the east, or 21 towns in northern India.

# Driving

The following info was sent in by our friend,   Richard Doring, who spent several months touring the Indian subcontinent in a camper.   Prerequisites are an international driver's licence,   an international registration (insurance!), and a Carnet de Passage.

**Carnet de Passage:**   This is a document issued by the automobile club in your home country guaranteeing that the import tax on the car will be paid should you sell the car in India,   lose it, make a present of it,   or otherwise run foul with Indian import restrictions. Obviously your issuing agency is going to want some kind of security to ensure that if they pay, you pay.

**Petrol:**   Regular (80-85 octane),   Super (96 octane) only available in cities;   Diesel is rationed but coupons are available in any city.

**Roads:** Generally in good to excellent condition, though frequently just one lane.   In rural areas,   traffic crawls behind slow vehicles,   bicycles, and pedestrians. 300 km to 400 km a day is tops. India has a good road system connecting major towns,   in three categories:

    **National Highways** - connect   major   cities:    Delhi - Bombay, Madras - Calcutta, and Madras - Bombay
    **State Highways** - connect major towns
    **District & Village Roads** - rural roads, rarely paved

**Drive On The Left:**    Pass on the right.   No maximum speed limit,
but in towns the speed limit is usually 30 mph (50 km/h).   Keep
in mind the speed variation between cars,   buses,   bikes,   ox
carts, and wandering cows. Standard international signs.

Spare parts are hard to find in India,   bring extra light
bulbs,   fuses,   spark plugs,   etc.   Need help, ask at any petrol
station or the automobile club, where you'll find maps & guides.

**The Automobile Association of Upper India,**    Lilaram Building,
14 F Connaught Pl., New Delhi 110001, tel.47565.
**Western India Automobile Association,**    Lalji Naranji Memorial
Building, 76 Veer Nariam Rd., Bombay 400020, tel.291192.
**Automobile Association of Eastern India,**    13 Ballygunj Circular
Rd., Calcutta 700019, tel.86121.
**Automobile Association of Southern India,**    38 A Mount Rd., P.O.
Box 729, Madras 600006, tel.474804.
**Uttar Pradesh Automobile Association,**    32 A Mahatma Gandhi
Road., Allahabad, tel.2445.

**Road Map Of India** (1 : 2.5 million), get it before you depart for
India;   and **Indian Subcontinent** (1 : 4 million) by Bartholomew.
Or just pick up a tourist map and route info at the automobile
clubs, see above.

**Distances:**   Amritsar – (450 km) – Delhi – (1510 km) – Kathmandu
(Nepal),   Srinagar (Kashmir) – (876 km) – Delhi – (1460 km) –
Bombay – (600 km) – Goa – (1285 km) – Cape Komorin,   Delhi –
(1495 km) – Calcutta – (1734 km) – Madras – (630 km) –
Rameswaram

**Camper Parking:**    In the country it's no problem to stay in the
yard of one of the public houses called **DAK–Bungalow,   PWD–Resthouse,   Circuit House,   Tourist Lodge,**   located every 30–50 km.
"Parking with shower and toilet" costs 5.-Rs to 10.-Rs.   Accommodations in major towns and tourist centers isn't as simple.   Ask
other camping globetrotters for recommendations.

# Shopping

**Books & Maps:**   For a real selection,   only the cities will do.  Besides commercial bookshops,   there is a number of shops connected
to left-wing political parties.   Books are cheap, but the quality is
poor.   Maps vary in quality,   but are free in the tourist offices.
Better material is difficult to buy;   try in Delhi at the Map Sales
Branch of the Survey Department.

**Souvenirs:**    Certainly worthwhile are arts and crafts,   available
everywhere.   Specialities include textiles,   metalwork, jewelry and
ritual objects.   For tips on buying musical instruments see Indian
Music. See Shopping in the regional sections.

**Endangered Species**:  Beware of the both India's export restrictions and the import restrictions of your home country.  Trade with ivory,  tortoiseshell,  fur and skin of endangered species is prohibited (both plants and animals)!  Be aware of the irreparable damage to nature (and humanity) thoughtless purchases entail.  Read the brochure, **Souvenirs, Souvenirs** by the World Wildlife Fund.

**Consumer Goods**:  No problem if you keep local conditions in mind. But you will need a lot of time.  Search, compare, bargain: many people enjoy it.  For clothes, India is perhaps the cheapest country in the world,  even for western clothes. But western duds are only available in major towns.  We found a large selection in Ahmedabad and in Delhi. See the regional sections.

# Activities

For sport facilities see the regional sections.  Like the beach? Visit Goa,  Kovalam Beach in Kerala,  Mahabalipuram (south of Madras),  Waltair near Vishakhapatuam in Andrha Pradesh,  and Puri in Orissa. There are other lovely beaches, less well known.
**Trekking**:  Permitted without a permit in much of the northwestern Himalayas.  For more info see Kashmir, Ladakh, Himachal Pradesh, Uttar Pradesh,  and Darjeeling.  The Nepal chapter also provides trekking tips.  In Ladakh, trek during monsoon season (this area isn't affected), otherwise October-November or March-April. The southern West Ghat mountains offer great hiking year round.

**Movies**: In a country with the world's greatest film production, be sure to see a movie. The best films are produced and shown in Calcutta.
**Dance**:  Performances are interesting in Madras and Ernakulum.
**Ashrams** (religious centers): Many people are attracted to India by spiritual needs.

# PASSAGE TO INDIA

## ARRIVING

I just spent ten minutes on the
phone listening to an Air India
ticket agent explain why she should
not give me latest price information
over the phone: in short, because
it is too complicated.

## Overseas Flights

"The prices that I can quote you
are official prices. But nobody with
intelligence flies at the official
rates (in parenthesis return to
Delhi). Go to a travel agency near
your home in London (£1050.-), New
York (US$1323.-), Toronto
(C$1500.-), Sydney (A$2300.-), or Auckland (NZ$2100.-), and ask
about cheap rates. Check the ads in the travel section of your
newspaper, and shop around!"

A regular fare ticket (return) Frankfurt - Bombay or Delhi
runs at 4100.-DM (US$2050.-), to Kathmandu 4550.-DM (US$2275.-).
Of course IATA cartel airlines only get these dream fares from
the rich and foolish. There are much cheaper fares available.

Try the Holiday Tariff: Frankfurt - Bombay (return) US$670.-,
but valid only on direct flights with Air India, Lufthansa or Pan
Am; tickets must be booked and paid 30 days in advance, no
stopovers en route (even if the plane hops along the way),
return tickets valid just three months.

Many cheap flights are only sold under the counter. Consider
crossing borders to save. Biman, the Bangladesh airline, offers
super discounts Amsterdam to Bombay via Dacca, Bangladesh's
capital, US$550.- (return). Or you can go on to Calcutta and
Kathmandu, US$580.- (return). But on Biman, expect delays.
We've met travellers who've spent the night in the Amsterdam
Hilton at Biman expense because the plane couldn't depart till
the next day. And don't be surprised if you miss your Dacca
connecting flight to Kathmandu. But Biman will put you up in
Dacca's luxury Purbani Hotel.

Air France offers Paris - Bombay,   US$560.- (return), minimum stay 14 days,  maximum three months. Book by Air France or any IATA travel agency.

PIA (Pakistan) offers cheap flights Amsterdam - Delhi (free stopover in Karachi).   Both Kuwait Airways and PIA offer Amsterdam to Bombay for US$550.- (return), tickets valid one year.

Russian Aeroflot flies from East Berlin,  Amsterdam,  Brussels, Luxembourg,  Zurich, and Vienna to India. Think US$480.- to Calcutta (return); to Delhi US$550.- (return).

And CSA will entice you with Prague - Bombay for US$550.- (return).

Munich to Delhi or Bombay:  US$525.- (return). Changing your return ticket from Delhi to Bombay or vice versa usually costs nothing.  From Munich try Syrian Arab Air or Egypt Air; the latter offers stopovers in Cairo.

The cheapest flights between Europe and southern Asia are Athens - Karachi,  Pakistan starting at US$160.-,  or with Egypt

Air, Bangladesh's Biman or other cheap airlines for US$200.- (one way).

Frequently embassies, consulates, and tourist offices of the country you plan to visit are willing to say which airline has the best momentary price; phone and ask!

If you're heading right to Nepal, you'll have to change planes in Delhi or Calcutta, unless you fly Biman from Amsterdam via Dacca to Kathmandu. For the connecting flight Delhi - Kathmandu, Indian Airlines and Royal Nepal Airlines charge US$142.- (one way - return is US$284.-). And should you get Aeroflot to Calcutta, calculate US$100.- (one way) to Kathmandu.

Cheap *flights to India, Nepal, and Sri Lanka aren't sold by every travel agency. Check the travel section of your major newspaper and particularly in magazines targeted to young readers. The latest info is vital because the market changes almost daily!

Don't buy a ticket at the first available agency. Shop around and compare prices, you're sure to save! And don't wait, start shopping a couple of months before your departure date. Mention this book when buying or booking your flight, perhaps you'll get a discount.

# Overland

Once upon a time the India-Pakistan crisis would occasionally close the border, keeping things exciting. Today the revolution in Iran adds spice, certainly for Americans. The war in Afghanistan has closed that country to freak buses, which once connected southern Asia to Europe. Today the southern route through Pakistan is open. But a Punjab crisis can close the Lahore - Amritsar border, or restrict traffic.

For hardy souls, here's a brief description of the cheapest route to India. Like politics, visa regulations change quickly, particularly for Iran - check at an Iranian consulate at least two months prior to departure.

**Time:** Munich - Delhi is 10,000 km; just the ride takes two weeks. If you want to learn anything about the countries you're passing through, plan at least one month, better two.
**Cost:** The overland trip costs US$150.- Munich - Delhi. Two-thirds

of this cost is within Europe to Istanbul, the first 2000 km. For food and lodging en route think US$10.- per day; Iran is the most expensive.
**Season:** Plan your departure to avoid the November advent of winter (deep snow) in Asia Minor. But don't arrive in Pakistan until October, after monsoon season.

## BY RAIL TO ISTANBUL

All aboard the Orient Express Paris - Istanbul (reserved seats required so book early), stops in Stuttgart and Munich; bring plenty of food and drink! Check for discounts off the regular fare, young people get Transalpino, Eurail, or Interail, compare!
    Save by hitchhiking to Zagreb in northern Yugoslavia, from there it's less than US$60.- to Istanbul. Bring your own food and a bit of Yugoslovian currency to pick up supplies en route.

## GREECE

Cheap flights to Athens are frequently available, ask at your travel agency. After a nice stopover in Greece, you can catch a ride or bus to Istanbul. The bus offices in Athens are located in the cheap hotel district, south of Syntagma Square. Riders and willing drivers meet at Aeropag, a hill near the Acropolis. In Salonika (Thessaloniki), a bus company also acts as a ride office: Bella Tour, Monastiriou 4, 1st floor, tel.525710.

Cabin Baggage

PRAY AND LEAVE THE REST TO HIM

## TURKEY

This is where your Asian adventure begins. From Bulgaria, you cross the Turkish border at Edirne (500 km from Nis in Yugoslavia), 230 km from Istanbul. From Greece, you cross at Ipsala, near Alexandroupolis (380 km from Salonika, 225 km from Istanbul).
    Shop in the tax-free shops at the border. No visa required for a stay up to three months. The Turkish Lira (TL), divided into 100 Kurus (Krs), is constantly losing value against hard currencies. Banks are open Mon-Fri 08:30-12:00 h and 13:00-17:00 h. Your ISIC student ID is good for discounts in Turkey on ferries, airlines, bus, and train; be sure to ask! Since 1985, Turkey is part of the Interail system along with Yugoslavia and Greece (but not Bulgaria). Turkey's city drugstores (Eczane) are well stocked. A hepatitis shot with 2 ml gammaglobulin costs 2000.-TL, without prescription.

## ISTANBUL - TEHERAN

In Istanbul, cheap accommodations (start at US$4.- for a double), information, and travel agencies near the world-famous Pudding

Shop in Sultanahmed (Ayasofia and
Topkapi Palace), 800 m south of
Sirkeci railway station. Here too is
the tourist office with free info and
maps. Poste Restante in the GPO
near Sireci Railway Station. Change
money Sat-Sun in Sireci railway
station, or at American Express in
the Hilton Hotel (Amexco mail service).

Budget buses to Teheran
(US$25.-) or Delhi (US$100.- but
unreliable and infrequent) depart
from Sultanahmed, or the agency
will provide a free taxi to the departure point (i.e. Topkapi); compare prices and bargain!

Iranian visas are available at
the Iranian consulate, corner of
Yerebatan / Ankara Caddesi, tel.
285053, Mon-Fri 09:00-13:00 h and
14:00-16:00 h. Due to the uncertain
political situation in Iran, it might
be best to get this visa before
leaving home.

If you still don't have a student ID card, pick one up in or
around the Pudding Shop, or from
a returning traveller who doesn't
need theirs any more.

Istanbul - Teheran by bus
takes 2 1/2 days (with a night's
rest), or 48 hours (nonstop). The
train takes 3-4 days, cold at
night, not recommended, and the
Turkish-Iranian border is now
closed to rail traffic.

If you're at your leisure, stop
along the way at Erzurum or Dogoubayazit at the foot of Mount Ar-
arat, 35 km from the Iranian border. Or from Ankara, make a detour via Samsun and Trabzon along
the Black Sea. There's a Tuesday
Istanbul - Trabzon ferry, takes
two days, costs 600.-TL. After
Erzurum, head on by bus to
Dogoubayazit. Buses pass through
at 05:00-08:00 h on the way to
Teheran. A minibus to the border
costs 350.-TL.

**IRANIAN BORDER**
In Turkey you'll get 3-4 times the official exchange rate for
Iranian Rials, changing black in Teheran: perhaps six times
(dangerous!).

Have a good meal and enough to drink before presenting yourself at the border; it could take all day. First fill out the Turkish exit papers, and have them stamped; show the guard, and
cross to the Iranian side. Set your watch 30 minutes ahead.

Fill out the Iranian entry papers and present them with your
passport. Don't let any of these papers out of your sight. Show
what currency you have; it will be noted in your passport. Before leaving, make sure you have a copy of your entry papers
and that your passport contains both the trapezoid-shaped entry
stamp and your currency declaration. Don't lose the entry paper,
you'll have to present it frequently at ID checks, and when
leaving the country.

The second customs building is 3 km further on. The Iranians
take the search very conscientiously. Don't get caught with any
drugs (or alcohol!). After the baggage check, look for a bus or
truck to Teheran. If you can't find one, get a taxi to Maho, a
village with a bus terminal in the center of town. You're about
900 km from Teheran.

**IRAN**
The monetary unit is the rial; ten rials are called a tuman.
Officially US$1.- = 90.-Rls. Changing money black on the street is
dangerous and harshly punished. Banks are open 08:00-13:00 h,
Thursdays till 12:00 h; Friday is Islam's day of rest.

During Ramadan, a month of daylight fasting each summer,
tourists are expected to conform strictly to Islamic edict: no
eating, drinking, or smoking between sunrise and sunset. Plus,
many shops and offices are closed.

**THE NUMBERS**
Written in Farsi, and unlike the script, read left to right:

| | | | |
|---|---|---|---|
| ) | 1 = jek | 30 = tschi |
| ٢ | 2 = do | 40 = tschel |
| ٣ | 3 = see | 50 = panscha |
| ٤ | 4 = tschahar | 60 = schaast |
| ٥,۵ | 5 = pansch | 70 = haaftad |
| ٦ | 6 = schisch | 80 = haschtad |
| ٧ | 7 = haaft | 90 = novad |
| ٨ | 8 = haascht | 100 = saad |
| ٩ | 9 = no | 200 = dosad |
| ٠, | 10 = daa | 1000 = hesar |
| | 20 = biist | |

You can get along in cities with English, French, or German.

## TEHERAN
Buses arrive at Terminal Azadi, or occasionally in the cheap
hotel neighborhood around Amir Kabir Avenue. Overlanders meet
in Amir Kabir Hotel ((S)300.-Rls or (D)400.-Rls) where you'll find
fellow travellers for the long road ahead, together with those
returning with the latest info. Other hotels nearby offer comparable prices. Amir Kabir Hotel guests can eat in the hotel, others
try the restaurant around the back.
  The GPO and bus company ticket offices are conveniently
nearby, to the north-west on Ferdowski Avenue. Book your departure tickets upon arrival;  most travellers put Teheran behind
them fast.
**Indian Embassy**:  166 Saba Street, tel.898814, Sat-Thurs 08:00-
15:00 h. A visa (3 photos required) takes one day.

## TEHERAN - PAKISTAN
After Teheran, it's a pleasure to reach Isfahan. Most of the
sights can be found in the center around Meidan-i-Shah Square.
Lodgings nearby on Chahar Bagh Avenue by the bus company
offices.
  The bus from Teheran to Isfanhan costs 600.-Rls. From here to
Zahedan, the last major town before the Pakistan border, is
1400.-Rls. The direct bus Teheran - Zahedan takes 26 hours,
costs 2000.-Rls, and departs from Khazaneh Terminal.
  Relatively expensive (since only foreigners use it) is the mere
100 km from Zahedan - Taftan. The bus (600.-Rls) only goes when
enough passengers will fill it. The alternative is 1200.-Rls for a
flat-bed truck.
  Iran's roads are in good repair; gas is cheap. A motor vehicle carnet for Iran can be expensive;  some countries require
double the car's worth plus several thousand dollars as security.
For cars without a carnet, Iranian customs will establish a con-
voy of up to four cars accompanied by a customs official, costs
US$400.-.

# Night Bus In The Desert

During the height of the Iranian revolution and Ramadan,
Matthew Brennan, a traveller from New York, looked at a
map, and figured the quickest route from Istanbul, Turkey to
India was via Iran. A few excerpts from his story:

  ... the journey was feasible as long as my conduct was
low keyed. No American flags should be flown from car
antennas...

Miles and miles of desert... passed by the bus window. Iranians to my front and Iranians to my rear... old men wearing western dress, some young men wearing mideastern robes...

An old man had been constantly screaming day in and day out through the radio speakers. If it was different men, the tone and style possessed amazing similarities. The language was Farsic which I knew not one word of. My language was English, in which I recognized three words repeated again and again... There I was on a bus in the middle of the desert with the only familiar words being "Jimmy Carter", "CIA", and "America". Brought via an old man screaming into an implement of western technology...

Specks in the distance... which became slowly recognizable as men, dressed in long flowing robes, carrying rifles. The bus stopped in front of a jeep which blocked the road. Who were these people... Clothed in baggy white cotton shirts, baggy white cotton trousers, brown leather sandals, and dirty white turbans, their presence was formidable.

The group's apparent leader stood in the middle of the road. As soon as the bus came to a halt he boarded the bus, followed by two other men... tall, and armed with... an old Colt .45 pistol, which dangled from his belt, he proceeded up the bus aisle examining the passengers' carry on luggage for contraband... A second man, who was also very tall, and had a remarkable resemblance to the late Malcom X, stood at the front of the bus and pointed a rifle at the passengers as... security...

The first man passed me nonconsequentially. I had no carry on baggage. Shortly thereafter the second man shouted... in Farsic which caused some passengers to rush off the bus. By that time the bus had been surrounded by a platoon of approximately sixty soldiers in a circular formation. A systematic search was then begun of the luggage stored in the undercarriage luggage compartments...

Customs had become a common occurrence to me. Initially, I was not alarmed when the man with the dangling revolver began to search the carry on luggage. However, when the luggage doors on the undercarriage of the bus began to open up, and the baggage began to come under close scrutiny, apprehension... my navy blue American passport located in a very accessible place in my royal blue, very western looking backpack, labeled "made in USA"... Would my final eulogy be delivered through a transistor radio speaker? An old man screaming "Jimmy Carter", "CIA", and "America", intermixed with other nice expressions in Farsic language? Would the end of my life occur as live target practice for a guerrilla band operating in the middle of the Balughistan Desert... A basic rule of life from the reality school of method acting... "Act like you belong there and the people will treat you as such." I stood up and walked off the bus, boldly going...

The bus driver quickly took notice... and whispered in broken English... "get back on the bus"... I quickly returned
to my seat.
    The search continued...
    Suddenly, a young Iranian... twelve years of age, was
standing in the bus aisle, next to my seat, yelling Farsic
words intermixed with the word "American". A younger mimic
of the old man's announcing style, without the polished
flair.
    The frequent mention of the word "American" was causing
some raised eyebrows among the bus passengers... The young
boy kept yelling and all I could do was... try an age old
trick... "If you want someone to stop bothering you just
ignore them until they go away." A scene between myself and
the boy would only bring more attention to me, the big guy
trying to blend into the woodwork...
    Next to me the young Iranian boy scout continued babbling
and drooling... the baggage compartment doors were closed.
My backpack had not been searched. The bus was given the
signal to proceed...

## PAKISTAN

Though the border between Iran and Pakistan sees little traffic,
the wait takes hours. Still, the process is no worry if you still
have your entry form, haven't overstayed the visa, and can
account for all the currency you brought in with you. The Pakistan side of the border is very relaxed. Be sure to get the entry
stamp placed in your passport; the building is a little off to the
side. You can stay for 30 days without a visa. Otherwise get a
three-month visa at a Pakistan consulate before departure.
    Change money in Taftan, mornings in the bank, afternoons on
the street; both rates about the same: US$1.- = 15.-Rs (Pakistani
Rupees). Advance your watch 90 minutes ahead of Iran.
    From the border, it's 130 km to Nok Kundi, poor gravel road,
7 h by car. Then 500 km of paved road to Quetta, think 11 h.
The bus, of course, takes 27 h, but costs just 100.-Rs.
    The train from the border, Taftan - Quetta, runs once a
week, Fri 12:50 h, and takes 1 1/2 days. Bring Pakistani rupees
and enough food and drink! Evening arrival. Accommodations in
the bazaar, US$2.-. A scooter from the railway station: 4.-Rs;
from the New Bus Stand: 6.-Rs.
    From Quetta there's a daily train to Lahore near the Indian-
Pakistan border. Departs Quetta 10:30 h, arrives in Lahore at
15:00 h the next day, costs 100.-Rs (Quetta-Express).
    Show your ISIC for a 50 % student discount on the train;
other tourists get a 25 % discount. Reductions in bus fare are
also possible, ask!

The best road from Quetta to Lahore runs via Sukkur and Multan. The 1200 km is completely paved. You can ship a VW bus from Karachi to Bombay for US$600.-, but it might be difficult to find in Bombay. Passenger rates are also cheap. The ferry runs twice a month.

There's talk of reopening the rail line and border between Hyderabad, Pakistan and Barmer in Rajasthan, India. Check! The Pakistani border town is Khakhropar; the Indian is Munabao. The border is reportedly open to locals.

Before independence, Lahore was the capital of all Punjab, but the split with India left it capital of just the Pakistan part. You'll find lots of cheap hotels not far from the railway station and bus terminal. If you're just staying one night, many beds start at 15.-Rs, or (better) 40.-Rs a double, in the neighborhood across from the railway station. The youth hostel is a distance away. Beware in the hotels of thieves and tricksters who might plant drugs and try to blackmail you! Safest are Clifton (only this spelling!), Parkway, the YMCA, and the YWCA.

All important facilities: the GPO, Tourist Office (in Faletti's Hotel), American Express, bookstores, restaurants, IA, PIA, YMCA, are on or near The Mall, today called Shahrah-e-Quaide-Azam, about 1 km from the railway station and bus terminal.

Pakistan is certainly worth a four-week stay, particularly in the Himalayas. A flight Rawalpindi - Skardu - Gilgid - Rawal-pindi costs just US$35.-. Fantastic treks are possible, but you need a permit: costs 100.-Rs from Ministry of Tourism, College Road, Islamabad.
**Tip:** On the return trip, your Iranian visa takes 3-5 weeks if you apply in Bombay, but in Islamabad the wait is two days. Overland buses Lahore - Athens cost US$150.-.

## PAKISTAN-INDIA BORDER

Get bus 12 from the bus stand or a minibus (3.-Rs) to the border. Careful, not all buses go all the way, make sure yours doesn't stop in Wagah, 3 km walk too short. The ride takes an hour.

The border is only open from 08:30-15:30 h on the Pakistan side. Border formalities take about an hour on each side. Expect very strict, thorough checks. The customs buildings are about 2 km from each other. From the Indian side of the border (Attari Road) buses bring you to the first Indian town, Amritsar.

There is one train daily between Lahore (departs 14:00 h) and Amritsar (18:30 h arrival). The customs formalities are at the Lahore railway station and at Attari Rd.

For Indian entry requirements, see Travel Tips. For the con-tinued journey, see Amritsar, and the local sections. You made it to India. Set your watch ahead 30 minutes.

## SRI LANKA
**By Air:** See Sri Lanka, Coming - Going. Book a cheap flight at one of the tiny travel agencies in Colombo Fort. Ask your innkeeper, perhaps, for a recommendation, but be sure he splits the commission with you. And bargain at the travel agency. A reduction of 500.-SLRs might be built into a long-distance ticket price. Sample prices: Madras (officially US$80.-), Trichy (US$55.-), Trivandrum (US$53.-), Bombay (US$170.-).
**By Ship:** The ferry from Talaimannar (Sri Lanka) to Rameswaram (India) runs Tues, Thurs, and Sat, no service in November, December, and the beginning of January. **No tickets available in Talaimannar!** Even if you arrive on time in Talaimannar, it's possible that overbooking will force you to wait 2-3 days for the next ship. You're better off flying and selling your duty-free whisky upon arrival in India (one liter brings 200.-Rs).

## THE MALDIVES
**By Air:** From Hulile International Airport, near Male, to Trivandrum US$65.-, takes two hours. 30 % discount if booked together with a domestic Indian flight. Airport tax US$7.-

## PAKISTAN
**By Air:** Indian Airlines and Pakistan International Airlines serve the Karachi - Delhi route for US$128.-. Daily flights to Bombay US$103.-. Lahore - Delhi US$83.- (travel agencies US$50.-).

## NEPAL
**By Air:** From Kathmandu, daily flights by Indian Airlines and Royal Nepal Airlines Corp. (RNAC) to Calcutta US$100.-, Delhi US$142.-, and Varanasi US$71.-. Cheapest is the flight to Patna US$41.-. Note: then continue on to Delhi for just US$128.- total; less than the US$142.- direct flight! Travellers under 30 get a 25 % youth discount off the dollar price (see Nepal).
**Overland From Nepal - Tibet:** See Nepal - Coming - Going.

## BANGLADESH
**By Air:** Bangladesh's Biman and Indian Airlines fly Dacca - Calcutta US$38.-, several times daily. Three times weekly Chittagong - Calcutta US$50.- (see Bangladesh).
**Overland:** See Bangladesh - Coming - Going.

## SOUTH-EAST ASIA
**By Air:** From Bangkok, Thailand to Calcutta US$170.-, Delhi US$230.-. Fly to Kathmandu for US$220.-, and spend seven days en route in Burma (advance visa required). From Singapore daily flights to Madras US$200.-, to Bombay US$250.-. From Penang, Malaysia to Madras flights are cheapest, but still US$200.-.

**By Ship:** The last regularly scheduled service ended in early 1985 when the good ship Chidambaram burned:  the end of an era! All that's left are freighters which carry vehicles,  but not passengers (see Madras).  Check with the shipping companies in Singapore or Penang.

# DEPARTING

## Overseas Flights

If you know from the beginning how you want to fly home, buy a round trip ticket with an open return date;  many are valid one year, but not all, check!

Cheap flights in India start at 3600.-Rs (one way),  but expect to pay 4000.-Rs.  King of the cheap flights is Russia's Aeroflot (round trip tickets also available).

Want a discount? Who doesn't? Many travel agencies require you pay full fare at a bank in hard western currency. You get your kickback from the travel agent in rupees. Leave yourself enough time to spend them.

In India, tickets are sold in cities with large international airports, i.e. Bombay, Delhi, and Calcutta (cheapest in Delhi!). For international flights an airport tax of 100.-Rs is collected at the airport (50.-Rs for neighboring countries).

## DELHI
With bargaining, the cheapest place to book flights in India! Cheap tickets are offered by the small travel agencies around Connaught Place, in Pahar Ganj (Main Bazar), and by touts in front of American Express.
**Student Travel Information Centre:** Imperial Hotel, Janpath (see Map, Delhi - Connaught Place).
**Yadav Travels:** Vivek Hotel, Pahar Ganj, tel.523015 & 521948.

## BOMBAY
Touts frequently wait in front of American Express on Flora Fountain and at the cheap hotels around Mereweather Road. Look for info brochures. We've heard good reports about:
**Spaceway Travels:** Nanabhoy Mansion, 4th floor, Sir P.M. Rd., Bombay 400 001, tel.255652, on the corner of Mody St., Mon-Fri 10:00-17:00 h, Sat 10:30-15:00 h. Spaceway also has agencies in Panaji and Calangute, Goa.

## CALCUTTA
Cheap flights are offered by several travel agencies in the cheap hotel neighborhood around Sudder Street, Chowringhee. Info too from the Lodges; ask Mr. Roy at Modern Lodge. Ask too at Bangladesh's Biman and Russia's Aeroflot airlines. Delhi prices.

## ASIA
For domestic flights, and international flights within Asia, see Coming - Going in local sections.

## SRI LANKA
Direct flights to the island from Kathmandu, Bombay, Madras, Tiruchchirappalli, and Trivandrum. If you're under 30, there's a 25 % youth discount on Indian domestic flights. The regular fare to Madras is US$137.- from Calcutta and US$110.- from Bombay. From Madras to Sri Lanka is another US$80.-, from Tiruchchirappalli and Trivandrum US$55.-. All flights land at Katunayake Airport, 30 km north of Colombo on the road to Negombo. Routes served by Air India and Air Lanka, 50.-Rs airport tax.

# By Ship From Sri Lanka

Between Rameswaram, an island town at the southeast tip of India, and Talaimannar, on the Sri Lankan peninsula, a ferry runs
three times weekly. More about Rameswaram in its local section.
The ferry is occasionally cancelled, due to riots; check!

Be sure to arrive in Rameswaram in the early afternoon, if
you want a chance of getting accommodations. All buses arrive
and depart at
Mandapam. Disem-
bark at the end-
station, next to
the railway sta-
tion, and get one
of 8 trains daily
(1.-Rs) to Rames-
waram (last stop);
there is no road.

If you can't
find a room, sleep
in' or around the
railway station,
but check your
bags in the cloak-
room at the sta-
tion, closed 21:00–
05:00 h. Tickets
for the ship, plus
to every railway
station on Sri
Lanka are avail-
able Mon, Wed,
and Fri 08:30–
11:00 h, at a spe-
cial ticket window
in the station.

You're best off buying your Sri Lankan train tickets here, saves
standing in line again later! Still, on the morning of departure,
you'll have to pick up a Boarding Card from the Shipping
Corporation Office. Without one they won't let you aboard. But
only in Sri Lanka can you reserve a seat for the return trip!

The ferry doesn't run due to poor weather conditions from the
end of October to the middle of January. Otherwise Mon, Wed, and
Fri, costs 125.-Rs, for upper deck (same price at the railway
station or harbour). The tickets window is open 07:00–11:00 h.

Customs is at the harbour (a 1 km walk), opens at 07:30 h,
but buy your ticket first. Harbour tax is 8.-Rs. Foreigners are
usually handled first by customs. The whole procedure takes at
least an hour. After customs, head to the dock where a leaky
bark brings you to the ship lying at anchor. After two strenuous

hours, you're aboard. If you start the wait at 08:00 h and are
on board at 10:00 h, the ship will weigh anchor about 16:00 h,
takes 3 hours.

But then you've lots of time to relax on deck. Someone might
pluck a guitar. And soon nobody will care if the ship is moving
or not; in fact it's fun. At 11:00 h, inexpensive food is served
on board. But be sure to have a bit of Indian money or a couple
of dollars. If all you've got are traveller's checks (not accepted), you hunger. Upper-deck passengers disembark first. Once
ashore, fill out the forms. If you're last off the ship, you miss
the last train.

In Talaimannar, money exchange and a small restaurant are
open when a ship puts in. A night's rest costs 25.-Rs per person, both here and in Mannar, the first railway station toward
Anuradhapura / Colombo (Traveller's Rest).


## THE MALDIVES
From Trivandrum, Indian Airlines and Maldives International
Airlines fly into Male, the capital (Hulule airport is on an is-
land), takes 2 hours, costs US$65.-, 50.-Rs airport tax. Colombo
- Male US$90.- (one way) US$130.- (return).

## PAKISTAN
Indian Airlines and Pakistan International Airlines (PIA) fly
daily to Karachi from Delhi US$128.- and Bombay US$103.-. To
Lahore from Delhi US$83.-, in travel agencies US$50.-.

## EUROPE - OVERLAND
For more info on the classic pancake route, see above.
**Visas:** No visa is required for Pakistan for stays up to 30 days.
Applying for an Iranian visa in Delhi can take up to six weeks,
but in Islamabad, Pakistan you have it in just one or two days.
An extension of your Iranian visa (7 or 14 days) is no problem
in Teheran at the Police Department, Office for Foreign Affairs,
Vila Street. Turkey doesn't require a visa.

It is cheapest to use local public transportation. Don't buy
any tickets across a border. This will keep your transportation
costs down to US$120.- Delhi - Munich. Buses, once common, have
become rare, costs from Delhi US$200.-, from Kathmandu US$220.-,
from Lahore US$180.-, Delhi to Athens US$150.-.

## CHINA - (TIBET)
Overland to China, the road runs through Kathmandu and Lhasa.

## SOUTH-EAST ASIA
There is no land route to South-East Asia. Burma is only accessible by air. The maximum stay in Burma is 7 days. The last
passenger ship from Madras to Penang, Malaysia, and Singapore
burned out in early 1985. Whether it will be replaced is a
question to ask in Madras.

# DELHI

India's capital (population 6 million) may well be your first expo-
sure to Indian culture; particularly
if you fly. So let's go into a bit
more detail to make things easier.

Recent excavations confirm earlier assumptions that the city was
founded around 1200 BC. In fact
Delhi is **Indraprashtra**, a city mentioned in the heroic Indian epic
**MAHABHARATA.** Our earliest historical records, however, date from
the 11th century AD when the city
was the seat of the Rajputan
princes.

Phrithviraj, the last Hindu
king, fell in battle against the
Muslims. Qutb Minar victory tower
dates from this era. Delhi remained
under Muslim rule until the days of British colonialism.

Delhi blossomed under Tughlak rule until, in 1398, Mongol
armies, under Timur Lenk, laid waste, killing over 100,000 inhabitants. The Sayyid and Lodi dynasties ran their course. In
1556 the Moghuls took over, building the Red Fort and Jama Mashid. The most famous of the great Moghuls were Akbar (Fatehpur
Sikri) and Shah Jahan (Taj Mahal). The Persian king Nadir Shah
raided Delhi in 1739, taking as spoils the famous Peacock Throne,
later used by the late Shah of Iran, Shah Reza Pahlevi.

The British East India Company established a trading post
here in the 18th century. In successive wars against Hindu armies attacking from the south, the British always allied themselves with the Moghuls, who survived numerous sieges of the
city. Only the Afghan King Ahmad Shah Durani succeeded in
plundering the city.

From 1804 on, the British ruled Delhi, although the Moghuls
retained both title and wealth. In 1857, the Rising, a mutiny
supported by troops of the Bengali army, temporarily overwhelmed
the British, in a terrible blood bath. Four months later the
British reoccupied the city. The British thereafter moved their
capital to Calcutta. Not until 1911 did King George V move the
capital back to Delhi, to reduce Muslim pressure for autonomy.

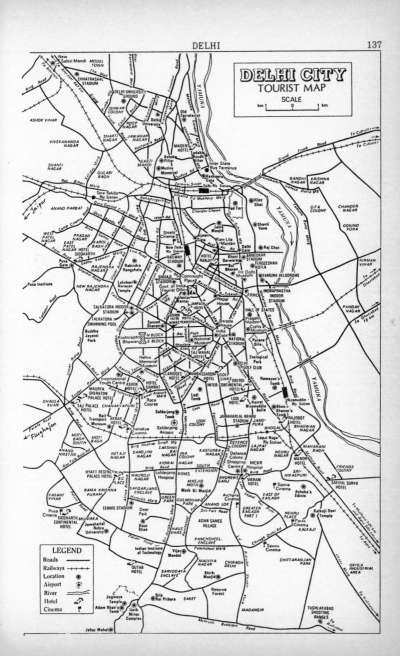

In the 1920s, New Delhi was founded south of the historic city center. Designed by British planners, dedication ceremonies were held in 1931. New Delhi remains the seat of the Indian government.

## COMING - GOING

For bus and rail connections, see under your destination. Since information is easy to procure in Delhi, just a few general tips.

**By Air:** Many of you will fly direct into Delhi. Indira Airport is 15 km south-west of town. After processing by customs and the bureaucracy, you can change money. The Information Window at the airport is open round the clock.

**Airport-City Connection:** Your cheapest ride into town is local Bus 780 to Connaught Place in the center of New Delhi. The bus to the airport departs from Super Bazar, costs 0.50 Rs.

The EATS airport bus departs half hourly, costs 8.-Rs to Connaught Place. To the airport, the bus departs from the Malhotra Building on Connaught, every 1-2 h, 04:30-23:00 h. A taxi costs 35.-Rs, a scooter 17.-Rs.

For domestic flights and to neighboring countries, you fly Indian Airlines. For information, bookings, confirmations, reservations, and information visit the Indian Airlines Office, Kanchenjunga Building, 18 Barakhamba Road, tel.3310052, open 09:00-19:30 h. There's a second booking office in PTI Building, Sansad Marg, New Delhi, tel.389168, Mon-Sat 10:00-17:00 h. At the Domestic Arrival Area in the airport, the office is open round the clock, tel.391250.

**International Flights:** The addresses of all the international airlines can be found at Indian Airlines, in the Tourist Office, at Airport Information, and in the brochure **Delhi Diary** (available in hotels, at news stands, and in bookshops).

Don't forget the airport tax, payable upon departure: 50.-Rs to neighboring countries, 100.-Rs to the rest of the world. If you want an early-morning taxi to the airport or Connaught Place, be sure to order it the night before.

**By Rail:** New arrivals should read our section on rail travel in India, see Country & Culture.

Upon arrival in New Delhi Railway Station, you'll find a number of cheap accommodations in Pahar Ganj, the main bazar. Walk down the left-hand road across the square from the station entrance.

Most trains to Delhi pass through Agra, Varanasi, Bombay. A tonga (horse cart) from New Delhi Railway Station to Connaught Place costs 1.-Rs, from Old Delhi Railway Station (Delhi Junction) 2.-Rs. Bus 6 runs between the two stations.

Around Old Delhi Railway Station, the cheap hotel region is Chandi Chowk (silver market); recommended if you're heading on to Jaipur, whose trains depart from Delhi Junction. A taxi to Connaught Place runs 12.-Rs, scooter 6.-Rs, tonga 3.-Rs.

Upon arrival at Hazrat Nizamuddin in southern Delhi, get a four-seater car rickshaw (2.-Rs) to Connaught Place.
For railway tickets, your two main stations are Old Delhi Railway Station (Delhi Junction) and New Delhi Railway Station. You can only book tickets, reservations, etc. from the actual station of departure! Some trains stop in both stations and can be booked at either 07:30-21:00 h. First class and AC tickets can also be booked at Northern Railway Reservation Office, State Entry Road, at the north end of Connaught Place, Mon-Sat 08:00-20:00 h, Sun & hol 08:00-13:00 h. Here too you can pick up an Indrail Pass.
If you're in a hurry, foreigners can usually get a reservation on the day of departure at the Railway Tourist Guide Office of Northern Railway in New Delhi Railway Station. Here, too, you can get information and advance reservations, Mon-Sat 10:00-17:00 h, closed every second Saturday of the month, tel.322135; Indrail Passes also available.
Connections to Delhi are discussed in the regional sections of your destination. Connections to Delhi are quickest via the wide-gauge line (Agra, Jhansi, Bhopal, Bhusawal) or (Agra, Kota, Vadodara, Surat). Trains through Rajasthan are slower, but there is a lot to see and do en route.
**By Bus:** Public overland buses arrive at Interstate Bus Terminal, Kashmiri Gate, 1 km north of Old Delhi Railway Station, and Delhi GPO. Get a scooter from the bus stand to Pahar Ganj (cheap hotels) and Connaught Place for 6.- or 7.-Rs; rickshaws cost 5.-Rs to Pahar Ganj. Local Bus 101 goes to Connaught Place.
Bus lines are divided according to the state of destination. Accordingly, there is a number of state transport agencies where you have to make the bookings. Bookings should be made 3-7 days in advance depending on the company and route. The bus companies include (booking time limit in parentheses): Haryana (7 days), Jammu & Kashmir (4 days), Rajasthan (6 days), Uttar Pradesh (3 days). The offices are open 10:00-17:00 h, some earlier, others later.
Buses to Agra depart hourly during the day, cost 18.-Rs; the more expensive de luxe buses less frequently, take 4 h. Direct buses to Dharamsala cost 54.-Rs, take 13 h; to Chandigarh (8 h, 25.-Rs), Simla (10 h, 30.-Rs), Amritsar (9 h, 44.-Rs).
Heading to Kashmir, you can get a bus direct to Srinagar, or get a train to Jammu, and from there on by bus. No matter what, you'll spend a night in Jammu.
Some luxury buses, headed in other directions, don't depart from Kashmiri Gate; ask!
Direct (freak) buses to Kathmandu, Goa, Kerala, or to Europe, from Tourist Camp, tel.278929, Nehru Marg, between Connaught Place and Old Delhi; go by and have a look.
**Around Town:** Delhi has an extensive local bus system, run by Delhi Transport Corporation (DTC), Scindia House, Connaught Place, tel.321367. The DTC office is open 07:00-20:30 h, pro-

viding information, maps (2.-Rs), and booking sightseeing
tours. The office is in the courtyard behind Central Court
Hotel. You can get discount day tickets for unlimited travel.
Taxis are expensive: 3.-Rs for the first km, 2.-Rs for each
additional. That is about double the stated price. Baggage
costs a few paisa extra. Between 23:00-05:00 h, there is a 25 %
night surcharge.

Scooters run about half the taxi price; here, too, you pay
double the posted price, and baggage and night surcharge are
extra.

Four-seater car rickshaws, powered by Harley-Davidson en-
gines, are a Delhi speciality. They can be found particularly
south of Connaught Place, near Regal Cinema. Most run established routes, and are quite cheap, e.g. to Chandni Chowk
(2.-Rs), or to Interstate Bus Terminal and Hazrat Nizzamuddin
(2.50 Rs).

Bicycle rickshaws are only licensed in Old Delhi, as are tongas (horse carts), running only as far south as northern Connaught Place.

## A NIGHT'S REST

It isn't easy to find a cheap room in Delhi, at least one that's
comfortable. There is a number of hotel regions where you can
have a look.

Pahar Ganj: Our first collection of cheap hotels is in the Main
Bazar, across from New Delhi Railway Station, north of Connaught Place. Have a good look around if you're planning to
spend a while in Delhi. According to our taste, this is the
region with the best price-quality ratio, and the best atmosphere in Delhi. And the location is good, particularly if you're
planning to head on to Agra or Varanasi. Most trains in this
direction depart from New Delhi Railway Station. Pahar Ganj is
a lively, bustling place with one shop after an other, inviting
you to shop on the way to your hotel.

We had a typical Indian experience in a hotel here. We returned from Connaught Place to find our room filled with a
strange odour. It apparently came from under the ceiling or
through the window from the neighboring room in the attic. Our
neighbours were gone. Fortunately the room had a window facing the hallway through which we could see inside. Nothing.
No smoke. A puzzle. We informed the hotel manager. Just as we
were beginning to speculate about a fire under the roof, our
neighbours, a Sikh family, returned. They, too, couldn't conceive of a reason for the smoke, until one thought to open the
closet by the window. In the closet, a bundle of incense sticks
was glowing peacefully in front of a picture of their guru. The
smoke rose up to the open window through which it was sucked
into our room. Indians say Puja. We began to laugh. Of all
the things you can imagine, who would have thought of that.
Pahar Ganj is full of such stories; that's why it's such fun.

**Hotel Vishal**, Main Bazar, tel.527629, **(S)**30.-, 35.-, **(D)**45.-, 65.-, upper priced rooms with bath, **(Dm)**15.-, friendly management, downstairs is **Lord's Cafe**, a nice restaurant with a view of the bazar bustle; if you want some quiet, stretch out on the roof (no shade).

**Hotel Vivek**, Main Bazar, tel.527629, **(S)**30.-, 35.-, **(D)**45.-, 65.-, upper priced rooms with bath, **(Dm)**15.-. **Hotel Sapna**, Main Bazar, **(D)**30.-, clean, simple. **Honey Guest House**, 1311 Sangtrashan, tel.523702, **(S)**15.-, **(D)**30.-, 80.-, **(Dm)**10.-, on a side street. **Hotel Chanakya**, on a side street by Imperial Cinema, **(S)**35.-, **(D)**55.-, clean, good. **Hotel Navrang**, 644-C Mohalla Baoli, 6 Tooti Chowk, tel.521965, away from the bustle, **(S)**15.-, 20.-, **(D)**20.-, 25.-. **Venus**, **(S)**25.-, very rundown.

Or try **Hotel King**, **Paramount**, **Sonu**, **Nataraj**, **Bright**, and others...

Market Street in Pahar Ganj, Delhi

Old Delhi: Upon arrival at Old Delhi Railway Station, the second
cheap hotel district, Chandi Chowk (Silver Market) awaits you.
This is a good location for those heading on to Jaipur, for which
trains depart from Old Delhi. Best known here are **Crown Hotel**
and **Khushdil**. The Crown charges **(S)**35.-Rs for an awful room
with one bed. The better rooms are much more expensive. If you
find any good cheap places in the area, let us know.
Downtown: Your third cheap hotel district is a small street south
of Connaught Place. It's a good location if you have to attend to
business; almost all travel agencies, banks, information offices,
etc. have offices on Connaught Place, Parliament Street, or Janpath. From here too, you have the best transport connections in
town. The cheapest hotels are on Janpath Lane behind Indian Oil
Bhavan, parallel to Janpath.

**Jains Guest House**, Janpath Lane, always to be recommended,
clean, safe, family atmosphere, **(D)**40.-. **Soni Guest House**, Janpath Lane, **(D)**40.-, **(Dm)**15.-, quality over the years, family
place.

If they are booked try **Tarra's Lodge**, near Regal Cinema,
**(S)**30.-, clean.

Lodgings by Scindia House, behind the Air India office, between Janpath and Kasturba Gandhi Marg are a bit more expensive, as is south of Connaught Place: **Ringo Guesthouse**, 17 Scindia House, tel.40605, **(D)**50.-, **(Dm)**15.-, popular among travellers, with a good reputation over the years. **Asian Guesthouse**,
14 Scindia House, tel.43393, **(D)**55.-. **Laguna Guesthouse**, Scindia
House, tel.42600, **(D)**55.-. Lots more lodges in the area in the
same price range.

Nearby on Connaught Place by Super Bazar: **Hotel Bright**, 1185
Connaught Place, **(D)**70.-, though the price has little relation to
what's offered, rundown, don't confuse with the equally rundown
**Hotel Bright** on Pahar Ganj. **Palace Heights Hotel**, D Block, Con-
naught Place, more expensive than Bright, but much better,
**(D)**85.-.

If you can afford more than **(D)**100.-Rs, try: **New Delhi YMCA
Tourist Hotel**, Jai Singh Road, tel.311915, with a lovely garden
and good restaurant. **YWCA International Guest House**, Sansad
Marg, tel.311561, all **(AC)**, **(S)**100.-, **(D)**150.-. **Ashok Yatri Niwas**,
Ashok Road, tel.344511, with and without **(AC)**, **(D)**120.-. **Nirula's**, L Block, Connaught Place, tel.35219, includes **Nirula Restaurant**, **(S)**200.-, **(D)**300.-, just **(AC)**.

In the diplomatic enclave, Chanakyapuri, are two reasonably
priced spots worth mentioning, but the bus ride is 20 to 30 min-
utes, get Bus 620 from Connaught Place, or Bus 662 from Old
Delhi Railway Station: **Youth Hostel**, Nyaya Marg, tel.376258,
**(Dm)**18.-, with YH-ID **(Dm)**15.-, Central Office of the Indian Youth
Hostel Association. **International Youth Center**, Vishwa Kendra,
Circular Road, with a good, reasonable restaurant, helpful man-
agement, **(Dm)**12.-, **(S)**25.-.

Popular among travellers is **Tourist Camp**, across from Irwin Hospital, Jawaharlal Nehru Marg, tel.278929, near Delhi Gate; any way you want to stay, this is the place, camping, campmobile, or in tiny bungalows, **(S)**26.-, 35.-, **(D)**36.-, 50.-, tent or camping-wagon 10.- plus 5.- per person, common showers, well-kept facilities, reasonable open-air restaurant, left luggage, nice personnel, 2 km from New Delhi Railway Station, 3 km from Old Delhi Railway Station, from Connaught Place 1.-Rs by four-seater auto rickshaw.

**Railway Retiring Rooms** in Old and New Delhi Railway Stations, usually booked out, **(D)**35.-, **(Dm)**5.-, 8.-. **Airport Retiring Rooms**, at Indira Airport, just for passengers with confirmed tickets, reservations by the Airport Manager, expensive.

**Paying Guest Establishments**, arranged through the Tourist Office, are expensive.

## REFRESHMENT

In Delhi you'll find something for every wallet and taste. Cold turkey or French pastry? No problem, it's here.

For good and cheap cooking, check around Pahar Ganj. Great fruit juices, fresh pressed, by the bazar facing the railway station. Otherwise, lots of foodstalls on the streets, tiny restaurants serving simple Indian food; i.e. masala dosa. Plus there are the restaurants in the hotels and lodges. **Lord's Cafe**, by Hotel Vishal, offers European and Chinese cooking. From here it's only a few more steps, left or right, to other restaurants with similar fare. Also in the Main Bazar is the more expensive **Metropolitan Restaurant**.

Around Connaught Place is a number of fast food places, icecream parlors, and snack bars. **Nirula's**, in L-Block, is particularly popular, offering everything you can imagine; downstairs are an icecream parlor (no seating), a fast food (hamburger) place, and pastries and cakes. Upstairs the Potpourri Restaurant is full of flowers, and friendly waiters. The cheapest pizza runs 16.-Rs (tomato and cheese), soups (7.50), chili con carne (19.-), and you can have a go at the salad bar for 23.-Rs per person no sharing).

Another fast food place is **McDowell's (!) Pizza King**, N 6, with a computerized cash register and western prices. Next to Regal Cinema on southern Connaught Place, not far from Gaylord's, at 16 Regal Building, is **Standard Restaurant**, featuring stucco ceilings, chandeliers, and fine German pastry (6.-Rs). **El-Arab**, 13 Regal Building, Connaught Place, offers an excellent Lebanese buffet dinner (32.-Rs), great since you can eat as much as you want. **Kwality Restaurant**, 7 Regal Building, is much too expensive.

**Sona Rupa Restaurant**, 46 Janpath, is excellent and reasonable, offering southern Indian food. Readers write in about **Restaurant Palace**, a luxury place on Janpath, AC, but still cheaper than **Volga** and **Host**. But you'll need your own definition of cheap.

In **Wenger House**, A-Block, next to Amexco or in **Central Court Hotel**, both on Connaught Place, you'll find cakes and sweets. Downstairs in the luxury hotel, **Oberoi International**, you'll find international meats and sausages.

You might shop in **Super Bazar**, on eastern Connaught Place; prices aren't super, but everything is here, open 10:00-19:00 h. Or try in (Maha) **Palik Bazar**, at the southern end of Connaught Place, entrance on Janpath.

## SHOPPING

Those who don't plan to travel too extensively through India, or who just want to pick up a few knick-knacks before returning home, can find a wide selection of Indian wares at reasonable prices. Four sections of town are of particular interest.

**Chandi Chowk**: The Silver Market, south of Old Delhi Railway Station and west of the Red Fort, offers a large selection of jewelry and consumer goods, silverware and other metal products, along with traditional Indian crafts.

**Pahar Ganj**: The Main Bazar, west of New Delhi Railway Station, north of Connaught Circus, features all traditional Indian goods, souvenirs (made for tourists), fruit and vegetables. This is the place to buy shoes and clothes cut to western taste, frequently with popular brand names made in India. Everything is super cheap, but still don't forget to bargain.

Right next to Hotel Vishal is a small shop with a large selection of incense, henna, and all types of perfume.

**Connaught Place**: And the surrounding area is the main business center of northern India, particularly domestic and international high finance. Everything is overpriced, but the quality is frequently good. In Mohan Singh Place, on the left coming from Connaught Place, you'll find a colorful mixture of eastern and western shops, black marketeers, money changers and pawnbrokers (fences). This is a place to bargain like crazy, where dream prices are possible, since few westerners venture in here.

**Super Bazar**: East of Connaught Place, junk of every sort, much made in the west. The department store is open on Sundays, closed on Mondays.

**Janpath**: On its western side, boasts numerous small shops where a bit of bargaining will get you tremendous prices, despite the ever-present "fixed prices" signs. For musical instruments, have a look in G-Block, near Marina Hotel. Or try in Panchkuin Road, behind Sant Sucheta Kriplani Hospital.

**State Emporia Complex**: This conglomerate of state-run shops from all the states of India offers a tremendous selection of every Indian ware you can imagine. All the wares of interest are concentrated in three buildings. Here, prices really are fixed, and a bit high. But then you can take your time shopping without any of the usual pressure to buy. This is a place where people with limited time can take a tour through all the crafts of India in half a day!

NEW DELHI
CENTRE

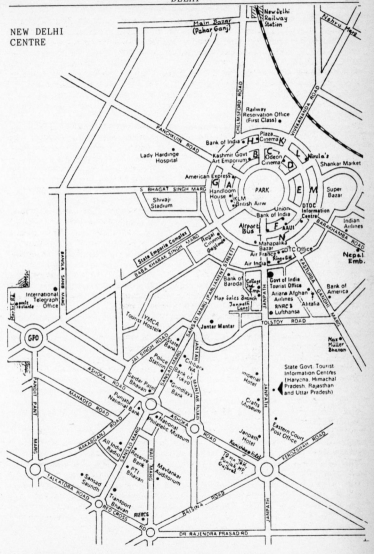

**The Gandhi Memorial Museum:**  Offers a variety of Gandhi-oriented literature. Lots of bookstores around Connaught Place.

**Map Sales Branch of the Survey Department of India:**  Maps are cheap, diagonally across from the Tourist Office on Janpath, open 10:15-17:00 h.

**Film:**  Developed by Kodak,  22 A Janpath,  tel.387215,  but just Ektachrome, not Kodachrome.

**Delhi Trade Fair:**  Held at the end of November,  beginning of December.  Exhibits by all the states of India provide a good overview of Indian industry.

**Sending Parcels Home:**  If you do any serious shopping,  at least part of your purchases will have to be sent home in parcels.  In Pahar Ganj is the excellent Parcel Packing Service,  tel.778298, across from Khanna Cinema,  info in Vishal Hotel.  You receive good and friendly advice.  A metal box,  or basket,  10-20 kg, costs 40.- to 50.-Rs.  In the shop are all types and sizes of packing material.  For packing and sewing, think 10.- to 40.-Rs, depending upon size.  The parcel cards can be filled out there; you bring it to the post office yourself.  The work is clean and orderly, takes an hour; there's nothing simpler!

## ACTIVITIES

**Swimming:**  It can get terribly hot in Delhi,  making a refreshing swim great. But the only swimming pools are in luxury hotels. In Hotel Imperial,  the fun begins at 25.-Rs,  ditto Ashoka Hotel. In Ranjit Hotel,  Maharaja Ranjit Singh Road,  3.-Rs by scooter from Connaught Place, use of the pool costs 12.-Rs.

**Delhi Diary:**  For cultural events,  have a look, costs 1.50 Rs, or ask in your hotel.  The magazine contains all important Delhi addresses.

**American Library and Reading Room:**  24 Kasturba Gandhi Marg, open 10:30-18:00 h.

**British Council's Library:**  AIFACS Building,  Rafi Marg,  is open 10:00-19:00 h.

**Max Mueller Bhavan:**  If you came to India to read German newspapers and magazines,  3 Kasturba Gandhi Marg,  200 m to the right,  coming from Connaught Place;  the Reading Room and Library are open Mon-Sat 11:00-18:00 h, with frequent events in the evenings.

## SIGHTS

Delhi has little you couldn't see elsewhere, i.e. in Agra.

**The Red Fort:**  Completed in 1648, enter through Lahore Gate. First you pass a collection of souvenir shops,  descendants of Meena Bazar,  run by relatively upper-class women for the moghul court. After the courtyard and gateway immediately following is the Public Audience Hall.  Within the well-kept grounds are the Private Audience Hall,  living quarters, a mosque, and Royal Baths. Evenings,  a slide show is presented,  costs 3.- or 5.-Rs.

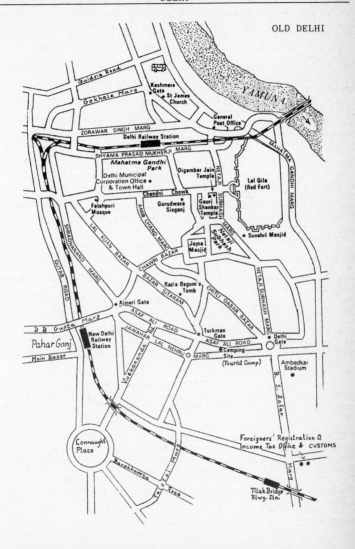

OLD DELHI

General admission is 0.50 Rs, open from sunrise to sunset. If you're short on time, and heading to Agra, then see its Fort instead.

**Jama Mashid:** The largest mosque in India. It was completed in 1658 under Shah Jahan. Regular prayers are still held today. For this reason, the courtyard is closed for brief periods during prayer time to non-Muslims. Entrance is permitted only without shoes. There's a nominal admission charge to climb the minaret. The mosque closes 20 minutes before sunset.

**Rajghat:** 1 km south of the Fort, the Tomb of Mahatma Gandhi, Father of the Country, a place of pilgrimage, particularly on the date of Gandhi's death, January 30th, when tens of thousands flock here. Nearby is Sangrahalaya, the **Gandhi Memorial Museum.** You'll find a number of these elsewhere in India, particularly in Ahmedabad, site of his ashram.

**Indira Gandhi's house:** Residence of the late Mother of the Nation, at 1 Safdarjung Road, preserved just as she left it. The spot on which she was shot is marked with a glass shrine. Open daily, except Mondays, 10:00-17:00 h.

**Lakshmi Narayan Temple:** Also known as Birla Temple, a sacred Hindu site, dedicated to Lakshmi, the Goddess of Fortune, and her husband, Narayan, an incarnation of the creator, Vishnu. The temple, however, also contains a Buddhist Prayer Room. The facility was dedicated in 1939 by Mahatma Gandhi. At the time, he was residing in nearby Birla House. Both 1 km west of Connaught Place.

All the above sites, and a few in between, are easily accessible by foot in one day, with the aid of an occasional tonga or bus. The following tour should be done by scooter, taxi or bus.

**The National Museum:** Like so many such museums, a bit stuffy. The concept confines itself to the exhibition of old, lovely, or valuable pieces. Everyday objects are rarely shown. Little background information is given. But in 1949, India had problems more important than developing a new museum concept. The facility features departments of Anthropology, Prehistory, Early History, Harappa and Maurya Cultures, the Guptas, Middle Ages, Bronzes, Manuscripts, and Miniature Paintings. Located 500 m west of India Gate, open Tues-Sun 10:00-17:00 h, costs 0.50 Rs.

**Lodi Garden:** Pleasant, quiet, and green, featuring lovely painted tombs dating from the 15th and 16th centuries.

**Hauz Khas:** A complex of buildings constructed during the early 14th century by Ala-ud-Din Khilji. It was designed as the seat of his Timur Lenks government after a victory over the Tughlaks. A

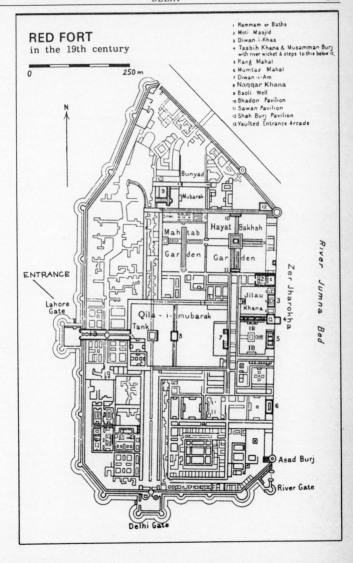

RED FORT
in the 19th century

0                250 m

N

1  Hammam or Baths
2  Moti Masjid
3  Diwan i-Khas
4  Tasbih Khana & Musamman Burj
   with river wicket & steps to this below it.
5  Rang Mahal
6  Mumtaz Mahal
7  Diwan-i-Am
8  Naqqar Khana
9  Baoli Well
10 Bhadon Pavilion
11 Sawan Pavilion
12 Shah Burj Pavilion
13 Vaulted Entrance Arcade

Bunyad

Mubarak

Hayat Bakhsh

Mahtab

Garden        Garden

ENTRANCE

Lahore
Gate

Qila - i - Mubarak

Tank

Jilau

Khana

River Jumna Bed

Zer Jharokha

Asad Burj

River Gate

Delhi Gate

Koran school was housed here too. Today, only part of the complex remains. A visit is only worthwhile in conjunction with a
trip to Qutb Minar; you're half-way there. Nearby is **Begum
Mosque**, also dating from the 14th century. Both are 8 km south
of Connaught Place, left and right of Mehrauli Road.

**Qutb Minar** (Kutab Minar): A 71 m high sandstone victory tower,
probably built to celebrate the victory by invading Muslims over
the Hindus around 1200 AD. Construction began in 1211, with
completion of the minaret by 1236. In the 14th and 15th centuries
it was restored and beautified, but an earthquake in the early
19th century damaged part. This damage could be repaired, but
to this day "the world's most perfect tower" still leans a bit.
Climb to the top.

**Quwwat-ul-Islam-Mashid** (Mosque of the Might of Islam): Constructed nearby from 27 Hindu and Jain temples torn down in
1193, according to an inscription above the east portal.

**The Iron Pillar:** Made of 99.75% pure wrought iron (hence rust-
free!), dates from the 4th century AD. It's thought to have originated in Bihar. Originally, it was likely crowned with a statue
of Garuda, messenger of the gods. If you can stand with your
back to the column, reach back around it, and are able to touch
your fingers, then you are a lucky person indeed; try! Located
15 km south of Connaught Place, get bus 504 or 505 from Super
Bazar at Connaught Circus. Bus 530 heads here half hourly from
Connaught Place, costs 1.50 Rs.

**Mausoleum of Humayan:** Dating from the 16th century, was the
architectural forerunner of the Taj Mahal in Agra. If you're
going to Agra, you've no need to visit here. But if you don't
have time to visit Agra, this sandstone monument, 48 m by 48 m
(38 m high), featuring marble inlay, is a must. Built by a widow in honor of her husband. In Agra, it's the other way
around. Located 5 km southeast of Connaught Place.

**Tours:** For 8.-Rs, a conducted tour departs from the Indian
Tourism Development Corporation, L-Block on Connaught Place.
Starting time is 07:15 h in the summer and 09:15 h during the
winter, takes 3 h. The price includes all admission fees. The
following monuments are visited: Jantar Mantar, India Gate, Mau-
soleum of Humayan, Lakshmi Narayan Temple, and Qutb Minar.
   Also offered are an Old Delhi Tour and a Museums Tour.
Bookings 06:30-22:00 h at Indian Tourism Development Corporation
(ITDC), L-Block, Connaught Place, tel.40982. A combined tour of
Old Delhi and New Delhi costs 16.-Rs, including all admission
fees.
   The same tour is offered by Delhi Tourism, N-Block, Connaught
Place, for 15.-Rs. A similar tour is offered by Delhi Transport
Corp., Connaught Circus, between Janpath and Kasturba Gandhi

QUTB MINAR
Quwwat–ul–Islam Mashid

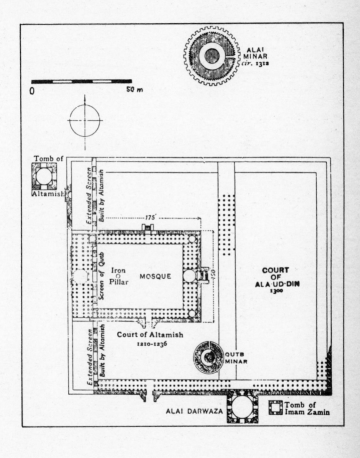

ALAI MINAR
*cir.* 1312

0                    50 m

Tomb of
Altamish

Extended Screen
Built by Altamish

175'

Iron Pillar

MOSQUE

Screen of Qutb

150

COURT
OF
ALA·UD·DIN
1300

Extended Screen
Built by Altamish

Court of Altamish
1210–1236

QUTB MINAR

ALAI DARWAZA

Tomb of
Imam Zamin

Marg, costs 10.-Rs.

**National Holiday:** January 26th, Republic Day is celebrated in Delhi with military parades, and a historic maharaja-style procession, featuring splendidly decorated elephants, horses, camels, marching bands, ethnic groups in traditional garments... a spectacle.

## AROUND DELHI

**Agra:** If you don't have a lot of time, but still want to see the Taj Mahal, then just take the tour. At the Tourist Corner in New Delhi Railway Station you can book a tour departing Delhi at 06:30 h, returning at 22:30 h. Your route includes: Sikandra, Agra Fort, Taj Mahal, Fatehpur Sikri, Mathura (Krishna's birthplace), costs 60.-Rs Deluxe, 80.-Rs Super Deluxe, 100.-Rs Video. During full moon, you return at 05:00 h the following day, costs 10.-Rs extra. Other tours are offered by various travel agencies. Agra tours for 45.-Rs are possible.

**Sohna:** 54 km south of Delhi toward Alwar, visit the sulphur springs, and stay at the Haryana Tourist Complex, set on a hill, **(D)**30.-Rs.

## TIPS
### Tourist Offices

**Government of India Tourist Office:** 88 Janpath, New Delhi 110001, tel.320005-8, 09:00-19:00 h, opens in the summer at 08:00 h. If you have any questions, ask at the Tourist Office on Janpath. On the left side of Janpath coming from Connaught Place, good information brochures and a wealth of information, particularly if you have unusual questions.

**Information Windows:** At the airport, open round the clock.

**Information Offices:** In Old Delhi and New Delhi Railway Stations, open 07:00-21:00 h.

**State Information Offices:** For the following states are located in the Chanderlock Building, 36 Janpath: **Haryana** (tel.344911), **Himachal Pradesh** (tel.345320), **Rajasthan** (tel.322332), **Uttar Pradesh** (tel.322251).

In the State Emporium Complex on Baba Kharak Singh Marg are the following State Information Offices (the letter-number combinations describe the stairway number): **Andhra Pradesh**-B6 (tel.343894), **Assam**-B1 (tel.321967), **Bihar**-A5 (370147), **Karnataka**-C4 (tel.343862), **Maharasthra**-A8 (tel.343774), **Orissa**-B4 (tel.344580), **West Bengal**-A2 (tel.343775).

Tourist Offices in Kanishka Hotel on Ashok Road: **Gujarat**, **Jammu & Kashmir**, **Madhya Pradesh**, and **Punjab**.

**Visa Extensions:** The Foreigners' Regional Registration Office, Hans Bhavan, Bahadur Shah Zafar Marg, tel.272790, 2 km east of Connaught Place, near Tilak Bridge, miserly about extensions! Open 10:00-16:00 h, four passport photos required.

**Income Tax Clearing Certificates:** Necessary for anyone staying longer than 90 days in India, should be filled out at the Foreigners' Registration Office. You'll need all your bank receipts to

CHANAKYAPURI
Diplomatic Enclave

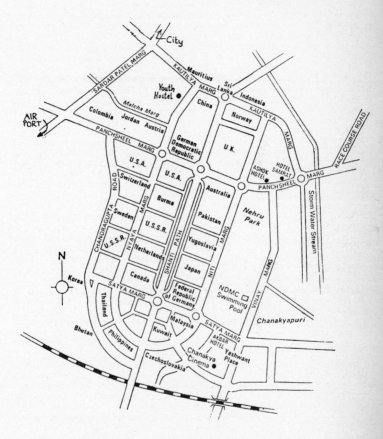

prove you changed money. It takes a half hour to get the certificate in the income tax foreign section. Tell the taxi driver to
take you to ITO near Tilak Bridge. You can pick up this certificate 14 days before your date of departure.

**Special Permits:** For the various restricted regions are available
at the the Ministry of Home Affairs, Lok Nayak Bhavan, Khan
Market, tel.611984, open just 16:00–17:00 h. The permit for Darjeeling is available at Foreigners' Regional Registration Office
(see above), in Delhi and in Calcutta, plus at Indian consulates
abroad, i.e. in Nepal.

Should the Punjab again require a special permit, check with
the Department of Interior, Undersecretary for Foreigners.

**Medical Attention:** Particularly good in Delhi; ask at your consulate for the name of a doctor (dentist) they recommend. If
you're into homeopathic medicine, visit Homeopathic Store, Connaught, across from York restaurant.

**International Student ID Cards:** Issued and extended at the Student Travel Information Centre, Hotel Imperial, tel.344789, Janpath, in a side building to the hotel, on the west side of Janpath, 300 m south of the tourist office.

**Cheap Flights:** To Europe and elsewhere are available on Connaught Place. You'll find a number of hawkers in front of American Express. Ask for their business card and compare. Most of
the travel agencies offering cheap flights are based around Connaught Place, so it's easy to shop around.

Two good addresses: **Vikas Travel** in Pahar Ganj, next to
Hotel Vishal; or try the **Student Travel Information Centre** (expen-
sive) in Hotel Imperial, on the west side of Janpath, tel.344789.
Think 3600.-Rs for a flight to Europe.

**Airlines:**
  Syrian Arab Airlines, 13/90 Connaught Circus, tel.343218, parti-
  cularly cheap flights to Europe.
  Aeroflot, Kanchenjunga Building, 18 Barakhamba Road,
  tel.42843.
  Air Lanka, Stic Travels & Tours, Hotel Imperial, Rooms 5 & 6,
  Janpath, tel.344789.
  Alitalia, Surya Kiran Building, 19 Kasturba Gandhi Marg,
  tel.351019.
  Indian Airlines, Kanchenjunga Building, 18 Barakhamba Road,
  tel.40084-6.
  Lufthansa, 56 Janpath, tel.343234.
  PIA, 102 Kailash Building, 26 Kasturba Gandhi Marg,
  tel.43161.
  Royal Nepal Airlines Corp., 44 Janpath, tel.321572.
  Thai Air, 12A, Connaught Circus, tel.343608.

**Banks:** Many have offices around Connaught Place and along
Parliament Street, making currency rate comparison simple.
  **American Express**, Wenger House, A-Block, Connaught Place.
  **Indian Overseas Bank**, Malhotra Building, Janpath, tel.42985.
  **State Bank of India**, Parliament Street, tel.312635.

Banks are generally open Mon-Fri 10:00-14:00 h, Sat until
12:00 h.
   **State Bank of India Evening Branch**, Mon-Fri 10:00-18:00 h, Sat
   10:00-12:00 h & 14:00-16:00 h.
   **Thomas Cook Exchange Booth** in Hotel Imperial gives good
   rates, unbureaucratic.

**Poste Restante**: GPO Old Delhi near Old Delhi Railway Station. All
mail ends up there which isn't specifically marked GPO New Delhi! The Post Restante window is open 08:00-18:30 h. Other windows are open Mon-Fri 10:00-17:00 h, Sat until 15:00 h.
In mid 1985, Poste Restante was moved to the Delivery Post Office
on Market Street, GPO New Delhi.

Poste Restante Address:
Name (underline family name!)
GPO
New Delhi 110001

**Amexco Clients' Mail**: Wenger House, 1st Floor, Connaught Place,
A-Block, New Delhi 110001, open 10:00-13:00 h & 14:00-16:00 h,
Sat 10:00-12:00 h, costs US$1.- for non-customers. In Delhi the
service is quite reliable.

**Amexco Clients' Mail Address:**
   Name (underline family name)
   c/o American Express Travel Division
   Wenger House
   1st Floor
   Connaught Place
   A-Block
   New Delhi 110001

**Telephone**: Calls to Europe or America are simplest through the
Overseas Communication Service, Bangla Sahib Road, west of Connaught Place, north of the GPO; expect a 1-2 h wait, costs
90.-Rs for 3 minutes to Europe.

**TIPS**
**Association of Voluntary Agencies for Rural Development** (AVARD):
If you're interested in being helpful, **The Directory of Voluntary
Action** could be of use to you. It's available from AVARD, 5 F.F.
Institutional Area, Deendayal Upadhayaya Marg, New Delhi
110002. AVARD, a coordinating agency, is located on the second
floor of the building. On the first floor is a Women's Department
with a small library run by helpful women knowledgeable about
social aspects of Indian life.
**The Gandhi Peace Foundation**: Across from AVARD, of interest to
those concerned with the philosophical aspects of development aid.

# PUNJAB & HARYANA

If you enter India via the land
route, there is no way around Amritsar, the main Sikh settlement.
Headed to Kashmir, you have to
pass through the Punjab; be sure to
plan a side trip to Amritsar. And
before you come, glance at our section on Sikhs and their history.

After Independence, the Punjab
was divided into a Pakistani half
with its capital in Lahore and an
Indian eastern half with its capital
in Amritsar. Since relations with
Pakistan were never cordial, it was
decided to have a new capital further from the border.

The famous French architect and
city planner, Le Corbusier, received
the assignment. Construction began
in the mid 1950s. Until the completion of Chandigarh, the British
summer capital, Simla, served as capital. When the Punjab was
divided in 1966 into the states of Haryana and Punjab, the
northern part, including the capital Simla, went over to Himachal
Pradesh.

Today, Chandigarh is an independent Union Territory, run by
the central government in Delhi. At the same time it serves as
capital of both Punjab and Haryana. Hindus are a majority here,
with Sikhs forming a large section of the population.

Despite repeated territorial division and destruction in the
wake of fighting between Muslims, en route to Pakistan, and
Sikhs, wandering east, this is the most affluent lowland state in
India. Certainly a testimony to the strength of the people!

Outside Amritsar, there are few sights of interest. And it
isn't unusual for Punjab to be closed briefly to tourism by unrest (as seen in 1984 and 1985).

## PUNJAB & HARYANA

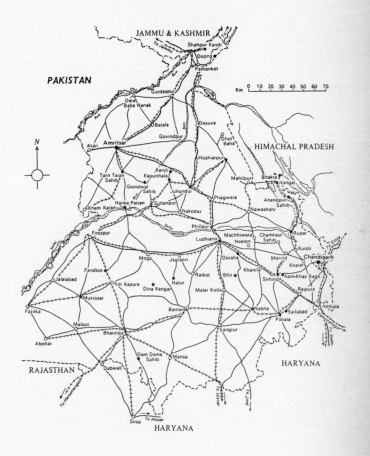

# Chandigarh

This town of 500,000 was built following the division of Punjab
between Pakistan and India to replace the historic capital, Lahore.  To the design of French city planner, Le Corbusier, the
town is spread comfortably over 47 Sectors.  It is simple to find
your way around.

However, many intended areas of green remain barren, lending
outlying areas a depressing appearance.

## COMING - GOING

**By Air:**  Direct flights to Delhi (256.-Rs).  Five flights weekly
via Jammu & Srinagar (400.-Rs) to Leh (450.-Rs).  Vayudoot
flies thrice weekly to Kulu (290.-Rs). The Indian Airlines office
is in Sector 17,  near the bus stand,  tel.40539.  If you've a
morning flight,  be sure to book a scooter the night before,
takes 40 minutes to the airport. There is no place to stay near
the airport.

**By Rail:** Chandigarh's railway station is so far from town, it's
simpler to get a bus to Kashmir,  Amritsar,  or Himachal Pradesh. Buses 6,  6A,  6B, and 37 connect the railway station to
the center of town.

**By Bus:**  The bus stand is in Sector 37.  The Tourist Office is
inside.  Buses from Delhi (depart from Interstate Bus Terminal
by Kashmir Gate) cost 24.-Rs,  take 5 h.  Deluxe buses cost
double, AC buses equipped with video 60.-Rs.

Buses to Simla (16.-,  5 h), Manali (42.-, 14 h), Kulu (36.-,
11 h),  Dharamsala (5 daily,  9 h),  Amritsar (5 h),  Hardwar
(30.-, 8 h).

## A NIGHT'S REST

**Youth Hostel,** **(Dm)**8.-, between Chandigarh and Pinjore, get the
bus. **YMCA,** Sector 11, tel.26532, **(S)**20.-.

The Tourist Office recommends state-run guest houses, and will
reserve a room by phone. The cheapest guesthouse is **Panchayat
Bhavan,** Sector 18, **(Dm)**7.-, **(D)**24.-. **Yatri Niwas,** in Sector 18,
**(S)**37.-,  **(D)**52.-. **State Guesthouse,** Sector 6, get Bus 11A or 17,
**(D)**110.-.

Also cheap are **Alankar,**  Sector 22,  near the bus stand,
tel.21303.  **Amar,**  Sector 22,  near the bus stand, tel.26608. Or
**Jullundur,** Sector 22, near the bus stand, tel.20777.

Lots of cafes and restaurants in Sector 17, downtown.

## SIGHTS

**The Secretary,  High Court,**  and **Assembly Hall:**  Must sees,  in
Sector 1,  in the north of town. Typical Corbusier buildings, very
pretty too.  From the top of the Secretary you've a great view of
the town.

**The Rock Garden:**  Not far away,  a trash-art-dream creation,
opens at 10:00 h, costs 0.25 Rs.

## CHANDIGARH

| | | | |
|---|---|---|---|
| A | Secretariat | H | Panchayat Bhawan |
| B | Vidhan Sabha | J | Jullunder Hotel |
| C | High Court | K | Yatri Niwas |
| D | Rock Garden | L | YWCA |
| E | Open Hand | M | Foreigners' Registration Office |
| F | Museum & Art Gallery | N | Banks |
| G | Rose Garden | O | Bus Stand & Tourist Office |
| | | P | GPO |

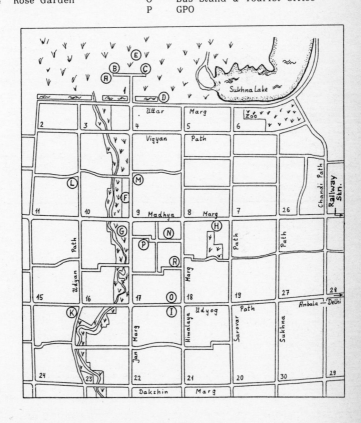

**Sukha Lake:**   Nearby,   artificial.   Boats are available for rent daily, except Mondays. To Sector 1 get buses 11A, 13, or 17.
**Rose Garden:** In Sector 16.
**Art Museum:**  Not far off in Sector 10,  offers a good collection of paintings and sculpture, open Tues–Sun 10:00–16:30 h.
**Chandigarh Shopping Centre:**  In the evening,  take a walk through,  in Sector 17,  where you'll find typical Punjab wares. Then have a bite in one of numerous restaurants or cafes.

Chandigarh is a very Indian town,  a good stopover on your way north.

## AROUND CHANDIGARH

**Pinjore Terrace Garden:**   20 km from town.  Well worth a look; in fact if you like luxury,  you might stay in one of the princely rooms **(D)**100.-Rs.  Spread over seven terraces,  on weekend evenings the fountain lights are turned on.  The gardens feature palm trees,  English lawns,  and animals.  Many consider this a real oasis.

# Amritsar

Located 440 km northwest of Delhi,  Amritsar (= pool of nectar) was founded in 1577 by the fourth great Sikh teacher,  Guru Ram Das.  This holiest of Sikh towns was destroyed in 1761 by Afghan armies under Ahmad Shah Durani, but rebuilt in 1764. The golden dome was crowned in 1802,  giving birth to the name "Golden Temple".
     During the fight for independence,  the British unleashed a terrible blood bath upon a group of peaceful demonstrators,  an act recorded by history as the Amritsar Massacre.
     The only land route between Pakistan and India runs between Lahore,  Pakistan and Amritsar.  Every overlander passes through here,  when the border (and Punjab) aren't closed.  Amritsar is nicknamed "Gateway to India".

## COMING –GOING

**By Air:**   Direct flights daily to Delhi (430.-).   Cheap flights twice weekly via Jammu (200.-) to Srinagar;   the rest of the week,  expect to pay 365.-Rs. Except in times of crisis, flights to the Afghanistan capital, Kabul.
     The airport is north of town;  the Indian Airlines bus costs 8.-Rs.  The Indian Airlines Booking Office on Mall Road at Albert Road is open 10:00–17:00 h.
**By Rail:** From the bus stand to the railway station costs 2.-Rs by rickshaw.  Good connections via Delhi and Agra,  along the Ganges Plains to Calcutta-Howrah.  Trains east,  via Lucknow, are ideal for those heading direct to Nepal or Darjeeling,  with

**AMRITSAR** TEMPLE DISTRICT

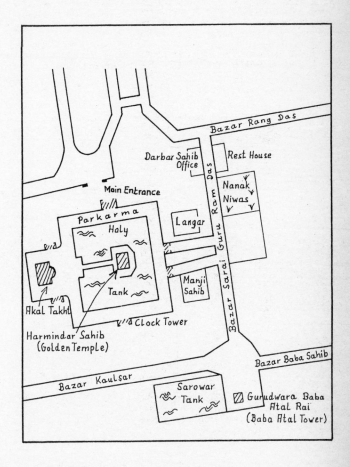

## AMRITSAR

| | | | |
|---|---|---|---|
| 1 | Golden Temple | 7 | Palace Hotel |
| 2 | Durgiana Temple | 8 | GPO & Telegraph Office |
| 3 | Jallianwala Bagh | 9 | Indian Airlines |
| 4 | Guru Ram Dass Sarai | 10 | Customs Office |
| 5 | Tourist Guest House | 11 | Punjab Government Emporium |
| 6 | Youth Hostel, | 12 | Kashmir Government Emporium |
|   | & Tourist Office | 13 | State Bank of India |

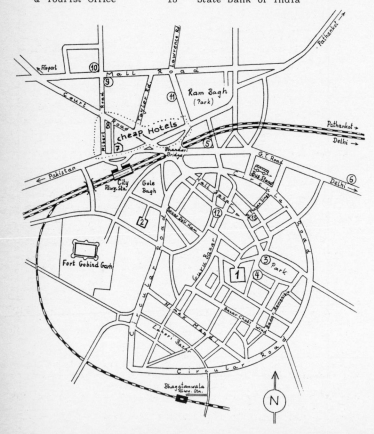

a side trip to Delhi. Buses connect Lucknow with the Nepal
border. The train from Amritsar to Lucknow takes 18-20 h,
costs 65.-Rs.
  Seven trains daily to Delhi, takes 7-12 h, costs 40.-Rs. One
daily at 09:00 h to Lahore in Pakistan.
**By Bus:** Good, hourly connections to Delhi-Kashmiri Gate, takes
10 h, costs 40.-Rs. To Chandigarh (5 h), Pathankot (3 h), and
Jammu (5 h). The most comfortable way to Srinagar is by direct bus, costs 75.- (ordinary) or 100.-Rs (deluxe). Buses at
least hourly to Wagah, the road border, where buses on to
Lahore, Pakistan await.

## A NIGHT'S REST
Cheap lodgings around the bus stand and across from the rail-
way station. Think **(D)**35.-Rs.
  The **Youth Hostel**, **(Dm)**8.- (members **(Dm)**6.-Rs), 1.5 km from
the bus stand, 2.-Rs by rickshaw.
  Worth a special mention is **Tourist Guesthouse**, G.T. Road,
near Bhandari Bridge and Hide Market, tel.46130, **(S)**20.-,
**(D)**30.-, **(Dm)**8.-.
  You can park your camper by **Tourist Hostel**.
  In the Temple District, lodgings range from cheap to free of
charge in various Sikh lodgings (see below).
  Cheap restaurants are collected around the inexpensive hotels.
The better and more expensive are along Lawrence and M.M.
Malviya Road in Ram Bagh, the new section of town, north of
the tracks.

## SIGHTS
**Golden Temple:** The religious center and main attraction, surrounded by the holy pool. The **GRANTH SHAHIB**, the Sikh's sacred
book, is preserved here, and recited from continuously. In the
room below, traditional religious music is played without end.
The Temple District is open to all, except in times of political,
police, or military conflict.
  Everybody is invited to free room and board for three days,
provided you conform to temple rules. The same goes for accommodations in the near vicinity. The atmosphere is agreeable.
**Temple Museum:** Be sure to visit, featuring a collection of gold
and silverware.
**Baba-Atal Tower:** Equally of interest, 42 m tall, covered with
fresco inside and out, depicting the life of Guru Nanak.
**Akal Takht Building:** Where religious councils are held.

## TIPS
**Tourist Office:** In the youth hostel, open Mon-Sat 09:00-17:00 h.
**Information Office:** Right of the entrance to the Golden Temple, is
happy to answer any questions about the Sikhs.
**Post Office** and **Telegraph Office:** Located across from the railway
station on Court Road.
**Indian Airlines:** Mall Road, the airport bus departs from here.

# JAMMU & KASHMIR

In the northwest of India, the state of Jammu & Kashmir is the largest and most densely populated portion of Kashmir, which sought local sovereignty after British withdrawal. During a revolt by Hindu volunteers and Afghan tribes against the Muslim leadership, both India and Pakistan got involved in the fighting. Negotiations under UN auspices led to the division of Kashmir into two zones, administrated by India and Pakistan respectively. The Indian zone, however, was annexed by India shortly thereafter, despite a UN resolution to the contrary. Kashmir's Prime Minister Sheik Abdullah was arrested.

Border conflicts with China between 1959 and 1962, left part of Ladakh occupied by the Chinese. Activity by Islamic freedom fighters resulted in the 1965 Indian-Pakistan War, which was settled under Soviet initiative, through UN sponsored negotiations at the Tashkent Conference in 1966.

Freedom of movement is greatly restricted in Indian Kashmir. The strategic highlands remain under army control. The pass roads connecting Srinagar and Leh / Ladakh often close for hours when a column of military vehicles rolls in the opposite direction: the pass roads are only one lane in spots. That means everyone off the bus at the control point, and wait. You can't even take a walk, because nobody knows when the road will reopen. Closed to tourism are the region north of the road and another road, not open to public transport, between Leh and Manali. To visit these regions, you need a permit. When trekking, be sure to avoid the closed military zones!

Almost the entire population of Kashmir is Muslim, though traditional habits aren't as strict here as elsewhere. Polygamy is rarely practised, women don't wear veils. People are relaxed about prayers and alcoholic consumption.

JAMMU & KASHMIR

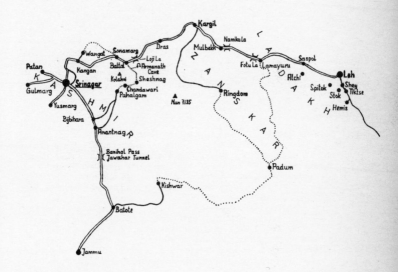

The Kashmir Valley is set between 1585 m and 2743 m. It is 152 km long and 56 km wide. High, snow-covered mountains, surrounded by green valleys are cut by raging streams full of trout. Lotus blossoms bloom in summer; the autumn is colored by fields of saffron. The air is clean, and crystal clear. There is no hurry; everyone has lots of time. On the way to Srinagar, notice the nomads, driving herds, with all their possessions borne on small ponies.

The landscape has special appeal. Sometimes Kashmir is called the "Switzerland of India", though there is little in common beyond the high mountains. Perhaps "Happy Valley" is better.

Jammu & Kashmir is a resort region where wealthy Indians escape the worst monsoon months from May to July. The monsoon rarely makes it this far. And thanks to the high altitude (Srinagar 1768 m), the climate provides refreshing relief from the heat and humidity further south. Jammu & Kashmir's popularity is reflected in higher prices. Even in cheap houseboats, don't be startled by the cost of food and drink.

# Srinagar

Set at 1768 m altitude, the capital of Kashmir is situated on Dal Lake (25 km²). The Jelum River flows through town. Srinagar is famous for its houseboats, first seen under the British. Canals crisscrossing town give Srinagar the name, "Venice of India".

Moghul emperors liked to spend monsoon season here. Gardens, ringing Srinagar, date from that era. The valley was transformed into a "Garden of Eden".

In mid 1983, a treasure worth US$400 million was discovered in the basement of the Ministry of Finance, where it had lain for 30 years. Over the course of three decades, a former employee of the last Maharaja, Hari Singh, regularly appeared secretly to check if the diamond-studded harness, cases of rubies and emeralds, splendid garments, swords, and priceless diamonds were still secure.

### COMING - GOING

**By Air:** The airport is 15 km from town. Daily flights to Amritsar (388.-Rs), Jammu (223.-Rs); five flights weekly to Chandigarh (571.-Rs); thrice weekly to Leh (334.-Rs); twice daily to Delhi (617.-Rs, by airbus 756.-Rs).

All tourists are greeted at the airport by officers of the Tourist Department and luxury bused to the Tourist Reception Centre (TRC), where hoteliers, houseboat owners, etc. await.

**By Rail:** The nearest railway station is Jammu Tawi, 305 km from Srinagar, at the foot of the mountains. This is the last stop of many express trains running from Calcutta, via Lucknow, Delhi, even Poona and Bombay. Only on the long runs is a train worth while.

SRINAGAR

1 TRC and Buses to Jammu & Leh      5 Raghunath Temple
2 GPO                               6 Pather Mosque
3 Museum                            7 Naoshband Sahib Mosque
4 Youth Hostel                      8 Jami Mashid

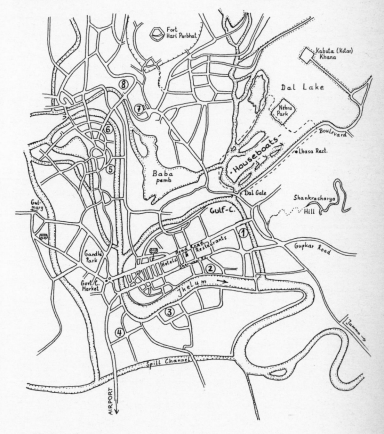

**By Bus:**   Direct buses from Old Delhi Kashmiri Gate,   several
times daily,   costs 60.-Rs to Jammu. Ashok Travel & Tours provides deluxe bus service from Delhi to Srinagar including a
night in Jammu,   departs daily at 07:00 h,   from Ashok Travel & Tours office,   L-1 Connaught Place,   New Delhi.   To Delhi
departs from Srinagar Tourist Reception Centre,   also at
07:00 h, costs 190.-Rs one way.

Direct buses to Amritsar-Jammu,  takes 5 h, costs 20.-Rs. From
Jammu Tourist Reception Centre at 07:30 h in A-Class buses
(wider,  more comfortable seats),  costs 37.-Rs. Buses, too, from
Jammu Tawi Railway Station,   should you be arriving by rail.
Buses with various classes of comfort await trains from Delhi,
and don't depart until all the passengers are settled.   So
there's no hurry getting a ticket!  It's not worth while spending an extra day in Jammu. There is little to see. A few cheap
lodgings are,   as usual, in the bazar near the bus stand. American Bar, shakes and juice are cheap.

There are no trains north of Jammu.  The bus takes 10-12 h to
Srinagar;  the scenery is varied and lovely.  You pass through
Jawarhar Tunnel connecting the Kashmir Valley to India during
the winter.  The double-tubed tunnel (2550 m) is in poor condition, dripping all the way. A toll is charged.

**Around Town:**  Your main transports are rickshaw,  taxi,  and
bus. Rent a bicycle for the day; it's cheap.

Along the canals you travel by **Shikara**,   the Srinagar gondola. You'll find them tied up at the ghats.

**Heading Back:**  Get a direct bus to Amritsar, or another nearby
town.  Or get the bus to Jammu, then head on by rail. You can
book rail tickets and reservations (at least four days in advance) through the Northern Railway Out Agency in the courtyard of Badschah Chowk,  near Lal Chowk Bus Stand,  Maulana
Road (about 1.5 km from the Tourist Reception Centre, which is
near a different bus stand from where sightseeing tour buses
depart).  If you aren't up to waiting hours for a ticket,  pick
one up at one of many Srinagar travel agencies:  for a few
rupees more, you save a lot of hassle.

Regional buses to Pahalgam (26.-Rs), Gulmarg (26.-Rs), Sonamarg (24.-Rs),  Yusmarg (22.-Rs),  Daksum (27.-Rs). There are
regular buses to Leh (see Leh).


## A NIGHT'S REST

Upon arrival in Srinagar,  you'll be mobbed at the Tourist
Reception Centre (TRC) by dozens of touts,  some of whom would
even stoop to physical means to drag you to their lodgings.
Your best escape is quick inside the TRC,  where you can book
accommodations at the window. Houseboat owners frequently wait
outside until called by microphone to pick up their guests.  Or
just pretend that you know your way around;   out of the bus

stand head right, then take another right over the bridge, and
then left along the water. On the variously numbered ghats
(docks), you can bargain in peace for a houseboat.
There are four classes, each with officially fixed prices. But
as business is poor (competition from new state-run hotels)
prices are often below the fixed rate. No problem finding a
place!
The top category is Deluxe Class, some featuring chandeliers
and hand-woven carpets. This is where rich Indians and Europeans stay. Globetrotters are rarely willing to pay 200.-Rs
(including meals). Then you have A-Class, B-Class, C-Class
((D)100.-Rs), and Donga Class (S)30.-Rs (including three
meals).
As an example, one of the simpler houseboats: **Houseboat
Martanda** / M. Jaquoob Goona, Dal Lake, Gate 2 (take a shikara), 40.-Rs per person including meals. Alongside, **Houseboat
Snowking** charges 60.-Rs per person with meals. Jaquoob's boat
is a globetrotter hangout. If he's occupied, he'll suggest
another. When you arrive, have him called out at the TRC.
Jaquoob looks after his guests, you'll hardly be bothered by
hawkers.
On most houseboats, don't be surprised if carpet peddlers, or
other tourist leeches hop aboard your boat in the morning, and
make no effort to leave until you buy something. Houseboat
owners pay little attention, after all, they get a commission
which you pay without knowing.
If you aren't careful, some boat owners have been known to
steal from their tenants. Many houseboats can't even be
locked.
Srinagar boasts hotels of every class, including the 5-star
**Hotel Oberoi (D)**750.-Rs. But if you've come all the way here,
stay on a houseboat.

### REFRESHMENT
Compared to the rest of India, food is expensive. But with all
the tourists, the quality and selection are good. You've a rich
selection of vegetables, fruit (tons of cherries in June and July), dried fruits, almonds, and nuts. Outstanding bread,
cakes, pies, and sweets make your mouth water. **Glocken Bakery** on a side street by Dal Gate has a good reputation. The
best local bakery is **JEE/ENN/SONS** on Hotel Road.
Most people prefer to eat on their houseboat. Still, have a
look along the Boulevard and around Dal Gate. If you can't
stand the sight of any more Kashmiri food, try Tibetan in **Lhasa Restaurant**. Srinagar boasts an amazing number of liquor
stores for a Muslim region. Good beer is expensive, but
available.

## SHOPPING

Your largest selection is along Residency Road, around Lambert's Market. Here too are the more serious shops. Head left from the TRC, then your first right along the park. You can satisfy any desire, provided the proper depth of wallet: carpets, hammered silver, papier mâché (visit the papier mâché factory to see how it's made), silk, embroidery, furs, leather goods, Kashmir scarves. The Kashmir wool you see in the west rarely originates in Kashmir, rather it represents a means of processing and quality. In Kashmir the wool is called "pashmina". Notice the wonderful **shatoo** scarves, woven so fine that a tremendous scarf will pass through a tiny ring. However, this quality is expensive, even for Europeans: over 1000.-Rs.

Prices are fixed in the state-run **Kashmir Government Arts Emporium.** You are best off wandering around and comparing prices. Don't let yourself be taken in by a tout, particularly if you're staying on a houseboat.

Be wary of the following offer: you pay a deposit for your souvenirs and they are mailed to your home address. The merchant has your bank address and account number. When your bank transfers him the balance of the money, you can pick up the wares at the customs office near your home. Naturally, many packages never arrive, and you lose your advance deposit. And be advised that you'll have to pay customs duty when picking up the goods, no matter how often the merchant denies it! Think again if you are tempted to use this means of getting your pretty things home.

One useful item to bring home is saffron, a valuable spice, garnered from the stigma in a type of crocus. It takes 15,000 blossoms to produce one kilo.

## SIGHTS

**Dal Lake** and **Nagin Lake:** A boat ride is certainly one of Srinagar's nicest experiences. The **shikara**, Srinagar's gondola, is your primary means of transport. Shikaras of every size and outfit await at the ghats. Helmsmen, frequently youngsters (sometimes just five years of age), are eager to invite you aboard, each cheaper than the other. You'll figure out fast what a ride is actually worth. Bargain!

Take a shikara excursion (think 10.-Rs per hour), through Srinagar's canals and the branches of Dal Lake or Nagin Lake. You'll see lovely plants, lotus blossoms, and rare wildlife including the kingfisher, teal, and golden oriole. A shikara ride can be a very romantic experience. And if you've hunger or thirst, just wink over one of the peddlers plying between houseboats with fruit, flowers, vegetables, sweets, drinks, smoke, groceries and souvenirs. Lay back in your shikara, catch some sun, and enjoy.

You might even take out a shikara on your own.  Ask your houseboat owner if he has one available,  and you're off.  Or perhaps not.  Steering a shikara requires special talent.  It takes a while before you're cruising as fast as a Kashmiri.

Dal Lake and Nagin Lake are connected by Chinar Bagh Canal.  Three islands in Dal Lake are popular among Indians for daytrips.

**Chasma-i-Shahi:**  The smallest moghul garden,  get the local bus from Dal Gate.  Get off at the crossroads to Raj Bhavan.  From here it is 3 km uphill past Nehru Park.  You've a great view of the lake,  particularly the lights at night.  Another moghul garden is in Nishat Bagh, 4 km further on.

**Shalamar Bagh:**  The prettiest garden,  built by Jehangir for his wife,  Nur Jahan.  From May to December,  a slide show is presented in the evening.

**Shri Pratap Singh Museum:**  In Lal Mandi,  open 10:00-17:00 h, daily except Wednesday, featuring exhibits from Kashmir.

**Hari Parvat:**  An 18th-century fort,  which can be visited only with permission from the Tourist Office.

**Two Mosques:**  Worth a visit are **Hazratbah Mosque**, which harbors a hair from the prophet's beard as a cherished relic.  **Jami Masjid** is Srinagar's most important mosque.  Its wooden ceiling is constructed with 300 wooden stakes.

**TIPS**

**Fishing Permit:**  Issued at the Tourist Reception Centre,  cost 75.-Rs per day and rod.  The best season is May to September, on the Lidder in Pahalgam,  Sindh in Sonamarg,  or Bringhi in Kokarnag.  There too,  you can get a fishing licence,  but apply in advance.

**Soura Hospital:**  10 km toward Leh,  a modern clinic,  open mornings for consultation.

**AROUND SRINAGAR & TREKS**

From Srinagar you've a number of bus excursion possibilities. You can take a mountain hike,  rent a pony and camping equipment,  or hire a guide. Jeep trips are offered.

**PAHALGAM**

An excellent departure point for treks,  Pahalgam is 96 km from Srinagar in the Lidder Valley.  Here you'll find ice-cold rivers with some of the best trout fishing in the world.  You can rent a fisherman's cottage;  local help is easy to recruit.  But only fish with a fishing licence!

**Amarnath Caves:**  From Pahalgam,  take a side trip to the snow-covered caves.

**Festival:**  During the July / August full moon,  a festival is held in honor of Shiva. A lingam made of natural ice is revered.

**TREK**
This trekking route from Pahalgam is considered of moderate difficulty; takes 5-6 days:
1st Day:    **Pahalgam – Chandanwari**,    13 km,    from    2150 m to
            2895 m, stay the night in PWD Rest House.
2nd Day:    **Chandanwari – Sheshnag**,    13 km,    climbing to 3718 m,
            PWD Rest House in Wavjan.
3rd Day:    **Sheshnag – Panchtami**,    15 km, 3657 m, PWD Rest House
            in Panchtami.
4th Day:    From    Panchtami    it's    another    8 km    up    to    4175 m;
            you'll have to camp in a tent.
Via Bal Valley is a path to Sonamarg.

The simplest trek runs from Pahalgam out onto Kolohai Glacier.
Your best trekking season is May to mid-October.
1st Day:    **Pahalgam – Aru**, 11 km, climbing to 2414 m.
2nd Day:    **Aru – Lidderwatt**, 11 km, up to 3000 m.
3rd Day:    **Lidderwatt – Kolohai Glacier**, 13 km, 3000 m.
4th Day:    **Lidderwatt – Tarsar**, 12 km, up to 3795 m.
5th Day:    **Lidderwatt – Pahalgam**.

**Cost:**    There are fixed prices for some treks.    The average price
for ponies is 30.-Rs per day, porters costs 25.-Rs per day.

**GULMARG**
This is a popular place to get away;    i.e. lots of tourists. Still,
it's worth a look;    Gulmarg (flower fields).    The valley is set at
2600 m, 60 km from Srinagar.
   The route here winds dangerously through green fields of
rice,    then golden mustard fields, followed by sweet-smelling pine
forest.
   A day tour departs TRC Srinagar at 9:00 h,    costs 39.-Rs,
return at 16:00 h.
   You can rent a horse,    and ride perhaps to Khilanmarg
(40 minutes uphill).    At the top you've a tremendous view across
the glaciers.    The    mountain    to    the    north    is    Nanga    Parbat
(8126 m).
**Golf:**    The highest golf course in the world, for low scores in the
thin air, is open May to October for the summer season.
**Skiing:**    During the winter this is a ski resort, featuring some of
the best runs in the world.    You can rent equipment;    classes are
offered. The lift facilities don't rank with those in Europe.

**A Night's Rest:    New Mountain View Lodge,    (S)**25.-Rs.    Lots of
   other lodges. Plan to stay a few days.

**SONAMARG**
En route from Srinagar to Kargil,    you pass through Sonamarg
(golden field),    where you can profitably spend a couple days.
Set at 2720 m,    all buses en route to Leh stop here; so expect

tourists! Riding is excellent without a guide; costs 30.-Rs per horse per day. But only if you're a good rider. Rooms are excellent in Tourist Bungalow, **(D)**20.-Rs, below town, perfectly quiet, comfortable, showers; book at the tourist office, or better in Srinagar to ensure a reservation.

**Trek:** An excellent trek runs from Sonamarg via **Krishensar** and **Vishensar Lake** to **Gangabal Lake**, and on to **Wangat.** From there, you've buses to Srinagar. Takes at least 5 days. Four of us took three ponies (40.-Rs per pony per day), and two pony driver-guides (5.-Rs per man per day plus food). The two did the cooking and supplied necessary utensils. We bought all our food in Sonamarg.

## KARGIL

Set at 2800 m, we are further on the way to Ladakh, 200 km from Srinagar. The awful bus ride takes an entire day, costs 30.-Rs (B-class). Along the way you cross a 3500 m pass, where even in summer it can be very cold (bring a sweater). All buses en route to Leh stop here for the night. Kargil is otherwise of little interest, so hurry on.

**A Night's Rest: Hotel De Luxe;** **(D)**20.-Rs, including shower, on the main road. **Hotel International,** most comfortable in town, **(S)**100.-Rs.
   A list of all local accommodations is available at the Kargil Tourist Reception Centre, by the bus stand.

# Leh/Ladakh

Ladakh is the highest-altitude inhabited region in India. Tourists are attracted by fascinating scenery: tall, barren, snow-covered mountains, jagged valleys, green oases. No less interesting are the picturesque Buddhist monasteries, colourful festivals and mask dance performances. And let's mention the warmth of the people, and their ancient Buddhist tradition.
   Ladakh is known as "Little Tibet" because of similarities with Tibetan culture. Many Tibetan refugees chose to settle in Ladakh. For more on Lamaism, see Nepal Country & Culture.
   Ladakh gets very little precipitation; few clouds make it over the Himalayas. However, recent years have seen some disturbing summer rains.
   Due to the high altitude (most towns in Ladakh are above 3500 m), the air is very thin. Lack of oxygen (compared to the lowland plains) can result in rapid pulse, shortness of breath, headache, etc, particularly if you've just flown up from Delhi: acute mountain sickness. It's advisable to adjust slowly at lower levels (Sonamarg, Kargil). If you have low blood pressure, don't forget your medication!

Leh, Ladakh's capital, is at 3500 m, with a population of 20,000.

The first thing you notice upon arrival by air or bus are tremendous military installations between the Indus and town. A closer look reveals a palace towering above town, and the gompa overlooking that. Pressed up against the foot of the palace are the twisting, tiny streets and passageways of the Old Town. Many houses are in decay. The newer part of town is less impressive.

Leh was an important junction on the historic trade route for silk from Sinkiang to western Asia and the Indian plains. Today Leh is a military site and tourist center.

## COMING – GOING
**By Air:** Leh's airport sees five flights weekly during summer season (June to October), in good weather. Twice from Delhi 741.-Rs) via Chandigarh (476.-Rs), thrice from Delhi via Srinagar (334.-Rs). Make your reservations well in advance. If your flight is cancelled, you'll be placed on the waiting list for the next flight. Fewer regular flights during the winter.
**By Bus:** The only road open to the public runs from Srinagar, via Sonamarg and Kargil. Depending upon snow conditions, the road is open June to October. B-Class buses (70.-Rs) depart Srinagar daily; with A-Class buses (90.-Rs) on Wednesdays and Saturdays; Deluxe buses (180.-Rs) from TRC Srinagar at 08:30 h. Reservations also available there, certainly necessary for an A-Class bus. B-Class buses are standard Indian; A-Class offers adjustable, single seats, set 2-2. Deluxe buses feature tinted glass. For the long ride, I recommend the A-Class, takes two days. At noon on the first day you stop in Sonamarg; just a quick break for lunch. The next stop is after Zoji La Pass in Drass. You'll have to fill out a Foreigners' Registration Form. Then on to Kargil. Here the buses stop, at least the A-Class and Deluxe buses, in the TRC yard (touts are kept outside).

In the TRC is a list of all accommodations including price. The cheapest category **(D)**20.-Rs, **(Dm)**5.-Rs, with common showers. Look for something near the TRC; morning departure time is 04:00 h! There are several restaurants on the main street.

From Kargil, you might make a side trip by truck or partly by bus to Zanskar. The ride to Padum takes two days.

Be sure to bargain with your host for a morning breakfast. The first and only stop the next day is at 11:00 h in Khalsi. Or make a few purchases so you have something to munch en route. And in the early morning, you'll need a flashlight.

The ride on the 2nd day takes 11-12 h. Just before Leh you'll have to fill out an army registration form. The bus stops in Leh near the TRC, not at the bus station. The entire drive is made by one driver, without a break.

LEH

1 Two-Star Guesthouse
2 Tsemo-La Hotel
3 Ladakh Ecological Development Group, Restaurant, Library
4 Hotel Sangrila
5 Himalaya Hotel & Camping
6 Antelope Guesthouse & Hotel
7 Camping Site
8 Tsemo Gompa
9 Old Tower
10 Palace
11 Somar Gompa
12 Padmasambhava Temple
13 Moravian Church
14 Hotel Klang-La-Chen
15 Swimming Spot
16 Syed Ali's Postcard Shop
17 Artou's Bookshop
18 Tibetan Restaurant
19 State Bank of India
20 Potala Hill Top Restaurant
21 Mosque
22 Jokhang
23 Fruit & Vegetable Market
24 Tourist Information
25 Post Office
26 Telegraph Office
27 Hotel Yak Tail
29 Relax Restaurant
30 Khangri Hotel & Restaurant
31 Library
32 Burmese Restaurant
33 Potala Restaurant
34 Bakery
35 Palace View Guesthouse
36 Chenrezi Gompa
37 District Commissioner
38 Palace View (Kidar) Hotel
39 Big Chörten
40 Handicraft Training Centre
41 Hotel Tibet
42 Petrol Station
43 Hotel Lha-Ri-Mo
44 Indian Airlines
45 Restaurant Snow-lion
46 Chapati Bakeries

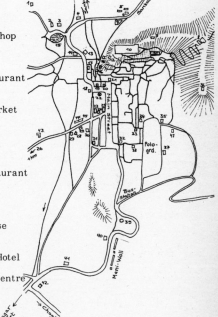

The return trip departs Leh at 06:30 h. Reservations only
begin the night before, at 17:00 h, at the Transport Office, by
the bus station. Normally, the Srinagar buses return the next
day, i.e. A-Class and Deluxe on Mondays and Friday.
**By Truck**: Ask around in Srinagar or Leh, costs about 50.-Rs.
Taxis charge outrageous prices, 1600.-Rs one way for five
people. But there are cheaper possibilities. Some readers have
ridden back from Leh in a returning taxi for 100.-Rs per
person.

The hardy might consider trekking to Ladakh. Try from Manali (Himachal Pradesh) or Pahalgam to Padum (Zanskar), and
from there to Hemis or Lamayuru.

## A NIGHT'S REST

The cheapest rooms generally begin around **(D)**30.-Rs without
bath or **(D)**35.-, 40.-Rs with bath. You'll find a number of
establishments in this and more expensive categories. The TRC
displays a list of all lodgings, their prices and a large city
map. Prices fluctuate greatly with supply and demand. This
list was put together during an off-peak period:

**Norla Guest House (D)**35.-, with bath, a bit below Leh in the
grain fields overlooking the Indus Valley to the Zanskar
Mountains (not all rooms), clean, new, nice people. Similarly
situated and equally new is **Pangong Guest House**, **(D)**30.-
without bath, 35.- with bath. **Choskor Hotel**, **(D)**40.-, with
bath. **Dehlex**, **(D)**30.-, no bath.

Or try **Sabila Guest House**, **(S)**20.-, **(D)**30.-, clean, friendly
family, roof-top terrace for sunning, great view, centrally
located by the polo grounds.

## REFRESHMENT

The shops and markets here offer just about everything you could
find in Srinagar. Expect slightly higher prices. Crispy **chaptis**
rolls are baked in the tiny bakery behind the mosque.

Restaurants feature reasonably priced Tibetan, Chinese, and
Indian food. But keep in mind that most dishes call for half-raw
vegetables, certainly of questionable hygiene. And water, at this
altitude, boils at 85° C; just a refreshing dip for many germs.

Most popular, and the best food, is **Dreamland**, next to the
generator; meals cost about 10.-Rs. **Snow Lion**, across the way,
is known for slow service, and food of lesser quality. More expensive, but tastefully decorated, with a good view of the Old
Town and Market Street is **Potala Hill Topi**, which shouldn't be
confused with the **Potala** by the Polo Grounds (also good).

For real Swiss Rosti, visit Monique in **Relax Restaurant**, behind Dreamland; sit out in the garden and enjoy the snow-covered mountains.

**SHOPPING**
Most souvenir shops are owned by Kashmiris living in Srinagar.
They offer all the usual northern Indian souvenirs at salted
prices. Tibetans from Dharamsala man street stalls, featuring
Tibetan jewelry, cups, religious artifacts, made for the tourist
trade, at relatively high prices.
    Keep in mind, it's illegal to export antiques over a century
old, though little actually is!

**SIGHTS**
**The Palace:** Built in the 16th century by King Singge Namgyal,
with 8-storeys, similar to the Potala in Lhasa, open 06:00-09:00 h
and evenings after 17:00 h. The interior is less interesting, but
the view from the palace is impressive.

**Leh Gompa:** Set above the palace with a lovely view of Leh and
the surrounding mountains. You can take the steep zigzag path
from the palace or a simpler path beginning by the Chörten behind the Himalaya Hotel, open 07:00-09:00 h.

**Jokhang Gompa:** Built in 1957, contains Buddha statues from
Tibet.

**Samkar Gompa:** Small, friendly monastery, 1 km from Leh. Ask
about the statue of Dukar with his 1000 heads, 10,000 arms, and
1000 feet; it isn't displayed automatically, costs 10.-Rs.

**AROUND LEH**
All excursion possibilities mentioned are accessible by bus from
Leh. You can also get a taxi (jeep), at high prices, to any
place in the region.

**Choglamsar** (9 km from Leh): Here you'll find a **Tibetan Refugee
Camp** with an SOS Children's Village, and an Arts & Crafts Center. The **School of Buddhist Philosophy** has an interesting library.

**Shey and Tikse:** At 08:00 h, you can get a bus for 2.-Rs to Shey
(15 km). Above the village is a small **Summer Palace**, built by
the first King of Ladakh. The **Gompa** is famous for its 11 m tall,
golden Buddha, admission 10.-Rs.
    Then walk across the fields (5 km) to Tiksa Gompa. Looking
from the top of Shey palace toward Tikse, you'll see two paths,
besides the road, to Tikse. Take the path on the right!

**Tikse Gompa:** Open all day, 10.-Rs admission. Over 100 monks, of
the yellow cap sect, belong to this gompa. The monks' houses are
built into the hill below the gompa. Notice the 15 m tall Buddha,
mural paintings, the prayer room, and the smaller rooms with
Thankas, pictures, and statues. By the crossroad of the car

road to the gompa is Skalzang Chamba Guest House and Restaurant; enjoy lunch or stay, **(D)**20.-Rs. Diagonally across, buses to
Leh stop (3.-Rs), departs at 15:00 h.

**Spitok Gompa** (10 km from Leh):  Set on a mountain overlooking
the Indus,  airport,  and military grounds,  costs 13.-Rs. About
120 yellow-capped monks live here.  Of the three main temple
prayer rooms,  the upper is most impressive.  Some visitors see
**Paldan Lamo Temple** as a chamber of horrors.

**Stok Palace** (16 km from Leh): Buses depart at 07:45 h (2.50 Rs).
The last stop is just below **Stok Gompa**,  admission 10.-Rs.  From
there, head back down the road by foot to Stok Palace. A number
of rooms in the still inhabited palace have been converted to a
museum,  admission 20.-Rs. You can see a number of royal family
heirlooms.  From Stok,  take the direct path by foot to the Indus
bridge,  to catch the afternoon bus at the crossroads.  Or head a
bit further toward Leh to Choglamsar Tibetan Settlement.

**Hemis Gompa** (45 km from Leh):  Several buses daily,  takes 3 h,
costs 10.-Rs. Hemis is the largest and most wealthy monastery in
Ladakh, famous for its **Masked Dance Festival**. Each year, during
the second half of June or early July,  tourists from all over the
world come for the two-day festival.  During the festival, special
buses run from Leh to Hemis. In one hotel restaurant a few rooms
are available.  But don't expect any room during the festival.
Otherwise,  you'll find tent accommodations.  If you have a tent,
there is a good camping area in Pampel Forest.  During the
festival,  lots of tent restaurants and souvenir stands are set up
around the monastery.
   Dance performances are held twice on both days, mornings and
afternoons.  Be there in the morning! Even if the TRC claims that
the first performance begins at 10:00 h,  it could easily be over
by then.  The dancers wear impressive masks,  and depict with
their dance Buddhist stories and teaching.  Present during the
festival is Gyalwang Drukchen Rinpoche,  leader of the Red Cap
sect.  He is very outgoing,  even holding audience with tourists.
And outside the festival,  be sure to visit the monastery rooms,
with their well preserved murals,  valuable Thangkas,  Buddhas,
and excellent library.

All the following gompas are on the road to Srinagar.  Worth visiting on your way back.

**Phyang Gompa** (24 km from Leh):  Founded as a monastery by
Lama Chhosje Damma in the early 15th century.  Fifty people reside here today.  Recent renovations have been complemented by
new construction.  An annual **Masked Festival** (since 1983) is held

in mid-July.  The atmosphere is nice;  tourism is low key.  Admission to the Gompa,  murals and Buddhas is 10.-Rs.  The new Guesthouse by the monastery offers a fantastic view.

**Alchi Gompa** (63 km from Leh):  Get a bus (2.5 h, 9.-Rs) to Saspol,  where you will find a Tourist Bungalow offering large clean rooms **(S)**25.-Rs.  From Saspol it's a 2 km walk to Alchi Monastery.  Head out of Saspol toward Srinagar and follow the road to the Indus bridge. Cross over,  and a serpentine footpath leads you up the mountain.  You can't miss the tiny town of Alchi.  The monastery isn't so easy to spot because it's not set on a small mountain,  in the usual gompa fashion.  Admission is 10.-Rs;  a monk will lead you through six temples,  spread over a wide area.  Notice the outstanding murals and Buddhas.  Alchi,  itself, has two Guesthouses and a camping area.  From Saspol,  you can also visit **Likir Gompa**.  The steep path begins behind the Tourist Bungalow.

**Lamayuru** (124 km from Leh): A typical monastery complex, set on a cliff,  at the foot of which the village and monks' quarters are located. The impressive murals have been restored recently.  In a cave next to the main building, Siddha Naropa is said to have meditated in the 11th century.  You've a number of lodgings:  try **Guest House**,  by the monastery,  or **Monastery Hostel**, **(Dm)**8.-Rs.

**Mulbekh** (40 km before Kargil):  Set on a hill,  high above the village are two monasteries. The climb is strenuous;  check if any monks are up in the monastery first.  By the road,  just beyond Mulbekh is a 7 m tall Buddha.

### The Gompas (Monasteries)

Almost every village in Ladakh has a monastery of some
note. Usually they are set fortress-like on high ground. Most
are now accessible by road. The monks reside in small
dwellings below the gompa. Every gompa is different: in
architecture and furnishings, but also in atmosphere and the
character of the monks. Many travellers, however, fail to
recognize the differences, and therefore restrict their visits
to only two or three.

Most gompas charge 10.-Rs admission. This may seem like a
lot of money to some travellers. But considering the restoration work financed with tourist money, the money is well
spent.

Frequently you
can participate
in ceremonies,
usually held in
the early morn-
ing and evening
hours. If you do
not want to miss
a sip of butter
tea, which is
almost invaria-
bly offered, then
bring your own
cup. Before en-
tering the mon-
astery build-
ings, you have
to remove your
shoes.

Some monasteries find it difficult to show you all the
rooms, because a different monk has the key to each room.
Don't be surprised if you aren't able to find a guide. Few
monks speak English, and their level of education is low.
The teaching monasteries in Tibet are now inaccessible. Occasionally a monk will ask you for a pen, or offer an artwork for sale.

**Sabu:** This is a good trek to test whether trekking in Ladakh is
really for you, spend a day getting in trekking condition, or
just take a day off from visiting gompas. A way beyond the Leh
Polo Grounds, a path leads off to the village, **Sabu** (ask!). The
path runs via two passes. After crossing over the first pass,
follow the jeep tracks up the valley. At the fork, head right,
and follow the somewhat disorderly trail up the slope. The rest
of the way is easy to see. Takes 2.5 h to 3 h to Sabu. You can't
buy food there, so bring ample provisions. From Sabu, you have
a choice of four ways back. First, you could take the same

LEH REGION

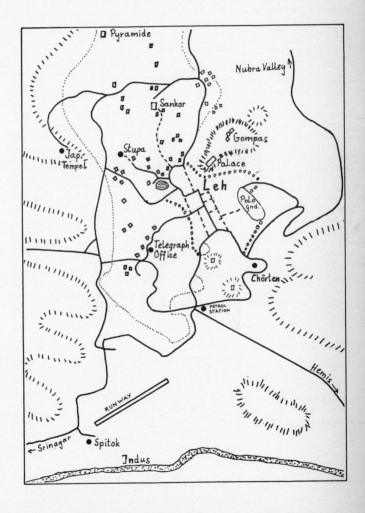

route. Second, just follow the road; takes 3 h. Third, get a bus;
ask ahead about departure times. Or fourth, by foot to the Tibetan refugee camp, Choglamsar, in the Indus Valley (ask the way),
and from there by bus.

**TIPS**
For locations of the TRC, GPO, and the State Bank of India, see
the map. Everything else is grouped together. You can get everywhere in Leh by foot. The TRC provides mimeographed maps of
Leh and vicinity, plus info on bus schedules, opening hours,
trekking tips, etc.
**Indian Airlines Office:** Keeps varied hours. Reservations are sup-
posedly only possible a week in advance, but even then you
aren't sure of a seat. The actual number of air passengers is
determined on departure day, depending on weather conditions.
**No Amexco Traveller's Checks are cashed in Leh:** Other well-
known brands are accepted!
**Library:** The only place in Leh where Indian English-language
newspapers (a few days old) are available. There is no place to
buy a paper. Otherwise, you'll find lots of literature in English
about Ladakh, Zanskar, and Tibet.
**Electricity:** Runs in Leh only from 20:00-24:00 h, if it's running
at all. A flashlight is a must! It is equally invaluable when
visiting the surrounding gompas. Without a flashlight, many murals are impossible to see.

# Trekking

Ladakh is frequently called a trekking paradise, though the
region is not a place for beginners. Most treks lead through
passes 5000 m or higher and require frequent river crossings, not lacking in danger. During the day, the sun burns
down on the barren countryside, where you'll find no shade.
Evenings are cold. Along with good physical condition,
you'll need the proper equipment. At high altitude, you can
expect snow, even in summer. We ourselves have seen the
mountains around Leh gleam with snow after an evening
storm in July. And don't forget to bring enough food,
including a stove and fuel. Along the way, you'll find no
wood, nor any place to pick up provisions. If you feel up to
the challenge, you've an excellent selection of treks in
Ladakh. For information and help picking guides, ponies, or
porters, ask at the TRC in Leh or Kargil, or at the Tourist
Office in Padam.

# HIMACHAL PRADESH

Himachal Pradesh is bordered by Jammu and Kashmir to the north, Tibet to the east, Uttar Pradesh to the south-east, Haryana to the south, and Punjab to the west. The state contains much of the western Himalayas, providing good skiing in Kufry or Narkanda, and excellent trekking in general. The 55,673 km$^2$ are home to 4.2 million people, 96 % of whom live in villages. Pahari is the primary language, followed by Hindi. Before 1947, Himachal Pradesh was divided among 30 tiny feudal states. Its present shape was created in 1966, when Punjab was split into Punjab and Haryana.

The state capital, Simla, was an important summer residence during the British colonial era. Each summer, Simla is crowded with Indian tourists, here to enjoy the pleasant mountain climate, lovely scenery, and tremendous forests.

The primary destinations for western tourists are the fertile Kulu Valley, and Dharamsala / Mc Leod Ganj. The focal point of tourism in Kulu Valley is the village of Manali. Dharamsala / Mc Leod Ganj, with its view of the snow-covered Himalayas, is the residence of the Dalai Lama, and many other Tibetans. This is an excellent place to get acquainted with Tibetan culture.

In the north, Spiti is a restricted region, as are parts of Lahaul. To travel the road from Manali to Keylong, you'll need a special permit from the Ministry of Home Affairs in Delhi, which we've found can take a while.

The five major tribes in Himachal Pradesh are the Gaddis, Gujjars, Lahaulis, Kinners, and Pangwals. The Gaddi herd sheep by tradition, while the Gujjar migrate with their herds of buffalo.

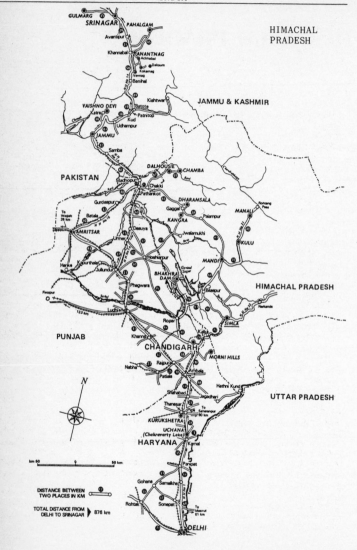

GULMARG
SRINAGAR
PAHALGAM
Avantipur
Khannabal
ANANTNAG
Achhabal
Daksum
Kokarnag
Verinag
Banihal
Kishtwar
VAISHNO DEVI
Katra
Batote
Patnitop
Kud
Udhampur
JAMMU
Samba

HIMACHAL
PRADESH

JAMMU & KASHMIR

PAKISTAN

DALHOUSIE    CHAMBA
Madhopur
Chakki
Pathankot
Gurdaspur
DHARAMSALA
Gaggal
Palampur
KANGRA
MANALI
Rohtang Pass
To Wagah
26 km
Batala
AMRITSAR
Urmar
Jwalamukhi
KULU
Hariana
Kapurthala
Jullundur
Hoshiarpur
Desuya
MANDI
Phagwara
BHAKHRA
DAM
Govind Sagar
Ferozpur
120 km
Ludhiana
Bilaspur
HIMACHAL PRADESH
Roper
Nalagarh
Khanna
SIMLA
Kalka
CHANDIGARH
MORNI HILLS
PUNJAB
Nabha
Rajpura
Ambala
Patiala
Hathni Kund
Shahabad
Jagadhari
Thanesar
Pipli
To
Saharanpur
90 km
KURUKSHETRA
UCHANA
(Chakreverty Lake)
HARYANA
Karnal
UTTAR PRADESH
Panipat
Gohana
Samalkha
Rohtak
Sonepat
To
Meerut
61 km
DELHI

N

km 50    0    50 km

DISTANCE BETWEEN
TWO PLACES IN KM

TOTAL DISTANCE FROM
DELHI TO SRINAGAR    ▶ 876 km

# Simla

The capital of Himachal Pradesh is set at 2100 m. A British officer, Rose, discovered the spot in 1819, spending his first summer
here in a tent. The first home was built by a Major Kennedy in
1822, but it was several decades before the town assumed its
standing as the British Summer Capital. The buildings around The
Mall are reminiscent of India's colonial past. The pleasant summer climate, lovely surrounding mountains, and winter sport facilities make Simla a popular resort area.

## COMING - GOING
**By Rail:** A narrow-gauge line from Kalka to Simla was built in
1904. In Kalka you have to change trains due to incompatibil-
ity of the wide-gauge and narrow-gauge tracks, lengthening
travel time considerably.
**By Bus:** Most practical, Chandigarh - Simla (5 h, 18.-Rs).
Regular buses to Delhi (369 km, 10 h), Kulu, and Manali. The
nearest airport is in Chandigarh.

## A NIGHT'S REST
Hotel prices fluctuate with the season (April to June, September
to October, December to February). Many hotels, but not the
cheapest, are around The Mall. An affordable exception is **Hotel
Cambermere**, The Mall, **(S)**20.-.
It's much simpler to find a room near the bus stand. **Sun
Hotel, (D)**36.-, 65.-. **Snow Hotel, (D)**35.-, 65.-. **Highway Hotel,
(Dm)**10.-, **(D)**40.-; close your windows before going out, the
local monkeys are extremely curious. Also recommended is the
**YMCA, (D)**30.-, 45.-Rs, clean, good food for 5.-Rs.
And around The Mall you'll find lots of restaurants and coffee
houses: **Alfa, Fascination, Goofa, Indian Coffee House**, etc.
Simla HPTDC runs the restaurant **Ashiana**, featuring a lovely
panoramic view, tinted glass, and stylistic furnishings, but
you pay for it. **Goofa**, downstairs in the cellar, offers thalis
in a dimly lit setting.

## SIGHTS
**The Mall:** All important offices are here including the Tourist
Office, Foreigners' Registration Office, and the GPO. Along with
restaurants, you'll find a number of elegant shops offering a
rich selection of souvenirs, clothes, and consumer goods. It's
more interesting and cheaper in the markets and bazars, spread
over the steps and steep alleyways running from the main road
(bus stand) to The Mall.
If the walk up is too strenuous, get a lift for 1.-Rs. The
Mall stretches out of town, transforming into a lovely promenade,
surrounded by luscious vegetation and splendid mansions. Here
too is the **Simla Rotary Club.**

## AROUND SIMLA

Near Simla, you'll find a number of outstanding spots for trekking. The tourist office offers convenient transportation to places furthest afield:

**Jakhu Hill** & **Jakhu Temple** (2 km): Simla's highest mountain, featuring a panoramic view. The temple is dedicated to the Monkey God, Hanuman. Perhaps that's why there are so many monkeys around here.

**Glen** (4 km): A popular picnic spot at 1830 m, near the Cecil Hotel and Kennedy House.

**Chadwick Falls** (7 km): Surrounded by thick forest, the 67 m tall waterfall is prettiest during monsoon season.

**Summer Hill** (5 km): A picturesque village, on the road to Kalka, inviting long walks.

**Prospect Hill** (5 km): A popular picnic spot, with a lovely view. The climb takes 15 minutes from Boileauganj. The temple is dedicated to Kamma Devi.

**Sankat Mochan** (7 km): At 1875 m, with a lovely view and a Hanuman temple. And head on to **Tara Devi** (8 km, 1851 m), where you'll find another temple.

**Skiing**: January to February in **Kufti**, 16 km away. On the way to Kufti, you pass **Wildflower Hall**; Lord Kitchner's former residence is no longer maintained, but the Himalaya view is excellent. Another ski resort is 64 km distant in **Narkanda**.

**Trekking** routes in the region are described in the brochure, **Trekking in India**, by Mr. Gyanchand, available for 35.-Rs in Minerva Bookshop.

# Dharamsala /McLeod Ganj

The world hardly took notice in 1959 when the Tibetan people
rose up in a fruitless fight to regain independence and political
autonomy from the People's Republic of China. With revolutionary
zeal, the Chinese set about extinguishing a culture whose roots
predate Buddhism. Tens of thousands of Tibetans died during the
flight to India and in poorly provisioned refugee camps.

A thaw in relations with
China has made it possible in
recent years for members of
the Tibetan government in exile to send official delega-
tions to Tibet.

Some of the exiles, in-
cluding the Dalai Lama, Tibet's spiritual and worldly
leader, have made a new
home in Dharamsala / Mc Leod Ganj.

With their own strength,
and international support, Tibetans have made impressive
social strides. Their residential areas are designed to
complement the natural environment. Education is available; schools are supportive
of the individual. Tibetan
medicine looks closely at the
origins and needs of the
patient.

Openness and tradition
find no contradiction in Tibetan life, unlike their Indian counterparts. Cultural
institutions actively nurture
and support Tibetan consciousness. These responsibilities
have largely been placed in the hands of the younger generation.
Equal rights for women are a reality.

# Dharamsala

### COMING - GOING

**By Rail:** Get the train from Delhi to Pathankot, where you head
on by bus. You sleep better aboard a train. The only way to
get a reservation to Delhi is if you book it right upon arrival.
The night train departs Pathankot at 18:33 h, arrives in Delhi
at 05.00 h.

**By Bus:** Dharamsala is a major junction, with the best bus connections in Himachal Pradesh: Manali (12 h, 40.-Rs), Kulu (10 h. 32.-), Pathankot (3 h, 17.-), Amritsar (7 h, 30.-). From Delhi (13 h, 54.-Rs) Interstate Bus Terminal at Kashmir Gate, night buses leave at 19:40 h from Gate 7a (attention: you may have to change buses at a stop around 02:00 h!), arrive about 10:00 h.

From Dharamsala to Delhi, you've morning, afternoon and evening departures. Video coaches also ply this route, though I've never met anyone who enjoyed riding video coaches. Make advance reservations in Dharamsala across from the bus stand.

To Chandigarh (8 h, 30.-Rs), five morning buses.

**Around Town:** Buses between Dharamsala and Mc Leod Ganj, hourly until 19:00 h, costs 1.50 Rs.

## A NIGHT'S REST

There are hotels in Dharamsala, but if you're interested in Tibet, head right on with the hourly bus uphill to Mc Leod Ganj. Should you miss the last bus, try **Tibet United Association Hotel**, (D)15.-, 20.-. Also good is **Rising Moon Hotel**, (D)15.-, 20.-. Both hotels have good food.

# McLeod Ganj

## A NIGHT'S REST

Marked on our sketch are several hotels in the (D)15.- to 25.-Rs category. All the hotels are near the bus stand.

In **Green Hotel** (Path 5), the best rooms, (D)18.-, face the valley; the sun wakes you in the morning to enjoy the lovely view; the food is good, and cake recommended. **Koko Nor Hotel** is one of the cheaper hotels. **Hotel Tibet** is more expensive, but still offers simple (D)20.-; the restaurant has a large menu, including great Indian food. The expensive **Bhagsu Hotel**, (D)60.-Rs, is a bit outside town.

Besides the above mentioned hotels and restaurants, there are lots more to discover on your own. Mc Leod Ganj is a place you can live.

If you are planning to stay a while, rent a cheap private room or house. A convenient place to stay is in **Rishi Bhavan**, above the Drama School. If you are here to do some studying in the Tibetan Library, you'll find lodgings nearby. And you can stay at the **Tushita Meditation Center**, or in the **Hindu Mehr Ashram** (Path 2), if you are interested in taking a meditation course.

## REFRESHMENT

The best momo soup, a Tibetan speciality, is served in **Yak Restaurant**, where many Tibetans eat. Another good place to try momo is in **Hotel Kailaish**; the restaurant upstairs overlooks the village bustle around the prayer wheel or out to the mountains. If you've been in India for a while, and want to try some real

Swiss cooking, for a change, order rosti with egg and cheese at
**Cafe Kangra**. The **Tibetan Himalayan Restaurant**, next door to
Green Hotel, has excellent food, and television.

If you want an alcoholic drink, try the bar in **Hotel Tibet**, or
in **Friend's Corner**, by the bus stand. Both alternate as a disco
on Saturday evenings. Next to Tashi Restaurant is a small Tibetan restaurant offering outstanding breakfast. The food is good in
**Om-Restaurant**, from the roof, you've a lovely view, and the
vultures are within reach.

## SHOPPING
Tibetans aren't permitted to sell anything other than handicraft
items, to prevent them from taking jobs from native Indians. In
the shops, you have lots of time to look over the wares. Tibetans

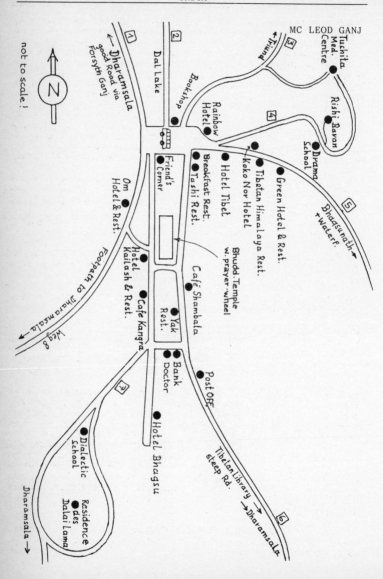

not to scale!

N

← Dharamsala
good Road via
Forsyth Ganj

Dal Lake

Bookshop

MC LEOD GANJ

Triund

Tushita
Med.
Centre

Rishi Bavan

Rainbow
Hotel

Drama
School

Green Hotel & Rest.

Tibetan Himalaya Rest.

Koko Nor Hotel

Hotel Tibet

Breakfast Rest.

Tashi Rest.

Friend's
Corner

Bhadsunath
+Waterf.

Om
Hotel & Rest.

Bhudd. Temple
w. prayer-wheel

Café Shambala

Footpath to Dharamsala

Weg 8

Hotel
Kailash & Rest.

Café Kangra

Yak
Rest.

Bank

Doctor

Post Off.

Dialectic
School

Hotel Bhagsu

Tibetan Library
steep Rd.

→ Dharamsala

Dharamsala →

Residence
des
Dalai Lama

won't usually pressure you to buy their wonderful products. Comparing prices is a must, because prices are high, and many traders would rather not make a sale, than lower their price.

Look for colorful bags, multicolored ribbons, jackets, shirts, vests of traditional design and unusual patterns. Rugs with large Tibetan symbols, products made of yak wool, colorful prayer flags, woven belts, apron cloth (used in traditional women's dress), sweaters, hand or machine woven cloth sold by the meter. Printed matter, multicolored postcard reproductions of Tibetan paintings, rice paper prints, various wood and metal wares including necklaces, earrings, bracelets. Carvings of buffalo horn and bone. Silver jewelry, some set with semiprecious jewels, is generally overpriced. Claims concerning silver content and weight are often exaggerated. The silver price is listed daily on the economics page of the newspaper.

Second-hand books are available in a small bookstall on Path 5. For a good selection of books in English, French, and German, visit Dharamsala Bookshop by the bus stand; most books are new, and the postcards are nice.

Recommendation: if you're heading on to Nepal, you'll find a larger selection of Tibetan wares there, at much lower prices!

## AROUND MC LEOD GANJ
The path numbers refer to our sketch; times are from Mc Leod Ganj.

**Path 1:** A heavily travelled road, via Forsyth Ganj. Take a walk to the **Old English Cemetery** (1 h).

**Path 2:** To the **Tibetan Children's Village** (50 minutes), Dal Lake is small and questionable for swimming, 75 minutes. **Mehr Ashram** (2 h) is open April to November, room and board is 30.-Rs. The aim of the meditation is to become conscious of Chakra and Kundalini energy. Only people serious about meditation need inquire.

**Path 3:** **Indian Mountaineering Institute** (15 minutes) provides reliable info about trekking routes, and sells maps. Triund, 3000 m altitude, takes 4-5 h, lodging 2.-Rs, bring warm clothes, sleeping bag, water, and all necessary provisions. This is your departure route for high mountain treks and pass crossings.

The first snow fields begin around 3400 m. If you take the crossroads right toward Triund, after 15 minutes you reach **Tushita Meditation Center**, which never closes. If you're interested in taking a meditation class, check in the center, or look for the posting in the Tibetan Library. You have to register in advance for the classes. From Tushita, you can walk back to Mc Leod Ganj via Path 4.

**Path 4:** To the **Tibetan Dance and Drama School**, 20 minutes, where you can observe classes in Tibetan music and dance. In 1984, one of the main school buildings burned down. To save on

reconstruction costs, students and teachers help with rebuilding
during their spare time. Donations are gratefully accepted. Those
interested in aiding Tibetan culture can join the Friends of the
Tibetan Institute of Performing Arts; a year's membership fee is
US$25.- or 200.-Rs. The school has an interesting film about Tibet
it will gladly show to groups of five or more; five people are
easily found in Mc Leod Ganj. And you help fill the school's
coffers.

**Path 5:** **Bhagsunath Temple** (40 minutes) Bhagsunath offers cheap
accommodations and Chai Shops with Indian food. The swimming
pool by the temple is only used by locals. A bit further is a
waterfall up on the mountain, and lots of small pools of water
where you can do your laundry quick.

**Path 6:** The **Library of Tibetan Works and Archives** is in a newly
constructed building complex below the road, 30 minutes walk
from town. An admission card is issued upon presentation of a
passport and 2.-Rs. The library, containing several thousand
works, is a treasure house for everything connected with Tibet.
Books and periodicals are available in local languages, as well
as English, French, German, Italian, and Russian. You'll find
picture albums, newspapers, plus **Time** and **Newsweek**; black-
boards and information about classes and events concerning Tibetan language, medicine, and Mahayana Buddhism. 20 minutes
downhill on the road to Dharamsala.

**Path 7:** The **Buddhist School of Dialectics** (15 minutes). The path
taking a circular tour around the hilltop and past the **Tibetan
Temple** takes 50 minutes. Before sunrise, numerous monks and lay
supporters make a pilgrimage to the temple. This too is the residence of the **Dalai Lama** when he is in Dharamsala.

**Path 8:** A direct footpath to Dharamsala, takes an hour.

# Kulu Valley

**MANDI**
The town is a junction for travel in the Kulu and Kangra Valleys. But the pretty countryside is peacefully situated at 750 m
on the Beas River. You can stay in Tourist Lodge, uphill from
the bus stand, **(D)**40.-, 120.-Rs, or in a six-bed **(Dm)**10.-Rs.
**Temple:** In town, a must see, with lovely stone masonry.
**Rewabar Lake:** 25 km, attracts Sikh, Hindu and Buddhist pilgrims; lodgings available.

# Kulu

The district capital is at 1220 m on the bank of the Beas River. The Kulu Valley stretches from Mandi, at 750 m, to Lahaul and Spiti, at 3915 m in the Rohtang Pass. The green, fertile valley is enclosed by forest-covered slopes, topped by snow-capped mountains. Kulu is a possible departure point for treks and excursions through the region, but Manali is more convenient.

If you're in northern India during autumn, be sure to experience the **Dussehra Festival**, lasting for seven days during the October full moon. Splendour and color galore, as depictions of the gods are paraded in a procession through the Valley of the Gods.

## A NIGHT'S REST

The Tourist Office, tel.7, is by the bus stand in the south of town. There are lodgings nearby around Dhalphur Maidan, or by the main bus stand in the north of town. On the road to Mandi, lodges charge **(D)**20.-. Other hotels ask **(D)**40.-Rs.

## COMING - GOING

**By Air:** Daily Vayudoot flights from Chandigarh (272.-) and Delhi (525.-Rs). The airport is 10 km south of town in Bhuntar.

**By Bus:** Direct buses to Delhi (17 h, 80.-), Chandigarh (12 h, 38.-), Simla (25.-), and Dharamsala. The buses pass through or continue on to Manali; Kulu to Manali (2-3 h, 7.-Rs). Buses take 2 h via the main road on the west bank, or a good 3 h by the less travelled east bank road, via Naggar, the former capital with a well preserved castle.

# Manali

Next to Dharamsala, this is the second largest attraction for travellers in northern India. As in Goa, many travellers stay for weeks or even months. And no wonder: set at 2200 m, surrounded by mountains over 4000 m tall, you've good accommodations in a picturesque setting. This is a great departure point for treks. Wool scarves, blankets and rugs are excellent buys.

## COMING - GOING

**By Bus:** From Delhi, Interstate Bus Terminal, Kashmiri Gate, reservations at counter 40, a day in advance; plus lots of private bus companies on Janpath Road.

From Manali you've direct buses to Delhi, Chandigarh, Dharamsala, Mandi, Manikaran, and Leh, via one of the highest roads in the world (4600 m), open just from June to August.

# Manali

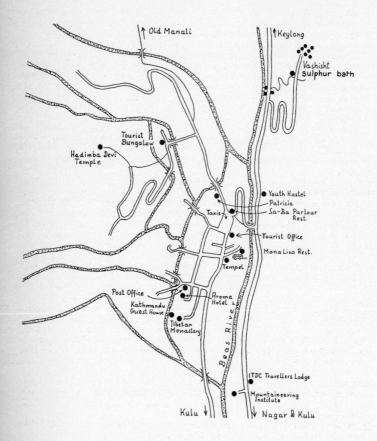

↑ Old Manali

↑ Keylong

Vashisht
**sulphur bath**

Tourist
Bungalow

Hadimba Devi
Temple

Youth Hostel
Patricia
Sa-Ba Parlour
Rest.

Taxis

Tourist Office

Mona Lisa Rest.

Tempel

Post Office

Aroma
Hotel

Kathmandu
Guest House

Tibetan
Monastary

Beas River

ITDC Travellers Lodge

Mountaineering
Institute

Kulu ↓

↓ Nagar & Kulu

Foreigners need a permit. There are regular buses between Kulu and Manali, on the main road, west of the Beas River, takes 2 h, costs 7.-Rs.

## A NIGHT'S REST

There's no problem finding lodgings in Manali, start at **(D)**10.-Rs. The tourist office provides a list of 55 places and prices, certainly incomplete. **Kathmandu Guest House**, near the Tibetan Monastery, **(D)**40.-. **Aroma Hotel**, near the Tibetan Monastery, **(D)**40.-. **Tourist Bungalow** (and other spots at the other end of town), **(D)**80.-. The outskirts of town is a bit cheaper. You can rent a house for 150.-Rs a month.

There are lots of Indian and Tibetan restaurants, along with a number of video cafes. **Monalisa Restaurant**, by the bus stand, is good, but expensive.

Near the post office, next to Rama Bakery, is **Patricia**, where you can pick up müsli, whole-grain bread (cheap), jam, and peanut butter.

## SIGHTS

**Hadimba Devi Temple**: On a hill, 2 km from the Tourist Bungalow. The goddess, Hadimba, plays an important role in Kulu Dussehra.

**Vashisht Sulphur Bath**: Across the Beas River and left, 3 km from Manali, are the hot springs and bathhouse. Twenty minutes in a single bath (large enough for two) costs 5.-Rs. A family bath is 7.-Rs. In the village of Vashisht, you can rent cheap rooms and houses. Departure point for short and long treks.

**Tibetan Monastery**: A monastery of recent origins, featuring some lovely paintings.

**Manikaran - Parbati Valley**: A sacred spot for Sikhs. Direct buses from Manali, Kulu and Bhuntar. The entire town is built above hot sulphur springs, by the Parbati River. Steam rises everywhere. Lots of public baths, accommodations in private farmhouses, many with their own sulphur baths, **(D)**10.-, 20.-. And the **Guru Nanak Ashram** provides room and board. Several Indian restaurants.

## TIPS

**Tourist Office**: On the main road, hotel lists, sightseeing tours by jeep or bus.

**Post Office**: Near Aroma Hotel.

**Mountain Office**: Across the Beas River, then right, a 2.5 km walk. Provides trekking maps, and fishing licences.

**Horses & Donkeys**: For treks, 50.-Rs per day; same prices as in Zanskhar.

# UTTAR PRADESH

The state of Uttar Pradesh, with 110 million people, is the most populous state in India. Its capital is Lucknow. The primary languages are Hindi and Urdu. Total area is 294,413 km$^2$. The borders stretch from the high Himalayas, through the foothills, the fertile north Indian plains, and the northern outcroppings of the Deccan highlands.

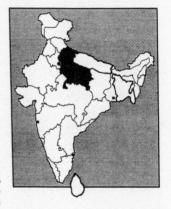

The fertile lowlands are irrigated by the Ganges and Yamuna River systems, which join in Allahabad, with the Ghaghara. The region ranges from 50 m to 200 m in altitude. Each year, heavy floods are catastrophic. But the floods do create rich soil. The plains are farmed intensively. The road system is good.

Tourists flock to Agra, and the Taj Mahal. Other popular towns include Fatehpur Sikri, Lucknow, and Varanasi. These Uttar Pradesh towns are included in our Ganges Plains chapter.

More tourists visit Uttar Pradesh than any other Indian state. The majority are Indian pilgrims, visiting holy sites.

We begin our tour in the mountains, embraced by Himachal Pradesh, Tibet, and Nepal. Primarily of interest are the pilgrim towns Hardwar and Rishikesh, the resort towns Dehra Dun, and Mussoorie, plus Nainital and the Garhwal Region.

The Garhwal Region contains several important Hindu pilgrim sites: Yamunotri, Gangotri, Kedernath, Badrinath, and the Valley of Flowers. This is also great trekking country.

## Hardwar

On the right bank of the Ganges, at the foot of the Siwalik Mountains, Hardwar is one of the most sacred Hindu towns in India. With its ghats, temples, ashrams, and many sadhus, Hardwar resembles a miniature Varanasi. The high point of life here is the **Kumbh Mela Festival**, held every 12 years, attracting

UTTAR PRADESH

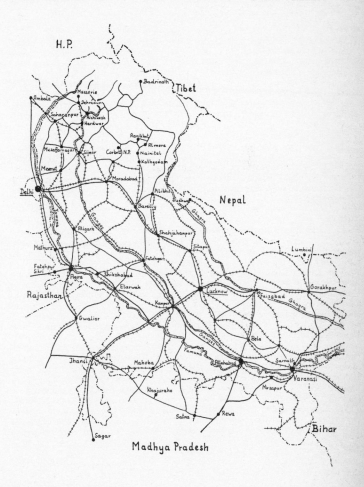

pilgrims and sadhus from all over India.   During the last festival,   in April 1986,   many people were trampled to death in the
crowds.

## COMING - GOING
Buses and trains from Delhi (256 km,   6-7 h).   The bus stand
and railway station are close together.   Direct buses to Agra
(365 km),   Chandigarh (263 km),   Simla,   Nainital,   Dehra Dun
(54 km),   Dharamsala,   and of course Rishikesh (30 km).

## A NIGHT'S REST
Lots of hotels near the bus stand and railway station.   **Deep
Hotel,**   Shravannath Nagar,   **(S)**17.-.   Plenty of other lodges
nearby.
   **Tourist Bungalow,** tel.379, in the outskirts, on the left side of
the Ganges,   **(D)**60.-,   **(Dm)**10.-.   **Railway Retiring Room, (D)**25.-,
**(Dm)**5.-.   Most travellers like to stay in Rishikesh and visit
Hardwar on daytrips.
   The Tourist Office (tel.19) is near the Lalta Rao Bridge,   on
the road to the bus stand and railway station.   The Post Office
is nearby.

## SIGHTS
**Bazar:** We enjoy just browsing through the streets by the Ganges,
or just sitting on a ghat by the bank of the Ganges.
**Ganges River:**   For a good view of the bustle,   have a look from
one of the bridges.
**Har-ki-Pauri Ghat:**   The most interesting by the sacred bathing
area.   Non-Hindus are permitted to visit this spot after removing
their shoes. Photography is prohibited. One of **Vishnu's Footprints**
is preserved in a temple.
**Parmarth Ashram:**   4.5 km from Har-ki-Pauri Ghat.   Features a
lovely depiction of the Goddess Durga;   **Sapt Rishi Ashram,**   and
**Sapt Sarovar.** Hindu mythology tells that the Ganges divides itself
here into seven (sapt) streams,   in order not to disturb seven
Rishis at prayer. Another path leads to **Beauty Point** (lovely view
of the city), and **Mansa Devi Temple.**
**Daksh Mahadev Temple:**   Four km downstream in Kankhal,   at a
sacred spot,   are a **Shiva Temple,**   and **Sati Kund.** According to
legend,   Sati Kund is the spot where Sati,   Shiva's first wife,
burned to death.   Her father,   King Daksha held a Yajna (fire
ceremony),   to which everyone except Shiva and Sati were invited.
Sati attended anyway.   But when she heard insulting remarks
about Shiva, Sati leaped into the sacred fire.

# Rishikesh

Famous for its many ashrams and yoga centers, Rishikesh even
attracted the Beatles, who visited Guru Maharishi Mahesh Yogi.
Today, many Europeans study yoga, meditation, and Hindu philosophy here.

Rishikesh is also your departure point for visits to sacred
spots in Garhwal Himal: Badrinath, Kedernath, Yamunotri, Gongo-
tri, and Gaumukh, the source of the Ganges.

The village, set on the Ganges, is surrounded by hills on
three sides. Most ashrams are in peaceful Muni-ki-Reti, across
Chandrabhaga River Bridge.

## COMING - GOING
From Delhi Interstate Terminal, Platform 28, buses depart
hourly from 05:00 h on, takes 6 h, costs 31.-. Buses hourly,
30 km, to Hardwar. Direct buses to Dehra Dun. One bus to
Simla, at 06:30 h. Rishikesh is equally accessible by rail via
Hardwar.

Locally, you get around by tonga (horse cart), scooter, or
bus.

## A NIGHT'S REST
The cheapest accommodations are in Muni-ki-reti. **Tourist Bungalow**, **(S)**20.-, 30.-, **(D)**25.-, 45.-, **(Eb)**15.-, Indian restaurant, lovely garden.

Also recommended is **Badooni Tourist Lodge**, Uttarakhand Colony, also known as French Colony (the first tourist was a
Frenchman), next to Omkarananda Hospital, above Yoga Niketan
Ashram, **(S)**8.-, **(D)**10.-, do your own cooking, or build a fire
out front, helpful owner, great view of town, good place if you
don't want to stay in an ashram.

The most expensive possibility is **Hotel Indralok**, Station Road,
**(S)**60.-, **(AC)**125.-, **(D)**75, 150.-, good restaurant.

**Hotel Meneka**, near the bus stand, **(S)**25.-, 65.-, **(D)**35.-,
125.-. **Tourist Home**, Dehra Dun Road, **(S)**25.-, 65.-, **(D)**35.-,
125.-. **New Tourist Lodge**, near the station, **(S)**25.-, 65.-,
**(D)**35.-, 125.-. **Laxman Jhoola Hotel**, near Laxman Jhoola
Bridge, **(S)**25.-, 65.-, **(D)**35.-, 125.-.

If you register in advance, you can stay and study yoga in
**Shivananda Ashram**. Rooms are available in **Hanuman Temple**,
on the bank of the Ganges, but don't look for luxury.

Around the scooter and tonga stand on Muni-ki-reti are chai
shops and tiny restaurants where you can eat cheap. Or get a
bite across on the opposite bank of the Ganges.

## SIGHTS
**Muni-ki-reti:** The town, particularly, has its appeal, in no way
reduced by the ashrams, pilgrims, and sadhus.

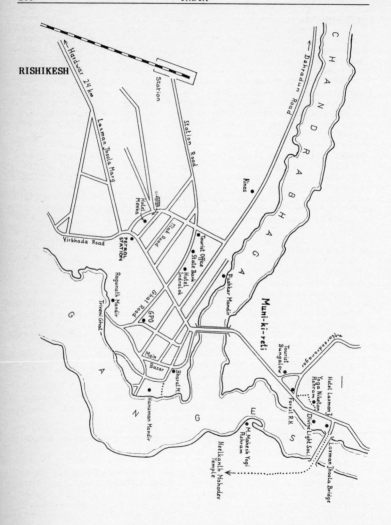

**RISHIKESH**

Hardwar 24 km

Laxman Jhoola Marg

Station

Station Road

Dehradun Road

C H A N D R A B H A G A

Kinas

Virbhada Road

Hotel Menka

PETROL STATION

Tourist Office

State Bank

Hotel Jandrlok

Ragunath Mandir

Ghat Road

Thid Road

Pushkar Mandir

Muni-ki-reti

GPO

Triveni Ghat

Main Bazar

Bharat M.

Hanuman Mandir

Tourist Bungalow

Narendranagar

Hotel Laxman J.

Yoga Niketan Ashram

Forest R.H.

Divine Light Soc.

Laxman Jhoola Bridge

G A N G E S

M. Mahesh Yogi Ashram

Neelkanth Mahadev Temple

**Early Morning Singing:** Be sure to join in the ashrams. For 0.50 Rs, you can get a boat across the Ganges, and visit the **Ashrams** and **Ghats** on the East Bank. A wide path leads to Laxman Jhoola Bridge, next to the multi-storey **Laxman Temple** (also Lakshman Temple).

Those who stay a while can dedicate themselves to intensive study of yoga and meditation.

**Yoga Classes:** Offered twice daily in **Shivananda Ashram**, at 05:30 h and 17:00 h, lasts 90 minutes. You can join at any time without any minimum requirement. Shivananda Ashram has an outstanding library. Every evening is Satsang, when ashram members get together with visitors to sing, and hear an occasional talk by Swami Krishnananda.

Yoga and meditation classes are also offered in **Yoga Niketan Ashram**. However, you are required to register in advance, and to participate for a minimum of several weeks. You can't just stop by for a look.

**Learn to Play an Indian Musical Instrument:** If you've always wanted to learn, you can get sitar, tabla, harmonium... lessons from one of the teachers in Muni-ki-reti, near Yoga Niketan Ashram.

**Bathe In The Ganges:** Don't miss the opportunity, in traditional dress, while visiting Rishikesh.

**TIPS**

**Tourist Office:** Between the railway station and Indralok Hotel on Railway Station Road, tel.209.

**The State Bank of India:** Next to Indralok Hotel, but for their own reasons, refuses to accept American Express traveller's checks.

**Doctor:** An excellent physician resides near the French Colony, and can be contacted through its owner.

# Dehra Dun & Mussoorie

Dehra Dun is the last stop on the railway line from Hardwar, and a good departure point for tours of the Garwhal Himal, particularly to Mussoorie, a hill station, 30 km away.

India's largest Forest Research Institute is in Dehra Dun. Tourists find little of interest beyond several picnic grounds and some nearby temples.

Mussoorie is a popular Indian summer resort. Set at 2000 m, you've a view of the Himalayas to the northwest. Its recorded history begins in 1827 with a visit by a Captain Young. The English heritage is still readily apparent. From Mussoorie, you can take excursions into the surrounding region, including the pilgrim towns of Gangotri and Yamunotri.

## COMING – GOING

**By Rail:** Dehra Dun is an important regional junction. The railway station is the last stop for trains originating in Bombay and Calcutta via Varanasi and Lucknow. Two direct trains from Delhi take 10 h, costs 33.-Rs.

**By Bus:** Additionally, the town has two bus stands. The bus stand by the railway station serves for regional buses. The bus stand beyond the clock tower serves for long-distance buses. Frequent buses to Hardwar, takes 90 minutes, costs 8.-Rs. To Chandigarh (24.-Rs), Delhi (6 h, 40.-Rs); direct buses to Agra, Simla, Nainital, and other locations.

## A NIGHT'S REST

Mussoorie has lots of hotels in every category. Prices vary greatly with the season (May to June and September to October). Check with the Tourist Office on Mall Road, tel.663, before booking a room. **Snow View Hotel**, Library Bazar, **(S)**30.-, **(D)**40.-. **Minerva**, Kulri Bazar, **(S)**30.-, **(D)**40.-Rs.

## SIGHTS

**Gun Hill** (gondola): The best views of the Himalayas.
**Lal Tibba:** Outstanding view, the highest peak in Mussoorie (5 km).
**The Municipal Garden:** Invites you to relax beside an artificial lake.
**Kempty Waterfall** is 15 km from Mussoorie.

# Garhwal Region

The major pilgrim attractions: Yamunotri, Gangotri, Kedarnath, Badrinath, and the famous Valley of Flowers. A trip through the region features lovely countryside and outstanding Himalayan views. Numerous pilgrims visit the temples; direct buses from Rishikesh and Hardwar to these sites, whenever road conditions permit. Accommodations are available all along the pilgrim route. The region is also great for trekking. Tours are organized, and info available from Vikas Nigam Muni-ki-Reti in Rishikesh, tel.372.

## YAMUNOTRI

Buses run as far as Hanuman Chatti (233 km from Haridwar). The last 13 km you'll have to do by foot. The path runs via Phoolchatti and Janikibaichatti (6 km), and then 7 km on to Yamunotri. The **Temple**, set at 3322 m is dedicated to the Goddess Yamuna. The sacred **Yamuna River** has its source in the icy regions at 4421 m. Near the temple, water from hot springs has been directed into several pools.

## GANGOTRI
Bus connections to Lanka
Chatti (259 km from Hardwar),
then 3 km by foot to Bhairon
Chatti. From here buses bring
you the last 10 km to Gangotri
(3140 m). The **Temple** on the
Bhagirathi River is dedicated
to the Goddess Ganga. The
Bhagirathi is a tributary of
the Ganges.

Gaumukh is revered as the
**Source of the Ganges.** Gaumukh, 19 km from Gangotri, is
accessible by foot via Chir-
basa and Bhojbasa. Rising
above Gaumukh is **Gangotri
Glacier.**

From Gangotri runs a quite
difficult **Pilgrim Trail** to the
sacred shrine in Kedernath.
The 132 km trail begins 75 km
from Gangotri in Mala Chatti.

## KEDERNATH
From Hardwar to Gaurikund, it's 235 km by bus. The last 14 km
from Gaurikund to Kedernath, you'll have to do on foot. Kedernath is set in a valley surrounded by snow-covered mountains.
**Kedernath Temple** is dedicated to the god, Shiva. In **Gandhi Sarovar,** 5 km from Kedernath, the ashes of Mahatma Gandhi found
their last rest in 1948.

## BADRINATH
Direct buses from Hardwar to Badrinath (324 km). The village,
set at 3122 m, is surrounded by snow-capped mountains. This is
an important site for Hindu pilgrims. Many stories are told about
Badrinath. In the main **Temple,** the god Badrinath is revered. In
a **Cave** by Mana, near Badrinath, it's said that Rishi Ved Vyas
wrote the **Bhagavad Gita.**

## VALLEY OF FLOWERS - HEMKUND
28 km from Badrinath, **Govind Ghat,** is your departure point for
the Valley of Flowers and Hemkund Lake.

From Govind Ghat (1828 m), it's 14 km uphill to Ghangariya
at 3200 m. You can stay at the **Forest House** and decide in the
morning whether to head 4 km to the Valley of Flowers, or to the
Hemkund Lake. The Valley of Flowers is a long stretching valley,
brimming with flowers. Over 1000 species are said to blossom
here, especially in July and August.

GARHWAL REGION

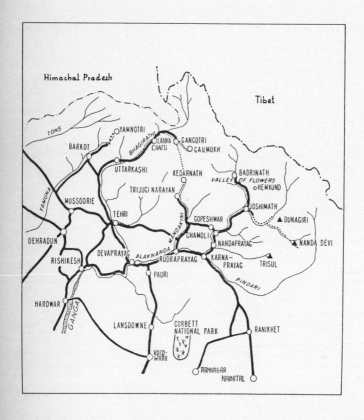

Sacred Hemkund Lake is famous as a spot where great religious teachers, rishis and sadhus have retired for meditation. Even the Sikh guru, Govind Singh is said to have meditated here.

# Nainital

At 1938 m, the Nainital is a popular resort area for Indian tourists during May and June. Set on a lovely lake, surrounded by mountains, Nainital's colonial heritage as summer residence of the Uttar Pradesh administration is readily visible.

April is a quiet month, just right for people looking to escape India's heat and bustle. On the lake you can take out small boats and paddlers. And you've great trekking in the vicinity. If you want a good view during your walk, be sure to get up early.

Several agencies offer one and two day excursions to:
**Ranikhet**, a mountain village with a Himalaya view, one day, 55.- to 75.-Rs.
**Almora**, a mountain village with the Kasar Devi Temple, one day, 50.- to 60.-Rs.
**Kausani**, famous for its view of the Himalayas, two days, 150.- to 170.-Rs.

**Tourist Office:** By the lake, provides reliable info, and helps you find a decent room.

## COMING - GOING
The nearest railway station is Kathgodam, where you have direct connections to Agra via Mathura and Lucknow (11 h, 37.-Rs). At the bus stand is an office where you can make rail reservations. Plus good bus connections to Ramnagar Railway Station, along with Almora, Kausani, and Ranikhet. See Corbett National Park.

## A NIGHT'S REST
You are best off in the beautifully situated **Youth Hostel**, **(Dm)**10.-, a bit out of town, clean, quiet. Otherwise several hotels: **Hotel Punjab**, **(S)**15.-, 50.-, **(D)**40.-, 90.-, on The Mall. **Hotel Coronation**, Mallital, **(S)**15.-, 50.-, **(D)**40.-, 90.-. The most expensive alternative is **Royal Hotel**, on The Mall, **(S)**100.-, 200.-, **(D)**150.-, 200.-.

## The Chipko Movement

Chipko (= hug) is an ecological movement which celebrated its first victory in Uttar Pradesh in 1973. The object was to hug trees to prevent them from being cut down by loggers thus further disturbing the fragile ecological balance in the Himalayas. Spokesman for the movement is Sunderlal Bahugu-

na, a supporter of Mahatma Gandhi, who was active in the
independence movement in his youth. In 1956, he and his
wife founded an ashram in Silyara.

The Chipko Movement sees its roots in the Bishnoi (Hindu)
sect in Rajasthan, who in 1730 used this method to prevent
the Maharaja of Jodhpur from felling trees they considered
sacred. In all, 363 people died, mostly women and children.
But their goal was achieved: the Maharaja, impressed by
their faith, took active measures to protect the trees. During
colonial rule, there were several examples of mass resistance, when forests were placed under state control.

Environmental catastrophes, including mountain slides in the
Garhwal Region, made people conscious of the damage
wrought by logging. In April 1973, several villages used
tree hugging to prevent logging by outside companies. The
movement began in support of local economic interests, but
with time evolved into an ecological movement. It became
increasingly clear, to ever more people, that the forest was
a basic necessity to maintenance of earth, water and clean
air. Further successes were achieved in 1978 and 1979, a
period which saw S. Bahuguna engage in a hunger strike,
and his imprisonment in Dehra Dun.

Demands of the Chipko Movement:
1. Prohibition of commercial logging of green trees in mountains above 1000 m, and on slopes of 30 % incline or
   greater. Only dead or dying trees can be removed, after
   local needs for wood have been satisfied.
2. Prohibition of the logging of precious woods, including
   white beech.
3. Thousands of pine trees are uprooted annually as a result of over-tapping resin. Trees which have been cut
   deeply for the harvesting of sap should be allowed a
   recuperation period.
4. Planting of trees for a minimum of 3 km around villages,
   including precious woods (building, fodder, firewood,
   fertilizer, fiber). These regions should be maintained and
   protected for the villages, even if they encroach upon the
   borders of private forest reserves.

Over 100,000 trees have been planted to date by members of
the Chipko Movement. Additionally, no trees have been felled
above 1000 m in eight districts of Garhwal Himal. In 1981,
S. Bahuguna began a 5000 km march, together with friends,
from Srinagar in Kashmir, across the Himalayas, to Kohima
in Nagaland. His tools consisted of a megaphone, a small
slide projector, several slides, brushes and paint. The slides
showed the results of logging: erosion, landslides, floods.
With brush and paint he left his slogans throughout the
countryside. Children, happy to learn his slogans and songs,
were an additional form of advertising.

The Chipko Movement provided the spiritual support for a
revolt against today's materialist civilization, whereby ris-
ing demand leads to the destruction of Mother Earth. (By
Ludmilla Tüting: **Hug the Trees: The Chipko Movement in
India**)
  If you're interested in learning more about the Chipko
Movement, contact: Sunderlal Bahuguna, c/o Chipko Informa-
tion Centre, Parvatiya Navjeevan Mandal, Silyara, Tehri-
Garhwal, via Ghansali, PIN 249155, U.P., India.

# Corbett National Park

The park is named for the hunter, conservationist, and author,
Jim Corbett. It was established in 1936, making it the oldest
animal reserve in India. The 520 km$^2$ is set between 400 m and
1100 m. The main attraction are the tigers, which, unlike in most
parks, are relatively easy to spot. Also finding habitats are
elephants, panthers, wild boar, deer, jackals, several species of
ape, various birds, and other animals. Admission for three days
is 30.-Rs, for students 2.-Rs; each additional day costs 6.-Rs.
  Dhikala is your best departure point for park excursions.
Elephant rides are offered for 13.-Rs, up to two hours. The best
times to see wildlife are in the early morning, and just before
sunset, when the animals come to water.
  It is possible to hire a guide for a tour of the park in your
own car. You are not permitted to tour the park on your own! In
1981, a local resident was killed by a tiger.
  The park is open from November 15th to June 15th. The best
time to visit is January to May when the elephant grass isn't so
high.

**COMING - GOING**
  **By Bus:** From Delhi Interstate Bus Terminal by Kashmiri Gate,
six buses daily, starting at 08:00 h, takes 8 h, costs 22.-Rs.
No reservations possible, so get to the terminal early. At
05:40 h, a de luxe bus (40.-Rs) departs.
  From Ramnagar, one bus daily to Dhikala, departs at 16:00 h,
takes 3 h, costs 9.-Rs. Be sure to book your lodgings in advance from Ramnagar (see A Night's Rest). Ramnagar is also
the nearest railway station.
  From Rishikesh and Hardwar, get the train to Mohradabad,
and then if necessary by bus to Ramnagar (3 h, 20.-Rs).
  From Corbett Park, you've direct connections to Nainital. Get
the morning bus to Ramnagar (3 h, 9.-Rs), then continue on
with the same bus to Nainital (4 h, 10.-Rs). For the return
trip, the bus departs Nainital in the afternoon.

**A NIGHT'S REST**
It's advisable to make advance reservations from Dhikala. Or
you might try in Delhi at the Uttar Pradesh Tourist Office.

CORBETT NATIONAL PARK

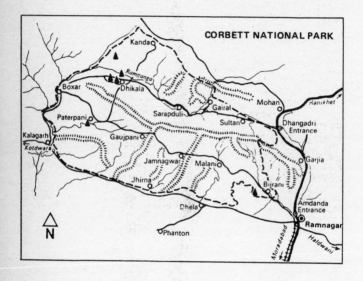

Otherwise,    reservations  in  Ramnagar  at  Corbett  Reservation
Centre.   Your cheapest accommodation is **Swiss Cottage (Dm)**6.-,
or in an old-fashioned tent 15.-Rs.   There is a river for swimming by the campsite.

In both **Forest Resthouses (S)**100.-.

You can eat in the chai shops,  or in the **Park Restaurant**
where a vegetarian dinner costs 12.-Rs. If you want to do your
own cooking,   pick up supplies in Ramnagar.   Open fires for
cooking are prohibited.

If  you  get  stuck  in  Ramnagar,   cheap  accommodations  are
available. Ask in one of the restaurants.

# GANGES PLAINS

When you think of the Ganges
Plains, you usually mean the nor-
thern-Indian lowlands and the Ganges River system, including its tri-
butaries, flowing down from the
Himalayas and the northern Deccan
highlands.

The Ganges Delta joins the Brahmaputra Delta where they mouth into
the Bay of Bengal. In the mire of
the two river deltas are the Republic of Bangladesh and the Indian
state of West Bengal with its capital at Calcutta.

This tremendous river system,
fed by countless meandering
streams, rises up toward the end of
the rainy season in September. Catastrophic floods leave untold dead
or homeless. And the road system is the first to go, leading to
irregularities in rail and bus connections. Delays and detours
are a way of life. Keep your schedule flexible during this
period.

If you are heading from Delhi on a quick trip to Kathmandu,
and still want to catch the sights in Agra, Khajuraho, and Varanasi, try Indian Airlines' Sightseeing Flights, offering stopovers
en route at any or all the above. The flights depart daily. And
you can book right through to Rangoon or Bangkok.

Politically speaking, the north-Indian lowlands include the
south and east of Uttar Pradesh, Bihar, and West Bengal (except
Darjeeling). We are also including the northern edge of Madhya
Pradesh, as this is frequently visited on a side trip. Our com-
mentary runs from east to west.

GANGES PLAINS

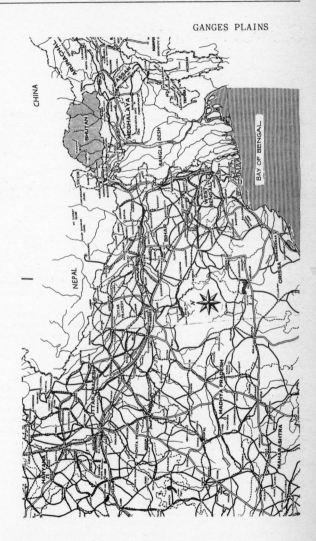

# Agra

India's biggest tourist attraction is the old moghul city on the west bank of the Jumna,   site of Love's most splendid monument, the Taj Mahal mausoleum.

According to legend,   Agra was founded by the first Aryan settlers,   and named "Arya Garh",   which with time was shortened to Agra.   This story finds support in the writings of an ancient Greek historian,   Ptolomäus,   who mentions an Indian town of this name.   Later Agra was probably inhabited by Rajputans.   The Muslims seized the town in 1131 AD.

In 1526,   the moghul dynasty became infected with an urge to build,   culminating under Emperor Akbar (1555-1605) and his ne-phew Shah Jahan (1627-1665) in construction of the Red Fort and the nearby city of Fatehpur Sikri.   The excesses of Shah Jahan, who invested his state's entire treasury in construction of the Taj Mahal and the Red Fort,   led to his disenthronement by his son Aurangzeb (1665-1706).

But the nation's decline could not be forestalled.   Hindus rose up repeatedly against Islamic rule,   until the English seized the town in 1806.   Agra's population of one million,   at the height of moghul rule,   declined to just 100,000.   Today the city houses 140,000, or 250,000 including its suburbs.

As elsewhere,   the buildings are threatened by air pollution. Sulphur from nearby refineries is eating at historic structures faster than repairs are possible.   A zone has been declared around Agra where no new industry is permitted to settle,   nor existing facilities expand.   Monitors,   to register pollution,   have been set up by the Taj Mahal and in Sikandra.   The green belt, around the Taj Mahal,   is being steadily expanded.   And new methods are being tested to clean and conserve the buildings. Only the future will show if they succeed.

## COMING – GOING

**By Air:** Agra is served by a daily flight from Delhi (191.-Rs), and via Khajuraho (331.-Rs) to Varanasi (499.-Rs).   The Indian Airlines office is in Hotel Shiraz,   tel.73434.   The airport bus costs 8.-Rs. Tell the driver to let you off along the way at the Tourist Office.   This is the cheap hotel district. Or continue on to the last stop,   and get a rickshaw to the cheap hotel district around the Taj,   costs 2.-Rs.

**By Rail:** Agra is on the two-track wide-gauge line,   heading south from Delhi to Bombay,   Hyderabad and Madras.   To the east you have connections to Kanpur,   Varanasi,   Patna,   and Calcutta. Connections are frequent,   and good.

The best connection from Delhi is the Taj Express,   departing New Delhi Railway Station at 07:05 h,   arriving Agra Cantt at 10:20 h,   costs 25.-Rs (2nd class).   If you plan to spend a night in Agra,   you can get one of the other trains,   which take 30 minutes longer,   but stop at Raja Ki Mandi Railway Station, near the Tourist Office,   and cheap hotels.

AGRA

1  Power House Bus Stand
2  Bank of Baroda
3  State Bank of India
4  Indian Airlines in Hotel Clarks Shiraz
5  ITDC Transport Unit in Laurie's Hotel
6  Registration Office
8  Kwality Restaurant
9  UP Tourist Bungalow & Ashoka Hotel

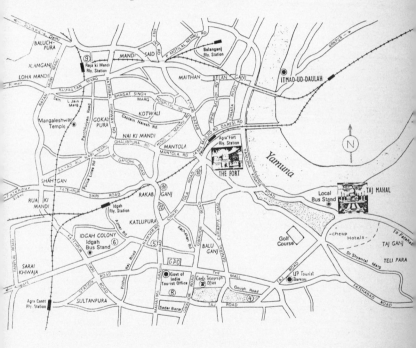

Coming from the east, get off at Agra Fort (Agra City), where you are closest to the cheap hotels around the Taj Mahal and downtown.

A rickshaw from Raja Ki Mandi, Agra Cantt, or Taj Mahal, to the Red Fort and Agra Fort Railway Station is 2.-Rs.

**By Bus:** You arrive near the Red Fort, or at Idgah Bus Station in Cantonment. From the Fort, get a rickshaw downtown to the cheap hotel district. Here too is the Tourist Office. Or for 2.-Rs to the Taj, where you'll find more cheap lodgings nearby. Buses depart half hourly to Fatehpur Sikri, and hourly to Jaipur from Idgah Bus Station, in the Cantonment, costs 30.-Rs.

## A NIGHT'S REST

There are three hotel districts. Near Raja Ki Mandi Railway Station at Delhi Gate in the northwest, try **Tourist Bungalow**, tel.72123, **(S)**60.-, **(D)**70.-, 4-bed rooms 105.-, **(Dm)**16.-, very quiet, clean, garden, restaurant, camper parking and camping area.

Around Delhi Gate are three other hotels, not quite as expensive: **Ashoka Hotel**, tel.75108. **Goverdhan Hotel**, tel.73313. **Shitaze Hotel**, tel.75106.

More convenient to the sights, are hotels downtown, or around the Taj Mahal, between the Red Fort and the Tourist Office. **Taj Mahal Hotel**, Daresi No. 1, tel.61616, across from Agra Fort Railway Station. **Bengal Lodge**, Rakabganj Road, near the State Bank of India, tel.72400, **(S)**15.-, **(D)**25.-. **Major (Retired) Bakshi Sardar Singh**, 33/83 Ajmer Road, tel.76828, **(S)**40.-, **(D)**60.-, clean bungalows, the guesthouse is now run by the son of the deceased Major. **Laurie's Hotel**, M. Gandhi Road, tel.77047, **(S)**65.-, **(D)**110.-, large rooms, swimming pool filled from a spring, extensive grounds, camper parking. **Hotel Priya**, Gwalior Road, Baluganj, tel.75405, **(S)**40.-, **(D)**50.-, **(AC)**double the price. **Tourist Rest House**, Baluganj, tel.64961, **(D)**25.- without bath, or **(D)**40.- with bath. **Mrs. Naval M. Franjee**, 16 Gropichand Shivhare Road (formerly Mansfield Road), tel.72205, **(S)**30.-, breakfast and meals are cheap, lovely old colonial house, right by the Tourist Office. **Hotel Akbar Jun**, 21 Mall Road, **(D)**45.-, 80.-. **Agra Caterer**, The Mall, tel.72271, **(D)**25.-, restaurant, clean. **Jaggi Hotel**, Sadar Bazar, tel.72370, **(D)**25.-, good restaurant.

The cheapest region is just south of the Taj Mahal, try: **Mumtaz-mahal**, **(S)**10.-, **(D)**15.-, **(Dm)**5.-, pleasant, sunny terrace, good food, 400 m from the Taj, by the tonga stand. **Indian Guest House**, near the South Gate to the Taj, **(S)**10.-, **(D)**15.-, simple, but clean and well kept. Around the corner, the **New Aishi Restaurant** is cheap and good. **Shanti Lodge**, same area, large, clean, sunny rooms, **(S)**10.-, **(D)**20.-, **(Dm)**5.-, and good food. **Akbar International**, Jasoria Enclave, Fatehabad Road, near the Taj, lovely garden, **(D)**20.-, 80.-, clean, the better rooms have rugs and bath, people gather evenings in the courtyard.

Camping: **Highway Inn**, Vibhar Nagar, 2 km south of the Taj, for two people and camper parking, 12.-Rs, a rickshaw to the Taj is 2.-Rs.

Other restaurants worth mentioning include **New Star Restaurant, Taj Mahal**, and **Southern Gate**, all clean, with good, cheap food.

## SHOPPING

**Sadar Bazar:** The ideal and cheapest shopping area in Agra, south of the Tourist Office. But there is nothing special, except **durries**, cotton mats with traditional patterns. Touts get 30 % commission if they bring you into a shop, and 1.-Rs even if you don't buy anything! Be sure to do your shopping alone; your bargaining power increases appreciably. Good buys are inlaid stonework, including marble chessboards, small jewelry boxes, etc. For good **pietradura** (marble with inlaid semiprecious jewels), you'll pay a fraction the price charged in European cities such as Florence. Around the Taj Mahal are a number of shops where you can compare prices. Keep in mind that marble can't be scratched with your fingernail!

Also recommended are musical instruments, particularly sitars; visit **Sweety Musicals**, tel.65680, 61 Gwalior Road, Naulakha Bazar (Sadar Bazar).

## SIGHTS

**The Taj Mahal:** Attraction number one in India, an architectural masterpiece, built in mosque style. The Taj Mahal was built in 1630 on the orders of Shah Jahan, in memory of his favorite wife and advisor, Mumtaz Mahal (crown of the palace), who died

giving birth to their 14th child. 20,000 workers and artists, some coming from Europe and Persia, spent 22 years working a monument of love wrought in sandstone, marble, and semiprecious jewels. Mumtaz Mahal rests in a tomb directly below the dome. An exact copy of her sarcopharg is placed at earth level, partly to foil thieves, but also to permit prayers for the deceased without disturbing her place of rest. The complex also includes a mosque facing west, a similar structure looking east, plus tombs for the royal family and court women. The main entrance was completed last, with 22 domes symbolizing the duration of construction. If you get the chance, visit the monument at full moon. During full moon week, the Taj grounds stay open until 24:00 h, costs 2.-Rs, free on holidays. No cameras of any type are permitted on the grounds. Measures are being tested to combat decay caused by air pollution.

**The Red Fort:** Built on the orders of Emperor Akbar and expanded by his successor Aurangzeb. Admission is only permitted via **Amar Singh Gate** in the south, costs 2.-Rs. Facing the river are a number of palace structures in red sandstone and white marble, many built by Shah Jahan. In **Saman Burj**, the eight-cornered tower, Aurangzeb imprisoned his father on charges of excessive spending. But he did permit his father a view of the Taj Mahal. Jahan was later buried next to his wife. The tower was built as an addition to the **Diwan-i-Khas**, a private audience hall constructed in 1637 by Akbar. **Moti Mashad**, the world's largest marble mosque, is another must see in the Red Fort.

**Itmad-Ud-Daulah's Tomb:** Where Shah Jahan's predecessor is laid to rest, was built on the orders of his wife, Nur Jahan (Light of the Earth). It is seen as the architectural forerunner of the Taj Mahal. The pietradura technique of marble inlay was first tried here. Nur Jahan's father was the grandfather of Mumtaz Mahal. The mausoleum is across the Jumna, to the right of the road leading from the bridge, admission is 2.-Rs.

**Chini ka Rauza** (The Chinese Tomb): 1 km to the north, a less well kept mausoleum. Inside rests the Persian court poet and teacher under Shajahan, Allama Afsal Khan Shukrullah, from Shiraz.

**Ram Bagh:** 1 km further north, a less than spectacular Moghul Garden, established during the reign of Babur in 1526. But the first of its kind.

**Akbar's Mausoleum:** 10 km north-west of the Fort in Sikandra, get Bus 22 from the Fort. The mausoleum's construction was begun under Akbar, and completed under his son Jahangir in 1613. The structure, set in a park, combines red sandstone and white marble in a work showing both Islamic and Hindu influences.

Akbar's actual tomb is in the crypt, though the room above contains an exact replica. Admission is 2.-Rs, no charge on Fridays, open all day.

## Sightseeing Tours

**UP State Road Transport Corp. (UPSRTC):** Offers a daily bus
tour 10:30-18:30 h departing from Agra Cantt Railway Station,
visiting Fatehpur Sikri (mornings), the Fort, and Taj Mahal.
You can also board by the Tourist Office at 10:00 h. Reservations at platform 1 in Cantt Station, or through the UPSRTC,
96 Gwalior Road, tel.72206, or from sales people aboard the
morning Taj Express from Delhi. You can make a day trip from
Delhi to Agra, see the major sights, and make the train back
that night. There are three classes: De Luxe 23.-Rs, AC Bus
43.-Rs. Tour price includes 6.-Rs admission. Tour price on
Fridays is 4.50 Rs cheaper. The AC bus with lunch and tea
costs 63.-Rs.
**ITDC Tours:** Depart from the Tourist Office, 191 The Mall, and
from the major hotels, costs 15.-Rs, 08:00-12:30 h, visiting the
Taj Mahal, the Red Fort, and Itmad-ud-Daulah's Tomb. From
14:00-18:30 h a tour visits Fatehpur Sikri and Sikandra, costs
20.-Rs.

## TIPS

**Government of India Tourist Office:** 191 The Mall, tel.72377, in
the center of town, 09:00-17:00 h, closed Sundays.
**UP Government Tourist Information Counter:** At Kheria Airport,
open just for incoming flights.
**Head Post Office:** The Mall, tel.74000, near the Tourist Office.
**Central Telegraph Office:** Nearby on The Mall at Gwalior Street,
tel.76914.
**Foreigners' Registration Office:** 16 Idgah Colony, tel.4167, on Ajmer Road at Malpure Road, also provides visa extensions.
**State Bank of India:** Rakabganj Road, tel.74061, Mon-Fri 10:00-
14:00 h, Sat 10:00-12:00 h.
**Allahabad Bank:** In Hotel Clarks Shiraz, Money Exchange Booth
open Mon-Fri 12:00-17:30 h, Sat 12:00-16:00 h, tel.72421.

# Fatehpur Sikri

A ghost town today, this village is an example of failed city
planning in the middle ages. A Muslim holy man, Salim Chisti,
who had retired here, was consulted by Emperor Akbar. The Emperor felt frustrated in his hopes for a son. The holy man is
said to have sacrificed his own six-month-old son, with the hope
that his son should be reborn in Akbar's Hindu wife. After Mar-
iam-uz-Zamani actually gave birth to a son, he was named Salim.
This son was later to be Akbar's successor, Jahangir. In thanks,
Akbar ordered local stone masons to begin construction of an
11 km long town wall. Five years later, the entire town was

FATEHPUR SIKRI

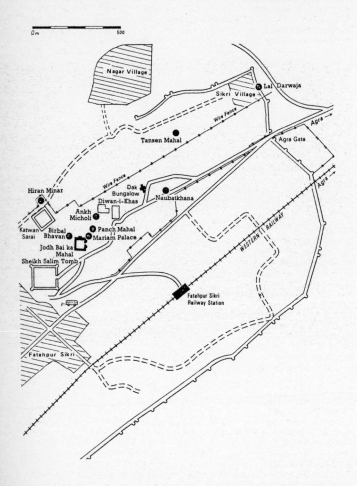

complete. Akbar moved his court here. The town grew so quickly
that the wells went dry, forcing abandonment of the town
16 years later. Akbar returned to Agra, and Fatehpur Sikri fell
into decay. In 1719 Mohammed Shah had the town restored. Today
only the village at the foot of the town hill is inhabited. The
town above awaits, just as it was built, 400 years ago.

Any more details would burst the bindings of this book, but a
visit is certainly worthwhile. The grounds are well kept, and
peaceful.

## COMING - GOING
Buses from Agra, Idgah Bus Station (1 h, 5.-Rs). Last bus
from Fatehpur Sikri Bus Stand (departures half hourly) to Agra, just after sunset.

## A NIGHT'S REST
**A.S. Resthouse**, (D)9.-, book through the Archaeological Survey
of India, 22 The Mall. Or in **Saras Tourist Complex**. Camper
parking 10.-Rs, in **Bharatpur Bird Sanctuary**.
In the village below, food and drink are available. At the
top you've just a few tidbits.

# Lucknow

Lucknow is capital of Uttar Pradesh, India's most populous state.
A number of interesting buildings date from the reign of the
Nawabs of Oudh. Few tourists pass through here. The town is
spread over a wide area with lots of well kept parks. During the
1857 Sepoy uprising, the British were defeated in heavy fighting.
Lucknow is conveniently situated on the Delhi, Sonauli, Pokhara,
Kathmandu route, or as a stopover on the Delhi, Agra, Varanasi
route.

## COMING - GOING

**By Air:** Daily to Delhi (400.-), Calcutta (805.-), Patna (410.-),
and Ranchi (645.-). Four times weekly to Bombay (1330.-), and
Gorakhpur (236.-). Three flights weekly via Allahabad (180.-)
to Varanasi (250.-Rs). The airport is 13 km from town. The
Indian Airlines office is in Hotel Clarks Avadh on M. Gandhi
Marg.

**By Rail:** Lucknow has two railway stations located side by
side. The largest and most obvious belongs to Northern Railway, serving trains to Delhi, Agra, and Varanasi. The smaller
railway station belongs to North-Eastern Railway, departures to
Gorakhpur.

There are two separate reservation offices, booking offices,
etc.

Good connections to Delhi (10 h, 45.-), to Varanasi (7-10 h,
32.-Rs), to Agra (8 h, 32.-Rs). Through Lucknow pass direct
trains to Jammu Tawi (for Srinagar) (24 h, 75.-Rs), to Ambala,
near Chandigarh (9-14 h, 50.-Rs), to Amritsar (18-20 h,
66.-Rs).

Five trains daily take 6-8 h to Sonauli, the border crossing
to Nepal's Bhairawa. From there you head on by bus.

If you want to travel fast from the southern freak center in
Goa to the northern in Nepal, get the 115 Gorakhpur Express,
from Bombay V.T. to Lucknow in 28 h, to Gorakhpur-Khalibad
in 35 h, costs 107.-Rs.

**By Bus:** Buses to Delhi, Agra, Gorakhpur, Allahbad, Varanasi.
To Mahoba (7 h, 27.-Rs). To Kajuraho (3 h).

## A NIGHT'S REST

Lucknow has lots of hotels, but still too few. It can take a
long time to find a room. There are cheap hotels around the
railway station where you can try your luck.

**RRR** in the railway station, **(S)**15.-. **Hotel Sharma**, **(D)**55.-,
right across from the station.

On the road diagonally across from the station: **Bengali Hotel**,
**(D)**30.-, no bath. **Hotel Mohan**, **(D)**70.-, with bath; **(Dm)**15.-,
restaurant downstairs. Next door **New Maharaja Restaurant** has
good cheap food. **Hotel Samrat**, **(D)**45.-, clean, quiet, tiled
bath. **Republic Hotel**, **(D)**25.-. **Hotel Apsara**, 25.-Rs. Lots more
hotels with similar prices.

LUCKNOW

| 1 | GPO | 8 | G. Buddha Park |
|---|-----|---|----------------|
| 2 | Zoo & Museum | 9 | Clock Tower Hussainabad |
| 3 | Botanical Garden | 10 | Jama Masjid |
| 4 | Tourist Bungalow | 11 | Chota Imambara |
| 5 | Kaiserbagh | 12 | Hotel Clarks Avadh |
| 6 | Residency | 12 | Indian Airlines |
| 7 | Haathi Park | 13 | Tourist Office |

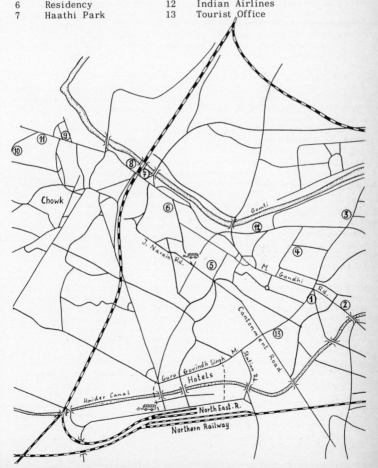

**Baba Tourist Lodge**, **(D)**25.-, left out of the railway station, across from the bus stand, clean, common showers, nice owner. **YMCA**, Rana Pratap Marg, tel.477227, **(S)**25.-. **Tourist Bungalow Hotel Gompti**, 6 Sapru Marg, tel.32257, 6 km from the railway station, **(D)**70.- with bath, tourist information window.

Cheap food as usual in the railway station restaurant, breakfast 5.-Rs, thali 3.50 Rs or 4.50 Rs. Across from the railway station and around the bus stand are lots of good Indian restaurants (mostly Punjabi), some quite expensive.

Much more expensive, but good, with a self-service buffet in **Hotel Carlton**, Shahnajaf Road at Rana Pratap Marg. A full course meal (soup, main dish, tea/coffee) costs 40.-Rs. If you're en route to Nepal, you might celebrate this as your last Indian meal.

## SIGHTS
Everything of interest is grouped close together, about 10 km north of the railway station; get local bus 27 (stops across from the railway station) and disembark by the medical college which resembles a palace.

**Bara Imambara** (bara = great): Also known as Asafi Imambara, built in 1784 by Nawab Asaf-ud-Dauka. The main hall is 50 m by 15 m and 15 m high. The unsupported ceiling is one of the world's longest. A stair leads to the roof and a lovely view. Upstairs is a labyrinth, be sure to take a guide. Admission is 2.50 Rs, a guide costs 5.-Rs. Generally he tries to get a larger fee, particularly from groups, so bargain. The lower levels are closed to the public. Open 06:00-17:00 h.

**Rumi Darwasa**: Next to Bara Imambara, this lovely arch was also built by Nawab Asaf-ud-Dauka in 1784. The gate is called the **Turkish Gate** because its design was based on an arch in Istanbul.

**Husainabad Imambara**: About ten minutes walk from Bara Imam-bara, by the Clock Tower, visible far and wide. The Husainabad, or Chhota Imambara, was constructed by Muhammed Ali Shah as a mausoleum. The lovely building is set in a garden centered on a tiny lake flanked by two copies of the Taj Mahal, open 06:00-17:00 h.

**Jama Masjid**: West of the mausoleum, impresses with its size. Construction also begun under Muhammed Ali Shah, only Muslims admitted.

**The Residence**: Or at least its ruins, 3 km east of Jama Masjid by foot or bicycle rickshaw. The British Residence was construct-ed between 1780 and 1800, and demolished in a siege during the

1857 battle of Lucknow. Across from the Residence, a simple column stands in memory of the victims of the decade-long struggle for Indian independence.

**Shahnajaf Imambara:** Further east, near the Tourist Bungalows, a mausoleum with an unusual dome.

TIPS
**Tourist Information Window:** In Northern Railways Railway Station, and in the Tourist Bungalow, books sightseeing tours. City tours depart daily from the railway station, 09:00-13:00 h, 15.-Rs plus admission charges.
**Indian Airlines Office:** In Hotel Clarks Avadh, Mahatma Gandhi Marg.

# Khajuraho

This village in northern Madhya Pradesh is famous for its beautiful temples. Today, 4000 souls make their homes in Khajuraho. From the 9th to 13th centuries it was capital of the Chandella Empire. The Chandellas derived their name from Chanirama, the God of the Moon. According to legend, Chanirama sired a son by Amaravati, the daughter of a priest. One of his descendants in Khajuraho required a sacrifice, and therefore built 85 temples, of which 22 still stand. These temples represent the peak of mediaeval Hindu architecture. The outer walls are decorated with Hindu deities, particularly in erotic pose, which shame most modern Indians. Along with the worship of Vishnu and Shiva, you'll find traces of Buddhism, Jainism, Sun Worship, and esoteric Tantraism.

The temples can be seen in three architectural groups. The Western Temples are the largest and the most beautiful. Additionally, there are an Eastern group and a Southern group.
**The Western Temples:** The main attraction, can be visited on foot in three hours. To visit the Eastern and Southern Temples, we advise renting a bicycle by the old bus stand, costs 1.-Rs per hour.
**Archaeological Museum:** Worth a look, featuring interesting and well preserved sculpture. The 0.50 Rs admission is valid for the museum and the Western Temples. The other temples have no admission charge.

**COMING - GOING**
**By Air:** From Delhi (467.-), via Agra (331.-), arrives and returns in the afternoon. Morning flights to Varanasi (331.-Rs). The airport is 5 km to the south.

**By Rail & Bus:**      There is a daily bus service to Agra and
Khajuraho via Jhansi.    Information at the Tourist Office.    The
daytime ride takes 12 h,   costs 55.-Rs,   including reservation.
Direct buses to Gwalior (8 h, 30.-Rs).

The rule of thumb is that when coming from Agra or Lucknow
you always change in Jhansi on the Delhi,   Agra,   Bombay rail
line.

From the railway station in Jhansi,   direct buses at 06:00 h,
07:00 h,   and 08:00 h,   takes 5 h, costs 20.-Rs. Buses also depart from the bus stand, 5 km from the railway station.

To Varanasi and the south (Jalgaon,   Ajanta / Ellora),    the
ride is simplest via Satna,   a railway station on the line from
Bombay to Allahabad and Varanasi.

Between Khajuraho and Satna are a morning and afternoon
bus,   takes 4 h,   costs 15.-Rs.   From Satna you can go on by
bus to Rewa,   or get a train to Varanasi,   takes 8 h,   slightly
longer by bus. The bus stand and railway station in Satna are
2 km apart.

To Lucknow,   your best connection is via Mahoba (also Ma-
howa) railway station on the Jhansi - Varanasi route,   south of
Kanpur.   From there you've both buses and direct trains to
Lucknow and Varanasi (12 h,   35.-Rs, short term reservations).
Mahoba is 3 h by bus north of Khajuraho (10.-Rs),   frequent
connections.   The bus stand and railway station in Mahabo are
6 km apart.

If you are forced to spend a night in Jhansi,   try RRR in the
railway station,   **(D)**40.-,   **(Dm)**10.-. Central Hotel, **(D)**20.-, left
out of the station and ten minutes walk along the street, tonga
1.-Rs. Sipri Hotel, next door, run down, **(D)**25.-, 35.-Rs.

In Satna there is absolutely nothing to see, but if you do get
stuck,   try right by the railway station,   Hotel India, **(S)**20.-.
Glory,   next door, **(D)**30.-, with WC and showers. Both are loud
with bus horns. Quieter in Hotel Samvat, Hanuman Chowk, rickshaws from the station 3.-Rs, **(D)**20.-Rs, bargain.

## A NIGHT'S REST

Cheap accommodations around the old bus stand: **Hotel Apsara**,
**(D)**15.-,   four-bed rooms 25.-,   nice owner. **Gupta Lodge**, clean,
**(D)**20.-,   good,   somewhat expensive food. **New Bharat Lodge**,
**(D)**20.-,   bath and WC,   good restaurant. **Sunset View**, a good,
clean establishment,   100 m from the lake,   **(S)**25.-,   **(D)**60.-,
**(Dm)**12.- (high season prices),   bargain! **Jain Lodge**, Jain Tem-
ples Road,   **(S)**35.-,   **(D)**50.- (high season),   bargain, nice view
from the roof.

The **Tourist Bungalow** isn't cheap any more,   **(S)**20.-,   40.-.
The two other state-owned hotels,   **Rahil** and **Hotel Payal** are
even more expensive.   **Hotel Pahal** does have a quiet camping
area,   6.-Rs. Camping too by **Tourist Bungalow**.

Besides the hotel restaurants, try **Madras Coffee House. Swiss Cafe** has a view of the temple to go with its excellent, but expensive food. For a cheap meal, try the local restaurants around the old bus stand, e.g. **Gupta Restaurant** featuring meals for 4.-Rs.

**TIPS**
**Tourist Office:** By New Bus Stand, 200 m south of the old bus stand. The maps provided are inadequate, as is the info. But they are informed about departures.
**Panna National Park:** 471 km$^2$, founded in 1984. Situated just a half hour from Khajurho: tigers. bears, wolves, hyaenas, jackals, and gazelles find habitats here. Jeep tours are organized by the hotels and travel agencies.

### TANTRAISM AND TANTRAIST RITUAL
Tantraism was widespread throughout India in the 7th century. From India, siddhis carried the practice to Nepal. A major aspect is the **Shakti Cult**, whereby the female is revered. Male gods can only achieve fulfilment with the aid of

female energy (Shakti). Tantraists see the entire world as a union of male passivism and female activism. That is why Maithuna (sexual intercourse) is so greatly revered.

The Chandella rulers were cult members, building richly decorated temples. Tantra rituals were performed in the temples at night. The ritual knows no caste differences.

The participants sit in a circle (Devi-Chakra = circle of goddesses) with their female partners, who may include temple prostitutes. In the center sits the ritual leader with his shakti. First the goddess, or her symbol is placed on the altar and worshipped. Oil lamps and joss sticks are lit. A female temple dancer performs before the goddess, clad only in her jewelry.

**The Ritual of Five Mukaras:** Performed as the next stage of the ritual, combining **Mada** (wine), **Matsja** (fish), **Mamsa** (meat), **Mudra** (roasted grain), and **Maithuna** (sexual intercourse). The wine is placed in a jug in the circle center. The ritual participants meditate about the union between God and his shakti. This union transforms the wine into a divine medicine. Mantras are chanted, and flowers laid down as a sign of reverence. The meat is nourishment for the body, provides energy, and stimulates intelligence. Fish and roasted grains are blessed with special gestures and mantras.

Fish establishes the connection to water, from which all life originates. The roasted grains place us in touch with the earth and preservation of life. Drinking of wine and eating of food are integral parts of the ritual. Even the sexual intercourse follows prescribed ritual. The man first places his hand above the head of his partner while chanting mantras for Kama, the Goddess of Love. Then he places his hand upon her forehead, neck, breast, heart, navel, yoni, and finally upon his lingam. At each stage various mantras are chanted a prescribed number of times, together with exactly prescribed gestures. During sexual intercourse an exact number of positions is assumed, and the shakti must become totally aroused. During orgasm, the man must chant the fertility mantras, while his thoughts, sink completely into the goddess.

Many parallels to Tantraism can be seen in Chinese Taoism.

# Varanasi

This town on the banks of the Ganges River is the most important of Hinduism's seven sacred cities. Varanasi was mentioned 3000 years ago in the heroic epics, **SKANDA PURANA** and the **MAHABHARATA**, making it one of the world's most ancient towns. Back then the town was called Kashi (= the light), a name still used by millions of pilgrims. While the British called the town "Benares", the present-day name "Varanasi" stems from the two rivers, Varu-

VARANASI

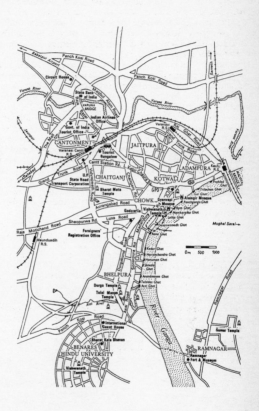

na and Assi, which join with the Ganges by the Old Town center.
Along the sacred river, Indians flock to ghats with sloping stairs
to partake in a sacred bath. As the sun rises over the water,
the faithful let the water wash away sins, and pray for release
from the cycle of reincarnations.

Over the course of repeated Muslim attacks and reconquest,
many temples were destroyed. But stable rule under the latest
maharaja dynasty has permitted the restoration or replacement of
every temple since 1738.

The Indian Government has allocated 2.15 million Rs in coming
years for restoration of temples and ghats. And work will begin
to combat environmental pollution of the sacred waters of the
Ganges. In 1986, 450 million Rs were appropriated to save the
Ganges.

## COMING - GOING

**By Air:** Daily flights to Agra (500.-), Bhubaneshwar (424.-),
Delhi (637.-), Lucknow (250.-, except Sundays). Thrice weekly
to Allahabad (156.-), Calcutta (601.-), and Gorakhpur
(160.-Rs) near the Nepali border. A direct flight to Kathmandu
costs US$71.-. The Indian Airlines office is in Mint House Mo-
tel, near Cantonment Railway Station, tel.43146, open 10:00-
17:00 h. The Airport is 23 km from town, buses from the Cantonment (20.-Rs).

**By Rail:**   Reservations for all classes in Cantonment Railway
Station, tel.64920, 08:30–15:30 h, 16:00–19:30 h. Excellent connections to major towns on the Ganges Plains via a two–track,
wide–gauge line.   The line to Gorakhpur is currently being
converted to wide–gauge. For connections to Nepal, see Nepal.
  Many direct connections run through the railway junction,
**Mughal Sarai,**   15 km from town. Get a bus, or the local train
from Varanasi Junction (Cantt.).    Trains to Agra (13–15 h,
50.–Rs).
**By Bus:**   Buses to the larger nearby towns in Uttar Pradesh by
UP State Transport Corporation, information, tel.63133, no advance reservations.   The bus stand is at Varanasi Jn. (Cantt.)
Railway Station.

**A NIGHT'S REST**
Upon arrival at Mughal Sarai get a bus or local train,  15 km
into town.   The bus will likely drop you off at Varanasi Jn.
Railway Station. Directly across from the station is **Governmental Tourist Bungalow,**   Parade Kothi, tel.63186, **(S)**30.–, **(D)**35.–,
with showers,   **(Dm)**10.–, lovely courtyard, garden, reasonably-
priced restaurant,   clean, friendly; Tourist Office in the building,   helpful tourist officer,   tel.63186. **Hotel Relax**, right next
to the Tourist Bungalow,   **(D)**25.–,   35.–, clean, friendly. **Hotel
De Paul**,   next door,   **(S)**15.–,   **(D)**20.–,   no bath, books direct

buses to Kathmandu (150.-Rs). **Hotel Amar**, **(S)**30.-, **(D)**35.-, rooms with bath, friendly management, clean, good. **Hotel Raj Kamal**, **(D)**25.-, bath. **RRR Varanasi Junction**, **(D)**35.-, the dorm is generally booked out.

More cheap hotels in the Cantonment behind the station, get a rickshaw. But be advised that rickshaw drivers in Varanasi often give misinformation about hotels, preferring to direct you to where they receive a commission, at your unknowing expense.

**Tourist DAK Bungalow**, with camper parking, The Mall, Cantonment, **(S)**45.-, **(D)**70.-, parking according to car size 5.- to 16.-Rs, nice, shady, restaurant. A caravan driver informs us that **Overlander Riverview Hotel** is better and cheaper for campers.

Lots of hotels between Varanasi Junction and the Ganges. **Hotel Blue Star**, **(S)**15.-, 25.-, **(D)**20.-, 50.-, **(Dm)**5.-, 10.-, near the station.

In Lohurabir district, southeast of the station, are a number of hotels, try **Natraj Hotel**, **(D)**30.-.

But more popular are the hotels in Chowk, running south from the ghats. **Hotel Maharaja**, Jangambari Road, near Chowk, Godowlia Crossing, tel.55089, rooms with bath, **(S)**15.-, **(D)**30.-, 40.-, plus a 10 % service charge; Mr. Gopha Sharma, the manager, is helpful and friendly. **Hotel K.M.M.**, Shyam Bazar, Machhodry, **(S)**20.-, **(D)**25.-, rickshaw from the station (3.-Rs), frequently recommended. **Central Hotel**, Dasawamedh, tel.62776, **(D)**40.-. **Yogi Lodge**, D 8/9 Kalika, Gali Varanasi, tel.53986, 50 m from Vishnuwath (golden) Temple, a popular place among travellers, but not among rickshaw drivers, who don't get a commission; some people therefore recommend you give the golden temple as your destination, and walk the last few meters; **(D)**25.-, 15.-, per bed in a 4-bed room, **(Dm)**7.-, friendly management, good restaurant, frequently booked up. **Golden Lodge**, next door, **(S)**15.-, **(D)**20.-, **(Dm)**6.-, no restaurant, but a roof-top terrace. **Tandon Lodge**, right on Gai Ghat, **(D)**20.-, terrace with a lovely view of the Ganges; again rickshaw drivers don't like this address, rickshaw 15.-Rs. **Ganga View Lodge**, **(D)**15.-. **Prakash Lodge**, **(D)**15.-. **Sri Vankateswar Lodge**, by Dasaswamedh Ghat, **(D)**20.-. Lots more accommodations in the area.

Two hotels recommended southwest of Chowk: **Hotel Yogesh**, C. 13/11, Aurangabad, a bit away from the bustle, **(D)**25.-, showers, WC, excellent, clean, cheap hotel. **Sun Shiv Hotel**, D 54/16 D Jaddumandi, Aurangabad, tel.52468, **(S)**15.-, **(D)**20.-, very clean, friendly, helpful owner, breakfast served on the lovely roof-top garden.

**International Guest House**, Benares Hindu University, 6 km south of town, if you are attending classes, you might try getting a room here.

**Hotel Imperial**, Luxmi Kund, near Luxa Road, but beware of thieves, we were burgled despite locking our door, as were several friends and acquaintances. This seems to happen frequently. There is a lot of thievery in Varanasi, some of it even by the local monkeys, so lock your windows before heading out.

## REFRESHMENT
Around the corner from Tandon Lodge, by Gai Ghat, are two small, friendly, reasonably-priced restaurants: **Priya** and **Street View**.

Reports concerning **Aces New Deal** abound with superlatives. Select from müsli, fruit salad, and excellent vegetarian food. A lovely garden and temple complete the scene. Well marked by signs in town, you can't miss it near Godowilia Crossing.

Nearby, but closer to the Ganges, is **Ayar's Cafe**, a good, cheap, southern Indian restaurant. **Restaurant Gangotri**, facing Central Hotel, offers a large selection of excellent food.

If you are up for some real Chinese, try **Mandarin Restaurant**, near the Tourist Bungalow. In Hotel India, Patel Nagar, Cantonment, the **Amber Restaurant** offers excellent Indian food in a pleasant atmosphere.

## SHOPPING
Varanasi is famous for its silk and scarves. In **Chowk** you'll find a tremendous selection of every type of cloth, saris, scarves, dhotis, blouses, shirts, and the familiar Indian scarf. But check a few prices first. Varanasi is full of touts out to sell you the cheapest and best silk. They'll even try to convince you that you can sell the silk, scarves, and other products in Delhi or Kathmandu for a profit. No way!

If you aren't heading on to Calcutta, this might be the place to pick up a traditional Indian musical instrument, especially sitars, see Traditional Indian Music.

Wolfgang Ruppnig writes to us that first class and inexpensive musical instruments, particularly sitars are available at **Ravi Classical Music Centre**, Dashaswamedh Road (in front of the lane of Central Hotel), 88, Terhi Neem, Varanasi, 221001. A family business, both father and son are excellent musicians (sitar and tablas). Instruction is offered, free if you buy an instrument. The atmosphere is pleasant. You can take your time choosing from a large selection of instruments, until you find one with the tone you like best. Upon request, a wooden box will be made for you, costs 45.-Rs, the best way to ensure your instrument gets home safely. First class service, fixed prices, but reasonable by comparison.

Ganja is sold in government shops in Uttar Pradesh, certainly in Agra, Khajuraho, and here in Varanasi. Many sadhus consider ganja a necessary ingredient in their religious life, in keeping with the example set by Lord Shiva.

## ACTIVITIES
**Swimming Pool:** If you'd enjoy a cool dip, try in Ashok Hotel, The Mall, tel.52251, costs 10.-Rs. Clarks Hotel also opens its pool, The Mall, tel.62021 for 20.-Rs.
**Music Lessons:** Varanasi is a good place to take lessons in Indian music, see Shopping.
**Yoga Institute:** In Benares Hindu University.

## SIGHTS
The entire town center is one big sightseeing tour of the Hindu religion: temple after temple, shrine upon shrine, ghat after ghat.

**At Sunrise:** Head down to the river and join in the religious activities. Be inconspicuous with your camera, or better, don't use it at all. Try to see with your heart. This is the holiest Hindu town, comparable to Mecca for Muslims, Jerusalum for Jews, or the Vatican for Catholics.

**Boat Rides:** Past the ghats along the Ganges (Ganga = river), particularly lovely at sunset. Good bargainers will pay about 10.-Rs per hour.

**Cremations:** Performed all day long, mainly at Manikarnika Ghat. Photography here is prohibited! Imagine what it would be like if at a burial ceremony, you started hopping around with a camera over the open grave: okay?

**Vishwanath Temple** (Golden Temple): Closed to non-Hindus. A guide will, however, for a little baksheesh, show you a spot where you can peer inside. Pooja is held in the morning and evening in honor of Shiva, the patron god of Varanasi. Here Shiva is also known as Vishwanath, hence the temple's name. Located near Manikarnika Ghat.

**Bharat Mata Mandir:** In this temple, an inlaid marble relief on the floor, depicting the Indian subcontinent, assumes the spot usually reserved for a depiction of the patron goddess or god. The temple was dedicated by Mahatma Gandhi in honor of "Mother India". Located 1 km south of the railway station on Vidyapeeth Road.

**Durga Temple** and **Tulsi Manas Mandir:** The Durga Temple, located 4 km south of town, dedicated to Shiva's wife, the goddess Durga, is frequently referred to as the "Monkey Temple" due to all the monkeys haunting the vicinity. The temple's tower, encompassing five shikkaras (storeys), symbolizes the five elements of earth. The last being Brahman. Via a small stairway you can reach the roof for a look at activity below. Beware of the aggressive monkeys! Next door is the less than original Manas Temple, completed in 1964, dedicated to Rama.

**Benares Hindu University**: 7 km further south, 8000 students study Hindu philosophy, culture, and religion, along with Indian history. It was founded in 1916 as a gift by Pandit, Madan Mohan Malaviya. On the grounds, **Vishwanath Temple** is dedicated to Shiva and open even to non-Hindus. Be sure to have a look at **Bharat Kala Bhavan**, the University Museum, with its lovely collection of Indian miniature paintings. The university grounds are laid out in a half circle.

**Sightseeing Tours**: To all the above sights, including the boat ride, can be booked at the UP State Road Transport Corporation, Varanasi Cantt, tel.63233, costs 10.-Rs, from 05:30-12:00 h. A tour to Sarnath and Ramnagar Fort costs 12.-Rs, from 14:00-18:00 h. Depart from the Tourist Bungalow and the Tourist Office, The Mall. Disappointed tour participants tell of being rushed in record tempo past the sights, only to be towed for an entire hour through sari and souvenir shops. After complaints at the Tourist Office, the afternoon tour was great.

**Ramnagar Fort** is the residence of the former Maharaja of Varanasi. Besides the **Palace**, be sure to visit the **Royal Museum**, open 10:00-12:00 h. 13:00-17:00 h, costs 1.-Rs. Located across the Ganges, get a bus to the northern edge of Benares Hindu University, then walk from the crossroads to the river, where you can get a ferry across.

**TIPS**
**Government of India Tourist Office**: 15 B The Mall, Cantt, tel.64189, manager is Mr. Ganguli, open Mon-Sat 09:00-17:00 h, until 13:00 h on holidays and the second Saturday each month.
**Uttar Pradesh (UP) Government Tourist Office**: Parade Kothi, Cantonment, Varanasi, tel.63186, in the Tourist Bungalow, very friendly and helpful, diagonally across from the railway station, Mon-Sat 10:00-17:00 h, closed every second Saturday. An Information Window is open for arriving flights at Babatpur Airport.
**Visa Extensions**: In the Foreigners' Registration Office, Ramapura, tel.63433, in southern Chowk, near the big crossroads.
**State Bank of India**: Two large branch offices. One is behind Varuna Bridge in northern Cantonment on Rajabazar Road, tel.62412. The City Branch is in the Chowk near Aurangzeb Mosque and Vishwanath Temple. Plus windows at the airport and in Varanasi Hotel. You can change money at bank exchange rates on Sundays in **Subhanali Brocat Factory**.
**GPO**: In the northern town center, Kotwali District, at the southern end of Kabir Chaura Road, 1 km north of Vishwanath Temple. **Poste Restante** Mon-Fri 10:00-18:00 h. Here too is the **Telegraph Office**. A second Post Office is in Cantonment near the Government of India Tourist Office and The Mall.

**Dussehra Festival:**  Held in September or October,  check for the
exact date during your year of visit.  This is the best time to
visit Varanasi.  The festival celebrates the victory by Rama over
Ravana,  as told in the **RAMAYANA.**  Scenes from the heroic epic
are depicted on stages erected throughout town.  Performances
often last through the night into the early morning.  Sometimes
impromptu scenes are added,  or the entire performance is done
extemporaneously!

## SARNATH

This is where Buddha,  after his enlightenment,  held his first
sermon for five followers.  It is considered the birthplace of
Buddhism.  Later, Ashoka founded several monasteries and stupas
here (see Buddhism).  Today the **Dhamaek Stupa** occupies the site
in the Deer Park.  Certainly worth a visit,  the village is 10 km
north by bus from Varanasi Cantt Station.  Rooms available in the
Tourist Bungalow,  **(S)**15.-, **(D)**30.-, **(Dm)**8.-Rs.

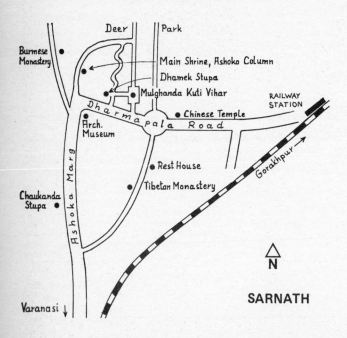

# Patna

Patna is capital of the state of Bihar, one of India's most populous and poorest states. Once upon a time, Patna was the capital
of an empire stretching to Afghanistan. The city is spread along
the Ganges, where its bridge provides good connections to Nepal's
border crossing, Raxaul / Birgunj (see Nepal).

## COMING - GOING

**By Air:** The airport is 8 km from town. Indian Airlines has an
office on Gandhi Maidan, tel.25936, in the hotel district. Daily
flights to Bagdograh (Darjeeling, 385.-), Calcutta (443.-),
Delhi (750.-), Lucknow (409.-Rs). On Mondays and Fridays, the
hour-long flight to Kathmandu costs US$41.-.

**By Rail:** Located on the double-track wide-gauge line from
Varanasi to the north-east and Calcutta. Good, frequent connections to Delhi along the Ganges Valley. Sample prices: Delhi
(73.-), Agra (63.-), Varanasi (24.-, most trains just to Mughal
Sarai), Calcutta-Howrah (41.-Rs).

**By Bus:** Convenient connections, e.g. the Raxaul-Patna express,
30.-Rs, 5 h, several times daily.

## A NIGHT'S REST

Sadly high prices; the most reasonable hotels are near the
railway station. **Hotel Welcome**, **(D)**35.-, bath, push-button
music in your room! **Hotel Shalimar**, **(D)**30.-, 35.-, bath, clean,
friendly. **Hotel Aadarsh**, **(D)**35.-, bath. **Hotel Meenaxi**, **(D)**35.-,
bath. **Tourist Bhavan**, near the bus stand, **(D)**40.-, bath,
**(Dm)**12.- (12 beds, bath); good tourist information in house,
and an expensive AC restaurant. **Central Hotel**, **(D)**30.-, no
bath, not recommended, dirty.

The best restaurants are on Gandhi Maidan, where you'll find
good southern Indian food.

## SIGHTS

**Hari Mandir** (Gurudwara): An impressive Sikh temple built on the
birthplace of the 10th and last Sikh guru, Gobind Singh. After
the Golden Temple in Amritsar, this is the second most important
Sikh temple. Though 16 km from the railway station, the temple
is easy to reach: go by bicycle rickshaw (3.-Rs) from the station
to Gandhi Maidan where an autorickshaw will take six passengers
for 2.-Rs per person to Hari Mandir.

Everyone is invited into the temple, though you must cover
your head (turbans may be rented), remove your shoes, and wash
your feet in the basin before entering the temple. Nobody will
ask you for baksheesh, no hassles about photography, but please
don't disturb the worshippers. It is so brightly lit inside, you
won't need a flash. The temple is richly furnished with lots of
gold; the floors are covered with rugs. Upstairs a gallery opens
out onto a lovely terrace (great view). Up another flight of
stairs is a **Museum** depicting Sikh history, the life of Gobind

Singh, and Sikh martyrdom; a rather gruesome story. Sikhs in the temple are happy to discuss their religion with you. Ask to speak to Dr. Shamsher Singh, whose office is in the building. He has a brochure about the Sikh religion, which he wrote himself in English. He offered us free room and board in the temple, but unfortunately we were short on time. He informed us that all Sikh temples accept guests free of charge. If you are interested, ask!

**The Pataliputra** (Kumhrar): The ruins are 7 km west of the railway station. The archaeological excavations are open 09:00-17:30 h, except Mondays.

**Patna Museum**: Features a large collection of fossils.

**Golghar**: Built by the British in 1786 as a base and fortress. Even today its use is largely unchanged. You can climb up to the top for a view of the Ganges and town.

**Martyrs' Memorial**: A life-size statue of seven men who were killed in August 1942 during the struggle for independence.

**Biological Garden**: A place to relax among the plants and animals.

## AROUND PATNA
At the Patna Tourist Office you can book a day trip to Nalanda, Pawapuri, and Rajgir (07:30-20:00 h, 30.-Rs per person), but the tours only go if at least 13 people book.
It is possible to visit all the above by bus on your own, particularly if you are heading to Bodh Gaya. But solo excursions are not recommended. Despite the short distances involved, connections are poor, making a visit to all three towns in one day impossible. You are best off spending a night in Rajgir.
Get a bus from Patna Bus Stand (last gate coming from the railway station) to Bihar Sharif (7.-Rs, 2.5 h). Get to the bus stand as early as possible; there are no fixed departure times. Each day at the stand, you decide whether to drive to Nalanda or Pawapuri first. Both rides take half an hour and cost 1.-Rs. You can check your bags in Nalanda, try in the Tourist Information Office, then visit Pawapuri and Nalanda (each can be done in less than an hour), then ride on to Rajgir.

## NALANDA
Coming - Going as described above. Several direct buses daily from Gaya (6.50 Rs, takes 3 h). Buses every half hour from Rajgir (1.-Rs, 30-40 minutes). From the bus junction, it's 3 km to the excavations, tonga or rickshaw 2.-Rs.
There are no lodgings in Nalanda. The Government Rest House does not seem to be in operation (you might be able to book a room through the Tourist Bhavan in Patna). The information brochures list a youth hostel, but it has disappeared. Its address

is occupied by the Tourist Office, next to the Museum. If you
still want to stay a night in Nalanda, ask for help in the Tourist Office.
**Buddhist Monastery** and **University**: Or the ruins, dating from the
5th to 12th centuries. Admission to the **Excavations** and **Museum**
across the road is 0.50 Rs. The complex is quite impressive,
particularly the well kept lawns and shrubs.
   In front of the entrance are a number of good, reasonable
restaurants. If you like tiny stone statues (Buddhas, Hindu gods,
elephants, lingams), or small stone boxes, the souvenir stands
are reasonable. The prices are aimed at an Indian market. In
Bodh Gaya you've the exact same selection, but the prices are
double.

## PAWAPURI
Direct buses from Gaya. The only accommodations are Jain Dhar-
amsalas for pilgrims.
   Pawapuri is a major attraction for Jain pilgrims. The holy
man, Lord Mahavir Jain lived and died here.
**Jalmandir**: A white marble temple marking the site where Lord
Mahavir was cremated.
**Samoshran**: Another Jain temple, directly adjoining. A third Jain
temple is 2 km further (visible from the lotus tank), get a tonga
(2.-Rs). The latter two temples are not particularly interesting.
All the temples are open to the public, but unfortunately, no
cameras!

# Rajgir

This village was also visited by Lord Buddha, as a large, Jap-
anese-built stupa reminds. Rajgir is also a resort town whose hot
springs attract numerous Indian tourists. Hence hotels in every
category, and lots of good, reasonably priced restaurants.

## COMING - GOING
**By Bus**: Buses from Bihar Sharif, Nalanda, Gaya (2.5 h, 12.-Rs),
occasional direct buses to Bodh Gaya (13.-Rs).

## A NIGHT'S REST
Lodgings begin in the **Burmese Temple**, very simple **(D)** (wooden
planks without sheets), a voluntary donation of 3.-Rs per person
is expected. **Hotel Pantona**, **(D)**30.-. **Hotel Anand**, **(D)**20.-. **Hotel
Hill View**, **(D)**45.-. **Hotel Mamta**, **(D)**40.-Rs. Lots more lodges in
town.
   Numerous restaurants invite with southern Indian, Punjabi, or
Bengali dishes. Excellent and reasonable prices in **Hotel Sarada**,
diagonally across from the Burmese Temple; egg curry (1.50 Rs),
fish curry (3.-), large servings, slow service. The **Burmese Temple** also has a restaurant, which is rarely open.

## FROM PATNA TO BODH GAYA

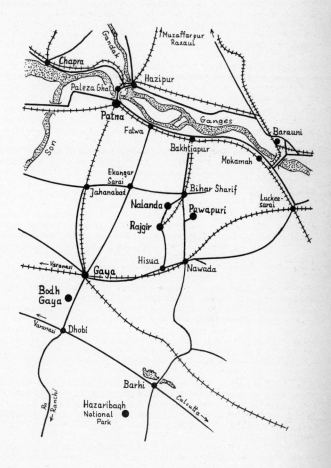

## SIGHTS
**Shanti Stupa**: On a hill, 5 km from town (rickshaw 10.-Rs for two passengers). A chairlift will take you up the hill (3.50 Rs), or you can walk up. At the top is a large, white stupa with a **Golden Buddha** facing in all four directions. The temple is manned by Japanese monks.

**Vultures Peak**: Lord Buddha is said to have preached here.

**The Cyclopean Walls**: Remains of the town wall, can be seen at your convenience as you wander about.

**The Hot Springs**: Indian style, 1 km from Rajgir, on the way to Shanti Stupa. The activity is certainly worth a look, but a bath is not recommended for western tourists. The atmosphere is less swimming pool and more temple.

**Swarna Bhandar Cave**, and **Saptaparni Cave**: Two temple caves, a bit outside town.

# Bodhgaya

If you are heading to Calcutta, be sure to stop in Gaya and make a side trip to Bodh Gaya. This is the village where Lord Buddha achieved enlightenment. Because Buddhists believe that Buddha will be reborn every 2500 years, which calculates out to 1957, a number of temples were built in 1957, in honor of Buddha, with donations from around the world.

Every winter (January or February) the Dalai Lama, who resides in Dharamsala, pays a visit accompanied by a number of Tibetan monks. Then Bodh Gaya becomes another Lhasa. If you want to be sure of the Dalai Lama's schedule during the year you visit, write: Office of His Holiness the Dalai Lama, Thekchen Choeling, Mc Leod Ganj - 176219, Kangra District, Himachal Pradesh. Include a self-addressed, stamped envelope, or international reply coupons. But expect to find large crowds of pilgrims. In 1986, 300,000 looked on as the Dalai Lama celebrated the dedication of Kalachakra.

And Bodh Gaya is a famous center of meditation. Several varieties are practised, and classes offered here (some free of charge, as in the Japanese Temple). Gaya is a major site for Hindu pilgrims; several temples in the region are worth a look.

## COMING - GOING
Several rail lines run via Gaya, heading for Calcutta (8-10 h). Be sure to book your reservations well in advance; this stop is only allocated 2 seat reservations on major trains. Coming from Nepal, get a bus. Ditto if your train doesn't stop in Gaya. In Gaya, get a bus (1.-Rs) or a taxi (2.-Rs per person) 11 km to Bodh Gaya. By tonga or rickshaw is much more expensive.

## A NIGHT'S REST

Gaya: There are a number of cheap hotels right around the railway station. **Punjab Rest House,** Station Road, tel.1082, **(S)**25.-, **(D)**30.-, 35.-. **Station View Hotel,** 33 Station Road, tel.512, **(S)**25.-, **(D)**30.-, 35.-, restaurant with good food and reasonable prices. **Ajat Shatu Hotel,** tel.1514, **(S)**50.-, **(D)**60.-, 70.-, good restaurant. **Hotel Satkar, (D)**25.-. **Hotel Saluja, (D)**40.-. **Ajit Rest House, (D)**22.-, with bath. **Hotel Madras, (D)**30.-, 40.-, looks better from outside than from inside.

Bodh Gaya: **Tourist Bungalow, (D)**30.-, **(Dm)**10.-. **Youth Hostel, (Dm)**8.-. Those truly interested in religion and culture may stay in a monastery. The rooms of the **Burmese Monastery** are very clean, and it has a library. If you stay the night, be sure to give the monastery a donation. You can ask in some of the other monasteries. In front of the Tibetan monastery are a number of restaurants serving Tibetan, Japanese, and Chinese food. Or try **Madras Coffee** for southern Indian dosas.

## SIGHTS

### Gaya

**Vishnupad Temple:** 4 km by collective taxi (2.-Rs) from Gaya Station. One of the most sacred sites for Hindu pilgrims, it was built in 1707 by Rani Ahilaya Bayee from Indore. Closed to non-Hindus.

**Brahma Yoni Hill:** 3 km southwest of the station, steps lead up to a Shiva Temple.

**Ramshila Hill:** 3 km northeast of the station, the site of another Shiva temple.

**Surya Temple:** Dedicated, as its name implies, to the Sun God, 2.5 km from the station.

### Bodh Gaya

**Mahabodhi Temple:** Inside, a gold-plated statue of Buddha, depicted in the pose of enlightenment, receives lots of food sacrifices.

**The Jewel Shrine of the Walk:** Marks where Buddha left a footprint, and a lotus blossom later blossomed.

**Bodhi Tree:** In the west of the temple, in whose shade the place of enlightenment is marked with a red stone slab. The present Bodhi tree is just 100 years old, but considered a direct descendant of the tree under which Buddha achieved enlightenment.

**Tibetan Monastery:** Nearby, a golden Buddha awaits up the first flight of stairs. The walls are richly decorated, depicting the life of Buddha. Downstairs is a tremendous Prayer Drum.

**Thai Temple:** An attraction if only for its splendid exterior, located several hundred meters further down the road, past the plain **Chinese Temple.** Inside is a third golden Buddha. As a small aside, the statue depicts the Mother (see above, the 2500-year reincarnation).

**Japanese Temple:** Right behind, looking quite plain from the outside. Inside, don't forget to look up at the fourth - black - Buddha. The temples are generally closed 12:00-14:00 h.

## ELSEWHERE IN BIHAR
**Sasaram:** The mausoleum of Shershah, an important military leader around 1500 AD.

**Vaishali:** The birthplace of Mahabir Jain, and a spot visited by Buddha. Visit the **Museum,** **Jain Temple,** two **Stupas, Ashokan Pillar,** 36 km from Muzaffarpur.

**Ranchi:** A hill station (2140 ft.) and resort. Waterfalls in the vicinity (distance in km from Ranchi): Hundru Falls (45 km), Jonha Falls (35 km), Dassamghagh Falls (34 km), and Hirni Falls (75 km). Ranchi Hills and Ranchi Lake.

**Neterhat:** Hill station (3700 ft.), 155 km from Ranchi. Sunrise view, sunset view (Mangolia Point), Upper Ghagri Falls, and Lower Ghagri Falls (10 km from Neterhat).

**Hazaribagh:** Canary Hill, Observation Tower. Hazaribagh is a health resort, and a departure point for the National Park, 25 km distant.

**Baidganathdam:** A Hindu pilgrim site, with lots of temples.

# Comments, Suggestions, Feedback To:
Tell us what you think of this book, and what you would like changed in the next edition. We respond!

David Crawford
P.O. Box 110232
1000 Berlin 11
Germany

# CALCUTTA

It won't be long before this city
of 10 million moves from the fourth
largest to the second-largest city
in the world!

Calcutta was founded in 1690
by Job Charnock on the banks of
the Hooghly River at the site of
the fishing village, Kalikala. He
was dispatched by the East India
Company. Calcutta grew quickly,
its convenient location by the sea
attracting trade.

Calcutta has achieved consi-
derable social progress in recent
years. The number of beggars living on the streets has been reduced substantially. But there is
still a tremendous gap between
rich and poor, modern and decay-
ed. But the city has a certain charm. The friendly Bengalis are
helpful. The markets and bazars seem endless.

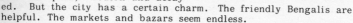

"To me, Calcutta is the craziest, most impressive city in
India. The absurdly small wooden coaches waiting at the
station must be from a fairytale. Who can describe a ride
with a hand-pulled rickshaw across Howrah Bridge into the
city center? It is an astounding mixture of people crowded
together: overloaded double-decker buses tilt ominously
around every turn, handcarts heavily laden with wares, two
baskets suspended on a pole across a bearer's shoulder;
loud, fuming trucks, chugging over the only Ganges bridge.
Downtown is disappointing, perhaps even worth avoiding.
Western mentality, architecture, clothes, shops: a legacy of
British colonialism. Around Howrah Bridge, you'll find a
bustling network of market streets. Streets of spices, fish,
grain, fowl, fruit, and vegetables project you back to the
middle ages. No cars disturb the narrow market streets, a
postcard picture of Asia. Old buildings, ornamented with
wrought iron; merchants sipping tea; artisans; factory workers; currymakers stained yellow from head to toe; children
playing; women sitting proud on their rickshaw...

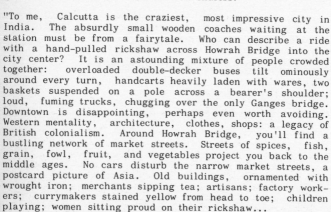

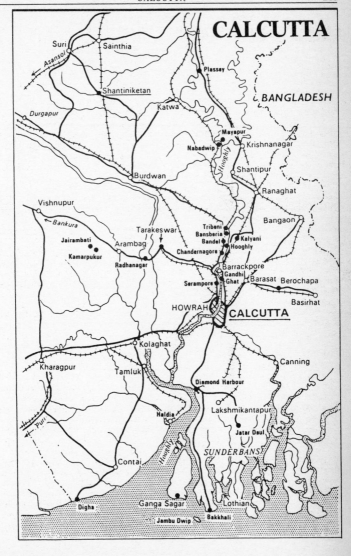

Boats are loaded in the Ganges harbour, alongside religious ceremonies in the water. A colorfully decorated paper goddess is pushed into the waves, accompanied by loud cheers. Wooden barges lie at anchor. Small flames flicker aboard the boats, ghostly lights on a sacred river. Lambs are sacrificed in the Kali temple: the lamb's head is placed between two iron bars, by the temple; a third bar is fixed above; a sable parts the neck. The tongue leaps forth; both halves shiver. Whew! The Faithful dip a finger into the blood to paint their forehead..." (Christian Spitzl).

The mail we receive about Calcutta is contradictory, like the city itself. Downtown, Peter's impression is that the British merely handed over administration to the Indians temporarily. Much remains very British. After all, Calcutta was the capital of British India for 52 years, until 1911.

Capital of West Bengal today, Calcutta remains the center of Indian high art. Rabindra Nath Tagore has left his mark. Calcutta is home to India's alternative film industry. The largest library in India holds one book for every resident (9 million in all). The Indian Museum testifies further to the love Bengalis have for art.

And Calcutta is important to travellers. Its major international airport offers budget flights to Europe and throughout Southeast Asia. For many travellers, Calcutta provides a first or last impression of India. You've cheap flights to Dacca in Bangladesh, or via Rangoon to Bangkok. And this is a convenient departure point to Nepal.

However, the city has lost much of its trading might: the jute trade with Bangladesh is now cut off by the border, and silt is slowly closing the Hooghly River.

## COMING – GOING

**By Air:** Upon arrival at Dum Dum Airport (named for the horrid ammunition produced here), pick up a map at the Tourist Information Booth, if it is open. Get Bus LB31 or Bus S10 (2.-Rs) to the bus terminal (last stop). Then make your way by rickshaw, taxi (6.-Rs), or foot to Sudder Street in the cheap hotel district. A taxi to the airport costs 40.-Rs from Sudder Street. The airport bus, from the Indian Airlines City Office costs 10.-Rs

The Indian Airlines Office is on Chittaranjan Avenue, in the large corner building on your left coming from the tram terminus, 08:00-21:00 h, tel.263390. Flights to Kathmandu (US$96.-), Dacca (US$38.-), Chittagong (US$49.-). Domestic flights to every major town in the north-east, and every city in the country. Sample prices: Bagdogra Darjeeling (420.-Rs), Bangalore (1383.-), Bombay (1370.-), Delhi (1142.-), Gorakhpur (615.-), Hyderabad (1166.-), Lucknow (805.-), Madras (1201.-), Patna (443.-), Varanasi (601.-Rs).

CALCUTTA

1   Bus Terminus & Sahid Minar
2   Tram Terminus
3   Foreigners' Registration Office
4   Bhutan Consulate
6   Bangladesh Consulate
7   Map Sales
8   YMCA, Banerji Street
9   Birla Planetarium
10  National Library
11  RNAC
11  State Bank Of India
12  Sitambara Jain Temple

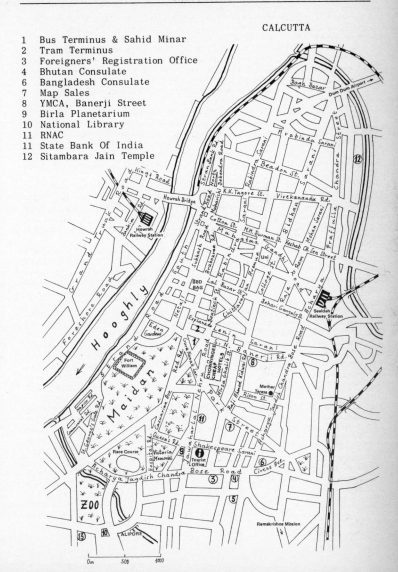

The Air India office is on J. Nehru Road,  around the corner from the Tourist Office.

Bangladesh Biman (BB) is at 1 Park Street,  tel.212864,  south of the Indian Museum. Flights to Dacca, Chittagong, and Kathmandu,  same prices as India Airlines but discounts possible. Via Dacca to Bangkok (1400.-Rs),  with a stopover in Rangoon (1500.-Rs), to Amsterdam (US$500.-).

Burma Airways Corporation (BAC) is at Esplanade Row East, via Rangoon to Bangkok (US$159.-).

Aeroflot is on the southern end of J. Nehru Road,  Saturday flights to Munich (US$430.-).

Several cheap flight agencies in the cheap hotel district around Sudder Street.  Look for S. Roy from Modern Lodge,  or Pan Asian Tours, 20 Mirza Ghalib Street, 2nd floor, tel.240814.

The Airport tax is 50.-Rs for neighboring countries,  and 100.-Rs for international flights.

**By Rail:** Upon arrival at Howrah Railway Station, get Bus 5 or Bus 6 or Tram 12A or Tram 13 to Sudder Street,  near the Indian Museum.  On arrival at Sealdah Railway Station, get a tram or bus to the tram or bus terminus,  then go on by rickshaw, taxi (6.-Rs) or foot to Sudder Street.  A taxi from Sealdah Railway Station to Sudder street is 12.-Rs.

The Eastern Railway Booking Office is at 6 Fairlie Place, near GPO/BBD Bagh,  tel.224356, Mon-Sat 09:30-16:30 h, Sundays and holidays until 14:00 h,  Information tel.222789, books 2nd class reservations and the Tourist Quota in the Tourist Booth,  for trains in all directions except south.

The South Eastern Railway Booking Office is in Esplanade Mansions,  tel.235074,  Mon-Sat 09:30-16:30 h Sundays and holidays 10:00-14:00 h,  Information tel.239530,  2nd class reservations and Tourist Quota for trains heading south,  near the tram and bus terminus / Chowringhee.

Most trains depart from Howrah.  A few trains north and north-east,  e.g.  to Siliguri, Darjeeling, depart from Sealdah, in the east of town.  In season (November to February),  the Tourist Quota on major trains is booked out five to ten days ahead.

**By Bus:** Except the direct bus to Puri,  there are few worthwhile long-distance buses. Reservations at the Esplanade Subcash office-cum-bus terminus, West Bengal State Transport, near Sahid Minar / Ochterlony Monument, 06:00-20:00 h, tel.231916. A night bus to Siliguri also departs from here,  costs 80.-Rs, connections from there on to Nepal and Darjeeling.

**Around Town:** Buses are hopelessly overloaded; minibuses little better.  All have their main stop in Chowringhee between Esplanade Row West and J. Nehru Road.

India's first subway opened in 1984 with two short stretches in Calcutta.  The Metro only runs at rush hour:  Esplanade to Bhowanipore (1.-Rs).  The tram system is unique in India; you can even get a seat.

Taxis are expensive, charging astronomical prices at rush
hour. Rickshaws are cheap. Calcutta does not have bicycle
rickshaws like elsewhere in India. They are pulled by a rickshaw wallah. But rickshaws are not permitted on several busy
streets, so expect detours.

Your best transport around Calcutta is by foot, except perhaps on Sunday when a Travel As You Like It Ticket costs just
1.-Rs.

## A NIGHT'S REST

If you are just here for a night before heading on by rail,
there are lots of cheap hotels around Howrah Station. Representative in price: **Natraj (D)**50.-. Or **Meghdoot, (D)**50.-.

The district with the largest selection of reasonable lodges is
Chowringhee, near the Indian Museum on Sudder Street. Every
taxi or rickshaw wallah knows the place. Taxis from Howrah
Station average 15.-Rs, from the airport 40.-Rs at most.

**Salvation Army Red Shield Guest House,** 2 Sudder Street,
tel.242895, **(Dm)**12.- in nine to twelve-bed rooms; **(D)**35.-, no
breakfast, usually full; bike rentals 1.50 Rs per hour; check-
-in at 09:00 h, not very quiet, baggage check. **YMCA**,
25 J.Nehru Road, tel.233504, very dirty, **(Dm)**40.- in a four
bedder, **(S)**90.-, plus 10.-Rs membership fee. **Hotel Paragon**,
2 Stuart Lane, tel.213115, **(S)**15.-, **(D)**25.-, 40.-, **(Dm)**8.-, on
the roof for 5.-Rs, clean, friendly, drinks, warm beverages
until 22:00 h. **Modern Lodge**, 1 Stuart Lane, tel.244960, same
prices, **(D)**40.-, four-bed room for 60.-Rs, friendly, clean, roof
garden, drinks, the dorm is a bit loud, Stuart Lane is a side
street off Sudder Street. **Tourist Inn,** 4-1 Sudder Street,
tel.243732, **(D)**50.-. **Hotel Paragon**, 2 Sudder Street, **(S)**20.-,
**(D)**30.-, **(Dm)**12.-.

Other cheap hotels in the surrounding side streets: try **Hotel
Neelam**, 11 Kyd Street, **(D)**50.-, clean inside, but not much
appeal outside. **Capital Guest House**, Chowringhee Lane, clean,
safe, **(D)**80.-.

And on Sudder Street are some better, and more expensive
establishments: **Fairlawn, (D)**300.-. **Lytton, (D)**300.-.

**Youth Hostel**, 10 J.Babu Ananda Dutta Lane, Howrah,
tel.672869, **(Dm)**8.-, just for members, get bus 52 or 58 from
the station to Shamarsi Movie House. **Rajasthan Guest House**,
tel.348153, 19 Zakaria Street, **(Dm)**8.-, northeast of BBD Bag.

If you want to get involved in Indian religion, and are
willing to live according to the rules of a particular religious
community, then the following dharamsalas (free pilgrim accommodations) might be recommended: **Bara Sikh Sangat Dharamsala**, 172 M.Gandhi Road, tel.335227. **Kalighat Gurudwara**,
31 Rash Behari Avenue, tel.411727. **Netram Bazar Dharamsala**,
25 Battala Street.

## REFRESHMENT

Lots of restaurants in the Chowringhee cheap hotel district cater to globetrotters. **Blue Sky Cafe,** Sudder Street at Chowringhee Lane is recommended as a popular meeting place. **Cafe 48** on Free School Street offers good, cheap food. Readers recommend **New Cathay Restaurant** between Oberoi and the YMCA, plus the snackbar there on a large balcony.

Across from the Esplanade, **Madras South Indian Restaurant** offers great southern Indian dishes like Masala Dosa. We've heard raves for the Chinese food in **Silver Grill** on Park Street. Equally recommended is **Kwality,** with good Indian and European food. Both are generally crowded.

A number of elegant restaurants feature food of every origin. Or try good Indian food with all the extras on Park Street, south of the Indian Museum, off J. Nehru Road, and the surrounding streets. Lighten your wallet, and loosen your gums. And there is more good stuff east of BBD-Bag (Dalhouse Square); try on Waterloo Street.

**Super Snack Bar** at 5 Old Court House Street (diagonally across from American Express) serves good southern Indian food, try massala dosa or uttapam; and quick service if you need to eat and run.

Buffet lunch is offered in many hotels, usually on weekends. If you really want to eat your fill, then this is your opportunity, all you can eat (around 50.-Rs). Watch for the newspaper advertisements, e.g. in the **Statesman.**

In Calcutta lots of oil is used for baking and frying. Along with various snacks, delicacies include puris, parathas, chapathi-vegetable curries, and of course fish. West Bengal is famous for sweets, offered everywhere.


## SHOPPING

You'll find a rich selection of cotton goods in the bazars:
**New Market:** Near Sudder Street, Chowringhee. "You can get everything from a sari to birthday cake", as a reader writes. Have a look!

Also good is the region north of BBD Bag around Old China Bazar Street, and south of Sealdah Station on Acharya J.C. Bose Road.

**Musical Instruments:** In and around Rabindra Sarani, north-east of BBD Bag, cheap prices. The quality of the sitars is better, but also more expensive on Rashbenari Avenue, further north. A wooden case for sending your sitar home costs 50.-Rs. See India Country & Culture before you buy a musical instrument. Be sure to judge your instrument not by the appearance - even pretty instruments can sound bad - rather by how it plays. A relatively long-resonating sound is a good indication. There should be 13 resonating strings, and seven picking strings. The woodwork should consist of no more than two pieces of wood, i.e. one piece for the entire neck.

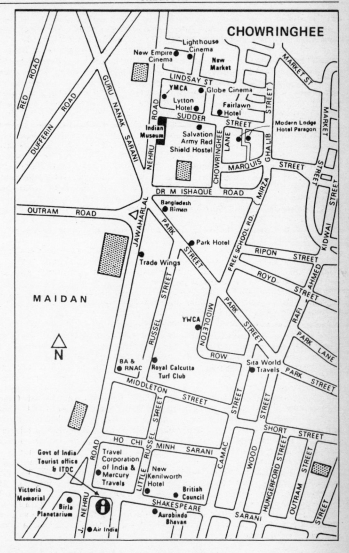

CHOWRINGHEE

Lighthouse Cinema
New Empire Cinema
New Market
LINDSAY ST
YMCA
Globe Cinema
Lytton Hotel
Fairlawn Hotel
Indian Museum
SUDDER
STREET
Salvation Army Red Shield Hostel
CHOWRINGHEE LANE
MARQUIS
STREET
Modern Lodge Hotel Paragon
DR M ISHAQUE ROAD
OUTRAM ROAD
Bangladesh Biman
Park Hotel
Trade Wings
RIPON STREET
ROYD STREET
MAIDAN
YWCA
ROW
N
BA & RNAC
Royal Calcutta Turf Club
Sita World Travels
PARK LANE
PARK STREET
MIDDLETON STREET
SHORT STREET
HO CHI MINH SARANI
Govt of India Tourist office & ITDC
Travel Corporation of India & Mercury Travels
New Kenilworth Hotel
British Council
Victoria Memorial
Birla Planetarium
SHAKESPEARE
Aurobindo Bhavan
SARANI
Air India

RED ROAD
DUFFERIN ROAD
GURU NANAK SARANI
NEHRU ROAD
JAWAHARLAL
PARK STREET
RUSSEL STREET
MIDDLETON
PARK STREET
FREE SCHOOL RD.
MIRZA GHALIB STREET
MARKET ST
MARKET STREET
KIDWAI STREET
RAFI AHMED
CAMAC STREET
WOOD STREET
HUNGERFORD STREET
OUTRAM STREET
LITTLE RUSSEL STREET
J. NEHRU ROAD

**Books:** New and used, on Park Street and Mirza Ghalib, branching off to the north (Free School Street). The Calcutta Information Brochure is also available (3.-Rs).

**Photo Equipment:** And repairs, passport pictures, photocopies, etc. on J. Nehru Road, mostly at the northern end. If you want to make sure your camera is functioning okay, you can get a roll of film developed within 24 hours (film: 15.-Rs, picture 3.-Rs) at North East Colour Photos Pvt. Ltd., Shop No 7-9, 14 Sudder Street, Calcutta 700016.

**Western Consumer Goods:** J.Nehru Road and the surrounding streets.

**Arts & Crafts:** In New Market, a tremendous, roofed bazar. For an idea of what prices to expect, visit some of the government-owned shops, most in Chowinghee. All are depicted on a map available at the Tourist Office. You'll also find wares from Assam, Manipur, and Tripura.

**Student ID Cards:** Sold in the lodges around Sudder Street for about 50.-Rs, ask around!

**SIGHTS**

**India Museum:** A must see; the best museum in India, conveniently located on J. Nehru Road, just south of Sudder Street. Features art from all over India, and natural history. Tues–Sun 10:00-17:00 h, admission 0.50 Rs, free on Fridays.

**Maidan:** Today a park, it was created in 1781, as part of jungle clearing, to improve the line of fire for **Fort William.** While the Fort still serves a military function, the park, stretching 3 km along the Hooghly River, invites peaceful activities: soccer, tennis, yoga, picnicking, etc.

**Sahib Minar:** At the northeastern end of the park, a 48 m tall tower, whose architecture shows Middle Eastern influences. Erected in 1928, in honor of Sir David Ochterlony (hence the former name, Ochterlony Monument), after his battles in the war with Nepal (1814-1816). To visit, you need a permit, provided free of charge from the police on Lal Bazar Street. The tower is open 10:00-16:00 h.

**Burmese Pagoda:** At the northwestern end of the park, in Eden Gardens, brought here in 1856, and rebuilt in the middle of a small lake.

**BBD Bag:** British buildings around Dalhousie Square, today Benoy Badal Dinesh Bag.

BBD BAG                              AROUND DALOUSIE SQUARE

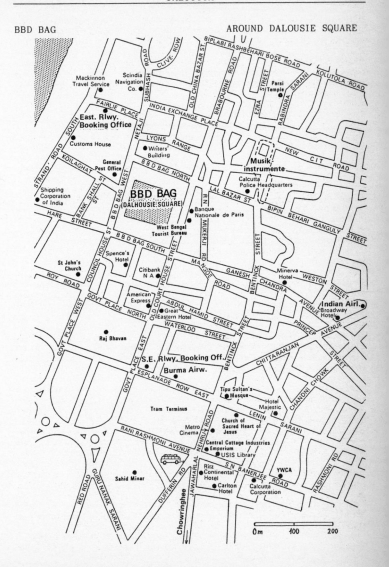

**Victoria Memorial**: At the southern end, a monumental marble structure, begun under the British Raj in 1906. The temple was completed in 1921. Inside is an exhibit on British-Indian history, including busts, paintings, prizes of war, etc; but also some lovely Indian art. Open Tues-Sun 10:00-17:00 h, admission 0.50 Rs. The **Victoria Memorial Gardens** is a large, splendidly landscaped park, a great place to escape from the hectic city and regain your bearings.

**St. Paul's Cathedral**: Nearby, built originally between 1839 and 1847, but severe earthquakes required reconstruction in 1934.

**Birla Planetarium**: On J.Nehru Road, visit after a tour of Maidan Park, tremendous, Mon-Fri 12:30-18:30 h, Sat 12:30-20:00 h, Sun 10:00-20:00 h, costs 5.-Rs, but worth it. Presentations in several languages.

**Minor Sights**
  **Zoo**: Way south in Alipore.
  **Jain Temple**
  **Kali Temple**
  **Howrah Bridge**: 450 m long, across the Hooghly River
  **Botanical Gardens**: On the Howrah side
More about these in brochures available at the Tourist Office. Two half-day tours can be booked at the Tourist Office (21.-Rs). If you book both tours on the same day, you pay just 26.-Rs for both. If you only plan to do one tour, then take the morning 07:30-11:40 h when the sights furthest from town are visited. Admission charges not included.

**OFF THE BEATEN TRAIL**
**Botanical Gardens**: Get Bus 59 from the Esplanade, or Bus 61 or Bus 62 from Howrah Bus Stand (Howrah Station) for an hour, to where they claim the largest Banyan tree in the world, a lovely palm house, an extensive system of paths and shady spots. Across the river are the Calcutta Docks.

Exit out onto Andul Road, where you came in, head left toward Andul. After three minutes walk, take a right in Dakhim Buxara, 1st By-Lane. Down 100 m on the left, in the Howrah South Point Building, is the Social Welfare and Community Centre, whose batik workshop offers lovely batik. Orders to your own design are possible. Heading back to Calcutta, either get a bus, or walk through the Botanical Gardens, and get the ferry across to the Docks. Walk through the port to the city center, or take a bus.

**Calcutta's China Town**: Where 8000 Chinese live and work, primarily in the tanneries. A way to get to know Calcutta, and tour the outskirts. Combine the tour with a meal at the best Chinese restaurant in Calcutta. Get Bus 24 or 24 A (from Howrah Station, Esplanade, or BBD Bag) to the last stop. At 47 South

Tangra Road, ask for the **China Restaurant**. You'll be led into
one of the better wooden huts where the Chinese like to eat, and
where cooking is an art form. Enjoy! If you're lucky, you might
be invited to visit a tannery.

## AROUND CALCUTTA
**Diamond Harbour:** Located three hours ride up the Esplanade in
the southern Ganges delta. Many people from Calcutta come out
here to relax, although there is no sandy beach. Hotels start at
**(D)**40.-Rs. The bus is cheap, just 2.-Rs, get Bus 12C or L3 E to
the last stop, then change onto the connecting bus. You pass
through endless paddies of rice, tiny villages, and palm forests.
A lovely outing into the Calcutta countryside, just get off at one
of the crossroads; a different world after the city bustle.

**Ganga Saga Island:** At the far south in the Bengali region of the
Ganges Delta, hundreds of thousands of pilgrims congregate annually in mid January. The object is to bathe in the Ganges where
it mixes with the Bay of Bengal. Due to the great danger of
infection, everyone who visits at this time is required to get a
cholera immunization (free injections at the checkpoints). Accommodations are practically impossible to find, so bring a tent.
    The Tourist Office of West Bengal offers bus/boat tours to the
Ganga Saga Islands, takes 15 h, costs 150.-Rs including meals.
This is a good way to meet some of the locals; few western tourists think to take this tour.

**Sunderban:** A tremendous wildlife reserve in the Ganges Delta.
Almost 300 tigers live in the wild. West Bengal is actively developing the area for tourism. A large lodge was completed on the
reservation in 1984. Several tiger towers are sited to provide a
view of wild tigers. Organized tours from Calcutta by bus and
boat, takes two days, costs 300.-Rs including food and lodgings,
or 150.-Rs for 12 h. You can't explore Sunderban on your own; it
consists of dozens of islands. During my two-day visit, all I saw
of the tigers were a few footprints. ·The only large animal was a
crocodile; very disappointing.

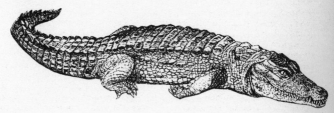

The Tourist Office in BBD Bag runs about ten additional tours. Ask for their latest selection.

## TIPS
**Government of India Tourist Office:** 4 Shakespeare Sarani, Calcutta 700071, tel.441402, Mon-Sat 09:00-18:00 h, holidays until 13:00 h, down the street across from Birla Planetarium. Information Windows at the airport and in Howrah Railway Station. ITDC City Tours, half day (21.-Rs), all day (26.-Rs).
**West Bengal Tourist Bureau:** 3/2 Benoy Badal Dinesh Bag, Calcutta 700001, tel.238271, Mon-Sat 09:00-18:00 h, Sun & hol until 13:00 h. On the east side of BBD Bag (Dalhouse Square), difficult to find in an arcade. Here too, you can book the same City Tours. At either Tourist Office, pick up a copy of the free brochure, **Calcutta This Fortnight**, featuring info on upcoming events.
**State Information Offices:** Maintained in Calcutta by the following Indian states: Assam, Bihar (26 B Camac St., tel.440821), Haryana, Himachal Pradesh, Jammu & Kashmir, Meghalaya, Orissa (55 Lenin Sarani, tel.245121), Rajasthan, Sikkim (3B Camac St.), Uttar Pradesh.
**General Post Office** (GPO): In the domed building on the west side of BBD Bag. **Poste Restante**, Mon-Sat 07:00-20:00 h, except holidays. Another Post Office is on Mirza Ghalib Street, New Market, near Sudder Street.
**Central Telegraph Office:** On the southern side of BBD Bag, tel.233942.
**American Express:** On the west side of 21 Old Court Street, two blocks south of BBD Bag, tel.232133, clients' mail service Mon-Fri 10:00-13:00 h, 15:00-16:00 h, Sat until 12:00 h.

## Banks
**State Bank of India:** Himalaya House, 38 J.Nehru Road. Another office at the airport is open round the clock.
**Bank of America:** Ruby Insurance Building, 8 India Exchange Place, tel.222327.
**Bank of Baroda:** International Business Branch, Ruby House, 1st floor, 8 India Exchange Place, Calcutta, 700001, provided us great service by international money transfers, very reliable.
**DUTT:** Money Exchange in New Market, at bank rates, perfectly legal, also traveller's checks.

**Foreigners' Registration Office:** 237 Agdisch J.V.Bose Road, tel.443301, processes visa extensions and Darjeeling permits, the latter takes at least a day, bring your passport and leave it here, no fees, no passport photos, Mon-Fri 10:30-17:30 h. Here too, permits for excursions to Kalimpong. Even in Calcutta, you can't get a Sikkim permit immediately!

**Writers' Building**: On Dalhousie Square, special permits also processed.  Same requirements as at the Foreigners' Registration Office,  friendly service. The Writers' Building is an absolute must
see;  hundreds of officials on long bench desks,  with tremendous
piles of official files,  a seemingly endless mass of work.  The
officials seem relaxed,  sit around,  drink tea, stare at the sky,
hold political discussions,  take naps. So if you're looking for a
bureaucratic paradise (some people call it hell)...the Writers'
Building.

**Income Tax Clearance**: Takes just an hour, no hassle in Calcutta.
Bring your passport and exchange receipts to the Tax Office,
Bentinck Street, near the Esplanade.

## Consulates
**Bangladesh**: 9 Circus Avenue, tel.445208.
**Bhutan**: 48 Tivoli Court, Pramothesh Barusa Sarani, tel.441301.
**Thailand**: 18B Mandeville Gardens, tel.460836.

**United Kingdom**: 1 Ho Chi Minh Sarani, tel.445171.
**United States**: 5/1 Ho Chi Minh Sarani, tel.443611.

## Cultural Institutes
**British Council**:  5 Shakespeare Sarani,  from the Tourist Office
300 m off J.Nehru Road, on the left.
**Max-Mueller-Bhavan**:  8 Pramatesh  Barua  Sarani,  Calcutta
700019,  tel.479398, 1 km southeast of the Foreigners' Registration Office and the Tourist Office.
**National Library**:  Belvedere House,  Alipore, the largest in India, 9 million books.
**Ramakrishna Mission Institute of Culture**:  Gol Park, tel.463431,
in far south of town,  library,  reading room,  and events of
interest to India's religious and culturally minded.

West Bengal and Calcutta in particular are cultural centers in of
themselves.  Every day,  you've theatre,  dance, or musical performances to choose from.  Special exhibits are presented in the
museums, literary readings are popular. Check any newspaper, or
at the Tourist Office;  pick up a copy of **Calcutta This Fortnight**.
Be sure to carry your student ID card;  discounts at many
venues.

## HELP
Travellers who,  at the end of their journey,  would like to put
their left-over first aid supplies to good use,  can donate them to
Missionaries of Charity,  54a Lower Circular Road, Calcutta 700016
(Mother Theresa).  One of the Children's Homes is at 78 Lower
Circular road.  You can go by and help (washing dishes or
laundry,  serving meals, etc.), but not just stand around in the
way.  Mother Theresa homes have taken 150,000 children off the
streets in the last 10 years.

If you enjoy nursing, help out as a volunteer for a couple of weeks in the Home for Dying People, near the Kalighat Fire Station. The nurses will integrate you quickly in the daily regime.

# Santiniketan

Located 150 km from Calcutta, Santiniketan is the site of a university founded by Tagore in 1921. Tagore established his experimental open-air school on the grounds of an ashram, visited by his father. Although many of Tagore's ideas have been put aside, this remains one of India's largest cultural institutes.

## COMING - GOING
**By Rail:** Howrah (06:00 h) - Bolpur (08:30 h, Kanchangana Express, 18.-Rs). Bolpur (17:20 h) - Howrah (20:00 h). This train is frequently delayed. Only get a train arriving in Bolpur before 20:00 h because you won't find a taxi leaving later. The alternative is Prentik (06:00 h) - Howrah (10:30 h).
**Around Town:** There are few cars in Santiniketan (a real relief after Calcutta). Bicycles and rickshaws are the main transport. From Bolpur, rickshaws to Santiniketan (3.-Rs).

## A NIGHT'S REST
**International Guest House, (Dm)**6.-Rs; you'll only get in here if you insist that there must be more room. Otherwise, ask at the Tourist Lodge.

## SIGHTS
**Kala Bhavan:** The College of Art.
**Sangit Bhavan College of Music and Dance:** Should be visited in the morning, when you can ask to look in on classes. Sitar, tabla, and singing are taught, with emphasis on Tagore music. In dance classes, Manipuri and Kathakali are taught. You'll find numerous Europeans studying music and dance. It is also possible to take private lessons. Closed Wednesdays.

**Prayer Hall:** Open to all religions, a Bengali religious service is held Wednesdays at 07:00 h.
**Tagore Museum:** Can only be visited in the accompaniment of a student; ask around.
**Sriniketan:** An agriculture and handicrafts college, 3 km distant. Get up early and have a drink of ice-cold coconut milk, sold freshly cut from a tree. Wonderful experience.

**Meela Festival:** Held from December 22nd to 24th. People from the surrounding villages flock to the carnival, sell handicrafts, and perform music (bauls).
**Sangit Bhavan:** Sponsors a number of special events ("functions") each year. Keep your eyes and ears open; perhaps you'll have luck.

# EASTERN HIMALAYAS

## Darjeeling

The town of Darjeeling is in northern West Bengal, just short of the
border to Sikkim, set on a mountain ridge at 2100 m to 2300 m. It
is famous as a British summer resort under colonial rule, for the
Darjeeling tea grown in the region,
and for fantastic Himalayan mountain views. The tallest mountain in
the vicinity is Kanchenjunga
(8584 m), on the border to Nepal
and Sikkim. As Sikkim is considered part of the Indian Republic, it is the largest mountain in
India.

For a better look at the mountains, a number of treks are possible. Trekking is most pleasant in
spring or autumn, but possible any
time, except during monsoon season from July to September.
December through February can be very cold.

Darjeeling has much to offer: even non-trekkers can enjoy a
visit. To visit Darjeeling you need a special permit.

### DARJEELING PERMIT

Let's begin with the exception: if you enter and exit via Bagdogra Airport (100 km from town), and stay for no more than
15 days, no permit required. The flight from Calcutta is 450.-Rs
one way.

Any other way you come and go, you need a special permit,
available at the Foreigners' Registration Office or in the Writers'
Building, Dalhouse Square, in Calcutta. Or get a permit in Delhi,
Madras, Bombay, or at an Indian consulate abroad (including
Nepal). Issued for seven days, the permit is extended for an
additional seven days free of charge (allow one day for processing).

Ask at the same time about a permit for Kalimpong. Permit
extensions (seven days) are free of charge, and available immediately at the Foreigners' Registration Office, Ladenla Road,
Darjeeling, tel.2261. Here, too, you can pick up a Kalimpong
permit, if you don't already have it.

FROM CALCUTTA
TO SIKKIM

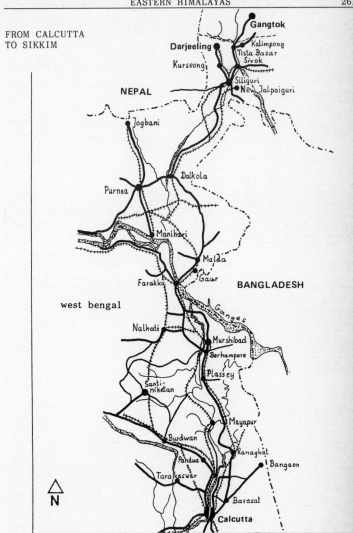

Gangtok

Darjeeling          Kalimpong
                    Tista Bazar
Kurseong            Sivok

NEPAL               Siliguri
                    New Jalpaiguri

Jogbani

                    Dalkola

Purnea

        Manihari

                    Malda

Farakka        Gaur        BANGLADESH

west bengal                 Ganges

Nalhati        Murshibad

               Berhampore

               Plassey

Santi-
niketan

                    Mayapur

        Burdwan

        Pandua      Ranaghat

    Tarakeswar               Bangaon

                    Barasat
N
            Calcutta

Trekking permits are free of charge at the Foreigners' Registration Office in Darjeeling. If you've arrived by air, you only
have to let them know a day in advance of your trekking plans,
i.e. no permit is required in this case.

## COMING – GOING
**By Air:** Afternoon flights from Calcutta (450.-Rs) to Bagdogra
Airport, 96 km from Darjeeling. Buses from the airport to Dar-
jeeling (3 h, 35.-Rs). Daily direct buses to Kalimpong. Indian
Airlines offices in Darjeeling, Kalimpong, Siliguri, and at the
airport. Daily flights from Delhi (1120.-Rs), Guwahati
(265.-Rs), Imphal (465.-Rs), and Patna (390.-Rs).
**By Rail:** Only three trains of interest: Calcutta (Sealdah,
19:15 h) – New Jalpaiguri (08:20 h), aboard the 43 Darjeeling
Mail. Calcutta (Howrah, 18:55 h) – New Jalpaiguri (07:35 h),
aboard the 59 Kamrup Express, costs 55.-Rs.
From New Delhi (31–36 h, 2nd class sleeper 120.-Rs) aboard
the Assam Mail. Enjoy a lovely serpentine ride on a narrow-
gauge whistle-stopper; hop aboard in New Jalpaiguri at 08:00 h
or 08:50 h, takes 9 h. Your Darjeeling permit is checked upon
arrival and departure at New Jalpaiguri Railway Station.
Tourist Reception Office inside.
Heading back, book a Jalpaiguri to Calcutta sleeper well in
advance, in Jalgaipuri or Darjeeling. Darjeeling (07:00 h or
10:45 h), arrives New Jalpaiguri (14:35 h or 18:20 h). The
trains from here to Calcutta depart at 19:15 h to Sealdah (arrival 09:00 h), and 20:50 h to Howrah (arrival 14:00 h).
**By Bus:** NBSTC buses nightly from Calcutta-Esplanade Bus Stand
to Siliguri, costs 60.-Rs. Bookings in Darjeeling at Bazar Taxi
Stand, or in Siliguri, takes 17 h.
From Siliguri and New Jalpaiguri up to Darjeeling, buses
(9.-Rs, 12.-Rs), jeeps (12.-Rs, 15.-Rs), overland taxis (15.-Rs,
20.-Rs), takes 3–4 h.
To Kathmandu, see Nepal: Overland from India. To Kalimpong
and Sikkim, see local sections. Buses, jeeps, and taxis depart
in Darjeeling from GPO and Cart Road.

## A NIGHT'S REST
Lots of lodges and hotels. Particularly nice is the **Youth Hostel**, at the top of a hill with a lovely view of the mountains,
clean and cheap in the dorms, **(Dm)**6.- (members), 8.- (nonmembers), **(D)**25.-, the hostel leader is friendly and helpful.
Dorms in the youth hostel (and elsewhere in town) are unheat-
ed, hence cold in winter. At the hostel you can build a fire:
firewood costs 9.-Rs per 10 kg. The youth hostel also has a
book where travellers can describe their trekking experiences.
And you can rent trekking equipment, deposit required. Nearby
are **Ratna Restaurant** and **Cafe-Tabac Snack Bar.**

DARJEELING

1   Tourist Office & Indian Airlines
2   Foreigners' Registration Office
3   Taxi Stand
4   State Bank of India
5   Hotels & Restaurants
6   Youth Hostel
7   GPO, Sikkim National Transport
8   Nirvana & Kadambari
9   Zoo
10  Mountaineering Institute
11  Chairlift to Singla Bazaar
12  Natural History Museum
13  Darjeeling Tourist Lodge
14  Dhirdham Temple
15  Tibetan Refugee Center

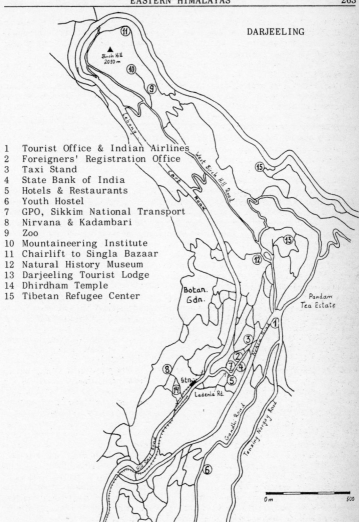

Lots of other lodges around the GPO: try **Shamrock**, **(D)**30.-.
**Timber**, **(D)**30.-. Left on the road below the railway station is
**Nirvana**, **(D)**40.-, 50.-. On the same street, **Kadambari**,
**(D)**40.-, 50.-; checkout time is 12:00 h.

**Broadway Hotel**, above the clocktower and movie house, offers
maisonettes with bath and five beds, (two downstairs, three
upstairs), pleasant, clean, friendly owner and personnel, hot
water in buckets upon request; we were a group of ten people
paying 40.-Rs per maisonette (bargained down from 60.-Rs);
**(S)**20.- big enough for a double, **(D)**20.-, 30.-; all rooms we
saw were with bath; you can check your excess bags at the
hotel while you go trekking (reader's tip).

Hotel prices fluctuate greatly with the season. At the Tourist
Office, pick up the brochure, **Hotel List Darjeeling**.

## REFRESHMENT

Lots of restaurants along and above Ladenla Road. We recommend:
**Cafe Himalayan Restaurant**, with Tibetan food, porridge, Tibetan
bread. During winter, a small stove is lit at your feet. Friendly
people; the owner has the adjoining sweater and souvenir shop.
**Glenarys** is a large, elegant restaurant, British in style, alcoholic beverages served, fireplace in winter, a bit expensive. **Janta
Restaurant**, H.D.Lama Road, in the market, hefty servings of
chowmien (6.-Rs). **Beni's Cafe**, side street off Ladenla Road, near
the GPO, Indian food, good, cheap. **Dreamland**, near the horse
stand, good southern Indian food.

For trek provisions and picking up groceries, two shops deserve mention; both are on the road connecting Ladenla Road with
the Tourist Information Office. The dairy, at the beginning of the
street on the left, with a roof-top restaurant (hot dogs 3.-, hamburger 4.-Rs, otherwise expensive due to the lovely view). Downstairs in the shop, milk (3.-Rs per liter, bring your own con-
tainer!), cheese (5.-Rs per 100 g), dried sausage (6.-Rs per
100 g,), plus fresh meat, bacon, breadmeats, butter. Further
along the same street, 100 m before the Tourist Office on the left,
is a wonderful bakery. A few stairs lead down into the shop.
Featured are brown bread (500 g loaf, 1.60 Rs), but sold out by
9 am; French bread (1.60 Rs), croissants, pastry, chocolate can-
dies, cheese.

## SIGHTS

**Tiger Hill** (2555 m, 11 km): You've a breath-taking view at sunrise of Kanchenjunga, the world's third largest mountain. There
is an observation platform (2.-Rs) and a VIP lounge (!), wind
sheltered, serving coffee (7.-Rs). Jeeps to T.H. depart Darjeeling
at 05:00 h, check the evening before, costs 20.-Rs to 30.-Rs per
person (off season 15.-Rs); cars (10 passengers 120.-Rs, offseason
90.-Rs). The alternative is to climb Tiger Hill from Ghoom. The
8 km makes a wonderful hike from Darjeeling. A night in the
Tourist Lodge costs 18.-Rs, excellent food. At the Tourist

Office in Darjeeling you can make reservations. Wake-up time is 04:30 h, then you've a 2.5 km hike to the summit. The view is tremendous, when it isn't fogged in. If it's clear, you can spy a wee peek of Mount Everest.

**Buddhist Monastery** (2438 m): In Ghoom the monks are members of the yellow-cap sect. Photography costs 10.-Rs per picture. There is a large statue of Maitreya Buddha, plus rare palm leaf and paper manuscripts in the Tibetan language.

**The Mountaineering Institute** (2 km from the Mall): The way here leads through the Zoo. Classes are held to get climbing enthusiasts in shape. A small **Museum** informs about regional mountains, flora and fauna, and features a relief model of the Himalayas. Open 08:30-13:00 h, 14:00-16:30 h, costs 0.50 Rs. The small **Zoo** really pens up its animals: Siberian tigers, pandas, llamas, deer, birds, admission 0.50 Rs.

**The Natural History Museum:** In Chowstra, features a collection of stuffed animals and pinned butterflies. The director is friendly and pleased to answer any questions you have on the subject of ecology. Ask him about deforestation in India. Open April-November 10:00-17:00 h, December-March 10:00-16:00 h, closed Thursdays.

**The Botanical Garden:** Features 2000 species of orchids in the Orchid House, 06:00-17:00 h, admission free.

**Gondola:** Spans from Northpoint down into the valley to Singla Bazar, 8 km, costs 16.-Rs return.

**Happy Valley Tea Estate:** 3 km, for a look at tea production, 08:00-12:00 h, 13:00-16:30 h, closed Sunday afternoons and Mondays.

**Dhirdham Temple:** A Hindu temple built in this century, emulating the style of Pashupatinath Temple in Kathmandu. The only one of its kind in India, look just below the railway station.

**Tibetan Refugee Self-Help Camp:** A lovely walk from town, features a number of workshops (weaving, wood cutting, etc.) where you can see local craftsmen at work. If you want to do some shopping, check the prices against those in the shops in Darjeeling.

**Shopping:** If you are not going to Nepal, Darjeeling offers a chance to buy Tibetan crafts, sweaters, (check in the Bazar!), jewelry, carpets, etc.

## TIPS
**Tourist Bureau, Government of West Bengal:** 1 Nehru Road, Darjeeling, tel.2050, upstairs in the Ambassador Hotel, Chowstra Square, Darjeeling maps (2.-Rs).
**Indian Airlines:** Same address, 1 Nehru Road.
**The Tourist Office:** Offers an information paper on Darjeeling, and an interesting brochure, **Himalaya Treks**, featuring maps and regional information no trekker should be without. Also info about Sikkim. The people in the Tourist Office are well informed, and friendly. At the railway station, the Information Office has some good tips.
**GPO, State Bank of India**, and **Foreigners' Registration Office:** All on Ladenla Road between the railway station and Chowrasta. Everything of importance to travellers is located between Ladenla Road and Cart Road to the south.

## TREKKING IN DARJEELING
The best seasons are April-May or October-November. In April and May the rhododendrons and magnolias are in full bloom. But occasional rains should be expected during this period, as in October. The best info on trekking can be found in the trekking book available for browsing in the Youth Hostel. Since it gets quite cold at this elevation, be sure to bring warm clothes.
**Equipment Rentals:** The Youth Hostel has a limited selection. Summit Tours, on Robinson Road, near Central Hotel, offers down sleeping bags (8.-Rs), Jackets (5.-Rs per day), hiking boots, etc. The Mountain Institute does not rent to foreigners.
   Be sure to book accommodations along your route at the Tourist Office before you depart, except for private lodges. Otherwise you might meet with a full house, or be charged double.

## DARJEELING TREKS
**Trek 1:**     (a) Darjeeling - Manaybhanjang - Tonglu - Sandakphu and return via the same route, 118 km.
               (b) Darjeeling - Manaybhanjang - Tonglu - Sandakphu - Phalut and return, 160 km.
**Trek 2:**     Darjeeling - Manaybhanjang - Tonglu - Sandakphu - Phalut - Ramam - Rimbik - Jhepi - Bijanbari - Darjeeling, 149 km.
**Trek 3:**     Darjeeling - Manaybhanjang - Tonglu - Sandakphu - Phalut - Ramam - Rimbik - Palmajua - Batasi - Manaybhanjang - Darjeeling, 180 km.

## TREKKING NOTES
   Jeeps cover the 26 km to **Manaybhanjang** (2133 m).
   From **Manaybhanjang** to **Tonglu** (3056 m) you have a vertical climb of almost 1000 m over an 11 km route.
   Instead of staying the night in **Tonglu**, why not make a quick side trip across the border into **Nepal** (no checkpoint), and spend a night in a Nepalese village!

TREKS IN DARJEELING

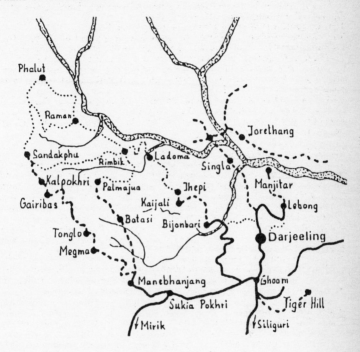

Between **Tonglu** and **Sandakphu** (3618 m), it's 24 km uphill and
downhill.
From **Rimbik**, a bus departs at 07:00 h to Darjeeling, check if
it is still running during your visit.

# Kalimpong

This lovely little mountain town (1250 m) is 51 km from Darjeeling. The ride here is an incredible experience, past tea plantations, bamboo forests, and a fantastic view of the confluence of
the Rangeet and Teesta Rivers. On Wednesdays and Saturdays,
farmers from surrounding villages gather in two bazars to sell
their wares. Lifestyles in Kalimpong show influence from Nepal,
Sikkim, Bhutan, and India. The colourful way of life and easy-
going nature of the people is refreshing. If the weather is clear,
you've a great view of Kanchenjunga. (Dieter Wettig)

**COMING - GOING**
Two buses daily from Darjeeling at 07:30 h and 13:00 h (3 h,
12.-Rs). Jeeps are faster (2 h, 20.-Rs), depart hourly from
08:00 h. En route your Kalimpong permit is checked. Buses from
Kalimpong Bus Stand to Siliguri, depart hourly from 07:00 h,
costs 11.-Rs including seat reservation. To Gangtok, Sikkim
Nationalised Transport (SNT) runs buses at 07:00 h and
14:00 h, takes 3 h, book early!

**A NIGHT'S REST**
Cheap hotels around the bus stand, try **Punjab**, **(S)**20.-,
**(D)**30.-, attached bathroom. **Sherpa Lodge**, side street off the
bus stand, by the sports field, **(S)**20.-, **(D)**40.-, hot water
provided in buckets. **Cosy Nook Lodge**, **(S)**20.-, **(D)**30.-, near
the bus stand.
  **Gampus Hotel**, Chowrasta, excellent (!), **(S)**25.-, **(D)**40.-,
**(Dm)**15.-, great food, try fried momos, chicken noodle soup, or
chowmien, alcoholic beverages served, nice manager.
  **Shangri-La** (Government Tourist Lodge), food only upon request, **(S)**25.-, **(D)**50.-, **(Dm)**11.-, at the entrance to town, tell
the driver in advance and he'll drop you off here. **Silver
Oaks**, **(D)**290.-, full board, running hot water.
  **Deki Lodge**, near the power house, Tripai Road, the extension
of Rishi Road, beginning north of Menla Ground (Bus Stand);
run by a nice Nepalese family, clean, pleasant rooms, 15.-Rs
per person or **(D)**20.-, bargain, good, reasonable breakfast,
evening meals in a family atmosphere.
  For a meal, try around Menla Ground in **Mandarin Restaurant**,
Tibetan and Chinese food, friendly, a bit expensive.

KALIMPONG

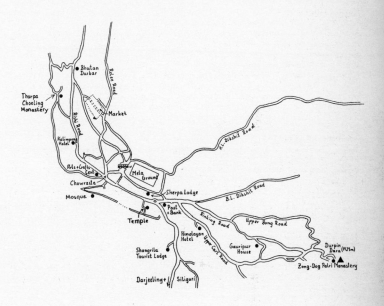

**SIGHTS**
**Bazar:** Wednesdays and Saturdays.
**Thapa Choeling Monastery:** A half-hour walk from the bus stand on Tripali Hill. Friendly monks are happy to show you inside the lovely Tibetan monastery. Plus there are several workshops where monks produce incense, etc., and a school for training monks. Established in 1937, the monks belong to the same yellow-capped Lamaist group as the Dalai Lama.
**Arts & Crafts Centre:** Near Gampus Hotel, you can observe carpet makers at work, showroom.
**Durpin Dara:** Lovely view of Kanchenjunga and the Buddhist Zangdog Patrifo Bang Monastery.
**Gauripur House:** Where Poet Rabindranath Tagore lived and wrote.
**Flower Nurseries:** This is an ideal climate, particularly for orchids. Open to the public are Sri Ganesh Pradhan Nursery, Standard Nursery, Shri LB Pradhan Nursery, Twin Brother Nursery, and Flowerwood Nursery.

**AROUND KALIMPONG**
**Leva** (2194 m): 32 km, lovely panoramic view, stay the night in Forest Bungalow.
**Lolay Gaon** (1676 m): 56 km, view of Kanchenjunga, Forest Bungalow.
**Rissisum** (1954 m): 20 km, Forest Bungalow.
**Takdah Orchid Centre:** 26 km drive, raises 110 species of orchid, buyers welcome.

# Sikkim

The once independent Kingdom of Sikkim was annexed by India in 1975. Its borders touch Nepal, Tibet, Bhutan, and West Bengal. Set right in the Himalayas, Sikkim features some fantastic views of India's largest mountain, Kanchenjunga. Measuring just 85 km by 85 km, Sikkim (= new palace) rises from 350 m to the peak of Kanchenjunga (8586 m), on the border to Nepal. For a close-up view, try the trekking route to Dzongri.
Most visitors are attracted by the mountains and monasteries. Just the bus ride from Darjeeling or Kalimpong to Gangtok is an unforgettable experience, taking you through Tista Valley, past rice fields, bamboo forests, and Buddhist prayer flags.
   Sikkim is a country of monasteries (called gompa, 67 in all), mountain streams, rice fields, and incredible mountain scenery.
   The people trace roots into the surrounding countries. Sikkim's aboriginal inhabitants, the Lepchas, probably came from northeast India. Arriving from West Bengal, you sense the difference in people here; not just in appearance, but in the aura they radiate, their openness, and easy-going way.

Many visitors see Sikkim as a living legend, the much herald-
ed mystical culture, hidden in the Himalayas. However, the
reality is less inspiring. Development for the Indian government
means road construction, concrete buildings, colour TV, and a
strong military presence.

## SIKKIM PERMIT
Entry requirements for foreigners have been relaxed, but still
entail a special permit. Apply 2-3 months in advance. Available
at Indian consulates abroad or from the Ministry of Home Affairs
in New Delhi. Some travellers have had good experiences at the
Ministry of Home Affairs in Delhi, receiving the permit within a
few days, for brief visits of 4-7 days. Then they extend the
permit at the Foreigners' Registration Office in Gangtok for a
total of two weeks. You'll have to present a plausible reason for
the extension: perhaps a visit to a monastery requires more than
one week due to poor bus connections. It is possible to have your
permit sent by the Ministry of Home Affairs to Darjeeling Foreigners' Registration Office, where you can pick it up during a stopover. Don't forget to have your Darjeeling permit extended for
15 days; otherwise there might be difficulties at the strict checkpoints. The Foreigners' Registration Office is 150 m below the bus
stand, open 10:00-16:00 h.

# Gangtok

Set at 1760 m, surrounded by mountains, including the dominating
presence of Kanchenjunga. From most hotels, you have a lovely
view of the tremendous mountain every morning. Winters can be
very cold, maximum daily temperatures hover between 2°-12° C.
The best times to visit are February to May and October to December. During summer, temperatures reach 25° C. The monsoon
does affect Sikkim!

## COMING - GOING
**By Bus:** Book early! From Darjeeling, Sikkim Nationalised
Transport (SNT) runs buses at 08:30 h, arrives at 14:30 h,
20.-Rs. North Bengal Service (NBS) leaves Darjeeling at
10:00 h, arrives 15:30 h, 20.-Rs. Your permit is checked at the
border. Minibuses cost 35.-Rs, jeeps 50.-Rs per person. To
Darjeeling, SNT departs at 09:00 h, arrives 14:30 h; NBS departs 10:00 h, arrives 15:30 h.
From Kalimpong, SNT departs 08:30 h, arrives 12:00 h or departs 14:00 h arrives 17:30 h, 15.-Rs. To Kalimpong SNT
08:30 h, arrives 12:30 h, or 13:30 h arrives 15:30 h.
From Sangem 07:00 h, arrives 11:30 h; return 14:00 h arrives
18:00 h. From Jaishree, 14:30 h arrives 18:00 h; return 09:00 h
arrives 14:30 h.
Crown Coronation, ask about departure times.

From Siliguri,   SNT 07:00 h arrives 11:30 h,   09:30 h arrives
15:30 h,   13:00 h arrives 18:00 h,   costs 20.-Rs.   NBS 06:00 h
arrives 10:30 h,   20.-Rs. Apsara (near Amardeep Hotel),  07:00 h
arrives 12:00 h.   Sikkim Beauty (near Amardeep Hotel),  06:30 h
arrives 11:30 h. Sikkim Glory, 08:15 h arrives 13:00 h,  09:00 h
arrives 14:00 h.
To Siliguri,   SNT,   07:00 h arrives 11:30 h,   09:30 h arrives
15:00 h, 12:15 h arrives 17:30 h. NBS, 12:00 h arrives 17:00 h.
Apsara 13:15 h arrives 18:00 h. Sikkim Beauty, 12:30 h arrives
18:30 h. Sikkim Glory, 14:15 h arrives 18:30 h, 15:00 h arrives
19:30 h.   Reservations near Central Bank,   10:30–15:00 h,   in
front of the bus stand.

## A NIGHT'S REST
Near the bus stand are several reasonable hotels:  **Woodlands**,
100 m below the bus stand,  **(S)**20.-,  **(D)**25.- (off season);
**(S)**40.-,  **(D)**50.- (season),  attached bathroom.  **Hotel Orchid**,
300 m below,  **(S)**20.-,  **(D)**25.- (off season),  **(S)**40.-,  **(D)**50.-
(season),   attached bathrooms,   cheaper without bath,  features
warm showers and a good restaurant,  ask for a room facing
front,  great view,  and warmer (south side) in winter.  **Shere
Punjab**,  across from the Orchid,  **(D)**30.- (off season),  **(D)**40.-,
50.- (season).  **Green Hotel**, above the bus stand, Mahatma Gandhi Road,  **(S)**25.-,  **(D)**25.- (off season),  **(S)**15.-, 20.- (season),
common bathroom,   **(D)**25.-,   30.-,   common bathroom,   **(D)**50.-,
90.- attached bathroom,   also **(Dm)**.  **Karma**,   Mahatma Gandhi
Road,  **(D)**25.- common bath,  **(D)**40.- attached bath (off season);
**(D)**30.- common bath,  **(D)**45.- attached bath (season),  restaurant.  **Deeki Hotel**,  **(D)**25.- bath (off season);  **(D)**35.-, 40.- (season).  **Tourist Lodge** (Government of Sikkim),  **(S)**30.-,  **(D)**40.-Rs.

## REFRESHMENT
**Orchid Restaurant and Bar**,  good, reasonable Chinese and Indi-
an cooking and alcoholic beverages,  i.e. Sikkim Whiskey, beer.
**Bamboo House**,   Mahatma Gandhi Road,   Chinese food.   Lots of
small restaurants around Lall Market with good cheap food:
Tibetan, Chinese, Indian.

## SIGHTS
**Tashi View Point:**  9 km uphill from Gangtok,  a 2 h walk along
the North Sikkim Highway.  If the weather is good,  you can see
Kanchenjunga and Phodong Monastery.  Those visiting Phodong
travel the same route,  and enjoy the same view from the bus (sit
on the left),   making an excursion to Tashi View Point
unnecessary.

**Enchey Monastery:**  5 km uphill, surrounded by a tiny forest. The
monastery was founded in 1840 by the 8th Chogyal Sidkeong Namgyal,  and belongs to the Nyingmapa sect (Mahayana Buddhism).
Ritual dances are performed in December. Open to the public.

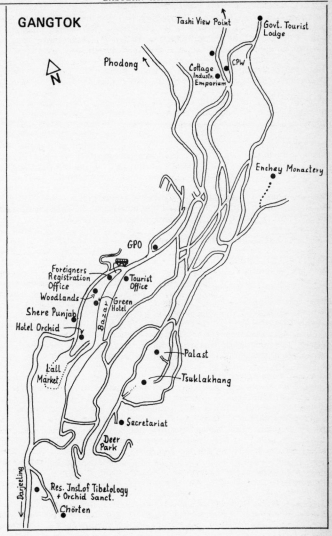

GANGTOK

N

Tashi View Point

Govt. Tourist Lodge

Phodong

Cottage Industr. Emporium

CPW

Enchey Monastery

GPO

Foreigners Registration Office

Tourist Office

Woodlands

Green Hotel

Shere Punjab

Bazar

Hotel Orchid

Lall Market

Palast

Tsuklakhang

Secretariat

Deer Park

Darjeeling

Res. Inst. of Tibetology + Orchid Sanct.

Chörten

**The Research Institute of Tibetology:**  4 km below the bus stand, founded by the Dalai Lama and J. Nehru.  The large library contains works on Tibet,  Buddhism,  Medicine,  Astrology, etc. It is an international center for the study of Buddhism.

**The Orchid Sanctuary:**  On the same grounds,  features over 250 species of orchid, in bloom April - May and December - January.

**Chorten:**  Just above the Tibetan Research Institute.  I enjoyed watching young lamas practising their musical instruments,  wonderful.

**Tsuklakhang** (Royal Chapel):  The main Buddhist temple where large ceremonies and festivals are celebrated.  For the exact dates,  ask in the Tourist Office. Notice the lovely paintings and wood carvings; photography, however, is prohibited.

**The Government Institute of Cottage Industries:**  Mon-Sat 09:30–12:30 h,  13:00-15:30 h,  closed on holidays, features hand-woven carpets and blankets with typical Sikkim patterns.

**The Deer Park:** Near the **Secretariat**, of little interest.

## MONASTERIES AROUND GANGTOK
**Phodong Monastery:**  38 km from Gangtok,  one of five major monasteries in Sikkim.  Get a SNT bus at 08:30 h,  14:00 h,  or 16:15 h, takes 2.5 h, costs 6.-Rs. Same day reservations opens at 07:30 h.  Return buses at 08:30 h, 10:00 h, 12:00 h. Enroute, ask to be dropped off at the spot where you have a 15 minute climb to the monastery.  If you are lucky,  a monk will be there to provide admission to the artfully restored interior. The monastery belongs to Rumtek Monastery.  Each year in late December,  over 200 lamas gather for two weeks of dance.

**Raprong Monastery:**  A 25 minute climb from Phodong Monastery. Along the way you pass the ancient ruins of a royal palace, although little remains beyond tremendous stone walls. Raprong is on the edge of a jungle still inhabited by tigers and bears.  The monastery itself is abandoned; only during the great dance festival in December do lamas venture here.  If you plan to spend a night,  return to the highway and continue uphill 1 km where you'll find several lodges in the village.

**Phensong Monastery:**  Between Gangtok and Phodong (12 km from Phodong,  buses 1.-Rs). At the end of November, colourful dances are performed. Check in Phodong.

**Rumtek Monastery:**  Just 24 km from Gangtok, poor bus connections require that you either spend a night (simple lodge across from the monastery,  5.-Rs per bed),  or fall back on more expensive

SIKKIM

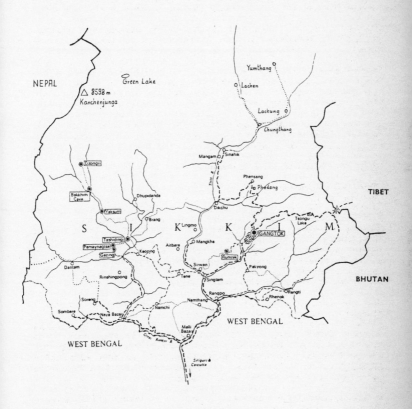

transport. Just one bus daily from Gangtok to Rumtek at 16:00 h, return at 07:30 h, costs 6.-Rs. An alternative is the Sightseeing Tour organized by the Gangtok Tourist Office, 13:30-16:30 h, costs 20.-Rs. Or find several friends to share a chartered taxi. The Green Hotel occasionally organizes rides for 5-6 people, the hour ride costs 140.-Rs. Otherwise a taxi costs 150.-Rs.

The head of the monastery is Gyalwa Karmapa, who fled Tibet during the Chinese occupation. He built the monastery as an exact replica of a Tibetan monastery. This provides an opportunity to see traditional Tibetan architecture, murals, and wood-carving. The monks are friendly and glad to show you around.

**Pemayangtse:** 115 km from Gangtok, in West Sikkim, board a bus toward Gyalshing, departs at 09:30 h and 15:30 h, costs 22.-Rs, reservations begin at 07:30 h. Founded by Gyalwa Chatsunpa of the Nyingma-ya sect, traditional lama dance is performed in January. Several other monasteries are within walking distance.

**Special Trekking Permit**
If you wish to head further north, you'll need a special permit, available from the Ministry of Home Affairs in New Delhi. You must form a group of 6-20 people, and an official public relations officer will accompany you as a guide. The best season to visit is March-April; permit processing usually takes 15 days.

**Trek**
**Pemayangtse - Yuksam:** 6 h, stay in the Forest Bungalow.
**Yuksam - Bakhim:** 5 h, through forest, rhododendron and magnolias, stay in the Tourist Hut.
**Bakhim - Dzongri:** 6 h, through valleys, mountain rivers, and fields of flowers, stay in the Tourist Hut. (D. Wettig)

For trekkers, the Gangtok Tourist Office rents backpacks (2.-Rs), sleeping bags (5.-Rs), tents (12.-Rs), and mats (2.-Rs) by the day.

**TIPS**
**Gangtok Tourist Office:** At the beginning of Mahatma Gandhi Road, by the bus stand; friendly, well informed personnel, brochures on Gangtok, Sikkim, trekking, handicrafts, West Sikkim, and Enchey Monastery. The Tourist Office runs tours, February-May and October-December, 09:30-12:30 h, costs 15.-Rs, visits Tashi View Point, Deer Park, Enchey Monastery, Royal Chapel, Secretariat, Cottage Industries Emporium, Research Institute of Tibetology, Chorten, Orchid Sanctuary. Organizes tours to Rummtek Monastery, 13:30-16:30 h, 20.-Rs. The tours show you all Gantok's sights, but time is limited at places of real interest, e.g. the Research Institute of Tibetology, while other stops, e.g. Secretariat are scarcely worth a visit.

# ORISSA

Orissa stretches along the east cost
of India, bordering Andhra Pradesh
in the south, Madhya Pradesh to
the west, and Bihar and West Bengal in the north. A northern outcropping of the East Ghats divides
the state. At the delta created by
the mouth of the Mahanandi River,
you'll find one of India's last
mangrove swamps.
   Puri, like Mahabalipuram, is a
major traveller stomping ground on
the east coast. Tourism is increasing at Gopalpur-on-Sea and nearby
Chilka Lake.
   The state covers 155,182 km$^2$,
and is home to 26 million. Primary
languages include Oriya, Bengali,
and Hindi. The capital of Orissa is
Bhubaneswar.
   Although few signs remain today, Buddhism flourished here
under Ashoka following the Kalinga War. Over the centuries Buddhism's influence waned, and Hinduism's regained vitality, which
can be seen in energic temple construction during the 8th
century, Orissa's golden age. The prettiest temples are in
Bhubaneswar, Konarak (including a 13th-century Sun Temple),
and in Puri (Jagannath Temple). Orissa's temples are famous for
their outstanding masonry. Non-Hindus are prohibited from
entering the major temples in Bhubaneswar and Puri, but you can
enjoy Konarak's erotic sculpture.
   Unfortunately, many 8th- to 13th-century temples were destroyed in military skirmishes with the moghuls. Undiminished remains
Orissa's unique style of dance, which has been danced in Jagannath Temple since the 12th century.
   Orissa is home to 62 separate tribes, each with their own
individual culture and language. Best known are the Kondh,
Koya, Bonda, Godaba, Paraja, Santal, and Juang. Among the
Bondas, boys and girls live together in youth houses, enjoying
free sexuality.

ORISSA

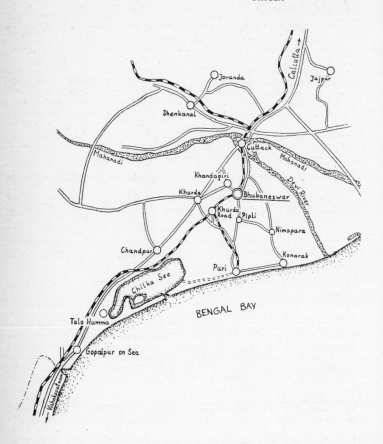

# Bhubaneswar

Orissa's capital is 437 km south of Calcutta. Tourists are attracted by the lovely Hindu temples, built between the 8th and 13th centuries. In the middle of the Old Town is **Bindu Sagar**, a holy pond, and place of Hindu pilgrimage. It is said to be connected underground to the Ganges. Also of interest are **Muktesh-war Temple** (10th century), **Raja Rani Temple** (12th century), and Lingaraj Temple (11th century). Unfortunately, admission to the largest and most important temple is closed to non-Hindus. You can have a glance into the Temple District from a platform overlooking the northern wall; from the entrance go right and around the corner. The district contains about 50 temples and shrines. The tallest temple tower is 46 m. Notice the contrast in Orissa-style architecture when compared to southern Indian Dravidian architecture, as seen in Madurai or Trichy. The Orissa style features an entrance hall, **Mandapam**, and the entire temple centers on the tall tower of the main shrine, called a **Deul**. In the southern Indian Dravidian style, the gate towers (Gopuram) rise high above the temples and walls.

In February-March, the Shivaratri Festival is held, attracting thousands of pilgrims to honor Shiva. And weather-wise, this is a great season to visit.

## COMING - GOING
**By Air:** The airport is just 4 km from town, buses 8.-Rs. Daily flights to Calcutta (343.-Rs), Delhi (1045.-Rs), Raipur (565.-Rs), and Varanasi (565.-Rs). Four flights weekly to Hyderabad (779.-Rs). The Indian Airlines Office is by the bus stand, tel.50533.
**By Rail:** Bhubaneswar is a major stop on the route between Calcutta and Madras. Since all the trains originate at stations far away, they are frequently booked out, here, weeks in advance, Bhubaneswar's allotment of reservations is small. Only toward Calcutta is there some hope: eight trains daily, takes 7-11 h, costs 44.-Rs. Four trains daily to Puri, takes 2-3 h.
**By Bus:** Regular buses to Puri (2 h, 8.-Rs) and Konarak. The drive to Konarak is prettier and faster from Puri.

## A NIGHT'S REST
**Panthanivas Tourist Bungalow**, housing the Tourist Office, near the main sights, **(S)**20.-, **(D)**35.-, **(Dm)**10.-, restaurant, by rickshaw from the bus stand (3.-Rs), from the railway station (2.-Rs). **Bhubaneswar Hotel**, by the railway station, **(S)**20.-, **(D)**35.-, **(Dm)**10.-. **Banaraswalla Hotel**, by the bus stand, **(D)**25.-Rs. You are best off staying in Puri!

# Puri

This beach and pilgrim town is 62 km south of Bhubaneswar, on
the Bay of Bengal. If you are travelling the east coast, Puri is
a must. The lovely beach lacks palms, in fact has no shade, but
it is one of the few globetrotter beaches on the east coast. And
as one of the four most important pilgrim towns in India, Puri is
a major attraction for domestic Indian tourism.

Puri has developed in recent years into a major tourist center
for both western and local tourists. Simple accommodations and
multi-star hotels are shooting up everywhere. Small shops and
restaurants are flourishing. Still, Puri hasn't lost its charm and
is a great place to relax, have a swim, or just wander around
the Old Town.

Indian tourists come primarily as Hindu pilgrims to Jagannath
Temple, or to the beach. The ocean surf is sacred; in the evening, hundreds gather to watch the sunset. Wander through the
streets of the Old Town and the Temple District, discover the
shops, shrines, merchants, pilgrims, ashrams and lodgings.

Even during monsoon season, a visit is fun: the renowned
Rath Yatra Festival (= wagon festival) is held in June or July.
tremendous (10 m by 10 m by 16 m) temple wagons are pulled
through town by an entourage of 4000 faithful, in honor of Jan-
gannath, God of the Universe. By the way, the popular theory
that people intentionally throw themselves under the huge wheels
is false. It is much more likely that they are trampled in the
commotion. Jagannath Temple contains the largest kitchen in the
world, serving mahaprasada daily to thousands of pilgrims. The
temple employs 6000 people in a variety of functions.

Jagannath Temple is off limits to non-Hindus. Even Indira
Gandhi was refused admission in the early 1980s, because she
married a Parsee (hence her name) and no longer practised Hinduism. From the roof of a building across Grand Road, you can
see over the walls. The temple complex dates from the 12th
century.

All around is a bazar where you'll find lovely souvenirs:
shells, necklaces, sculptured stone. Good, fixed prices in Art &
Craft Centre of the Workers' Cooperative Society, Grand Road,
across from the temple. At least check prices here before bargaining in the bazar.

## COMING - GOING

**By Rail:** Puri is end of the line from Khurda Road on the Calcutta - Bhubaneswar - Madras route. Every train along the
route stops at Khurda Road, except the Choromandel Express,
which only stops in Bhubaneswar. Good bus connections, takes
2 h, costs 4.-Rs to 6.-Rs.

Direct trains to Howrah-Calcutta (11 h, 44.-Rs), and via
Jhansi and Agra (39 h, 120.-Rs), to New Delhi (36 h, 130.-Rs),
and to Varanasi (23 h, 77.-Rs).

PURI

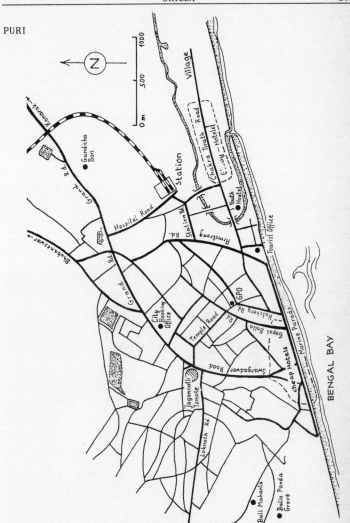

Direct connections south from Khurda Road and Bhubaneswar,
see there.  Heading south,  reservations are limited. North from
Puri to Calcutta or Delhi, you can usually find an empty seat.
The City Booking Office of S.E. Railway usually has a few
reservations available when the railway station quota is booked
up. Much simpler by bus from Bhubaneswar and Khurda Road.
**By Bus:**    Direct bus connections to Calcutta (13 h,   50.-Rs),
reservations via HIJLI,  Swargadwar Road,   near Sea Beach
Road.  Buses to Bhubaneswar (2 h,   8.-Rs) and Khurda Road
(1.5 h, 5.-Rs).

To Konarak, regular connections by bus, minibus, or jeep. All
depart from the bus stand, the latter when a full load of passengers has assembled (45 minutes, 5.-Rs).

Reservations at the bus stand in Grand Road, 09:00-11:00 h.

## A NIGHT'S REST

Get a rickshaw to the beach from the bus stand (3.-Rs) or
railway station (2.-Rs). Here are **Panthinivas Tourist Bungalow**
with Tourist Information,  the **Youth Hostel**,  and just beyond a
motley    group    of    globetrotter    hotels    and    restaurants

almost right on the northern edge of the beach. Tell the driver
to bring you to Chakra Tirath Road, a bit beyond South
Eastern Railway Hotel; everyone knows the place. At least five
new hotels have opened there recently. More are planned in the
fishing village. **Hotel Shankar,** (D)20.-, 30.-. **Seashore,**
(D)20.-, 30.-. **Milli,** (S)20.-, (D)30.-, 40.-, very clean,
friendly, tel.2335. **Sea Foam,** (D)20.-, (Dm)8.-.

A bit further toward the fishing village: **Hotel Z,** (D)20.-,
30.-. **Travellers Inn,** (D)20.-, 30.-. **Derby,** (D)20.-, 30.-.

In the fishing village: **Hotel and Restaurant Queen,** (D)15.-,
20.-. **Fakir Lodge,** (D)20.-. **Raja Lodge,** (D)20.-. **Balajee,**
(D)20.-.

Good restaurants include **Shaboo** and **Xanadu.** Kalia and Queen
deserve less praise. The seafood is good and cheap; try grilled
fish or lobster (order in the morning, deposit required).

**Jaganath South Indian** on Grand Road has good southern Indian food. **China Restaurant Cung Wah,** Gopal Road (side road by
Puri Hotel), 11:30-13:00 h, 18:30-22:30 h, good Chinese food, a

bit more expensive.

Most Indian tourists stay near Beach Sea Road where hotels charge 50.-Rs including meals: **Sea View Hotel**, tel.2117, attached baths, full boarding, **(S)**40.-, 50.-, depending on room location. **New Victoria Hotel**, attached baths, full boarding (bed, tea, breakfast, lunch, afternoon tea, dinner) 60.-Rs, in season (October-November), but hopelessly booked, and caution: checkout time is 06:30 h!

**Somali Restaurant** on Sea Beach Road has good cheap Indian food. On Swargadwar Road, near Sea Beach Road is the **Diplomat Liquor Shop**. Puri has several Government Ganja Shops. North of Puri in Mohinipur, 8 km toward Konarak, is the **Toshali Sands Village Resort Hotel**, tel.2888, **(D)**325.-Rs, comfortable facilities, air conditioning. The opposite end of the price scale is **Camping Coaches**, by the railway station, where you can stay in a shelter for 2.-Rs per person.

## TIPS

**Kriya Yoga Meditation:** Lessons in Karar Ashram on Swargadwar Road, a side street between Pulin Puri Hotel and Sonali Hotel, on Sea Beach Road.

**Used Book Store:** Across from Mill Hotel, 09:00-12:30 h, 15:00-17:00 h, except Thursdays, also rentals.

KONARAK

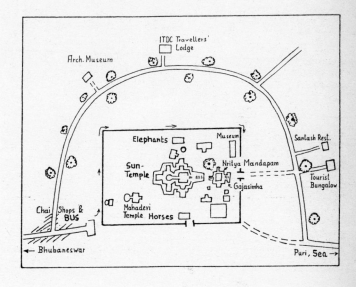

**Dangerous Currents**: Swimming is dangerous! During my 10-day stay, two people drowned in the undertow. One couldn't really swim; the other was stoned. Still, **Beware**! Professional lifeguards do serve on the beach, but who rescues them?

# Konarak

This village is by the ocean, 68 km south-east of Orissa's capital, Bhubaneswar. Besides a lovely sandy beach, and fertile tropical scenery, the Sun Temple dates from the 13th century.
**Black Pagoda**: Seafarers, of days long past, named the village after the structure visible far out to sea. Some charts still mark it as such today. The Sun Temple has been excavated in this century, and the interior filled out to prevent further decay. It was built in the shape of seven horses pulling the splendid chariot of Surya, the Sun God. The stone masonry is outstanding, including many erotic scenes, similar to those in Khajuraho. The facility is worth an excursion from Puri; very impressive.

You can stay in Tourist Bungalow **(D)**60.-Rs, and ITDC Ashok Travellers' Lodge, **(D)**100.-Rs. It's cheaper 3 km down the ocean road in Labanya Lodge, or in the lodges around the bus stand.

Since completion of the road from Puri, bus connections are good (see Puri). And good connections to Bhubaneswar (5.-Rs).

# RAJASTHAN

With a total area of 342,272 km$^2$, Rajasthan is the second largest state in India. The 34 million inhabitants speak Rajasthani or Hindi. Rajasthan is surrounded by Pakistan to the west, Punjab, Haryana and Uttar Pradesh to the north and north-east, Madhya Pradesh to the west, and Gujarat to the south. Rajasthan's capital is Jaipur, famous as the Pink City.

Rajasthan is the state which best fits the India cliché: the Thar Desert and the Aravalli Mountains; palaces, forts and warlike Rajputs. The Rajputs are famous as heroic warriors, who preferred to die than admit defeat, and legendary women, who preferred a death by fire to a life of submission. You can still see this pride in Rajasthanis today.

Rajasthanis are easy to recognize by the way they dress. The men wear bright turbans. Instead of saris, the women wear skirts and blouses, along with a large cloth which they stick in their skirts, and pull over their heads like a sari.

The major tourist towns are Jaipur, Chittorgarh, Ajmer, Pushkar, Bikaner, Jodhpur, Jaisalmer, and Udaipur. You might like to experience the desert for a few days by visiting Jaisalmer and perhaps even taking a Camel Tour. A stay in the Fort, with its lovely stone masonry, is a wonderful experience. To escape the heat, visit the heights of Mount Abu (1220 m), where you can learn more about the Jain religion. Mount Abu is an important spot for Jain pilgrims. And Rajasthan is famous for its colorful festivals. Don't miss the Pushkar Festival each summer.

Another less inviting chapter in the history of Rajasthan deserves mention. India tested its first atomic bomb near the Pokhara Railway Station on the rail line from Jodhpur to Jaisalmer.

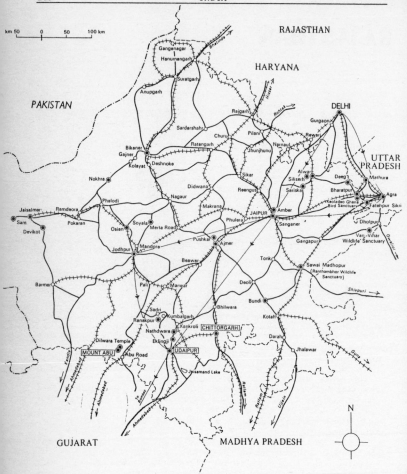

# Jaipur

The Pink City will probably be your first stop heading south, if you are coming from Agra and Delhi in the north. This city of one million marks one of the high points of every trip to India.

Jaipur was founded in the early 17th century by Maharaja Jai Singh II as a fortress city. According to ancient Hindu tradition, the streets were laid out in chessboard form. The yellow-brown colour of the buildings, which shines a warm rose colour in the evening sun, gives it the name, "The Pink City". The Old Town is surrounded by a thick wall which is completely intact. Entry is possible through just one of seven splendid gates. Inside you'll find the Maharaja Palace, the Jantar Mantar Observatory, and Hawa Mahal - Palace of The Winds.

In March / April, the Gangaur Festival is held, while the Teej Festival is celebrated in August. Both feature splendid processions of elephants and camels. For the coming years the following dates are planned: 1-2 April 1987, 29-30 July 1987, 20-21 March 1988, 15-16 August 1988, 8-9 April 1989, 4-5 August 1989.

## COMING - GOING

**By Air:** Two flights daily to Delhi (222.-), Jodhpur (280.-), Bombay (800.-Rs). Daily to Ahmedabad (460.-), Aurangabad (650.-), Udaipur (288.-). Vayudoot flies several times weekly to Agra, Bikaner, Kota, and Jaisalmer. All flights can be booked in the Indian Airlines Office, tel.72940, on Ajmer Road. And the Indian Airlines bus runs between the office and the airport, 14 km from town.

**By Rail:** Your fastest connection from Delhi is the Pink City Express, from Old Delhi Railway Station (05:50 h, Jaipur 11:00 h), costs 33.-Rs. Make reservations! The train continues on to Ajmer (13:42 h). The return trains runs Ajmer (14:00 h), Jaipur (17:00 h), Old Delhi (22:07 h).

Other direct trains run to Delhi, Agra (5-10 h, 26.-Rs), Ahmedabad (11-15 h, 53.-Rs), Abu Road (8-13 h, 41.-Rs), Jodhpur (8-10 h, 32.-), Ajmer (3-4 h, 16.-Rs), Udaipur (12 h, 40.-Rs), Bikaner (11 h, 36.-Rs) and Jaisalmer.

Reservations are possible round the clock for major trains, except 05:30-06:30 h, 13:30-14:30 h, and 21:30-22:30 h. Queues are shorter at night.

**By Bus:** Direct buses within Rajasthan are generally faster than by train. Regular De Luxe buses from Delhi via Agra and Fatehpur Sikri, 50 % more expensive than 2nd class rail, but a lot more comfortable.

**Around Town:** Lots of rickshaws, taxis, and a good bus system, which includes Amber.

## A NIGHT'S REST

In Jaipur, as elsewhere, be sure to appear at your lodging
without a rickshaw or taxi driver. The drivers get a very high
commission which you pay unknowingly.

**Teej**, Tourist Bungalow II, Beni Park, tel.74206, **(S)**30.-,
**(D)**40.-, 60.-, no bath, large **(Dm)**12.-, **(AC)(S)**100.-. **Evergreen
Rest House**, Mirza Ismail Road, in a small lane across from the
GPO, **(D)**20.-, **(Dm)**7.-, good restaurant. **RRR**, **(S)**15.-, **(D)**25.-,
45.-, **(Dm)**6.-. **Swagat Tourist Bungalow**, **(S)**20.-, 40.-, **(D)**30.-,
55.-, new, state-run, clean, reasonable, near the railway station. **Paradise Hotel**, Station Road, across from the railway
station, **(D)**15.-. **Govind Hotel**, **(D)**25-, nearby. **Assam Hotel**,
Station Road, tel.68474, **(S)**25.-. **Vikram Hotel**, **(D)**20.-, 25.-,
right of the bus stand 50 m, a reader warns against leaving
valuables at the reception. **Hotel Sadhana**, across from the Raj
Mahal Palace Hotel, near the railway station, **(D)**50.-, recommended by several readers. **Youth Hostel**, SMS Stadium, Bhawani
Singh Marg, tel.66433, members **(S)**6.-, **(D)**15.-; nonmembers
**(S)**25.-, **(D)**35.-, **(Dm)**8.-. **Jaipur Inn**, B 17 Shiv Marg, Beni
Park, tel.66057, **(D)**30.-, **(Dm)**15.-, clean, well managed, reasonable food, dinner for 12.-Rs as much as you can eat. **Hotel
Mahendra**, Kanti Nagar 1, near Polo Victory, between the rail-
way station and the GPO, 5 minutes from the bus stand,
**(S)**15.-, 25.-, **(D)**20.-, 40.-, helpful management. **Circuit
House**, M.I. Road, tel.74455, **(S)**38.-, **(D)**50.-, hot water, wonderful, not just anyone accepted in this state-owned establishment, look your best. Other lodgings in the same price range
and lots more expensive.

## REFRESHMENT

Good cheap food in **Jaipur Inn**, B 17 Shiv Marg, Beni Park, where
you'll meet lots of travellers to exchange info with. Also good in
**LMB Hotel**, 1 km south of Hawa Mahal in Johari Bazar, all vegetarian, excellent! Several restaurants on M.I. road including
**Kwality**, **Niro's Restaurant**, and the restaurant in **Circuit House**.
Near Evergreen Rest House, **Bambino Restaurant** is recommended.
**Restaurant Moonlight**, near Hotel Sadhana is very reasonable, and
spices so hot, tears run down your cheeks. Otherwise, lots of
other cheap restaurants which you stumble past during a walk
through town.

## SHOPPING

**Silver Jewelry** and **Silverware**: Wages are so low here that they
hardly have any effect on price. The daily silver price has to be
posted in every shop.
**Mirror Work**: Cloth, bags, tapestries, clothes, in which tiny mirrors are woven into the pattern are popular.

Three shops across from Hawa Mahal feature: Brass, stones
and jewels, painted cloth, printed cloth (blankets), stone figures
and vessels, puppets. This is one of the nicest cities in northern

JAIPUR

1 Teej Tourist Bungalow
2 Swagat Tourist Bungalow
3 Jaipur Inn
4 Rajasthan Handicraft Emporium

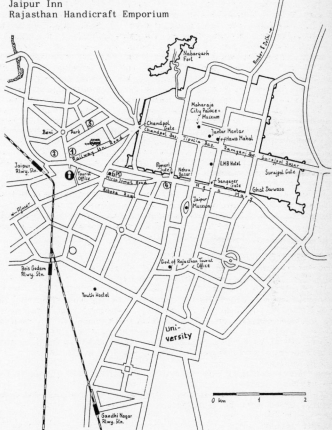

India for shopping! Don't forget to bargain. Check out prices in advance at Rajasthan Government Handicrafts Emporium on M.I. Road, where you'll find a large selection.

If you want to buy precious jewels in Jaipur, you'd better know something about them before you come! Here you'll find the largest selection in India.

Never let yourself be steered toward a shop by a rickshaw driver or a tout. In fact, don't even let them know which shop you plan to visit! Otherwise you'll end up paying a commission they pick up after you've gone.

## SIGHTS
**The Maharaja Palace:** Covers one-seventh of the entire Old Town. The Maharaja of Jaipur resided here until Independence in 1948. The palace consists of several buildings. The **Chandra Mahal** is the splendid seven-storey main building. A newer palace, the **Mubarak Mahal**, dates from the 19th century. Be sure to visit the **Textile and Garment Museum,** **Weapons Collection,** and other exhibits, admission 6.-Rs, students 3.-Rs.

**Observatory Jantar Mantar:** Jai Singh II, founder of Jaipur, and a famous astronomer, had observatories built throughout India, of which the Jantar (Yantra) Mantar is the largest and best preserved. The accuracy of the instruments is astounding. You can set your watch according to the sun, accurate to within a minute, but keep in mind the geographical difference to today's Indian Standard Time. Astronomy enthusiasts should be sure to take the tour. Admission 1.-Rs, 09:00-17:00 h, Mondays free.

**Hawa Mahal** (Palace of the Winds): A five-storey, fantasy palace, just the fassade, which you can climb inside for a lovely view of the city, admission 1.-Rs, 10:00-17:00 h.

**Jaipur Museum** (Albert Hall Museum): In the New Town in Ram Nivas Gardens. Exhibits of weapons, jewelry, traditional arts & crafts, garments, musical instruments, carved ivory, precious stones (including a collection from Idaroberstein), admission 1.-Rs, Mondays free, 10:00-17:00 h. In **Ram Nivas Gardens** there is a **Zoo**, and a restaurant serving good Indian food.

**City Tour:** Run daily by Rajasthan Tourist Office, departs from the railway station. Another daily tour by ITDC departs from State Hotel. Both visit all above-mentioned sights, plus the Amber Palace, 08:00-13:00 h, costs 15.-Rs.

## AROUND JAIPUR
**The Amber Palace:** 11 km north of Jaipur, a must see, challenging the beauty of the Jaipur palaces. For 600 years, Amber was the capital of the Rajput Empire, before the capital was moved to Jaipur. A bus departs from Hawa Mahal, costs 1.-Rs. After the lovely drive, over a small pass, you can ride an elephant up to

the residence,  costs 65.-Rs per elephant, sits up to four. On the way up you have a lovely view of the **Moghul Garden**. The palace buildings date from the 17th century and are amazingly well preserved. The rooms are decorated with mirror ceilings and the finest inlay. Admission 1.-Rs, Mondays free.

**Gaitor:**  8 km from town,  toward the palace gardens. Here you'll find the incredible marble tombs of the maharajas of Jaipur, decorated with wonderful reliefs.

# Ajmer

This ancient pilgrim town,  130 km south-west of Jaipur,  is the site of the Tomb of the Muslim holy man Khawja Muin-ud-Din Chisti,  who died in 1236. Lots of Christi pilgrims, but a visit is still worthwhile.  Like Jaipur,  the Old Town is surrounded by a wall.

Ajmer has had an eventful history. It was founded in the 11th century by the Chauhan Rajput Ajaipal,  but was conquered in 1192 by Mahmud of Ghauri.  This marked the beginning of 200 years of Muslim rule.  The reign was passed through several dynasties until the town's conquest by Akbar in the 16th century.

The Marathen took power in 1734 before handing over power to the British in 1818. Most of the sights date from the era of Islamic rule.

## SIGHTS
**Akbar's Palace:** Near the railway station, built in the 16th century, with a **Museum** inside.
**The Red Temple:** Built by the Jains in the 19th century, features an impressive model of scenes from Jain mythology, and a **Jain Model of the World.** Admission 0.50 Rs.
**Achai-Din-ka-Jonpra Mosque:** Also of interest, particularly if you take time for in-depth study, dating from the 12th century. The precise stone masonry of the columns, which are all different, and of the seven large archways, is only visible upon closer examination.
**Anasagar Lake:** In the north of town, man-made, with a lovely park, invites a stroll.

## COMING - GOING
**By Rail:** Ajmer is at the fork junction of the meter-gauge line from Delhi and Jaipur to Abu Road, Ahmedabad, or to Chittorgarh. Good but slow connections to Delhi, Agra, Jaipur in the northeast, and Chittorgarh, Udaipur, Abu Road, and Ahmedabad in the south. There are two direct trains via Indore to Secunderabad. See Jaipur. Reservations 08:30-13:30 h & 14:00-16:30 h; the Tourist Quota is distributed at the reservations desk.
**By Bus:** Excellent bus connections to Jaipur (3 h, 20.-Rs), Jodhpur (5 h, 30.-Rs), Udaipur, Chittorgarh, and Abu Road / Mount Abu. Buses to Pushkar rarely depart from the bus stand, but frequently from the railway station at the other end of town, 1 km, 2.-Rs by rickshaw.

## A NIGHT'S REST
Lots of hotels within 10 minutes of the railway station in Prithviraj Marg on the left behind the GPO: **Ratan, (D)**40.-, 50.-, fan, bath, bargain. **Anand, (D)**40.-, 50.-, fan, bath, bargain. **Raju, (D)**40.-, 50.-, fan, bath, bargain. **Payat, (D)**40.-, 50.-, fan, bath, bargain. **Bhola Hotel, (D)**40.-, 50.-, fan, bath, bargain. Bargaining can save 10.-Rs at any of the above. **Hotel Minar, (D)**20.-, clean, across from the railway station in the bazar.
  A few minutes from the bus stand in the north of town is **Tourist Bungalow** with Tourist Information, **(S)**30.-, 70.-, **(D)**40.-, 100.-, **(Dm)**10.-, restaurant.

# Pushkar

Pushkar, 11 km west of Ajmer on Sacred Pushkar Lake, has become a Mecca for long-term travellers, a place to recuperate from the stress of the road. There is no car noise, but people are friendly, and the lodgings are clean. For Hindus, Pushkar is a sacred pilgrim town.

## SIGHTS
**Brahman Temple:** Legend tells that the **Lake** was created by Brahman, for whom a rare temple stands at one end. It is the most sacred of all temples, because this is said to be the only spot on earth where Brahman has manifested himself. Pushkar has over 100 temples and ghats along the lake.

**Kartik Purnima:** If you're in Rajasthan in November, be sure to visit Pushkar for the tremendous fair. Features camel races, riding contests, and a large livestock market attracting over 100,000 visitors each year. The Pushkar Fair will be held 2-5 November 1987, 20-23 November 1988, and 10-13 November 1989.

## COMING – GOING
**By Bus:** From the railway station in Ajmer, buses and mini-buses to Pushkar, costs 3.-Rs. From Pushkar, direct buses to Jodhpur, 25.-Rs.

**A NIGHT'S REST**
   **Pushkar Hotel,** **(S)**15.-, **(D)**20.-, De Luxe **(D)**50.-, **(Dm)**6.-, on
   the roof **(Dm)**4.-, camping 4.-, popular, good location by the
   lake, swimming, garden restaurant, friendly staff, tel.1 is well
   earned.
   **Sarovar Tourist Bungalow,** next to Pushkar Hotel, by the lake,
   **(S)**16.-, 25.-, **(D)**30.-, **(Dm)**4.- no sheets, **(Dm)**8.- with sheets;
   the building once belonged to the Maharaja of Jaipur. **Lake
   View Hotel,** **(S)**15.-, **(D)**20.-, lovely view from the roof of the
   lake and town. **Krishna Guest House,** **(S)**8.-, **(D)**15.-, pleasant
   atmosphere. **Hotel Peacock,** **(S)**10.-, clean, simple.
   Plus there are lots of other lodgings which you'll learn of by
   word of mouth. Find just any place at first then pick the right
   spot for you more slowly. It is high season during the Pushkar
   Fair, so expect higher prices.

**REFRESHMENT**
No problem! On the main street, you'll find brown bread, curd,
good milkshakes, excellent lassi shakes, Indian food, whatever
you want. Plus many lodges have a restaurant. Of course it is
nicest to find a spot next to the lake; try in **Sunset Restaurant,**
next to the Tourist Bungalow.

**SHOPPING**
Pushkar is a good spot to pick up some souvenirs, and perhaps
get a tailor-made suit. Since most people stay here for a while,
you'll quickly get a feel for prices.

# Jodhpur

Until a few decades ago, Jodhpur was capital of the Marwar Empire. The town's name stems from the name of its founder, Rao
Jodha, who in 1458 was leader of the Rathora Clan of the Rajputs, a group which traces its roots back to Rama, the princely
incarnation of Vishnu, and hero of the **RAMAYANA** epic. The Fort,
set on a 120 m high sandstone hill, is visible far and wide. The
town itself is surrounded by a mighty wall.
   Although the town contains lots of trees, plants, and several
artificial lakes, the arid Rajasthan desert is just a few steps
away. The location, combined with a tremendous Fort, lend Jodhpur an unbelievable uniqueness, a dream city in a moon-like
landscape. Jodhpur is known as the "Gateway to the Desert". It
is your departure point for a 10 h train ride to Jaisalmer: ten
hours in a time zone centuries past.

## COMING - GOING

**By Air:** The Indian Airlines Office is in the Tourist Bungalow, tel.20909. The airport is 5 km from town. Flights twice weekly to Delhi (406.-), Bombay (705.-Rs), Jaipur (280.-). Daily flights to Ahmedabad (376.-Rs), Aurangabad (640.-Rs), and Udaipur. Vayudoot flies three times weekly to Jaisalmer.

**By Rail:** Because Jodhpur is served by the meter-gauge rail system, train connections are slower than buses. Most convenient are the trains thrice weekly to Delhi (12 h) overnight in the Mandore Superfast; the Jodhpur Mail takes 16 h costs 53.-Rs. To Jaipur, get the Marudhar Express, takes 8 h, costs 32.-Rs. Connections to Jaisalmer.

**By Bus:** Bus information tel.22906. Six buses daily to Jaipur, plus super deluxe buses at 16:00 h and 22:30 h. Eight buses to Ajmer plus a super deluxe bus at 16:00 h. To Udaipur at 07:30 h, 11:30 h, 21:00 h, super deluxe 22:30 h. Four buses to Bikaner plus a super deluxe bus. To Jaisalmer at 06:00 h and 13:30 h. To Ahmedabad 06:30 h. To Abu Road 06:00 h, 06:30 h, and 11:30 h. To Delhi 06:00 h and super deluxe at 16:00 h.

## A NIGHT'S REST

**Tourist Bungalow,** High Court Road, tel.21900, **(S)**40.-, 120.-, **(D)**50.-, 150.-, **(Dm)**5.-, 10.-, near town, Tourist Information, and Indian Airlines inside. **DAK Bungalow,** tel.21638, and **Cir-**

cuit House are both state-owned lodgings.
  Railway Retiring Rooms (RRR), by the station, (S)10.-,
(D)15.-. Plus several cheap lodges near the station (S)10.-,
20.-, (D)20.-, 50.-.
  Shanti Bhawan Lodge, (S)20.-, 30.-, (D)30.-, 40.-, across
from the railway station. Kalinga Hotel, next door, (D)80, good
restaurant. Prithvi Hotel, Station Road, (D)35.-Rs, with bath.
Hotel Aruna, tel.20238, (D)35.-, clean, friendly staff, 10 min-
utes from the railway station by Sojati Gate.
  Jodhpur's most expensive hotel is Umaid Bhawan Palace,
(S)330.-, (D)425.-Rs, mostly of interest for its swimming pool
(use 15.-Rs), and perhaps for dinner.

## REFRESHMENT
By the railway station are the excellent Kalinga Restaurant and
Renuka Restaurant. Near Sojati Gate and Sadar Bazar, you'll find
a number of spots for cheap Indian food, tasty lassis and
snacks. Try in Coffee House and Agra Sweet House. Another possibility is the restaurant in Tourist Bungalow, where breakfast is
served 08:00-10:00 h, lunch 12:00-14:00 h, and dinner 18:00-
20:00 h; just snacks outside these time slots.
  You might try the princely fair in Umaid Bhawan Palace Hotel, where 60.-Rs buys an excellent, well rounded, multi-course
meal.

## SHOPPING
All types of embroidered gold and silver, embroidered shoes, fine
embroidered kerchiefs, worn by Rajput women. Simple paintings on
paper and cloth are cheaper in Jaipur.

## SIGHTS
Old Town: Surrounded by a wall 10 km long.
Fort Meherangarh: Set on a hill overlooking the town. A road
leads up to the fortress in the north-east.
Lohapol Gate: The last gate before the fortress, here you can see
fifteen handprints. It is assumed that six of them belong to the
six wives of Maharaja Man Singh, who in 1843 burned themselves
to death upon the late Maharaja's funeral pyre. "Sati", or ritual
death by burning of wives upon their husbands' pyres has been
forbidden in India for 150 years, although it is still practised
occasionally.
  Inside the fortress are several palaces dating from the 16th to
18th centuries. In the Maharaja's apartment are exhibits of
weapons, miniature paintings, musical instruments, garments, etc.
A guide opens the doors behind which the treasures are hidden.
Admission is 10.-Rs, a photo permit costs an additional 10.-Rs
(15.-Rs for a flash). Open 09:00-17:00 h. The view from the Fort
down onto the town is lovely. Near Chamunda Temple, several
cannons are upon display. The holes left by cannonball hits can
be seen by the Fort entrance gate.

**JODHPUR**

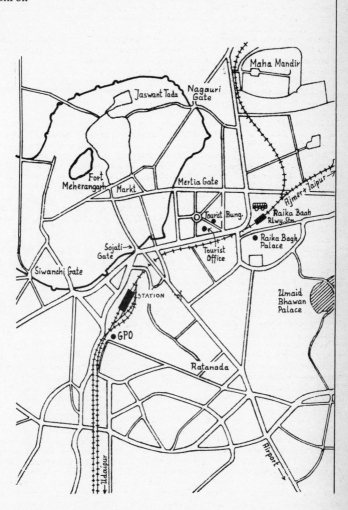

Maha Mandir
Jaswant Tada
Nagauri Gate
Fort Meherangarh
Markt
Mertia Gate
Ajmer + Jaipur
Tourist Bung.
Raika Bagh Rlwy. Stn
Sojati Gate
Raika Bagh Palace
Tourist Office
Siwanchi Gate
STATION
Umaid Bhawan Palace
GPO
Ratanada
Udaipur
Airport →

**Jaswant Thada**: North of the Fort, a few hundred meters downhill, is a tomb of white marble, in memory of Maharaja Jaswanth Singh; admission is free.
**Umaid Park**: Features a **Zoo** and a **Museum**, nominal admission, open 10:00–17:00 h.
**Umaid Bhavan Palace**: 2 km from the park, completed in 1943, admission 3.-Rs. Only nine rooms are open to the public because the palace has largely been turned into a hotel.
**Marwar Festival**: A splendid time for all. Dates for coming years: 6–7 October 1987, 24–25 October 1988, 13–14 October 1989.
**Town Tours**: Run by the Tourist Office, cost 15.-Rs.

## AROUND JODHPUR

**Mahamandir**: 3 km from Jodhpur, the interesting temple town features a town wall and a **Shiva Temple** with 100 columns. Direct buses from the Tourist Bungalow.
**Balsamand Lake & Palace**: Where Indians like to get away, 7 km north of town. The artificial lake was constructed in 1159 by Balak Rao Parihar. A tremendous park and palace complete the scene.

**Kailana Lake**: Another man-made lake with a park, 10 km west of town.
**Mandore**: 9 km from town, this was the Marwar capital before it was moved to Jodhpur. The richly decorated tombs of the Jodhpur rulers can be seen in a park. Equally of interest is the **Shrine of 330 Million Gods**, including a **Hall of Heroes** containing 15 bigger than life Statues hewn from solid rock. Buses from the bus stand, 1.-Rs.
**Osian**: The Old Town, 58 km north of Jodhpur, contains the ruins of 16 **Hindu** and **Jain Temples**, dating from the 8th to 11th centuries. The temples are richly decorated with sculpture. Buses and trains from Jodhpur.

# Bikaner

This town of 200,000 is an oasis, 380 km northwest of Jaipur in the sands of the Thar Desert. Founded in 1488, a 7 km wall surrounds the town.

## SIGHTS

**The Fort:** Built between 1588 and 1593 under Raja Rai Singh, shelters a lovely palace. Admission to the Fort is 3.-Rs; photo permit 10.-Rs. The **Museum** is also worth a look.

**Lalgarh Palace:** 3 km from the Old Town, you can see the Maharaja's family photos, and other royal exhibits. Here, expect a 10.-Rs charge for a photo permit.

**The Camel Research Institute:** 7 km from town, run by the Indian Government. Bikaner is famous for breeding camels. To visit, get a scooter (25.-Rs) or rent a bicycle (sandy roads). Your best chance of seeing a camel in its stall is around 17:00 h.

## COMING – GOING

**By Air:** Vayudoot offers three flights weekly from Delhi via Jaipur.

**By Rail:** The meter-gauge rail line via Bathino to Amritsar or conversely Ambala and Chandigarh is now being converted to wide gauge. Still, connections to Punjab remain poor for the moment.

There is a night train to Jaipur, takes 10 h, costs 36.-Rs. To Delhi are a slow night train, Bikaner Mail (12 h), and a day train, Bikaner Express (11 h), costs 42.-Rs.

Night train to Jodhpur (8 h, 28.-Rs) and Marwar Junction (junction for lines to Ajmer and Abu Road, Ahmedabad, and the Jodhpur and Udaipur line).

**By Bus:** Direct buses to all major towns in northwestern Rajasthan including Jaisalmer and Pokaran on the Jaisalmer – Jodhpur rail line. The express bus to Jaisalmer departs daily at 05:00 h, takes 10 h, costs 40.-Rs. Reservations the day before. The bus stand is by the Fort.

## A NIGHT'S REST

Near the railway station: **De Luxe Hotel**, tel.192, **(S)**15.-, **(D)**25.-, 35.-. **Green Hotel**, tel.296, **(S)**15.-, **(D)**25.-, 35.-. **Roopan Hotel**, tel.373, **(S)**15.-, **(D)**25.-, 35.-. **Delight Resthouse**, **(S)**15.-, **(D)**25.-, 35.-.

**Circuit House**, tel.142, **(S)**35.-, **(D)**50.-, large pleasant rooms, quiet, lovely garden. **Dak Bungalow**, tel.151, **(S)**5.-, **(Eb)**1.-. **Tourist Bungalow**, **(S)**60.-, 100.-, **(D)**75.-, 125.-.

You can eat at most hotels, or in **Amber Restaurant**, good Indian food, or medium priced continental food, on Station Road, across from De Luxe and Green Hotel. Curds, sweets, and biscuits are particularly good in Bikaner.

## AROUND BIKANER

**Camel Safari:** Bikaner has lots of camels: ask around in the hotels and shops first to compare prices! Ask about the itinerary; are meals included in the price? Will there be any extras you have to pay for? We've heard of people in Bikaner paying 125.-Rs per person per day, everything included. In Jaisalmer the price is just 50.-Rs! A safari to Phalodi Railway Station takes six days. To Jaisalmer takes 12 days.

**Jeep Safaris:** Offered to groups of eight, including guide, costs 300.-Rs per day per passenger.

**Dev Kund:** 8 km from town, here rest the tombs of the kings in the Bika Dynasty. The white marble tomb honors Maharaja Surat Singh.

## DURGA MANDIR (The Rat Temple)

Westerners might consider it strange to worship hundreds of rats, wandering free through a temple. Several Sadhus perform this exotic form of worship, even inviting the rats to eat from their bowl. But like so many other strange things in India, there is a

story which explains everything. The Rat Temple, also called Durga Mandir, is dedicated to Karni Ma, a holy woman. She is seen as an incarnation of Durga, the Giver of Life, Mother Goddess. Karni Ma is said to have reached the biblical age of 160 years. On her death bed, she assured her followers that she would always remain in this place, reincarnated as a rat! Karni Ma belonged to the Charan Clan, who are famous as professional poets. It is assumed that after their death, every Charan is reincarnated in the Temple of Karni Ma as a rat. Every rat which dies is reincarnated in its next life as a Charan. Be especially careful not to step on a rat. Such behavior is strictly punished. It is considered good luck if the rats walk over you. 30 km from town in Deshnok, buses hourly from the bus stand (4.-Rs), photo permit 5.-Rs. We wish you good luck!

**TIPS**
**Jain Meditation Centre:**  In Ladnun, between Bikaner and Sikar on
the road to Jaipur.  Westerners, too, are invited to learn medita-
tion.  Write:  Jain Vishva Baharati,  P.O.  Ladnun 341306, Distr.
Nagaur, Rajasthan.
**Tourist Information:** By the Fort entrance.
**Bank of Bikaner and Jodhpur:** Cashes traveller's checks, near the
Tourist Office.
**Head Post Office:** At the bus stand by the Fort.

# Jaisalmer

Out here in the desert,  by a perfectly intact Fort,  live 20,000
people who trace the founding of their town back to 1156 AD and
the Bhatti Rajputs under Rawal Jaisal.
   The town's intricately decorated buildings and friendly people
make a visit to Jaisalmer,  a trip into the past,  unequalled by
any museum.
   Only recently have electricity and the railway reached town.
The Indo-Pakistan War lent the border region new strategic importance,  spurring the quick construction of new infrastructure.
Notice the good paved roads and the many military bases in the
region,  including an airforce base. Soldiers are the best customers in Jaisalmer.  But in recent years,  tourism has increased
substantially.  The first edition of this travel guide is partly to
blame.

So many visitors have discovered the picture book mediaeval
town: camel safaris are now booked
as complete tours,  and souvenir
shops accept all the major credit
cards.
**The Fort:**  Dating in its present
form from the 16th century,  sits on
rock,  80 m above the desert. Both
the Fort and the parts of the New
Town at its feet are built of a
warm-coloured,  yellow sandstone.
In the Fort,  visit the **Raj Mahal**
(town palace) and several **Jain
Temples.** Open just in the morning,
photography is prohibited.  A **Library** in one of the temples contains valuable,  old manuscripts,
written on palm leaf,  open 10:00-
-11:00 h.
**Haveli:**  Below the Fort,  notice the
splendid homes,  built for wealthy
merchants in the 18th and 19th
centuries.  The most impressive

include **Salim Singh ki Haveli**,  the **Patva ki Haveli**,  and the **Natmal ki Haveli**, all located near the market.
**Camels:** Sights further from town are best visited by camel.

## COMING – GOING
The railway station and bus stand are by the two gates located at opposite ends of the lower town.
**By Air:** Thrice weekly to Delhi via Jodhpur and Jaipur.
**By Rail:** Day and night trains to Jodhpur, takes 10 h, costs 32.-Rs. Reservations 10:00–13:00 h & 14:00–16:00 h, but not for the night train. For a couple of rupees, the staff at your lodge will pick up your reservation.

To Jaipur, get the night train and change to the connecting train in Raikabag, just before Jodhpur. But frequent delays can cause you to miss your connection. We take the bus.

If, after a side trip into the Thar Desert, you want to continue on from Jodhpur by rail, be sure to make reservations upon arrival, before heading on to Jaisalmer. Otherwise you have little chance of getting a reservation upon return.
**By Bus**: Buses to Bikaner, Jodhpur, Ajmer, Jaipur (15 h), and Barmer. Reservations are not possible in Jaisalmer.

## A NIGHT'S REST
As the number of visitors increases, so too, does the number of lodgings. Most are located in the lower town, between the Market and Amasagar Gate, i.e. the State Bank of India. Think **(S)**10.-, or **(D)**15.-, 20.-.
  **Rama Guest House**, **(D)**15.-, 20.-, popular, downtown, near the market, good restaurant, friendly staff, a bed on the roof, including a lockable box costs **(Dm)**5.-, jeeps from the railway

Raj Mahal

JAISALMER

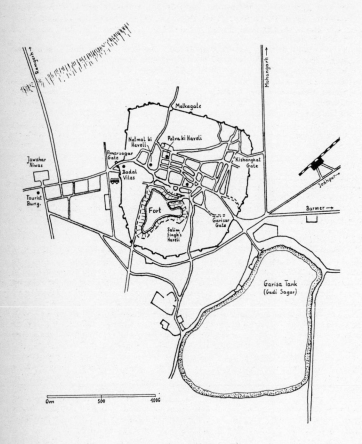

station 2.-Rs, free camel safaris for hotel guests.
  **Golden Rest House,** (D)20.-. **Sun Ray Hotel,** (S)10.-, (D)15.-.
**Hotel Swastika,** (D)20.-. **Hotel Green,** (D)15.-.
  **Fort View Hotel,** Central Market, tel.214, (D)15.-, 30.-, helpful manager, arranges camel safaris, jeep tours, etc., roof
terrace with a view of the Fort and excellent vegetarian food,
no butter or eggs served because the family is strict Brahman;
great place!
  You might also stay in the Fort: **Hotel Laxi Niwas,** near the
Jain Temple, (S)10.-, (D)15.-, clean, friendly, camel safaris.
**Jaisal Castle Hotel,** nearby, (D)80.-, 100.-, expensive, baths,
restaurant, panoramic view over the desert from the roof terrace. **Shree Nath Palace,** in the Fort across from the Jain
Temple, (S)35.-, (D)50.-, lovely old rooms, great view from the
roof terrace.
  Outside the town walls to the west: **Moomal Tourist Bungalow,**
tel.92, (S)60.-, (D)75.-, (Dm)8.-, restaurant. **Dak Bungalow,**
tel.60, across from Tourist Bungalow.

## REFRESHMENT
We've received multiple recommendations for **Kalpana** and **Gaylord
Restaurant,** near the State Bank of India. Also good are the restaurants and lassi shops around the market. Otherwise try the
hotel restaurants, or the restaurant in **Tourist Bungalow** (expensive). The tasty snacks and spicy-hot specialities are great!

## CAMEL RIDING
These days there is hardly a hotel in Jaisalmer which doesn't
organize or offer small camel safaris. Prices can vary, so be
sure you check exactly what is offered. The cheapest rate we've
seen is 30.-Rs for a day trip without food or lodging. For 45.-Rs
you can expect a simple snack, just chappati and dal. For
65.-Rs and up, expect good Rajasthani cooking and lodging.
  If you are planning to take a longer tour, be sure to plan a
day tour first, just to get used to the idea. Camel riding is
strenuous activity for most people. On your brief tour, you are
sure to pass the town's water reservoir. On its banks, notice the
several small temples and an entrance gate from which stairs
lead down to the lake. It was said to have been built by a
prostitute, against the will of the King. She succeeded by
adorning it with a picture of Krishna.
  We particularly recommend a two-day tour, during the off
season (March to October) for riding novices. Your seat and back
are in for an experience. I've met travellers who, after one day,
were so wounded that they considered turning around.
  Don't forget the Vaseline and wound cream. Light, loose fitting pants are a must, jeans invite discomfort, as do shorts. For
18.-Rs you can buy the necessary cloth, and for 8.-Rs a tailor
will sew you a pair to measure. Your safari kit must also contain a water bottle, water purification tablets, head cover (tur-

ban,   2 m for 16.-Rs),   flashlight,   sunglasses,   suntan lotion,
knife, fork spoon, fruit, lemons. A sleeping bag and tent are not
necessary.

The price of a safari should include camel and driver,  food
except fruit, blankets, etc.

You pass by desert villages,   abandoned settlements and temples,  former caravan camps. You'll be surprised how much activity goes on in the desert.   Enterprising merchants have even
opened soft drink bars in old ruins,   out in the middle of the
desert.

The camel drivers cook food and tea.  Speak with the manager
when booking the safari so you have some input as to what types
of food he buys.   All along the route are springs with fresh
water.

If you suffer from motion sickness (camel rocking),   pick up
the necessary medication at a druggist in Jaisalmer (i.e. Metoclo-
pramide).

Be sure never to photograph women.  Remove your shoes before
entering temples and water holes.

Most tours offered last four days.  A popular destination are
the sand dunes at Sam,   41 km from Jaisalmer. You ride past the
unwalled,   and well-kept **Mool Sagar** Garden. You return via **Lod-
ruva**,  a village with a Jain Temple,  and **Amar Sagar**,  a lake
featuring temples and a garden.

**AROUND JAISALMER**
**Sam:** Accessible by bus, or jeep (20.-Rs) from Fort View Hotel.
**Khuri:** 45 km south-west of town, on the road to Myajlar, get a
bus, (2 h, 5.-Rs), departs at 12:30 h, return 17:00 h. In Mama's
Guesthouse, excellent Rajasthani food. This is right in the middle
of the desert sands. You can visit surrounding villages by camel.

**TIPS**
**Tourist Office:** In Tourist Bungalow, tel.106, outside the Old Town
in the west of town.
**State Bank of India:** Near Amarsagar Gate, tel.98.
**Desert Festival:** Dates for coming years 31 Jan-2 Feb 1988, 18-20
Feb 1989.

# Chittorgarh

Chittorgarh's history is characterized by fighting between the
Rajput princes and the Moghul kings. Founded in the 7th century AD, the town was stormed three times in the 14th and 16th
centuries. The story is told that during each attack, the female
residents voluntarily submitted to jauhar (ritual death by fire),
when the men were overcome by the enemy. In 1303, the first
attack against Chittor under Ala-ud-Din Khilji was made by the
Sultan of Delhi, to capture the beautiful princess Padmini, wife
of Bhim Singh. But she too preferred ritual death by jauhar. In
1535, Sultan Bahadur Shah from Gujarat stormed the fortress. In
1567, Emperor Akbar conquered the Rajputs. Maharana Udai Singh
fled to Udaipur, where he founded a new capital.

**COMING - GOING**
  **By Rail:** Five trains daily to Ajmer (4-5 h, 22.-Rs), twice via
Indore to Secunderabad (37-49 h, 82.-Rs). From Delhi via Jai-
pur and Ajmer on Wednesdays, Fridays and Sundays with the
Pink City Express or Garib Nawaz Express; continues on to
Udaipur. On other days get the Chetak Express to Udaipur,
takes 4 h, costs 15.-Rs, the railway station is 8 km from the
Fort!
  **By Bus:** To Udaipur, Ajmer, and beyond. Unless you get an
express train, buses are faster to Udaipur (3 h, 16.-Rs), and
Ajmer. From the bus stand it is 5 km to the Fort, to the rail-
way station a good 3 km.

**A NIGHT'S REST**
  Not a very good selection: **Panna Tourist Bungalow,** **(D)**40.-
with bath, clean, with soap, towels, toilet paper, 1 km from
the railway station toward the bus stand and Fort. **Janta Avas
Grih Tourist Guest House,** run by RTDC, Tourist Information,
**(D)**20.- no bath, **(D)**25.- with bath, near the railway station.

Other hotels near the railway station on Station Road, try:
**Hotel Savaria,** (**S**)15.-. Also of interest: **Dak Bungalow, Circuit House,** and **RRR.**

## SIGHTS
**The Fort:** Set 160 m above the desert on a hill, everything of interest is inside: temples, towers, and ruins. 8 km from the railway station. The Fort is big, just wander about to get a feel.
**Tours:** Organized twice daily by the Tourist Office, 08:00-13:00 h and 15:00-18:00 h, costs 12.-Rs, depart from Tourist Bungalow, the railway station, and the Tourist Office. Or organize your own tour by tonga (horse cart). Groups can hire an auto-rickshaw for 20.- to 30.-Rs, if the driver is willing to act as guide. You might also just rent a bicycle. Signs in English describe most of the sights. The Fort is said to have been built in keeping with the legend of Bhim, one of the Panduva heroes in the **MAHABHARATA.**
**Ran a Kumbha Palace:** Partly in ruins, particularly the Elephant Stalls, Audience Hall, and Shiva Temple. In a cellar, the first Jauhar is said to have been performed.
**Fateh Prakash Palace:** A **Museum** inside displays historical finds from the Fort.
**Mira** and **Kumbha Shyam Temple:** Mira Bai is a mystical woman, revered by the Hindus. She composed verse and song in honor of Krishna. She was married to the eldest son of Maharana Sangram Singh. The Mira Temple, built in Indo-Aryan style, is dedicated to her. The Kumbha Shyam Temple, built in the 15th century, is dedicated to Vishnu.
**Jai Stambha** (The Victory Tower): Nine storeys tall (37 m), the climb up costs 0.50 Rs. From the top you've a lovely view. The richly decorated tower was built by Rana Kumbha to celebrate a victory over the Sultans of Malwa and Gurat in 1440.
**Mahasati Sithala:** Site where the Ranas were ritually burned to death. It is assumed that the second Jauhar took place here.
**Sammiddhiswara Madadeva Temple:** It is unclear if this was originally a Jain or a Shiva Temple.
**Gaumukh Reservoir:** The basin is fed by an underground spring, whose water flows out of the rock through the jaws of a cow. This is said to be the entrance to a series of underground caverns where Padmini burned in her death by Jauhar.
**Kalika Mata Temple:** Constructed originally in the 8th century as a Sun Temple. In the 14th century it was converted to a Kali Temple.
**Padmini Palace:** Actually a pavilion by a small lake. There is a legend, of which various versions are told, about this spot. All stories agree that Ala-ud-Din, conqueror of Chittorgarh, was enticed by reports of Padmini's beauty, and was determined to see her. She, however, only permitted him to see her reflection in a mirror which is situated today in the palace building so that a

CHITTOGARH

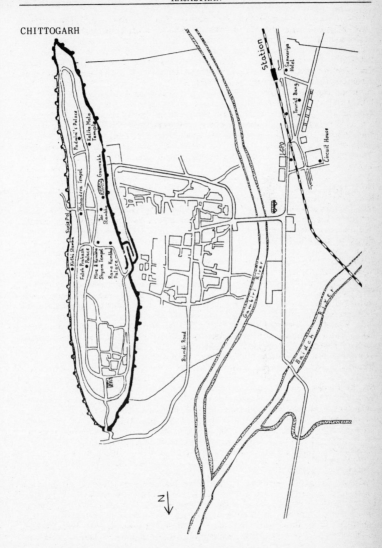

view of the pavilion can be seen.  Ala-ud-Din was overwhelmed
and put all his power to win her.  He kidnapped the Maharaja
and demanded Padmini as ransom. According to the most humorous
version,  Padami sent her brother,  disguised with a veil,  to the
wedding in her place.  The Sultan married a man for the first
time.  His majesty was not amused when the joke was uncovered.
Trumpets please.

**Kirthi Stamba** (Tower of Fame):  The 22 m tall tower was built by
a wealthy Jain merchant in the early 14th century in honor of
the first Tirthankar Adinath.  The seven-storey tower is decorated
outside with depictions of the Tirthankar and other ornaments. A
stair leads to the top; careful, the doors are low!

This is by no means a listing of all the sites.  The grounds are
laid out with paths, lawns, bushes, and trees.

# Udaipur

Rajasthan's "Lake City" is considered by some to be the most
romantic spot in all of India.  Located at 580 m above sea level,
you've good connections by air, bus, or rail from Bombay, Delhi,
Jaipur, or Ahmedabad.

According to legend,  Maharana Udai Singh met a sadhu (holy
man) while hunting,  on the bank of a lake.  The king allowed
himself to be blessed by the sadhu,  and received the advice,  to
build his capital around the lake.  It was a good spot,  with a
group of green hills protecting the lake.  So it was that the town
of Udaipur was founded in 1559.  After his flight from besieged
Chittorgarh in 1568,  Maharana Udai Singh moved his capital to
Udaipur.  As leader of the Sun Clan of the Rajputs,  the Maharana's coat of arms contains the Sun as its symbol. Udaipur became
known as the "Town of the Rising Sun".

On Lake Pichola,  Udai Singh ordered construction of his in-
credible palace, Jag Niwas. Upon the reported advice of Jaqueline
Onassis,  the palace was converted into the Lake Palace Hotel.
Even without the lake,  the City Palace,  and the Lake Palace
Hotel,  Udaipur is a bustling town with lots of tiny bazars. It is
a lot of fun just to wander about exploring.

In all,  it is a lovely town with an interesting history, seem-
ingly out of 1001 Nights.  No wonder Udaipur has so many names:
"City of the Rising Sun",  "Fairytale Town of Marble Palaces",
"Venice of the Orient", etc.

## COMING - GOING

The bus stand and railway station are close together,  outside
the town wall.

**By Air:**  The airport is 25 km from town.  Since there isn't an
airport bus,  calculate 40.-Rs extra for a taxi into town. Going
out, drivers demand 60.-Rs. It's a 35 minute drive. No cameras
are permitted aboard planes departing Udaipur,  strict searches
(military facilities).

UDAIPUR

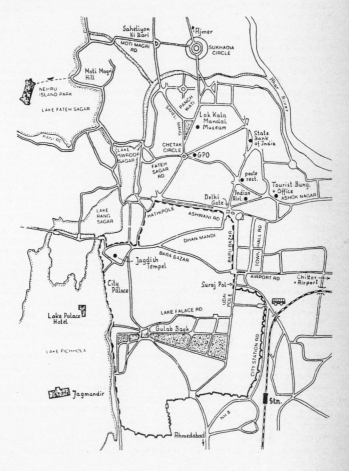

The India Airlines Office is by Delhi Gate, tel.2513. Daily
flights to Delhi (483.-), direct or via Jodhpur (214.-), and
Jaipur (288.-). Daily to Aurangabad (523.-Rs) and Bombay
(578.-Rs).
**By Rail:** The fastest trains are the Pink City and Garib Nawaz
Express, Mon, Wed, Fri, and Sun from Old Delhi (05:50 h) via
Jaipur (11:20 h), Ajmer (13:57 h), and Chittorgarh (18:25 h),
arrives at 21:35 h. Returns on Tues, Thurs, and Sat. Daily
from Delhi the Chetak Express takes 21 h from Delhi or 12 h
from Jaipur, costs 60.-Rs or 40.-Rs respectively. Other trains
are considerably slower. Just one good night train to Ahmedabad, takes 9 h, costs 30.-Rs. In Udaipur there is no Tourist
Quota, but there is a VIP Quota; speak to them, big shot.
**By Bus:** Six connections daily to Ahmedabad and Jaipur, twice
daily to Ajmer and Abu Road, or direct to Mount Abu (20.-Rs).
The day bus takes 7 h, the night bus requires 10 h. Reservations up to two days ahead. Frequent connections to Chittorgarh (3 h, 15.-Rs). Daily to Jodhpur (10 h, 40.-Rs).

## A NIGHT'S REST
**Kajri Tourist Bungalow**, Shastri Circle, tel.3509, **(S)**30.-, 120.-,
**(D)**40.-, 150.-, **(Dm)**10.-, Tourist Information Office inside,
lovely situation **Alka Hotel**, also on Shastri Circle, tel.3611,
**(S)**20.-, **(D)**30.-.
Plus lots of cheap lodgings in town: **Railway Retiring Rooms**,
in the railway station, **(Dm)**5.-. **Hotel Apsara**, City Station
Road, tel.3400, **(S)**15.-. **New Yoti**, Station Road, tel.3539,
**(D)**20.- with bath. **Hotel Natural**, Fateh Sagar Road, **(D)**20.-,
30.-, clean, right at Rang Sagar, across from the Old Town.
**Dak Bungalow** and **Circuit House** are nearby.
**Hotel Keerti**, Saraswati Marg, an especially popular traveller
stomping ground, **(S)**10.-, **(AC)(D)**80.-, **(Dm)**6.-. Also owned by
Hotel Keerti is **Country Inn**, 6 km from Udaipur, a farm with
horses, camels, and chickens, **(D)**15.-, 25.-, swimming pool and
free riding lessons during the first three days, free transport
into town to Keerti Hotel several times daily by jeep or tonga;
food is expensive, but excellent, order your dinner early.
Occasional events include day trips to Chittorgarh (50.-Rs when
enough are interested), and horseback treks (also expensive);
a lovely spot to relax. Please don't confuse Keerti Hotel above
with Keerti Tourist Hotel, which tries to steal customers with
its similar name.
**Hotel Chandra Prakash**, Lake Palace Road, quiet, clean,
**(D)**30.-, praised by readers. **Hotel Rang Niwas**, quiet, lovely
courtyard, **(D)**40.-, 60.-. **Lal Ghat**, clean, quiet, lovely view
of Lake Pichola, **(S)**15.-, **(D)**25.-, behind a Jagdish Temple.
And let's not forget **Hotel Lake Palace**, in the middle of Lake
Pichola, **(S)**300.-, **(D)**375.-Rs, for the select few, a boat out
for a quick look costs 20.-Rs, not cheap, even if cookies and
drinks are included.

## REFRESHMENT
There are several restaurants around Chetak Circle, try **Kwality**.
On Shastri Circle, try the restaurant across from Tourist Bunga-
low. Across the street is a stand selling outstanding fresh-
pressed fruit juices. **Lovers' Paradise Restaurant**, by Hathi Pole
Gate is particularly recommended.

## SHOPPING
Similar wares to Jodhpur, including silver handicrafts and dolls
(50.- to 80.-Rs). Everything here is more expensive than in
Jaipur.
**The Old Town:** Here you'll find an entire street where only
craftsmen catering for weddings live and work: musicians,
tailors, silk merchants, light bearers, horse rental... Perhaps
they can cater to your needs?

## SIGHTS
**Old Town:** Surrounded by a **Town Wall**, set west of the lake,
entry is through seven gates.
**Lake Pichola:** Over 4 km long and 3 km wide. The island in the
south is the site of **Jag Mandir Palace**, built in the 17th century.
**Jag Niwas Palace:** On the northern island, known today as the
Lake Palace Hotel, including swimming pool and all the frills.
Movie fans are familiar with the scene from the James Bond film
Octopussy, which was filmed here. A quick look is not cheap, a
boat out costs 20.-Rs including a free drink and cookie.
**City Palace Museum:** In the Old Town, above Lake Pichola, built
in several stages with granite and marble. In the palace rooms
you can see the famous **Peacock Mosaic**, and inlay featuring tiny
mirrors. Admission is 3.-Rs, a photo permit another 3.-Rs, open
09:30-16:30 h.
**Jagdish Temple:** North of City Palace, the city's largest temple
was built in 1651 under Maharana Jagat Singh I in Indo-Aryan
style.
**Gulab (Rose) Bagh:** No charge to visit this park and its tiny
**Zoo**.

## Walking Tour
Outside the town wall, wander between the two lakes, **Rang
Sagar** and **Swaroop Sagar** to the large lake in the north:
**Fateh Sagar:** Featuring **Nehru Island Park**, boats out to the
lovely island and restaurant (1.-Rs), tremendous at sundown
when the fountains are turned on.
**Japanese Rock Garden:** From the jetty, head through the park
to the Japanese Rock Garden on Moti Magri Hill.
**Saheliyon Ki Bari** (Fountain Garden): A bit further on, well
tended beds, pools, fountains, marble elephants, open 09:00-
18:00 h, nominal admission, originally built for the Ladies of
the Court.
**Sukhardia Circle:** Heading south, large fountain.

**Bhartiya Loka Kala Mandal Museum**: A folklore museum for dance, puppets, and puppet theatre performances, admission 1.-Rs, students 0.50 Rs, exhibits include musical instruments, costumes, masks, and other examples of folk art.

**City Tours**: Offered by the Tourist Office, tel.3509, depart from Tourist Bungalow, daily, 08:00-13:30 h, costs 15.-Rs, visits all the major sights in town.

## AROUND UDAIPUR

**Regional Tour**: The Tourist Office offers a daily tour from 14:00-19:30 h, costs 30.-Rs including visits to Eklingji, Nathdwara, and Haldighati.

**Eklingji**: 21 km from town, a marble **Shiva Temple**, dates from the 15th century.

**Nathdwara**: 48 km from Udaipur, a popular pilgrim town with a famous **Krishna Temple.**

**Haldighati**: 42 km from town, this was the battlefield where Maharana Pratap faced the moghul army. A Monument for **Chetak**, the Maharana's horse, is nearby (3 km).

**Jaisamand Wildlife Sanctuary**: 48 km from Udaipur, near Jaisamund Lake, ask in the Tourist Office.

**Kumbhalgarh Fort**: 85 km from Udaipur, near Ranakpur, the Fort dates from the 15th century.

## TIPS

**Tourist Office**: In Kajri Tourist Bungalow, Shastri Circle, tel.3506, 10:00-17:00 h.

**Tourist Information**: At the railway station 07:30-10:00 h, the Information Window at the airport is only open for incoming flights.

**General Post Office**: Chetak Circle.

**Poste Restante**: Not in the GPO! At the corner of Hospital Road and Mandi Road, 200 m north of Delhi Gate and east of Chetak Circle.

**Barber**: Good, cheap, (haircut 3.-Rs), right of Tourist Bungalow.

**Bicycle Rentals**: Start at 4.-Rs for 24 hours.

**Tummy Troubles**: The Anil Clinic on Hospital Road performs good medical tests, liver test, examination of faeces, blood test, etc., results within 5 h.

**Tribal Research and Training Institute**: On Ahar Road, of interest to ethnologists and India specialists. The tremendous Library is open to the public, if you are interested in India and related subjects. The institute staff are extremely friendly. They can provide you with a list of all similar institutes in India. This is an important stop for anyone interested in tribal culture and the "lower castes".

**Mewar Festival**: Dedicated to Parvati, held 1-2 April 1987, 20-21 April 1988, and 8-9 April 1989.

# Ranakpur

On the bus route from Udaipur to Jodhpur, Ranakpur is famous for its lovely **Jain Temples** in which puja is still held today.
**Chaumukha Temple** (= Four Faces): Foremost, built in 1435.
**Adinathji:** Dedicated to the first Jain holy man. No two of the 1444 temple columns are alike.
**Parshwanat Temple:** Also interesting. Lovely landscape only underlines the beauty of the temples. The temples are open to the public 12:00–17:00 h. Remember, no leather objects may be taken into the temples.

## COMING – GOING

**By Bus:** Connections to Udaipur, Mount Abu, and Jodhpur. To Udaipur (6 h), you may have to change in Sadri for the last 10 km (1.-Rs extra). A taxi from Sadri is 25.-Rs. Marwar Junction is not far, on the rail lines to Ajmer, Abu Road, and Jodhpur.

## A NIGHT'S REST
**Tourist Bungalow.** Or you can sleep on the floor at the pilgrim sites. A small donation is expected. For 3.-Rs you receive an excellent vegetarian meal.

# Mount Abu

Mount Abu, at 1220 m, is Rajasthan's only hill station, making it a popular spot where people from Rajasthan, Gujarat, and Maharasthra get away from desert or dry season heat. The number of Indian tourists far outweighs western tourism. In season, mid-March to late June and mid-September to mid-November, temperatures are only 25° C. It isn't as much fun up here during monsoon season (July to mid-September), and it can get quite cold from December to mid-March. But during off season, prices plummet to one-fourth the high season rates. The town's name stems from Rishi (wise man) Arbuda. Mount Abu is an important spot for Jain pilgrims.

## COMING - GOING
No matter how you arrive, you'll have to pay a toll, 3.-Rs for each car, taxi, or bus passenger.
**By Rail:** The nearest railway station is 25 km in Abu Road. Frequent bus connections from Mount Abu to the railway station. Reservations through the Railway Outpost, which administers Abu Road's allocation, but book early.
  Seven trains daily to Ahmedabad, takes 3-5 h, costs 22.-Rs. There is a midnight train to Jodhpur, takes 6 h. Four trains to Ajmer (5-7 h, 31.-Rs), and Jaipur (8-11 h, 41.-Rs), and Delhi. Calculate another 5.-Rs for the bus ride to Mount Abu.
**By Bus:** The bus stand is on the secondary road to Abu Road. The Tourist Office is directly opposite. Bus connections are generally preferable to rail, because then you don't have to change in Abu Road. Regular connections to Ranakpur, Ahmedabad, (6 h, 27.-Rs). To Udaipur, takes 7 h (day bus) or 10 h (night bus), costs 30.-Rs. One bus daily to Jodhpur (13 h, 36.-Rs). Prices vary slightly between public and private bus companies.

## A NIGHT'S REST
**Shikar Tourist Bungalow,** tel.69, has become expensive in season, **(S)**45.-, 120.-, **(D)**60.-, 150.-, **(Dm)**12.-, 50 % discounts in off season. **Tourist Guest House,** below Tourist Bungalow, **(D)**20.-, **(D)**30.- with bath. **Devi Bhavan Hotel,** from the main road go right just before the bazar, nice manager, **(D)**15.-. **Youth Hostel,** **(D)**12.-Rs, cheap, but just for boys, not very nice rooms. **Nataraj Hotel,** 10 minutes walk from the bus stand, **(S)**15.-, 25.- (off season **(S)**10.-, 15.-), **(D)**20.-, 30.- (off season **(D)**15.-, 20.-). **Sudhir,** 1 km further, **(S)**15.-, 25.- (off

MOUNT ABU

season **(S)**10.-, 15.-), **(D)**20.-, 30.- (**(D)**15.-, 20.-). More cheap
lodges in the same price range along the road to Abu Road and
around the Golf Course.

## REFRESHMENT
**Nina Refreshment** on Sunset Road has good food, in the woods,
with a lovely quiet garden. **New Shere Punjab Hotel,** next to
Shere Punjab, by Subzi Market, has an excellent restaurant, rich
selection of cheap food.
   **Abu Restaurant,** by the Golf Course, is cheap, but poorly
motivated. Tourist Bungalow Restaurant has a lovely location by
the lake, but reports are poor.

## ACTIVITIES
**Walking:** A great region just to wander about.
**Rowing:** Take out a rowboat on Nakki Lake. According to legend,
the lake was created by a God using just one fingernail
(= nakk).
**Yoga Classes:** Offered free of charge at the Brahma Kumaris Universal Peace Hall.

## SIGHTS
**The Dilwara Temples:** 5 km from town, buses (1.-Rs), open 12:00-
18:00 h, photo permit (5.-Rs). No leather is permitted within the
Temple District! Mount Abu is one of Jainism's five most important
places of pilgrimage.
   **Vimal Vasahi Temple:** Built of white marble in 1031 AD, famous
   for its outstanding marble carvings. Its most sacred object is
   the seated statue of Jainism's first Tirthankar, Adinath. In
   52 cells, surrounding the temple courtyard, are statues of other
   Jain holy men.
   **Tejpal Temple:** Also remarkable for its marble craftsmanship.
   39 cells contain statues. Three other temples are of interest.
**Adhar Devi Temple:** 3 km from the Tourist Office, in the north of
town. Over 200 m of steps lead up to this Hindu temple, built
into the rock.
**Museum & Art Gallery:** Across from the GPO on Raj Bhawan Road,
open daily, except Fridays 10:00-17:00 h.
**Sunset Point, Honeymoon Point,** and **The Crags:** Popular spots for
viewing the sunset.

## AROUND MOUNT ABU
**Regional Tour:** Run by Tourist Office, 08:00-13:00 h or 14:00-
19:00 h, costs 15.-Rs. Visits far off villages including Achalgarh
and Guru Shikhar, a good idea. Be warned against private tour
operators with poor buses.
**Achalgarh:** 11 km, with a legendary **Shiva Temple,** considered the
most ancient on Mount Abu. Unlike most Shiva Temples, instead of
worshipping a lingam, the focal point is a hole in the ground
which was bored by Shiva with his big toe. This stabilized the

geological unrest in the mountain region. In fact, he bored so enthusiastically that the hole reaches all the way down to the center of the earth!

**Gaumukh Temple:** 8 km from town, the holy man, Vashistha, reportedly lived here. The four Rajput Clans were created from the Sacred Fire, which he lit next to the water in Agnikund Basin. A marble Nandi (bull, Shiva's vehicle) stands beside a small stream flowing from the jaws of a marble cow (gaumukh = cow jaw).

**Guru Shikhar:** At 1722 m, the highest spot on Mount Abu, 15 km from town. A temple is dedicated to Swami Dattatreya, an incarnation of Vishnu. Dattatreya's footprints have left an eternal mark in the form of caves. During the dry season, you've a great view across the flatlands to the distant forests beyond.

**TIPS**
**Tourist Information Centre:** Across from the bus stand, tel.51.
**GPO:** Raj Bhavan Road, downtown.
**Mount Abu, The City of the Sunset:** An informational brochure, available everywhere, 3.-Rs.
**Summer Festival:** Each year, 1-3 June, lots of folklore events.

# GUJARAT

The State of Gujarat, with an area
of 195,984 km², is bordered by Pakistan and Rajasthan in the north,
Madhya Pradesh in the east, with
Maharasthra and Arabian Sea to the
south and west. The coastline
covers 1290 km, its length increased
by the deep cuts of the Gulf of
Khambhat and the Gulf of Kutch.
Adjoining is the swamp region,
Little Rann of Kutch. Together with
the Great Rann of Kutch, stretching
along the Pakistani border, they
occupy a quarter of the area. Other
regions in the north belong to the
Thar Desert.

Gujarat has enjoyed a lively
history, with roots looking back
4000 years to the Harappan culture
in the Indus Valley. Until 1961, the regions of Daman and Diu
belonged to Portugal.

Gujarat's 34 million people speak Gujarati, Marathi and Hindi. The capital is Gandhinagar, 25 km from Ahmedabad. Like
Chandigarh, it was designed by the French architect Corbusier in
a chessboard pattern.

Gandhinagar was named for Mahatma Gandhi, who was born in
Gujarat, and later led the struggle for independence from an
ashram in Ahmedabad. Ahmedabad is an important textile center.

A large part of the population is Muslim. And Gujarat is also
a Jain stronghold. Palitana, a Jain temple town, is the major
tourist attraction in Gujarat. Also worth a visit is Junagadh,
which, after Independence, voted to join the Indian Union.

Gujarat was never part of the British Empire. After Independence its duchies were added to the then state of Bombay. In
1960, this was divided into the two present states of Maharasthra
and Gujarat.

GUJARAT

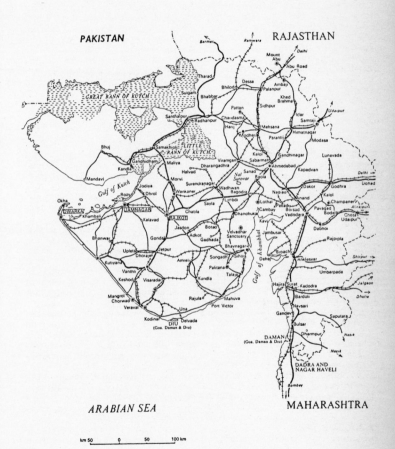

PAKISTAN

RAJASTHAN

*GREAT RANN OF KUTCH*

*Gulf of Kutch*

ARABIAN SEA

MAHARASHTRA

km 50    0    50    100 km

# Ahmedabad

The town used to be one of the prettiest in India, but that must have been shortly after its founding in the 15th century. Today this is a dirty industrial city with little to offer which couldn't be seen elsewhere in India, beyond cotton and the Harijan (Gandhi) Ashram. With 2.6 million inhabitants, Ahmedabad is the metropolis of the Jain and Muslim state, Gujarat. The administrative center, Gandhinagar, 30 minutes by bus to the north, like Chandigarh, was designed by Corbusier.

## COMING - GOING

**By Air:** The Indian Airlines Office, tel.391336, is in the city near Nehru Bridge. Several flights daily to Bombay (385.-), Delhi (653.-). One flight via Jodhpur and Jaipur. Three flights weekly via Bangalore (1075.-) to Madras (1170.-). The airport is 10 km north-east of town.

**By Rail:** A railway junction via which almost all trains from Rajasthan and Gujarat to Bombay run. The railway station, overland bus stand, and city bus stand are grouped within 1 km.

Very fast connections on the wide-gauge rail line to Bombay, seven times daily, 9-15 h, costs 45.-Rs. To Rajasthan, you've several very slow trains, mostly to Udaipur and Abu Road.

There is one train to most major towns in southwestern Gujarat: Palitana, Veraval (Somnath), and Junagadh; aboard the 45/46 Ghandigram Express, which carries cars with side destinations. The 46 Down departs Ahmedabad (22:50 h), Sihor (Palitana, 05:58 h), Bhavnagar (07:00 h), or Junagadh (08:00 h), or Veraval (10:00 h). The 45 Up returns Veraval (17:10 h), Junagadh (19:10 h), Bhavnagar (23:00 h), Sihor (23:00 h), Ahmedabad (06:05 h).

The alternative is Ahmedabad (21:45 h), Junagadh (10:06 h), Veraval (12:50 h). Or departing Veraval (14:10 h), Junagadh (16:37 h), Ahmedabad (05:30 h) on the 24/23 Somnath Mail.

The Reservations Desk is open 08:00-13:00 h and 13:30-16:30 h. The Tourist Quota is administered by the Station Superintendent, opens at 10:00 h.

**By Bus:** At least to Rajasthan, buses are much faster than trains. See under your destination. Reservations 07:00-19:00 h for ordinary and from 09:00-12:00 and 13:30-21:00 h for luxury trains.

## A NIGHT'S REST

Generally difficult to find. Try on the two roads across from the railway station, Relief Road and Gandhi Road, and walk from one flop house to the next. As you can tell, we don't really like Ahmedabad. Perhaps because it breaks the fairytale vision of India we bring with us from Rajasthan.

The Tourist Office by the railway station,  open 06:30–09:30 h
and 19:00–22:00 h,  will help you find a room. Have them make
the reservations for you.
By Gandhi Ashram is a **Tourist Bungalow, (D)**60.-.

## REFRESHMENT
Excellent thali (hmmm, I'm hungry), in **Payall Hotel (AC)**, in the
Purohit Hotel Building on Gandhi Road,  300 m beyond the large
gate on the left.  You can eat good and cheap in the **Railway
Station Restaurant**,  upstairs.  On Relief Road,  try **Kwality** or
**Chetna Restaurant**.

## SHOPPING
Ahmedabad is an excellent spot to pick up any kind of cotton
products, even for export, cheap.
**Cotton Bazar:**  Between Relief Road and Gandhi Road.  There are
lots of shops where you can pick up a shirt for 15.-Rs to 20.-Rs.
And there is a rich selection of local handicrafts.
**Packet Post Office:** Near Cotton Bazar.

## SIGHTS
**Harijan Ashram:**  In the northwestern district,  Sabarmati,  buses
from the railway station or Lal Darwaja bus terminus.  This is
where Mahatma Gandhi lived while he led the non-violent resistance against British occupation.  Of interest is his home,  which
has been converted into a **Museum**, including an extensive
**Library**,  **Picture Gallery**, and a pictorial depiction of the life of
the pacifist,  philosopher,  and statesman. A small bookshop sells
handmade paper.  See the **Slide Show** in English,  Sun, Mon, Wed,
and Fri at 20:15 h.
**Shaking Minarets:** Near the railway station, the two thin minarets
are worth the climb (1.-Rs).  It is considered great fun,  when
you are sitting at the top, if someone starts shaking the tower...
**Calico Museum:**  Calico Hill,  near Jamalpur Gate,  a tremendous
collection of old textiles,  open April to June 08:30–10:30 h,  July
to March 11:00–12:00 h, and 15:00–17:00 h, free admission.
**City Tour:**  Run by the Ahmedabad Municipal Transport Service at
08:00 h and 14:00 h from Lal Darwaja bus terminus,  takes 3 h,
costs 12.-Rs,  but not worth it.  Better just go on your own to
Gandhi Ashram and spend some time there.
**Lothal:**  80 km from town,  buses bring you to the excavation site
of a 4500–year–old trading and harbor town,  of the Harappan
culture.

## TIPS
**Tourist Office**
   **Ahmedabad Tourist Association:**  Municipal Corp.,  Sardar Patel
Bhawan, south of Gandhi road, tel.365611.
   **Information Window:**  In the railway station (just mornings and
evenings), and at the airport.

**Tourist Information Bureau:** Tourist Corp. of Gujarat Ltd., H.K.
House, Ground Floor, behind Jivabhai Chambers, Ashram Road,
tel.449683.
**City Center:** GPO, State Bank Of India, restaurants, icecream
parlours, bus stand, hotels, bazar, shops...
**Tribal Research & Training Institute Museum:** Ashram Road, open
16:30-17:30 h, closed Sundays and holidays, for people interested
in ethnology and Indian studies.
**Auto–Rickshaws:** In Ahmedabad they have a
separate kilometer counter which has to be
reset before each ride. The driver carries a
table of calculations to determine the fare.

# Palitana

Everyone comes to see the sacred Jain temple
town, located nearby on **Shetrunji Hill**. To the
temples, get a tonga (5.-Rs) to the foot of the
hill. Then follow the stairs, 3309 steps as I

*Shaking Minaretts*

count them. But the exercise (we needed 90 minutes to climb 600 m in altitude) is worth the reward: a unique complex of 863 temples. Many are open and can be visited without special permission. Occasionally we were asked to show our photo permit, available from the manager of the Tourist Bungalow without formality.

## COMING - GOING
Trains from Sihor (see Ahmedabad), then change to Palitana (1 h, 3.-Rs). Hourly buses to Sihor and Bhavnagar.

## A NIGHT'S REST
**Tourist Bungalow Hotel Sumeru Toran,** Station Road, tel.227, en route from the railway station (400 m) toward town, 100 m before the bus stand, **(S)**40.-, **(D)**60.-, **(Dm)**10.-, restaurant. **Readyman Guest House.**

## BHAVNAGAR
Not an absolute must see. But it could be planned as a day trip or stopover.
**Takteshwar Temple:** You've a lovely view of town.
**Gandhi Smirti:** A Gandhi memorial with an extensive photo documentation about his life. This is where the future Mahatma went to college.
You can eat in Apollo Hotel across from the bus stand, **(AC)**, good, but not cheap.

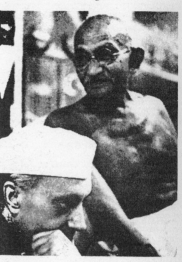

Gandhi at his Alma Matre

# Diu

At the southern tip of Gujarat is the island Diu, which belongs to the Union Territory Goa, Daman, and Diu, and is administered from Panaji, Goa. Today this is a peaceful, somewhat forgotten spot, with some lovely beaches in the west by Nagoa. The island has 31,000 inhabitants.

Of interest in the town of Diu is the old Portuguese Fort, dating from 1547, and two churches, one of which lies in ruins since a bombardment by the Indian Airforce in 1961 in the fight to end Portuguese colonial rule.

The district serves as an alcoholic paradise for "dry" Gujarat, as it awaits discovery by western tourism. The best travel
season is October to March. After November, the mosquitoes are
gone, and evenings are pleasantly cool.

## COMING – GOING
**By Bus:**  Direct buses to Veraval (10.-Rs) and Bombay (125.-)
via Baroda and Daman. But surprisingly, there are no direct
connections to Ahmedabad or Palitana. From Palitana, it is a
struggle by bus via Talaja, Mahuva, Port Voctor, Una &
Ghoghla, where you get a ferry, rarely possible in just one
day. It is much simpler to head first to Veraval / Somnath,
and from there on by bus.
At the state border between Gujarat and Diu, your passport
will usually be checked. Within Diu, a few private bus companies connect the town of Diu and Nagoa. In Diu you can rent
a bicycle for 5.-Rs per day.

## A NIGHT'S REST
In the town of Diu: **Apana Guesthouse,** large roof terrace,
**(S)**25.-, **(D)**35.- no bath, **(D)**50.- with bath, 70.- with a bal-
cony, reasonable restaurant. **Nilesh Guest House,** Dr. Kelekar
Road, near the Bank of India, **(D)**20.- no bath, **(D)**30 with
bath. **PWD Rest House,** by the Fort, tel.63, **(S)**10.-, **(D)**15.-.
In Nagoa by the beach: **Gangasagar Guest House cum Restaur-
ant,** **(S)**10.-, **(D)**20.-, **(Tr)**30.-, all with common showers.
Palm-leaf huts 500 m from the beach rent for 50.-Rs per month.
The walls are partly of clay.

## TIPS
**Tourist Office:**  Near the bazar and the ferry on the road to
Nagoa.
**Post Office:** Right by the bazar.
**Goa Travels:** By the bazar, sells bus tickets to Bombay.
**State Bank of Saurashtra:** Cashes traveller's checks.

# Veraval & Somnath

Veraval is a fishing port of little interest to tourists. Travellers
are here to visit Somnath, 5 km to the east, accessible by bus,
scooter, or foot.
**Shiva Temple:** Somnath's pride is right by the sea. The present
structure, built in 1950, replaces a legendary, thousand-year-old
temple, which was destroyed by Aurangzeb in 1706 AD. Unfortunately, little of this legend remains to be seen, even if this is
one of the twelve most important Shiva Shrines.
**Archaeological Museum:** Remains of the ancient temple are on display. Admission is 0.20 Rs, open daily, except Wednesdays,
09:00-12:00 h and 15:00-18:00 h.
**Beaches:** Very stony, and / or public toilets; definitely not where

you want to swim!

**Sasan Gir** (Gir Forest): This National Park is 55 km north of Veraval amd 60 km south of Junagadh. Within its 1400 km$^2$ grounds live the last 200 free-roaming lions in Asia. The best time to visit is November to early June, particularly toward the end of the dry season. The park is closed during monsoon season. For the jeep ride to the park, calculate 20.-Rs to 50.-Rs, depending on the number of passengers and travel time. If you want to learn more about the park, pick up the brochure **Gir, Last Home of the Asiatic Lion** at the Forest Department.

## COMING - GOING

For rail connections, see Ahmedabad. Direct buses to Diu (10.-Rs) and Porbandar, Gandhi's birthplace. Between Veraval and Somnath get a bus (1.-Rs) or scooter (10.-Rs).

One interesting form of transport are the **Dhow**, two-masted ships with trapezoid sails, built here, as by the ancient Arabs, without blueprints. They serve as trading ships on coastal routes to Arabia and Africa.

## A NIGHT'S REST

In Veraval: **Tourist Bungalow, (D)**40.-, by the lighthouse, 3 km from the railway station, west of town. **Satkar Hotel, (S)**25.-,

**(D)**30.-,   **(Dm)**15.-Rs,   and more expensive,   by the bus stand,
restaurant.

# Junagadh

Junagadh is one of the few regions which joined the Indian Union
a while after Independence.   The Muslim Nawab (ruler) wanted to
integrate his little realm into Pakistan,   but when a vote was
taken,   the Hindu majority elected to join India.   The last Nawab
of Junagadh thereupon fled to Pakistan where he lives in exile.
     The main attractions are an ancient Uparkot Fort and the
Girnar Hill temples. The present population is 100,000.

## COMING - GOING
   Rail connections,   see Ahmedabad.   Hourly buses to Veraval
   (10.-Rs). Daily buses via Rajkot to Ahmedabad.

## A NIGHT'S REST
**Vaibhav Hotel**,   **(D)**80.-,   near the bus stand.   **Sharada Lodge**,
**(S)**10.-,   **(D)**20.-,   **(Dm)**5.-,   near the railway station. **Relief Hotel**,
**(D)**30.-,   40.-Rs,   downtown. Other hotels and guesthouses are on
Kaval Chowk,   a good km from the bus stand or 2 km from the
railway station.   **RRR** in the railway station.   Good food in
**Annapurna Hotel** on Kalva Chowk,   in **Relief Hotel**,   or **Vaibhav
Hotel**.

## SIGHTS
**Maqbara Mausoleums:**   Here rest the Nawabs,   the last rulers of
Junagadh.
**Uparkot Fort:**   Ancient,   with an eventful history.   In addition to
the mighty walls,   you can see a huge cannon, a mosque, and two
cisterns. A Buddhist cave temple dates from the 4th century AD.
**Sakarbaug Zoo:** Admission 0.50 Rs, have a look at the Asian lion.
The small **Museum** on the Zoo grounds (nominal admission) is
nothing special. English-speaking guides are available.
**Durbar Hall Museum:**   Possessions of the former Nawabs are on
exhibit.
**Girnar Hill:**   A sacred site for Jains (others include Mount Abu
and Palitana) and for Hindus.   The stairs up begin 6 km from
town,   or take a scooter (7.-Rs).   The path up to the temples
contains 3800 steps,   a 2 h climb.   The temple complex,   dating
from the 12th century is open to the public,   cameras prohibited.
Notice the lovely mosaics on the roofs and domes.   The marble
floors and sculpture are pretty.   There are other temple districts
on Girnar Hill.
**Ashoka Edicts:**   En route to Girnar Hill is a boulder on which
edicts by Emperor Ashoka and later rulers are inscribed.   Unfortunately the stone is walled in by an unattractive building.
**Tourist Office:**   On Diwan Chowk,   provides maps and other
information.

# BOMBAY

Bombay (Mumbai since 1981) is India's most western city, providing
an interesting contrast: English
colonial buildings, and modern Indian skyscrapers; temples, churches, mosques, endless slums, a tremendous business district; begging
artistic troupes, and western movies. Bombay is the real capital of
India, and with a population of 8.5
million, the second-largest city (after Calcutta).

Bombay is the state capital of
Maharasthra. Handling 50 % of India's freight, the 8 km$^2$ harbor
with a 10 m draught makes Bombay
the busiest port on the subcontinent. For more than a century,
cotton trade and textiles have dominated the economy.

Bombay experienced two centuries of Islamic Gujarat rule before being occupied by the Portuguese in 1534. As part of her
dowry, Princess Catherine of Portugal gave the city to the
English king, Charles II. The city was shortly thereafter leased
to the British East India Company for an annual fee of 10 English pounds. From 1708 to 1773, the city served as the company's
administrative seat. Bombay later became the most important port
for trade to England. After railway construction provided access
through out the subcontinent (in 1853), the city gained the dominant position it enjoys today.

In 1862 a tremendous land reclamation project saw completion.
Seven swampland islands were combined into one great island.
The island is connected by several bridges to the mainland. In
the low-lying northern region, salt is produced by evaporation of
salt water. Further south, population levels increase drastically.
First are the districts housing various Indian ethnic groups.
Even further south are the Fort, business and banking districts,
where strong European influence is reflected by large numbers of
foreign residents. The highrise buildings on Narimam Point could
easily be found in any European city. The best known cheap
hotel district is inside the Fort, near the Gateway of India, in
Colaba District, just south of the former Fort.

GREATER BOMBAY

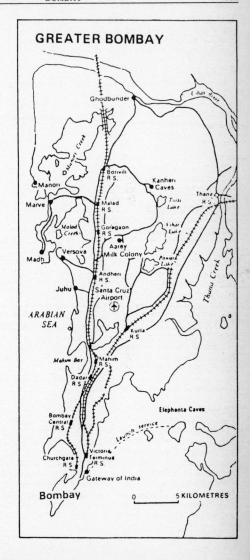

**INTERNATIONAL ARRIVALS**
Many of you will experience Bombay as your first Indian city,
via a cheap flight. Political uncertainty has made the air route
more popular than the overland route.

### Airports
**Sahar International Terminal** (2): Connected with the city via
the relatively expensive EATS buses, takes an hour, costs
25.-Rs to the Air India office at Nariman Point, 1 km from Taj
Mahal Intercontinental, near Gateway of India and the cheap
hotel district. There is a Tourist Office Information Booth in
the Taj Mahal. A taxi into town costs 90.-Rs. The return trip
to the airport on the meter runs at just 60.-Rs.
**Santa Cruz Terminal** (1): Even further from town, used exclusively for domestic flights. You've connections between the two
terminals by taxi or by EATS bus (5.-Rs) which stops en route
to or from town.

The cheapest way into town from Santa Cruz is to get the red
local Bus 321 for 1.50 Rs to Vile Parle Railway Station, takes 20
minutes. From Track 2, there is a local bus every 15 minutes to
Churchgate (3.-Rs, 35 minutes). The bus stop is diagonally to the
left of Santa Cruz Terminal, 200 m from the arrival entrance.
    Or get red city Bus 338 for 1.-Rs (scooter for 8.-Rs) to An-
dhari Railway Station, where you've four local trains hourly to
Bombay-Central (3.-Rs), and on to Churchgate (3.50 Rs), takes
an hour and a half in all.
    Or get a city bus to Sion Station, and change buses to Elec-
tric House or Colaba Bus Station, near the cheap hotel district
(see map). From Sion, you can get a local bus via Dadar to
Victoria Terminus Railway Station.
    The Federation of Hotels & Restaurants of India has an Infor-
mation Booth at Sahar Terminal (Bombay Airport), open round the
clock, helpful with hotel bookings.
    In both terminals, Tourist Information, Post Offices, and other
services are open round the clock.

### Railway Stations
**Bombay Central**: Connected by city buses 70 and 124 (1.-Rs) to
Colaba (cheap hotel district). Your train ticket is valid for
continuing on by local train to Churchgate!
**Victoria Terminus**: Buses 1, 3, 4, 6 Ltd., 9, 45, 65, 69, 101,
103, and 124 take you to Colaba / Electric House.
**Dadar Railway Station**: The last stop for several trains from
the south, east, and north. Continue on by local train to
**Churchgate Terminus**: Your long-distance ticket is still valid,
Government of India Tourist Office; get city Buses 45, 132, or
133 to Colaba / Electric House.

## Wharfs
Upon arrival at **New Ferry Wharf**, i.e. with the steamer from Goa, get Buses 42 or 48 to the railway stations or cheap hotel district, costs 1.50 Rs. Bus 42 also passes Mahatma Phule Market and Sandhurst Road Station (local trains to Victoria Station). Or get Bus 41 to Central Railways Goods Depot and then Bus 43 to Colaba.

## Bus Stands
The state-run buses usually arrive at the bus stand by Bombay Central Railway Station. For local bus connections from there, see Railway Stations.

Private buses generally put in near the GPO and Victoria Terminus; for local buses see Railway Stations.

MTDC buses arrive at the Maharasthra Tourist Office next to Air India on Madame Cama Road, 1 km from the cheap hotel district, get buses 45, 132, or 133; taxis cost 5.-Rs to Colaba.

The Lunch Wallahs by Churchgate Station at noon. These men collect cooked lunches from the homes of office workers and deliver them to the workers in their offices in town. Although most of the lunch wallahs are illiterate, they manage to deliver the correct lunch to the correct office.

BOMBAY

1  Government of Hary-
   ana Tourist Office,
   Air India, Indian
   Airlines, Airport Bus
   Departures
3  MTDC, Bus Tours de-
   part here
4  National Centre for
   Performing Arts
5  Quantas Airlines
7  Air Lanka
8  Garuda, KLM
10 Bangladesh Biman
11 Aeroflot
13 Income Tax Office
14 American      Cultural
   Office
16 Rajasthan      Tourist
   Office
17 Amexco Travel Agen-
   cy,    Clients' Mail,
   Thomas Cook.
18 Space Travels
19 Fernandez       Guest
   House
21 YWCA   International
   Guest House
22 Salvation Army

BOMBAY

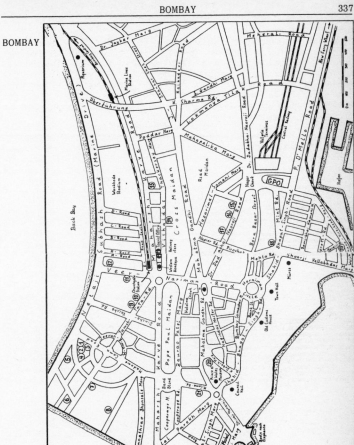

INDIA

## COMING - GOING

As the administrative and business center of India, Bombay is well connected to the rest of India. For connections see listings under the and regions and towns you plan to visit. Information and bookings are astoundingly simple.

During the monsoon months, May and June, many Indians take their holidays, crowding every means of transport. You are then advised to use secondary routes, e.g. to Goa via Poona, Sholapur, Bigapur, Badami, and Hubli.

**By Air:** For domestic flights consult Indian Airlines, Air India Building, Nariman Point 20, Bombay 400021, tel.2048382-84 (24 hours), at the airport tel.536363. On the main routes, supplementary flights are provided by Air India, which you can also book through Indian Airlines. Sample prices (in Indian Rupees):

Ahmedabad (385.-), Bangalore (730.-), Calcutta (1290.-), Cochin (881.-), Delhi (946.-), Goa (375.-), Hyderabad (600.-), Jaipur (800.-), Jodhpur (705.-), Madras (900.-), Mangalore (625.-), Poona (150.-), Trivandrum (1020.-), Udaipur (580.-Rs). Numerous other towns are served daily or several times weekly.

International flights to Europe run at least 3650.-Rs one way. Air India, Air India Building, Nariman Point, Bombay 400021, tel.2024142, and in Taj Mahal Hotel. Air Lanka, Mittal Towers, C-Wing, Ground Floor, Nariman Point, Bombay 400021, tel.223299, official price to Colombo 1530.-Rs, or US$168.-. Aeroflot, 87 Stadium House, Veer Nariman Road, tel.221743. Bangladesh Biman, Airlines Hotel Building, 199 J.Tata Road, Bombay 400020, tel.221339, flights to Dacca 1400.-Rs or US$158.-. Czechoslovakia Airlines, 308/309 Raheja Chambers, 213 Nariman Point, tel.220736. Egypt Air, Near Ritz Hotel, Churchgate, 7 J.Tata Road, Bombay 400020, tel.221415. Lufthansa, Express Towers, Nariman Point, Bombay 400021, tel.2023430. Pakistan International (PIA), Hotel Oberoi Towers, Nariman Point, Bombay 400021, tel.2021372, airport tel.535491, flights to Karachi 930.-Rs or US$102.-. LOT Polish Airlines, Maker Arcade, Shop No.6, Cuffe Parade, tel.211440. Singapore Airlines, Air India Building, Nariman Point, Bombay 400021, tel.2023365. Syrian Arab Air, 307 Ritz Hotel, Churchgate, Veer Nariman Road, tel.226043. Thai International, World Trade Centre, Cuffe Parade, Bombay 400038, tel.219191.

**By Rail:** Central Railway runs trains to the south and east, plus to nearby stations in the north: Victoria Terminus (Bombay V.T.), reservations 08:00-13:00 h, 14:00-20:00 h. The Railway Tourist Guide administers the Tourist Quota, where you can often get a reservation or sleeper after everything is booked out, tel.264321.

Western Railway has trains to the north and north-west: 2nd class reservations in Bombay Central Station, 08:00-13:00 h, 13:30-16:00 h, tel.375986. 1st class reservations in Churchgate

Station, 08:00-13:45 h, 14:45-20:00 h, tel.291952. The Tourist
Quota for Western Railway is distributed in Churchgate Station.
Some trains depart from Dadar Station in northern Bombay.
**By Bus:** State Transport Terminal, across from Bombay Central
Station is open 08:00-23:00 h, bookings up to seven days in
advance, tel.374272.

Buses to Ganeshpuri daily at 19:00 h, plus Sun 07:00 h.

Private buses can be booked near the GPO and Victoria Terminus Station. Depart and arrive at State Transport Terminal.

Direct buses to Mangalore, Panaji, and Margao, Goa; Bangalore, Hyderabad, Poona, Aurangabad, Surat...

**By Ship:** For the ferry to Goa, New Ferry Wharf is accessible
by local train (1.-Rs) from Victoria Terminus to Sandhurst Road
Station, then get Bus 42 to Ferry Wharf. Or get Bus 42 from
Bombay Central Station. From Mahatma Phule Market (get there
with Buses 1, 3, or 4), you can get Bus 41 to the harbor.
Bus 43 runs from Colaba to Central Railways Goods Depot; then
change to Bus 41 or 42 to New Ferry Wharf. A taxi from the
Fort to New Ferry Wharf costs 25.-Rs.

Book Deck-class reservations six days in advance, 10:00-
13:30 h, 14:00-15:00 h, closed Mondays, tel.864071. The main
office of Mogul Line Ltd. is at 16, Bank Street, Bombay 400023,
tel.256835. Sample prices: Owner's Cabin 300.-, De Luxe A
260.-, De Luxe B 235.-, First Class 220.-, Upper Deck 75.-,
Lower Deck 50.-. Departs daily, except Tuesday, at 10:00 h,
crowded Wednesdays. The ferry doesn't run during monsoon
season from early June to early October.

Ferry bookings (same price) also by Maharasthra Tourism
Development Corporation, Madame Cama Road, tel.2026713,
10:00-12:00 h, 14:00-15:00 h, see Goa. Other connections by
ship are listed in **Daily Shipping Times.**

There is a monthly ship connection to Karachi, Pakistan, costs
700.-, takes two days.

**Getting Around:** Bombay is known for its hair-raising rush
hours (if there is even any room for that). Try to avoid the
crunch, or at least enjoy the show from the top of a
double-decker bus.

**City Buses:** Good, cheap, and only crowded at rush hour.
The buses are run by Bombay Electric Supply and Transport
(BEST), for info tel.446521. Schedules are displayed at the
major stops, and available in shops and stands. You might
also pick up a copy of **Latest Bombay Guide** (2.-Rs), or a
BEST busline brochure (1.-Rs). **Ltd.** = Limited Stops: faster,
more expensive, stops less frequently. For 2.-Rs you can
take a tour through Bombay City on Buses 132 or 133, no
transfer necessary, a great way to gain a first impression.

**Local Trains:** Cheap and fast to the northern suburbs from
Churchgate, Bombay Central or Victoria Terminus, to Dadar.

**Taxi:** Very expensive in Bombay. Whatever the meter says is multiplied by an ever-changing rate. Drivers also have a calculation chart. Downtown there aren't any scooters or rickshaws.

## Travel Agencies
**Students Travel Information Centre**, Hotel Bombay International, 29 Marine Drive, Bombay 400020, tel.233404.
**Space Travel**, Nanabhay Mansion, 4th Floor, Sir P.M. Road, Bombay 400001, tel.255652, other branches in Calangute and Anjuna Beach, Goa.

## A NIGHT'S REST
Those of you experiencing Bombay as your first Indian city, be advised, you are starting with the worst lodgings India has to offer. Reasonably priced isn't even whispered here, and cheap implies loud, filthy, unfriendly or dangerous. After 10:00 h you've no chance of finding a place without a tout!

Most cheap hotels are near Mereweather Road behind the Taj Mahal Intercontinental Hotel, near the Gateway of India and the Electric House bus stand in Colaba: **Red Shield Hotel**, Salvation Army, tel.241824, 30 Mereweather Road, Bombay 400039, the hottest tip in Bombay, but always full, **(Dm)**40.- includes three meals a day(!), **(D)**100.- (three meals too), queue up well before check-in starts at 09:00 h!. **Rex** and **Stiffles** in the same building on Ormiston Road, **(D)**80.- (filthy), **(AC)**160.-, full of Arabs here to see what rain looks like, worth a try. **Carlton**, 12 Mereweather Road, **(D)**90.-, breakfast, so-so. **India Guest House** 1-49 Kamal Mansion, Arthur Bunder Road (way at the southern end of Mereweather Road), **(S)**30.-, **(D)**60.-, **(Eb)**30.-, best on the fourth floor, but more expensive. **Sea Shore Hotel**, 1-49 Kamal Mansion, Arthur Bunder Road (same building as India Guest House) good **(D)**90.-. **Cowie's Guest House**, diagonally across on Walton Road between Arthur Bunder Road and Salvation Army, **(S)**100.-, **(D)**200.-. **Oliver Guest House**, same building, **(Dm)**30.-. **Strand Hotel**, P.J. Ramchandani Marg (Strand Road), **(S)**100.-, **(D)**150.-. **Kerawella Chambers Guest House**, same building, **(D)**80.-. **Whalley's Guest House**, Mereweather Road, **(Dm)**20.-, **(S)**50.-, **(D)**100.-. **Take Off Travels**, Mereweather Road at Mandlik Road, **(D)**80.-. **YMCA International Guesthouse**, 18 Madame Cama Road, Bombay 400039, tel.2020445, **(Dm)**30.- (four bed), **(S)**71.-, **(D)**139.-, plus 10 % service and 10.-Rs membership fee. **YMCA Central Branch**, 12 Nathala Parekh Marg (formerly Wodehouse Road), tel.2020079, cheap but just men. **Hotel Prosser's Boarding House**, 2-4 Henry Road, near Red Shield Hotel, 30 PJ, Ramchandani Marg, tel.240229, **(S)**90.-, 105.-, **(D)**120.-, 135.- (without **AC**), almost twice the price with **(AC)**, breakfast, plus 5 % service. **Bentley's Hotel**, 17 Oliver Street (near Garden Road), tel.241733, without **AC (S)**75.-, **(D)**120.-, 130.-, 50.-Rs more with **(AC)**, **(Eb)**45.-, plus tax.

COLABA

1  Salvation Army Red Shield Hostel
2  Rex, Stiffles, Diplomat
3  Carlton
4  Cowies's Guest House
5  Oliver Guest House
6  Strand Hotel & Kerawella Chambers
7  Hotel Prosser's Boarding House
8  Whalley's Guest House
9  Bentley's Hotel
10 Apollo
R  Restaurants & Fruit Juice

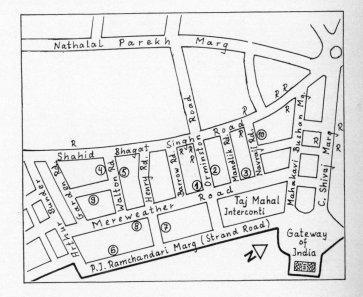

On Shahid Bhagat Singh Road is a number of hotels: **Royal Guest House**, 5 Shahid Bhagat Singh Road, 1st floor, **(D)**80.-. **Apollo**, Shahid Bhagat Singh Road, across from Colaba Police Station. **Hotel Volga**, in Causeway House, 3rd floor, 33 Shahid Bhagat Singh Road, tel.2026320, **(Dm)**30.-, **(S)**40.-, **(D)**60.-.

In Colaba there are also higher-priced hotels. In the medium category try **Hotel Godwin**, Garden Road, **(S)**250.-, **(D)**300.-. **Hotel Garden**, Garden Road, **(S)**250.-, **(D)**300.-.

The best, and most expensive hotel is **Taj Mahal Intercontinental**, **(S)**700.-, **(D)**800.-, but don't book a room just to peek inside.

More accommodations in and around (south-east of) Victoria Terminus: **RRR Victoria Terminus**, tel.264503, **(Dm)**20.-. **Fernandez Guest House**, Balmer Lawrie Building, 3rd floor, Ballard Estate, tel.260554, **(S)**40.-, **(D)**70.-, with breakfast. **Narsimha Guest House**, near Victoria Terminal, tel.262972, **(S)**32.-, **(D)**85.-, restaurant. **Empire Hindu Hotel**, across from V.T., tel.262789, **(S)**33.-, **(D)**76.-, restaurant. **City Guest House**, across from V.T. main entrance, **(D)**95.-, showers.

Not far from Victoria Terminus on P.D. Mello Road are a number of cheap hotels: **Hotel Manora**, 245 P.D. Mello Road, tel.257509, **(S)**50.-, **(D)**80.-,100.- **(AC)(D)**150.-. **Hotel Rupam**, 239 P.D. Mello Road, tel. 267203, **(S)**70.-, **(D)**105.-, **(AC)(D)**150.-.

A third cheap hotel district is around Bombay Central Station: **RRR Bombay Central Station**, tel. 377292, **(Dm)**46.- (24 hours). **YMCA International Guest House**, 18 YMCA Road, (Club Back Road), tel. 8911191, **(S)**88.-, **(D)**190.-, 10 % extra with breakfast, 20.-Rs membership fee. **Solidarity House**, Seva Niketani, (Jesuits), Sir J.Jeejabhai, tel.372395, **(Dm)**15.-, 30.-. **Salvation Army**, Maulana Azad Road, **(Dm)**10.-, **(D)**25.-.

**Youth Hostels** are open to members during summer holidays: **Bhavan's College**, Versova Road, Bhavan's Camp, Andheri, tel.572192. **University Hostel**, L.A. Kidwai Road, tel.472425.

**Padar College Of Commerce Hostel**, 193 Sion-Koliwada Estate, tel.472414.

At Juhu Beach in the north of town you can find **(D)**100.-, ideal for air passenger stopovers! At the airport, ask for a reservation at the hotel information counter. Other cheap accommodations are also available out here.

Medium priced accommodations, particularly on Marine Drive (Netaji Subhah Road) and around Churchgate Station. Prices for doubles run 250.-Rs, without the rooms being worth it. But that is the norm in Bombay. Write us and let us know how you fared in The Great Bombay Cheap Hotel Hunt!

Paying Guest Accommodations are available in private households, though relatively expensive. For information and bookings contact the Government of India Tourist Office, 123 Maharshi Karve Road, Churchgate, tel.293144. The Tourist Office is also happy to help if you can't find accommodation on your own. They know the problem! Open Mon-Sat 08:30-17:30 h.

## REFRESHMENT

It's never a problem finding a good restaurant in Bombay. Just head for the hotel districts, Colaba, Marine Drive, around the railway stations, or the Gateway of India.

In Coloba: **Leopold Cafe & Store** is a hangout for Arabs, whores, and high-class beggars. **Olympic Coffee House** and **Cafe Apsara** are nearby. Also nearby are **Apollo Restaurant Laxmi Vilas** and **Cantene**, a juice centre next to the Durbar Hotel. Juice Center stops are always more expensive than planned; it tastes so good.

Right across from Electric House is **Dipti's Pure Drinks.** Cheaper than **Ananda Punjabi** is the vegetarian restaurant on Shahid Bhagat Marg, across from Electric House, very clean, excellent thalis (6.-Rs).

The side streets are generally cheaper than the main roads. You have an excellent selection between the Prince of Wales Museum and the Gateway of India. The **Sahakari Bandar Canteen** in the department store, across from Regal Cinema, offers good, cheap vegetarian food. **Delhi Durbar**, also near Regal Cinema, is good, northern Indian cooking.

**Reserve Restaurant**, Nanabhay Mansion, Sir P.M. Road is pleasant and cheap, most meals under 5.-Rs, thali 3.-Rs. **New Empire Restautant** boasts a garden, across from V.T. Station, next to Empire Cinema.

If you can afford it, try one of the five restaurants in Taj Mahal. You'll find Indian, continental, Chinese, and French cooking. For 40.-Rs, you can enjoy great Indian cooking.

On Marine Drive are several good, but expensive, restaurants, e.g. **Talk Of The Town**, famous for its seafood specialities.

## SHOPPING

Western consumer goods? If you want them, you can find them!
**Indian Musical Instruments**: Check Sardar V. Patel Road, north-

east of Chowpatty Beach and south-east of Bombay Central Station.

**Flea Market:** At the corner of Maulana Azad Road.

**Crawford Market:** For clothes, come to Naoroji Road at L.Tilak Road. But keep in mind, silk garments are cheaper in Madras.

**Film:** Developed by Kodak, tel.262604, on D.N. Road, between Victoria Terminal and Flora Fountain. The quality is good but you wait, generally two weeks. Within India you can have the film sent to you by mail, free of charge. Several other photo shops on the same street. We've had good experience with the developing, but were disappointed by the mailing.

**State Governments' Emporia:** Several states maintain handicraft shops here, offering good quality at fixed prices. A number of the shops are located on D.N. Road.

**Mahatma Pule Market:** Fresh fruit, vegetables, and fish are available in the bazar building (built in 1867) on D.N. Road.

**Bora Bazar:** A produce market, south of Victoria Station.

**Books:** Thacker Co. Ltd., on D.N. Road, offers the best selection in Bombay of both eastern and western literature. Also excellent is Nalanda Bookstore in the Taj Intercontinental Hotel, where you'll also find foreign magazines.

## ACTIVITIES

**Movies:** More movies are produced in Bombay than in any other city in the world. No wonder there are so many cinemas. Be sure to see a typical Indian box office hit, featuring: love, dance, tears, and violence. They are colorful, but loud, a taste as acquired as hot curry or sweet tea. But then, Indians can't stomach western cooking either...

Many cinemas run English-language films, e.g. Eros, by Churchgate Station, or Regal, south of Prince of Wales Museum, both downtown. For the latest schedule, check any newspaper; for film criticisms, give **Bombay Magazine** a glance.

**Swimming:** Chowpatty Beach is closed to bathers. Those few intrepid souls willing to risk a dip at Juhu Beach can get Bus 4 Ltd. or Bus 84 from Hutatma Chowk (Flora Fountain) or the local train from Churchgate to Santa Cruz; from here get Bus 182, 231, or 253 to Juhu Beach. But be warned: big-time pollution. We recommend a swimming pool.

Try **Mahatma Gandhi Memorial Swimming Pool**, Shivaji Park. Or as a temporary member in **Beach Candy Swimming Pool**, Bhulabhai Desai Road, by the sea, west of Central Station. Plus there's the **YMCA Swimming Pool**, Bombay Central, tel.230079.

## SIGHTS

**Gateway of India:** The wharf where passenger ships from Europe once put in. The 26 m high arch, built in Gujarat style, was dedicated at Christmas 1924, in honor of a 1911 visit by King George and Queen Mary. From here you can take a harbor tour, or get a boat out to Elephanta Island; see Around Bombay.

**Prince of Wales Museum:** Established in 1914, features Art, Archaeology, and Natural History departments. Open Tues-Sun 10:00-18:00 h, admission free.

**Jehangir Art Gallery:** Founded in 1952, on the museum grounds, occasional special exhibits, worth a visit. Here too is Somovar Snack Bar.

**Western Railway Headquarters, Churchgate Station,** and **Victoria Terminus:** Classic examples of imperial architecture. V.T. was built in 1888 in Italian-Gothic style.

**Municipal Corporation Building:** Another neo-Gothic structure nearby, completed in 1893, features an 84 m high tower.

**Marine Drive:** Still the local name for Bombay's promenade, even after post-colonial Indianization changed the name to Netaji Subhash Road. Here you'll find hotels, splendid apartments, cafes, restaurants...

**Taraporewalla Aquarium:** Also on Marine Drive, daily, except Mon, 11:00-20:00 h, costs 1.-Rs.

**Chowpatty Beach:** Closed to swimmers due to pollution, but it's still an evening showplace for activities ranging from sand castle building to artistic performances, and just making the scene. Lots of food stands offer Bhelpuri, a tasty local speciality.

**Mani Bhawan:** The house where Mahatma Gandhi lived from 1917 to 1934. This is where he organized his first newspaper. Today, as a Gandhi Museum, it features a photo exhibit and library. Open 09:30-18:00 h. On Labernam Road, left off Pandita Ramabai Street, coming from Chowpatty Beach.

**Malabar Hill:** Further north, offers a great view of Marine Drive, whose lighted lanterns are known as the Queen's Necklace.

**Raj Bhavan:** Also on the hill, former residence of the British Resident.

**Walkeshwar Temple:** On the other side of the headland, pilgrims have flocked here for a thousand years.

**Hanging Gardens:** Up on the hill, established in 1880, in a water reservoir, redesigned in 1921.

**Kamala Nehru Park:** A children's attraction, from where you have the best view of the Back Bay.

**The Towers of Silence:** The Parsee burial towers are nearby, though out of sight, closed to non-Parsees. There is a scale model in the Prince of Wales Museum.

**Mahalaxmi Temple:** On the other side of the hill, further down by the water, attracts thousands of pilgrims on special holidays; Laxmi is the Goddess of Luck & Wealth.

**Jaji Ali Dargah:** A Muslim tomb by the sea. Only at low tide can you cross the 300 m long connecting dam past hundreds of beggars. So be sure to visit one of the money-changing wallahs in advance to change a few rupees into paises - for a fee, of course.

Coming or going, get Bus 124, 132, or 133 from Electric House. Or get Bus 103 or 107 from Electric House to Walkeshwar. Buses 81, 83, 84, 85, 86, 87, 88, 89, 90 all run from Hutatma Chowk to Vatsalabai Desai Chowk.

346                          INDIA

Bus 101 runs from Prince of Wales Museum to Walkeshwar Temple. Get Bus 106 from Hutatma Chowk to Kamala Nehru Park.
**Sightseeing Tip:**    Hop aboard a double-decker bus heading north from downtown. Notice the contrast between the modern city center, and the older quarters, and slums, in the outskirts. It's particular fun during rush hour, when you can sit upstairs above the chaos: but don't be in a hurry.

Other second-class sights are noted in any Tourist Office brochure, and in tiny Bombay guides available at any bookstall. There you'll also find a bus map and other useful info.

## AROUND BOMBAY
Those of you, who, like Barbara, can't stand Bombay, are hardly likely to use it as a departure point for regional excursions. But if you're like Peter, and can't get enough of this contrast-rich city, or just get stuck, a few ideas.
**Elephanta Caves:**    Out in the Bay on Elephanta Island, accessible by boat from the Gateway of India. Actually there isn't much left to see after the Portuguese destruction. And if Ajanta or Ellora are on your itinerary, there's no need to come. The trip in an ordinary launch costs 15.-Rs, de luxe boats charge 25.-Rs, depart daily 08:30-13:30 h, 10 km, takes an hour. During monsoon season only de luxe boats go out, and then just mornings. Tickets are available at the Gateway of India in the stands on the left. Avoid the trip at weekends. Enjoy a nice walk and a good restaurant.
**Matheran:**    100 km or 2 h by rail toward Poona, get off at Neral. Here you change trains for a 2 h serpentine ride up 700 m in altitude to the resort. Up here you won't find any cars, just rickshaws, yet a road is under construction. The hiking trail up from Neral is 11 km. The Tourist Office by the station has lots of lodgings to suggest, but the best deal in town is Laxmi Hotel, by the Post Office, not far from the station. There is no train during monsoon season. Second-class tickets cost 20.-Rs. Instead of returning to Bombay, plan a stopover on the way to or from Poona.

The Tourist Offices in Bombay have lots of brochures enticing you to tour the countryside. But apart from **Basein Fort**, there is nothing special. Interesting side trips from Bombay include **Muktananda Ashram** (see Ganeshpuri) and the **Caves** at Karla and Bhaja (see local sections).

## TIPS
**Tourist Offices:**    Provide info on all parts of India. Offices are maintained by the central government and all the states individually.
   **Government of India Tourist Office:**    123 Maharshi Karve Road, Churchgate, Bombay 400020, tel.293144, Mon-Sat 08:30-17:30 h, till 12:30 h on holidays and the second Saturday each month. Next to the Delhi office, this is the largest selection of brochures in India, friendly, next to Churchgate Station.

**Government of India Tourist Counter:** Taj Intercontinental Hotel, tel.297755,   Mon–Sat 08:30–15:30 h,   as above,   excellent bookstore.
**Government of India Tourist Counters:**   In Sahar New International Passenger Terminal, tel.6325331,   and in Santa Cruz, Bombay Airport (domestic flights),   tel.6149200,   open round the clock.

**Hotel Information:**   At Sahar Airport Terminal,   run by the Federation of Hotels and Restaurants of India,  open round the clock, helpful with bookings.

**Maharasthra Tourism Development Corporation** (MTDC):  Madame Cama Road,  Bombay 400020 (Churchgate),  tel.2026713, books bus tours of Bombay and surrounding Maharasthra and the ferry to Goa.

**Government of Gujarat Tourist Office:**  Dhantaj Mahal, Chhattrapati Shivaji Maharaj Road, Bombay 400001, tel.2026866.

**Government of Goa,  Daman & Diu Tourist Counter:** Bombay Central Station, tel.396288, in the main hall.

**Government of Jammu & Kashmir Tourist Office:**  In the World Trade Centre, Cuffe Parade, tel.216249.

**Government of Uttar Pradesh Tourist Office:**  In the World Trade Centre, Cuffe Parade, tel.215497.

**Government of Himachal Pradesh Tourist Office:**  In the World Trade Centre, Cuffe Parade, tel.219191.

**Government of Madhya Pradesh Tourist Office:**  In the World Trade Centre, Cuffe Parade, tel.219299.

**Sikkim Centre:**  5th floor,  Air India Building,  Nariman Point, tel.233777.

**Haryana Tourist Office:**  Air India Building,  Nariman Point, tel.234239.

**Government of Rajasthan Tourist Office:**  230 D. Naoroji Road, tel.267162.

**The Times of India Information Service:**  Only by telephone, tel.268271.

**Brochures:**  Available free of charge in the Tourist Offices,  or cheap at the street stands and bookstores around the Fort.  Pick up **Latest Bombay Guide** (3.-Rs) and the white **BEST** brochure (1.-Rs) featuring a good bus map.

## Consulates

**Afghanistan:** 115 Walkeshwar Road.

**Indonesia:** Lincoln Annexe, 17 Altamount Road (S.K. Barodawala Marg), tel.368678.

**Iran:** Baldota Bhavan, M.Karve Road.

**The Philippines:** Industry House, Churchgate, tel.2026340.

**Sri Lanka:**  Trade Commission,  Sri Lanka House,  Homi Mody Street, tel.255861.

**Thailand:**  Krishnabad Building,  Bhulabhai Desai Road, across from Mafat Lal Park, tel.8226417.

**Austria:**  Taj Building,  3rd floor,  210 D. Naoroji Road, tel.262044.

**West Germany:** 10th floor, Hoechst House, 193 Backbay Reclamation, Nariman Point, tel.232422, just mornings.

**The Netherlands:** 16 M.Karve Road, tel.296840.

**Switzerland:** Manek Mahal, Veer Nariman Road (also Swiss Air), Bombay 400020, tel.293550.

**United Kingdom:** 2nd floor, Mercantile Bank Building, M. Gandhi Road, tel.259981.
**United States:** Lincoln House, Bhulabhai Desai Road, tel.363611.

**Visa Extensions:** In the **Foreigners' Regional Office**, Commissioner of Police, Dadabhai Naoroji Road, tel.268111, by Crawford Market (Mahatma Pule Market).

**Banks**
 **American Express:** Dr. Dadabhai Naoroji Road (D.N. Road), Clients' Mail Service Mon-Fri 11:00-13:00 h, 15:00-17:00 h, Saturdays just mornings, but it doesn't work well! Traveller's checks cashed 11:00-15:00 h. Another Amexco banking office is on D.N. Road, at Hutatma Chowk (Flora Fountain), both on the right coming from Victoria Terminus.
 **Black Market:** If you are up to the risk, look in front of Amexco at Flora Fountain, rates 25 % above official cash rates are offered.
 **State Bank of India:** Samachar Marg, from Flora Fountain, head down Nariman Road, east to Horniman Circle, then go right (south), tel.295765.
 **Money Exchange:** After 14:00 h in the Air India Building, (Pheroze Framroze & Co.); here too is Bank of America, tel.2021678.

**General Post Office** (GPO): By Victoria Terminus on Nagar Chowk at D.N. Road, Mon-Sat 08:00-20:00 h, Sun 10:00-17:00 h, holidays 10:30-17:30 h, packages are accepted next door on the right. You can have your package sewn, sealed, and addressed according to regulations in front of the Post Office. The Post Offices in the ticket halls at Sahar and Santa Cruz Airports are open round the clock.

**Central Telegraph Office:** Hutatma Chowk (Flora Fountain); the Overseas Communications Service is open round the clock.

**Automobile Club:** For info on road conditions, petrol prices, shipping vehicles, maps, etc., check with the Western India Automobile Association, Lalji Narainji Memorial Building, 76 Veer Nariman Road, tel.291085.

# MAHARASTHRA

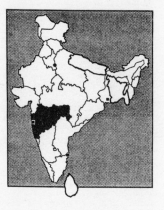

Maharasthra (population 63 million) covers an area of 307,762 km$^2$, running as a fertile coastal strip along the Arabian Sea. To the north are Gujarat and Madhya Pradesh. Andhra Pradesh is to the south-west, while Goa and Karnataka are to the south.

All along the coast, tremendous plantations of coconut trees hug the slopes of the West Ghats and their evergreen rain forest. Further east, the Deccan Highlands spread out with fields of wheat and cotton, plus forests of precious woods.

The southwest monsoon drops its water over the steep slopes of the West Ghats. The great expanses of the Deccan Highlands lie in the rain shadow, receiving little rain as the clouds are forced to dump their precipitation when crossing the mountains. But rivers flowing east, including the Krishna, Bhima, and Godavi, provide water for extensive irrigation for agriculture.

The principal language is Marathi, along with Gujarati and Hindi. The state capital is Bombay, where 8.5 million people make their homes, primarily in suburban slums. Bombay, also called "Gateway of India", is an important point of arrival for travellers to India. It is the most modern, but also the most expensive Indian city. Maharasthra is India's most industrialized state.

In the 3rd century AD, Maharasthra was part of the Maurya Empire. The artistic achievements of this period are still visible in lovely frescoes adorning the Ajanta Buddhist caves. After the fall of the Maurya Empire a succession of ruling dynasties followed. In the 13th century, Islamic rulers took command, until Chatrapati Shivaji unified the Marathas in the 17th century.

Besides Bombay, major tourist attractions include Aurangabad as a departure point to Ajanta and Ellory, the Lonavla and Karla Caves, and Poona.

MAHARASTHRA

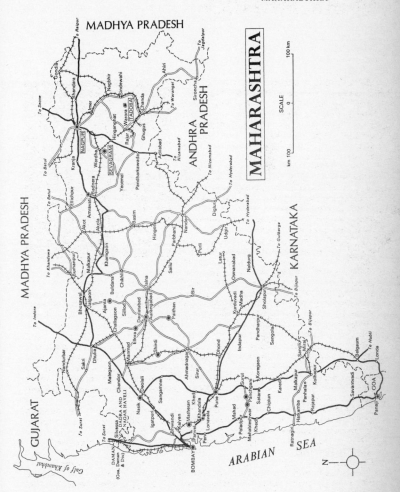

# Ganeshpuri

Ganeshpuri, 90 km north of Bombay, attracts visitors to the Vaj-
reshwari Hot Springs and Muktananda Ashram. En route you might
visit an ancient Portuguese fort, 5 km off Bassein Road.

## COMING - GOING

**By Rail:** From Bombay, get a local train from Churchgate or
Central Station for the hour-long, 90 km ride to Bassein (also
written Vassei). From there it's another 30 km by bus. From
Victoria Terminus, get the train to Thane, then 35 km by bus
to Ganeshpuri.

**By Bus:** Direct buses daily from Bombay Central Station at
19:00 h to Ganeshpuri, Sundays at 07:00 h.

From Ganeshpuri to Bombay, daily buses at 06:30 h and
11:15 h, plus Sundays at 16:00 h, costs 15.-Rs.

### The Ashram

Ganeshpuri is home to the loveliest and most splendid Ashram in
all of India. Swami Muktananda began teaching here in 1956. The
Ashram is reminiscent of a maharaja palace. The tremendous well-
kept garden features statues of the best-known indian deities and
wise men. Everyone is welcome, but it is best to register in
advance. The address: Gurudev Siddha Peeth, Ganeshpuri 401206,
Thane District, Maharasthra.

Before leaving his body in 1982, Swami Muktananda made a
number of trips abroad. The Ashram hosts more Europeans, Americans, and Australians than Indians. Besides the canteen, where
Indian food is served, a cafeteria offers western snacks, at western prices.

Anyone staying longer than three days has to perform at least
four hours of Guruseva (work) for the Ashram. The Ashram keeps
a very strict schedule, waking at 03:30 h and lights out at
21:15 h. Everyone is expected to join the temple singing.

Occasionally, classes are offered in Siddha Yoga, completed
with a test. A stay at the Ashram is relatively expensive, plan
at least 60.-Rs per day.

In the Ashram you'll see many statues of Nityananda, Muktananda's guru. From the Ashram you can take a walk to the
nearby village of Ganeshpuri where Nityananda lived. Gaze from
the road in front of the Ashram to the mountains toward Ganeshpuri; they form Nityanada's silhouette.

# Aurangabad

Located at 500 m altitude, about 400 km east-north-east of Bombay on the rail line between Manmad and Secunderabad (another
530 km). Aurangabad is best known as a departure point for
visits to the temple caves of Ajanta and Ellora. But this should
not detract from the town's own touristic attractions. After all,

Aurangabad is home to the Taj Mahal's little sister, smaller perhaps, but no less beautiful. So if you are only here to see the Ajanta and Ellora caves, be sure to not to miss Bibi ka Maqbara. By the way, the town gets its name from the Muslim ruler Aurangzeb.

## COMING - GOING
To Ajanta and Ellora, you have to go by road, see their sections and the map. The bus stand is 2 km from the railway station, scooters charge 3.-Rs.
**By Air:** The airport is 10 km east of town. Daily flights to Bombay (280.-), Delhi (806.-), Jaipur (650.-), Jodhpur (640.-), and Udaipur (522.-Rs). Three flights weekly to Nanded (150.-Rs) and Poona.
**By Rail:** From Bombay, 38.-Rs, takes 10 h, change trains in Manmad.
Travellers coming from the north can get a train to Jalgaon and Bhusawal, then head on by bus (stopping en route in Ajanta) to Aurangabad.
From Gujarat, you usually change in Surat; only one train daily to Jalgaon and Manmad, costs 48.- or 57.-Rs, takes 13 h. Coming from Rajasthan, change in Khandwa to Jalgaon.
The train is really only worthwhile coming from the southeast, i.e. in 12 h overnight, 45.-Rs from Hyderabad.
**By Bus:** Anyone coming from the north will generally get a bus via Ajanta, see Ajanta. But your best connections from Bombay or Poona are also by bus. The Maharasthra State Transport Luxury Coach from Bombay takes 10 h, costs 80.-Rs, ordinary coach just 55.-Rs. Bookings and departure at Bombay Central Station. There is a MTDC-AC bus from the Maharasthra Tourist Office, Madame Cama Road, Bombay to the Holiday Resort by the railway station in Aurangabad, costs 112.-Rs one way. The MTDC in Bombay also offers organized tours of Aurangabad, Ajanta, and Ellora; a 4-day ticket runs 465.-to 860.-Rs depending on accommodations.
**Around Town:** In town your best connection from the railway station or bus station to the tourist attractions is Bus 1. To Bibi-ka-Maqbara, get off at the town hall and walk 1 km across the river and to the right. On the same side, 1 km south of the Mausoleum is the 200-year-old Panchakki Water Mill. From there, cross the middle bridge back into the town center, where you can head on with Bus 1.

## A NIGHT'S REST
The best address in town is the **Youth Hostel**, Padampura at Station Road, tel.3801; conveniently located between the railway station to the south and the bus station to the north, costs **(Dm)**10.-Rs, 6.-Rs for members; taxi and rickshaw drivers won't like to bring you here because they don't get a commission (at your expense and without your knowledge), often claiming it is full; dinner costs 5.-Rs, camper parking 4.-Rs.

On the same street (Station Road), running from north to
south, **Kathiawad Hotel**, **(D)**25.-. **Tourist Home (D)**20.-, tel.4212,
both by the ITDC Tourist Office tel.4817. **Hotel Natraj (D)**35.-,
tel.4260. **Municipal Traveller's Bungalow (D)**30.-, tel.3356.
**Dwarka Hotel (D)**25.-, bath. **RRR** in the railway station
**(S)**15.-, **(D)**25.-, tel.4815.

Left around the corner (from the station on the left side of
the road heading off to the right) is **MTDC Holiday Resort**
(Holiday Camp), **(S)**35.-, 65.-Rs, MTDC Tourist Office.

Good food around the station, try in **Hotel Guru** or **New Punjab
Hotel**. Across from the railway station is a stand with lovely
fruit juice.

## SIGHTS
**Bibi-ka-Maqbara:** The main attraction, the mausoleum, modelled
on the Taj Mahal, is considered the prettiest example of moghul-
era architecture in the Deccan. Emperor Auranzeb had it built in
1679 in memory of his wife Rabia-ud-Daurani; admission 0.50 Rs.
**Panchakki:** A 17th-century water mill. The water, piped from a
mountain spring still had enough pressure to turn the wheel.
Adjoining the mill is the tomb of the Muslim holy man Baba Schah
Musafir, a whitewashed monument with an arched gateway and
onion towers, 0.50 Rs admission.
**Juna Bazar:** Lots of colourful tiny shops to browse through.
**Aurangabad Caves:** 3 km north of Bibi-ka-Maqbara, if you have
not had your fill of caves after Ajanta and Ellora. Of Buddhist
origin, work began in the 6th and 7th centuries. Caves number 3
and 7 are most interesting.

## AROUND ARANGABAD
**Daulatabad:** A mediaeval fortress, 13 km toward Ellora, whose
victory column is visible far and wide. It was built in 1187 AD
at the command of Bhilama Raja, a ruler in the Yadava dynasty.
It is considered the oldest intact fortress of the Hindu era. In
1308 AD, however, it was taken over by the Sultan of Delhi. In
1338 AD, Mohammed Tuglak declared it the capital of India, but
only for three years. The citadel is accessible via a drawbridge
and a dark stairway. From the top you've a lovely view of the
surrounding fortress and Deccan hills.
**Khuldabad:** A small village, notable as you drive through for its
old town wall, numerous mosques, and tombs, 26 km from Aurangabad on the road to Ellora. The main attraction is Aurangzeb's
tomb, quite modest, compared to that of his wife. More interesting
is a walk down the village street past mediaeval buildings interspersed with modern. You can get off the bus at one end of town
and get back on at the other.
**Shirdi:** A major pilgrim town, 136 km west of Aurangabad, just
off the rail line connecting Manmad and Dhond to Poona, best
visited en route to or from. The nearest railway station is Kopar-

gaon, 13 km. From there get a taxi or tonga. Direct bus connections to Aurangabad, Poona, and Bombay. Lots of reasonable restaurants and accommodations.

Shirdi was the home of Shri Sai Baba who on 15 October 1918 went over into Samadhi. He is considered an incarnation of Sathya Sai Baba in Puttaparthi, AP. On religious holidays, especially the Dussehra Festival in October or November, lots of pilgrims arrive. Several aatis (religious services) are held daily.

**TIPS**
**Government of India Tourist Office:** Krishna Vilas, Station Road, tel.4817, open 08:00-19:00 h. Information at the airport for passengers on incoming flights, tel.8320.
**MTDC Tourist Office:** Holiday Resort, tel.4713, 10:00-17:00 h, the window at the train station is open daily except Mondays 06:00-09:00 h, 18:00-22:00 h.
**State Bank of Hyderabad:** Railway Station, tel.3423, Mon-Fri 08:00-10:30 h & 16:30-18:30 h, Saturday just mornings, branch office with normal hours in Shanganj.
**State Bank of India:** Kranti Chowk, Mon-Fri 10:30-14:30 h, Sat 10:30-12:30 h.
**Bus tours:** Can be booked at the MTDC Tourist Office or by MSRTC at Central Bus Stand 08:00-10:00 h, 14:00-21:00 h; Sample prices: Aurangabad, Daulatabad, and Ellora 17.-Rs (MSRTC) to 38.-Rs (MTDC luxury bus). To Ajanta 39.-Rs (MSRTC) or 54.-Rs (MTDC).
**Indian Airlines:** Anvikar Building, Adalat Road, tel.4864, 07:00-15:30 h, information at the airport (15 km from town), tel.8223.

# Ajanta & Ellora

The temple caves and monasteries of Ajanta and Ellora are considered the most important of this type. The Ajanta caves are also remarkable for their paintings. A visit is the perfect stopover on the north-south route, to or from Bombay. Check the map and around Aurangabad. More interesting than the side trips around Bombay.

**COMING - GOING**
**By Rail:** Ajanta is 60 km south of Jalgaon and 80 km from Bhusawal. All express trains running the Bombay - Itarsi or Surat - Nagpur routes stop in one of the two towns. Sample prices (from Jalgaon): Bombay (6-9 h, 40.-Rs), Ahmedabad (11 h, 48.-Rs), Agra (18 h, 70.-Rs).
**By Bus:** Buses between Jalgaon and Ajanta every 60 to 90 minutes beginning at 06:00 h, departs from stop 7 at New Bus Stand, 1 km from the railway station, costs 2.-Rs by scooter (one bus at 06:30 h from the railway station). The bus to Ajanta via Holiday Camp Fardapur takes 20 minutes, costs 9.-Rs. Last bus back at 17:30 h.

Numerous buses daily between Ajanta and Aurangabad, takes
2 h (105 km), costs 15.-Rs. Direct buses from Ajanta to Sola-
pur, from where you have connections to Bijapur and Hampi).
Three buses daily to Poona or Bhusawal.
Ellora - Aurangabad depart half hourly, 4.-Rs for the 30 km.
For excursions to the caves see Aurangabad.

## A NIGHT'S REST
Jalgaon is situated in the middle of a tremendous cotton-grow-
ing region. If that is your interest, this is the place. Many
people get stuck here because of bad rail connections. It's
much nicer staying around the caves or in Aurangabad.
Jalgaon: Cheap hotels around the railway station, try **PWD-
Travellers Bungalow (D)**35.-, Station Road, tel.103. **RRR
(S)**12.-, **(D)**25.-Rs, in the railway station.
Ajanta: Or better said, the village of Fardapur, 5 km from the
caves, regular buses 1.-Rs: **MTDC Holiday Resort (D)**40.-, bath.
**MTDC Traveller's Bungalow (S)**30.-, **(D)**50.-, right behind the
resort. **Forest Rest House (D)**20.-. **Fardapur Guest House
(D)**50.-. **Circuit House (D)**35.-Rs.
Ellora: **Kailas Hotel (S)**60.-, **(D)**90.-Rs, tel.43, near the caves.
Great spot for camper parking in front of the cave entrance.

## SIGHTS
For an in-depth look at the caves, at the entrance pick up a
copy of the brochure **Aurangabad, Daulatabad, Ellora & Ajanta** by
Prof. Dr. S.Siddiqui.
**Ajanta:** The Ajanta caves are of pure Buddhist origin. Twenty-
four monasteries and five temples were founded over an 800-year
period between the 2nd century BC and the 7th century AD, all
cut into the same rock. Notice the development of Buddhism as it
develops from its pure original forms to a concept approaching
Brahmanism.
    The painting continued until into the 8th century AD. The
artistic techniques are much more advanced than those seen in
Europe at the time. There are some signs that Persian artists
lent a hand with several of the murals.
    The most important caves are numbered 1, 2, 9, 10, 16, 17,
19, and 26. Caves 9 and 10 fit into ancient Hinayana tradition.
They are spread in a half circle along the 80 m high cliffs
overlooking the Waghore River.
    The complex is open 09:00-17:30 h, costs 0.50 Rs. A group of
20 people can share a **Light Ticket** (5.-Rs), whereby the lights
are turned on in the caves with the most exciting paintings. You
can check your bags at the entrance (1.-Rs). The sunlight in the
complex is best during the morning.
**Ellora:** These 34 caves are not as ancient as those in Ajanta,
and unlike their counterparts, include caves of Buddhist, Hindu,
and Jain origins. Roughly said, they stretch along the west side
of a chain of hills running from north to south. The best time to
visit is during the late afternoon sun.

AJANTA & ELLORA

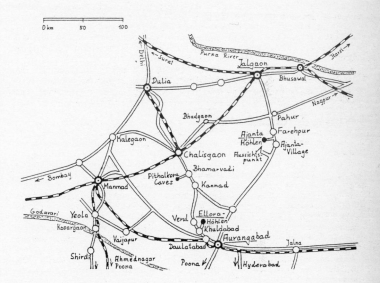

The numbers run from south to north, generally following the order of creation. The first 12 caves are Buddhist monasteries, only no. 10 is a temple. They were opened between 600 AD and 800 AD. Most interesting are caves nos. 5, 10, 11, and 12.

Caves 13 to 29 are of Hindu origin and the most important here. Be sure to get a glance in caves 14, 15, 16 (Kaila's Temple), 21, and 29. Most exciting is Kaila's Temple, perhaps the largest monolithic structure in the world. It was cut into the rock in the late 8th century AD, and unlike its predecessors was opened from the outside. The rock enclosure is 50 m wide, 90 m long and 35 m high. The temple itself covers 54 m X 35 m.

The group of Jain caves (nos. 30 to 34) are 500 m north of the last Hindu cave. They were hewn most recently, from 800 AD to 1000 AD. They impress less with their size than with their loving detail. Spend most of your time in no. 32.

Admission is 0.50 Rs, the grounds are open from sunrise to sunset, Kaila's Temple from 09:30-17:30 h. Visit as a day trip from Aurangabad.

# Lonavla & Karla Caves

On the route from Bombay to Poona are the highland resorts of Lonavla (Lonavala) and Khandala, good departure points for visits to Karla Cave and Bhaja Cave. Much fewer tourists are attracted here than to the famous Ajanta and Ellora caves. Still, we don't advise visits on weekends or holidays.

**COMING – GOING**
All express trains between Bombay and Poona stop in Lonavla. Only the Bombay - Poona Passenger stops in Malvali. Second class from Bombay costs 16.-Rs, from Poona 8.-Rs. Both buses and trains take 3 h to cover the lovely 130 km climb from Bombay through the West Ghat mountains. From Poona think 2 h for 64 km. The two villages, the Holiday Camp and Karla Cave are connected by bus.

**A NIGHT'S REST**
If you just want to see the caves and move on quickly, stay in the **Holiday Camp**, tel.30, near the branch off to the cave, **(Dm)**5.- (no bed) or 25.-Rs per person and bed. Accommodations in Lonavla near the railway station and around the bus stand start at **(S)**20.-Rs.

**SIGHTS**
Set at 625 m altitude, Lonavla and Khandala Highland Resorts and sanatoriums were founded in 1871 after their discovery by Sir Elphinston, then Governor of Bombay.
**Lohagad Fort** (6 km from Malvali) and **Rajmachi Fort**: Nearby, the two Forts were built by the famous Mahrati King Shivaji.

LONAVLA & KARLA CAVES

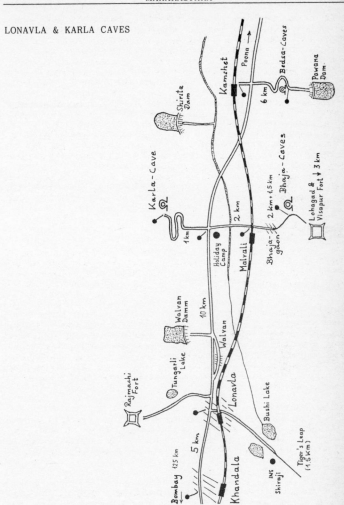

**Lakes:** There are a number of artificial lakes and scenic views, including that from the top of a 650 m drop, **Tigers Leap** (bus to INS Shivaji) and **Duke's Nose.**
**Rajmachi Point:** Offers a view down onto the winding rail line to Bombay.
**Karla Caves:** Even more famous, of course, 11 km from Lonavla toward Poona (see map). Regular buses run between Lonavla via Holiday Camp and the caves.
**Chaitya Hall:** Part of a holy Buddhist grotto, 160 m long, 15 m wide, and 16 m high, dating from 160 BC. It is one of the largest temple caves in India. The teak braces supporting the ceiling have been here since the very beginning, over 2000 years. Dedicated to Hinayana Buddhism, the cave is famous for its very puristic style, typical of the period. The sunning window and the stone masonry of the interior columns are particularly lovely. Small admission charge.
**Bhaja Caves:** South of the village of Bhajagaon, 3 km from Malvali Station. The 18 caves date from 200 BC. Cave 12 is similar to Karla Cave. The cave furthest south contains the famous dancing pair.
**Bedsa Caves:** 6 km south of Kamshet, these are the least well known. The ceilings of the main caves were probably painted. The complex dates from the first century BC.

# Poona

Situated at an altitude of 560 m, Poona has 1.7 million inhabitants. Mountains rising up in all directions keep the monsoon season moderate. Hence many people flee here from Bombay during the rainy season. Poona is both a university and industrial town. Its major attraction for foreigners was lost perhaps in 1981 when Bhagwan Shree Rajneesh moved to Oregon (he was deported from the United States in 1985). The once famous ashram in Koregaon Park, an upper class residential area, is run today by several Indian Bhagwan followers.

## COMING - GOING

**By Air:** Indian Airlines offers two flights daily to Bombay (147.-Rs). Daily service to Bangalore (686.-), and Delhi (1065.-). Three flights weekly to Hyderabad (461.-Rs), Aurangabad, and Indore. The airport is 9 km north of town. The Indian Airlines office is in Amir Hotel, Waswani (Connaught) Road, tel.61541, airport tel.65312.
**By Rail:** Poona is a junction where the rail line from Bombay Victoria Terminus branches east via Daund, Solapur, and Wadi to Hyderabad and Bangalore, and branches south to Miraj. The fastest connection to Bombay is the Miraj Express, takes 3 h. The 15 other daily trains need 4-5 h to cover the 192 km, costs 21.-Rs, a a wonderful ride through lovely West Ghat scenery.
    The Poona-Jammu Express to Kashmir, via Delhi, departs each

evening, arriving at noon two days later in Jammu. During
monsoon season, many Indians flock to Kashmir, so reserve a
seat at least 3 days in advance, unless you want to be one of
four people crouching in the baggage rack, next to us perhaps, costs 130.-Rs.

**By Bus:** The bus stand is right at Poona Railway Station. Direct buses to Bombay (5 h, 40.-Rs), Goa, Mahabaleshwar, and
Solapur. From Shivaji Nagar Bus Stand (at the railway station
of the same name) buses depart to Aurangabad (6 h, 230 km)
and Lonavla.

A private bus company sells tickets at Ambika Petrol Depot on
Connaught Road, near the railway station.

**By Overland Taxi:** Taxis from Poona to Bombay (80.-Rs per
person), book at Tourist Taxi Service Centre, Poona Railway
Bus Stand, tel.28258, or at Poona Taxi Union, Poona Railway
Station, near National Hotel, tel.28360. The taxis are only
permitted as far as Bombay-Dadar, where you have to get a
bus, local train, or city taxi on into town.

**Around Town:** Bicycle rickshaw, tonga, auto-rickshaw, bus, taxi, and masses of bicycles! The meter has to be used by the auto-rickshaws in Poona. Every driver has a price list which he is required to show you if his meter is broken. The rickshaw drivers have developed some pretty amazing tricks to take advantage of western tourists. Don't fall for the evening tariff after 18:00 h, or pay a triple rickshaw price for what is actually a double.

## A NIGHT'S REST
Since the flood of European tourists has dried up, there are lots of empty beds, to the detriment of hotel owners, and the joy of government officials. Just cross the railway station square and you'll see the first mostly reasonable hotels. If you don't find what you want around the station, get a rickshaw further into town or to Koregaon Park where numerous hotels and lodges surround the Rajneesh Ashram. Many are now defunct, but you are sure to find something in your price class. Try **Sunderban Hotel** or **Shakti Lodge.** Keep in mind that Poona is cheaper than Bombay, but more expensive than the rest of India.

## REFRESHMENT
There is good Indian food across from the station on the left. You will have no trouble finding a nice spot to eat here. You'll find numerous Chinese restaurants, i.e. **Nan King.** Rickshaw drivers are happy to bring you there. European food can be found on Mahatma Gandhi Road, even brown bread.

## SHOPPING
Like any large town, Poona has a number of shopping districts. The center includes Laxmi Road and Deccan Gymkhana in the city, or Mahatma Gandhi Road in Camp.
**Tailor:** Off M. Gandhi Road on Center Street is a tailor who'll sew packets fast and cheap. A few houses further on the corner is an excellent Chai Shop.
**Souvenirs:** Of every description from clothes to silver jewelry, hand-made lamps, rugs, etc.
**Sari Bazar:** Where you can get used saris for just a few rupees. There are several bazars around town.

## SIGHTS
Poona is set at the joining of the Mula River and the Mutha River, which logically flow on as the **Mula-Mutha River.**
  Poona reached its peak toward the end of the 18th century when, until 1817, it was the capital of a mighty empire. Later it became the seat of the British Resident, attracted by the pleasant highland climate.
**Agha Khan's Palace:** In 1942, Mahatma Gandhi was interned here along with other leaders of the Indian National Congress. Surrounded by a lovely garden.

**The Samadhi of Kasturba Gandhi:** Open to the public. She died here during the internment. By the way, the Hindu radical who assassinated Gandhi also came from Poona.
**Peshwa Palace:** The seat of the Maratha Kings, no longer in very good condition, but still worth a look.
**Pataleshwar Temple:** Over 1000 years old.
**Parvati Temple:** In the outskirts of town, accessible via steep stairs, once the personal shrine of the Peshwar King. Wonderful view of the region.
**Bund Gardens** (Mahatma Gandhi Udyan): 2 km northeast of the station on the right bank of the Mula-Mutha River.
**Empress Gardens:** Covers 24 ha with huge trees, lovely plants and flowers, a paradise in the center of town.
**Racetrack:** Across the way, the ponies are a popular sport in Poona.
**Raya Kelkar Museum:** Features fantastic examples of traditional Indian art. It is the private collection of Shri Dinkar Kelkar, who presents his treasures as if you were his personal guest.
**Rajneesh Ashram:** In Koregaon Park, a well-kept residential area. The ashram has seen better days; after all, Rajneesh is gone. Plans call for the ashram to remain open to visitors with daily meditation. Groups are scheduled for the 11th to 20th of every month. You can stay in a guest house for 5.- to 25.-Rs.
**City Tours:** Offered by the Tourist Information Counter, Railway Station, costs 20.-Rs. Depart from the station, 08:00-11:30 h and 15:00-18:30 h.

## AROUND POONA
Of course, the caves (see above).
**Mahabaleshwar** (1350 m): Also fun is a trip past waterfalls, strawberry fields, and a small lake. The 120 km journey costs 15.-Rs by regular bus. Direct buses from Bombay charge 30.-Rs for the 260 km. The village is the highest resort in Maharasthra.

## TIPS
**Divisional Tourist Office:** Government of Maharasthra, Central Buildings, tel.26697, southeast of the station.
**Tourist Information Counter:** In the railway station.
**Travel Agency:** In Hotel Blue Diamond, 11, Koregaon Park, offers good connections everywhere. Or in Hotel Amir, 50 Sadhu, Waswani Road, Travel Corporation of India, tel.22260, connections within India. Here too are the Indian Airlines office and a good snackbar.
**Currency Exchange:** In Blue Diamond Hotel, after banking hours, poor exchange rate.
**Central Bank of India:** 317 M.G. Road, tel.20538.
**Bank of Baroda:** B.J.Medical College Building, No. 1, tel.20083.
**General Post Office** and **Central Telegraph Office:** 1 km southeast of the railway station.
**City Post Office** & **Telegraph Office:** Shivaji Road at Laxmi Road.

# GOA

Heaven for the 1960s flower power people is a former Portuguese colony. Now under direct Indian central government rule, the Union Territory of Goa, Daman & Diu is administered by a governor sitting in Panaji.

The people are friendly, and only quick to anger when conversation turns to the question of the union territory's special rights. Social conflict, too, is discussed much more publicly than in less developed parts of India. Goans are proud of their Indian-Christian culture. Many elderly Goans still speak Portuguese, though the colonial era ended in 1961.

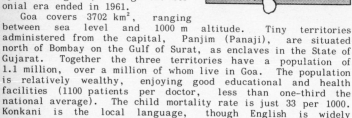

Goa covers 3702 km$^2$, ranging between sea level and 1000 m altitude. Tiny territories administered from the capital, Panjim (Panaji), are situated north of Bombay on the Gulf of Surat, as enclaves in the State of Gujarat. Together the three territories have a population of 1.1 million, over a million of whom live in Goa. The population is relatively wealthy, enjoying good educational and health facilities (1100 patients per doctor, less than one-third the national average). The child mortality rate is just 33 per 1000. Konkani is the local language, though English is widely understood along with some Portuguese.

A comfortable tropical climate provides temperatures ranging between highs of 33° C (91° F) and lows of 21° C (70° F) in January and 24° C (75° F) in June. Rainfall during the June to September monsoons reaches 1300 mm. Your best travel season is December to February. Even then, tourists and globetrotters are concentrated along just a few hundred kilometers of Goa's fine sandy beach. Christmas and Carnival are famously celebrated. Anjuna Beach hops over Christmas and New Year with a tremendous festival, featuring rock groups and dancing in the waves. Even Sikhs let their hair down!

During monsoon season swimming is extremely dangerous, with high waves and tricky currents.

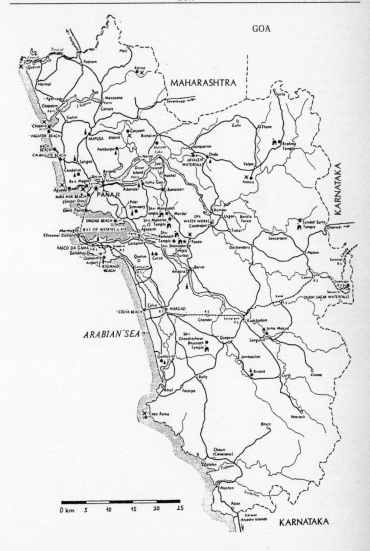

Fenny (coconut liquor) and other alcoholic beverages are freely available. A sign during a demonstration against former Prime Minister Moraji Desai, "Moraji, drink your piss, we want our Fenny!" Good food, featuring a variety of seafood, is still affordable. A godly cool 0.65 l beer, costs just 9.-Rs.

Thieves are at home among the freaks in Goa. Careful! Your greatest risk is at the beach, in restaurants, and while you are away from your lodgings.

## HISTORY

The Greek historian Ptolomäus mentioned this place during the 2nd century AD. Ancient Arabs called it Sindapur. From the 6th to 8th centuries, the region was ruled by the Chalikyas of Badami. Later the Kadambas of Goa succeeded to reign, moving their capital to Goapuri (Goa Velha) in 1052 AD. The city developed into a major maritime and trading center. Brahmanism and Jainism were the primary religions. The Kadamba dynasty met its end when Islamic armies marched south in the 13th century.

In the 14th century Goa was annexed by the Vijayanagar kings who used the port to import Arab cavalry horses. In 1488 the Shahs of Bijapur took sway, using Velha Goa occasionally as a second imperial capital.

After Vasco da Gama landed on the Malabar Coast, the Porguguese established a trading settlement at Cochin in present-day Kerala. But continued resistance by the Zamorine of Calicut moved the Portuguese to seek a safer foothold further north. This they found in Goa's strategic coast where outcropping headlands protect the entrance to navigable rivers. In 1510 AD, Afonso de Albuquerque defeated the army of the newly installed Ismail Adil Shah. Thereafter the Portuguese expanded their influence. The Marathas resisted forcefully, even besieging Velha Goa at one point.

A malaria epidemic in 1543, and an even worse epidemic in 1635, killed or dispersed most of the population. Still, the city continued to grow. At its heyday, the population reached a quarter million, challenging even the splendour of Lisbon. Fear of the Inquisition drove many people to flee the city toward the end of the 16th century, causing a decline. In 1759 the Portuguese viceroy moved his residence to the former Adil Shah palace in Panjim, today the Secretariat. In 1843, Panaji became the official administrative capital of Goa. After the Portuguese government prohibited several Christian orders, Old Goa fell into decay. Today, only the churches remain.

With time, the British established themselves as the dominant force on the subcontinent. As British allies, the Portuguese retained control of Goa, which in 1954 included Nagar Haveli (on the border to Gujarat and Maharasthra, near Daman) in addition to Daman and Diu.

In the 19th and 20th centuries, Panaji was the administrative and trading center of Portuguese colonies in the east, including Timor and Macao; and seat of a Roman Catholic bishop.

On 19 December, 1961,   the Portuguese colonial era came to an end in the wake of a coup d'état supported by the Indian army.

## COMING - GOING

Coming from Bombay, we recommend going by ship, otherwise by bus.   Only a secondary,   narrow-gauge rail line reaches here from Londa on the Miraj - Hubli line,   where you have to change trains.

**By Air:**   Indian Airlines offers daily flights to Bombay (375.-Rs),   Bangalore (430.-),   Cochin (daily except Fri, 561.-), Delhi (1240.-), and Trivandrum (686.-Rs).

Publicly owned,   Kadamba Transport Corp.   Ltd.   provides an airport bus service between the Indian Airlines office,   Dempo House,   Dayanand Baudodkar Marg, Panaji, tel.3826, and Dabolim Airport (30 km,   costs 20.-Rs).   If you want to head south from the airport (Margao / Colva),   get off at Cortalim and get the next bus to Margao (1 h, 2.-Rs).

The Air India office is in Hotel Fidalgo,   18th June Road, tel.4081.

**By Rail:**   From Bombay your fastest daytime connection is the Miraj Express,   or evenings the Sahyadhri Express,   takes 12 h to Miraj.   Fastest is the night Laxmi Express,   just 9 h.   From Miraj,   Mandovi Express connects with both night trains,   or in the evening get the Gomatak Express.   The former takes 11 h, the latter 12 h to the last stop,   Vasco da Gama,   or get off an hour before in Margao.   Calculate an entire day for the trip, costs 62.-Rs second class.

To Madras,   think a day and a half via Hubli and Bangalore. You'll definitely have to change trains in Bangalore.   If you aren't sitting in a through car,   between Goa and Bangalore, you'll have to change trains in Londa.

It's wonderfully scenic between Margao and Londa or Hubli. To Mysore and vicinity,   disembark in Arsikere,   and change trains or go on by bus.   Better connections make Margao much more convenient than the last stop,   Vasco da Gama.   Train reservations at the railway stations in Margao or Vasco da Gama 09:00-11:00 h,   16:00-17:00 h. The Railway Out Agency in the G, D & D Tourist Office,   near the bus stand in Panaji (see map), tel.2673,   is open Mon-Sat 10:00-12:30 h,   14:30-17:00 h, holidays 09:30-12:30 h for second-class reservations.

**By Bus:**   Thanks to its touristic importance,   Goa enjoys excellent long-distance bus services,   with connections to all major towns in the region.

From Bombay State Transport Terminal,   tel.374272,   near Bombay Central Station are five state-owned buses daily to Goa, costs 70.- to 110.-Rs depending upon bus and route.   Takes 17 h to Mapuca (Calangute, Vagator, etc.) and 18 h to Panaji. The direct bus to Margao takes 19 h.   Most buses drive through the coastal mountains,   along a catastrophic road.   So resign yourself to the jolts, and forget about sleep.

Private buses depart from Mahapalika Marg, near Victoria Terminus and the GPO, where you'll find their booking offices. Costs 110.-Rs to 130.-Rs, takes 17 h, book well in advance!

From Poona, direct buses daily, 14 h in the ordinary, or 12 h in the De Luxe.

From Bangalore, several super De Luxe buses daily (just nights), takes 14-16 h to Panaji, 13-14 h to Margao, costs 90.- to 110.-Rs. If you're on a bus to Panaji, and want to change for Margao or Colva, be sure to change in Ponda (don't confuse with Londa!). Frequent connections on to Margao.

More direct connections from Londa, Hubli (7 h, 20.-Rs) and Mysore. From Mangalore, costs 60.-Rs, takes 11 h.

Prices vary occasionally in opposite directions over the same route!

Private buses from Panaji to Bombay (110.- de luxe) and elsewhere in Maharasthra depart from the Boat Jetty, near the booking offices. Comparing prices is simple, hence they vary only by a couple rupees. Book well in advance!

Other private buses head for Margao; book in the tiny shops near the Municipal Building. In Mapuca, you've bookings and departures at the bus and taxi stands. There are two buses daily (day and night) to Bombay.

State-run buses from Panaji to Bombay depart from Old Bus Stand, bookings 09:00-12:00 h, 13:00-15:00 h. Luxury buses depart at 15:30 and 18:00 h. Direct buses to Poona depart at 07:30 h, takes 12 h. Laxmi Bus Company seems to have the best buses, MTDC the worst.

Buses to Bangalore and elsewhere in Karnataka also depart from the Old Bus Stand in Panaji, situated on the river bank, behind the buildings across from the GPO. The ticket office is open 08:00-09:00 h, 09:45-10:45 h, 15:00-17:00 h, bookings three days in advance. Super de luxe buses to Bangalore via Londa and Hubli at 14:30 h, arrives at 06:00 h, costs 90.-Rs.

An ITDC bus departs Margao each evening for Bangalore, takes 13 h, costs 110.-Rs, book well in advance at M/S George Travels, across from Tourist Hotel, Belavita, shop No.16, Margao.

There are direct day and night buses between Margao and Mangalore, costs 60.- to 75.-Rs depending on bus and company. Book the blue buses at Mahabaleshwara Tourist Corporation, Kamath House, near the Municipal Building (see map) from 16:30 to departure at 20:00 h reserve a week in advance.

From Margao, hourly daytime public buses to Karwar (3 h, 7.-). From there connections with public transport to Mangalore (7 h, 35.-Rs), 20.-Rs cheaper than other alternatives, see Mangalore.

**By Freak Bus:** These young European businesses have become rare since the closing of Afghanistan to tourism. Irregular connections at best.

Sample prices:   New Delhi-Connaught Place (US$45.-),   Bombay
(US$20.-),   Madras (US$20.-),   Kerala (US$45.-),   Rameswaram
(US$45.-), Kathmandu (US$85.-), Pokhara (US$85.-).
**By Ship**: The prettiest and most popular way to get to Goa from
Bombay, particularly as the land route is less than scenic.
  Outside monsoon season (June to October),   there is a daily
(except Tues) state-owned Mogul Lines ship from New Ferry
Wharf in Bombay to Panaji, Goa,   departs at 10:00 h,   arrives
08:00 h the next morning,  if it isn't delayed. Reservations are
possible six days ahead for Deck Passage.   Cabins can and
should be reserved even earlier.  Book at the pier building by
New Ferry Wharf,  tel.256835, daily (except Mon) 10:00-15:00 h.
Or book more comfortably at the Maharasthra Tourism Development Corp.  on Madame Cama Rd.,  tel.2026713,   10:00-15:00 h.
Returns to Bombay daily (except Wed) from Pajani Steamer Jetty
at 10:00 or 11:00 h,   takes 22 h.   Book at the agency office
Dempo & Co., tel.2257, across from the pier, daily (except Wed)
07:30-12:30 h,   14:30-17:00 h, bookings only for Deck Passage in
the afternoon.   Costs:   (Deck) 50.-, (Upper Deck) 75.-, (Double
Cabins) 250.- to 350.-Rs per person.  Food is cheap on board.
For connections to New Ferry Wharf,  see Bombay.  Deck seats
are reserved by coolies,  who are allowed on board before the
passengers,  and for 3.-Rs will place a blanket on your spot.
The deck cleaners are also happy to oblige. If you don't storm
on board as one of the first passengers,  the benches are all
reserved, and you'll have to sleep on the floor, which isn't so
bad as it might seem.

# Getting Around In Goa

Your main junctions in Goa are the capital Panaji (pronounced
'panshi' or 'panshim'),  the main town in the north is Mapuca
(pronounced 'mapsa'),  and in the south,  Margao (pronounced
'margo') also called Madgaon.
  Within Panaji there's a minibus from Steamer Jetty to New Bus
Stand (-.80 Rs), from where all other buses depart.
  Mapuca is your departure point for the beaches in the north,
e.g. Calangute, Anjuna, Chapora / Vagator, and Arambol. Margao is the departure point for trips to Colva and Benaulim
Beach.
**Panaji – Mapuca**: Buses half hourly, costs 1.50 Rs. Three buses
daily via Mapuca to Chapora.  Other buses direct to Calangute
and on to Baga,  costs 1.80 Rs,  takes 40 minutes.  Otherwise
regular buses between Mapuca and the beaches.
**Panaji – Margao**:  The direct route across the new bridge takes
an hour, costs 4.-. By the old route via Velha Goa and Ponda,
you'll need two hours, 5.-Rs to cover the 45 km.
**Panaji – Velha Goa**: A 30-minute ride, half hourly, (1.-Rs).

**Panaji – Marmagao / Vasco:** Get the bus to Dona Paula, and from there by boat for 1.50 Rs on to Marmagao, and then by bus to Vasco da Gama (end of the rail line), Cortalim (20 minutes, 1.50 Rs) or Margao. A second possibility from Panaji is by bus via Agacaim and Cortalim to Vasco and Marmagao.

**Margao – Benaulim – Colva:** Some buses head first for Benaulim then Colva, some the other way around, costs 1.-Rs, takes a half hour. The last bus departs at 20:00 h. Taxis charge 2.50 Rs per person (bags -.50 Rs each) Margao to Colva, from the bus stand, see map.

**Panaji – Velha Goa:** Frequent connections, takes 25 minutes, costs 1.50 Rs.

**Margao – Mapuca:** Just a few direct buses, costs 8.-Rs.

**Calangute – Anjuna:** Direct, but infrequent buses.

You've an extensive and adequate system, with regular buses, which obey no schedule, 06:00–20:00 h. Of course there are lots more lines than these mentioned above. The local people are happy to fill you in, ask.

**Overland Taxi:** You'll see them often on the short routes, e.g. Margao to Colva (2.50 Rs), Panaji to Calangute (10.-Rs), Mapuca to Calangute or Vagator (8.-Rs). Up to seven passengers are the rule.

**Scooters and Motorbike Taxis:** Usually get you to the beach, costs 1.-Rs per kilometer.

**Motorcycles and Bicycles:** Rent for 60.-Rs and 5.-Rs per day respectively. A motorbike for an entire month at runs 700.-Rs depending on the quality. More during high season, when rentals are often restricted to an entire month.

# Panaji

Panaji (also Panjim), as administrative capital of the Union Territory Goa, Daman & Diu, is primarily a stop on the way to the beach. Sights include the **Church of Immaculate Conception** and the **Mahalaxmi Temple**, see map.

## A NIGHT'S REST

Few people stay long in Panaji, so here's a quick look at the hotel district: between the Secretariat, Post Office, bridge to the bus stand, and the roads behind the Post Office. **Goa Tourist Lodge**, (S)20.-, (D)25.-. **Republica Hotel**, (S)20.-, (D)25.-. **Safari Hotel**, (S)30.-, (D)40.-, 60.-. **Tourist Hostel**, (S)30.-, (D)40.-, 60.-, centrally located. New is **Tourist Home**, (Dm)8.-, in the same building as the G, D & D Tourist Office and the Railway Booking Office between the GPO and New Bus Stand behind the bridge on the right. **Youth Hostel**, at Miram Beach, (Dm)8.-.

## PANAJI

| | | | |
|---|---|---|---|
| 1 | Hotel Venite | 7 | Goa Tourist Lodge |
| 2 | Moghul Lines | 8 | Republica Hotel |
| 3 | Karnataka Tourist Office | 9 | Aroma & Safari |
| 4 | Andhra Pradesh Tourist Office | 10 | Indian Airlines |
| 5 | GPO & Poste Restante | 11 | Bazar |
| 6 | Tourist Hostel | 12 | Godinho Restaurant |
| | Maharasthra TO | 13 | Hotel Mandovi |
| | Automobile Club | | Book Shops |

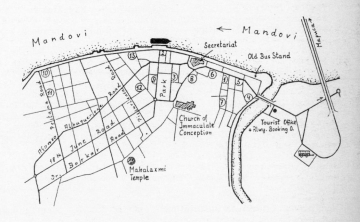

## REFRESHMENT

Around the park are a number of nice, cheap restaurants. Try **New Punjab Restaurant** or the restaurant in **Hotel Aroma** in the west of town. Further north is a dairy bar, and in the south an icecream parlor.

Plus there is the restaurant in **Hotel Venite** in the hotel district behind the GPO. Or for the feudal touch, try **El Gazelle** in Miramar.

Hot tips are the roof terraces at **Tourist Hotel** and in **Godinho**. See the map.

## TIPS

**Tourist Offices:** Panaji has no lack, for what they're worth.
**Department of Tourism**, Government of **Goa, Daman & Diu**, Tourist Home, Patto, Panaji 403001, tel.5715, Mon-Sat 10:00-12:30 h, 14:30-17:00 h, holidays 10:00-11:30 h, bus tours (9.- to 25.-Rs), guides, between the bridge and New Bus Stand.
**Tourist Information Bureau**, Government of **Maharasthra**, Tourist Hostel, tel.3572.
**Tourist Information Centre**, Government of **Karnataka**, Velho Building by Municipal Park, tel.4110.
**Tourist Information Office**, Government of **Andhra Pradesh**, Ourem Road, by the tiny Ourem River.
**G, D & D Tourist Information**, by New Bus Stand in Panaji, in Margao, in the Joshi Building in Vasco da Gama (tel.2673), at Daolim Airport (tel.2644), and at Bombay Central Railway Station Bombay 400008, tel.396288.

**Head Post Office:** Panaji 403001, Goa, India (address for efficient Poste Restante 14:00-18:00 h), tel.3704, other business Mon-Fri 09:30-13:00 h, 13:30-16:00 h, Sat 09:30-13:00 h, 13:30-15:00 h.
**Poste Restante:** Also in Margao, Colva Beach, Vasco da Gama, Mapuca, and Calangute.

**Banks:** Here and in all major Goan towns, i.e. Bank of India, Bank of Baroda. In Panaji, Commercial Bank is conveniently near Municipal Park. When banks are closed, some hotels are willing to change money.
**West India Automobile Association:** Tourist Hostel, Panaji, maps and info on road conditions.
**Book Store:** Good in Hotel Mandovi on the main street, just west of the boat jetty. Other bookshops in the lobby of the Tourist Hostel, and in Hotel Fidalgo, 18th June Road.
**Police:** Dr. Pisurlenkar Road at Afonso de Albuquerque Road, near the center of town.
**Foreigners' Registration Office:** Junta House, 18th June Road.

# Velha Goa

Portuguese political-economic conquest went hand in hand with fanatic missionary activities. It isn't surprising that the Franciscans established the first Christian order in Goa in 1517 AD, followed by numerous orders from other European countries.

Most of Goa's churches were built in the early 17th century, based on architectural models in the Catholic homeland. In Italy, the Renaissance had reached its ultimate, seen in rigid classical forms. In reaction, opulent Baroque was predestined to spread slowly, firstly through church interiors. Late Gothic influences can also be detected.

For coming and going, see Getting Around In Goa. There are no accommodations here, but lots to eat in the chai shops and stands.

## SIGHTS

All that remains of a once splendid capital are a few churches, mostly dating from the 16th and 17th centuries. Velha Goa is the only important sightseeing attraction in the region.

**Basilica of Bom Jesus:** Built by the Jesuits between 1594 and 1605 AD. It shelters a silver sarcophagus containing the last remains of St. Xavier. Upstairs is a collection of modern paintings.

**The Professed House:** Next door, completed in 1585, then partially destroyed by fire in 1663, before reconstruction in 1783.

**The Convent of St. Monica:** 100 m further up the same (southern) side of the street toward Panaji. The convent was built in 1627. Since 1964 it's home to Mater Dei Institute for Nuns.

**Our Lady of the Rosary:** At the tip of Holy Hill, 50 m to the west, was built in compliance with a solemn vow by Afonso de Albuquerque. From this hill he commanded the battle against the Sultan of Bijapur. Construction began after his death, with completion in 1549.

**Sé Cathedral:** Between the road and the Mandovi River is the largest remaining structure. Its 14 altars are certainly worth a look. Construction lasted from 1562 until 1619; the altars were finished in 1652.

**The Archbishop's Palace:** Connects the cathedral with the **Church of St. Francis of Assisi.** The church dates from 1517 when eight Franciscan friars built a chapel here. The present church dates from 1661.

**The Archaeological Museum:** Established in 1964, housed in the church of the adjoining convent. The exhibits feature the pre-colonial era, as well as the period of Portuguese rule.

**Chapel of St. Catherine:** Right next door, built immediately after the Portuguese conquest of Goa in 1510, making it Goa's oldest church.

**St. Cajetan's Church:** A replica of St. Peter's Cathedral in Rome. Construction was carried out by Theatine monks in the late 17th century. Located near the River, 100 m north of Sé Cathedral.

VELHA GOA

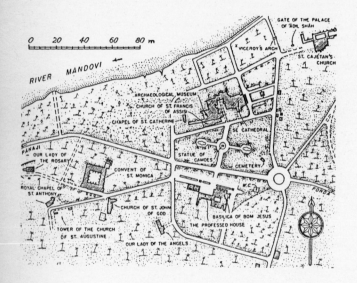

Plan several hours for your visit, perhaps an entire day. For an in depth look, pick up a copy of the 50-page brochure, **Old Goa**, by S. Rajagopalan, published by the Archeological Survey of India in 1975, available in the museum.

# Northern Goa

Along the coast north of the capital are the best known beaches. We intentionally avoid mentioning individual lodgings because conditions change quickly, and it's easy to find a place to fit your taste. All too often we've seen hot tips become the opposite, as overrunning leads to raised prices, unfriendly service, and difficulty getting a room.

### CALUGANTE BEACH
This was the first beach opened to tourism, and remains the most touristy. But don't expect the French Riviera. There are a num-

ber of reasonable accommodations. In season, near the beach, with a shower, think at least **(D)**30.-. During low season, further from the beach, **(D)**20.-Rs is reasonable, depending on comfort. Private rooms and houses run for 250.- to 600.-Rs per month.

Calangute's infrastructure includes banks, a Post Office with Poste Restante, lots of shops, vendors, fruit and fish markets, chai shops, pubs and restaurants. Particularly popular are **Wilson** on the beach for its food, **Alex** by the statue for its music, and **Modern Tavern** for cheap drinks. But you'll find your own favourites.

## BAGA BEACH
This long, sandy beach is just north of Calangute, a 3 km walk. Buses from Calangute and Mapuca. Lodgings are cheaper than in Calangute. The atmosphere is more relaxed; the beach is nicer.

## ANJUNA & CHAPORA / VAGATOR
These are the two most popular beaches in Goa, where it's happening. The scene hangs out in cheap rooms starting at **(S)**8.-Rs, or in huts running 250.- to 500.-Rs per month, depending on location, comfort and season. Among all the pubs and dope are some sad people. Theft is rampant as a few junkies and stoned heads try to get by at the cost of others. This isn't just us talking; each year we receive countless letters on this theme. But here too you'll find an odd assortment of wonderful, and very original people. The two beaches are separated by a 3 km walk.

Chapora (also Vagator) is the prettier of the two with small inlets separated by outcroppings of rock. Beyond, the plateau rises 20 m. The **Fort** at the top is quite interesting.

**Flea Market:** Wednesdays at 14:00-19:00 h, held at the southern end of Anjuna Beach where both travellers and locals buy and sell. The locals are interested in trading for or buying your jeans, watch, walkman, or camera. This is a good place to unload unnecessary weight in your

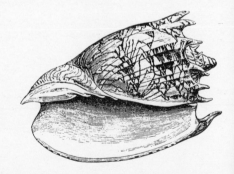

backpack, perhaps on another traveller.

**Full Moon:** Famous parties are held, though as one reader ventures, they've deteriorated into just another disco. Careful, Full Moon Nights are infamous for burglar activity.

# Narcotics seizure

### By A Staff Reporter

PANJIM, Feb 6: Narcotics and prohibited drugs worth over Rs 41,000 were siezed by the Goa police during series of raids held along beaches, last month.

The police arrested at least 50 persons, mostly foreigners, in connection wi.h the seizures and 46 cases have been registered against them. The items seized included over 27 kgs of charas 2.65 kgs of ganja, 800 grams of hashish, 3.5 grams of heroin, 5.5 grams of morphine and 5 grams of opium.

The raids were conducted at Calangute, Anjuna, Baga, Vagator and Arambol. Among those arrested are 12 Britishers, 9 Frenchmen, ten Germans, five Swiss nationals, two each Americans Australian and Dutch.

Three each Indians and Italians, and one Yugoslavian. Police said some Indian na ionals were hand-in-glove with foreign drug racketeers.

Police also claimed that in view of the series of raids on the residences occupied by foreigners, the hippy menace in the territory has been curbed to a large extent. The drive against the drug peddlers launched by the Calangute and Pernem police is continuing.

## ARAMBOL
Goa's northernmost beach is the least touristy, with fewer crowds and cheaper prices. Rooms, if you aren't choosy, start at (S)10.-Rs. You can eat in a chai shop for 5.-Rs. Accessible in 3 h by bus from Mapuca via Pernem and Harmal.

## MAPUCA
The union territory's third largest town is the center of trade and transport in the north. You'll find a State Bank of India, Post Office, and a large market every Friday (a boon to your provisions). Mapuca (pronounced 'mapsa') is also a good departure point for long-distance buses to northern India, including Bombay. Accommodations aren't very attractive, but if you must, try Tourist Hostel, near the bus and taxi stands, (D)33.-Rs.

# Southern Goa

This is our kind of Goa, but what accounts for taste? The north
has much more happening. In the south, it's peaceful. You find
beaches devoid of people, 20 km in all. Outside the two main
towns, we don't want to mention any names. Find your own little
hideaway!

# Margao (Madgaon)

The southern district capital (Selcete) is trading center for a
large inland region, and your stop on the way to southern
beaches. All important services can be found around Aga Khan
Park, where the buses arrive.

For rail and bus connections outside Goa, see Coming – Going
above. From Kerela, see Mangalore / Karnataka, an important
stopover en route. From northern Goa, get a bus via Panaji. If
you arrive in Goa by rail, disembark right in Margao, see Getting Around Goa.
   Bus stands and booking offices for long-distance buses are
near the Municipal Building, see map.
**Note:** The last bus to Colva departs at 20:00 h. A taxi to Colva
(departs when full) costs 2.50 Rs per person without bags, or
3.-Rs with luggage.

### A NIGHT'S REST
   Nobody stays here unless they get stranded. Near the bus stand
   is **Goa Woodlands**, tel.3121, Minguel Loyola Furtado Road,
   **(S)**20.-.
   Lots of lodges and hotels behind the bus stand and State
   Bank of India, or try on the other side of the park.
   The cheapest hotels are near the railway station on the side
   streets off Station Road, e.g. **Sangam Boarding**, **(S)**10.-. **Milan
   Kamat Hotel (S)**10.-. **Vishranti Lodge (S)**10.-. **Centaur Lodging
   (S)**10.-.

### REFRESHMENT
   Around the park are restaurants of every class. Try **Kwality
   Restaurant**, near the Tourist Office. On the east side of the
   park are nice cafés, icecream and dairy shops. Hmmm, computer off, lunch break.

### TIPS
**Tourist Information Centre:** Government of Goa, D & D, Tourist
Hostel, behind the Municipal Building, tel.2513.

i  Tourist Office
   in Municipal Building
1  Buses & Collective Taxis
   to Colva Benaulim
2  Telegraph Office
   Poste Restante
3  State Bank of India
4  Booking Office for
   Long-distance Buses
5  Kwality Restaurant
6  Restaurant, Café
   Dairy & Icecream
7  Hotel & Restaurant
   Woodlands
8  Lodges & Cheap Hotels

MARGAO

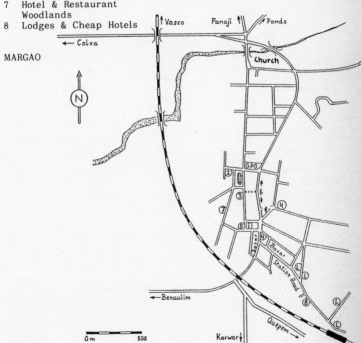

**Head Post Office:** At the northern end of the park. **Poste Restante** is behind the Telegraph Office, 300 m from the Post Office, up the hill to the left, 08:00–11:30 h, 15:00–18:00 h.

**Book Shops & Pharmacies:** On Station Road.
**Bazar:** Right and left of Station Road, behind Municipal Building, features vegetables along with used goods; the prettiest in Goa.

# Colva Beach

About 6 km from Margao, half an hour by bus, is the prettiest beach in Goa. Colva Beach, running 20 km, is also the longest. Construction has increased along the beach in recent years. But considering its size, the people to sand ratio is pleasant, particularly in the off season (starting late January). In March, you might even feel lonely!

### A NIGHT'S REST

Right by the beach are expensive hotels and bungalows, **(D)**50.-. But when demand is low: **Sukh Sagar Beach Resort**, a **(D)**85.- room goes for **(D)**45.-Rs, or **(Dm)**15.-Rs, tel.3661.

Other top addresses (also price) include the **Silversands**, and **Mar e Sol** by the bus stand, the **Whitesands Hotel**, and state-owned **Tourist Cottages**, further north, **(D)**50.-, off season **(D)**35.-Rs.

COLVA
VILLAGE

BENAULIM
VILLAGE

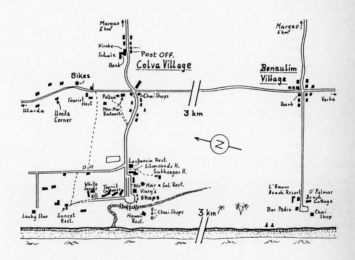

The simplest rooms and huts run **(S)**15.- per day.  Better in
Colva Village,   clean,   sunny rooms,   spring water,  1 km from
the beach,   near the church,   **(S)**10.-,   15.-,   **(D)**20.-,  30.-Rs,
depending on how long you stay.   Near the beach calculate
**(S)**20.-Rs.  Then you usually stay in a nice family home,  easy
to find, ask around, have a look, bargain!
Entire houses can be rented for just 300.-Rs per month,   but
only if you stay a while; ask.

By the last bus stand are a number of cheap pubs,  and
icecream and drink stands.  More pubs across the bridge by the
beach,   and north of the square in the palm grove.   Even
Mar e Sol is reasonably priced considering what's offered.
**Lactancia** and **Lucky Star** in Colva Beach and **Men-Mar** and
**Unita Corner Bar & Restaurant** in Colva Village are popular
among the scene.  `

At the Colva Village Crossroads,  by the bus stop,  are a number
of chai shops,  a motley collection of stores,  and a police station.
Next to the church is a branch office of Bank of Baroda.  Across
the way is a Sub Post Office providing Poste Restante.  Next door
is a stationery shop.  Bicycles rent for 1.-Rs an hour,   ask in

your hotel or in Colva Village, see map.

Fish is dried along the beach, creating an awful smell, that fades away after 500 m. Up here the flow of bus tourists (particularly on weekends) is reduced to nil. In Colva, itself, the buses stop for about an hour.

## BENAULIM
About 3 km south of Colva is the even more peaceful Benaulim. You might stay in Amour Beach Resort, large, clean rooms, **(D)**30.-Rs, restaurant. Facing across is O Palmar Beach Cottages, running 40.-Rs per cottage. In Liteo Cottages, on the road into town, **(D)**60.-Rs, fan, showers, toilet.

Popular among travellers is Bar Pedro by the bus stand, good food. You can eat and drink well in L'Amour and in the chai shops by the beach.

In the nearby village, by the church, is a bank branch office, a tiny Post Office and a mailbox. The nearest Poste Restante are in Colva Village or Margao.

Buses run Margao, Colva, Benaulim, and return. You can easily cruise by bicycle between Colva and Benaulim along the beach.

# KARNATAKA

Karnataka borders Goa and Maharasthra in the north, Andhra Pradesh in the east, Tamil Nadu and
Kerala in the south. To the west is
the Arabian Sea. Total area is
191,791 km$^2$. The West Ghats cast a
rain shadow over 90 % of the country (rain is prevented because
clouds can't make it over the mountains without losing their water in
the cool upper atmosphere). Several
major rivers provide tremendous water reservoirs. The coastal strip
and the West Ghats receive the
brunt of the summer monsoons.

Karnataka, formerly Mysore, is
home to 37 million people. The primary language is Kannada, along
with Urdu and Tamil. The capital
is Bangalore, a surprisingly modern and western-oriented city.

The region has experienced various powerful dynasties, including the Kadambas, the Chalukyas, and the Hoysala. Starting
in the 14th century, Islamic influence took hold. Bijapur became
an important capital. You can still admire examples from this era
today. A high point was achieved under Sultan Hyder Ali in the
late 18th century. He made Srirangapatna his capital. His son,
Tipu Sultan, died in fighting with the British. Under British
rule, the region was turned over to a Hindu dynasty.

Due to its long, eventful history, there is a lot to see in
Karnataka. Of primary interest to travellers: Bangalore, Mysore,
Badami, Bijur, Hampi, Hassan, Belur, Halebid, and Sravanabelagola. Mysore and its Maharaja Palace are a must. From here you
can easily visit Srirangapatnam (Hyder Ali's capital) and
Somnathpur, with its famous temples. Karnataka's natural beauty
is revealed at Jog Falls and in Bandipur National Park.

# KARNATAKA

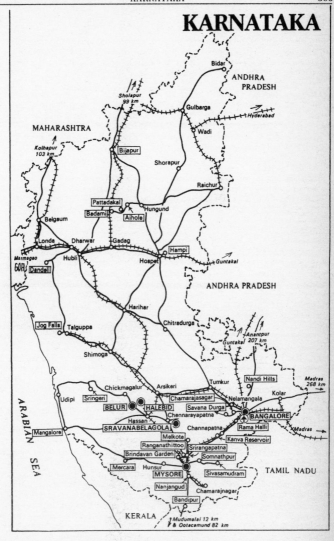

# Bijapur

Bijapur, as a Muslim town, boasts numerous mosques, mausoleums, and palaces. It experienced its peak from 1490 to 1686 AD as the capital of the Adil Shah Dynasty which originated in Turkey. The town, set at 600 m, is surrounded by a mighty wall.

## COMING - GOING

Bijapur is on the Solapur-Gadag rail line in northwestern Karnataka. Either change trains in Solapur, or get the bus, an inviting idea since Bijapur Bus Stand is centrally located while the railway station is in the outskirts. Connections to Badami and Hampi are also best by bus.

## A NIGHT'S REST

Simple hotels on Station Road: **Hotel Midland (S)**15.-, **(D)**20.-. **Mysore Lodge (D)**15.-. **Hotel Adil Shahi** (KSTDC), **(S)**25.-, **(D)**40.-, tel.934. **Traveller's Lodge** (ITDC) **(S)**50.-, **(D)**80.-, tel.401.

## SIGHTS

**Gol Gumbaz:** The most famous and imposing structure in town is the tomb of Adil Shah (1627-1657). The tremendous mausoleum **dome** is second in size only to the dome of St. Peter's Cathedral in Rome. Via one of the four eight-sided, seven-storey towers rising from the building's corners, you enter the **Whisper Gallery** where even the slightest whisper carries or echoes with undiminished volume over great distance. As at the Taj Mahal in Agra, the sarcophagus in the domed hall isn't the actual place of burial. The emperor rests in a **Crypt**, accessible from the west door, open 06:00–18:00 h, small admission, remove your shoes! The **Archaeological Museum** opens at 10:00 h

**Jami Masjid** (Friday Mosque): Offers a place of worship to 2000 faithful within an 11,000 km² complex. The harmonic structure is less ornamented than similar mosques in northern India; only the prayer ornaments facing Mecca are decorated with golden Arabic calligraphy. Construction took well over a century. The start was begun by Ali Adil Shah I, who reigned until 1580. Completion was celebrated in 1686.

**Ibrahim Rauza:** Beyond the town walls to the west, the mausoleum was built by Ibrahim Adil Shah II (1580 - 1627 AD) for himself and his family. It boasts lovely stone masonry and slim minarets. Adjoining is a matching mosque.

**Malik-e-Maidan:** A 4.5 m long cannon captured as a prize in battle, mounted on the town wall, not far from Ibrahim Rausa. At the mouth you can see a lion's jaws swallowing an elephant.

**Asar Mahal:** Built as a courthouse in 1646, boasts lovely painted ceilings. Its main attraction are two beard hairs preserved from the Prophet Mohammed.

## KARNATAKA ALPHABET

| aa | aa | ee | ee | u |
|---|---|---|---|---|
| ಅ | ಆ | ಇ | ಈ | ಉ |
| oo | ru | roo | ai | ai |
| ಊ | ಋ | ಋೂ | ಎ | ಏ |
| eye | o | ou | ow | um |
| ಐ | ಒ | ಓ | ಔ | ಅಂ |
| aha | | | | |
| ಅಃ | | | | |

| ka | kha | ga | gha | ngna |
|---|---|---|---|---|
| ಕ | ಖ | ಗ | ಘ | ಙ |
| cha | chha | ja | jha | ingnya |
| ಚ | ಛ | ಜ | ಝ | ಞ |
| ta | ttha | da | ddha | na |
| ಟ | ಠ | ಡ | ಢ | ಣ |
| tha | thha | dha | dhha | na |
| ತ | ಥ | ದ | ಧ | ನ |
| pa | pha | ba | bha | ma |
| ಪ | ಫ | ಬ | ಭ | ಮ |

| ya | ra | la | va | sha |
|---|---|---|---|---|
| ಯ | ರ | ಲ | ವ | ಶ |
| shha | sa | ha | la | ksha |
| ಷ | ಸ | ಹ | ಳ | ಕ್ಷ |

**The Citadel**: In town, surrounded by a water moat, containing a number of interesting buildings. Many, however, are in ruins. Be sure to see **Gagan Mahal** (Heaven's Palace), the audience hall, the harem palace **Anand Mahal**, the tiny **Mecca Masjid**, the ancient **Mosque**, **Sat Manzali Palace**, and **Jal Mandir**, an ornamented water pavilion.

# Badami & Aihole

The district capital Badami is set on a rectangular reservoir. Rocky cliffs towering over the town are mirrored in the green water. This is an enchanting town in picturesque surroundings.
It was once capital of the Chalukyan Empire (6th–8th centuries), which ranged from Kancheepuram in Tamil Nadu to Orissa in the north-east and over to the west coast. Today it is famous for its Dravidian architecture, particularly cave temples spread across the realm, founded in honor of Hinduism, Jainism, and Buddhism.
50 km further, Aihole was capital before Badami in the 4th to 6th centuries. Here the first experiments in Dravidian temple architecture can be seen, including the surprisingly round Durgigudi Temple. Later examples can be seen in Pattadakal on the road between Badami and Aihole.
For more info on the area, pick up the brochure **The Cave Temples of Badami**, costs 5.-Rs in front of the cave temples.
Because of its better connections, you're best off staying in Badami. Or you might try the Tourist Bungalow in Aihole, but not in Pattadakal.

## COMING – GOING
**By Rail**: The Badami Railway Station is several km from town, connected by an hourly bus. A tonga costs 3.-Rs at most. The rail line from Solapur runs via Bijapur, then heads on via Gadag west to Hubli and Goa, or east via Hospet, Hampi, and Guntakal to Bangalore or Madras.
Departing Bijapur at 07:30 h, arrives in Badami at 11:30 h, costs 8.-Rs. Four slow trains daily in each direction. You'll definitely have to change trains at Solapur in the north, likewise at Gadag or Hubli in the south.
**By Bus**: From Solapur via Bijapur (arrives at 10:00 h, takes 4 h, 14.-Rs), and Badami (bus stand in town center) to Gadag. Morning buses to Bangalore, afternoon buses to Hospet. Several buses daily to Hubli. Direct buses to Goa.

## A NIGHT'S REST
Not a big selection: **Sri Mahakuteswar Lodge (S)**8.-, **(D)**12.-, 15.-, right next to the bus stand. **Tourist Bungalow (S)**15.-, **(D)**30.-, from the bus stand, behind the tonga stand, then

right.  **Hotel Chalukya** (KSTDC) **(S)**25.-, **(D)**40.-Rs, tel.46. There
are places to eat along the main road between the bus stand
and tonga stand.

# Hampi & Hospet

The tiny village of Hampi,  and the ruined city and temples,  are
remains of a famous temple city,  Vijayanagar (city of victors),
capital of a Hindu kingdom ruling southern India from 1336 to
1565.  Once upon a time half a million people inhabited a city
covering 30 km$^2$.  The most important ruler of the day was Krishna Devaraya, a patron of the arts. The decline of the empire was
sealed in 1565 in a battle at Talkota against the combined armies
of several Deccan sultans.  Islam gained admission to much of
southern India. Sightseeing is most convenient if you find accommodations southwest of the Hospet ruin fields.

## COMING - GOING
   **By Rail:**  The town is east of Goa on the rail line connecting
Hubli,  Gadag,  and Bellary to Guntakal and Gooty. From Vasco
da Gama in Goa (21:20 h) or Margao (22:00 h) to Hubli
(06:00 h),  reserve a seat several days in advance!  Departs
Hubli (09:30) arrives Hospet (15:00 h);  the train continues on
to Bangalore.  In Hospet get a rickshaw (2.-Rs) to the bus
stand.
   **By Bus:** Quicker and more frequent connections. Buses to Hospet
from Panjim,  Bangalore,  Badami (20.-Rs),  Hyderabad,  and
Hubli.
   From the bus stand in Hospet,  there is an hourly bus 13 km
north up the river to Hampi Bazar or to Kamalapuram at the
southern end of the ruined city. Here, or in Hampi, you should
rent a bicycle,  since distances are wide,  you have to cover at
least 8 km.  You might even pick up a bike in Hospet just to
make sure.  Taxis run between Hampi and Kamalapuram,  costs
1.50Rs per person.

## A NIGHT'S REST
Hampi has few accommodations,  and Kamalapuram is little better.  In Hampi Bazar,  you might try to stay in **Virupaksha
Temple** for 3.-Rs. And outside pilgrim season, rooms are avail-
able in some of the ashrams.
   Your simplest solution,  however,  is to find a place in Hospet
and make day trips to Hampi.  If the following are full,  check
at the Tourist Information Office on Station Road,  across from
New Bus Stand.  **Hotel Mayura (S)**10.-,  **(D)**20.-, Gandhi Chowk,
by the GPO,  restaurant. **Pampa Lodge (S)**10.-, **(D)**20.-, Station
Road.  **Hotel Sandarshan (S)**15.-,  **(D)**30.-, Station Road. **Malligi
Tourist Hostel (S)**15.-,  **(D)**30.-Rs, near the road to Hampi, more
comfortable.

You can eat in the above hotels and in numerous Hospet restaurants. Hampi and Kamalapuram offer only chai shops; likewise at the ruin field, but they are cheap.

## SIGHTS
The most important sights in Hampi, i.e. Vijayanagar include:
**Vittala Temple:** With its **musical columns** hammered from a single
rock 8 m high. In front of the temple is a large map.
**Hazarama Temple:** Boasts lovely stone tiles. The fruit stands are
a welcome relief in the heat.
**Purandaradasara Mandapam:** The ruins of an ancient stone river
bridge.
**Ruins:** Including the **Elephant Stalls**, the **Lotus Mahal**, the **Royal
Bath**, and **Achutaraya Temple**. The Museum and archaeology office
have little to offer besides a useful map (1.-Rs). The ruins are
scattered across lovely countryside, dotted with tremendous rocks.
Just a walk through this scenery is worth a visit to Hampi.

# Jog Falls

This peaceful village offers lovely views of four waterfalls: Raja,
Rocket, Rani, and Roarer, on the Sharavati River. Outside the
rainy season they impress more with their height (253 m) than
with their trickle. Still, these are the highest falls in India.
Take the nice walk down the serpentine path to the river (sturdy
shoes, not slippers!). A number of pools invite a swim. Bring
along something to eat and drink, you'll want to spend a while.

## Coming - Going
**By Bus:** Direct buses to Karwar (7 h, 20.-Rs), south of Goa,
or on to Margao. Lots of buses head southeast to Shimoga
where you have connections to Bangalore, Mysore, Hassan,
Arsikere, Hampi, etc. For other connections ask in any hotel,
i.e. Woodlands.
**By Rail:** The nearest railway station is Talguppa, last stop on
the line to Arsikere. The afternoon train has a wagon going
all the way to Bangalore and Mysore: Talguppa (16:50 h),
Bangalore (06:15 h), Mysore (10:15 h); 921 Passenger. From
Bangalore (21:30 h) with the 201 Mail, Mysore (19:40 h) with
the 968 Passenger, arrives at Talguppa (10:10 h), from here
buses to Jog Falls.

## A NIGHT'S REST
**Hotel Woodlands (D)**20.-, 25.-, right at the bus stand. **Inspec-
tion Bungalow. Youth Hostel (Dm)**8.-Rs.
Food in the hotels and in the three tiny chai shops.

# Hassan

A good departure point for cultural excursions through the Sravanabelagola, Belur, and Halebid triangle. If you plan to spend some time in Belur and Halibad, get a room there. You can book into the Tourist Cottages through the Tourist Office near the railway station.

## COMING - GOING
**By Rail:** Hassan is on the metre-gauge line connecting Mysore with Arsikere. Three trains chug daily in each direction. The railway station is outside town.
**By Bus:** Buses every 45 minutes to Belur 06:00-20:00 h, takes 1.5 h, costs 4.-Rs.

Ten buses daily to Halebid, takes 2 h, costs 3.-Rs. Good connections between Belur and Halebid, half an hour, 1.50 Rs.

Just three buses to Sravanbelagola (05:30 h, 09:00 h, and 18:30 h), takes 1.5 h. The alternative is to get a bus to Channaraya Patna and then change to Sravanbelagola, but it takes longer. From Sravanbelagola direct buses to Mysore (13:00 h).

Good bus connections to Bangalore, Mysore, or Arsikere (90 min., 4.-Rs). The bus stand is in the town center.

## A NIGHT'S REST
Near the bus stand are a number of cheap hotels running **(D)**15.- to **(D)**25.-Rs with bath. Try **Hotel Dwaraka** or **Hotel Sathyaprakash**, 90 m right of the bus stand exit. Alternatives are **Hotel Madhu Nivas**, **Hotel Hassan**, etc. Or go all the way to **Ashoka Hotel (S)**100.-, **(D)**150.-Rs.

Since Hassan is popular among pilgrims as a holy place, it's often difficult to get a room in the afternoon, so start early.

**Cafe Shanbag** offers good, cheap Indian food. Lots of food stalls and chai shops near the bus stand. Readers recommend **Three Star Lodge** as a place to meet for a drink.

# Belur

800 years ago, this was a thriving town in the Hoysala kingdom, whose kings, from the 11th to 14th centuries, ruled present-day Karnataka. Temple architecture achieved new heights during this era. The prettiest examples of architecture from this period can be seen in Belur, Halebid, and Somnathpur.

The Hoysala style is marked by a star-shaped foundation and rich ornamentation. Chennakesava Temple was built in Belur in the 12th century. The construction celebrated the conversion of Hoysala's King Vishnu Vardhana from Jainism to Hinduism. The outer walls are decorated with wonderful sculpture and orna-

ments based on Hindu mythology. Take enough time to see everything well, no two of the 28 windows are the same. Admission is
0.50 Rs, closed from 13:00-14:30 h.

## COMING - GOING
**By Bus:** Connections everywhere in Karnataka. Sometimes you
have to change in Hassan or Arsikere. Express buses every two
hours to Mysore; to Hassan hourly. To Halebid you've both
buses and minibuses. The nearest railway station is Hassan.

## A NIGHT'S REST
Two hotels on the main road near the bus stand: **Vishnu
Prasad (D)**20.-, restaurant. **Gyathri (D)**20.-, restaurant. **Trav-
eller's Bungalow (D)**30.-. **Inspection Bungalow (D)**30.-. **Tourist
Cottages (D)**30.-Rs.
   Food and accommodations are no problem, particularly as most
travellers elect to stay 40 km away in Hassan.

# Halebid
Also called Halebeedu, the last capital of the Hoysala kingdom is
just 16 km from Belur. Once upon a time, the complex of temples
and palaces was spread over a large area. In 1310 AD the town
was captured and plundered by a Muslim general. In 1326 another Muslim army destroyed the town completely. Two temples are
the main tourist attractions.
**Hoysaleshwara Temple:** Was designed to be the largest and most
splendid in its realm. Construction continued for 86 years, but
was never completed. Still, it overwhelms the temples in Belur.
There is hardly a stone which hasn't been wonderfully worked.
**Kedareswara Temple:** Also of interest, with its finely worked reliefs and sculpture. The Museum has little to offer.

## COMING - GOING
Halebis is connected to Belur by bus and minibus. Bus connections to Arsikere and Hassan.

## A NIGHT'S REST
**Tourist Cottages (D)**30.-. **Inspection Bungalow (D)**30.-. Both
right by the temple in a well-kept garden.

# Sravanabelagola
This town is important to the Jains, whose religion blossomed
under the Hoysala realm.
**The Statue of Gomateswara:** The main attraction is the Jain's holy
man. At 17 m it's the tallest monolithic statue in the world.

**12 Year Festival:** Once every dozen years, Jains come from all over India. At the high point of the celebration, priests (standing on a scaffold built just for this purpose) pour coconut milk, kum-kum water, fruit, seeds, ghee and other valuable sacrifices over the statue. The statue, which recently celebrated its 1000th anniversary, was cut from a single block of stone in 983 AD.

Sravanabelagola has a long history dating back to the 3rd century AD. Bhadra Bahu, the Jain holy man, lived here then with his follower Chandragupta Maurya, a king who withdrew from the world to live the life of an ascetic. Even Gomateswara, depicted by the statue, is said to be a prince who chose to suffer asceticism as a Jain holy man.

Six hundred granite steps lead up Indragiri Hill to the statue. Near the stairs is the Tourist Office, which likes to be helpful. But don't expect quiet observation. For that you'll have to visit the smaller Chandragiri Hills where you'll find less well known, but no less interesting **bastis** (sacred temples) from which you have a wonderful view of the entire complex.

**COMING - GOING**
  Regular bus connections to Hassan, Mysore, and Bangalore.

**A NIGHT'S REST**
  Just a modest selection at best. Simple accommodations in the Dharamsalas (pilgrim accommodations) and in the teahouses for just a few rupees. **Traveller's Bungalow** is usually booked up. Plan your visit on the way between Hassan and Mysore.

# Bangalore

The capital of Karnataka, formerly Mysore, was a British summer resort during the colonial era. At 1000 m altitude, the climate is comfortably cool. Three million people live here today. An important administrative, university, and industrial city (precision mechanics, electronics, metals, motors, and aerospace industries), Bangalore is one of the cleanest and most peaceful cities in India, featuring tremendous gardens and parks. Though lacking in sights of its own, this is a good departure point for trips to interesting sites in the region.

**COMING - GOING**
  Bangalore City Railway Station, Bangalore Bus Station, the city bus stand, and numerous private bus companies are grouped together in the west of town, just south of the cheap hotel district (500 m to 1200 m).
  **By Air:** At least one flight daily to Delhi (1332.-), Bombay (725.-), Calcutta (1300.-), Cochin (331.-), Coimbatore (222.-), Hyderabad (460.-), Goa (430.-), Madras (260.-), Mangalore

(290.-), Poona (686.-). Four times weekly to Madurai (321.-), and Tirupati (211.-). Thrice weekly to Ahmedabad (1073.-), and Trivandrum (510.-Rs).

The airport is 10 km from town, no airport bus. Insist that the taxi driver uses the meter, costs 60.-Rs. The Indian Airlines City Office is in the CBAB Building, Kasturba Gandhi Road, tel.29769.

**By Rail:** Almost every train, particularly night trains, is booked out well in advance. For Indrailers, and those with endless spirit, a few tips:

You've good connections to Madras Central. The fastest trains take 7-8 h over the 360 km.

Mysore is served six times daily 06:00-18:00 h, takes 4 h along an enchanting route, 18.-Rs.

The Bangalore Express to Bombay takes 24 h, ending at Dadar in the outskirts of Bombay, running via Poona (78.-Rs), Wadi, and Guntakal. The Mahalaxmi Express runs to Bombay V.T. via Poona and Miraj. There you can change to the meter-gauge line via Londa (connection to Goa), and Arsikere (connection to Hassan, Belur, and Halebid), to Bangalore, takes 26 h, costs 86.-Rs.

Heading for Goa, change trains in Londa! Takes 20 h, costs 50.-Rs, wiser by bus.

From Delhi Hazrat Nizamuddin there's an express train via Agra (135.-), Jhansi (124.-), Bhopal, Manmad, Daund, Wadi (connection to Hyderabad), and Anatapur (27.-Rs), takes 43 h, costs 143.-Rs. From New Delhi Railway Station, the Karnataka Express runs twice weekly via Jhansi, Nagpur, Secunderabad, Anantapur, takes 40 h.

Plus direct connections to Ahmedabad, Trivandrum, and Tiruchchirappalli.

**By Bus:** As trains are frequently booked out weeks in advance, it's advisable to use state-owned or private long-distance bus companies running luxury AC buses featuring reserved seats. State buses "S" can be booked and depart from Bangalore Bus station, across from the railway station on the right. Private buses (denoted here with "P") can be booked around the railway station and bus station, generally on the city-side of the square on the road by Sangsam movie theater. Ask about the departure times.

The main routes include: Mysore (S, 18.-, 3 h, hourly, nonstop), Madras (S & P, 50.-, 60.-, 8 h, thrice daily), Salem (S, 26.-), Trichy (S, 38.-), Pondy (S, 35.-, 07:00 h), Tiruvanamalai (S, 26.-), Madurai (P, 62.-), Ernakulum (P, 80.-), Trivandrum (S, 108.-, 18 h), Hyderabad (S, 102.- / P, 220.-, 24 h), Ooty (Ootacamund), Vellore, Kanchipuram, Hubli, Belgaum, Poona, Mangalore, Puttaparthi.

BANGALORE

1 Government of Karnataka Tourist Office
2 Public Utility Building
  Kaveri Arts & Crafts
3 Central Telephone Office
4 Indian Airlines
5 Long-Distance Buses
6 Air India
7 Sudha Lodge
8 British Library
9 Max Mueller Bhavan
10 Government Museum
  Technological Museum

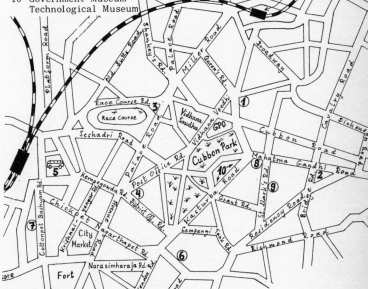

To Goa and Bombay: Panaji (Old Bus Stand) 17:45 h, Bangalore 09:00 h, S & P, 95.-Rs. Return Bangalore 22:15 h, Ponda
13:00 h, Panaji 14:00 h. Several buses daily from Bombay Central, takes 24 h, costs 220.-Rs (P), the 14:00 h bus (S) costs
250.-Rs. Buses to Poona via either Hubli or Belgaum.
**Around Town:** You've a good local bus system, plus taxis and
scooters.

## A NIGHT'S REST

Most of the cheap accommodations are 500 m to 1200 m south of
the railway station and bus stand along Cottonpet Main Road
(Cottenpet Bashyam Road) heading directly south from the bus
stand and railway station. More are a bit east on Sri Narsimharaja Road south of City Market, near Tipu's Fort.
**Sudha Lodge,** 6 Cottonpet Bahashyan Road, Bangalore 520053,
tel.605420, **(S)**20.-, ·**(D)**30.-, **(Tr)**35.-, **(Eb)**5.-, showers, "Service is Friendly" is the motto, clean, five minutes from the
railway station. **Sri Ganesha Lodge,** Cottonpet Main Road,
tel.609144, just a couple of steps further, **(S)**15.-, 18.-,
**(D)**25.-, 28.-, **(Tr)**30.-, **(Eb)**6.-.
Heading on to Sri Narsimharaja Road (ask!), 15 minutes from
the railway station, similar prices prevail. Somewhat higher
prices around the bus stand and on Gandhi Nagar (**(S)**25.- to
50.-, **(D)**40.- to 90.-).
**Nanda Hotel,** Gandhi Nagar, request the **(S)**25.-. **Hotel Hindustan,** Gandhi Nagar, tel.23063, **(S)**25.-, **(D)**45.-. More expensive
at **Hotel Lakshmi,** 11 First Cross Road, Gandhi Nagar,
tel.274247, **(S)**50.- and higher.
**Bombay Ananda Bhavan Hotel,** 10 Grant Road, tel.54581 is
worth a special mention, real family atmosphere, a lovely old
house with a small garden and good kitchen; the owner, Mr.
Gupta (Senior) is wonderfully helpful, and a follower of Sathya
Sai Baba, so lots of people from Puttaparthi stay here. Set on
a quiet, but centrally located residential street, think **(D)**65.-;
family rooms for 4 to 6 guests available, say hi from Barbara.
**Hotel Rama,** Lavelle Road, tel.53381, **(D)**140.-, fine restaurant,
near Bombay Ananda Bhavan Hotel. **Shilton Hotel,** St. Mark's
Road, tel.568184, **(S)**105.-, **(D)**140.-, 160.-, just around the
corner from Bombay Ananda Bhavan Hotel, good food.
**Ashoka Hotel,** Race Course, **(S)**350.-, swimming pool 25.-, and
other luxuries including a hairdresser, and good restaurants,
drinks around the pool run at 8.-Rs.

## REFRESHMENT

Besides all those Indian restaurants, you'll find western and
Chinese food. Try downstairs in Sangam Moviehouse by the bus
stand, or in **Hotel Blue Star** on Gandhi Nagar by Tribhuvan Cinema. Otherwise have a look on M. Gandhi Road, Residency Road,
or further south on Brigade Road. On M. Gandhi Road we recommend **Rice Bowl,** for Chinese food. You can dine expensively but
well in **Shilton Hotel** on St. Mark's Road. The restaurant in **Hotel**

**Rama** on Lavelle Road is worth a try. If you're out for something expensive but fine, head for Ashoka Hotel where you can breakfast in **Restaurant Lotus**, or feast on Chinese in the **Mandarin Room**, or in **Hibiskus Bar**. The Buffet in Restaurant Lotus is well worth the 45.-Rs.

## SHOPPING
A large selection of wares! Interesting shops along Mahatma Gandhi Road.
**Kaveri Arts and Crafts Emporium:** On Mahatma Gandhi Road, featuring a tremendous selection of southern Indian wares, sandalwood and rosewood, inlay, silk. Not cheap but best quality. Similar to Mysore.
**Books:** Also on M.G. Road are left-wing bookstores offering underground literature you'll not see anywhere else in India.
**Cloth** and **Clothes:** Excellent and cheap on pedestrian Commercial Street near M.G. Road.
**City Bazar:** For second-hand goods; also check out Chickpet District.
**Supermarket:** On M.G. Road.

## SIGHTS
**Tipu's Fort:** Interesting, but little remains.
**Tipu Sultan's Southern Palace:** Ruins, open 06:00-18:00 h.
**Bull Temple:** At the southern end of the street of the same name.
**A Monolith Nandi:** Similar to the one in Mysore.
**Lal Bagh:** The Botanical Garden, founded in the 18th century, is in the south of town along with all the above sights. Be sure to take a walk through the 100 ha grounds.
**Cubbon Park:** The second largest, in the center of town, north of K.Gandhi Road.
**Government Museum:** In Cubbon Park, some of the exhibits are 5000 years old! Open daily, except Wed or Fri 08:00-17:00 h.
**Vidhana Soudha:** The newest building is also the most interesting, at the north end of Cubbon Park, housing the **State Parliament** and government. The neo-Dravidian structure is open to visitors after 17:30 h if you get an advance invitation from the Department of Personal & Administrative Reform, tel.79401. The structure is illuminated on Sunday and holiday evenings.

**Tours:** All the above are on the agenda of tours conducted by private bus companies and the KSTDC, take all day, cost 25.- to 35.-Rs. Day tours are also offered to Mysore, Sriangapatnam, and Brindavan (start at 65.-Rs). Tours during the dry season to Belur, Halebid, and Sravanabelagola cost 75.-Rs and up. Plus day trips (daily May to June, otherwise on weekends) to the Nandi Hills, a hill station. Overnight tours are also offered.
**Sai Baba:** When he's in Bangalore, Sai Baba stays in suburban Whitefield, in his **Brindavan Ashram**. For more info on his ashram in Puttaparthi, see Puttaparthi, Andhra Pradesh.

**The Kolar Gold Fields:**  100 km from Bangalore, are the richest in India.  Some of  the mines,  at 3000 m, rank among the  deepest in the world. Visits are possible if you get an advance permit.

**TIPS**
A number of inefficient tourist information offices provide varied material, of little real use.

**Karnataka State Tourism Development Corporation:**  Badami House, across  from  the  corporation  offices,  Narasimharaja  Square, tel.74711, sightseeing tour bookings.

**KSTDC:** 10/4 Kasturba Road, Bangalore 1, tel.578753.

**KSTDC:**  Karnataka State Tourist Counter,  Public Utility Building (ground floor), Mahatma Gandhi Road, tel.52377, near Mayo Hall.

**KSTDC Head Office:**  9 St. Mark's Road,  corner Kasturba Gandhi Road and Mahatma Gandhi Road,  Bangalore 560001,  tel.579186; plus windows at the main railway station,  in the City Market Building, and at the airport.

**Foreigners' Registration Office:** Shankey's Road, near the GPO.

**Max Mueller Bhavan:**  12 Museum Road,  POB 5058,  Bangalore 560001,  tel.52135,  between Residency Road and Mahatma Gandhi Road.

**British Library:**  Mahatma Gandhi Road at Kasturba Road, English newspapers.

**State Bank of India:** St.Mark's Road, tel.55629, other major banks in Gandhi Nagar and south of Cubbon Park.

**State Bank of India:** Overseas Branch, 6/1 Infantry Road.

**Ashok Nursing Home:**  18/4 Cambridge Road Cross,  Ulsoor, recommended in case of  illness,  run by a  German-Indian couple, Dr.Mundra.

**GPO, Poste Restante, Central Telegraph Office:** On Cubbon Road at Vidhana Vidi,  on the northern end of Cubbon park,  across from Vidhana Soudha (Secretariat).

**Fortune Teller:**  Your future isn't cheap, so if you aren't low on cash (150.- 300.-Rs) visit Sri Narayana Sastry,  House no.35, 5th Main Road,  Chamrajpet,  Bangalore 18, phone for an appointment tel.601971.

**Con Artists:**  "At the bus stand in Bangalore I met an Indian speaking educated English with the standard story:  His money was stolen,  his brother in Madras would pay me back.  I didn't really believe him,  but the 25.-Rs was worth having an address in Madras.  'Ravi' was about 40 years old,  and seemed respectable." (Reader's letter).  The trick has a  great tradition in Bangalore, as numerous letters testify!

# Mysore

The former capital of the former empire and state of the same name (now Karnataka) has a touristic importance far exceeding Bangalore. The last Maharaja, His Highness Krishnaraja Wodeyar IV, died in 1981. During his lifetime, he turned his palace home into a museum and cultural center.

This town of 400,000 is one of the most beautiful in the south. Situated at 770 m, it enjoys a moderately tropical climate. The fertile surrounding countryside is intensively cultivated. The jungles to the south are rich in wildlife. Certainly, this is one town no visitor to southern India should miss. Be sure to come at the beginning of October during the ten-day Dassara (Dussehra) Festival. A great place to shop, Mysore is an excellent departure point for excursions to Sriangapatnam and Somnathpur, both attractions in themselves. Nearby Chamundi Hill (1160 m) features a temple and tremendous Nandi.

## COMING - GOING

The railway station and bus stands are near the cheap hotels. City Bus Stand is right next to the Maharaja Palace. Central Bus Stand has been moved to Church Road. Everything is accessible by foot.

**By Rail:** Only worth it to and from Bangalore (see Bangalore), takes three hours. Or to Arsikere on the meter-gauge line, 150 km west of Bangalore. Arsikere or nearby Hassan are good departure points for Belure, Halebid, and Sravanabelagola (discussed individually above). Heading north-west, again change trains in Arsikere. Trains depart Mysore for Arsikere, takes 5 h, at 07:00 h, 14:15 h, 16:45 h (the latter with a car to Mirij). There is a Southern Railway Booking Office in Mysore across from the Kaveri Arts & Crafts Emporium.

**By Bus:** The numerous overland buses are the faster and more comfortable public transport here. Direct buses with seat reservations to Bangalore (3 h, 18.-Rs, nonstop, departure on the hour), Arsikere, Sravanabelagola (5 daily), Bellary (connection to Hampi, 21:00 h), Hassan (20 daily), Calicut (8 daily), Ernakulum (08:00 h & 10:00 h), Srirangapatnam (half hourly, 2.-Rs). To Ootacamund (Ooty), costs 22.-Rs, takes 5 h, 6 daily, last at 15:00 h. Midway along the 160 km route are the nature reserves, Bandipur and Mudumalai (Theppakadu). Bring warm clothes; it can get cool along the way.

**Around Town:** To Chamundi Hill, get Bus 101 from City Bus Stand (hourly, 1.50 Rs). Buses 1 or 1a bring you to the Governmental Sandalwood Oil Factory. Otherwise go by foot or scooter.

## A NIGHT'S REST

Most cheap accommodations are around Gandhi Square (see map), and on the southern side of Dhanwantari Road.

**Geetha Lodge**, Gandhi Square, **(S)**20.-, **(D)**30.-, loud! **Central Hotel**, Gandhi Square, **(S)**20.-, **(D)**30.-, 40.-, better. **Hotel Durbar**, Gandhi Square, tel.20029, **(S)**15.-, **(D)**25.-, private bath 40.-, clean, friendly, rooms facing front are loud, Indian restaurant and dairy open till 18:00 h, pleasant roof-top restaurant. **Hotel Satkar**, Gandhi Square, **(S)**20.-. **Hotel Dasapraksh**, tel.24444, most expensive on Gandhi Square, also **AC**, **(S)**40.-, 75.-, **(D)**60.-, 125.-, just vegetarian food in the restaurant. **Hotel Srikanth**, tel.22951, Gandhi Square, **(S)**30.-, **(D)**60.-.

On Dhanvantari Road are three equally good hotels, each with a restaurant serving standard Indian food. **New Gayathri Bhavan**, tel.21224, Dhanvantari Road, **(S)**20.-, 25.-, **(D)**30.-, 40.-. **Agarwal Lodge**, tel.22730, Dhanvantari Road, **(S)**20.-, 25.-, **(D)**30.-, 40.-, clean, set back from the road, quiet. **Indra Bhavan**, tel.23933, Dhanvantari Road, **(S)**20.-, 25.-, **(D)**30.-, 40.-.

Elsewhere in Mysore: **Sri Rama Lodge**, Srirampet, tel.23348, **(D)**30.-, clean, 7 minutes from the bus stand. **Hotel Mona**, next to Prabhat Cinema, **(D)**40.-, very clean, side street, quiet. **Park Lane Hotel**, tel.30400, Curzon Park Road, near the K.E.B. Buildings, north of Hardinge Circle (statue circle), follow the signs, centrally located, quiet, nice restaurant, friendly service, **(S)**30.-, **(D)**50.-, booked up by noon. **Chasmundi Guest House**, tel.21152, Jhansilaksmibai Road, Mysore 570005, recommended for people with campmobiles, lovely parking, 5.-Rs. And for those of you who've never slept in a maharaja palace: **Lalitha Mahal Palace**, tel.23650, T.Narasipur Road, Mysore 570005, the pleasure runs at **(S)**325.-, **(D)**425.-Rs.

## REFRESHMENT

Many cheap hotels have an adjoining restaurant. On Dhanvantari Road, there's good food in **New Gayathri Bhavan** or in **Agarwal Lodge**. The restaurant in **Regent Hotel** by the golf course is quite simple, but the food's good, excellent breakfasts. The **Punjabi Restaurant** may truly be "the only one in town" with good Punjabi cooking, but expensive. **Kwality Restaurant** can sometimes be considered among the best.

If you're staying at Gandhi Square, you have a large selection of restaurants. Hotel Durbar offers Indian food in its downstairs **Restaurant / Dairy**. The roof-top restaurant is open evenings. Across the street in **Shilpashtri Restaurant**, you've a large selection of not just vegetarian dishes, served on the roof-top terrace. The restaurant in **Hotel Dasaprakash** deserves a mention for its reasonably priced vegetarian food. Excellent, and not too expensive is the **Bamboo Grove** by Hotel Hoysala, Jhansi Lakshmi Bai Road. Also good is the restaurant in **Hotel Park Lane**, 2720 Curzon Park Road. Expensive, but good, try **Gunhouse Imperial**, across from the main palace gate.

MYSORE

1 Kavery Arts & Crafts
Tourist Information
2 S. Railway Booking Office
3 Ashok Book Centre
Punjabi Restaurant
4 Kwality Restaurant

5 Shilpashtri Restaurant
6 Hotel Durbar
7 City Bus Stand
8 Central Bus Stand
Long-Distance Buses
9 Indian Airlines

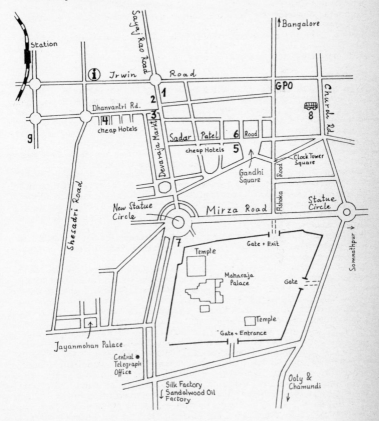

## SHOPPING
Mysore is famous for inlaid rosewood and sandalwood products,
silk saris, and incense.
**Kaveri Arts & Crafts Emporium**: You'll find a large selection,
Sayaji Rao Road, daily, except Thursdays and holidays, 10:00–
14:00 h, 15:30–19:30 h, but Sunday just mornings. You can pay
in foreign currency, but the exchange rate is poor. They will
pack and send it for you. A visit is certainly worthwhile, if
only for a look and comparing prices.
**Sandalwood Oil Factory** (see map): For the best deal on incense.
**Devaraja Market**: Be sure to take a walk through the colourfully
bustling market.
**Books**: And visit the bookstores, e.g. **Ashok Book Centre**, next to
Punjab Restaurant, at the beginning of Punjab Road or **Geetha
Book House** on New Stature Circle (see map).

## SIGHTS
**Maharaja Palace**: Breathtaking, in itself worth the trip, admission to most parts just 2.–Rs, 10:30–17:30 h. The palace, set
behind fortified walls, was built in Indo-Saracenic style as a
replacement for the old palace burned down in 1912. The palace
grounds feature two Hindu temples and a parade ground. In
keeping with the last wishes of the late maharaja, the palace
has been converted into a museum and cultural center. The palace is illuminated on Sunday evenings 18:30–19:30 h.
**Devaraja Bazar**: This vegetable market, stretching endlessly along
Sayaji Rao Road offers a variety of wares and colorful spectacle.
**Kaveri Arts & Crafts Emporium**: This state-owned store offers a
tremendous selection (though sloppy presentation) of local rosewood and sandalwood products including inlaid wares, surely a
sight, (see shopping).
**Jaganmohan Palace**: featuring the **Sri Chamarajendra Art Gallery**
with paintings, handicrafts, and musical instruments, 08:00–
17:00 h, costs 1.–Rs.
**Chamundi Hill**: At 1160 m, this is a great place for morning
walks. Way at the top is the Maharaja of Mysore's summer residence (now a hotel), and Sri Chamundaswari Temple (founded 2000
years ago), featuring a 40 m high gopuram, open 09:00–12:00 h,
17:00–21:00 h. Chamundi was the patron of the royal family. From
the top you've a great panorama of Mysore and the surrounding
hills. Buses up the 13 km to the top cost 1.50 Rs, takes 30 minutes. Along the way, on the plains to the left, notice the huge
white Lalitha Mahal (today an ITDC Hotel **(S)**325.–, 425.–Rs). A
path leads down from the top to the largest **Monolithic Nandi**
(Shiva's mount was a bull), 5 m high and almost 8 m long. The
walk from the top into town is 5 km. Be sure to start early due
to the temple's limited hours and the tremendous heat. Get
Bus 101 from City Bus Stand, by the palace.
**Sandalwood Oil Factory**: See the production of incense 09:00–
11:00 h, 14:00–16:00 h, daily except Sunday (also sales), get
Bus 1 or 1a.

**Government Silk Factory:** Sari weaving can be seen 07:30–11:30 h, 12:30–16:30 h, daily except Sundays.

**Dussehra (Dassara) Festival:** This ten-day festival, held at the beginning of October, celebrates Chamundaswami's victory over the demon Mahishasura. Evening performances feature dramatic dance, folk dancing, tournament games, fireworks. The high point on the tenth day is a procession of elephants, horses, troops in historic uniforms and coaches through the town. During the day enjoy the sports and exhibits.

**Sightseeing Tours:** Offered by all three tourist offices (see tips) and numerous travel agents in the cheap hotel district. All important spots in the region can be visited by organized bus tours; ask.

## AROUND MYSORE

**Sriangapatnam:** About 15 km from Mysore on the road to Bangalore (another 125 km), the 18th-century capital of Hyder Ali and Tipi Sultan is on an island in the Cauvery. Unfortunately, not much was left of the town after its capture by the British in 1799. The ruins of the fortifications, mosque and temple do give a good indication of the wealth and power of the empire. Outside the Fort are Tipu's Summer Palace and Mausoleum. The palace now houses a small museum, open 09:00–17:00 h. Get Bus 125 (1.60Rs) from Mysore City Bus Stand. Buses too from Bangalore.

**Brindavan Gardens:** Get Bus 150, from Mysore, 19 km west. The well-tended gardens are below Krishnarajasagar Dam. In the

evening the grounds are lit by a thousand colourful lights, with
soft music via the sound system. A computer switches the fountains and lights in time with the music's rhythm. The spectacle
attracts both local and traveller interest, as testified by our
mail. Opinions vary from lovely, to wonderful, or kitsch, costs
2.-Rs.

**Somnathpur:** Built on stay-shaped foundations around 1260 AD,
this Hoysala temple features three Vishnu shrines and a courtyard. The Channakeshara Temple is covered with reliefs depicting
the great Indian epics, and the lives of the great Hoysala kings.
Notice the frieze of animals and mythical figures.

You might stay at the KSTDC Tourist Home with adjoining restaurant, excellent, **(D)**35.-Rs. Buses from Mysore Central Bus Stand
(change buses in Tirarasipura; costs 5.-Rs, 45 km) or from
Sriangapatnam (change buses in Bannur) direct buses are rare.

Or take a long day trip by bus (90 km) to Sravanabelagola
(see Sravanabelagola).

**TIPS**
There are three tourist offices, but a visit isn't worth it, if all
you want are brochures. But they do serve as booking offices for
sightseeing tours.
**Tourist Reception Centre:** In the Old Exhibition Building, Irwin
road, tel.23251, Mon-Sat 10:30-13:30 h, 14:15-17:30 h.
**KSTDC:** 2 Jhansi Lakshmi Bai Road, tel.23652.
**Tourist Office:** In Kaveri Arts & Crafts Emporium.
**GPO:** Ashoka Road at Irwin Road, see map.
**Central Telegraph Office:** By the palace, see map.
**Indian Airlines:** Hotel Mayura Hoysala, Jhansi Lakshmi Bai Road.
**Railway Booking Office:** Conveniently in the town center, see map.

# Bandipur National Park

Eighty km down the road from Mysore to Ootacamund (Ooty), Tamil Nadu, this 874 km$^2$ wildlife sanctuary is a habitat for elephant, bison (gaur), deer, monkeys, leopards, and even tiger,
which are naturally rarely seen. Together with Mudumulai
(320 km$^2$ in Tamil Nadu) and Wynad (Kerala), the sanctuary
stretches over 2000 km$^2$. The best seasons to visit are May to
June and September through November.

**COMING - GOING**
Several buses daily run from Mysore to Ooty via Bandipur and
Mudumalai (Theppakadu). The first bus departs Mysore at
05:00 h; the last bus leaves Bandipur at 17:30 h, takes 3 h,
costs 10.-Rs; likewise to and from Ooty. From Theppakadu,
you've direct buses to Hassan. The Reception Office, at the

parking lot entrance, has information about exact departure times. You'll have to board the buses along the street; they stop wherever there's space.

In Bandipur and Mudumalai, boats, jeeps, and elephants are your primary sources of transport.

## A NIGHT'S REST
Accommodations are reasonable. For Bandipur, book in advance in Mysore (!) at Field Director Office, Project Tiger, Government House, Mysore 570010, tel.20901. You stay in comfortable

bungalows, with two doubles, bath, each with a tiny living room and a room for the 'housekeeper'. All this luxury costs **(D)**25.-Rs. Meals are served in the bungalows. Very quiet and friendly.

**Elephant Rides:** Cost 30.-Rs per hour for at most four riders. Minibus trips through the park (15 km) cost 5.-Rs per kilometer, divided according to the number of passengers.

You can't make reservations for Theppakadu / Mudumalai in Karnataka; rather, speak with the Forest Office in Ooty.

# Mangalore

The town is on the west coast near the border to Kerala, at the northern end of the rail line from Trivandrum and Ernakulum. Once a major seaport, today this is an important junction, of interest as a place to stay the night and change transport. Most travellers passing through are en route between Goa and Kerala.

Mangalore is the primary embarkation point for cashew nuts and coffee. As the former shipbuilding center for Hyder Alis, you can still see remnants of the past, including a battery of cannon. Equally of interest are the lighthouse, frescos in the St. Aloysius College Chapel, the Mangaladevi Temple, and the Temples of the Seven Tanks.

If you're interested in the Jain religion and architecture, you'll find a number of spots to visit between here and Belur / Halebid, including Venur, Karkala, and Dharmastala.

## COMING - GOING

A ten-minute walk separates the railway station and the down-town KSRTC Bus Stand. For connections to Goa, see Goa.

**By Air:**  Mangalore has an airport served by Indian Airlines daily from Bangalore (288.-Rs) and twice daily from Bombay (622.-Rs).

**By Rail:**  Direct trains along the Malabar Coast heading south to Ernakulum and Trivandrum. To Salem and Madras, you may have to change in Shoranur. The fastest connection south is the Malabar Express, takes 11 h to Ernakulum, 16 h to Trivandrum (56.-Rs 2nd class).

**By Bus:** Regular buses to Bangalore and Mysore, plus along the coast north.

At 08:00 h, 13:30 h, and 20:30 h, direct buses to Karwar at the southern border of Goa. A ride in the public bus takes 7 h, costs 35.-Rs, private buses charge 40.-Rs.

In Karwar, since completion of the bridge to Sadashivgarh, you've buses to Goa, depart hourly, takes 3 h to Margao, costs 7.-Rs. The earliest bus departs around 06:00 h. A state-run Kadamba bus runs from Goa via Mangalore to Panaji, departs Mangalore at 10:00 h, costs 65.-Rs. There is a night bus direct to Panaji. In Karwar, five lodges offer cheap accommodations.

**By Ship:** Sporadic connections along the coast between Bombay and Cochin, stopping in Mangalore. Perhaps you'll be lucky.

## A NIGHT'S REST

Several reasonable lodges by the bus stand start at **(S)**15.-Rs; try **Venkamtash** or **Nirmal Lodge**. By the bus stand, try a meal in **Taj Mahal Restaurant**.

Further from town, accommodations 3 km out at Kadri Hill in **Tourist Home**, **(S)**12.-, **(Dm)**6.-.

Ten km south of town, near Chotamangalore (fishing village) is **Summer Sands Beach Resort**, **(S)**110.-Rs, **(D)**130.-, **(Eb)**25.-Rs, a shady bungalow complex with swimming pool, lounge chairs, restaurant; the only one in Karnataka.

# ANDHRA PRADESH

Three million people make their
homes in the capital of India's
poorest state, Andhra Pradesh
(60 million people, 277,000 km$^2$,
local language: Telugu). A long
Islamic tradition, dating back to
Hyderabad's founding by Mohammed
Quli in 1590, is visible in the
architecture, though only 15 % of
the population are Muslim.

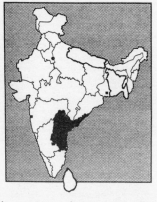

After Aurangzeb's victory over
the Qutab-Shahi dynasty in 1687, he
installed a Nizam (= viceroy) as
ruler over this remote addition to
his kingdom. But the Nizams made
themselves independent after Aurangzeb's death in 1707, without
British interference. Not until one
year after Indian Independence did
the Indian Union march troops into the region, forcing the last
Nizam of Hyderabad, the richest man in the world at the time, to
agree to annexation of the territory by the Indian Republic.
Later the Telugu-speaking parts of the then Madras State (today
Tamil Nadu) were added, creating present-day Andhra Pradesh.

Only those interested in Islamic architecture should plan an
extensive visit. There's little else to see in this part of the
Deccan and Andhra Pradesh.

ANDHRA PRADESH

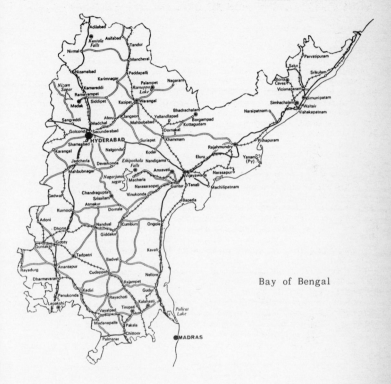

Bay of Bengal

# Hyderabad & Secunderabad

Hyderabad, together with its twin city Secunderabad, forms a single metropolitan area. Secunderabad is most important for travellers passing through.

## COMING - GOING

Secunderabad is the most important of many railway stations; most trains begin, pass through, or end here. Heading south, however, trains also stop in Kacheguda, which is closer to the hotels and sights in Abids. The City Bus Stand (all major inter-city connections) is just south-east of this region on the Musi River. Because trains are frequently booked out, buses are a good alternative.

**By Air:** Hyderabad airport enjoys several flights daily from Bangalore (400.-), Bombay (525.-), Calcutta (970.-), Delhi (900.-), Madras (410.-), Nagpur (340.-), Tirupati (390.-), Vijayawada (230.-), and Visakhapatnam (420.-). Plus several flights via Bhubaneswar (690.-) to Calcutta.

The Indian Airlines office is in Saifabad, near the Secretariat, tel.36902.

**By Rail:** Secunderabad is a major junction in the Deccan rail system. The quickest connections to Delhi (120.-) are Andhra Pradesh or Karnataka Express via Nagpur, Jhansi, and Agra, takes 24 h. The New Delhi - Hyderabad Express takes 34 h. The Karnataka Express goes on to Bangalore (65.-), the Andhra Pradesh continues to Madras (47.-).

Numerous other connections require changing trains in Kazipet, 130 km east of Hyderabad on the two-track main line from New Delhi to Madras Central. Connections to Bombay and the south often require changing trains in Wadi, 195 km west of Hyderabad on the wide-gauge route between Bombay and Guntakal / Gooty; branches too to Madras and Bangalore.

Two direct trains from the west are the Minar and the Bombay-Hyderabad Express via Poona (50.-), takes 14 h, to Bombay 18 h, 65.-.

Two direct trains to Rajasthan, the faster runs twice a week, the 69-Express or 70-Express. Even so think 42 h on the narrow-gauge track to Ajmer, costs 90.-.

The Ajanta Express between Aurangabad and Secunderabad takes 12 h, costs 45.-.

Five express connections daily to the east and north-east, to Vijayawada (40.-) on the east coast route between Calcutta and Madras. Direct connections via Waltair (65.-) to Bhubaneswar / Orissa (85.-Rs), twice daily. No direct connection to Calcutta, go via Vijayawadar, Waltair, or Bhubaneswar.

**By Bus:** Direct De Luxe or Super Express buses to Bangalore (82.-, 13 h), Puttaparthi (50.-, 11 h), Madras (85.-, 17 h), Vijayawada (35.-, 6 h), Waltair (75.-, 15 h), Tirupati (70.-Rs, 15 h), Poona (13 h), Bombay (17 h).

HYDERABAD / SECUNDERABAD

1   Tourist Office
2   Secunderabad
    Railway Station
3   Kacheguda
    Railway Station
4   Hyderabad
    Railway Station
5   Bus Stand
6   GPO
    Telegraph Office
7   Hotels
8   Youth Hostel
9   Charminar
10  Mecca Mosque
11  Salar Jung Museum
12  Archaeological Museum
13  Birla Mandir Temple

No direct buses to Orissa and Calcutta! Almost all tickets are available on day of departure. A bit more expensive than by rail, but faster, and you're guaranteed a seat. It is a well organized booking system.

**Around Town**: Buses are agonizingly crowded. Some of the major lines include Line 2 between Charminar and Secunderabad Railway Station; Line 7 from Secunderabad to Abids (cheap accommodations); and Line 119 from Hyderabad Railway Station to Golconda Fort. At City Bus Station, you can buy a schedule and city map. Otherwise stick to scooters or rickshaws.

## A NIGHT'S REST

Almost all cheap accommodations are situated in the area between the GPO and the Abids district and by Hyderabad Railway Station on or near Station Road. You might try **(S)**10.- no shower, to **(AC)(D)**50.- with shower: **Super Hotel**, **Super Lodge**, **Royal Hotel** (tel.221020), **Royal Lodge**, **New Royal**, **Gee Royal**, etc. All are grouped together on a quiet courtyard, except a few rooms facing Nampally High Road (say that destination to your scooter or rickshaw driver so he won't know to ask for a commission on the lodgings at your expense). Some rooms are good, others shabby, have a look first, restaurant available. **Paradise Lodge**, Abids, **(D)**30.- fan, shower, toilet. **Sri Brindavan Hotel**, Station Road, tel.220820, better rooms, **(S)**50.-, **(D)**70.-, shower, fan, centrally located, but quiet, good restaurant. **Hotel Imperial** (a bit cheaper) and **Hotel Apsara** (a bit more expensive) also on Station Road. **Youth Hostel**, tel.220121, on the northern bank of the Hussain Sagar in Secunderabad, offers **(Dm)**8.-, outside town, near Secunderabad Railway Station.

## REFRESHMENT

The HYDERABAD GREAT RESTAURANT HUNT is still on. To date nobody has found one worth a mention. So try any restaurant, lots around Hyderabad Railway Station near the GPO.

## TIPS

**ITDC Tourist Office**: Lidcap Building, 3-6-150 Himayat Nagar, tel.220730, best of all info offices. Info too in the two major railway stations, and in Diamond House, Liberty Road. The booth marked on many maps west of the GPO is wrong!
**GPO**: With **Poste Restante** and the **Telegraph Office**, Abids Road at the corners of Nehru, Gandhi, and Station Road.
**Foreigners' Regional Registration Office**: Commissioner of Police, Purana Haveli, Hyderabad, tel.30191.
**Bazar**: Best buys, south of the river, near Charminar, where you'll find the famous Hyderabad Bangles (bracelet).

## SIGHTS

South of the Musi River, everything's close. It takes just one long day to see everything.

**Charminar**: A gate tower on the main road into the old town, now a lively bazar. The structure was constructed under Mohammed Quli Qutab Shah in 1591 as part of the city's founding. You can climb the 53 m minaret of this city landmark, costs -.50.

**Mecca Masjid**: Mosque constructions from 1614 to 1687 AD saw fruit in tremendous arches, hewn from granite blocks weighing tons, and dragged here across 11 km by 1400 oxen.

**Salar Jang Museum**: Near the bridge, north of Charminar, houses perhaps the world's largest and most valuable private exhibits, featuring pieces from all over the world, spread over 36 halls. It was put together by Prime Minister Mir Yusaf Ali Khan (Nawab Salar Jang III) in the court of the last Nizam, 10:00-17:00 h, costs 1.50.-Rs, crowded Sundays.

**The Archaeological Museum**: Located in the Public Gardens north of Hyderabad Railway Station, open daily (except Mondays) 10:30-17:00 h, costs -.50, frequently closed for construction.

**Naubat Prahat** (Birlar Mandir / Kala Pahad): A lovely modern Hindu temple of white marble on one of two hills south of Hussain Sagar, free admission.

## AROUND HYDERABAD

**Golconda Fort**: 11 km west of town, first construction dates back to the 13th century. The fortress served as capital for the Qutub Shahi dynasty from 1525 until its defeat at the hands of Aurangzeb in 1687. Only after eight months of siege did the fort fall. The fortress, built on a 120 m granite hill, went into slow decay after the viceroys, named by Aurangzeb, declared Hyderabad the new capital. However, the fortifications, including an 11 km outer wall, and interior fortifications featuring eight gates, are still preserved. The structures inside the facility are in sad condition. But reconstruction, albeit slow, is underway.

**Qutub Shahi Tombs**: 1 km north of Colconda, the Qutub Shahi dynasty kings are interned in tombs of intricate stonework, costs 0.25 Rs, plus 2.-Rs photo permit. Think in terms of a half day, better a whole day, for this excursion. Bus 119 connects Hyderabad Railway Station with Colconda Fort.

**Nehru Zoological Garden**: Worth the -.50 Rs admission, daily (except Monday) 09:00-18:00 h.

All these sights are included in the conducted tours offered by the tourist offices (AP and ITDC) in Himayat Nagar. They last from 08:00-18:00 h, cost 25.- to 30.-Rs. Besides the above, the tours visit Osmania University and Gandhipet Lake (Osmansagar).

# Waltair & Visakhapatnam

The earliest written references we find to this double town (pop.
400,000) date from 1068 AD,  but it is certainly much older.  The
region has a long Buddhist tradition,  as part of the Ashoka Empire.  Its development into a major industrial and port town (Visakhapatnam) on one hand,  and as a beach resort (Waltair) on
the other, is still in full swing.

The harbour was founded just 50 years ago,  but it's become
one of the most important harbors in southern Asia. Its protective
harbor (important in a country plagued by monsoons) shelters
India's only submarine base. It is the deepest harbour in southern Asia,  housing India's only dry dock.  The lighthouse is the
second largest in the world (with the white light).  And there is
a tremendous radar installation.

Major industrial projects,  including a refinery,  fertilizer
factory, ore-shipping facilities, and steelworks, make this section
of Andhra Pradesh relatively wealthy and well organized.

There isn't much to see; just a nice town with a 2 km sandy
beach along Beach Road in Waltair. In addition, you can swim in
Lawson's Bay,  3 km north of Waltair,  or 20 km further north in
Bheemunipatnam (India's only long beach).

By the way,  this is the only major town in India where I've
never seen foreign tourists,  and where I've never been spoken to
on the street. While this is not a town you go out of your way to
visit,  it is certainly the most pleasant spot to take a break
between Orissa and Madras.

## COMING - GOING

**By Air:**  Calcutta (590.-),  Madras (460.-), Raipur (310.-), Vijayawada (240.-).  Indian Airlines office,  Waltair Main Road,
tel.62673. The airport is 15 km from town.

**By Rail:**  All trains between Madras, Bhubaneswar and Calcutta
stop in Waltair Junction from where you have frequent bus
connections to Visakhapatnam Bus Stand (15 km).  The quickest
east coast connection is the Coromandel Express between Calcutta-Howrah and Madras Central (5 additional trains).  Three
trains daily to Secunderabad / Hyderabad.

**By Bus:**  Visakhapatnam Bus Stand is situated 2 km outside the
town center.  Direct buses to Hyderabad (08:00 h,  75.-, 16 h),
Vijayawada (10 h,  connection to Madras), Puri (06:00 h, 52.-,
14 h), and Guntur (09:30 & 20:00 h).

## A NIGHT'S REST

Although the region isn't set up for foreign tourists, there is a
surprising number of pleasant places to stay, some with all the
perks.  Here too is Andhra Pradesh's only 5-star hotel, a sure
sign of the importance of domestic tourism!  **Hotel Apsara,**

(S)55.-, (D)90.-, 12-1-17 Waltair Main Road, tel.64861, lots of
pleasantry for the money, centrally located with three restaurants in all price classes; offices inside include the regional
Tourist Office, Indian Airlines, and a travel agency. **Hotel
Ooty**, (S)30.-, (D)60.-, Daba Gardens, centrally located in
Visakhapatnam. **Hotel Marina**, (S)30.-, Beach Road, Visakhapatnam, tel.4345. Around Hotel Ooty in Daba Gardens are numerous
cheap accommodations, (S)15.-, (D)25.-, e.g. **Hotel Annapurna**
(in hot Andhra Pradesh, cool names are in!), **Hotel Jupiter**,
and **Hotel Manorama**. **Municipal Traveller's Bungalow**, just
(S)15.-Rs, Beach Road, near Ramakrishna Mission, tel.2301.
**Circuit House**, near Hotel Apsara.

## REFRESHMENT
For a change, try a restaurant with a lake view - **Kwality**, on
Beach Road, almost in the middle, Indian and Chinese food,
soft drinks and ice cream, dinner runs 12.- to 18.-Rs including
drinks and ice cream. **Hotel Apsara** has good food in all price
classes, western food evenings only in Seven Star restaurant,
costs 18.-Rs. Good but expensive at the north end of Beach
Road in **Park Hotel** or **Palm Beach**. Try pies and cakes in **Gulmarg**, near Hotel Ooty, Daba Gardens. Indian restaurants are
everywhere. Roasted corn on the beach in the evening.

## AROUND WALTAIR & VISAKHAPATNAM
**Simhachalam:** 20 km north of Visakhapatnam. On a hill (300 m) is
**Simhachi Narasimhaswamy Temple** (Vahara Narasimha Temple),
dedicated to Vishnu, dating from the 11th century, Orissa in
style. Stay the night in Tourist Rest House, reservations at the
Tourist Office, Waltair Main Road.

## TIPS
**Regional Tourist Office:** Waltair Main Road, next to Hotel Apsara.
**Indian Airlines & Travel Agency:** Same building.
**State Bank Of India:** Main branch(!), the only place in town
which cashes traveller's checks, near the Old Post office in Vi-
sakhapatnam center.

# Puttaparthi

In southern Andhra Pradesh, in Anantapur District near the
Gooty - Bangalore Road, this Deccan village would hardly deserve
a mention, were it not for one of the most important ashrams in
India, surrounding the Avatar (incarnation of God, comparable to
Krishna) Bhagavan Sri Sathya Sai Baba.
    Hundreds of pilgrims stay at the ashram, including numerous
foreigners. A room costs 5.-Rs, with a toilet, but without any

furniture. Food is cheap in and around the ashram. And all your
daily needs can be purchased.    A State Bank of India (which
cashes travellers checks), and a Post Office are in town.

**Ashram Address**:   Prasanthi Nilayam, Puttaparthi, Anantapur District, PIN 515 134, Andhra Pradesh. You might telegraph ahead to
ask when Sai Baba will be there.

## COMING - GOING
**By Bus**:   From Bangalore at 13:00,   16:00,   and 17:00 h, takes
5 h,   costs 30.-.    Bus to Hyderabad at 19:30 (50.-,  11 h), return at 20:15 h.   Frequent connections via Anantapur,   change
there,   i.e. to Madras, costs 50.-Rs. Eat in Anantapur in Hotel
Bheema, on Srikantam Road.
**By Overland Taxi**:   From Bangalore,   costs 400.- to 500.- pro
vehicle.   Find other riders by S.Babu,   Hotel Cauvery,   11/37
Cunningham Road,   tel.29350,   Bangalore.   Babu's taxi service
frequents the Bangalore Puttaparthi route.

Puttaparthi
Street Scenes

# MADRAS

Over four million people live in the
capital of India's southeasternmost
state, Tamil Nadu. But India's
fourth largest city isn't the metropolitan giant you might expect (except in a few spots).

The city's written history began
in the 16th century when the Portuguese founded a small settlement in
what is now Mylapur. The village
first achieved importance in 1639
when Francis Day, for the East India Company, negotiated a treaty
with the Raja of Chanragiri (the
last ruler of the Hampi Kingdom),
founding the first trading center in
India. The stage was set for 300
years of British exploitation in
India.

Completion of Fort St. George in 1653, gave rise to a settlement called Georgetown, which forms the center of Madras today.
After independence for the British administration on Java in 1683,
the village was given a town charter by King James II in 1688.
From that day on, British influence increased greatly, spurred by
competition with France. France occupied the town as part of its
bid for control of the Deccan Plateau. But Clive managed to push
the French back into insignificant enclaves such as Pondicherry.
In the 19th century, Madras became one of four regional capitals
under the British Raj.

Today it is a major industrial city (textiles, metal works,
auto industry). Along with Bombay, this is the home of the Indian film industry. Madras sports many names, including, "India's Gateway to the South" or "India's Hollywood".

Additionally, the city serves as the spiritual and cultural
center of the south, with numerous schools, universities, ashrams,
and cultural institutions.

## COMING - GOING

Madras is the traffic junction of southern India, if only because it receives so many visitors. Several international
flights, make it a major point of arrival. Plus, there's a
shipping line from Singapore via Penang, Malaysia.

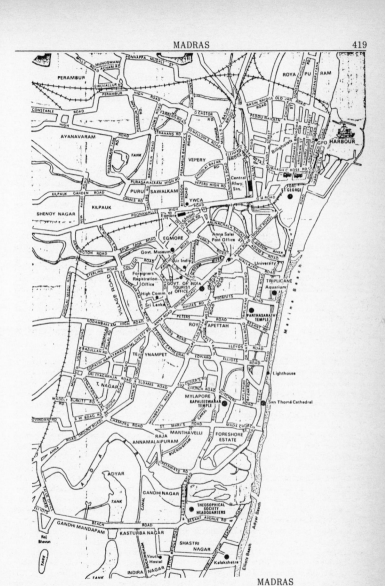

MADRAS

The airport is far south-west of town. All the major bus and
train stations are grouped close together along the east-west
artery, Poonamalle High Road, and its eastward extension toward the harbor, G.H. Road. Here too are countless budget
hotels.

**By Air:** Madras is served by numerous international airlines,
albeit less frequently than Bombay, Delhi, or Calcutta. Prices
here are higher.

Daily flights to Colombo, Sri Lanka with Air Lanka or Indian
Airlines for 710.-Rs (US$78.).

Maldive Airways flies into Madras on Sundays with its DC-8.
Agent: Cross World Tours, 7 Rosy Towers, Nungambakkam
High Rd., Madras 600 034, tel 471497.

Besides domestic flights, Air India offers a service to
Singapore, Kuala Lumpur, and Sharjah (Abu Dhabi). Other
major international carriers serve Madras at least weekly.

Sample prices: Bangalore several times daily 228.-; Bombay
several times daily 790.-; Calcutta daily 1000.-; Cochin daily
380.-; Delhi twice daily 1200.-; Hyderabad twice daily 410.-;
Madurai daily 325.-; Port Blair, Andamanen Wed & Sun 980.-;
Tiruchirappalli (Trichy) daily 240.-; Trivandrum daily 470.-Rs.

Air India, 19 Marshalls Road, Egmore, Madras 600008,
tel.847799, 09:30-17:30 h.

Indian Airlines, 19 Marshalls Road, Egmore, Madras 600008,
tel.847522 & 847098, 09:00-19:00 h, closed Sun.

Singapore Airlines, 167 Mount Rd., tel.86156-58, twice weekly to
Singapore.

Air Lanka, Hotel Connemara Annexe, Binny's Rd., Madras
600002, by Mount Road, tel.87432: Colombo and Kuala Lumpur.

For airlines without an office in Madras, e.g. Syrian Arab
Airlines, Thomas Cook Ltd. will book you by telex, 112 Nungambakkam High Rd., Madras 600034, tel.473092 or 475052.

Info on arriving and departing flights: tel.433131 & 433954.

The Airport Hotel costs 75.-Rs in a comfortable room. You have
to present a confirmed ticket.

Meenambakkam Airport is situated well south-west of town. The
airport bus departs half-hourly 04:00-24:00 h, in the night just
hourly. By request it will stop at the major hotels, perhaps
even make a slight detour. The ride, 1 h maximum, runs between Egmore Station and the airport, stopping at the India
Airlines office on Mount Road and a number of hotels along the
way, costs 15.-Rs. A taxi from Adyar Bridge costs 20.-Rs,
Egmore 27.-Rs, Parry's Corner 30.-Rs. Baggage costs 5.-Rs
extra. Scooters are a bit cheaper.

**By Rail:** Almost all Southern Railway trains, plus the Kerala
Line and Tamil Nadu Line, stop at Egmore Station. All other
trains, i.e. those from northern and western India, put in at
Madras Central Station. The two stations are a good kilometer
apart on Poonamallee High Rd.; get a scooter for 3.-Rs.

1st-class tickets are sold in the respective train stations. For
2nd-class tickets, Southern Railway has a booking office on the

northern end of Mount Rd. (Anna Salai), tel.85642, open 10:00–
18:00 h. The tourist quota for Southern Railway is distributed
to foreign tourists at Egmore Station in the Superintendent's
Office.

The ticket windows for both stations are open 06:30–13:00 h
and 13:30–20:30 h for 1st and 2nd class, Sunday 07:00–13:00 h.

To Bombay your three fastest connections are the Dadar-Mad-
ras Express (27 h), Janata Express (29 h), and the Mail
(31 h).

The two fastest trains to Delhi are the Grand Trunk Express
(36 h) via Agra and Jhansi, and the Tamil Nadu Express
(33 h, four times weekly).

To Varanasi get the Ganga Kaveri (38 h) on Tuesdays and
Sundays.

To Calcutta-Howrah get the Coromandel Express (27 h) daily,
along the east coast, booked out days ahead, just 1st class.
Or get the 4 Howrah (33 h) or the 3 Madras Mail (33 h).

To southern India, buses are best.

**By Bus:** All local and long-distance bus stations are grouped
together east of Madras Central Station between G.H. Road and
Netaji Subhash Bose Rd., in an area still called Parry's Corner. City buses also depart from here. The entrances are on
Esplanade Rd. (which connects the two above-mentioned roads).
There are two overland bus stations: Tamil Nadu State
Transport Bus Stand on Broadway, and a bus stand for the
private Tiruvalluvar Transport Corporation Ltd. The combined
bus systems provide better transport through southern India
than by rail!

Buses to Mahabalipuram (19 A and 68) and Kanchipuram depart from State Transport Terminal. Schedules are usually
written in Tamil, but young boys will be glad to help you find
your bus for a 30 paisa tip. You might even just ask.

From Tiruvalluvar Bus Stand, tel.25044, buses to Bangalore
(nine times daily, 30.- to 50.-); Mysore (09:00 h, 9 h); Coimbatore (five times nights, 12 h, 38.- to 48.-); Trichy (hourly,
25.- to 31.-); Madurai (twice mornings, six times evenings,
34.- to 45.- via Trichy); Nagercoil (ten daily, 15 h, 52.- to
65.-); Kanyakumarin (four daily, 53.- to 67.-); Mandapam /
Rameswaram (five daily, 42.-, 52.-); Tanjavur (12 daily, 25.-
to 31.-); Trivandrum (16 h, 74.-); Mettupalayam (a stop on the
narrow-gauge railway to Ooty, 17:30 h, 50.-); Pondicherry (six
daily besides those to Nagapattinam, 4 h, 13.- to 20.-); Chidambaram (six daily, 20.-Rs).

Bookings can be made ten days in advance, 06:00–20:00 h;
prices vary according to route and comfort.

Several buses daily to the pilgrim town, Tirupati (AP), costs
14.- to 17.-Rs.

Buses to several locations in Andhra Pradesh depart from
Basin Bridge Bus Stand, i.e. Hyderabad (15:30 h, 84.-); or
Ananthapur (21:00 h, 10 h, 50.-Rs, 2 h beyond Puttaparthi).

**By Ship:** Several shipping companies are located around Par-

ry's Corner, the bus stands and Armenian Street: Binny & Co.,
tel.26894 (same building as Amexco). Indo Malaysia Shipping
Agency, tel.24525. K.P.V. Shaikh Mohamed Rowther & Co., official agency of the Shipping Corporation of India. Boats to Port
Blair, Andaman Islands, Penang / Singapore. Located at
202 Linghi Chetty Street (corner Thambu Chetty Street), Madras
600001, tel.25756, 10:00-13:15 h, 14:00-17:30 h. Until the M/S
Chidambaram burned out in 1985, there was a ship every three
weeks via Penang, Malaysia to Singapore; talk of a replacement ship abounds; ask!

Monthly service to Colombo, Sri Lanka; sporadic service to
Trincomalee, Sri Lanka.

There is a ship every three weeks to Port Blair, Andaman
Islands, costs 100.- to 600.-Rs. But plan your trip early, many
islands require an entry permit, detailing your exact travel
plans. Apply at least six weeks in advance at the Ministry of
Home Affairs in New Delhi, or at an Indian consulate abroad
(see Andaman Islands).

**Around Town**: The cog of local transport is Municipal Bus
Stand, Parry's Corner, near Express Bus Stand, on Netaji Subash Bose Road. For a look at all the bus lines, pick up a
copy of **Madras City Tourist Guide**, costs 2.50 Rs. Mount Road
(Anna Salai) runs north - south: lots of offices, banks, airlines, shops, tourist offices, and terrible air pollution. Traversing the entire length are Buses 5, 5A, 9, 10, 11, 11A, and
18F.

After 21:00 h, service is limited to a small night bus system.

The Indian airlines airport bus connects Egmore Railway Station and the Indian Airlines office with the airport, costs
15.-Rs. Upon request it stops at major hotels, tel.841284, takes
an hour.

There is an efficient local train system. Most interesting are
the lines heading south: departing from Beach Station (GPO),
via Egmore and Saidapet (buses to Adyar / youth hostel), to
Ninambakkam (10 minutes walk from the airport).

Taxis cost 3.- for the first kilometer, and 1.-Rs for each
additional, but you'll still have to bargain. Scooters are little
cheaper; the kilometers are less expensive, but you won't get
a ride for less than 5.-Rs (too short). And in Madras it's
traditional that few scooter drivers are willing to use the meter. If you hear "the meter is not working", don't argue, just
look for a new scooter. A rickshaw costs 1.-Rs per kilometer.

# A NIGHT'S REST

While reasonable lodgings can be found all over town, most are
concentrated in three regions: Madras Egmore, Madras Central,
and in Adyar in the south of town.

In Egmore: **Hotel Impala**, across from the railway station,
**(S)**25.-, **(D)**40.-, showers, good friendly. **Tourist Home**, 20
Gandhi Irwin Road, tel.844079, **(S)**40.-, **(D)**65.-. **Hotel Imperial**,
1A Gandhi Irwin Road, tel.847076, **(S)**60.-, **(D)**100.- (plus),

restaurants, bars. **Hotel New Victoria**, 1 Kennet Lane,
tel.847736, near Hotel Imperial, **(S)**80.-, **(D)**135.-, restaurant.
**Hotel Majestic**, Kennet Lane, across from Hotel New Victoria,
**(S)**15.-, 30.-, **(D)**30.-, 40.-. **People's Lodge**, near Egmore
Street, **(S)**30.-, **(D)**60.-, popular, frequently booked out. **RRR**
in Egmore Railway Station, **(S)**20.-, **(D)**30.-, **(Eb)**5.-, usually
full. **YMCA**, Ritherdon Road, Vepery, **(D)**25.-, showers, toilet,
fan, open to men and women, north of Egmore Railway Station.
**YWCA** Guest House & Camping Ground, 530 Poonamallee High
Road, tel.39920, **(S)**25.-; Camping: 5.- per vehicle, 3.- per
person, 2.- per tent, restaurant. **World University Student
Center**, Spur Tank Road, tel.663991, near the Government Museum, student ID required, **(S)**10.-, showers, **(Dm)**5.-, a male
dorm: not recommended for single women!

Near Egmore, across Mount Road, facing Star Cinema on Triplicane High Road, try **Broadlands**, 26 Vallabhu Agraharam
Street, tel.845573, lots of readers praise this travellers' spot,
**(S)**17.-, 25.-, **(D)**34.-, **(Tr)**44.-, **(Dm)**10.-, two shady courtyards with plants and palms, several roof terraces, peaceful
atmosphere, pleasant rooms, clean, friendly. **Traveller's Home**
and **Hotel Eswari** are located between Egmore and Central Station.

In the Georgetown District, between Madras Central Station
and the harbour to the northeast, near the GPO and bus
stands: **Malaysia Lodge**, 44 Armenian street, best-known spot in
Madras, crowded, **(S)**12.-, **(D)**15.-, 25.- (bath), **(Dm)**5.-, restaurant, but at these prices you get what you pay for (Reader's Tip: filthy mattresses and sheets, slime in the showers,
"the most miserable in India"). **Hotel Rolex**, tel.24236, across
from the fruit market, 190 Netaji Subash Bose Road, looks from
outside a lot nicer than it is, but except for morning market
noise (out front) we liked it, **(D)**35.-, good expensive AC restaurant, full of luxury tourists (Reader's Tip: real India lurks
in the Rattan Market behind the building). **YMCA**, Esplanade 223, on N.S. Bose Rd., Parry's Corner, tel.23941, just
men, **(Dm)**10.-, **(S)**20.- (bath). **RRR**, in Central Station,
**(S)**20.-, **(D)**30.-, **(Eb)**5.-. **Sri Rama Bhavan's Boarding Home**,
Thambu Chetty Street, **(D)**15.-. **Hotel Jayalakshmi**, Kondi Chetty
Street, **(S)**25.-, **(D)**35.-, showers. **Hotel Surat**, Popham's Broadway, near the YMCA, **(S)**20.-, **(D)**30.-, 50.-Rs.

And away from the city smells, in the southern districts of
Mylapore and Adyar (Bus 19 M): **Gupta's Ajanta Hotel**, 32 Roy-
apettah High Road, tel.845223, **(S)**35.-, **(D)**50.-. **New Woodlands
Hotel**, 72-75 Dr.Radhakrishnan Salai, Mylapore, tel.831111,
**(S)**35.-, **(D)**50.-. **Karpagam Hotel**, 19 South Madha Street, Mylapore, tel.72388, by Kapaleswar Temple, a real Indian hotel,
front rooms have a nice view of the temple and pond, **(D)**50.-.
**Tourist Hotel**, Andhra Mahila Sabha, 38 Adyar Bridge Road,
tel.76001, **(S)**25.-, **(D)**40.-. **Youth Hostel**, Indira Nagar, Adyar,
tel.412882, just **(Dm)**7.-, members have preference and pay
half, if it's booked, you can sleep on the floor for 4.-Rs, last

stop on Bus 19M or Buses 19S,    23A,  half hour from town, near
Elliots Beach,   quiet,   clean,    much more pleasant than in the
inner-city heat.
  Members of the Theosophical Society can sleep on the grounds
with advance reservations.
  In the southern Thyagaraya district: **Transit House**,   26 Ven-
kataraman Street,   Madras 600017,  tel.441346, owned by Silversands in Mahabalipuram,   luxury dorms (just women) **(Dm)**35.-,
**(S)**200.-,  **(D)**250.-.
  The most expensive hotels, **(S)**350.- plus, are worth mentioning
because they have swimming pools,  good hairdressers,   and
change money at any odd hour.
  **Holiday Inn Adyar Gate**,   132 Mowbraya Road,   Madras 600017,
tel.444676,  hairdresser,  lunch and dinner buffet.  **Hotel Taj
Coromandel** (Reader's Tip),  17 Nungambakkam Road, tel.848888,
the most expensive hotel,   swimming pool,   good food,   features
free dance performances.  **V.G.P. Golden Beach Resort**,   East
Coast Road,  Madras 600041 (Enjambakkam),  tel.412893,  beach
cottages 150.-,   the entire complex is built in Indian fantasy
style,   attracting tourist groups,   moderate prices in the restaurant,   friendly,   but swimmers seem to attract crowds of
onlookers.
Note:  During the Pongol Festival in January,  all the downtown
lodgings are booked.  Don't even imagine arriving in the afternoon and finding a bed!  Only in the morning do you have a
chance.  When all else fails,  there are still the most expensive
accommodations. Let the Tourist Office phone around, or reserve
well in advance!

## REFRESHMENT
If you insist on western food,  this is a place where you can
pig out on unaccustomed fare.  In Buhari Hotel,   3/17 Mound
Road, diagonally across from the post office, 07:00-01:30 h, try
chicken with cheese sauce,   veal,   etc.,  good, affordable, but
not if you're saving,   also on Poonamallee High Road by Moore
Market and on Beach Road in Marina Beach.  There is a good,
reasonable restaurant in Spencer's Building on Mount Road.  If
you like typical Gujarati and Rajasthani food, try the restaurant in Safire Theater Building at 614 Mount Road.  Across from
Abbots Bury (Sai Baba Centre,  Mount Road) is **Chitchat**,  a
small café where you might risk real icecream and cake.  Or
try **Woodlands Drive-In Restaurant**,  Cathedral Road at Mount
Road,  good,  cheap.  Also recommended in Wheat Hotel,  near
popular Broadlands Hotel (200 m down Triplivane Road,   then
left).  Good restaurants in the hotels around Egmore Station,
ranging from Indian vegetarian to Chinese and western.  Try
Chinese in **Chunking** on Mount Road,  where you'll find everything from fast foods to garden restaurants and icecream
parlours.
  **Ganga Vegetarian Restaurant**,   57 Armenian Street, Georgetown,
with that special touch,   moderate prices.  **Ramakrishna Vege-**

**tarian Restaurant**, nearby, by Parry's Corner and the YMCA.
Good restaurants in Adyar at the corner of Elliots Beach Road
and Adyar Bridge Road.

## SHOPPING
**Western Consumer Goods**: Primarily on Mount Road.
**Spencer's**: Has just about everything, but the package shipping
department has closed.
**State-Owned Emporia**: Offer local handicrafts at fixed prices, i.e.
**Poom Puhar**. Lots of private shops offer the same selection. In
Madras buy hand-woven cloth carpets for 20.-Rs, and lovely bath
mats for 5.-Rs, silver jewelry, and silk saris.
**Silk**: South of Panangal Park (S.M. Usman Road), in Spencer's,
and in Mylapore near the temple. We've never seen southern In-
dian silk cheaper than in Madras.
**Bazars**: Two other places to shop include the **Rattan Bazar** at
Broadway and Esplanade, north and east of Central Railway Sta-
tion (silk, jewellery, silver). And look between Mount Road and
Parthasarathy Temple. For more info pick up the brochure, **Where
To Buy**, at the Government of India Tourist Office.
**Bookstores**: On Mount Road, you've a good selection of Indian and
foreign books and magazines in English. The largest bookstore in
southern India is **Higginbothams Ltd.**, tel.86556. Or try **Kennedy
Book Stall**.
**Film**: Will be developed within two weeks by the **India Photo-
graphic Company** (formerly Kodak Ltd.), 129 Greames Road, Madras 600006, tel.472918, 09:30-13:00 h, 13:45-17:30 h, good service, western developing coupons are not accepted.

## ACTIVITIES
**Sport**: Keeping fit in Madras is organized by clubs for the middle
and upper classes. Cricket, tennis, golf, and billiards, are pop-
ular.
**Swimming**: For a swim, you might head out to Elliot Beach, 10 km
from downtown, or visit one of the pools. Most expensive (25.-Rs)
in the luxury hotels: Holiday Inn Adyar Gate, 132 Mowbrays
Road, Madras 600018, and in Taj Coromandel, 17 Nungambakkam
Road. Or try the Dolfins Pool in Hotel Connemara, Binny's Road;
in Hotel Sudarasan International, Egmore; Woodlands Swimming
Pool, Mylapore; the YMCA, Saidapet (closed Mon); Anna Swimming
Pool and Marina Swimming Pool (just Sat, Sun, Mon) at Marina
Beach.
**Movies**: Madras is a movie town. There are five movie theaters
just in the Safire Building, 614 Mount Road. Check any newspaper
for the latest listings. Be sure to see at least one Indian film.
After all, more films are made each year in India than in any
other country in the world, bringing important foreign exchange
(mostly from Asian countries). Madras follows only Bombay in
numbers of films produced. The best films, however, are made in
Calcutta. Here in Madras, the classical Indian film motif "Lost
and Found" featuring pain, heartbreak, and song is still strong.

## CULTURAL INSTITUTES

**British Council:** Local Library Authority Building, Mount Road.
**Alliance Française de Madras:** 40 College Road, Nungambakkam, tel.812650.
**Theosophical Society:** Near Adyar Bridge, in the south of town, library, reading room, various events.
**Max Mueller Bhavan:** Express Estate, Old Club House Road (off Mount Road), Madras 600002, tel.811315, reading room, library, German magazines, films, exhibits, events.
**Kalakshetra's Auditorium:** During the Pongal Festival in January an **Art Festival** is held in Kalakshetra, featuring Indian music, dance and dramatic dance. The spiritual life of the artists is reflected in their performances. Anyone truly interested in understanding India should attend, costs 5.- to 25.-Rs, best tickets are 10.-Rs for the floor in front of the stage, starts at 18:00 h. Address: Kalakshetra's Auditorium, Thiruvanmiyur, Madras 600041, tel.411836, get Bus 19E, 19G, 19M, 19S, 21A, 21F, 23A, or 23E; buses await after the performance.

## SPIRITUAL FULFILMENT

**Krishnamurti Foundation India:** Vasanta Cihar, 64/65 Greenways Road, Madras 600028, tel.73803, north of Adyar Bridge.
**Theosophical Society:** World Headquarters, near Adyar Bridge, if you are interested in the religious and spiritual movements, here is a place you'll find information, people to talk to, a bookstore, library, all in a lovely park.
**The Ramakrishna Mission:** Near the Kapaleshwara Temple in Mylapore, friendly, open people.

### Hatha Yoga Lessons.

**Prof.T.Krishnamachary's Yoga Mandiram,** 10B, 4th Cross Street, Ramakrishna Nagar, tel.72416.
**Adyar Yoga Research Institute,** 15 III Main Road, Kasturbai Nagar, Adyar.
**Shivananda Yoga Institute,** Yogiraj Kashyap Ramanth, 78 C.P.Ramaswamy Iyer Road, Alwarpet, Madras 600018, yoga classes for Indian and foreign students, 07:00-09:00 h and 17:00-19:00 h, 50.-Rs for a ten-day course.
**Kaivalyadhama Yogie Health Centre,** Yoga Brotherhood, Express Estate, Club House Road, Madras 600002.
**Manisha Rajneesh Meditation Centre,** 33 Landons Road, Kilpauk, Madras 600010, tel.663118.

**Sathya Sai Baba:** During January, he can usually be found in Sundaram Temple, Greenways Road, or in Abbots Bury.

## SIGHTS

**Fort St. George, Fort Museum, Secretariat, The Lighthouse, St. Mary's Church** (founded on October 28, 1680, the oldest Anglican church in India): All the above, at the northern end of South Beach Road, provide a good introduction to the history of the British East India Company and India's colonial era. The company's trade representatives began work on September 24, 1641, after completion of the Fort. The East India Company exploited the Indian subcontinent unchallenged from 1600 to the mid 18th century, the early days of British imperialism. Military support by the British crown began in 1759. In 1857 the mightiest company in the world, ruling one-fifth of all humanity, was nationalized by the British parliament. The Government of Tamil Nadu Tourist Office provides an interesting brochure about the Fort, featuring a map. The Fort is open 09:00-17:00 h, free admission.

**Marina Beach:** Just south of the Fort. The **Promenade** invites a walk past **Madras University**, and the **Aquarium**, 14:00-20:00 h, nominal admission.

**Parthasarathy Temple:** Off to the side a bit further south on Triplicane High Road. The temple was built by the Pallavas and dedicated to Krishna in the 8th century. In the 16th century, it was rebuilt by the Vijayanagar dynasty.

**St. Thomas Cathedral:** After the lighthouse, rises at the southern end of South Beach Road, on the spot where the last remains of the apostle are said to reside. The church was built originally in 1504 and rebuilt toward the end of the 19th century.

**Kapaleswara Temple:** Nearby in the district of Mylapore, with a large lotus blossom pond, and a typical Dravidian **Gopuram** (a richly decorated gate tower).

**Theosophical World Headquarters:** The tremendous grounds follow south of Adyar Bridge.

**Botanical Gardens:** Nearby, featuring a huge **banyan tree** (70 m tall and spreading its boughs 75 m), worth a visit, open 08:30-10:30 h, 14:00-16:30 h.

**Guindy Deer Park:** In the southern district of Guindy, near the Raj Bhavan. Inside this National Park, you can observe wild Indian antelope and other rare animals. The snakes in the **Reptilium** can be seen from 09:00-18:00 h, costs 1.-Rs.

**Agri-Horticultural Society:** St. George Cathedral Road; on the grounds is another **banyan tree** large enough even to walk around in. Other unusual plants are offered for sale.

**Government Museum & Art Gallery:** Downtown, Pantheon Road, Egmore, 08:00-17:00 h daily except Fridays, free admission. Most interesting are the bronze department and gallery of paintings featuring both ancient and modern exhibits.

**City Tours:** All the above and more are on the bus itinerary of Sightseeing Conducted Tours by the ITDC and TNTDC (TN Tourist Office), depart daily 14:00-18:00 h, costs 25.-Rs.

## AROUND MADRAS

There are a number of interesting excursions, though the distance involved, and the charm of Mahabalipuram, make it a better departure point for excursions. For sights in the region see the town descriptions, e.g. Mahabalipuram, Kanchipuram, Tirukkalikundram, etc.

Convenient to visit from Madras is the world's second largest
pilgrim town, Tirupati. Only Rome hosts more pilgrims each year.
Situated north-west of Madras in Andhra Pradesh, the town
centers around a temple hill, Tirumala, which is primarily dedicated to the god Venketeramana. Buses from Madras depart hourly
05:00-20:30 h, takes 4 h express, costs 14.- to 17.-Rs. Tours to
Tirupati are organized by both tourist offices on Mount Road
(Tamil Nadu and the Government of India tourist offices), takes
12 h, departs 06:00 h, costs 100.-Rs.

The Government of India Tourist Office, 154 Mount Road,
tel.86240, organizes day trips to Kanchipuram, Tirukkalikundram,
Mahabalipuram, and to the Crocodile Farm. But it is really more
a wild goose chase than a day trip. Just of interest to people
who are truly in a hurry, departs at 07:30 h, return 18:00 h,
costs 40.- (bus), or 55.-Rs (AC De Luxe coach).

## ARTISTS' VILLAGE CHOLAMANDAL

On the road to Mahabalipuram, 20 km from downtown, or
10 km from Adyar is the artists' village of Cholamandal,
founded in 1966. Around 35 painters and sculptors live and
work here in relative peace and seclusion.

Their works are sold by a cooperative via a permanent
exhibit for reasonable prices, providing the creative independence every artist needs. The cooperative is self-admini-
stered, by a council elected annually. Alternative lifestyles
are possible in India! A nearby beach offers a refreshing
finish to the outing.

Address: Cholamandal Artists' Village, Madras 600041,
tel.412892, get Bus 19C, 119A from Broadway Bus Stand, or
Bus 19 from Indira Nagar near the youth hostel.

## TIPS

**Government of India Tourist Office:** 154 Mount Road (Anna Salai),
tel.86240, 09:00-17:00 h, best brochures, etc.
**Tourist Office at the Airport:** Open round the clock, tel.431686.
**Government of Tamil Nadu Tourist Office:** 134 Mount Road,
tel.840752, 10:30-17:00 h, at the airport, tel.433969, 08:30-
21:30 h, and in Central Railway Station tel.33351, 07:15-19:15 h.
**Automobile Association of Southern India:** 187 Mount Road,
tel.86121, helpful if you're driving, sells maps, provides parking
(5.-Rs) and lodgings **(D)**40.-Rs for members of foreign automobile
clubs.

## CONSULATES

**High Commission for Malaysia:** 23 Khader Nawaz Khan Road, Madras 600006, tel.473534, 08:00-15:00 h.
**Sri Lanka High Commission:** 9D Nawab Habibullah Avenue, Anderson Road, Madras 600006, tel.475316, Mon-Fri 09:00-17:30 h,
visa office 09:30-12:00 h for same day completion by 17:00 h, two
passport photos required; it is simpler to get a three-month visa
here than upon arrival!

MADRAS                                                    429

**Japanese Consulate:** 60 Spur Tank Road, Chetput, tel.665594.
**Federal Republic of Germany:** 22 Commander in Chief Road, Mico
Building, Madras 600105, tel.82125.
**The Netherlands:** 739 Anna Salai, tel.86411.
**Great Britain:** 24 Anderson Road, tel.83136.
**United States:** 22 Anna Salai, Gemini Circle, tel.83041.

**Visa Extensions:** Foreigners' Regional Registration Office, 9 Village Road, Madras 600034, tel.85424, 10:00–17:00 h, parallel
street west of Nungambakkam High Road.

**Income Tax:** Foreign Section, 121 Nungambakkam High Road; if
you stay longer than three months, you'll have to present a tax
clearance certificate upon departure. They'll want to see your
money exchange receipts.

**Banks:** Most of the major banks are on Mount Road, including
Bank of America, Bank of Baroda, Grindlays. Best exchange rates
are offered by the State Bank of India, tel.89393, or occasionally
the Indian Overseas Bank, tel.82041, each facing the other on
Mount Road, so check both. The Money Exchange Window at the
airport is open 06:30–20:00 h. American Express in Madras is just
a travel agency, doesn't cash or replace checks (Armenian Street
by Binny's)! Money exchange in the major hotels.

**First Aid:** We know from experience how difficult it is to get a
doctor to make a house call in a hotel. One came once and we
never saw him again. In case of emergency, visit a hospital
immediately. The following nursing homes are good, but each
requires immediate payment for treatment, certainly unhealthy for
your travel budget.
  **H.M. Hospital,** 50 St. Mary's Road, Madras 60008, tel.73979.
  **Lady Willingdon Nursing Home,** 4 Pycrafts Garden, Madras
  600008, tel.86993.
  **Apolo Hospital,** Greams Road, Madras 600006, tel.811268, cheaper
  than most.
  **Government General Hospital,** Park Town, Madras 600003,
  tel.39181.

**Pharmacies:** Found everywhere, a good place to seek advice about
the proper remedy. If symptoms persist, visit a hospital immediately where you can have tests done, etc.

**Post Office:** GPO and Poste Restante near the harbor in Georgetown, across from Madras Beach Railway Station. Address: General
Post Office, Poste Restante, First Line Beach, Madras 600001,
tel.29011, open Mon–Sat 07:00–18:00 h. There is another large Post
Office on the northern end of Mount Road.
**Telephoning Overseas:** Best from the Overseas Communication Centre behind the GPO.

# TAMIL NADU

At the eastern edge of southern India, Tamil Nadu's 48 million population live in a total area of
130,069 km$^2$. To the west is Kerala;
Karnataka and Andhra Pradesh are
to the north. To the east is the
Bay of Bengal. Enclosed within Tamil Nadu is the former French territory, Pondicherry, which is administered as a separate Union Territory. Tamil Nadu stretches from
the West Ghat Mountains through
the East Ghats to the Coromandel
Coast. The northeast monsoon
brings most precipitation from October through December on the coast
and the West Ghats. The Cauvery
River provides life-giving irrigation water to agriculture.

Many Tamils work abroad in east and southern Africa, Mauri-
tius, Malaysia, and Sri Lanka. Tamils have made headlines in
recent years with demands for their own Tamil nation, and
through unrest on Sri Lanka.

In addition to Tamil (a Dravidian language), ethnic languages include Telugu, Malayalam, and Kannada. Tamil Nadu's
capital, Madras, with 4.5 million people, is second only to Bombay as the second largest film production center in India.

Tamil Nadu's history is relatively free of outside influence.
The local Dravidian culture was able to maintain its own development. English colonialism had little importance in Tamil Nadu.
The state in its present form dates from 1956. It was created
from the former state of Madras.

Tourists are primarily attracted to Tamil Nadu by its terrific
temples. Your main points of interest include Kanchipura, Mahabalipuram, Chidambaram, Tiruchchirappalli, Madurai, and Ooty.
Mahabalipuram has developed into the main traveller gathering
spot on the east coast.

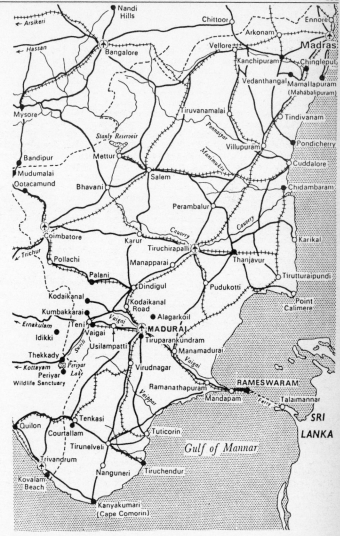

# Mahabalipuram

This beach town of 5,000 is 60 km south of Madras on the Bay of
Bengal. Founded during the 7th century as a harbor and second
capital of the Pavalla Kingdom, Mahabalipuram is considered the
cradle of Dravidian temple building in southern India. The numerous finished and unfinished monoliths are renowned, along with
a huge relief, and coastal temple.

The ancient art of sculpture flourishes anew; local craftsmen
are busy constructing new buildings and restoring old temples (in
India and abroad).

A long, palm-lined beach, and pleasant atmosphere, invite
you to relax; certainly no secret among travellers. Complementing
the lovely beach, thriving crafts, reasonably priced food and
lodgings, is an outstanding cultural event calendar.

## COMING – GOING

**By Air:** The nearest airport is south of Madras (see Madras).
An airport transfer from Mahabalipuram is planned, expected
cost 40.-Rs, ask at the Silversands Hotel in Mahabalipuram, or
at Safire Theatre, 614 Mount Rd., Madras 600006, tel.477444.

**By Rail:** The nearest station is Chingleput (Chengal Pattu),
60 km south of Madras on the route to Tiruchchirappalli (or
Trichy and other spellings), frequent connections, costs 7.-Rs.

**By Bus:** From Chingleput, get express Bus 212 H, thrice daily,
to Mahabalipuram. Regular connections to Chingleput aboard
buses connecting Mahabalipuram and the temple town of Kanchipuram (70 km southwest of Madras). From Mahabalipuram, get
Bus 212 H (express) at 8:30, 13:50, and 16:30 h via Chingleput
and Thirukkalikundram to Kanchipuram; excursions and onward
connections possible, costs 5.-Rs. From Madras, get Bus 68 or
19 A from Broadway Bus Stand, or a private bus. Depart
hourly, takes 2 h, costs 6.-Rs. The last bus in either direction
is at 20:00 h. Direct buses to Pondicherry at 07:30 and
18:30 h, takes 3 h, costs 8.-Rs, Bus 188.

## A NIGHT'S REST

Reasonable prices in the lodges near the bus stand, 10.-,
15.-Rs per person. **Mamalla Bhavan (D)**25.-, very clean, but
sometimes loud due to the bus stand and an excellent restaurant downstairs. **Mamalla Lodge (D)**12.-, 20.-, 25.-, with bath.
**Marina Lodge (S)**12.-, **(D)**15.-, 20.-. **Royal Lodge (S)**15.-,
**(D)**15.-, 20.-. **Pallava Lodge (S)**15.-, **(D)**25.-. **N.C.G. Lodge
(S)**15.-, **(D)**25.-. **Chitra Lodge,** West Raja St., **(S)**10.-, 15.-,
**(D)**20.-. **Madras Cafe (S)**12.-, 15.-, **(D)**15.-, 20.-. **Seaview
Lodge (D)**25.-. The higher prices above include a bath. But
don't expect comfort at these prices. Be sure to ask for fresh
sheets.

MAHABALIPURAM

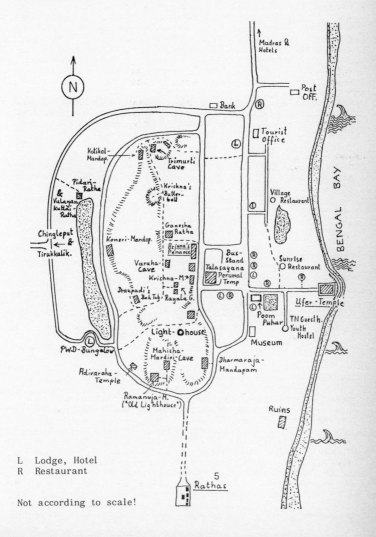

L   Lodge, Hotel
R   Restaurant

Not according to scale!

It's even cheaper in a family home.  Most private accommodations are away from the action,  near the Five Rathas.  Think
50.-Rs per week. You might be asked on the street.
The new **Tamil Nadu Youth Hostel** is popular,  along with the
**Guesthouse** to the right of the street between the bus stand and
the Shore Temple. The dormitory runs at **(Dm)**8.- with a locker.
The Cottages are very clean, cost **(D)**35.- (with bath).
Also reasonable is **Silver Inn** (actually a middle-class hotel),
lovely rooms with bath from February to November just **(S)**35.-,
**(D)**55.-.

Middle-class hotels (heading toward Madras):  **ITDC Temple Bay
Beach Resort** tel.51,  the most expensive hotel featuring pool,
bar,  etc.  **(S)**315.-,  **(D)**390.-, Cottage **(S)**265.-,  **(D)**340.-, Suite
750.-,  Camper parking 30.-. **TTDC Beach Resort Complex** tel.35,
Cottage  **(D)**75.-,   **(AC)**100.-,  as in many government hotels,
complaints about morale among employees. **Silversands**,  tel.28,
well  tended  grounds  with  individually  equipped  Cottages,
friendly,  helpful management, prices fluctuate with the season,
high season December/January,  cheapest season April/June,
**(S)**75.-,   100.-,  **(AC)**135.-,  200.-, Deluxe 200.-,  300.-; **(D)**110.-,
140.-,  **(AC)**175.-,   275.-,  Deluxe 250.-,  375.-,  Beach Villa
**(Suite)**350.-,  500.-,  expensive rooms with all the extras,  excellent restaurant,  disco,  films,  cultural events - see Activities,  free transfer to airport for guests of 3 days (but not for

Silver Inn residents on the same grounds), if you want to stay in comfort without too much expense, this is the place, costs February - November **(S)**35.-, **(D)**55.-. **Golden Sun** tel.45, **(S)**120.- **(AC)**155.-, **(D)**155.-, 200.-, (Suite)400.-. **Ideal Beach Resort**, tel.40, smallest hotel, **(S)**50.-, **(D)**70.-, **(AC)** costs double.

### REFRESHMENT

Good Indian food costs little by the bus stand in **Mamalla Bhavan**. On Shore Road by Shore Temple, try good European food in nice **Rose Garden Restaurant**. Not far away, set back from the street on the left is **Sunrise Restaurant**, books and magazines for browsing. Two other popular restaurants are **Village Restaurant** and **Bamboo Hut**. Stay a while and you'll know them all. Plus a few chai shops and other small restaurants. It is exquisite, but expensive, in the middle-class hotels.

### SHOPPING

This center of granite and soft stone craftsmanship is home to the **School Of Sculpture** including the **Government Sculpture Training Centre** and the Directorate Of Technical Education, tel.61, near the bus stand. Let them teach you something about masonry and sculpture (including realistic prices) before you visit any shops. Surprisingly, the government-owned **Poom Puhar** offers reasonable

prices, 09:00-13:00, 14:00-18:00 h, daily except Tuesday. And take a rewarding shopping excursion to the silk market in Kan-chipuram.

## ACTIVITIES
**Swimming**: The main attraction in town. Stick close to the major hotels.

**Caution**: Don't bathe near the Shore Temple; dangerous currents cause frequent drownings.

You might rent a catamaran from a fisherman (or arrange for one through your hotel). Bike rentals in town, or at Silversands for its guests.

A committee has been established by several hotels, lodges and restaurants to improve tourist activities. Every evening during high season, cultural events include classical Indian dance, sitar or flute concerts, and folklore, costs 10.-Rs, free transportation for lodge residents. Tours are organized by Club Mamallapuram. For information, ask at Silversands, tel.28.

## SIGHTS
Dating from the 7th century, everything is concentrated around three spots, easy to reach by foot.
**Descent of the Ganges**: A 27 m long and 9 m high stone relief (the largest bas-relief in the world), near the bus stand, has been said to depict Arjuna's Penance from the **MAHABHARATA**, but most archaeologists see it as a depiction of the mythological creation of the Ganges River in **RAMAYANA**. According to legend, the split in the middle represents the Ganges, a theory supported by remains of a water tank feeding from above into the split. A third theory sees a depiction of the Jain mythology.
**Cave Temples** (two are important)
  **Krishna Mandapam**: Near the relief, features a depiction of Krishna, holding Govardhama Mountain over his friends to protect them against the Rain God, Varuna.
  **Mahishasuramardhini Cave**: Southwest of the lighthouse, boasts three shrines. In one, the Goddess Durga (Kali) destroys the demon Mahishasura (with the buffalo head). A second relief shows Vishnu in cosmic sleep (Ananthasayanam) on a bed of snakes.
**Lighthouse Hill**: Eight temples are dug into the rock; two were never completed. It's assumed these were test models for other temples built in southern India. Working methods haven't changed much over the ages. See the example at the School of Sculpture, tel.61, 09:00-13:00, 14:00-18:00 h, daily except Tuesday.

**The Five Rathas**: A good kilometer south of the lighthouse are five monolithic temples shaped like a magnificent carriage, which served as models for much of later Dravidian architecture. Three other rathas can be found north and west of the temple hill.

**The Shore Temple:** Just a kilometer from town, right on the beach, this is the first fruit of experimentalism. The temple, featuring two shrines dedicated to Shiva and Vishnu in the 7th century, was the first non-monolithic building by Pavalla artists. It served as a prototype for all other temples of the same style.

## AROUND MAHABALIPURAM
**The Crocodile Farm:** 14 km north of Mahabalipuram, on the road to Madras, crocodiles are bred for release in animal reserves. The 1000 creatures can be visited by bus (half hourly) or bike, costs 1.-Rs.

**Vedanthangal Bird Sanctuary:** Worth an afternoon visit after the rainy season (November to January), when migratory and water fowl can be studied from observation towers. Located 40 km south of Chingleput, get a bus.

**Tours:** Organized by Clùb Mamallapuram (Hotel Organization), Kanchipuram 60.-, Pondicherry 100.-, Tirupati 125.-Rs.

For other ideas, see Kanchipuram & Thirukkalikundram. The Tourist Office offers brochures on many spots in Tamil Nadu.

## TIPS
**Bank:** Accepts traveller's checks, on the secondary road to Chingleput, north of the Tourist Office, heading west.
**Post Office:** Poste Restante (sub post office), tel.30.
**Library:** Small, English literature, at the Tourist Office.
**Nuclear Power Plant:** The monstrosity on the beach, 10 km south of town.
**Weather:** Lower temperatures here than in Madras, average highs 30-36° C, average lows 20-22° C.

# Tirukkalikundram

Also called Thirukazhukundram, pilgrims flock to the town 15 km west of Mahabalipuram, on the road from Chingleput to Kanchipuram. It's renowned for two eagles which, since time remembered, land here every morning at 11:00 h to be fed by the priests. According to legend, they are gods breaking their daily flight from Varanasi to Rameswaram. The feeding place is up on a hill. On the road below is a large complex of rarely visited Shiva temples, tremendous gopurams (gate towers), and tanks (large water reservoirs dammed with earth or brick).

## COMING - GOING
**By Bus:** Hourly on the way from Kanchipuram and Chingleput in the west and Mahabalipuram in the east (stop upon request).
Worth visiting by bike as a day trip. No lodgings.

# Kanchipuram

This town of 134,000, 70 km west of Madras, is famous for its hand-woven silk. The art developed and preserved here, originally catered to the royal courts of the Pavallas, Cholas, and the Rayas of Vijayanagar (Hampi), who in succession maintained a capital here. During the 7th century, 1000 temples were said to have been built here (only 120 remain). Most are dedicated to Shiva, four are particularly interesting. One of India's seven holy cities, Kanchipuram is a pilgrim town.

## COMING - GOING

**By Rail:** Difficult to reach by rail.

**By Bus:** Disembark at the large bus stand (baggage check), surrounded by cheap accommodations and most sights. From Madras Broadway Bus Stand, get Bus 134, 76 B, or 76 C, half hourly during the day. To Madras, get Bus 134 and 73 B (both express), costs 6.-Rs, takes 3 h, last bus 19:30 h. From Mahabalipuram, via Thirukkalikundram and Chingleput (railway station on the route Madras - Tiruchchirappalli) with Bus 212 H, direct, at 08:30, 13:50, and 16:30 h, takes 2 h, costs 5.-Rs (same heading back). Other buses transfer in Chingleput. Last bus to Mahabalipuram at 18:30 h. Direct buses to Vellore, Bangalore, Salem, Tiruvanamalai, and Pondicherry.

**Bike Rentals:** At the bus stand, costs 2.-Rs for half a day.

## A NIGHT'S REST

Near the bus stand on the corner of Kamaraj Street and Nellukkara Street are 3 cheap lodges: **Sri Rama Lodge (D)**15.-, 30.-, tel.2395. **Raja Lodge (D)**15.-, 30.-. **Town Lodge (D)**15.-, 30.-. In the bus stand building are rooms for 10.- per person. **Municipal Rest House (S)**10.-, **(D)**15.-, Nellukkara Street (toward the station), tel.2301 (Tourist Information in the building). **ITDC Ashok Travellers Lodge And Restaurant (S)**75.-, **(D)**115.-Rs, Rama Bhavan, 78 Kamakshi Amman Sannathi Street, right at the station, tel.2561, reservations possible from ITDC in Madras: 135 Anna Salai (Mount Rd.) tel.87621, Madras.

## REFRESHMENT

Expensive, but good in **ITDC Ashok Travellers Lodge.** If you want to save, try **Rama Cafe**, left of Raja Lodge, cheap and good. Otherwise, have a look around the bus stand.

## SHOPPING

**Silk:** Quality, hand-woven silk is offered by several weaving cooperatives. A meter of hand woven silk costs 100.- to 500.-Rs, depending on quality. Should you be in the market for Indian silk, be sure to inform yourself first. It can be very confusing with such a tremendous selection. Machine-woven silk is a better buy in Varanasi or Bangalore, where it's made. Madras, too, offers an excellent selection of both hand-woven and machine-

KANCHIPURAM

L     Lodges
i     Tourist Information

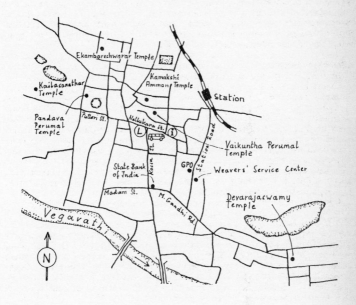

made silk (in Rattan Bazar, near Central Railway Station). For
top quality, hand-woven silk, you're best off here in
Kanchipuram.

## SIGHTS
Five temples get most of the praise.
**Eskambareswara Temple:** A large Shiva temple, in five parts,
dating in its present form from the 16th century, though its origins look back to the Pallavas. Covering almost 10 ha, the temple boasts massive outer walls and a 59 m high gopuram (gate
tower). Richly decorated, you've a lovely panorama from the
upper level. The facility includes a 1000-column hall. The great
Hindu holy man, Sri Sankara Acharya (788-820 AD), is also remembered; photo permit, 1.-Rs.
**Kailasanath Temple:** Another Shiva temple, in the west of town.
Dating from the 7-8th centuries, this is one of the most ancient
Dravidian temples, constructed upon models developed in Mahabalipuram. Later it was altered and expanded. Inside, the depictions of Shiva on the walls are remarkable.
**Vaikuntha(natha) – Perumal Temple:** Dedicated to Vishnu, completed around 800 AD, marks a further development of Dravidian
architecture. The colonnade of lion columns inside the ring wall
is considered a forerunner of the 1000-column halls popular later.
**Sri Kamakshi (Amman) Temple:** Nearby, dedicated to Parvati. This
is one of three holy places for Shakti venerators in India, and
center of a great car festival in January or February. Just a
short walk from Sakkiswarar Temple.
**Varadaraja Swami Temple:** Also called Devarajaswamy Temple, or
Varadaraja Perumal Temple, this temple of many names was constructed in the 12th century and dedicated to Vishnu. It is on a
small hill, 3 km toward Chingleput. Built under the Vijayanagar
Kings, the temple features outstanding sculpture and a 1000-col-
umn hall. A stone chain is carved from a single stone. There is
a modest admission price and photo permit fee.

Visit the sights on a rickshaw day trip (20.-Rs), or by bike.
Bike rentals near the bus stand, costs 4.-Rs per day.

## AROUND KANCHIPURAM
Most people flock here from Mahabalipuram, see Around
Mahabalipuram.

## TIPS
**Tourist Information:** By the Municipal Commissioner, in Municipal
Rest House, Nellukkare St., tel.2301.
**GPO:** On Railway Station Rd., tel.2534.
**State Bank Of India:** Cashes traveller's checks, M. Gandhi Rd.,
at Kamaraj St., tel.2521.
**Weavers Service Centre:** 20 Railway Station Road, tel.2530, near
the GPO, here you can see and have explained how silk is hand
woven, plus get info about prices; friendly, patient people.

# Tiruvannamalai

Tiruvannamalai is a temple town counting over 100 sacred sites.
**Arunachala Temple:** Lovely, one of southern India's largest temples, with a 65 m gopuram.
**Ashram:** Tiruvannamalai is primarily known for an ashram founded by Sri Ramana Maharshi, at the foot of Arunachala Mountain. Sri Ramana Maharashi left his body in April 1950, but his presence is still felt. If you wish to live here a while, write in advance.
**Gingee:** Half-way along the drive between Tindivanam to Tiruvannamalai, you pass Gingee, visible from afar. The mighty 13th-century fortress is spread over three hills.

## COMING - GOING

**By Rail:** Tiruvannamalai is situated on the Tirupati - Vellore - Villupuram rail line. But there's only one express in each direction, passing through late at night.
**By Bus:** Accessible from Mahabalipuram via Chingleput and Tindivanam. From Pondicherry, head first for Tindivanam (on Highway 45 from Madras to Trichy). Regular buses from Tindivanam to Tiruvannamalai.

# Pondicherry

While the whole territory contains 500,000 people, the town of Pondicherry (or Pondy) boasts 100,000 inhabitants on 6.2 km$^2$, situated 160 km south of Madras on the east coast. Since withdrawal of the French administration in 1954, the former colony has been ruled as a union territory under direct Indian central government rule. Like the former Portuguese colony, Goa, people in Pondy seek to maintain their unique character, combining southern Indian and European cultures. Besides Tamil, many people speak fluent French, which is taught in local schools. A treaty signed with France in 1962 stipulates that French culture should be preserved here. Gandhi would have smiled upon an uprising unleashed when the Indian

**Sri Aurobindo**

central government considered uniting Pondicherry with its neighbor Tamil Nadu. Certainly citizens of Tamil Nadu saw little to be gained by the unification. French culture traditionally enjoys a drop of alcohol, a freedom prohibited in dry Tamil Nadu.

Pondy's two main attractions are Sri Aurobindo Ashram and the international town of Auroville, situated on its own territory outside Pondicherry. Both are named after the great Indian philosopher and freedom fighter, Sri Aurobindo, who lived in Pondy together with a French-born woman, known as the Mother.

## COMING – GOING

**By Air:** The nearest airport is in Madras, 160 km away, offering domestic and international flights.

**By Rail:** Connections to Madras and Madurai, to Tirchirapalli and Rameswaram (ferry to Sri Lanka). But you have to change trains at Villupuram. Lots of buses and a few trains between Villupuram Junction and Pondy.

**By Bus:** To Madras get Bus 83 B or 87 A for 15.- (express), takes 4 h, from Bus Stand Pondicherry. Direct buses to Chidambaram (ten daily, 14.-), Coimbatore (twice daily, 30.-), Bangalore / Thiruvanamalai (three daily, 32.-), Mahabalipuram (three daily, 10.-), Kanchipuram (three daily, 11.-), Madurai (four daily, 28.-), Tanjore (twice daily, 2 h, 17.-), Nagercoil (over night, 50.-Rs).

## A NIGHT'S REST

Near the beach promenade are a number of lodgings of varying class, the most reasonable: **Shanti Guest House**, Rue Suffren, near the State Bank of India by the park, **(S)**20.-, **(D)**30.-, 40.-, cheaper by longer stays. **Society Guest House**, 15 Romain Rolland Street, **(S)**15.-, **(D)**25.-, 35.-, guests can buy a food pass here for the ashram canteen (8.-Rs), cheaper by longer stays. **Park Guest House**, Goubert Salai (southern end), **(S)**30.-,

Mother

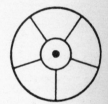

Auroville

**(D)**40.-, 100.-, quiet, pretty, on the ocean, bike rentals (5.-Rs daily), food pass available. **International Guest House**, 17 Gingy Salai, by the GPO on the canal, **(S)**18.-, **(D)**25.-, 50.-, clean, food pass. For info and reservations at other Sri Aurobindo Ashram guest houses, check with the ashram secretary.

PONDICHERRY

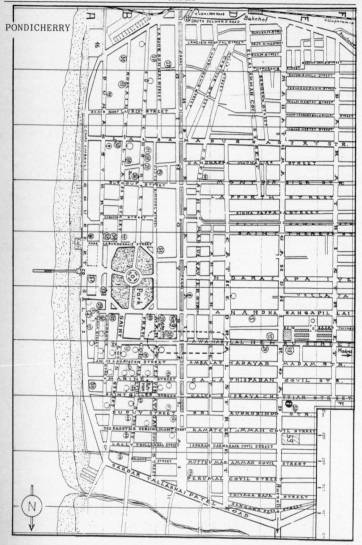

## MAP LEGEND

| | | | |
|---|---|---|---|
| 1 | Sri Aurobindo Ashram Ashram Reading Room | 28 | Vietnamese Restaurant |
| | | 29 | Kindergarten |
| 2 | Auroville Information | 30 | Aurosarjan Shop |
| 3 | Sri Aurobindo Society | 31 | Aurosarjan Factory |
| 4 | Visitor Service | 32 | Library of Physical Education |
| 5 | Anchra Bhavan | 33 | Romain Rolland Library |
| 6 | Cottage Guest House | 34 | Public Library |
| 7 | Colconde | 35 | Aurotravels |
| 8 | Good Guest House | 36 | Foreigners' Registration Office |
| 9 | International Guest House | 37 | Home Department, Visa Applications |
| 10 | Karnataka Nilayam | 38 | State Bank of India |
| 11 | Grand Hotel d'Europe | 39 | Head Post Office |
| 12 | New Sweet Home | 40 | Telephone Exchange |
| 13 | Orissa Guest House | 41 | Aurovedic Section |
| 14 | Oriya Nilayam | 42 | Dentist |
| 15 | La Paix | 43 | Pharmacy |
| 16 | Park Guest House | 44 | Homeopathic Medicine |
| 17 | Sea Side Guest House | 45 | Healer |
| 18 | Shelter | 46 | Eye School |
| 19 | Society Guest House | 47 | Physiotherapy |
| 20 | Standard Guest House | 48 | Ananda Emporium |
| 21 | Shanti Guest House | 49 | National Medicals |
| 22 | Government Guest House | 50 | Dr. C.J. Vyas |
| 23 | Ashram Dining Room | 51 | Hospital |
| 24 | Hotel Aristo | 54 | French Consulate |
| 25 | Sri Aurobindo Library | 55 | Police |
| 26 | Equals One | 57 | Lighthouse |
| 27 | Vietnamese Restaurant | 58 | Gandhi Memorial |
| | | 59 | Vedapuriswarar |

Unnumbered Circles Mark Auroville or Ashram Facilities

**Municipal Travellers Bungalow**, 6 Rue Suffren (across from the State Bank of India), **(S)**15.-. **Quality Hotel And Restaurant**, 5 Labourdonnais Street, **(S)**20.-. **Government Tourist Home**, Uppalam Road, near the railway station, **(S)**10.-, 20.-, **(D)**20.-, 40.-, **(Dm)**3.-, quiet, garden, camper parking 5.-Rs.

If you plan to stay a while, why not rent a house for 250.-Rs a month. It's easy to stay here a very long time. Lodges throughout town are reasonable. Also worth recommending is the **Youth Hostel**, 2 km north of Pondy, right on the beach in Solaithandavankuppam, lovely, peaceful, **(Dm)**8.-.

Another hotel district is Sereneti Beach, 5 km north in Kottakuppam, rickshaws from Pondicherry Bus Stand 8.-Rs, up M.G.Road, toward Auroville: **Vicky Hotel**, safe, clean, **(D)**15.-, bike rental 3.50 Rs per day. **Full Moon Resthouse**, **(S)**7.-, small rooms, good omelettes. **Chez Mohan**, huts with hammocks, **(S)**5.-, 10.-Rs. **Shiva's Garden**, huts with hammocks, **(S)**5.-, 10.-. A Frenchman has set up a complex of variously furnished huts, right on the ocean, starting at **(S)**12.-Rs, restaurant (closed Mondays), large croissants and french bread.

## REFRESHMENT
Your cheapest meal is in the **Ashram Canteen**: three meals for 8.-Rs. If you're staying at an ashram guesthouse, pick up a meal ticket there. Breakfast is early, 06:40-07:45 h, lunch 12:00-12:30 h; dinner time is posted on the blackboard.

Good European food in **Maison D'Auroville**, Lally Tollendahl Street, run by Auroville people. More good food in five tiny Vietnamese restaurants in White Pondy, on Nehru Road and on M.Gandhi Road.

A nice garden restaurant in **Hotel Aristo** on Nehru Street is not cheap. Try Swiss-German Rösti in **Sunshine Restaurant.**

## SHOPPING
Ashram residents have set up numerous shops and boutiques offering clothing, leather goods, handicrafts, and other fun items. **Hidesign's Boutique:** If leather is your thing, at 31 Nehru Street, featuring the latest designs in handbags, shoes, pants and clothes. The same wares are more expensive in Delhi's most exquisite shops.

**Priya Sales:** On Nehru Street, traditional Indian handicrafts, Saris, Punjabis.

**La Boutique d'Auroville:** Also serves as an Auroville Information Centre. In Pondicherry, you've a good selection of spiritual literature.

## CREATIVITY
**Music:** This is a great place to learn **yoga**, **sitar**, **tabla**, etc. Ask in the ashram secretariat, and check with people who've been living here for a while.

## SIGHTS
**Sri Aurobindo Ashram:** A center of integral yoga, attracts thousands of visitors each year, from all over the world. Ashram activities center around the teaching of Aurobindo and the Mother. Farming, handicrafts, and light industry, plus art & culture, round out Ashram life. Tours (6.-Rs) depart from the ashram at 08:30 h, ten stops. Pilgrims gather in quiet prayer around the tomb of the philosopher who founded the ashram in 1920. Evenings at 19:00 h, everyone is invited to meditation. You need a Visitor Pass to visit many ashram events, available in ashram guest houses or at the Ashram Visitors' Office (see map). Meal tickets for the Ashram Canteen also available.

**Library & Museum:** On Rue Capucine, French and Indian culture are united, named for the great French Sanskrit expert, Romain Rolland.

**Shiva Temple:**   A colorful Dravidian structure, on M.Gandhi Road,
near the Main Bazar.
**Aquarium:**   In the **Botanical Garden** on Lal Bahadur Sastry Street
at West and South Boulevard, across from the bus stand.
**Beach Promenade:**   Invites a walk; here too is the Tourist Office.
No real sights in Pondicherry.

## AROUND PONDICHERRY
**Tours:**   The Tourist Office, on Goubert Salai (beach promenade),
offers a sightseeing tour through Pondy, including a visit to
Auroville (3 h). The entire tour lasts 09:00-18:00 h, costs 7.-Rs;
departs when enough people are interested.   Tours run by Auroville residents (18.-Rs) depart Mon, Wed, Sat, from La Boutique
d'Auroville, Nehru Road, at 15:00 h, return at 18:00 h.

## TIPS
**Tourist Office:**   On the beach promenade, Goubert Salai, maps,
brochures.
**Ashram Beach Office & Auroville Information Office:**   Also on Gou-
bert Salai.
**La Boutique d'Auroville:**   Your best Auroville information office.
**Hairdresser (Women) & Children's Haircuts:**   Nirmal Hair Style
Centre, 26 A Romain Rolland Street, 08:00-12:00 h, 15:00-18:00 h,
10.-Rs, run by a Vietnamese woman.
**Medical Attention:**   Excellent in Pondicherry, one reader writes:
"If you're going to get sick in India, then Pondicherry is the
place." The ashram doctor was able to recommend the wonderful
**Ashram Nursing Home,** fantastic treatment.

# Auroville

Based upon the ideas of Bengali freedom fighter and philosopher,
Sri Aurobindo (who fled from the British to French-ruled Pondicherry), and Mirra Alfassa, a French woman, known as the Mother, a town of 50,000 is planned (present population 4000, with
600 full-time residents). A resolution of the Sri Aurobindo society
called for the construction of a spiral-shaped town centred upon
a spherically-shaped meditation center.
   The center consists of the **Mantri Mandir** (meditation center,
still under construction), an amphitheatre (at the center of which
is an urn containing a handful of earth from 121 countries), and
an ancient banyan tree.   The future town is divided into four
sectors: residential, cultural, production, and international. The
entire town will be surrounded by a green belt producing healthy, natural foods.
   Construction of this experimental, international town receives
support from various organizations, including UNESCO. Following
the Mother's death, however, progress slowed due to quarrels
between the ashram and the Aurovillians. The Sri Aurobindo Society stopped the flow of money to Auroville. An audit taken in

1980 couldn't account for 10 million Rs. The Indian central government assumed administrative control, with Auroville's consent,
and work has renewed. After ten years of construction the outer
shell of the Matri Mandir has been completed. Forty settlements of
varying size have been established.

Be sure to pay a visit. Pick up the latest Auroville map in
La Boutique d'Auroville, at 12 Jawaharlal Nehru Street in Pondicherry, Auroville's official information center.

## COMING - GOING

**By Bicycle:** From Pondicherry, an easy way to get around.
Either cruise up Nehru Street toward Jimper or take M. Gandhi
Road north. Aurovillers usually recommend the route up the
coast road, bringing you right to Aspiration, Auroville's
largest settlement.

## A NIGHT'S REST

Several settlements maintain guesthouses: Aspiration, Fraternity,
Center Field, Djaima, Kotta Karai, Revelation, etc. Depending
on your tastes, think 30.- to 40.-Rs per day for room and
board. If you plan to stay a while, register in advance:
Auroville Cooperative, Auroville, Post Office Kottakuppam
605104, India. Or ask at one of the three information offices.

## SIGHTS

Coming along Old Madras Beach Road, 5 km beyond Pondicherry,
head left by the chai shop. Soon you're in Auroville's largest
settlement.

**Aspiration:** Home to 100 residents. Aspiration is the educational
center of Auroville, providing a kindergarten, school, library,
health center, sport facilities, and numerous workshops.

**Fraternity:** The neighboring settlement, this is Auroville's handicraft center with emphasis on weaving and carpentry.

**Utility, Two Banyans,** and **Fertile:** After Aspiration, head right
(north) off the main road to the farming settlements. These
settlements are very active in regional reforestation.

**Certitude:** Further up the main road.

**Abri** and **Forecomers:** Agriculture-oriented settlement, just before
Certitude, take the road to the right.

**Auroville Center:** From Certitude, another 2 km. Here you'll find
**Matri Mandir,** the **Amphitheatre,** and a **Banyan Tree.** The settlement, once depicted here on Auroville maps is gone; just a camp
for people helping with Matri Mandir construction.

**Plant Nursery:** Nearby, open to visitors. Notice how experimental
strains of plants are cultivated.

**Bharat Nivas:** Here is the Auroville Information Center, one of
three Auroville info centers.

**Udavi:** Heading back toward Certitude, with an incense production
workshop.

**Hope** and **Auro Orchard:** Further on, a large farm with 60 acres
of land. Now you are back on the road to Pondicherry.

The map of Auroville has changed greatly in recent years as new settlements are added. Conversely, other settlements are no longer shown, e.g. Hope and Auroson's Home. Following the dispute over Auroville construction money, some settlements, which supported the Sri Aurobindo Society in Pondicherry, are no longer considered part of Auroville by other settlements.

The Matrimandir in Auroville

## THE CHARTER OF AUROVILLE

1. Auroville belongs to nobody in particular. Auroville belongs to humanity as a whole.
   But to live in Auroville one must be a willing servitor of the Divine Consciousness.
2. Auroville will be the place of unending education, of constant progress and a youth that never ages.
3. Auroville wants to be the bridge between the past and future. Taking advantage of all discoveries from without and within, Auroville will boldly spring toward future realizations.
4. Auroville will be a site of material and spiritual researches for a living embodiment of an actual Human Unity.

February 28, 1968, The Mother

AUROVILLE

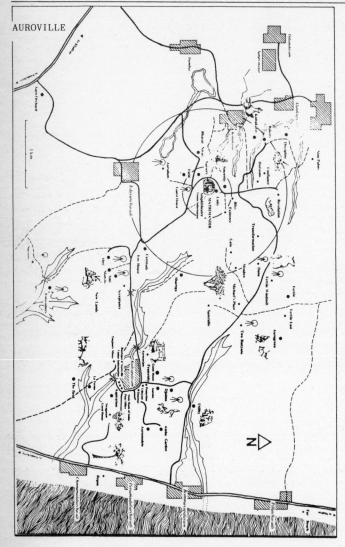

**TIPS**
**Auroville Information Center:** In Bharat Nivas, Auroville.
**Auroville Literature:** Many books have been written about the Auroville experiment. Browse through any bookstore in Pondy, or spiritual bookstores outside India.

# Chidambaram

The temple town is 230 km south of Madras, boasting some of the most ancient temples in southern India.
**Nataraja Temple:** The primary attraction, dedicated to the cosmic dancer, Shiva. The 13 ha temple complex is surrounded by two high walls. Four gopuram (gate towers), two 48 m high(!), are built into the inner wall. The east and west towers are decorated with sculpture depicting Shiva in the 108 Bharatha Natyam (Indian classical dance) positions. The main temple features a statue of Shiva dancing. The roof of the most sacred shrine is shingled with pure gold. The temple complex contains temples dedicated to other deities: a 14th century Parvati temple, a Subramanya temple, the Govindaraja temple (dedicated to Vishnu), and a small Ganesh temple. There are five

columned halls: Nritta Sabha, Deva Sabha, Kanaka Sabha, Chit Sabha, and Raja Sabha. The latter is a 1000-column hall, 103 m long and 58 m wide. In Chit Sabha, the Akasha Lingham is revered. Even non-Hindus are permitted inside. Most interesting at puja time, evenings around 18:00 h.

**COMING – GOING**
  **By Rail:** Chidambaram is on the rail line between Madras and Tiruchchirappalli. The Cholan Express and the Rameswaram Express stop here (see Thanjavur).
  **By Bus:** Chidambaram is served by Tiruvalluvar Express buses from Pondy, Thanjavur, and Tiruchchirappalli.

## A NIGHT'S REST
Several reasonably priced hotels in the streets surrounding the temple, ask at Tourist Information next to the Tourist Bungalow. In **Railway Retiring Room, (Dm)**10.-. Or try **Tourist Bungalow Hotel Tamil Nadu (D)**40.-Rs with adjoining restaurant, both recommended.

## AROUND CHIDAMBARAM
**Backwaters of Pichavaram:**　Make a wonderful 16 km excursion, buses from the bus stand.　You might rent a boat and take a lovely ride through the mangrove swamp.　These waters are completely different from the canals in Kerala.　Lodgings are available in relatively new bungalows, ask in Hotel Tamil Nadu or at the Tourist Office.

# Thanjavur

This popular town, also called Tanjore (pop. 180,000), had its golden age between the 10th and 14th centuries.　During the reign of the Chola Kings, Thanjavur was one of southern India's

most important political, cultural, and religious centers. The
Chola dynasty controlled major parts of southern India and Sri
Lanka. Victories were celebrated with the construction of a
temple, financed by the defeated. Its riches grew with the
damming of the Cauvery River. Life-giving water gave birth to a
major rice-growing region. The district is known as the rice bowl
of Tamil Nadu. Brihadeeswara Temple was the most important of
70-odd temples, constructed under Raja Raja (985-1014 AD) in just
12 years. In October, the birthday of Raja Raja is celebrated
with a festival.

## COMING - GOING
**By Rail:** Thanjavur is on Southern Railways main line from
Madras to Rameswaram. Only a few trains are of interest, i.e.
Cholan Express from Madras Egmore via Chingleput (Mahabali-
puram), Villupuram (Pondy), and Chidambaram to Thanjavur,
and on to Tiruchchirappalli. Also important is the Rameswaram
Express, between Rameswaram and Tiruchchirappalli (Trichy).
**By Bus:** Tiruvalluvar Express buses provide direct connections
between most important towns in Tamil Nadu. Public transport
buses half hourly to Tiruchchirappalli.

## A NIGHT'S REST
Cheap accommodations **(S)**7.-, 9.-, or **(D)**12.-, 15.-Rs, include
four Municipal Rest Houses near the bus stand: **Rajah's Rest
House**, Gandhiji Rd. **Ajanta Lodge**, 1306 South Main St. **Sri
Krishna Lodge.** The **Railway Retiring Room** costs **(Dm)**15.-.
**Tourist Bungalow Hotel Tamil Nadu (D)**50.-, big clean rooms,
restaurant and bar, tel.601, Gandhiji Rd., 400 m north of the
railway station (Tourist Information - friendly). **Ashok Traveller's Lodge (S)**60.-, **(D)**100.-Rs, tel.356, Vallam Rd., restaurant
serves Indian, European, and Chinese food.

## REFRESHMENT
Wander along Gandhiji Road, you're sure to find a restaurant
you like. If you're tired of looking, try the restaurant in
**Tourist Bungalow**, also on Gandhiji Rd.

## SHOPPING
Tanjore is famous for lovely handicrafts: brass and copper inlaid
with traditional silver motifs.
**Poompuhar Handicrafts Emporium:** On Gandhiji Road offers a fine
selection of souvenirs, including silk, rugs, and musical instruments.

## SIGHTS
**Brihadeeswara Temple:** Built between 985 - 997 AD, one of India's
most remarkable and splendid temples. Departing from traditional
construction (whereby gate towers are the highest part of a temple complex), a 65 m high tower above the main shrine dominates
all other buildings. A massive dome, carved from an 80 ton block

of granite, crowns the temple. The granite block was raised to
its resting place upon a 6 km ramp (a technique utilized by
Egyptians building the pyramids). The entrance is guarded by a
6 m high Nandi, the mount ridden by Shiva. Notice too the frescos, reminiscent of the cave paintings at Ajanta.

**The Palace:** Inside the fort, built in the 16th century. It houses
the **Saraswati Mahal Library** (30,000 palm-leaf and paper manuscripts, 09:00-13:00, 15:00-17:00 h), an **Art Gallery** (lovely bronze
and granite statues from the Chola era, 09:00-13:00, 15:00-
17:00 h), and **Sangitha Mahal** music hall.

**The Schwartz Church:** In a garden between the temple and palace. It was built in 1799 by a Maratha king for the Danish missionary, C.V.Schwartz.

**AROUND THANJAVUR**

**Tiruvaiyyaru** (11 km): Birthplace of the holy man, poet, and
composer, Sri Thayagaraja. A large music festival is held every
January in his honor.

**Thirukandiyur** (10 km): Two sculpture-rich temples to visit.

**Kumbakonam** (36 km): Sarangapani, Kumbeswarar, Nageswara, and
Brahma temples are famous for sculpture and stonework. Every 12
years, the Mahamaham Festival is held here, see you in 1992! A
bath in Mahamaham Tank on Maham Day is said to wash away all
sins.

# Tiruchchirapalli

Also written Trichy, and other spellings, this sprawling 25 km$^2$
town (pop. 350,000) is situated 80 m up on the southern bank of
the Cauvery River. The provincial capital's attractions include
the famous Rock Fort Temple in the north of town and the tremendous temple district Srirangam, on an island in the Cauvery
(rarely visited by foreigners).

The town's history stretches back before the birth of Christ,
when a Chola fortress held sway here. During the first millennium AD, this was the scene of repeated fighting between the
Pandyas and Pallavas, who alternated conquest and rule. The
Chola regained control in the 10th century. After the fall of the
Chola Kingdom, the Hampi Kings seized control, until they were
defeated by the Muslim Sultan of Deccan.

The present-day town, Rock Fort Temple, and the temples in
Srirangam were built under the Nayaks of Madurai in the 18th
century. The temple complex has seen a number of alterations and
expansions since then, though its origins lie in the 13th century.
Even today, construction, or reconstruction, continues.

During the 18th century, heated battles were fought over the
town between the British and French, both seeking to dominate
the Indian subcontinent.

TIRUCHCHIRAPALLI

i     Tourist Office & Bungalow
1     State Transport Buses
2     Tiruvalluvar Buses
3     General Post Office
4     State Bank of India
5     Indian Airlines
6     Air India
7     Hotel Aristo
8     Hotel Anand
9     Vijay Lodge, Guru H.
10    Rock Fort Temple
11    Teppakulam Tank
12    Church
13    Bus Stop Bus 1

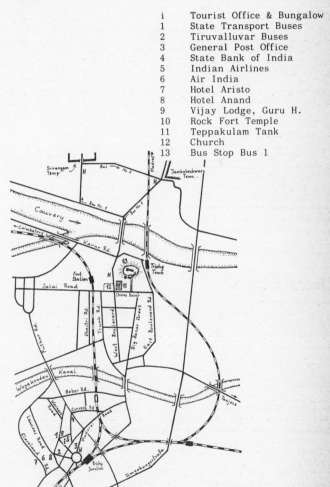

Trichy is important as a provincial capital, pilgrim town, trading center, and junction.

## COMING – GOING
**By Air:** Indian Airlines offers direct flights to Madras (240.-), Trivandrum (230.-), and Colombo (Sri Lanka). Air Lanka flies in from Colombo, costs US$50.-. 300 m across from the reception building, get Bus 7 to the bus stand in town.
**By Rail:** Trichy is a major station on the Madras and Madurai rail lines to Rameswaram or Quilon. Good connections everywhere. Most important are the Rameswaram Express and the Cholan Express (see Thanjavur), or the Quilon Mail from Madras Egmore via Trichy and Madurai to Quilon and return. The train to Villupuram (2nd class) costs 15.- (then on by bus on to Pondy, 4.-). Trichy Junction Railway Station is situated near the hotel district.
**By Bus:** There are two bus stands, just 200 m from one another in Cantonment, the cheap hotel district, near Trichy Junction Railway Station, by the Tourist Office. Always disembark at the bus stand. Express buses usually depart from Tiruvalluvar (Expressbus) Stand. With a bit of exertion, you might even get a seat aboard one of the hourly buses serving the main routes. Reservations are only possible on the longer routes. Direct buses via Villupuram (3.5 h) and Chingleput (6 h) to Madras (8 h). Via Madurai (3 h) to Nagercoil (change to Trivandrum and Kanyakumarin) and Coimbatore. Ask too at State Bus Terminal!
**Tip:** The empty seats go to those standing closest to the entrance when the bus arrives.
**Around Town:** Tiruchchirappalli boasts a good bus system. Bus 1 connects the bus stands in Cantonment with the Rock Fort Temple and Srirangam, every 10 minutes, costs 1.-.

## A NIGHT'S REST
Most cheap lodgings are concentrated in the Cantonment, the new part of town, near the bus stands, Trichy Junction, the GPO, and the Tourist Office. In other words, get off, look at the map, and within 5 minutes walk, you're there. **Hotel Tamil Nadu** (Tourist Bungalow) **(S)**30.-, **(D)**40.-, with bath, extra bed 5.-, **(Dm)**8.-, **(AC)(S)**60.-, **(AC)(D)**90.-, tel.25383, clean, quiet, restaurant, camper parking 4.-. **Guru Hotel**, Royal Road, tel.25327, **(S)**20.-, **(D)**30.-, **(Eb)**5.-, showers, upstairs De Luxe Doubles, not much better (quieter) 40.-, downstairs insist on a room in the back (loud restaurant), good Indian food. **Vijay Lodge** tel.24311, next door, **(S)**20.-, **(D)**30.-, showers, quieter than Guru, lots of travellers outside in Restaurant Uma Shankar. **Ashok Bhavan**, next to Express Bus Stand, **(S)**12.-, **(D)**20, okay. **Selvam Lodge**, Junction Road, tel.23114, simple, **(S)**12.-, 20.-, **(D)**20.-, 30.-, showers, roof garden restaurant, good food, between the bus stand and railway station. **Sarada Lodge** (across from Tourist Bungalow), tel.23216, **(S)**20.-, **(D)**30.-,

(Tr)40.-, showers, quiet, clean. **Hotel Anand**, 1 Ragult Court
Lane, tel.26545, **(S)**25.-, **(D)**45.-, showers, lots of nice rooms,
restaurant.
Further from town: **Hotel Aristo**, 2 Dindigal Rd., tel.26565,
**(S)**50.-, **(D)**150.- (and between). **ITDC Travellers' Lodge**, Kaja-
malai, Race Course Road (between the airport and the Canton-
ment), tel.23498, **(S)**50.-, **(D)**80.-. **Sangam Hotel (S)**120.- plus,
**(D)**170.-Rs, bar.

## REFRESHMENT

Good southern Indian food in **Guru Hotel**, next door in **Uma
Shankar Hotel**, at **Vijay Lodge**, and in the roof-garden restaur-
ant at **Selvam Lodge**. Several European dishes served at **Hotel
Anand**. Breakfast with toast, eggs, marmalade in the restaurant
next to the Tourist Office and Tourist Bungalow. Good food in
**Hotel Ashby**, 17 A Junction Road.

## SIGHTS

**Rock Fort Temple**: In the north of town, rising 83 m above the
banks of the Cauvery, crowning a steep cliff. But let's start at
the bottom. The entrance to the temple complex is south of the tip
in Chinna Bazar (see map). Leave your shoes here and give the
watchman 10 paisa later when you pick them up. First off you
meet the temple elephants. If you place a coin in their trunk,
they pass it back to their master, and thank you with a soft tap
on the head.
**The Climb**: Be ready for a strenuous climb up 434 steps carved
into the cliff. Almost the entire path is roofed, providing relief
from the sun.

**Sri Thayumanaswamy Temple:** Two-thirds of the way up, dedicated
to Shiva and Meenakshi. Only Hindus are permitted entrance.
After a few more steps, you reach a platform with refreshment
stands, a shade-giving tree, and a tremendous view. Great spot
to rest.

**Ganesh Temple:** Up at the top, you can enter if properly dressed.
For a small temple donation, get a **tika** (a spot of color on the
middle of your forehead, representing the third eye!), and some
sacrificial flowers. Admission -.10 Rs, photo permit 5.-Rs, try a
telephoto shot of the gopurams in Srirangam.

**Panorama:** Outside the temple. To the north are the temples in
Srirangam, to the south-west **Teppakulam Tank** (water reservoir),
and beyond a gothic church **Lady of our Lourdes**, built in the
18th century under C.V.Schwartz. Bus 1 stops here.

**Sri Ranganathaswamy Temple:** In Srirangam, at 250 ha, the largest Hindu temple complex anywhere! Bus 1 stops near the first
southern gopuram, pass through the outer wall into the quadratic
temple district. Seven walls boasting 21 gopurams encircle the
most sacred temple in the center (closed to non-Hindus). According to ancient Hindu scripture, only Brahmans are permitted to
live inside the quadratic town. Have a look at the bazars, if you
like, then press through slowly to the 4th wall, where you have
to leave your shoes (costs -.10 Rs) to the right of the gopuram,
open 06:00-13:00 h, 15:00-19:00 h. Inside the next section is a
1000-column hall (actually 960, during the Car and Thai Pongal
festival 40 bamboo poles are added to make the number round). A
photo permit for this section costs another 5.-Rs. Across from the
shoe depot is a Museum (hardly worth visiting). For -.50 Rs, get
a ticket to climb the small platform on a building affording a
view over the entire temple complex. You aren't permitted to
photograph the golden dome! The main shrine below is dedicated
to Vishnu.

**Sri Jambukeshwarar Temple** (also Thiruvanaikkaval): In Srirangam, almost as interesting, and even less crowded. The temple
district includes five walls and seven gopurams, dedicated to
Shiva. Also dating from the 14th to 18th centuries, open 06:00-
13:00 h, 16:00-21:30 h, take Bus 1.

**TIPS**

**Tourist Office:** Government Of Tamil Nadu, between the bus stands
and railway station, 10:00-17:00 h, tel.25336, friendly.

**Tourist Information:** A counter outside Trichy Junction Railway
Station, 06:30-10:00, 17:00-20:30 h, across from an info chart
showing lodgings and prices!

**GPO:** Madurai Rd., tel.25717, also Telegraph Office.

**State Bank Of India:** 10:00-14:00 h, tel.25172, in Cantonment, see
the map.

**Indian Airlines:** Dindigul Rd., tel.23116, airport tel.27563.

**Air Lanka:** Dindigul Rd., tel.23116, same building.

**AROUND TIRUCHCHIRAPPALLI**
**Ashram Shantinavar:**   30 km from Trichy in Taneerpalli,   near
Kulithalai,  is a Christian ashram.   Founded by Father Bodo Grif-
fith,   integrating Indian religious thought;   small,   beautifully
situated, nice atmosphere.

# Ootacamund (Ooty)

Situated at almost 2300 m,  the flavour of British colonialism still
clings to this resort town (pop.  70,000). Today, primarily Indian
tourists seek refuge here from the heat before and after the
southwest monsoon.   Winter temperatures are reminiscent of a
European autumn. The highest mountain in the surrounding Nilgiri
mountains is Dondabetta (2633 m).   During the summer,   average
temperatures range between 10° C at night and 25° C during the
day.
     The Nilgiri is home to a number of tribes,   each with its own
independent culture,  i.e.  the Todas,  Kotas,  Kurumbas, Irulas,
and the Panias (who lived as serfs until 1976).
     The mountains of southern India harbor tremendous forests,
but are also covered with tea and coffee plantations.   Also important are crops of herbs,   natural remedies,   medicinal plants,
and spices.  Have a look at the Botanical Garden,  2 km east of
the railway station.

## COMING - GOING
   **By Air:**   The nearest airport is 70 km distant in Coimbatore,
   daily connections to Bangalore (180.-),   Bombay (680.-),   and
   Madras (380.-).
   **By Rail:** A cog railway runs here, north from Mettupalayam (at
   the end of the branch line from Coimbatore);   departs Mettupa-
   layam at 08:00 h,   returns at 11:20 and 14:00 h.   Coming up
   takes 4 h,  going back just 3 h, costs 6.-Rs (2nd class). From
   Mettupalayam,   you've connections via Coimbatore to Kerala or
   Madras.   Coimbatore to Trivandrum takes 9-11 h,   costs 40.-Rs.
   The railway station and bus stand are conveniently close.
   **By Bus:**   Direct buses to Mysore 08:00,   09:00,   13:30, 15:30 h,
   costs 15.-,   takes 5 h; via Mudumalai and Bandipur (get off at
   Theppukady),   takes 3 h, costs 10.-. To Bangalore at 06:30 and
   10:30 h in 9 h,   costs 30.-.   To Hassan at 08:00, 11:30, 14:00,
   and 17:00 h.   Buses to Calicuta,   Erode,   Coimbatore (every
   15 minutes,  costs 26.-),  Palghat (07:00,  08:00, 14:00, 16:30,
   takes 5 h, costs 12.-), from here to Ernakulum (5 h, 18.-Rs).

## A NIGHT'S REST
   Only stay the night in Ootacamund if you really have warm
   clothes.   The cheap hotel district is on the road between the
   bus stand,  town center (Charring Cross),  and bazar, i.e. between Commercial Road and Hospital Road.   Numerous, somewhat

dingy lodges **(D)**25.-. All prices below for off season from the beginning of March to mid June, and less so in September or October. High season doubles the price.

**Gaylord**, behind the railway station and Central Bus Stand, **(S)**20.-, 50.-, good food in the restaurant. **YMCA**, Ananda Giri Ettines Road, tel.2218, **(Dm)**25.- (boys and girls), extremely clean, peacefully situated by the race track, expensive food. **Nahar Tourist Home**, Commercial Road, across from the Tourist Office in Charring Cross, **(S)**50.-, **(D)**75.-, showers, clean, modern. **TTDC Hotel Tamil Nadu**, tel.2544, on the hill behind the Tourist Office, **(S)**40.-, **(D)**70.-, **(Dm)**12.-, clean, quiet, friendly, restaurant. **Hotel Woodland**, from the bus stand 500 m toward the YMCA, right above the race course, **(D)**50.-, warm water, lovely rooms. The most expensive hotels include: **Fernhill Palace**, tel.2055, the Maharaja of Mysore's former summer residence, 70 luxurious rooms and suites, lots of recreation activities, **(S)**150.-, **(D)**200.-, 250.-. **Hotel Savoy**, tel.2572, expensive, rooms start at 250.-Rs.

## SIGHTS
**Botanical Garden:** Founded in 1847, and is one of India's prettiest today. Open 07:00-19:00 h, nominal admission; seeds are sold in the office. Budget half a day, and take one of the lovely charted hikes. Everything else is easily visible on a walk through town, which is spread over several hills.

## AROUND OOTACAMUND
**Dodabetta:** 2633 m, get the bus to Kotagiri, hop out at Four Road Junction. From here, you walk. Think half a day for the excursion.

**Kotagiri** (28 km): You might spend the night. Great hiking in the area.

**Tours:** If you're into organized tours, check at Kings Travel, Commercial Road, in Nahar Tourist Home.

**Mudumalai Sanctuary:** On the road between Mysore and Ootacamund. Be sure to reserve accommodations in advance.

## TIPS
**Tourist Office:** Commercial Road, Charring Cross, tel.2416, Mon-Sat 10:00-17:00 h, not very helpful, maps.
**Supermarket:** Same building, all your daily needs.
**Bookstore:** Same building, Higginbotham's.
**GPO:** Between the Tourist Office and Botanical Gardens, Havelock Road & Woodhouse Road.
**Wildlife Warden:** Mahalingam Building, Coonoor Road, tel.3114, reservations for Mumumalai Sanctuary, Mon-Sat 10:00-17:00 h.
**Horses:** Ride along the northern bank of artificial Ooty Lake, 15.-Rs per hour, according to demand, seasonal rates, bargain!

**Boats**: Depending on outfitting and season, 3.- to 25.-Rs an hour, no such thing as a fixed price.
**Bazar**: Go!
**Brochure**: Other attractions are described in **Welcome To The Nilgiris**, found in any Ootacamund bookshop; lists lodgings, connections, taxi prices, plus info on other villages in the mountain region, including Coonoor and Kotagiri, costs 3.-Rs.

# Kodaikanal

Situated at 2133 m, Kodaikanal (pop. 20,000) is a pleasant mountain village in the Palani Hills with a refreshing, cool climate. During the hot days leading up to monsoon season, wealthy Indians flee to Kodaikanal, driving prices up. Besides the climate, visitors are attracted by lovely forests, panoramic views, and tossing waterfalls.

## SIGHTS
**Cascade Falls**: On the route to Madurai.
**Kodaikanal Lake**: You can row a boat, or rent a horse to ride.
**Bryant Park**: Flourishes near the lake.

**Shenbaganur Museum:** For the botanically minded, provides an introduction to local flora and fauna, located 6 km from the lake near Sacred Heart Convent.
**The Observatory:** Founded in 1898, open to visitors from April to June, 10:00-12:00, 19:00-21:00 h.
**Coaker's Walk:** If you want to observe the Kodaikanal region through the eyes of a telescope. Or wander near Kurinji Andavar Temple.

Expect rain in Kodaikanal from mid October to December. The best time to come is April to June. Second best: September-October, but prices take a leap.

## COMING - GOING
Kodaikanal isn't accessible by rail; the nearest station is 80 km-distant Kodaikanal Road on the line connecting Madurai and Trichy. Still there's a Railway Booking Office in town.
**By Bus:** From Kodaikanal Road you've a lovely ride, 7.-Rs to Kodaikanal. Plus frequent connections to Madurai (takes 4 h). At 09:00 h there's a direct bus to Trichy, takes 6 h. Regular buses to Kumuli / Thekkady at Periyar Wildlife Sanctuary, and in season to Coimbatore.

## A NIGHT'S REST
Cheap accommodations on Bazar Road **(S)**12.-, **(D)**20.-Rs, but much higher in season from April to June, still bargain! **Lodge Everest**, Bazar Road. **Amar Hotel**, Bazar Road. **Sri Guru Lodge**, end of Bazar Road, simple, clean, **(D)**20.-, 50.-. **Youth Hostel**, at Hotel Tamil Nadu, 10.- per person. **Subedar Hotel**, Woodville Road, (low season) **(D)**40.-, (high season) **(D)**150.-, 200.-, separate toilets, kitchenette. **Jai Hotel**, Lloyds Road, **(S)**35.-. **Chiffton Hotel**, **(D)**100.-. **Hotel Tamil Nadu**, Fern Hill Road, **(S)**40.-, 60.-, **(D)**70.-, 110.-. **Carlton Hotel**, Boathouse Road, certainly the best hotel in town, but in high season you pay **(D)**300.-Rs.

## REFRESHMENT
For a simple restaurant with good but cheap food, try **Silver Inn Restaurant** on Seven Road. Nearby are **Tibetan Brother's Restaurant** (and several other restaurants) on Hospital Road.

## TIPS
**Post Office:** On Post Office Road, tel.241.
**Bazar Road:** Here you'll find the bus stand, a small bookshop, Railway Booking Office, and the Indian Bank, all conveniently close (on and surrounding).

# Madurai

Ancient records by Greek and Roman merchants doing trade with
the Tamils testified to Madurai's 2500-year history (population
today 600,000). At that time Madurai was used as capital by the
Pandavan kings, who were deposed in the 10th century. The Pandavan dynasty regained power 200 years later in the 12th century, but was conquered for good in the 14th century by the
Muslims under Malik Kafur. Later the Vijayanagar kings (Hampi)
assumed control for a short period, before the Nayaks conquered
Madurai in 1565 and held the city until Britain took control in
1781.

Midway through Nayak rule (about 1650 AD), Madurai flourished as the center of late-Dravidian architecture. Meenakshi Temple
is the main attraction in this bustling, but nice town. The former
old town center is marked by rubble from a fort razed by the
British, creating a rectangular slice through the city, with
convenient streets (ring roads) for processions, the present-day
Veli Streets. These ring roads were built in accordance with Hindu architectural tradition. Earlier epochs remain recognizable in
the foundations, from inside to outside. Avani and Masi Streets
are named for the directions faced (North Masi, East Masi, South
Masi, and West Masi Streets.

You might go on from here by rail or bus into the mountains
of southern India, or to Kerala. The scenery is tremendous. Be
sure to travel during daylight hours.

## COMING - GOING

Just 1 km apart (rickshaw, 1.-Rs) on West Veli Street are Madurai Junction Railway Station and Central and Tiruvalluvar
Express Bus Stands. The two bus stands are directly across
from the Tourist Office and the Tourist Bungalow.

**By Air:** Direct flights daily to Madras (375.-) and Cochin
(250.-), four times weekly to Bangalore (321.-Rs). The Indian
Airlines office is north of the station on West Veli Street,
tel.26795.

**By Rail:** Your quickest connection north is Valgal Express from
Madras Egmore Railway Station, via Chingleput, Villupuram,
and Trichy. The Quilon Mail runs from Egmore via Kodaikanal
Road to Kerala.

To Rameswaram there are day and night trains. The night
train arrives early in the morning in Rameswaram, in time to
catch the ferry to Sri Lanka. The 160 km takes over 6 h, costs
20.-Rs. If you want, book in Madurai all the way to Colombo,
Sri Lanka (but you still will have to reserve a seat on the
ferry!). So prepare to queue in Rameswaram.

**By Bus:** Good connections to Pondicherry (6 nightly), 30.-,
7 h), Bangalore (5 daily, 40.-, also private buses), Madras
(hourly, 40.-), Mysore, Dindigul (10.-), Rameswaram,

Periyar Wildlife Sanctuary / Thekkady, Kottayam (4 daily,
30.-, 8 h), Trivandrum (02:30 h, 07:30 h, 38.-), Ernakulum,
Nagercoil / Kanyakumarin (hourly, 30.-, 5 h), Coimbatore.
**Around Town:** Depart from Central Bus Stand, good info there
and at the Tourist Office, plus rickshaws or scooters. Get
Bus 4 to Gandhi Museum and Theppakulam Tank.

## A NIGHT'S REST

As so often in India, almost all the reasonable lodgings are
located near the sights and transport, i.e. Town Hall Road,
West Perumal Maistry Street and West Masi Street.
   **New College House,** Town Hall Road, tel.24311, **(S)**15.-,
**(D)**30.-, showers, **(Eb)**5.-. **Saraswathi Lodge,** Town Hall Road,
tel.25873, **(S)**20.-, **(D)**30.-. **Hotel Midland,** West Masi Street,
**(D)**20.-, **(Eb)**5.-, not as good as its reputation. **Hotel Arima,**
**(S)**20, **(D)**30.-. **Hotel Apsara,** 137 West Masi St., tel.31444,
**(D)**35.-, showers, clean, friendly, restaurant. **Ravi Lodge,**
**(S)**20.-, 12 Mandayan Asari St., tel.22493, quiet, clean,
friendly, from the railway station go down Town Hall Rd.,
toward downtown, then go right at Hotel Amutham. **TM Lodge,**
West Permumal Maistry St., **(S)**20, **(D)**45.- bath. **Krishna Hotel,**
**(S)**15.-, **(D)**25.-. **Uma Lodge,** West Perumal Maistry St. (near
Town Hall Rd.), tel.26621, **(S)**15.-, **(D)**20.-. **Rubi Lodge,** Kun-
dram Rd., **(D)**20.-, with fan, shower, toilet. Numerous similarly
priced hotels in the same neighborhood; have a look.
   **RRR,** **(S)**15.-, **(D)**20.-, **(AC)**40.-. **Hotel Tamil Nadu** (Tourist
Bungalow), West Veli St., tel.31435, right across from Express
Bus Stand, just 1 km south of the railway station, **(S)**30.-,
**(D)**60.-, **(AC)**150.-, **(Eb)**10.-, showers, clean, quiet, pleasant,
good Indian restaurant, egg and marmalade breakfast included
in price. **Hotel Tamil Nadu,** Alagarkoil Rd., easy to confuse
with the cheaper Hotel Tamil Nadu (above), **(S)**75.-, **(D)**100.-,
**(AC)**100.-, 150.-, restaurant serves international, Chinese, and
Indian food, bar. **Madurai Ashok,** tel.42531, the most expensive, and best hotel, all **(AC)**, **(S)**250.-, **(D)**325.-Rs.

## REFRESHMENT

Numerous Indian restaurants in the hotel district and around
Meenakshi Temple. **Hotel Amutham,** 30 Town Hall Rd., good food,
acceptable prices.

## SIGHTS

**Sri Meenakshi Sundareswarar Temple:** The main attraction, and
rightly so, is the newly rejuvenated Meenakshi Temple, featuring
five tremendous gopuram (gate towers). The tallest is 55 m,
richly decorated with 1055 breathtakingly colorful carvings depicting both religious and mythological themes. The tallest, the
**Southern Gopuram,** can be climbed (1.-Rs) for a view of the temple complex and Madurai. High walls surrounding the temple lend
peace to the 300 m X 270 m enclosure. One temple is dedicated to

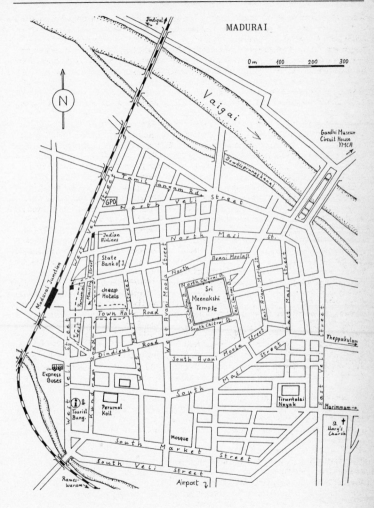

MADURAI

**Shiva**, the other to **Meenakshi**, a princess he married: a reincarnation of his wife Parvati. ·The **RAMAYANA** story is depicted in the Wedding Hall.
**Festival**: Every April and May the Marriage of Meenakshi and Sundareswara is celebrated by thousands of pilgrims.
**1000–Column Hall**: ·Houses an **Art History Museum**, but just 997 columns (count them!?), costs -.50 Rs.
**Musical Columns**: Also here, each sounds a note in a musical scale when struck (played).

Only Hindus are admitted to the most sacred of the two temples, and from 13:00-16:00 h the whole complex is closed. A photo ticket is only worthwhile if you have a flash. No charge for photos taken from the south gopuram (06:00-17:00 h).

**Thirumalai Nayak Palace**: In ruins, in the southeast of town, 1 km from Meenakshi Temple (rickshaw 2.-Rs), built in Indo-Saracenic style. The main section and entrance hall have been restored, 08:00-17:00 h, costs 40.-. Evenings at 18:40 h there is a Sound and Light Show, costs 1.- to 3.-Rs.
**Gandhi Museum**: 09:00-13:00 h, 14:00-18:00 h, dedicated to the life of Mahatma Gandhi, colonial history, and the struggle for independence, plus an exhibition of handicrafts from southern India.
**Float Festival**: Held at **Teppakulam Tank** (reservoir), 5 km outside town on Ramnad Road every January or February. Religious figures are pulled on flower-covered rafts through Teppakulam Tank to a tent in the middle of the tank. The festivities are in celebration of Thirumalai Nayak's birthday, builder of Thirumalai Nyak Palace and Teppakulam Tank.

**TIPS**
**Tourist Office**: (Buses 4, 4a, 15), tel.22957, across from Express Bus Stand on West Veli St., just 1 km from the railway station, 10:30-17:00 h (closed the 2nd Saturday each month). Info window in the railway station, tel.24535, 07:00-20:00 h, Sat-Sun 07:00-10:30 h, 17:00-20:00 h.
**State Bank Of India**: On the small street across from the railway station (corner building).
**Indian Airlines**: Northwest of the railway station at the north end of West Perumal Maistry St.
**GPO**: 300 m north of the railway station on Scott Rd., Mon-Sat 07:00-18:00 h, Sun 10:00-18:00 h, Poste Restante.
**Bookstores**: On West Veli St., some quite good.
**Automobile Association Of Southern India**: West Masi St., helpful for shipping cars to Sri Lanka, plus road information.

**FESTIVALS**
The major Indian festivals are celebrated in Madurai:
**Chithirai Festival:**  April–May,  Madurai's largest festival, celebrating the wedding of Lord Shiva (Sunareswarar) to Meenakshi,
lasts 10 days.

**Float Festival**:   January–February,   godly figures are pulled through Teppakulam Tank on rafts.
**Avanimoolam Festival:**  Celebrated in August–September in honor of Lord Sundareswarar.

# Rameswaram

Besides a ferry connection to Sri Lanka (Talaimannar Pier),  this island town (pop.  15,000,  but 35,000 on the island) is home to one of the most valuable examples of Dravidian temple art, Rama-natha Swamy Temple, dating back to the 12th century. Rameswar-am is India's second-largest pilgrim town (after Varanasi). Until completion of the road bridge,  the island is accessible primarily by rail from Mandapam (where all bus connections end).  Due to the influx of pilgrims, accommodations are difficult to find.

## COMING – GOING
**By Rail:**   Most important is the Rameswaram Express:   Madras Egmore 19:50 – Chingleput 21:05 – Villupuram 23:50 – Thanjavur 04:35 – Trichy 06:30 – Rameswaram 14:00 h.  Rameswaram 13:35 – Trichy 21:25 – Thanjavur 22:38 – Villupuram 04:30 – Chingle-put 06:40 – Madras Egmore 08:10. To Madras costs 50.-Rs (2nd class).  Chingleput is the railhead from Mahabalipuram and Kanchipuram. Change in Villupuram for Pondicherry.
   Coimbatore 22:15 – Dindigul 03:05 – Madurai 05:40 – Rames-waram 11:10 (165 Rameswaram Exp. / Pass.). Rameswaram 15:00 – Madurai 22:10 (166 Coimbatore Pass. / Exp.).
There are other local trains, particularly to Mandapam, where the buses depart, and to Madurai.
**By Bus:**  It is quicker and simpler to get a bus to the state of Kerala.  From Trivandrum Central Bus Stand by the railway station, you've  hourly buses to Nagercoil (10.-, 3 h) the first major bus stand in Tamil Nadu. From Kovalam Beach at 06:45, 09:50,   13.45,   18:40, direct buses to Nagercoil (10.-, 3 h) and Kanya Kumari (12.-,  3 h). If you're only coming this far, make departure reservations upon arrival.  From Nagercoil at 04:00,   07:30,   10:30,  16:45,  20:45. From Mandapam at 03:45, 07:30,   14:00,   17:00, and 22:00 h (30.-, 8 h). From Kanya Ku-mari (see Cape Comarin) buses 30 minutes later,  28.-. Express buses from Tiruvalluvar Transport Corp. Ltd.,  from Madurai, Trichy,  Villupuram (Pondy).  Departs Madras five times daily from Express Bus Stand,  Esplanade,  tel.25044, bookings three days in advance, costs 50.-Rs.
**Around Town:**  All important locations are close together.  You can get around by foot, or by tonga (horse cart) for 3.-Rs.
**By Ferry:**  To Sri Lanka, see Passage to India.

## A NIGHT'S REST
As a pilgrim town,  lodgings are tight.  If possible,  arrange advance reservations from a  Tourist Bungalow or  Tamil Nadu

Tourist Office elsewhere.

**TNTDC Tourist Bungalow** (Hotel Tamil Nadu),  tel.77,  **(S)**45.-, **(D)**70.-,  **(Eb)**15.-,  balconies with lake view. **Nadar Mahajana Sangam Lodge**,  New Street,  **(D)**15.- showers. **Alankar Tourist Home**,  West Car St.,  **(S)**15.-,  **(D)**25.-,  showers. **Michael Lodge**, near the railway station,  **(S)**15.-. **Maharaja's Tourist Home (S)**12.-,  **(D)**25.-,  bath. **Hotel Maharaja**,  **(S)**20.-,  **(D)**40.-, **(AC)**75.-,  all rooms with bath. **RRR**,  in the railway station, **(S)**12.-, **(D)**20.-, **(DM)**7.50, almost always packed!

Tip: If everything else is booked, try **Lakshmi Lodge**, you can sleep on the roof (no frills) for 5.-Rs.  Or try in the railway station,  where you can secure your baggage in the Cloak Room (closed 21:00-05:00 h). Other lodges charge **(D)**20.-Rs.

Food is no problem.  Rameswaram,  as a pilgrim town,  boasts lots of cheap vegetarian restaurants.

## SIGHTS
**Ramanatha Swamy Temple:**  The main attraction for pilgrims and tourists.  It is famous for the longest columned corridor in India: 1,200 m.  Construction began on the present temple in the 12th century.  Over time, it has been expanded, and is now considered an example of late Dravidian temple architecture.

**Aguitheertham:**  A pilgrim bathing area,  on the coast near the temple.

### HISTORY – LEGEND
Part of the sacred epic **RAMAYANA** tells of the creation of the chain of islands and sandbars between India and Sri Lanka.

Hanuman,  the monkey god, and his monkey army are said to have thrown rocks in the water and hopped across to Sri Lanka (also the Island's name in the story),  where they rescued Sita,  wife of the god Rama, from her imprisonment by the evil king, Ravana.

According to another legend,  Adam crossed the sea here after being driven from paradise, en route to the royal island of enlightenment where he settled.

Geologically speaking, the island chain across the Straits of Palk is a sunken landbridge which once connected the island with the Indian subcontinent. At the nearest point the two

are just 36 km apart.

After successfully freeing his wife,  Rama returned to present-day

Rameswaram. He assigned Hanuman to honor Shiva by marching forth with his army in search of a lingam (phallus) from the legendary mountain, Kailas. When Hanuman was delayed, Sita made her own lingam out of clay, which she worshipped. Hanuman, after finally returning, was so disappointed at his wasted effort, that Rama placed Hanuman's new lingam a bit north of Sita's recently installed lingam, and stipulated that Hanuman's lingam should have precedence over Sita's. Ramanatha Swamy Temple is located right on the spot. On the southeastern tip of the island, at a spot marked by Kothandaraswamy Temple, Vibishana, brother of the demon king Ravana, is said to have surrendered to Rama.

## AROUND RAMESWARAM
**Kothandaraswamy Temple:** At the southern tip of Rameswaram Island, a heavy storm in 1964 destroyed the village of Danushkodi, sparing only the temple. You'll find depictions of Rama, Sita, Lakshman (Rama's half-brother), Hanuman, and Vibishana.
**Padam of Rama:** A bit north of the temple in Rameswaram is the northernmost point on the island featuring a lovely view. Pilgrims flock here to worship the "Foot of Rama".
**Swimming:** Near town are coral reefs and beaches.

## TIPS
**GPO:** Between the railway station and harbor on your left.
**Tourist Information Center:** In the railway station (poor).
**Clams:** Taste good, try them.

## THE FERRY
Besides the sights, tremendous temples, and pilgrim town, Rameswaram offers the cheapest route to Sri Lanka. For all the formalities see Passage to India and Sri Lanka.

# Nagercoil

A major junction (pop. 100,000) for bus traffic between Tamil Nadu and Kerala, but of little touristic interest. Nagercoil is a good departure point for day trips, or an alternative place to stay when visiting Kanyakumarin.

## COMING – GOING
**By Rail:** Just two trains of interest, i.e. the Jayanti Janata running via Trivandrum, Quilon, Cochin, and Madras to Bombay. And the Him Sagar Express via Trivandrum, Quilon, to Delhi and Jammu Tawi, the longest run by rail in India: 4,000 km.
**By Bus:** There are two bus stands, one for local buses, and one for long-distance buses. From the local bus stand, you've connections to the day trip possibilities below. The overland buses provide connections all over Tamil Nadu, e.g. Madurai

(5 h),  or Rameswaram (8 h).  Nagercoil serves as a transfer
point and end station for buses to Kerala,  Kovalam (2 h),
Trivandrum, and Quilon.

**A NIGHT'S REST**
**Sri Swaminatha Lodge** by the long-distance bus stand. **Kumar
Lodge** by the stadium, **(D)**20.-.
   Two cheap but good restaurants near the bus stands: **India
Coffee House** and in **Hotel Ashok**.

**AROUND NAGERCOIL**
**Kanyakumarin:** At the southern tip of India (1.50 Rs, 1 h).
**Padmanabhapuram** (20 km):  Get a bus to Thukalay,  then change
buses, 3 km to the palace.
**Muttom:**  Another 20 km excursion brings you to this fishing village,  featuring a lighthouse and an old cathedral set on the
rocks, great view, costs 1.-Rs.

# Kanyakumarin

Also called Cape Comorin (pop.  12,000),  the most southern point
on the mainland in the Indian Republic is popular among
pilgrims and travellers.  This is the only place in India where
you can see the sun both rise and set over the ocean,  an
experience which attracts thousands, particularly at full moon.

**COMING - GOING**
   **By Rail:** Last stop on the route from Trivandrum (90 km).
   **By Bus:** Certainly the quickest and most comfortable way to get
   here.  From Trivandrum or Kovalam Beach (06:45 or 13:15 h,
   8.-,  2 h), direct or via Nagercoil (20 km from Kanyakumarin,
   1 h). Nagercoil is the main bus stand in the area, connections
   half hourly (see Nagercoil).  Direct buses to Rameswaram, Tuti-
   corin,  Madurai,  Trichy,  Salem,  Cochin,  Villupuram,  and
   Madras.

**A NIGHT'S REST**
   **Hotel Tamil Nadu** (Tourist Bungalow), tel.57, **(D)**50.-, **(Eb)**15.-,
   showers,  **(Dm)**10.- (7 beds),  restaurant. **Cape Hotel** (TTDC),
   tel.57,  **(D)**60.-,  **(Eb)**10.-, all rooms with showers, restaurant,
   bar. **Kerala House**,  tel.29, **(S)**20.-, **(D)**25.-, **(Eb)**6.-, all with
   bath,  but plus 5 % luxury tax, restaurant. Several new lodges
   charge **(S)**20.-,  **(D)**30.-, e.g.: **Shree Bhagavati Lodge**, **(S)**20.-,
   **(D)**30.-,  East Car St. **Kaveri Lodge**, **(S)**20.-, **(D)**30.-, Kovalam
   Rd.  Pilgrim accommodations by people in town for 5.-. **Youth
   Hostel**, recently opened by TNTDC, 34 beds, costs 8.-Rs.

**SIGHTS**
**Full Moon:**  Plan for the spectacular rise of the full moon in
conjunction with the setting sun. Schedule your visit accordingly!

**Kanyakumari Amman Temple**: Dedicated to Parvati in her incarnation as Devi Kanya, whereby she is said to have unsuccessfully
asked Shiva for his hand in marriage, and then sworn to remain
a virgin (Kanya). By the temple, pilgrims bathe in the ocean at
the foot of Kumari Ghat. Open 04:30-11:30 h, 17:30-20:30 h; non-
Hindus are not appreciated inside.

**The Gandhi Memorial**: Precisely constructed so that on October 2nd
(Gandhi's birthday) a ray of light falls on the spot where the
urn holding the founding father's ashes lay (near the temple).

**Vivekananda Memorial**: On a rock off the coast, marks the spot
where the Indian philosopher Swami Vivekananda meditated in
1892 before beginning his journey as a teacher throughout India.
The pavilion was constructed in his memory in 1970, uniting
architectural styles from all over India. Inside is a statue of
Vivekananda. Boats depart 07:00-11:00 h, 14:00-17:00 h, costs
3.-Rs in good weather. No photos allowed, admission 1.-Rs; long
lines for the ferry, but the view of the two coasts separating is
worth it.

## AROUND KANYAKUMARIN
**Kolachal Beach**: One of the most beautiful beaches in southern
India; half way between Nagercoil and Kovalam.

**Vattokotai**: 6 km from Kanyakumarin is an 18th-century fort offering great swimming and view of the sea.

**Padmanabhapuram**: Capital of Travaneore until 133 AD. Visit the
fort and its temple; located 45 km from Kanyakumarin toward
Trivandrum.

Also see Around Nagercoil.

## TIPS
**Tourist Information**: Near the bus stand and in Hotel Tamil Nadu,
tel.76, 10:30-17:00 h.
**Post Office**: In the town center.
**State Bank Of India**: In the town center.


What is your favourite spot in Tamil Nadu? Write us, tell us; we
are interested.

David Crawford
Barbara Rausch & Peter Meyer
India - Nepal - Sri Lanka
P.O. Box 110232
1000 Berlin 11
Germany

# KERALA

India's southwesternmost state occupies a fertile coastal strip, and the
steep western slopes of the Ghat
mountains. Don't come here expect-
ing cultural-architectronic attractions. This is your invitation to
nature: highland forests, tremendous nature reserves, rich wildlife.
Boat rides through palm-lined
canals (kerala = land of coconuts!)
along the coast are popular, as are
the beach inlets surrounding Trivandrum, the capital. Sightseers,
conversely, flock to the twin cities,
Cochin and Ernakulum.

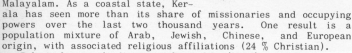

A population of 30 million occupies just 40,000 km$^2$, 625 people
per km$^2$! Kerala's state language is
Malayalam. As a coastal state, Ker-
ala has seen more than its share of missionaries and occupying
powers over the last two thousand years. One result is a
population mixture of Arab, Jewish, Chinese, and European
origin, with associated religious affiliations (24 % Christian).

Relatively equal division of wealth (land), and intensive
working of agriculture, including two-thirds of India's coconut
and spice production, is reflected in reduced poverty, better
health care, and higher educational standards. Kerala's literacy
rate is 60 %, three times the national average, and rising (also
unusual)!

Kerala, as a state, was founded in 1956. The world's first
freely-elected communist state government was elected here in
1957. Left-wing parties still hover around the 50 % mark in the
polls, even if they can't always form a ruling majority.

Numerous family fathers (and some women) work today in Arab
countries.

Kerala is easiest to reach by bus. If you're coming from Goa,
use the bus line Panaji - Margao - Mangalore (Karnataka); from
Margao 75.-, 20:00 h, 9 h. Lots of trains and buses connect
Mangalore and Ernakulum. For other connections see the local
sections. We will work through Kerala from north to south.

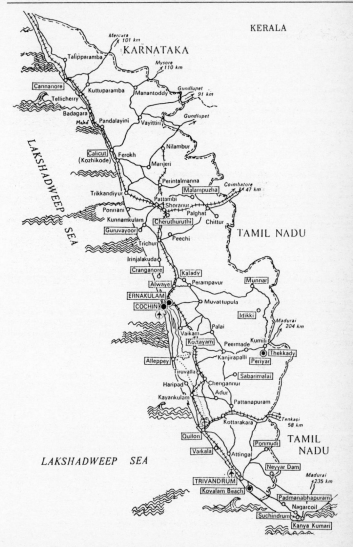

KERALA

KARNATAKA

*Mercara 101 km*

Talipparamba

Cannanore
Tellicherry
Badagara
Mahé
Kuttuparamba
Manantoddy
*Mysore 110 km*
*Gundlupet 91 km*

Pandalayini
Vayittiri
*Gundlupet*

Calicut
(Kozhikode)
Ferokh
Nilambur
Manjeri

Perintalmanna
*Coimbatore 47 km*
Trikkandiyur
Pattambi
Malampuzha
Ponnani
Shoranur
Palghat
Kunnamkulam
Cheruthuruthi
Guruvayoor
Chittur
Peechi
TAMIL NADU
Trichur

Irinjalakuda
Cranganore
Kalady
Alwaye
Perampavur
Munnar
ERNAKULAM
COCHIN
Muvattupula
Idikki
Palai
*Madurai 204 km*
Vaikam
Kottayam
Kumili
Alleppey
Peermade
Kanjirapalli
Periyar
Thekkady
Tiruvalla
Sabarimalai
Haripad
Chengannur
Adur
Kayankulam
Pattanapuram

Kottarakara
*Tenkasi 58 km*
Quilon
TAMIL
NADU
Varkala
Ponmudi
Attingal
LAKSHADWEEP SEA
Neyyar Dam
TRIVANDRUM
*Madurai 235 km*
Kovalam Beach
Padmanabhapuram
Nagarcoil
Suchindrum
Kanya Kumari

LAKSHADWEEP
SEA

# Mahé

The tiny enclave of Mahé doesn't belong to Kerala administrativ-
ely (just to begin with the exception), but to the former French
colony of Pondicherry. The village is situated 60 km north of
Calicut and 40 km south of Cannanore. Many maps neglect to
show it. Mahé's real claim to fame stems from its special status:
alcoholic beverages are cheap here. Are we actually writing a
guide to inebriation? The village, and fort, have changed hands
frequently over the centuries. In 1683 this was the first permanent British trade settlement on the Malabar Coast. The East India
Company built a fort in 1708. Later the French took over the
10 km² including three villages outside Mahé.
   In mid-October, a Christian festival is celebrated in honor of
Saint Theresa.
   The village is on the main rail line and road along the Malabar Coast. You've good bus connections both north and south.

# Calicut

Despite Calicut's (also Kozhikode) colorful past, there is little
left to see. So just a few words on the village's history.
   In 1498, Vasco da Gama landed here, becoming the first European to reach India by ship around the Cape of Good Hope (Cape
Storm at that time). The Portuguese failed in two attempts to
capture the town in 1509 and 1510. In 1513, however, an agreement was reached with the reigning Zamorin Raja, permitting the
founding of a settlement. In 1616 the British arrived, putting an
end to Zamorin rule. But constant unrest plagued the British
until 1789 when Tipu Sultan of Deccan turned the town to ash and
rubble. In 1792, the British regained the upper hand.

## COMING – GOING
   All trains between Ernakulum and Mangalore stop here, as do
   buses. Buses to Ooty at 06:00 h, 06:30 h, 07:00 h, costs
   20.-Rs, takes 8 h, lovely ride, but chilly.

## A NIGHT'S REST
   Hotel Imperial, (D)22.-, showers, restaurant. Hotel Maharani,
   (D)30.-, tel.76161. Beach Hotel, more expensive, (D)75.-, Beach
   Rd., tel.73851. Alagapuri Guest House, (S)30.-, (D)40.-Rs, Jail
   Rd., tel.73361. Or in the Tourist Bungalow.

# Cochin Ernakulum

This twin town (pop. 500,000) harbors all the touristic sights
Kerala has to offer. Culturally aware travellers don't just pass
through; they stay a couple of days. Even the location is interesting. Ernakulum is on the mainland, serving as a junction for

rail and bus connections.  Cochin is spread over several islands:
Willingdon Island,  Fort Cochin / Mattancherry,  Bolghatty,  Vypeen,  and Gundu; all connected by ferry. Only two main islands
are accessible by road to the mainland:  Willingdon Island (airport,  Malabar Hotel,  Tourist Office), and Fort Cochin / Mattancherry (Fort,  St. Francis Church,  the grave of Vasco da Gama,
Mattancherry Palace,  Chinese fishing nets,  synagogue, and Jewtown). The other islands provide harbor facilities.

Cochin boasts an interesting and varied history.  One look at
the town and its people confirms this.  Some of the high points:
Christianity has deeper roots here than in most parts of Europe.
Apostle Thomas (the Doubter) brought word of Christ here in
52 AD.  From the beginning, the Syrian-orthodox community played
a major role in trade.  When the Portuguese arrived after the
landing of Vasco da Gama in 1498 (see Calicut),  their missionaries were surprised to find Christianity already firmly entrenched.  The Portuguese put their energy into converting the faithful
to Roman Catholicism, with mediocre success.

The Jewish community is as ancient as the Christian.  The
synagogue in Jewtown dates from 1567.  Emigration to Israel has
reduced the white congregation to 40 mostly elderly members.

Equally influential were Kerala's contacts with Chinese and
Arab merchants and seamen.  Even today, Chinese fishing nets are
still in use.

The Portuguese built St. Francis Church in 1503.  Vasco da
Gama was buried here in 1524.  It is the oldest European church
in India.

In 1663,  the Dutch conquered the settlement. Dating from this
era is Bolghatty Palace,  built in 1744 on Bolghatty Island.  It
became the seat of the British Resident (today a hotel),  after
Britain took the town in 1795.

All Cochin's occupiers have left their mark in local architecture. Notice the 500-year-old Portuguese houses in the fort.

## COMING – GOING

Grouped together in Ernakulum,  the mainland section of Cochin,
are Ernakulum Junction Railway Station,  the bus stand,  the
Tourist Reception Centre,  the State Bank of India, boat jetties,
and most hotels and restaurants.

**By Air**:  The Indian Airlines office is located on Durbar Hall
Road, tel.32065, south of the Tourist Reception Centre.
Bangalore (331.-), Bombay (880.-), Delhi (1650.-), Goa (561.-),
Madurai (250.-), Trivandrum (180.-Rs).

**By Rail**:  All trains along the west coast stop here (eight daily).  Most important is the Malabar Express (time,  2nd class
price):  Mangalore (16:00 h,  38.-) – Ernakulum Junction
(03:05 h) – Quilon (06:05 h,  18.-) – Trivandrum (07:40 h,
23.-Rs).  Ideal for travellers from Goa,  via bus to Mangalore.
Trivandrum (16:00 h) – Quilon (17:35 h) – Ernakulum Junction
(21:05 h) – Calicut (01:55 h) – Mangalore (07:30 h).  From
Mangalore, get a bus on to Margao / Panjim in Goa.

COCHIN / ERNAKULUM

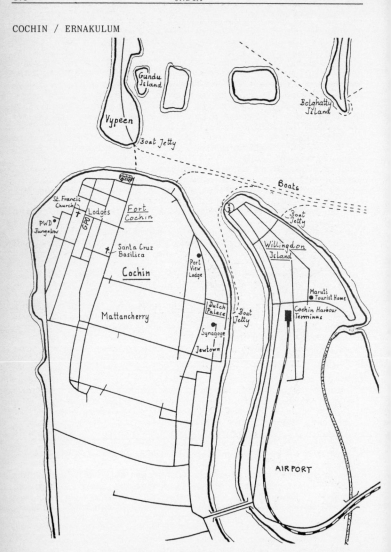

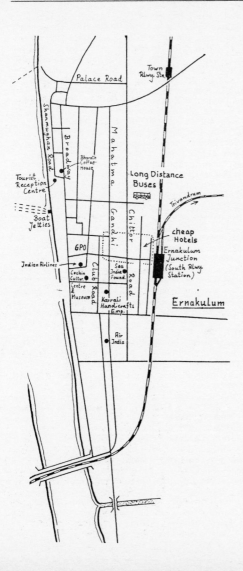

**By Bus:** Ernakulum Bus Stand is one of southern India's major junctions. Lots of connections, if we don't mention times then at least hourly. Trivandrum, Quilon, Kottayam, Alleppey (every two hours), Palghat (on the route to Ooty), Trichur, Calicut, Bangalore via Mysore (05:00 h, 07:00 h, 20:00 h), Cannanore (02:00 h, 09:30 h, 15:00 h, 22:30 h).

Several connections daily to Madurai via Periyar Wildlife Sanctuary, from Thekkady. Daily to Madras (60.-Rs).

**Around Town:** Besides buses, taxis, and scooters, your primary transport is by sea! Kerala State Road Water Transport Corporation provides ferry connections (-.50 Rs to 1.-Rs). You can rent a rowboat (3.-Rs). Or the Tourist Office organizes comfortable tours (10.-Rs). But don't carry a lot of baggage.

Regular ferries between Ernakulum - Fort Cochin; Ernakulum - Vypeen; Vypeen - Fort Cochin; Ernakulum - Willingdon Island - Mattancherry. In Ernakulum, all ferries depart from the Boat Jetty (see map). The ferry to Fort Cochin is crowded, otherwise okay. The three jetties on Cochin / Mattancherry aren't directly connected. And there is no no direct connection between Cochin Fort and Willingdon Island. You might get a rowboat for 3.-Rs per passenger. But there is a Mattancherry - Willingdon Island connection. Willingdon Island is called **Terminus** on some schedules. All ferries run at least hourly 06:00-21:00 h. Buy your tickets on land; they are twice as expensive on board!

Buses and taxis are not recommended due to idiotic routes, or high prices (unless you know where you're going, e.g. Cochin Jetty to Ernakulum Railway Junction, -.70 Rs. Otherwise, within Ernakulum and Fort Cochin, you have scooters, which run on a meter).

## A NIGHT'S REST

Budget hotels are located in two areas: in bustling Ernakulum, near the railway station, or by the Boat Jetty and Tourist Reception Centre. Other hotels are concentrated around Fort Cochin and St. Francis Church. In Ernakulum, moving away from the railway station:

**Tourist Bungalow**, on the street, right of the railway station, on the left-hand side, **(S)**20.-, **(D)**30.-, showers, restaurant acceptable. **Premier Tourist Home**, same street, just before Tourist Bungalow, **(S)**20.-, **(D)**30.-, showers, clean, friendly, relatively quiet, popular. **Central Lodge**, across from the railway station, straight ahead left, **(S)**14.-, **(D)**20.-, showers, only if the above two are booked! **Sangeetha**, Chittor Road (left), tel.36742, **(S)**32.-, **(D)**60.-, good restaurant (Ranjim!). **Hotel Sealines**, on the right between Chittor Rd. and M.Gandhi Rd., **(S)**20.-, **(D)**30.-, showers, good hotel, less good restaurant. **Anand Bhavan**, M.Gandhi Rd., west side, **(S)**15.-, **(D)**30.-, 50.-. **Woodlands**, M.Gandhi Rd., tel.31371, **(S)**45.-, **(D)**65. **International**, M.Gandhi Rd., tel.33911, **(S)**55.-, **(D)**100.-.

The closer we get to the Jetty and Tourist Reception Centre, the higher the class (and price!) of hotels. **Hotel National**, Canon Shed Rd., by the boat jetty, **(S)**10.-, **(D)**20.-, just a common shower, but quiet, friendly, popular! **Basoto Lodge**, Press Club Rd., **(S)**10.-, **(D)**20.-, clean, friendly, not as full as National. **Sea Shell**, Shanmugham Rd., tel.33807, **(S)**15.-, **(D)**30.-, showers, · a bit loud. **Hakoba**, Shanmugham Rd., near Sea Shell, tel.33933, **(S)**20.-, **(D)**30.-, excellent, view of the harbor, restaurant. **Breeze Hotel**, Shanmugham Rd., **(D)**20.-, toilet, shower. **Blue Diamond**, Market Rd., tel.33221, **(S)**30.-, **(D)**60.-, shower, see map. **Tourist Home Biju's**, Market Rd., quiet, clean, good beds, **(D)**30.-.
Near the bus stand: **YWCA**, Chittor Rd., Tel.35558, **(D)**8.-. **Ninan's Tourist Lodge**, **(S)**20.-. **Luciya**, Stadium Rd., tel.34433, **(S)**25.-, **(D)**45.-. **Bus Stands Retiring Rooms**, tel.32033, **(Dm)**5.-. Lots more lodges in the area!
On Willingdon Island are hotels higher in class and price, try: **Malabar**, **(S)**220.-, **(D)**250.-, all **(AC)**, near the boat jetty, Tourist Office inside, good info, friendly, tel.6045, Mon–Sat 09:00–17:00 h (except holidays and 2nd Saturday each month).
Or if you want to stay a while, try near Fort Cochin, though the selection isn't as large: **XL Hotel**, north-east of Fort Cochin GPO, on the same street, **(S)**8.-, **(D)**15.-, showers, only for long stays, restaurant downstairs for everyone. **Elite Hotel**, near the GPO, see map, **(S)**6.-, **(D)**12.-, just a common shower, another good restaurant. **YMCA**, by the GPO, tel.25288, **(S)**5.-, **(D)**15.-, often full! **PWD Inspection Bungalow**, Dutch Cemetery Rd., tel.25797, **(S)**12.-, **(D)**16.-, common showers, great for the price, but often crowded, nice view of the sea. **Port View Lodge**, outside town, but nicely situated, see map, according to furnishings, **(S)**10.-, 15.-.
If you're looking for something special, but don't want to spend too much, there is only **Bolghatty Palace**, Bolghatty Island, Ernakulum, tel.35003, **(S)**35.-, **(D)**60.-Rs, showers, toilet; built by the Dutch in 1744, later home to the British Resident; peacefully situated on tremendous grounds featuring lawns, golf course; restaurant and bar; upon arrival, make reservations at the Tourist Reception Centre in Ernakulum, and ask which boat to take.

## REFRESHMENT
Most hotels have an adjoining restaurant. In Ernakulum, we recommend the good, but cheap, **Ranjim Restaurant** in Hotel Sangeetha, Chittor Rd. Good, reasonably-priced Chinese food in **Golden Dragon**, Mahatma Gandhi Road, across from Grand Hotel. On Mahatma Gandhi Rd., good food in the restaurants in Hotel Woodlands, and Hotel International, though the latter is expensive. For a snack, try some of the good food and coffee in an Indian Coffee House, on Market Road, or the main street along the sea. In the fort, we have to mention the good, reasonably-priced restaurant in **Hotel Elite**.

## SIGHTS

Everything of interest is on the two main islands, Fort Cochin / Mattancherry. Willingdon Island is an artificial island which was created with sludge, dredged during harbour expansion.

**Fort Cochin:** Many buildings are 500 years old, dating from the Portuguese colonial era.

**St. Francis Church:** The oldest European-built Church in the Far East, dating from 1503. After capturing the Fort, the Dutch made the church Protestant. Later, under the British (1795), the church became Anglican.

**Santa Cruz Cathedral:** At the southern tip of the Fort, a modern Roman Catholic church.

**Chinese Fishing Nets:** Placed in the water on wooden frames, and pulled back out, hopefully full. North of St. Francis Church, along the coast, have a look at the rows of nets. They were brought here by seamen and traders from the court of Kublai Khan.

**Mattancherry:** This district. is very old.

**Jewtown:** The **Synagogue** dates from 1568 (renovated in 1664). The hand-painted floor tiles came from Canton, China in the 18th century, as does the **Clock Tower.** The synagogue is open Sun-Fri 10:00-12:00 h, 15:00-17:00 h, except Jewish holidays.

**The Dutch Palace:** Built by the Portuguese in 1557 as a gift for the Raja of Cochin, Veera Kerala Varma (bakshish), the Dutch renovated and expanded it after assuming control. In the courtyard is a **Hindu Temple.** On the second floor is a hall in which the rajas were crowned. In numerous other rooms, the 17th century walls are painted with scenes from the **RAMAYANA** (excellent!), 09:00-17:00 h, no flash photography.

**Kathakali Dance:** Another very special attraction are ancient temple dances based on the heroic epics **RAMAYANA** and **MAHAB-HARATA.** They were almost forgotten before being rekindled by western interest. While performances of the original 110 dances (some 2000 years old) took an entire night to perform in full ceremony, shortened, 90-minute versions are offered here. The dances could only be performed by upper caste temple members. Traditional training began at the age of five and lasted at least twenty years. If you want to learn more about this tradition, arrive a good hour before the performance:

**Theosophical Society Hall:** Shree Shankara Lodge, Churchlanding Road, near Pallimukka Bus Stop, Ernakulum South, tel.36238, performances from 19:00-20:45 h.

**See India Foundation:** Kalathi Parambil Lane, P.O. Box 1740, Ernakulum (see map), behind Laxman Theatre near Chittor Rd., tel.31871, daily performances 19:00-20:30 h, costs 25.-Rs, including photo permit.

**The Cochin Cultural Centre:** Durbar Hall Ground (by the Museum), tel.33732 (office) and tel.37866 (theatre), performances 18:30-20:00 h.

Other performances, some of greater length, are held irregularly, ask at the Tourist Office, or in the daily paper, cost 15.-Rs plus 10.-Rs photo permit.

## TIPS
**Government of India Tourist Office:** Malabar Hotel, Willingdon Island, tel.6045, Cochin, 09:00-17:00 h, except holidays and 2nd Saturday each month, excellent advice, good material, maps cost 2.50 Rs.
**Tourist Reception Centre:** Shanmughan Rd., tel.33234, Ernakulum, 08:30-17:30 h, friendly, but fewer brochures, books motorboat tours to all the sights 12:30 h and 14:00-17:30 h from Sealord Boat Jetty Ernakulum, 20 minutes later from Willingdon Island Tourist Office.
**GPO:** Fort Cochin, tel.24247, Poste Restante (see map).
**Head Post Office:** Ernakulum, Shanmugham Rd., Tel.31610.
**Bookstores:** Pai & Co. or Broadway on Shanmugham Rd.
**State Bank of India:** Shanmugham Rd., Ernakulum, tel.31184.
**Indian Airlines:** Durbar Hall Rd., tel.32065.
**Shopping:** M.Gandhi Rd., Ernakulum.

## LACCADIVE / LAKSHADWEEP ISLANDS
If you have the time, why not get a ship out to the Laccadive Islands, 200 km off the Malabar Coast? Together with the Amindivi Islands, Cannanore Islands, and Minicoy Island (at the southern border to the Maldives), these islands form the Lakshadweep Union Territory, with an administrative capital in Bingaram (other spellings include Bangara). The total area of the 23 atoll islands is 32 $km^2$. Nine of the islands are populated by an Arab-Indian Muslim population.

Foreign tourists are only permitted to visit the Islands of Bangara and Suheli, and then only with a special permit issued by the Interior Ministry in Delhi. To make arrangements, contact: Sports, C/O Lakshadweep Office, Wellingdon Island, Harbour Road, Cochin 3. Here they arrange the special permit and book ship passage and lodgings.

The passage by ship (2 days) costs at least 200.-Rs. For food and board in the state-owned bungalows, think US$50.- per person per day. Write us, and tell us how you liked it!

# Periyar Sanctuary

This 777 $km^2$ wildlife reserve is situated at 1000 m - 2000 m altitude, making it pleasantly cool on winter nights. Your best time to visit is November to March. Reasonably-priced boat rides in the early morning and late evening across Periyar Lake (created a century ago for irrigation) provide convenient transport to animal observation points. You'll find elephants, gaur (wild bovine), otter, sambar deer, wild boar, and a wealth of birds.

PERIYAR NATIONAL PARK

0 km            5

A   Wildlife Preserve Office
B   Periyar House
C   Araniya House
D   Forest Rest House
E   Forest Rest House
F   Periyar Dam
G   Forest Rest House
H   Forest Rest House

    Observation Tower

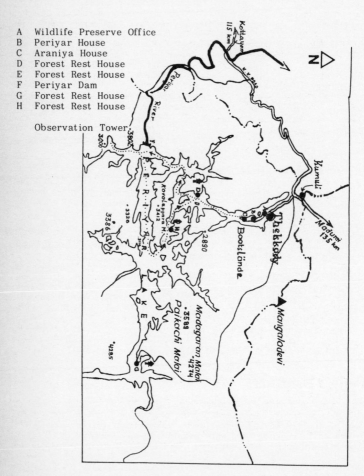

Get the hourly boat (6.-Rs, plus 1.-Rs admission, students -.50 Rs) at 07:00 h for the two-hour ride across the lake. When water behind the dam is low, ghostly tree stumps rise from the lake. Early morning and evening are best (depart 15:00–17:00 h). This is when elephants come to drink, taking little notice of the boat (5 m, close-up, photography).

**Elephant Riding:** For 20.-Rs an hour, you can ride an elephant, departing from the boat jetty. This is certainly the cheapest place in India to enjoy elephant riding, and a great view.

**Treks:** Some mornings, groups set off with a guide from the Info Centre. Individual treks are officially prohibited, but tolerated.

## COMING - GOING

**By Bus:** Express and Fast Passenger (F.P.) buses from Madurai, Ernakulum, Kottayam, Quilon, and Trivandrum.

Madurai - Thekkady, Express Bus 544 from Express Bus Stand at 05:00 h and 09:00 h (cheapest), 15.-, 4 h, connections on to Kottayam.

Thekkady - Ernakulum, 05:45 h, 09:10 h, 14:30 h, direct, 22.-, 8 h, return 06:30 h, 14:30 h.

To Quilon at 05:15 h, takes 6 h.

To Trivandrum at 08:00 h, 13:30 h, 14:30 h, takes over 8 h.

**Around Town:** Between Hotel Periyar House in Thekkady and the bus stand in Kumili, costs 1.-Rs. Most long-distance buses go via Thekkady.

## A NIGHT'S REST

You can stay in the small lodges or with a village family in Kumili (or Kumuli) for 5.- to 8.-Rs. **Hotel Woodlands, (D)**15.-, quite good. **Lake Queen Lodge**, Kumili, **(D)**25.-, 35.-, comfortable, warm, reasonable food.

More expensive around the lake. **Periyar House**, tel.26, **(S)**18.-, 25.-, pairs 25.-, **(D)**30.-, 40.-, two pairs 45.-, **(Dm)**8.- (no bed), service 10 % extra, simple restaurant. **Aranya Nivas**, tel.23, near the jetty, **(S)**100.-, restaurant, money exchange. **Holiday House, (S)**15.-, **(D)**30.-Rs.

Try in **PWD Inspection Bungalow, (D)**10.-, or in the watch towers for 5.-Rs per person; bring your own food; the park officer often claims the towers are occupied when it isn't true.

# Kottayam

Your departure point for motorboat rides through Kerala's flatland canals via Alleppey (see there) to Quilon, and for bus rides to Periyar Wildlife Sanctuary (Thekkady) and on to Madurai. This district capital is 75 km from Cochin, at the foot of the West Ghats, on the main road through southern Kerala.

## COMING - GOING

**By Rail:** Kottayam is a railway station on the west coast line between Trivandrum and Ernakulum. Twelve trains daily. Two trains north to Mangalore, and south to Kanyakumarin.

**By Bus:** Hourly connections north and south. Plus daily buses to Thekkady (Periyar Wildlife Sanctuary, 15.-Rs, 5 h) and Madurai.

**By Boat:** About 1 km from the bus stand (scooter 4.-Rs) is the jetty for boats to Alleppey; costs 3.-Rs (3 h), through palm-lined canals, departs hourly. Get off at the last stop in Alleppey. Last boat at 21:00 h.

## A NIGHT'S REST

There isn't much to see in Kottayam and vicinity, travellers just stay one night: **Tourist Bungalow** (Government Guest House), **(S)**20.-, **(D)**26.-. **PWD Rest House**, **(S)**6.-, **(D)**8.-. **Hotel Ambassador**, KK Road, tel.3293, **(S)**20.-, **(D)**25.-Rs.

# Alleppey

A lovely town with a large beach (3 km from the boat jetty) used unfortunately as a public toilet. This is your departure point for boat rides through the tremendous canal system, e.g. to Quilon.

**Snake Boat Races:** On the 2nd Saturday in August, the largest of Kerala's famous Snake Boat Races is held, featuring 20 men in the thin boats. There has been talk of moving these races and the great elephant processions to fit in with the main tourist season at the beginning of January. So ask at the Tourist Office if you are interested.

**Hindu Temple:** Lovely, take a left on the road from the bridge heading into town.

## COMING - GOING

This is one of the few places in India where getting there is a lot nicer than being there. So let's start with boats.

**By Boat:** Depart Quilon at 10:00 h and 20:30 h, depart Alleppey at 10:00 h and 22:30 h, takes 9 h, costs just 5.-Rs! But a boat out of service can reduce this frequency considerably; ask. Tickets are sold on board the large vessels, no reservations.

Many people visit Kerala just to enjoy the 80 km cruise through palm forests, stopping at numerous tiny villages, sometimes long enough for a quick meal. Along the way your eyes never tire of the lovely, ever-changing scenery: side canals, rowboats, sail-rigged barges, Chinese fishing nets, and villages full of laughing children stretched along the water-side. At full moon, the night boat is particularly nice. Bring your own food; you've just quick stops for tea on the night boat.

Boats to Kottayam depart hourly 05:00–21:00 h, takes 3 h, 3.–Rs. Just after midnight, there's a freighter to Ernakulum, takes 8 h, costs 2.–Rs, return in the afternoon.
**By Bus:** The bus stand is near the boat jetty and several cheap lodgings. Buses hourly to Trivandrum, Ernakulum, and Quilon.
**Bicycles:** Rent for 4.–Rs per day.

## A NIGHT'S REST

Near the boat jetty and bus stand: **Hotel Komala,** including **Lodge Nalanda,** (across from the boat jetty) has been remodelled and is now quite expensive, good restaurant. **Sheba Lodge,** behind the Omala, new, good, **(S)**15.–, **(D)**30.–. **Karthika Tourist Home,** clean, large rooms, showers, toilet, **(D)**25.–, 30.–, across the bridge from the boat jetty, then 150 m to the right. **Krishna Bhavan,** **(S)**8.–, **(D)**16.–, simple, but okay. **Mahalekshmi Lodge,** **(S)**10.–, **(D)**16.–, right by the boat jetty, a bit shabby. **Municipal Sathrom,** near the boat jetty, **(S)**6.–, **(D)**10.–, but not very good, on the same level as Mahalekshmi Lodge and Krishna Bhava.

In town: **Raja Tourist Home,** **(S)**9.–, **(D)**15.–, showers, clean, head toward town on the road by the bridge to the boat jetty, 2nd road to the right, on the right. **Danalekshmi Lodge,**

tel.2138, **(S)**9.-, **(D)**15.-, so-so, on the same street from the
bridge (Mullakkal), after the 2nd road to your right. **Sarada
Tourists Home**, Mullakkal, **(S)**15.-, **(D)**25.-, near Danalekshmi
Lodge, recommended. **St. George's Lodge**, **(S)**15.-, **(D)**25.-,
friendly, clean, sorry a long walk, same street from the bridge
to the next canal then right at the corner, 800 m from the boat
jetty. **PWD Rest House**, Beach Road, 3 km from the boat jetty,
near the beach, clean, quiet, **(S)**7.50, **(D)**15.-Rs, but expensive
restaurant.

## REFRESHMENT
Lots of Indian restaurants on the road from the bridge into
town, and the 2nd street to the right, near Raja Tourist Home.


# Quilon
Like every town on the Malabar coast, Quilon (70 km north of
Trivandrum) has had an eventful history, changing hands frequently. Today, however, it's a town to pass through quickly in
anticipation of the popular **Backwater Cruise** through Kerala.

## COMING - GOING
**By Rail:** All express trains along the Malabar coast between
Trivandrum and Ernakulum stop here. Plus a few very slow
local trains, and trains via Madurai to Madras Egmore. The
railway station is 3 km from the bus stand and the boat jetty.
**By Bus:** Buses are faster, and the bus stand is conveniently
located near the boat jetty and many cheap hotels. Connections
at least hourly to Trivandrum (9.-, 2 h), Alleppey, Ernakulum,
etc. Many buses continue on to Quilon railway station. In Kerala you are advised to book seat reservations for the red
KSRTC buses an hour before departure in the larger bus stands
(no charge).
**By Boat:** Quilon is your departure point for the lovely cruise
to Alleppey (see Alleppey), departs daily 10:00 h and 20:30 h,
takes 9 h, costs 5.-Rs. Boats from Alleppey arrive at 18:45 h
and 07:30 h, allowing convenient bus connections on to Trivandrum at 19:00 h or 19:25 h. The bus stand and boat jetty are
adjoining.

## A NIGHT'S REST
**Hotel Sudarsan**, Paramaswar Nagar, at the circle 700 m from
the boat jetty, your best tip for both accommodations and food,
**(S)**25.-, 30.-, **(D)**40.-, 50.-, showers, friendly, clean, quiet.
 All other recommended hotels are further in town near the
clocktower and temple. From the boat jetty or railway station,
3.-Rs by scooter: **Sika Lodge** (behind the Post Office right of
the bridge), **(S)**15.-, **(D)**20.-, showers, restaurant (Hotel Apsara, southern Indian), good, clean. **Traveller's Bungalow**,
across the river bridge, **(S)**10.-, **(D)**15.-, showers.

Chinese-Style Fishing Nets

**Tourist Bungalow**, lovely, but far (10.- by scooter), **(S)**15.-, **(D)**30.-, peaceful, great view, food a bit expensive.
If you aren't particular, try by the boat jetty: **Hotel Mahalakshmi**, quiet despite the bus stand, clean, **(D)**20.-. **Kopalakrishna Lodge**, **(D)**10.-, simple, cheap, clean, friendly. Lots of places to stay in town, nothing special worth mentioning, **(D)**15.-Rs.

Restaurants around the boat jetty offer average quality and prices. Or have a bite in Mahalakshmi Lodge near the bus stand.

# Varkala

A beach town, 19 km south of Quilon, on the Quilon – Trivandrum rail line.
**Maharaja's Summer Palace**: The Kerala Communist Government has expropriated the palace, and built a number of bungalows, all

super clean. From the gardens, you've a great view across the
rice terraces and ocean. Breakfast is served in an open salon,
spread over two terraces. The bungalow apartments come equipped
with toilet and shower. All reserved, of course for government
officials, who are rarely seen. Four friendly employees await
your needs, including an excellent cook (tall as a tree).
**(D)**25.-Rs.

If the palace is booked up, certainly possible, there are several
smaller accommodations 2 km below on the road into Varkala. But
what can compare with a maharaja's palace?

**Sacred Stream:** Irrigating the rice terraces, it flows through the
valley to the sea. It pours out of a pipe above the sandy beach,
providing a heavenly, freshwater shower after a quick dip in the
ocean.
**Fishing Villages:** There are several fishing villages in the region. The nets are pulled in around 9 am, when the entire town
is up and about. The markets are picturesque.

A bus to the beach stops across from the exit at the railway
station. Taxis charge horrendous prices for the same trip.

# Trivandrum

Kerala's state capital (pop. 500,000) is the most peaceful in
India. The town doesn't have many sights.
**Padmanabhaswamy Temple:** Closed to non-Hindus.
**Beaches:** Trivandrum is a good departure point for trips to Kerala's beaches and mountains.
**The Town Center:** In accordance with Hindu tradition, is built
quadrilaterally around the central temple, oriented toward the
four points of the compass.
**Park:** In the north of town is a park, featuring a **Museum** and
**Sri Chitra Art Gallery**, 08:00-18:00 h, except Mon & Wed, free
admission. The architecturally interesting building houses bronze
statues, wood and stone carvings. The art gallery supplements a
collection of Indian paintings from various schools and epochs
with works of Chinese, Japanese, and Tibetan origin.
**Zoo** & **Botanical Garden:** Nearby, 08:00-18:00 h, nominal admission. The zoo grounds include lakes, meadows and lawns, reputedly among the prettiest in Asia.

## COMING - GOING
**By Air:** Trivandrum's small international airport provides dir-
ect flights to Colombo US$53.- (IA or Air Lanka), Male US$63.-,
Dubhai and Abu Dhabi on the Persian Gulf and in Kuwait.

Bangalore (thrice weekly, 510.-), Bombay (1020.-), Cochin (180.-), Delhi (1805.-), Goa (680.-) Madras (535.-), Trichy (280.-Rs).

**By Rail**: Trivandrum Central Railway Station was until recently the end of the Southwestern Rail Line. An extension to Kanyakumarin is now in operation. The railway station and Central Bus Stand adjoin in the cheap hotel district, near the Tourist Reception Centre (see map). The most important express trains include: 12 trains to Ernakulum, two of which continue on to Mangalore. All these trains stop in all the Malabar Coast towns found in this book, except Mahé and Alleppey; their nearest railway stations are Badagara and Kottayam.

Two trains daily to Nagercoil and Kanyakumarin.

Express trains direct to Delhi, Bombay, Madras, Calcutta, and all major stops en route.

Sample prices: Ernakulum 24.-, Mangalore, 51.-, Madras 68.-, Kanyakumarin 10.-, Bangalore 64.-, Bombay 122.-Rs, all 2nd class mail or express.

**By Bus**: Central Bus Stand, for long-distance buses, is right next to the railway station. Budget hotels and the Tourist Reception Centre are nearby. You've express buses direct to Madras at 14:00 h, 16:00 h, 18:30 h, and 21:00 h, 75.-Rs, 16 h, Madurai, and Trichy.

Karnataka State Road Transport Corporation (KSRTC) offers a
Deluxe Bus Service between Bangalore and Trivandrum,    departs
16:00 h, 110.-Rs, 18 h.
To Kanyakumarin via Nagercoil five times daily.   Quilon and
Alleppey 30 times daily;   Kottayam and Ernakulum 15 times.
Buses here are faster than trains.
Thekkady (Periyar Wildlife Sanctuary) 03:30 h and 08:45 h.
Buses to Rameswaram.   To Kovalam Beach from City Bus Stand
by East Fort.
You can reserve seats at the Enquiry Point for -.50 Rs on the
long-distance buses.
**Around Town:**   Buses run particularly along the north-south
axis,   Mahatma Gandhi Road and via the railway station
square. Taxis and scooters use meters.

## A NIGHT'S REST

If Trivandrum lacks sights, at least budget hotels are conveniently close to Central Railway Station and Central Bus Stand;
most tourists just pass through. **Sreevas Tourist Home**, tel.2769,
**(S)**18.-,    **(D)**30, Railway Station Road. **Venkateswara**, tel.63968,
**(S)**18.-,    **(D)**30, Railway Station Road. **Hotel Arulakam**, **(D)**25.-,
Station Road,  very clean.  **Corporation Guest House**,  tel.22867,
by the railway station,    **(S)**8.-, 10.-, **(D)**10.-, 16.-. **Mini Tour-
ist Home**,   Manjalikulam Road,   **(S)**10.-,   **(D)**18.-. **Baba Tourist
Home**,  next door on Manjalikulam Road, **(S)**10.-, **(D)**18.-. **Siva-
da Tourist Home**,   tel.5320,   Manjalikulam Road (see map),
**(S)**15.-, **(D)**25.-, clean, quiet.
More hotels in and around East Fort:    **Nalanda Tourist Home**,
**(S)**25.-, **(D)**30.-, clean, friendly.
North-east of the railway station:   **Hotel Aristo**, **(D)**16.-, quiet
and cheap, bugs. **Sree Kumar Lodge**, **(S)**15.-, **(D)**25.-. **Green-
land Lodging**,   **(S)**15.-,   **(D)**25.-. **Shreevi Tourist Home** **(S)**15.-,
**(D)**25.-.   **Grand Udipi Lodge**,   cheapest,  **(S)**7.-, **(D)**12.-. **Shali-
mar**, **(D)**50.-, but better than the above.
Further north up Press Road are more cheap lodgings:   **YMCA**,
**(S)**12.-,   **(D)**20.-. **International Tourist Home**, **(S)**12.-, **(D)**20.-.
**Devi Tourist Home**, nearby, **(S)**10.-, **(D)**15.-, 20.-Rs.

## REFRESHMENT

Try **Ceylon Restaurant** on MG Road.  Or **Azad Restaurant**, across
from Nalanda Tourist Home on MG Road,  south of the railway
bridge.

## TIPS

**Tourist Information Office:**  Parkview,  Trivandrum,  10:00-17:00 h,
tel.61132, by the Zoo, Museum, and Observatory, at the north end
of MG Road, 3 km from the railway station.
**Tourist Reception Centre:**  Right by the railway station and Central Bus Stand, just books sightseeing tours:
**City Tour:**   East Fort,  Padmanabhaswamy Temple,  the Aquarium,
the Secretariat,   Museum,   Art Gallery,   Zoo,  Neyyar Dam, Kova-

TRIVANDRUM

i   Tourist Information
i   Tourist Reception Centre
1   KSRTC Bus Stand
2   City Bus Stand
    at East Fort
3   British Council
    Library
    YMCA
    International
    & Devi
    Tourist Home
4   Ceylon Restaurant
5   State Bank of India
6   Indian Airlines
7   Zoo

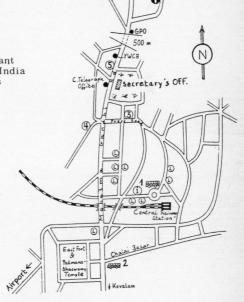

lam Beach; daily, except Monday, 08:00-19:00 h, 25.-Rs.
**Kanyakumarin:** Daily, 07:30-21:00 h, 35.-.
**Periyar Wildlife Sanctuary:**   Saturday 07:00 till Sunday 21:00 h,
85.-Rs, plus sleeping accommodations.
**State Bank of India:**   And other banks,   between the Secretariat
and University College,   MG Road,   only the State Bank changes
traveller's checks.
**GPO:** Has moved to MG Road, by St. Joseph's Church.
**Telegraph Office:** MG Road, across from the Secretariat.
**Indian Airlines Booking Office:**   Mascot Junction, near the Tourist
Office in the north, 10:00-17:00 h.
**Note:**   Kovalam Beach doesn't have a bank or post office.   But
there is a small branch office 3 km away in Kovalam Junc-
tion. You can change money at Kovalam Beach Resort.

# Kovalam

Half an hour south of Trivandrum is the travellers' spot in
Kerala:   the palm beaches on the Bay of Kovalam.   Crowds are
light despite the popularity of a large ITDC Kovalam Beach
Resort.   This is well off the usual tourist trail in the north or
south-east. The two southernmost inlets are nicest.

## COMING - GOING
**By Bus:** From Trivandrum City Bus Stand by East Fort, get Bus
15,   costs 1.50 Rs, departs half hourly from Platform 19, 06:00-
21:00 h,   early buses are packed,   last bus to Trivandrum at
22:00 h, takes half an hour.
From Trivandrum KSRTC Central Bus Stand,   by the railway
station,   Fast Passenger Buses (also stop at East Fort) depart
hourly,   3.-Rs,   but only stop in Kovalam Junction,   3 km from
the beach. The last bus is at 21:15 h.
From Kovalam,   you've direct buses to Ernakulum at 07:30 h,
to Nagercoil and Kanyakumarin at 06:30 h,   09:50 h,   13:45 h,
18:30 h, takes 3 h, costs 10.-Rs.
**By Taxi:** From City Bus Stand, costs 4.-Rs, departs when seven
passengers are willing.

## A NIGHT'S REST
The ideal place to rent a house with a couple of friends and
relax a while.   Those not staying long can choose from a number of hotels and lodges,   some up on the street where the bus
runs,   others down at the second inlet between the cliffs and
the lighthouse where the globetrotter scene hangs out.   The
further you live from the beach,   the less you pay for the same
comfort.   And prices change with the season;   i.e.   a room in
season runs at 30.-Rs, or half that at low season.
In recent years a number of new lodges (and restaurants!)
have opened along the beach.   As they change ownership,   the
names and standards of quality fluctuate.   So take your time

## KOVALAM

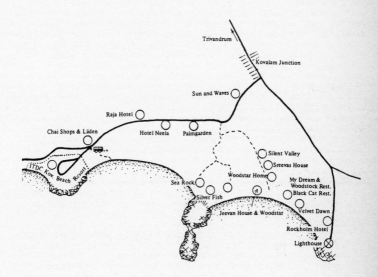

choosing where you want to stay. The prices and comments are only for orientation, certainly not the final word.

Up on the street, but far from the beach are: **Palm Garden**, **(S)**20.-, **(D)**35.-. **Sea Queen**, **(S)**20.-, **(D)**35.-. **Sun And Waves**, **(S)**20.-, **(D)**35.-. Also nearby, **Hotel Blue Sea** receives rave reviews despite its distance from the beach; a lovely, white, colonial-style building, in perfect condition, friendly owners, good garden restaurant, **(S)**25.-, 100.-Rs depending on comfort. **Raja Hotel**, further down the road, **(S)**35.-, 50.-, **(D)**50.-, 60.-, restaurant, bar, evening entertainment, money exchange.

And on to the beach where prices range from **(S)**15.- to **(S)**40.- depending on season and comfort, with or without bath, etc. These lodges are concentrated at the second beach. At the end, by the lighthouse are several middle-priced hotels: **Hotel Orion Hotel**, **(S)**30.-, 50.-. **Katvitha Hotel**, **(S)**30.-, 50.-. **Holiday Home**, **(S)**30.-, 50.-. Among the lodges, a few have maintained their standards over the years: **Sea Rock Lodge**, restaurant, **(D)**15.-, 40.-. **Jeevan House**, **(D)**15.-, 40.-. **Sreevas House**, **(D)**15.-, 40.-.

Private rooms, and several houses can be rented by and behind the lighthouse; look, ask, bargain!

**Rockholm Hotel**, on the same cliff as the lighthouse, **(D)**165.-, terrific, huge, wonderfully furnished, separate bath, toilet, ocean view (waves pounding below your window).

**Kovalam Beach Resort**, tel.3031, luxurious, **(S)**450.-, **(D)**500.-Rs; even if you aren't staying here, you can use the services, money exchange, sailing, motorboats, yoga, massage, swimming pool; one of the prettiest hotel grounds in India.

## REFRESHMENT

Lots of good places, many recently opened, particularly by the beach. You'll find your own favorite. Just a few of the spots which have maintained high standards over the years: **Silent Valley**, **Sea Rock Restaurant**, **Sreevas House**, **Woodstock** (formerly Wood Star), **My Dream**, and **Velvet Dawn**. The last three are right on the beach. Equally recommendable is **Padma Restaurant** in Hotel Blue Sea, though far from the beach. The restaurant in **Hotel Rockholm**, by the lighthouse, is excellent in line with its price.

In **Raja Hotel**, you've a large selection of Indian, Chinese and European dishes. Everything is more expensive, but far better in **Kovalam Beach Resort**.

By the beach, women from the obligatory head shops offer bananas, papayas, pineapple, oranges, nuts, and sweets. And don't forget the fruit juice stands. By the bus stand, a number of chai shops serve rice curry, and you can pick up your daily needs: detergent, soap, toothpaste, cigarettes, cookies, or suntan lotion. Beer, fenny, and toddy are sold at Kovalam Junction, where you'll find a Post Office and Bank.

# ANDAMAN ISLANDS

Situated off the Southeast Asian
mainland, the Andaman and Nicobar
islands have been only recently
discovered by international tourism.
Tourists still require a special permit. Apply for the permit at an Indian consulate abroad. If you need
to get the permit while you're in
India, you can pick one up at the
Ministry for Home Affairs in New
Delhi, but expect a couple of
weeks' wait. In Madras the permit
is available within a few days from
the Chief Immigration Officer, 9
Village Road, no charge.

Even with the permit, several
regions and islands remain closed.
But the restrictions are being relaxed. Except for tribal areas
established by the Indian government for several hundred Ongres,
Sentinelese, and Jarawas, the major Andaman islands and the
smaller islands surrounding Port Blair are open. A permit is
issued upon landing just for the city and Jolly Boy Island.

There isn't much to see on the islands. This is a place to
relax, enjoy nature, and do some skin diving. Underwater photography is prohibited. Year round, the water temperature is
24° C. Air temperatures hover between 20° and 30° C with extremely high humidity, but there is a constant ocean breeze.

ANDAMAN ISLANDS

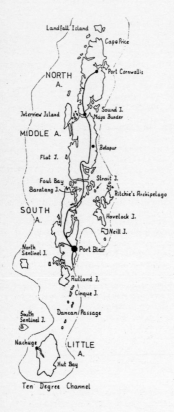

# Port Blair

Of the 200,000 island inhabitants, one-third make their home in Port Blair.
**Cellular Jail:** The island was a prison colony under the British, who incarcerated countless prisoners and freedom fighters there. Today it has been declared a national monument. Only three of the seven original prison wings have been preserved.
**Chatham Saw Mill:** On a small island, many types of rare woods are exhibited.
**Anthropological Museum**
**Oceanic Museum**
**Cottage Industries Emporium:** As in many small businesses, you can see craftsmen at work, or make a purchase.

**The Tourist Office:** Middle Point Road, Port Blair, 744101, tel.3006, runs City Tours, daily (5.-Rs). On weekends a Regional Tour is offered (20.-Rs). On Saturdays there is a tour to **Corbyn's Cove Beach** (10.-Rs), the closest beach to town, where a night's rest costs US$12.-.

## COMING - GOING
**By Air:** The airport is 3 km from Port Blair. Three flights weekly to Calcutta (1166.-Rs) and Madras (1178.-Rs), takes 2 h.
**By Sea:** The Shipping Corporation of India heaves anchor for Madras every ten days. The cruise takes two to three days and costs 69.-Rs (bunk class) or 558.-Rs (deluxe). Every 20 days there is a ship to Calcutta and Visakhapatnam. Tickets are only sold to those on a passenger list maintained by the Shipping Corporation of India in Port Blair; so be sure to get on the list early. Tickets are only sold on the mainland, i.e. from the agency in Madras: M/S K.P.V. Shaik Mohamed Rowther and Co. Pvt. Ltd., 202 Linghi Chetty Street, Madras 600001, India. You can also make reservations through this agency, but book several weeks in advance. Food on board is cheap.
Ferries ply between the islands, departing from Fisheries Ferry in Port Blair at 06:00 h, 12:00 h, and 15:00 h, via several small harbors to South Andaman Island. To other islands, there is just a weekly scheduled line. To charter a boat, speak to the Harbour Master, tel.528.

## A NIGHT'S REST
In every major settlement there is a state-run lodging, Circuit House, Dak Bungalow, or Guest House. The price is set at **(D)**20.-Rs. For a list, check with the Tourist Office, Middle Point Road.
In recent years a number of expensive hotels have been built, charging 100.-Rs per person and up.

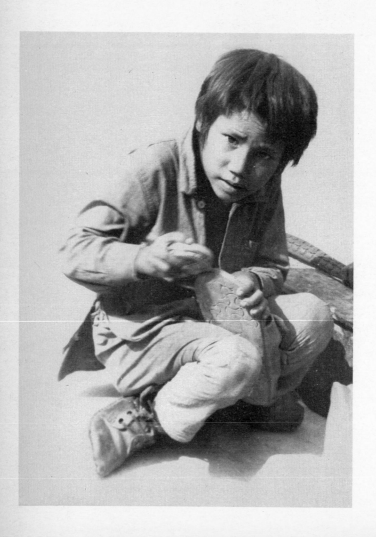

# NEPAL

# COUNTRY & CULTURE

## GEOGRAPHY

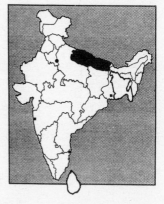

Situated at the northern edge of the Indian subcontinent from 80° 15' to 88° 15' East longitude, and 26° 15' to 30° 30' North latitude, we're as far north as the Canary Islands. Nepal is surrounded by the two most populous countries in the world: to the south and west is India, to the north is the Tibet region of the People's Republic of China. On the eastern border is the Kingdom of Sikkim which has been annexed by India. Nepal contains three altitudinal zones: the Himalayan mountain peaks, the foothill region before the high mountains, and the Terai, a fertile strip on the border with India. The two major valleys are Kathmandu Valley (1400 m) and Pokhara Valley (900 m). Nepal is about 900 km long and between 100 km and 240 km wide. Of Nepal's 144,000 km$^2$, the Terai covers one-third, KTM Valley just 5 %.

On average, this is the highest country in the world: besides Mount Everest, Nepal boasts nine mountains over 8000 m. Twenty-two peaks tower over 7000 m, and 250 mountains are 6500 m! Ten percent of the country is above 5000 m, 30 % above 3000 m, 25 % between 1000 m and 3000 m. Just 35 % of the country is below 1000 m in altitude. Still the lowest point in the Terai is only 70 m above sea level!

The highest mountains are Mt. Everest (8848 m, called Sagarmatha in Nepali and Chomolungma in Tibetan), Kanchenjunga (8584 m), Lhotse (8501 m), Makalu (8475 m), Yalung Kang (8420 m), Lhotse Shar (8363 m), Dhaulagiri (8167 m), Manaslu (8156 m), Cho-Oya (8153 m), and Annapurna (8090 m).

There's snow year round above 5000 m. Barley and potatoes are harvested up to 4300 m (the treeline).

NEPAL

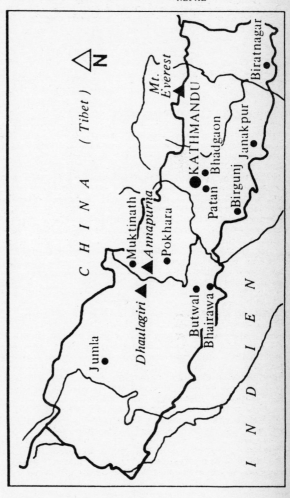

Formed within the last 70 million years, the Himalayas are a
chain of relatively young tertiary folded mountains. Over millions
of years, numerous rivers flowing down from Tibet have dug deep
gorges. Kali Gandaki, with a drop of 6000 m, is the world's
greatest. All these rivers feed eventually into the Ganges.

Before the Chinese occupation of Tibet, the traditional trading
routes between Tibet and India ran along Nepal's valleys. Today
they are popular trekking routes, along with the major mountain
passes; the best known is Nangpa La (5715 m), north of Namche
Bazar.

# Climate & Travel Seasons

Seasons, i.e. summer / winter, really don't exist here, but there
is some variation. The monsoon season is from July to September.
Your ideal travel season is after the rains, from the beginning of
October to the end of November. Visibility is clear (what good
are pretty mountains if they're fogged in?), and temperatures are
comfortable with average highs of 25° C and average lows of
10° C in KMT. Through till early summer, there's little rain.
December and January are relatively cold (19° / 2°). Springtime
is marked by cloudy, foggy weather, but everything is in bloom!
The best trekking season is October / November, the second best
March / April.

In the low-lying Pokhara, certainly in the Terai, it's warmer. The mountains are cooler. Plan for three climates: tropical in
the Terai, subtropical in the central mountains, and alpine in
the northern high mountains.

# Flora & Fauna

Due to its peculiar geographical structure, tiny Nepal has three
climatic zones, creating three separate biological regions.
**The Terai:** A subtropical climate with altitudes ranging from 90 m
to 300 m.
**The Central Highlands:** Altitudes range from 300 m to 2750 m. In
Pahar you'll find a moderate and tropical climate. The two fertile valleys, Kathmandu and Pokhara, are spread over this
region.
**The Himalayas:** An alpine and arctic climate with altitudes up to
8840 m.

**FLORA**
The Terai hosts a variety of useful plants. Foremost is the sal
tree, from whose wood, windows and doors are carved, an art
you can admire throughout Kathmandu Valley. It is a very sturdy
wood, capable of withstanding monsoon winds. Also of interest are
the banyan tree with its hanging spices, and the bodhi tree, under one of which Buddha achieved enlightenment. The coconut

palm is also well represented.   In the jungles of the Terai grows
a variety of tropical creepers.   Other plants include bamboo, elephant grass,   numerous herbs,   mimosa, and jasmine. There is not
a great variety of fruit,   mostly bananas or mangos,   plus oranges, grapefruit, and lemons.

In the central highlands,   the most common tree is the rhododendron in altitudes of 1500 m to just over 4000 m.   The rhododendron tree blossoms dark red to light red,   even pink and
white.   Magnolia also bloom in April.   Four varieties of oak, and
eucalyptus trees,   imported from Australia,   also thrive. In the
higher altitudes,   conifer grows.   And along your treks you are
certain to admire the orchids.

In Kathmandu gardens,   you'll find a number of familiar flowers including begonia,   dahlia, gardenia, geranium, jasmine, and
hibiscus.

Fruits in Kathmandu include bananas,   mangos,   oranges,
grapefruits, lemons, peaches, guava, pineapple, and papaya.

In the alpine region,   rhododendron trees are found up to
4000 m.   Also plentiful are   conifer,   pines,   cedar,   and other
evergreens.   Plus there is a variety of alpine plants;   even edel-
weiss is said to grow in the Langtang region.

## FAUNA
Nepal provides a habitat for 30 species of large animal,   over
800 species of bird, 80 species of mammal, and countless species
of insects and butterflies. The tiger population has been decimat-
ed in recent years;   just 30 to 40 survive today.   The one-horned
rhinoceros fares little better, and is closely guarded.

In Chitwan National Park you'll need real luck to see any of the
above.   The Himalayas are home to several species of deer.   In
isolated regions,   bears and snow leopards are reported,   though
rarely seen.   Also found in highland regions is the yak,   which
finds good use among the Sherpas and Tibetans.   Jungle cats,
jackals, fox, and hyaenas are also about.

Along your trekking routes you'll spot peacocks,  coocoo birds,
crows, eagles, hawks and other species of bird.

Less fun are the blood leeches which attack from the trees.
Mosquitoes and other insects are difficult to avoid.   But you will
be rewarded with the sight of colorful butterflies.

Snakes are rarely seen.   You will just have to get used to
pestering monkeys.   In Swayambunath and Pashupathinath are
countless rhesus  monkeys,  most fresh enough to steal right out
of your pockets.   The langur monkey,   with a black face surrounded by grey and white hair, is much more shy.

# PEOPLE

Nepal is home to almost 16 million people. While overall population density is 113 per km$^2$, keep in mind that only 60 % of the
country is inhabitable (just 17 % can be cultivated). Real population density is 190 people per km$^2$: in Terai 800 per km$^2$, and
in Kathmandu Valley where 800,000 people live on 560 km$^2$, it's
1400 per km$^2$. Over 16 % of the countryside supports a density
greater than 200 people per km$^2$; half the country has greater
than 100 per km$^2$.

Kathmandu, with 360,000 inhabitants, has neighborhoods where
50,000 people pack 1 km$^2$: without any high-rise buildings! Two
other major towns in Kathmandu Valley are Bhadgaon and Patan.
In Terai, Biratnagar has 50,000 and Nepalgani 35,000 inhabitants. Other important towns are Birjani in Terai and Pokhara in
the 900 m high Pokhara Valley.

**Life Expectancy**: At birth averages 45 years. Infant mortality is
15 %; 20 % of all children die before the age of five! The 1980
birth rate was 42 births per thousand inhabitants; the death rate
was 20. This produces a yearly population increase of 2.2 %. In
Terai the population increases at 4 % annually, partially due to
immigration from India and the job-poor hill country. Population
in the highlands is increasing at 1.8 %; in the mountains at just
1.2 %, but emigration into Terai keeps this figure down.

**Literacy**: Blesses 19 % of Nepal's population. Only 4 % of Nepal's
women can read, just 28 % of the men. In 1951 only 1 % could
read! Even in Kathmandu, half the adult population is illiterate.
Only in three other districts does literacy touch 25 %; in some
districts just 5 %. These statistics are certain to change soon, as
82 % of all children attend school, though frequently just for a
couple of sporadic years. Only 3 % of Nepalese youth goes on to
higher education.

The population belongs to two major language and ethnic families: Tibeto-Burmese in the north, and Indo-European in the
south. Altogether, about 25 different ethnic groups are counted.

## Ethnic Groups & Languages

The official national language is Nepalese, also known as Gork-
hali or Parbatiya, closely related to Hindi. Like Hindi, Nepalese
writing uses the Devanagiri script developed from Sanskrit, even
for numbers, unlike Hindi. Nepali is spoken by 55 % of the population, 4 % speak Newari, while 1 % speak Tibetan. The Terai is

POPULATION DENSITY

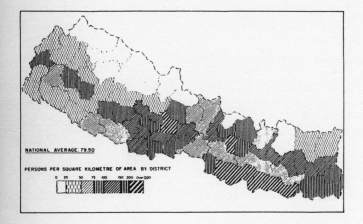

crisscrossed with numerous dialects of the Indo-Aryan language family, but in a small region Dravidian languages are spoken. In the mountains, Tibeto-Burmese languages and dialects predominate.

Thickly settled Kathmandu Valley is firmly in Newar hands, whose language thrives. The Newar are a mixed race people (though an ancient one) whose ancestors immigrated into the valley over the ages.

Also well known are the Sherpas (often falsely translated as mountain guides), due to their great tradition as wandering merchants. A Sherpa mountaineer, Tensing, was one of the first men to climb Mount Everest, along with Hillary. Originally the Sherpas migrated here from eastern Tibet.

In the north, Tibeto-Burmese languages are spoken by the Magar, Gurung, Tamang, Rai, Bhote, Chepang, Dolpo, Limbu, and the Thakali. Ethnic groups in the south speaking Indo-European languages include: the Danwars, Satars, Tharus, Khas. Other languages were brought by immigrating Brahman (called Bahun here), and the Kshatriyas, mostly from Rajasthan (called Chetris here). By the way, English is also an Indo-European language!

The world-famous Gurkhas aren't necessarily from the town of that name, rather mercenaries from almost all the tribes of northern Nepal, though mostly Gurung and Tamang. Once in British service, today they also serve in India, and as policemen in Singapore, or as private guards. Their pay and pensions are a regular source of income for many villages in Nepal, keeping Nepal's balance of payments in the black.

Consider how long a people has to remain isolated in order to develop its own language, and how many different languages flourish in this tiny country. For centuries the Himalayan mountains have protected these peoples from outside influence and invasion. These are truly ancient peoples!

# Tribes

The various tribes, such as Newar, Tamang, Tibetans, Sherpa, etc. differ greatly in their way of life, clothing, work habits, and festivals. Here are just a few examples.

## THE NEWAR

These are the most ancient inhabitants of Kathmandu Valley. It's easy to tell a Newar from other mountain tribesman when there's a load to carry: only the Newars use a bamboo pole with baskets fixed to ropes at both ends, slung over the shoulder. Other mountain tribesmen shrewdly carry the load in a basket on their back, supporting the weight with a tumpstrap (a long leather band strung across one's forehead). The Newar are monogamous, certainly not the rule in Nepal. Newar women can divorce their husbands in a simple ceremony, by returning the betel nuts received from their husbands in the marriage ceremony. At the age

of seven or eight, all Newar girls are symbolically married in a
Yihee ceremony to the God Narayan (an incarnation of Vishnu).
This is symbolized by a gold statue.  Shiva, himself, is witness
at the ceremony in the form
of Bel fruit.  This gives all
Newar women married status.
This marriage with the God
Narayan is considered the
only proper marriage, lasting
a lifetime.  Any marriage just
to a Newar man is therefore
easily dissolved.

For this reason, there
would never be a question of
Newar committing Suttee (wid-
ows burning themselves on
their former husbands' pyres,
a traditional Hindu practice,
now theoretically illegal in
India).  After all, the Newar
woman's true husband is im-
mortal.  They can return
without shame to their parents' home and remarry with
pride. Peasant women usually
wear black saris with red
trim.  Men wear traditional
cotton pants, wide at the top
and tight below. Around their
waist they wrap a cotton
cloth as a belt.  Newar don't
carry the Kukhri, a knife
worn by other tribes at the
belt.  I still remember the
sensation I had when first
leaving Kathmandu Valley on
a trek in the Hekambu re-
gion.  I actually felt threatened by all the Nepalese who
seemed armed to the teeth.
Kathmandu is tremendously
different.

## THE TAMANG
This Tibetan-Burmese tribe is a fairly recent arrival.  Many came
originally as horse traders from Tibet, before turning to farming,
particularly on mountain slopes.  The Tamang are mostly Lamaist
Buddhists;  Lamaism with marked influences of the Bon religion.
They also celebrate Hindu festivals and honor Hindu gods.  But
they don't practise the caste system.  Other caste-oriented Hindus
consider them members of a very low caste.  They live in the

eastern and central mountains
of Nepal, and a small propor-
tion (5 %) make their homes
in Kathmandu.

## THE THAKALI
Another Tibetan-Burmese tribe,
again mostly Buddhist. You'll
surely see them if you do the
Jomosom trek, since they're
settled all along the Kali
Gandakis. Ghasa and Tukuche
are the most important Thakali villages.

## THE SHERPA
This people can be seen on
the Helambu trek in Malenchi
and Tharkegyang, or in the
Solu-Khumbu region. They immigrated here 600 years ago

from Tibet. The Sherpa language is closely related to Tibetan.
They are Buddhist, usually belonging to the red-cap group. A
woman can be married to several men, usually brothers. The men
often have as an additional name the day of the week on which
they were born.

## THE TIBETANS
Tibetan men are easy to recognize, their long hair is braided
with red wool. In traditional dress, men wear long robes, whereby the right arm and shoulder remain free. Women wear a small
apron over a dark robe. Tibetans live mostly as traders, are
excellent craftsmen, and wonderful at weaving rugs. They live in
Swayambunath in Kathmandu Valley, Jawalakhel, and Bodnath,
where you'll also find a number of Tibetan shops. They are also
found near Pokhara and in the Solu-Khumbu Highlands together
with the Sherpas.
     Tibetans usually receive two names at birth. The first is the
name of the lama who helped to pick a proper name. The second
is a name designed to bring luck, i.e. a religious name, or a
name pointing to long life.

You'll find excellent books about all these ethnic groups in
Kathmandu bookshops.

# A Few Words of Nepalese

The official national language, Nepalese, uses Devanagiri script, derived from Sanskrit, without any universal agreement on spelling. The result is a motley selection of spellings for places and names, which is also reflected in this book.

Only about 55 % of Nepal's population are conversant in Nepalese; just 40 % use it as their mother tongue. You can get by just about everywhere with English; only on treks are a few words of Nepalese necessary. So we'll restrict ourselves to just a few words and the numbers.

Keep in mind that this language has no "F" sound, which people here pronounce as "P", giving rise to the famous "pipty" for fifty. If an "H" follows a consonant, it is strongly aspirated so remember to emphasize the "H" sound.

## NUMBERS

| | | | | | |
|---|---|---|---|---|---|
| 1 | ९ | ek | 16 | | sora |
| 2 | २ | dui | 17 | | satra |
| 3 | ३ | tin | 18 | | ath(a)ra |
| 4 | ४ | tschar | 19 | | unais |
| 5 | ५ | panch | 20 | | bis |
| 6 | ६ | tschaa | 30 | | tis |
| 7 | ७ | saat | 40 | | tschalis |
| 8 | ८ | aath | 50 | | patschas |
| 9 | ९/ε | nau | 60 | | sathi |
| 10 | १० | das | 70 | | sattari |
| 11 | | eghara | 80 | | assi |
| 12 | | bera | 90 | | nabbe |
| 13 | | tera | 100 | | (ek)say |
| 14 | | tschandra | 200 | | dui say |
| 15 | | pandra | 1000 | | hajar |

## HELPFUL WORDS

| ENGLISH | NEPALESE | ENGLISH | NEPALESE |
|---|---|---|---|
| hello | namestè | where? | kahan? |
| goodbye | namestè | (not) pretty | ramro (na) |
| thank you | dhanyabad | path | bato |
| yes (it is) | ho | river | khola |
| no | hoina | | naadi |
| there is | tscha | bridge | pul |
| there isn't | tschaina | hill | parha |
| okay | tschiktscha | mountain | parbat |
| | hunchha | mountain crest | lekh |
| what is it? | yo ke ho? | forest | ban |
| don't understand | budschina! | water | pani |
| how much? | kati? | house | ghar |
| here | yahan | tea house | tschia pasal |
| pay | tirnu | lodging | bhatti |

| | | | |
|---|---|---|---|
| money | paisa | rest area | tschantara |
| too expensive | tere mahango | tscha | |
| shop | pasal | friend | saathi |
| fast | tschito | innkeeper! | eh baba! |
| difficult | garo | waitress! | eh ama! |
| | | | |
| simple | sajilo | boy! | oh bhai! |
| dry | sukkha | girl! | oh didi |
| wet / cold | tschiso | guide | sirdar |
| (very) little | ali ali | porter | kuli |
| much | dherei | wood | dhaura |
| | | | |
| sick | biraami | | kath |
| closed | banda | fire | ago |
| now | bharkhar | festival | jatra |
| today | adscha | food | khana |
| yesterday | hidscho | drink | piunu |
| tomorrow | bholi | sleep | sutnu |
| | | | |
| morning | bihana | wait | pharkanu |
| afternoon | diuso | enough | pudschio |
| evening | belukka | in front | agaari |
| | | | |
| night | raat | behind | padschari |
| day | din | near | nadschik |
| | | | |
| how many days? | kati din? | high | aglo |
| how many hours? | kati ghanta? | low | hodscho |
| | | | |
| when | kahilai? | right | daya |
| I | ma | left | baya |
| you | timi | stop! | roka! |
| | | | |
| rice (boiled) | bhat | tea | tschai |
| linseed porridge | dal | | tschia |
| eggs | phul | sugar | tschini |
| milk | dudh | cookies | kek |
| yoghurt | daho | vegetable | tarkari |
| | curd | meat | masu |
| | | | |
| butter | nauni | bread | tschapati |
| | ghi | potatoes | alu |
| salt | nun | fruit | phalphul |

# RELIGION

Nepal is the world's last Hindu Kingdom. The King is considered an incarnation of Vishnu, called Narayan. Hinduism is the national religion. Other religions are permitted, though missionary activity is prohibited. About one-fifth of the population is Buddhist, while 3 % practise Islam. But there are strong regional variations in these numbers.

Buddhism was once much stronger here. The rulers and conquerors, however, have remained Hindu, giving Hinduism an advantage. Over the ages, Hinduism and Buddhism have intermixed. One result is that some of the major shrines are visited by worshippers of both faiths. The same deities are worshipped under different names; the same festivals are celebrated for different reasons. The intermixing is so great in Kathmandu Valley that the faith of an individual is often only apparent if one checks whether a Hindu or Buddhist house priest is employed. A Hindu Newar feels much closer to a Buddhist Newar than to another Hindu who has a different language and ethnic background. Marriages between Buddhists and Hindus of the same caste are no problem.

Nepal's religions can really be understood only if one looks first at Nepal's religious history. The ideas personified in early Hinduism and early Buddhism have little to do with today's religions. Under religious history, we will also look at Tantrism and Shaktism, both of which have been catalysts toward religious fusion.

## History

The changing history of Kathmandu Valley has dominated the course of religion. Religious conceptions have been moulded by the close proximity and fusion of various religious schools, trends and theories. Hinduism, Buddhism, Tantrism, plus remains of ancient Animism play a role.

**Animism:**  According to Animism, everything has a soul: good and evil spirits are everywhere.
**Buddhism:**  Buddhist thought probably gained its first foothold with the conquering Indian Emperor Ashoka (200 BC). The people formally converted to Buddhism, while the rulers remained Hindu. Under north-Indian influences, Buddhism in the Kathmandu Valley evolved into Mahayana-Buddhism around 100 BC.

**Tantrism:** Around 500 AD in northern India, a yoga-oriented cult took Mahayana-Buddhism in a direction called Tantrism today. Their teachings and practices were collected in the **TANTRA** (scriptures). Tantrists seek salvation through magical rites, including orgiastic practices.

**Shaktiism:** Toward the end of the 6th century AD, new interpretations of the Tantra led to Shivaist mysticism (worship of the female deity Shakti - usually seen as the wife of Shiva). According to Shaktiism, the female element carries the world's primal energy. The highest deity is seen as being female (Durga, Kali). Male deities can act only with the aid of the female energies (shakti). The Shaktiist congregation consists of two parts: the rites of the Right Hand of Shakta are open to all, while the rites of the Left Hand are secret and open only to the initiated. Important elements of the rites include the five mukara: mada (wine), matsja (fish), masma (meat), mundra (roasted grain), maithuna (sexual intercourse). Shaktiists break Hindu taboos, not for the sake of indulgence, but in pursuit of sacred goals. Temples of this faith can be seen at Khajuraho in Madhya Pradesh, India. For description of a ritual, see Khajuraho.

**Shaktiist Vajrayana:** Influenced by Hindu-Shakti ideas, Tantrist-Buddhism took a new direction, whereby the union of the male and female energies was seen to lead to the ultimate reality. These ideas arrived in Nepal during the 10th century. Shankaracharya, a great Hindu reformer, without ever setting foot in Kathmandu Valley, is said to have forced Buddhist monks and nuns to marry, because they didn't live ascetically, and participated in sexual rites. Thereafter, animal sacrifices were required to be made to Buddhist deities. Shankaracharya is said to have destroyed sacred Buddhist books. Hindu-Brahmanist ceremonies were given rebirth. Buddhism lost influence, evolving with time. Increasing emphasis on ritual and mysticism led to the Shakti Vajrayana cult.

**Intermixing:** In Nepal this evolution served to bring Shivaists and Buddhists closer together, through a mutual cult of worship. Orthodox Hinduism and Mahayana-Buddhism experienced a visible common ground in their religious practice through the rituals of Tantrism. Common ritual made it possible for each religion to integrate deities from the other faith into its own. Shaktiist ideas are said to have been brought by yogis to Nepal between the 7th and 10th centuries AD. Both the Buddhist and Shivaist traditions honor the 84 great yogis or Siddhas.

**Caste Laws:** Under caste laws instituted by King Jayasthiti of Mala, which affected both Hindus and Buddhists, the trend started by Shankaracharya continued. Monks and nuns were still required to marry. Monks became housekeepers, continuing to live with their families in monasteries, and undertaking the profession of gold- or silversmith which was thereafter inherited. Former

monks became family priests,  receiving liturgical office in Buddhist temples.  The result was a Buddhist rank of priest with the
same function as its Brahman counterpart.  When the Rana clan
came to power in 1846,  they championed radical Sanskritization
and radical Hinduism, a trend lasting until 1951.

Hinduism became a must for the social elite.  Particularly the
Newars of the merchant caste converted to Hinduism.  Even today
it is important for members of the upper class to emphasize their
religious affiliation.  Among lower classes the distinction carries
less weight.

# A Melting Pot of Religion

Religious fusion is most apparent in Kathmandu Valley.  Don't be
surprised to find depictions of Hindu gods in Buddhist temples,
or Buddhist stupas in Hindu temples.

The Shivaist fertility symbol,  the lingam (phallus), supported
by the yoni (female organ),  is referred to by Buddhists as the
"flaming lotus at the sacred source".  Hindus see the lingam and
yoni as the fundamental elements of male and female energy,
dating from before creation.  In the most important Hindu temple,
Pashupatinath,  the Shiva lingam is covered once a year by a
mask of Buddha.

In Swayambhunath,  Hindus worship the god of Swayambhunath
as Sambu (= Shiva),  even though a quick look at the huge stupa
would lead one to think it was Buddhist,  after all for Buddhists
Swayambu = Buddha.  In Pashupatinat and Swayambunath,  the
most sacred spots in Kathmandu Valley,  the God of Eternity is
worshipped.  Adibuddha and Adishivia are united in Adinatha, a
god accepted by both faiths.

Male deities tend to be depicted as Lekesvar / Matsyendra-
nath, a mixture of Shiva, the holy yoga Matsyendranath, and the
Bodhisattva Avalokitesvara.  Female deities fuse in the Shivaist
Kali / Durga,  or the Buddhist Tara (the most important female
Bodhisattva).

The goddess Guhyesvari is worshipped by Newar of all faiths.
For Buddhists she is the high goddess,  on a plain equal with
Adi-Buddha (Swayambu).  Female goddesses are frequently depicted
as variations of the Great Mother,  an idea championed by
Tantrism.

# The Caste System

Not until the 14th century,  under King Jayasthitimalla (1382 –
1395) in the wake of strict Hinduization,  was a universal caste
law instituted.  Till then,  caste laws affected only immigrant
caste members from India.  One result of the new law was the

creation of a Nepalese society, quite different from all its neighboring countries. As in India, there are four main castes: Brahman (in Nepali = Bahun), Kshatriya (in Nepali = Cheitris), Vaishya, and Sundra, and numerous lower castes. One's caste affiliation is reflected in one's name. Nepal's King Birendra Bir Bikram Shah Dev must belong to the Chetri caste because of the name "Shah". Kings are traditionally members of the warrior caste. Even Buddhists are integrated into the caste system. There are pure Buddhist and pure Hindu castes, but also castes encompassing both faiths.

**The Newar:** In an intra-ethnic caste system, Hindus and Buddhists are integrated equally under the caste system, with religious preference playing no role in social status. Traditionally professions are reserved for members of certain castes; membership is inherited from father to son (patrilineal). In Nepal, castes have never been as strictly isolated from each other as in India.

**Climbing Castes:** It is even possible to climb up a caste through marriage. This is only possible in the peasant and merchant castes, however. The reason is that merchants have been hit hard by the loss of trade with Tibet, while the peasants have maintained their relative affluence. For an upper-caste merchant, it's advantageous to marry a rich, albeit lower-caste, farmer's daughter. The children receive the higher merchant caste, while the wife retains her former caste status. Since caste membership includes strict culinary etiquette, the upper-caste husband is forbidden to eat any food cooked by his wife for fear of losing his caste affiliation. It would be interesting to see how that works in practice.

# Mahayana Buddhism

Mahayana Buddhism is based on the belief that the historical Buddha (see India Country & Culture) was preceded by numerous incarnations of Buddha, in which he proclaimed the same teaching. Additionally, Mahayana Buddhists, like Hindus with their Kalkinavatar (an incarnation of Vishnu), are awaiting a reincarnation of Buddha, the Maitreyabuddha.

**Adi Buddha:** Mahayana Buddhism perceives the essence of Buddha, from which Five Dhyani Buddhas originated. The Dhyani Buddhas are seen as the Five Elements from which the Cosmos is created, or the primary form of Buddha's energy.
**Five Dhyani Buddhas:** Vairocana, Aksobhya, Ratnasambhava, Amitabha, and Amoghasiddha.

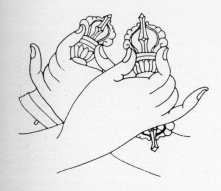

Each of the Five Dhyani Buddhas heads a family, consisting of
his Buddhashakti (female Buddha), and the Bodhisattvas (sons of
the Dhyani Buddha and his Buddhashakti). Family members of a
Dhyani Buddha decorate their heads, as a symbol of recognition,
with a miniature depiction of their respective Dhyani Buddha.

## THE TIBETAN BOOK OF THE DEAD (BARDO THÖDOL)
This interesting work offers a mostly psychological explanation,
which also serves as a guide to meditation, to aid in understanding of the Five Dhyani Buddhas. Suffering stems from dis-
belief in one's self, resulting from lack of consciousness and
uncertainty of one's true self. The Five Buddhas stand for Five
Wisdoms, which, through misinterpretation, can easily be
perceived as five poisons, or lost sensations. The **BARDO THÖDOL**
helps recognize these projections, and the dissolution of self
perception into the Light of Reality.

   **Vairocana Buddha:** Symbolizes the basic poison, the Blindness
   of Misunderstanding, intentionally refusing to understand, from
   which all other poisons are derived. Its Wisdom is "the perception of the endless space in which everything exists,
   exactly as it is".
   **Aksobhya:** Depicts the poison of Aggression and Hate, which
   can be turned into the Wisdom, "Let all things be reflected
   without criticism as they are".
   **Ratnasambhava:** Presents the poison of Pride. Its antidote is
   "The Wisdom of equality and equanimity".

**Amitabha:** Personifies Passion, Desire, and accompanying Greed. It carries with it the Wisdom "Differentiate between consideration and unleashed demands, with which passion is altered to compassion".

**Amoghasiddha:** The poison of Jealousy is accompanied by the Wisdom, "The enlightened viewpoint is the absolute Truth".

Through confrontation with the Five Buddhas, the Buddha within yourself can be awakened.

**Bodhisattva:** An enlightened being, which has achieved the great deed of enlightenment (Bodhi). In its endless compassion for humanity, the Boddhisattva declines to accept release into absolute Nirvana, but chooses to continues to aid others in achieving enlightenment, until all mankind is freed from the wheel of reincarnations.

**Great Vehicle:** Mahayana Buddhism is also called the Great Vehicle, because it seeks the enlightenment of all people.

**Hinayana Buddhism:** The converse or Small Vehicle, looking only to the enlightenment of individuals.

**Contrast:** Unlike Hinayana Buddhism, Mahayana Buddhism looks to the legend of the historical Buddha who, upon achieving enlightenment, is tempted by Mara to go over to Nirvana. But Buddha chose to continue work, to the benefit of all. In essence Buddha himself was a Boddhisattva, as depicted by Mahayana Buddhism.

# Lamaism & The Tibetans

The religion practised by 8000 Tibetans in Nepal is a mixture of
Mahayana Buddhism and the pre-Buddhist Bon religion. Buddhism
was brought to Tibet in 632 AD, where it mixed with Bon's belief
in spirits, demons, and gods of nature. Even today, these elements are clearly depicted on murals in Tibetan monasteries. Mahayana Buddhism differs from Hinayana Buddhism (see India-
Religion) in that it believes enlightenment will be attained by
many and not restricted to the Buddha (Mahayana = large vehicle). Furthermore, the enlightened seeks to aid others to achieve
salvation, and is therefore eternally reincarnated into this world
as a Boddhisattva. Lamaism is a monk-oriented religion. The
abbot of a Lamasery (monastery) is often considered an
incarnation a deceased spiritual teacher.

Until the 15th century, religious practice remained firmly in
the hands of the red-caps. A hierarchical system with the Dalai
Lama and Panchen Lama at the top came later. A reform movement
pushed by the yellow-caps created a hierarchical order. The
Dalai Lama and the Panchan Lama shared worldly and spiritual
powers, which began to concentrate in the hands of the Dalai
Lama.

From 1912 until the founding of the People's Republic of China
on 1 October, 1949 Tibet was an independent country under the
13th Dalai Lama who died in 1933. China laid increasing claim to
Tibet. Tibetan resistance was put down, and the 14th Dalai Lama
(inaugurated in 1940) fled to India in a great trek on 31 March,
1959. The man, viewed by Tibetans as their head of state, lives
today in Dharamsala in northern India. About 80,000 Tibetans
fled to Nepal and India; about one-third continued on to the USA,
Canada, Switzerland, and Great Britain. Many exiled Tibetans
still hope some day to return to their homeland. Tibetans living
in Nepal feel they aren't treated as full-fledged Nepalese
citizens.

Outside the refugee camps, Tibetans live as craftsmen, merchants, or restaurant owners in KTM. Tibetan tradition differs
greatly from Hindu Nepalese: women in Tibet are greatly honored,
and sexually liberated. It is accepted practice for women to have
several husbands. Similar habits can be seen among the Sherpa,
Thakali, and Mustang peoples.

Tibetans take their religion very seriously. To experience this
first hand, join the Tibetans at Swayambu in the morning and
evening as they finger prayer wheels, chant mantras, and round
the hill three times. Or go with them up to Swayambunath
Temple.

Astrology plays an important role at birth, Buddhist christ-
ening (= ceremonial name giving), and burial. The horoscope is
always made by a lama.

The most important tools for achieving enlightenment are meditation and knowledge of the Tantras, the sacred books. Lamaism has developed a number of techniques and methods of meditation. In Nepal, you can visit a lamasery and learn meditation. Another excellent place to increase your knowledge of Lamaism and meditation is in Dharamsala. Helpful for meditation are mantra and mandala. Mantras are phrases of Sanskrit words or syllables whose sound expresses the essence of a deity, its characteristics or power. Mandalas are pictures of deities or their symbols. The goal of any form of meditation is the recognition of one's own projection, and separation from this projection; not the recognition of any supernatural being or god.

# Om mani Padme hum

# Nepalese Festivals

As befitting a country of Nepal's ethnic diversity, countless festivals are celebrated in Nepal, many just locally. It would be very difficult to visit Nepal without experiencing at least one festival. Our list includes just a few of the most important festivals, some of which we know from India. The exact festival dates are difficult to predict. The moon calendar on which they are based has a leap year every three years. Dates can spring by weeks from year to year. It is important to know the Nepalese month in which a particular festival is celebrated. Nepalese months change in the middle of our months.

| | |
|---|---|
| **Baishakh:** | 14 April to 13 May. |
| **Jestha:** | 14 May to 13 June. |
| **Asadh:** | 14 June to 13 July. |
| **Shrawan:** | 14 July to 13 August. |
| **Bhadra:** | 14 August to 13 September. |
| **Aswin:** | 14 September to 13 October. |
| **Kartik:** | 14 October to 13 November. |

| Mangsir: | 14 November to 13 December. |
| Poush: | 14 December to 13 January. |
| Magh: | 14 January to 13 February. |
| Falgun: | 14 February to 13 March. |
| Chaitra: | 14 March to 13 April. |

Always ask several people when a festival will be celebrated. Even reconfirm information from Tourist Offices. The following list is presented in accordance with the Nepalese calendar.

**BAISAKH** 14 April to 13 May
  **Bisket:** New Year is celebrated in April throughout Kathmandu Valley with singing and dancing. Processions are held in Bhaktapur and Thimi.
  **Bhoto Machhendar Nath:** One of the most important Buddhist festivals, celebrated at the beginning of monsoon season; prayers are made to the gods for ample rain. At Patan, you can see a splendid wagon procession in which the god Machhendra Nath is pulled through the town in a temple wagon five times.
  **Buddha Jayanti:** Buddha's birthday is usually celebrated in May. The gompas in Swayambunath and Bodnath are decorated with hundreds of lamps. Pilgrims from all over Nepal journey to Swayambunath. Rituals are performed by lamas dressed in lovely costumes, accompanied by music and dance.

**JESTHA** 14 May to 13 June
  **Sithinaka:** The birthday of Kumar, god of War, and brother of Ganesh, is celebrated. Corn is planted in the villages. On the seventh day, at Hanuman Dhoka, a statue of the god's likeness is carried through the town accompanied by musicians.

**SHRAWAN** 14 July to 13 August
  **Ghanta Karna:** Evil spirits which might disturb the harvest are driven away. Straw puppets are set up to represent demons. In the evening the puppets are thrown in the river or burned.
  **Naga Panchami:** The Snake Festival is held on the fifth day of the waxing moon. Snakes (Nagas) are revered as gods whose power determines the monsoons. For this reason, farmers make sacrifices on this day: milk, sweets, kum-kum, and flowers are placed on spots frequented by snakes.
  **Janai Purnima:** On Full-Moon Day, all Brahmans renew their holy string.
  **Gai Jatra:** On the day after Janai Purnima, everyone who has died in the last year is remembered. During the day, boys and girls wear cow heads made of papier mâché. Only a cow can open the gates to the Court of Justice, where the God of Death, Yama, places everyone who has died within the last 12 months. In the evening the atmosphere turns carnival with masks, music, and dance performances.

**Krishna Ashtami:** Toward the end of the month, Krishna's birthday is celebrated. Statues of Krishna are displayed throughout Nepal. The focal point of the festival is Krishna Mandir in Patan.

## BHADRA 14 August to 13 September

**Teej:** A festival celebrating the joining of Husband and Wife. The festival is based on a legend in which Parvati, with the aid of her girlfriends, succeeded in foiling her parents' attempt to marry her to Vishnu instead of Shiva. On the first day a tremendous meal is prepared for husbands and married daughters. Women take to the streets in their wedding saris and jewelry. They sing and talk until 24 hours of fasting begin at midnight. The women remain together and walk in a morning procession to Pashupatinath Temple.

**Indra Jatra:** Usually celebrated in early September, the festival lasts eight days. This is one of Nepal's most important festivals, with major celebrations in Kathmandu at Hanuman Dhoka. A likeness of the god Indra is displayed. The festival culminates with a procession in which the Kumari, a living goddess, is accompanied by two boys, representing Ganesh and Bhairava. The King is present to receive the Kumari's blessing, a tika on his forehead.

## ASWIN 14 September to 13 October

**Dasain - Durga Puja:** This is the most important national festival. The first nine days of the ten-day festival are dedicated to the goddess Durga or Bhagavati. The Nepalese visit the goddess's temples and bathe in sacred rivers. On the seventh day the main festivities are held in Kathmandu: a state procession by the King's priests, troupes through town. At night in the Hanuman Dhoka courtyard over 100 buffalo and goats are slaughtered in a sacrifice to Durga. The head must fall at the first blow, or it is a bad omen. The last day is celebrated among family and relations. Officials and the King's astrologers hold court with the King.

## KARTIK 14 October to 13 November

**Deepawali - Tihar:** A festival lasting five days. On the first day crows are worshipped, as they bring news from Yama, the god of Death. On the second day, dogs are decorated with a tika (spot of color on the forehead) and flowers, and given something special to eat, as they guard Yama's gates. On the third day, cows are worshipped, decorated with flowers, and their horns painted. In the afternoon, Lakshmi, the goddess of Wealth, is revered. Candles and electric lights are lit. Every street and house is illuminated. Children romp, singing, from house to house, receiving sweets as a reward. The last day is dedicated to the veneration of brothers and sisters.

**Haribodhini Ekadashi:** The awakening of Vishnu is usually celebrated in early November. Thousands of pilgrims make their way to Budhanilkantha.

**MANGSIR** 14 November to 13 December
**Shatateejaropanam:** Thousands of singing pilgrims walk barefoot around sacred Mrigasthali Hill, near Pashupathinath. The sacrifice of seven seeds, and the visiting of an ancient depiction of Ganesha are said to aid the deceased.
**Vivaha Panchami:** On the 26th of November in eastern Terai in Janakpur, the marriage of Sita and Rama is celebrated.

**POUSH** 14 December to 13 January
**Seto Machhendranath:** This festival is celebrated by both Hindus and Buddhists. The celebration, in honor of the god Machhendranath, takes place in the Golden Temple in Old Kathmandu, between Asan and Indra Chowk Streets. Flowers are offered, and the foot of the god's likeness is kissed. After a temple ritual, the statue is carried from the temple on a richly decorated platform. The arrival of the living goddess, the Kumari, is accompanied by music. Then the statue is bathed in water, milk, oil, and finally with hot water.
**The King's Birthday:** On the 28th of December; the festivities include a tremendous Royal Parade in Tundikhet.
**Tribhuvan Jayanti:** On 11 January, the late King's Birthday is celebrated with a national festival. King Tribhuvan ended rule by the Rana regime in 1951.

**MAGH** 14 January to 13 February
**Shree Panchami:** A festival in honor of Saraswati, the goddess of Wisdom and Learning. At the same time the beginning of Springtime is celebrated. In a Ceremony of State, with the King, high officials, and Royal Priests participating, the blessings of Spring are proclaimed.

**FALGUN** 14 February to 13 March
**Shivarati:** New Moon Night is dedicated to Shiva. Thousands of pilgrims journey to Pashupatinath, to fast, honor Shiva with sacrifice and song, and bathe in the sacred waters of the Bagmati River. Guns fire a royal salute for the King during the afternoon on the Parade Ground in the centre of Kathmandu.
**National Day:** Celebrated on 18 February with parades and processions.

**CHAITRA** 14 March to 13 April
**Holi:** A week-long festival begins on Full-Moon Day, celebrating the coming of Spring. Men and boys romp, singing, through town throwing red powder on anyone conveniently close. A pole is raised on which strips of cloth are bound. They symbolize

the saris of the Gopis who kidnapped Krishna while he was
bathing.   The burning of the mast symbolizes the end of the
year.
**Chaitra - Dasain:**   The goddess Durga or Bhagvanti is pulled
though town on a four-wheeled wagon by thousands of men.
Buffalo and goats are slaughtered in her honor.

# Town Culture

The three towns in Kathmandu Valley (Kathmandu, Patan, and
Bhaktapur) demonstrate the high state of Newar town culture with
their own individual style.  The towns feature tiny, paved, winding streets, reminiscent of mediaeval Europe, with sturdy three-
storey buildings, temples, and temple squares. The buildings are
lattice-work (with brick filling), and the black, wooden skeleton
is of long-lasting sal wood, richly decorated with carving. Door
and window frames are particularly pretty.  Since the towns for
centuries have traditionally thrived on trade with Tibet (now
lost), there's always a shop or workshop on the ground floor.

The kitchen is directly under the roof to prevent anyone outside from desecrating the ritual purity of the kitchen.   There is
no chimney;  smoke escapes through the joints in the roof,  which
is usually covered with fired
brick or slate.   The houses
are built around a courtyard
which can also be entered
from the street.

In the towns' heyday,
there were extensive sewage
and ingenious water supply
systems based upon wells.
Unfortunately, these systems
were allowed to decay. Streets
and courtyards substitute for
adequate garbage removal.
Attempts have been under-
taken recently, however, to
improve hygiene.  Trash containers placed around town
quickly overflow as everyone
takes the opportunity to rid
their neighborhood of un-
wanted garbage.  Certainly the
trash isn't an expression of
the Asian mentality;  it results from lack of
organization.

On street corners you'll
still find ancient wells and
small cult sites.  At particu-

larly dark corners and other spots, you might find red-painted
fieldstones. Because spirits and demons still haunt local
superstition, warning stones are set at spots where spirits and
demons are known to meet. In Kathmandu, spirits like to collect
at Simhasattal, the oldest part of Kathmandu, so you'll find
many such stones there. However, since the introduction of
electric light in Kathmandu, the warning stones have been
greatly neglected.

The architecture used in Nepalese pagodas probably was inherited from ancient northern India in the 5th - 7th centuries AD. From Nepal, this architectural style passed on via
Tibet to China and Japan. Nepalese pagodas are often
multi-storey, towerlike shrines, dedicated to two Hindu or
Hindu-Buddhist deities. There are very beautiful pagodas in
Bhaktapur and Patan.

## Arts & Crafts

Religion and caste affiliation determine job choice and practice,
along with the forms expressed by artists and craftsmen.

Architecture accommodates itself to the climate and lifestyles of
numerous groups. Frequently, you can recognize a village's
ethnic make-up from a distance by observing architecture.

Every piece of workmanship tells the artistic history of its
craft. Marvellously developed are metalwork, woodworking, textiles, and the art of knotting carpets. Most handicrafts are
strongly influenced by the cultures of India and Tibet; often
they're identical.

# HISTORY

Once upon a time an earthquake turned a huge lake into the fertile plains of Kathmandu Valley. Settlers were attracted, creating over the centuries an ethnic mixture, the Newar. Relative ease working the land left the Newar with plenty of time to develop a high state of arts and crafts, as testified to by numerous artifacts. Buddha, during the 6th century BC, and later the great Indian ruler Ashoka, visited this famous cultural center.

At the beginning of the 6th century, Rajput Amshuverma founded the Thakur Dynasty and solidified the kingdom after receiving the royal title from his stepfather. A Tibetan king, Strong Dtasan Sgam Po, married Amshuverma's daughter in addition to a Chinese princess who converted him to Buddhism. That's why they are honored today as saints in Buddhist temples.

Highly acclaimed Kathmandu craftsmanship impressed China, leading to the introduction of pagoda-style architecture in both China and Japan. At one time, the Chinese imperial court looked to Nepal for many of its architects and master builders.

After centuries of Indian Rajput rule, a Newar, Jayassthiti Malla, united the Kathmandu Valley in the 14th century. His grandson Yakasha Malla expanded the kingdom further. Kathmandu's golden age, experienced during Yakasha Malla's 40-year reign, ended when his sons divided the kingdom amongst themselves. Later these kingdoms were further subdivided. At one point there were three kingdoms in Kathmandu Valley alone, with Kathmandu, Patan, and Bhaktapur as capitals.

The Gurkha king, Prithvia Narayan, conquered the valley in 1768 ending the Newar Kings' reign. 1814–1816 saw conflict with the British East India Company. In the treaty of Segauli, the present-day borders with India were set. Britain recognized the Gurkha kingdom.

In 1846, Jang Bahadur Rana seized power in a massacre, founding a dynasty of hereditary prime ministers, who paid nominal respect to the royal house while ruling as they saw fit. Until this day, a Rana daughter is the only acceptable bride for the crown prince. From 1846–1951 the Rana prime ministers held absolute power, isolating Nepal from outside influences, and maintaining close relations with Britain.

In 1951 King Mahendra deposed the Rana prime minister. But by 1955, the King tired of a constitutional monarchy, choosing to rule without a parliament. Four years later he was forced by the Congress Party to hold elections, which Congress easily carried. In 1960, however, the King retook power, banning all political parties. Instead, the Panchayat system was expanded to national level.

When he died in 1972, Crown Prince Birenda, who'd been raised in India, England, and Japan, assumed power. Though the new King promised greater consideration for development of democracy, the partyless panchayat system (a hierarchy of advisors) was retained.

During student unrest in 1979, students were shot in several incidents. A referendum on the panchayat system (forced by the unrest) was held in early 1980. The King won by a slim majority.

On May 9, 1981, elections were held, which for the first time offered the electorate a choice of candidates. Only those candidates were permitted to stand, however, who at least verbally supported the panchayat system. With only low turnout at the polls, many official candidates "lost their fat" and were defeated by younger candidates.

# GOVERNMENT

Till the mid 1950s this mountain country was an island of poverty. Today the government is run without political parties as a
constitutional Hindu monarchy (the world's only), based on the
panchayat system. King Shri Panch Maharajadhiraja Birenda Bir
Bikham Shah Dev (official title: King Birenda) was born 28 December, 1945 and has ruled since 1972. The monarchy is hereditary. Today's king is the 62nd in his dynasty. Traditionally
the king takes a Rana woman as his wife; no exception is Queen
Aishwarya Rajya Laxmi Devi (born 11 November, 1947). They were
married in 1970 and crowned on 24 February, 1975.

Crown Prince Dipendra Bir Bikram Shah Dev was born on
27 June, 1975. The queen's two younger sisters are married to the
king's two younger brothers.

Head of government since July 1983 is Lokendra Bahadur
Chand. According to the constitution of 1962, the king makes all
important decisions. However, since 1979, the king has made some
concessions to the panchayat parliament in keeping with the constitutional changes of 1975.

The panchayat system was confirmed at the polls on
2 May, 1980 by a majority of 55 %. Turnout at the polls was
68 %. Five percent of ballots cast were invalid. The urban vote
particularly favored a multiparty system.

Nepal has been successful in maintaining a policy of neutral-
ity between the world's two most populated countries: 1 billion
Chinese and 750 million Indians. Both countries are pleased to
have Nepal as a buffer. In 1979, the border with China was confirmed in a joint statement. Both India and China have invested
large sums in development aid for Nepal, one of the world's
poorest countries.

Nepal has no military draft; just 1 % of GNP goes to defence.
The armed services, including a minuscule airforce, boast 22,000
servicemen. Nepal has 12,000 police.

## Panchayat System

The panchayat system is a form of village self-administration,
long practised in Nepal. It was constitutionally instituted on a
national level in 1962. The lowest level of administration is the
Village Panchayat (representing 2500 to 3000 people), or the Town
Panchayat (over 10,000 people). Each panchayat has 9-11 members, and acts as the executive office of the local assembly.
Members of the Village Panchayat form the District Assembly and
elect the District Panchayat. At the top (since 1980) is the National Panchayat. Since 1981, the 112 members of the Rashtriya
(national) Panchayat are directly elected by popular vote;

28 members are appointed by the king. In a break with the past, the prime minister is no longer chosen by the king from the members of parliament. Instead the parliament elects one of its own with a 60 % majority. If the parliament can't decide, the king chooses from among three candidates. The king enjoys veto powers against unwanted legislation, and heads the executive branch.

The Panchayat Constitution is based upon decentralization: of responsibility, of development initiative, and of all political forces including parties and trade unions. Instead, class organizations have been established representing farmers, workers, women, students, graduates, and children. While rejecting the concept of class struggle, these organizations work to reduce social tensions, and create an exploitation-free society. The class organizations play an important role at panchayat elections. The panchayat is often assigned responsibility for local development projects, sometimes well beyond its capabilities.

**Country:** Sri Nepala Sarkar (Kingdom of Nepal)

**Flag:** Two triangles, one above the other, red with blue fringe, with a white moon in the upper and a white sun in the lower triangle. Nepal boasts the only national flag which isn't rectangular!

**Capital:** Kathmandu (Kantipur)
Founded in 723 AD, at 1400 m altitude, 360,000 people. Frequently shortened to KMT, the international airline abbreviation.

# ECONOMY

As a landlocked, mountainous country, lacking basic infrastructure, Nepal's economic development goes slow. A trade agreement with India, implemented in 1980, has eased trade with Nepal's major trading partner (55 %). Exports include jute (35 %), rice, pelts, goatskin, tobacco, spices, medicinal plants, rare woods, other agricultural products, souvenirs, wool carpets. Tourism is Nepal's primary source of foreign exchange (30 %); 180,000 tourists spend US$ 60 million annually.

Nepal's large foreign debt increases by the year. GNP is US$2 billion (i.e. US$140 per capita) with little growth.

About 57 % of national income is earned in agriculture where 93 % of the population is employed.  13 % of GNP is produced by industry which employs just 2 % of the work force. Less than 10 % of Nepal's population live in towns. Despite enormous advances, Nepal's standard of living is decreasing in comparison to developed countries.

## AGRICULTURE

93 % of Nepal's work force is engaged in agriculture, mostly in backbreaking production of terraced rice (annual production 2.5 million tons).  Just 17 % of the country is used for agriculture, 30 % is forest. 55 % of agricultural land produces rice, 25 % corn, and 12 % other grains. Potatoes are also popular. The primary economic unit is the self-sufficient village. Nepal supplies most of its own nutritional needs.  However, the north-west and north-east are only poorly developed.

## INDUSTRY

What very little industry you'll find arrived via development projects in the 1960s: two cement works (with all the accompanying pollution), beverages (Starbeer and soft drinks), cookies, tea, and cigarettes. There are steel works, jute processing, and textiles, along with small cottage industries. German aid provided a brewery, Switzerland sent a cheese factory.

Rich, but largely unexplored mineral reserves, including copper, gold, iron, lead, and coal are suspected. But without the necessary infrastructure, exploitation will have to wait. Quarries for limestone and mica are active.

The road system runs to 4000 km, but only a part is paved and open year round.

# Health

Health care in Nepal is inadequate.  For a population of 15 million, just 3,000 hospital beds are available (most concentrated in Kathmandu Valley).  Averaged over the entire country, that makes one hospital bed for every 5,000 citizens (West German ratio 1 : 120).  But don't forget that in 40 % of all districts there isn't a hospital, i.e. in the entire north-west and large sections of the east. Due to poor communications, immediate medical attention can mean several days' walk, perhaps on the back of a porter. Even Kathmandu has just one bed for every 430 people.

Practising physicians are even harder to find: on average just one per 25,000 inhabitants.  But some regions have no doctors, others find one doctor for 300,000 people.  Even relatively

prosperous Kathmandu Valley counts 1400 people to every doctor.
Altogether, Nepal boasts just 500 doctors, plus 2000 nurses and
midwives! Only an optimist would waste time looking for a
dentist.

Just 2,500 l of bottled drinking water are available annually.
In the northwest and in some Terai districts, there isn't any
clean drinking water. No wonder hepatitis and tuberculosis are
endemic.

# The Education System

Only one-third of Nepal's children (almost 1 million 6-15-year-
olds) actually attend school. Just 20 % of all girls get a chance.
Overall illiteracy is 81 %! Even in Kathmandu, just 40 % of the
adult population can read. And in the rest of the country, there
isn't one district where literacy exceeds 25 %. Worst off are inaccessible mountain regions where adult illiteracy runs at 93 % to
96 %.

These statistics reflect the regional distribution of grade
schools. In rural areas schools are few, and hard to reach. The
ratio of school-age children to distance from school is worst in
the north-west. On the national average, there are 30 pupils to
every teacher, but Nepal needs many more teachers, schools, and
children attending class.

Almost 25,000 students attend classes at Nepal's 30 universities, technical schools, and colleges. Emphasized are the humanities and social sciences including pedagogics, technology, business management, and economics, in that order. Most institutions
- all subordinate to Tribhuvan University in Kathmandu - are
concentrated in Kathmandu Valley, Pokhara, and the Terai. Less
than 20 % of the student body is co-ed. There are 12,000 students
in Kathmandu. Job training is most extensive in Kathmandu
Valley, in the near west (greater Pokhara), and in the far south
and east, reflecting regional development.

# Mass Media

**THE PRESS**
Officially, press freedom reigns, but in practise no criticism of
the royal house, domestic & foreign policy, the military, or the
police is tolerated. Among many newspapers are several English-
language publications. Check by the big Vishnu tree on New Road
in Kathmandu.

**Rising Nepal** is the largest paper, featuring domestic news, mixed
with reports from abroad. It's frequently available for browsing
in hotels and restaurants. Also available are **Motherland** and
16-page **Everest Weekly.** The only foreign magazines we've seen

are **Time** and **Newsweek**. All are available at the newspaper tree, at Nepal Book Sellers on Darma Path, in the arcade by Hotel Annapurna on Durbar Marg, or in Thamel.

Available in KTM is the latest edition of the **International Herald Tribune** (via satellite, 10.-Rs), plus several Indian papers. And don't forget the number of Nepalese and Indian topical magazines, all in English.

**TELEVISION**
The new age is coming...

**RADIO**
The news is broadcast in English daily at 08:00 h and 20:00 h. Friday and Saturday evenings at 21:15 h,· there's western music. With UNESCO aid, Nepal is expanding its regional radio network.

The BBC World Service drifts in on short wave. For exact time and frequencies (varies from season to season) write: BBC / Bush House / London WC2B 4PH / Great Britain.

Other international programming is available in English given proper reception conditions. Try your luck!

# Aid

Just 41 % of the Nepalese national budget is generated domestically through taxes, duties, etc. Filling the breach is international aid. US$171 million (half in loans and half as gift) were booked in 1981. The major creditors include the World Bank, Asian Development Bank, International Development Agency, and several UN sub organizations (e.g. UNESCO, WHO, and FAO).

Most donating countries know Nepal couldn't repay a loan. Major donor countries include: India 24.8 %, People's Republic of China 16 %, USA 15 %, Great Britain 14.5 %, West Germany 7,3 %, Japan 6.2 %, Kuwait 6.1 %, Switzerland 3,7 %.

Development projects eat up 70 % of Nepal's annual budget. Major projects include hydropower and electrification, road and bridge building, irrigation, education, agriculture, health, drinking water purification, mining and industry, forestry and reforestation.

Major projects completed in the 1980s include roads from Gorkha via Mugling to Narayangarh / Chitwan, from Butwal to west Nepal, from Lamosango to Jiri; plus several major hydropower plants making blackouts less frequent.

**Addresses**
  **United Nations Information Centre:** Lazimpath, tel.11939, Kathmandu.
  **Peace Corps** (USA): Lal Durbar, 11692 Kathmandu.
  **SOS Children's Village:** Samo Thimi (near Bhadgaon), tel.15391.

# TRAVEL TIPS

## Visa

Every visitor requires a visa, ob-
tainable in your country of origin,
en route to Nepal, or at the
border. Two extensions are possible
in Kathmandu or Pokahar, each for
four weeks. The maximum length of
stay is three months.

**At Home:** Phone or write your nearest Nepalese embassy or consulate
for a visa application. Some travel
agencies also have applications on
hand. Apply at least four weeks in
advance. Fill out the applications
and submit with your passport, two
passport pictures, processing fee
(about US$10.-, check for the rate
in your country), and a stamped
self-addressed envelope for registered mail. Takes about a week
in Europe, by mail. If you go to the consulate in person, you
receive the visa immediately. Usually issued for 30 days.

**In Asia:** The same proceedure, but appear in person. In India,
it costs 110.-Rs, you pick up the visa the next day, valid for
four weeks.

**At Kathmandu Airport:** A seven-day visa is issued quickly, grab
a visa application at the Immigration Counter, change money, fill
out the application and present yourself with passport, passport
pictures, and US$10.- or the equivalent in Nepalese currency. You
can change money at the next counter. Then continue on to
customs.

**At the Land Border:** Upon entry overland, visa processing has the
same duration and costs. Extension for the first full month in
Kathmandu costs just 1.-Rs.

**Validity:** A tourist visa is valid only for KTM Valley, Pokhara
(Kaski), Chitwan National Park, the Chinese road to Kodari, and
all access roads and connecting roads in between, plus all auto
roads! Anywhere else, no matter how you get there, you'll need a

trekking permit. A visa is valid for entry up to three months after the date of issue. If you are taking the overland route to Nepal, don't get your visa too early.

**Visa Extensions:** Apply at the Immigration Office in Kathmandu, 2 km toward the airport at Dilli Bazar, open Sun-Fri except holidays, 10:00-16:00 h, in summer until 17:00 h. Bring your passport and passport photos, fill out the applications, turn it in, pick your visa up the next afternoon. Costs 75.-Rs per week in the second month and 150.-Rs per week during the third month.

If you were issued only a seven-day visa upon entry, you can extend for three weeks (to one month total) at no additional weekly charge. The extension is just a formality, costing only a small paperwork charge. The visa can be extended just twice, for four weeks each.

If you apply for a trekking permit at the same time you extend you visa, you only have to pay for the trekking permit, the visa extension is free of charge.

### Regulations Change Frequently

**Money Exchange Requirement:** Usually you will be required to prove you have changed money, at least US$5.- per day, when applying for a visa extension. Only 10 % of the money you exchange into Nepalese Rupees can be re-exchanged upon departure.

# Trekking Permit

A trekking permit is required no matter how you get around, be it by air, bus, or foot, if you want to travel in regions other than those listed on your visa (see above). You will be required to show your trekking permit from time to time.

Permits are available from the Immigration Office, at Dilli Bazar in Kathmandu. You can also pick up a trekking permit in Pokhara, at the police station between the airport and the lake.

You must fill out an application and present two passport photos. The permit costs 60.-Rs per week during the first month and 75.-Rs per week during the second month. If you apply for a visa extension at the same time you apply for a trekking permit, the visa is free of charge! Processing takes one day; apply together with your visa extension.

The trekking permit is valid for just one route and its offshoots, which you'll have to list in your application. If you want to go on two different treks without returning to Kathmandu, then apply for the second permit immediately upon receipt of the first trekking permit. Should you be delayed during the trek by illness, injury, forced stays, or detours, perhaps due to bad weather, bring comfirmation of this from a doctor or a checkpoint, particularly if your visa has expired!

## NEPALESE CONSULATES
**Bangladesh:** 248 Dhanmondi Road, No. 21, Dacca.
**India**
  **New Delhi:** Barakhamba Road, New Delhi 110001, Near Connaught Place, tel.386592, Mon-Fri 09:00-13:00 h.
  **Calcutta:** 19 Sterndale Road, Alipore, Calcutta, 700027, south of the Zoo, tel.452824, open 10:00-16:00 h.
**Sri Lanka:** Dr. Subhash Chawla, Hon. Royal Consul General, 92 Chatam Street (Fort), Colombo 1, a small shop with no sign.

**Burma:** 16 Natmauk Yeiktha (Park Avenue), Post Office Tamwe, POB 84, Rangoon.
**People's Republic of China**
  **Beijing:** No. 11 San Li Tunxiliujie, Beijing.
  **Tibet:** Norbulingka Road 13, Lhasa, Tibet.
**Pakistan**
  **Islamabad:** No. 506, 84th Street, Attaturk Avenue, Ramna 6/4, Islamabad.
  **Karachi:** Mr. Kassim E. Chapra, Honorary Royal Con. Gen., 23 Karachi Memon Coop., Housing Society, Block 7-8, Modern Club Road, Karachi 29.
**Thailand:** 189 Soi Puengsuk, Sukhumvit 71, Bangkok, tel.912885.

**United Kingdom:** 12A Kensington Palace Garden, London W8 4QU.
**United States:** 2131 Leroy Place N.W., Washington D.C., 20008.

## FOREIGN REPRESENTATIVES IN NEPAL
**Bangladesh:** Naxal Bhagwati Bahal, tel.410012, 07:30-14:00 h.
**India:** Lazimpath, tel.211300, open Mon-Fri 09:30-12:00 h, visa and permits for Darjeeling, Assam, and Shillong, crowded, numbers distributed, be there by 09:00 h.

**Burma:** Pulchowk, Lalitpur, tel.521788, open 10:00-17:00 h.
**People's Republic of China:** Baluwatar, tel.412589, open 09:00-13:00 h, 15:00-17:00 h.
**Pakistan:** Panipokhari, tel.211431, open Sat-Thurs 09:00-13:00 h.
**Thailand:** Jyoti Kendra Building, Thapathali, tel.213910, open 10:00-12:00 h.

**Australia:** Thapathali, tel.2132666.
**United Kingdom:** Lainchaur, tel.211588, 09:00-17:00 h, Fridays until 14:00 h.
**United States:** Panipokhari, tel.211199, open 08:00-17:00 h.

## CULTURAL INSTITUTES
All libraries listed below offer books for reading in the reading room only, not for removal from the building.
  **American Library:** New Road at Khichpokhari, open Mon-Sat 11:00-19:00 h, latest US newspapers and magazines.

**British Council Library:** Kanti Path, open Sun-Fri 11:00–18:00 h, tel.11304, excellent facilities, events.
**French Cultural Centre:** Bagh Bazaar, first side street on the left, tel.14326, library and reading room, French films almost daily, sometimes with English subtitles.
**Goethe Institute:** Gnabbahal, POB 1103, Kathmandu, tel.12263, open Sun-Fri 14:00–19:00 h, near Bhimsen Pillar and DAS Photo Shop, library, large reading room, German newspapers, films, concerts, lectures, upon request you can be admitted to the better library upstairs; the Nepal Research Institute and the Carl Duisberg Ges. also have offices here.
**International Buddhist Library:** Swayambhu, up on the hill, in a building behind the stupa, upstairs, open Wed-Mon 12:00–17:00 h, not very extensive, but some good books about Buddhism in English!
**Kaiser Library:** Kanti Path, left, next to the new Royal Palace, features a great collection of books about Nepal, Tibet, and India, for deeper study.
**University Library:** Kirtipur.

## INFORMATION OFFICES
Written questions from abroad may be addressed to His Majesty's Government of Nepal, Department of Tourism, Tripureswar, Kathmandu, Nepal. In Nepal, check with any of the following addresses:
**Tourist Information Centre:** Gangapath, Kathmandu, tel.215818, between Durbar Square and New Road, on the left.
**Tourist Information Centre:** Tribhuvan International Airport, Kathmandu, tel.215537, open for incoming flights.
**Information Offices:** Smaller offices in Birgunj, Bhairawa, Kakarvitta, Janakpur (border crossings), and at Pokhara Airport.
**Export Information:** Information and Licensing for the export of antiques (objects over 100 years old, or which might be), consult the Department of Archaeology, or the customs office in the Foreign Post Office, north of the GPO.

Equally helpful are the managers of hotels and lodges, along with the staff of travel agencies and trekking agencies. For information abroad, check with your nearest Nepalese Consulate.

# Calendar & Time Differences

**The Nepalese Year:** Begins in April, dating from 57 BC, (1 B.S. also spelled 1 V.S.) when King Bikrramaditya Samvat achieved a decisive victory.
**April 1988:** Begins the year 2045 B.S. or V.S.
**April 1989:** Begins 2046 B.S.
**April 1990:** Ushers in 2047 B.S.
**Saturday:** The weekly day of rest.

**MONTHS**
   **Baisakh:** April / May
   **Jestha:** May / June
   **Asadh:** June / July
   **Shrawan:** July / August
   **Bhadra:** August / September
   **Aswin:** September / October
   **Kartik:** October / November
   **Mangsir:** November / December
   **Poush:** December / January
   **Magh:** January / February
   **Falgun:** February / March
   **Chaitra:** March / April

**Nepal Sambat:** The Newar calendar, begins in October. The year 1109 begins in October 1989.
**Tibetan Calendar:** The year 2115 begins in February 1988.

**Gregorian Calendar:** But the western Gregorian calendar is also used, along with another calendar which saw 1978 as the year 2000. In all official calendars and documents, the date is stated in Nepalese in B.S. or V.S. and in English using the Gregorian calendar.

**Nepal Standard Time:** 5 hours and 45 minutes ahead of Greenwich Mean Time, and 15 minutes ahead of Indian Standard Time.

# Business Hours

The official day of rest is Saturday. Many shops close in keeping with their own ethnic holidays, and for national holidays. Shops are generally open 07:00 h or 08:00 h to 19:00 h or 20:00 h with a long noon break. Government offices are open 10:00–17:00 h, in winter just until 16:00 h.

## BANKS

Open Sun–Thurs 10:00–14:00 h, Fridays 10:00–12:00 h. The government-owned Nepal Rastra Bank has a Money Exchange Booth on New Road, open Tues–Sat 12:00–18:30 h, and Sun 12:00–13:30 h, closed Mondays. A Money Exchange Window opens at Kathmandu Airport to meet incoming international flights.

**International Money Transfers:** Takes two weeks, only possible through Nepal Rastra Bank. Each day a list noting fund arrivals is posted, so you can look to see if your expectations have been fulfilled. You can ask for the money either in rupees or traveller's checks.
**Receipt:** Get a receipt each time you change money, or have the transaction noted on your Foreign Exchange Transaction Form which you sometimes receive at the airport. Otherwise the re-exchange of unspent rupees is not permitted upon departure. Frequently you have to present your money exchange receipts when applying for a visa extension.

# Money

| | |
|---|---|
| **USA:** | $1.– = 24.–Rs |
| **UK:** | £1.– = 39.35Rs |
| **AUS:** | $1.– = 17.20Rs |
| **India:** | 1.–Rs = 1.72Rs |
| **Sri Lanka:** | 1.–Rs = 0.83Rs |

**Nepalese Rupee:** Denoted as NRs or NC (Nepal Currency), or simply as Rs. A rupee contains 100 Pice (P). All prices listed in our Nepal chapter are in Nepal currency unless specifically noted otherwise.

**Coins:** 1, 2, 5 Pice (aluminium). 10 P (brass). 25 P (light-coloured alloy). 50 P, 1.–Rs (same but larger).
**Banknotes:** 1, 2, 5, 10, 50, 100, 1000.–Rs. They are easy to confuse, always look at the numbers exactly!

**Prices:** Tea 1.-Rs, egg 2.-Rs, Coke 4.-Rs, meal 8-30.-Rs, apples
6-10.-Rs per kilo, pie 5-6.-Rs, soap 3.-Rs, shoes 50-100.-Rs. A
bus ride (10 km) costs 2.-Rs. Toilet paper is exorbitant at
10.-Rs. For lodgings think **(Dm)**5.- on Freak Street, and up to
**(D)**100.-Rs in Thamel.

**Wages:** Female workers in Kathmandu earn 5.-Rs per day. A male
workers gets 10.-Rs per day. Teachers or artisans earn 450.-Rs
to 650.-Rs per month. The average family yearly income is
1300.-Rs. Compare that to the prices above, and how much money
you spend during your stay. Then it is easy to understand why
any western traveller is seen as a rich person in Nepalese eyes.
And think too, whether bargaining away the last half rupee profit is a good idea. A female worker in Nepal needs an hour to
earn what you earn at home in 20 seconds. The price of airfare
to Europe is two years' wages for a teacher in Nepal, for the
average family, ten years!.

# Mail

There are several places you can receive mail.
**American Express:** Clients' Mail Service, Jamal Tole, Kathmandu.
The mail service by the small lake in the park is open 14:30–
17:00 h, no charge for Amexco customers who can show traveller's
checks or a credit card, non-customers pay US$1.-. Forwarding
costs US$3.-.

**Poste Restante:** Kathmandu GPO, open Sun-Fri 10:00-16:00 h, bring
your passport. Because mail is sorted only by the first letter of
the family name (or what the official deems as such), processing
is slow. Have them check under your first name and titles if
necessary. No charge.
   Mail from Europe to Kathmandu takes two (!) to ten days, and
four to twelve days from Kathmandu to Europe. Sometimes a letter
sent three days later arrives first. Occasionally a letter is lost
altogether. See Mail in India Travel Tips.

## SENDING MAIL
The General Post Office (GPO) Kathmandu is on the Kanti Path
near the big, white, round tower, Bimsen Pillar, south of the
New Road. Open Sun.-Fri. 10:00 h-14:30 h, summer till 17:00 h.
The litle side window outside in the courtyard to the left of the
main entrance is open 8:00-10:00 h and afternoons until 18:00 h.

**GPO:** Handles all létters, including postcards.
**The Foreign Post Office:** Next door, only responsible for packages
(see below).

**Buying Stamps:** If lines are long behind the "stamps" window, go
into the Philatelic Bureau on the left behind the entrance. Here
they have particularly pretty stamps. Aerogrammes, however, are
only to be had at "stamps".
**Registered Mail:** All important mail should be sent Registered;
queue again, costs 6.-Rs.
**Cancellation:** Have your letter cancelled in your presence! That's
the only way to be sure that no postal employee will remove the
stamps for resale and throw your letter away! So never simply
put your letter in the mailbox or leave it at your hotel desk!
**Aerogrammes:** Blue sheets of airmail paper that can be folded to
a letter and envelope in one, but which may not enclose anything
additional. The stamp is printed on the sheet, and thus can't be
removed. Add additional stamps to meet higher rates. Available
at the "stamps" window.
**Airmail Postal Rates to Europe:** Postcard 3.-Rs; letter (per 20 g)
6.25 Rs; aerogramme 3.50 Rs. Mail to Europe takes 4-12 days,
usually a week.

**Tip:** Give urgent letters and exposed film to returning tourists in hotels, restaurants or at the airport. To this purpose, bring stamps from home and pre-addressed film mailing envelopes.

**Packages:** Must be sewn, which you can have done at the Foreign Post Office. First they will be customs-inspected at the FPO, then sewn, sealed, and franked. By land or sea, your things will take 3-4 months ("seamail"). 10 kg cost about 400.-Rs. 5 kg airmail cost about 700.-Rs. Insuring your package costs 3.- for the first 500.-Rs and another 3.- for each additional started 200.-Rs. The customs fee is 5.-Rs.

## SHIPPING
To get your souvenirs home, you can use a private shipping company. List contents (with a copy for yourselves), turn over your things with the list, pay, and don't worry about sewing, customs formalities, or insurance. Try, Sharmasons Movers, Kanthi Path, POB 508, tel.12709, Kathmandu (next to the German consulate). Plenty of others are in Thamel and around Freak Street. Shipping companies charge 75.-Rs more than the Post Office.
**Note:** Only personal effects and Nepalese products may be shipped. Carpets must be shown personally at customs in the Foreign Post Office or at the airport! Antiques over 100 years old may not be exported!
**Air Freight:** The most expensive and the surest way of getting your things home. Prices are the same on all airlines. Calculate eight days to Europe. Formalities (Foreign Post Office) and packing are your responsibility. The freight must be picked up at the destination airport or delivered at further cost by a shipping company. Freight costs can also be paid on delivery at the destination. Air freight is much cheaper than the charge for overweight luggage (1% of a 1st class ticket per kg!).

## TELEPHONE & TELEX
Telegrams can be sent from the Telecommunication Office at Kanti Path, south of the GPO on the same side just before the stadium. Open 06:00-00:00 h. You can telephone from here as well. Midday is best. Don't forget time differences! Connections are usually made in five minutes. Three minutes cost about 200.-Rs.

## ELECTRICITY AND WATER
**Electricity:** 220 Volts AC, 50 Hz, but voltage and frequency waver greatly; power cuts are common. The same electric plugs are used as in India. In rural areas there is no electrical system and very rarely a generator.
**Water:** Piped water exists only in a few urban areas, and even there it is not drinkable. It is absolutely necessary to boil water for 15 minutes or treat it chemically! On long visits, filter out the mica.

# The Travel Adventure

There is little private transportation. Except for the short rail-
road in Terai and a freight cable-railway between Hitaura in
Terai and Kathmandu, transportation of goods in Nepal is restricted to trucks and - in many rural areas, solely - the backs
of porters and pack animals.
  Passenger service is by bus and minibus (somewhat more expensive) on the country roads and by trolley-(O-)bus line between Kathmandu and Bhadgaon. In the dry season, a few unpaved roads are driven by jeep. In the cities there are taxis
and rickshaws, and, in Terai, tongas (horse-drawn wagons). In
Kathmandu there is a city bus system. In the countryside, you
walk.

## Hitching A Ride

Aside from the buses and the lively truck traffic, there are few
private vehicles underway on the main roads in Nepal. Hitch-
hiking as we know it is hardly possible. But it is possible to
pay to ride on a truck. Trucks often park in bus stops, or drive
by, and the man sitting next to the driver shouts the direction
they're headed. Ask what their destination is. A seat in the
cabin costs about 75 %, in the open about 50 % of a bus ticket
for the same stretch. We've had good experiences. The drive
takes no longer or little longer than with the bus. On a long
drive, the trucks always stop at good, cheap taverns. In Kathmandu, trucks park at the bus station Bagh Bazaar and in the
western part of the city, Tahachal. You're not insured, of
course, but then you probably aren't in the bus, either.

## Domestic Flights

Nepal has had domestic air service for 30 years; today chiefly
with Avro and Twin Otter machines. You can also charter.

All domestic flights are made by the Royal Nepalese Air Corporation RNAC. The main office with information and ticket windows is
at the archway at Kanti Path, New Road corner, tel.214511. Airport buses also depart from here. RNAC also has offices at Kathmandu airport and other smaller landing strips.

Offices Abroad
**New Delhi**: RNAC, Janpath 44, New Delhi, tel.320817 & 321572
(Janpath Hotel); and at the airport, tel.391155.
**Calcutta**: RNAC, 41 Chowringhee Road, Calcutta 71, tel.244434.
**Patna**: RNAC, Hasan Manzil, Fraser Road, Patna, tel.23205.

**Bangkok Thailand**: RNAC, 8-8 1/2 Silom Road, Bangkok, Thailand, tel.2333921, 2334892; and at the airport.
**Colombo**: RNAC, 434 Galle Road, Colombo 3 (Kullupitaya in the south of the city), Sri Lanka, tel.28945, open 08:30-16:30 h.

Except for the Kathmandu airport, all landing strips in Nepal are, to the best of my knowledge, mere grass or earth strips. Airports in the mountains are called STOL-strips (short take off and landing).

**From Kathmandu:** The following destinations are flown to regularly, with flight minutes in the parentheses: Baglung, Bhadrapur (60), Bhairawa (Lumbini/40), Bharatpur (Chitwan/Sauhara), Biratnagar (55), Birgunj (Simra/30), Dang, Dhangadi, Gorkha, Janakpur (45), Jiri (25), Jomosom (60), Jumla (95), Lamidanda, Lukla (Everest trek), Mahendranagar, Manang (55), Meghauli/Tiger Tops (25), Nepalgunj, Phaplu (near Everest trek/35), Pokhara (35), Silgadi,Simra (Birganj/30), Surkhet, Tumlingtar.
**From Pokhara:** Bharatpur, Jomosom (25).
**From Nepalgunj:** Jumla
**From Biratnagar:** Lukla.

In addition to the current air fares calculate an airport tax (20.-Rs) and perhaps the airport bus fare of 7.-Rs, or in Kathmandu a taxi for 15.-Rs.

**Weight Limit:** 15 kg luggage is free, above that, each kg costs another 1 % of flight price.
**Reduced Fares:** Students, up to age 26, pay 75 %, children to age 12 pay 50 %, infants to age 2 pay only 10 %. No reductions on return fares!
**Book Early:** Always book far enough in advance and be sure to confirm return flights as soon as you land. Something often goes wrong anyway, so plan two days leeway!

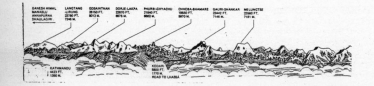

# Charter Flights

Charter flights fly to all STOL fields, and helicopters to even more places. Details at RNAC.
**Price:** In US$ per machine per hour (passengers, US$): Twin Otter (15, $675.-), Pilatus Porter (6, $390.-), Avro HS-748 (44, $1720.-), Boeing 727 (100, $6560.-), Alouette helicopter (5, $650.-), Puma helicopter (9, $1700.-). With more luggage, of course, fewer passengers than indicated can fly. These are rough estimates; get a concrete offer!

# Mountain Flights

RNAC offers organized flight tours every morning along the Himalaya range at 15 km to 20 km distance, in a 44-seat Avro HS-748. It's really something in clear weather! The flight lasts about an hour, your altitude is 6000 m, costs from Kathmandu $60 US or the equivalent in Rs.

You are sometimes invited into the cockpit. You will see Mount Everest (8848 m), Nuptse, Lhotse, Makalu, Kanchenjunga, and more. At the beginning of the flight, you may receive the chart printed below, which will help identify the peaks. Pay attention to seating! Rows 4-5-6 have almost no view, and two rows don't have windows!

A mountain flight leaves Pokhara on Tuesdays and Fridays. It lasts 50 minutes and costs US$50.-, flying over the central Himalayas, including Annapurna, Dhaulagiri, Manaslu, etc.

There are several charter flights offered from Kathmandu, to Gorkha and Lumbini, to the Helambu region, into Langtang Valley, the Everest region, and to Chitwan National Park. Ask at RNAC!

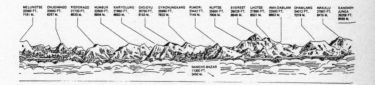

# First Aid

**Emergency**: Bir Hospital, Kanti Path, Kathmandu, tel.211119, provides emergency admission and accident treatment.  Christine, a
German nurse, works without pay in the emergency admission. She
asks that unused medication and other items from your travel
first-aid kit,  like scissors,  tweezers, etc., be personally turned
over to her.  Ask to see her yourself,  or your things will disappear in dark channels and end up in the black market.
**Vaccinations**:    Only offered at Bir Hospital 11:00-13:00 h,  good
service, Cholera-typhus combination costs 10.-.
**Pharmacies**:  In the center of Kathmandu are a few well-stocked
druggists;  try Indrachowk Drug House, Sukra Path, tel.211612, at
the monument on the New Road going north into the bazaar,  50 m
up on the right side.  They have everything you need to take on
a trek.
**Trekkers' Aid Post**: At Pheriche between Namche Bazaar and Everest Base Camp.  The Post is maintained by the "Himalaya Rescue
Association" and provides first aid.  The Association plans to
develop a system of such stations.  More information at Transhi-
malaya Tours, Durbar Marg.
**Trekking**:  As for medical care during a trek:  you're on your
own! Careful. More in the trekking chapter.

# Bookstores

There are a number of bookstores in the center around New Road
and going north in the bazaar. Some buy and sell used books.
   **International Book Centre**: Kamalakshi toward Kanti Path on the
   left (Asan Tole).
   **Ratna Pustak Bhandar**: Bhotahity, near Kanti Path, parallel to
   Ratna Park, good selection.
   **Nepal Book Sellers**: 6/78 Darma Path, near the monument on the
   New Road. A large selection includes magazines and maps.
   **Himalayan Book Centre**: Bhotahity,  maps and travel guides,
   books on the country, and postcards.
In Thamel / Kathmandu are plenty of smaller bookstores with
used as well as new books.  Good selection of photo-books,
trekking maps,  and other books on Nepal,  as well as Eng-
lish-language literature.
In Namal Tole,  north of Rani Pokhari,  are also lots of good
bookstores. See the map of Kathmandu as well.
In Pokhara there are many stores by the lake that buy and sell
used books. Sometimes there are quite good books available.

# Souvenirs & Sensible Buying Habits

Until 30 years ago,  Nepal remained shut off from the world, preserving its culture and rich tradition.  Worthy souvenirs that we

enjoy are traditional utensils still in daily use today. The immigration of many Tibetan refugees has enriched the spectrum
even greater. Culture and religion are closely intertwined in
Nepal. Almost all objects have religious significance if they
aren't directly religious cult objects. Aside from the outer beauty, an understanding of the symbolism of these objects will
increase their personal value to you. And be sure to bargain,
compare prices, and always be patient. But that's nothing new in
Asia! Some suggestions.

**Hand-woven Carpets:** Stool-carpets begin at 60.-Rs. Runners (90cm
by 180 cm) in Patan cost 800.-Rs (5-coloured, 4 threads per knot,
highest quality!). A carpet of this size weighs about 8 kg, calculate 250.-Rs for seamail. Only one carpet per package is allowed. You must be present at customs!

   **Check Quality:** Feeling and bending will tell you something
   about the thickness of the weave; compare. Be sure that
   patterns are cut for light and shadow effects. Look for as
   many threads per knot as possible, four if possible! On the
   back, the fewer chain.threads showing, the better; i.e., the
   knots should be as dense as possible. The chain threads
   shouldn't be patched in too often, as is often the case when
   too many light knots show on the back. Such carpets pull out
   of shape easily.

**Woven Jackets:** With linen lining cost about 200.-.
**Pullovers:** Grey with brown patterns, about 200.-.
**Pants & Shirts:** Made of cotton in traditional drawstring form or
custom freak-productions, about 40.-.
**Shoulder Bags:** Made of woven strips, sewn together. These can
be used as backpacks.
**Passport Bags:** And other small silk bags, available in various
qualities and prices.
**Prints:** On rice-paper, dirt cheap.
**Thankgas:** Religious paintings on cloth, of all qualities and
prices, with or without cloth borders and coverings, cost 200.-Rs
and up.
**Silver Jewelry:** Rings with stones, from 25.- up. Compare prices
and bargain. I took ten days to buy 60 rings, visiting at least
30 silversmiths and shops in Kathmandu, Badgaon, Patan, and
Bodnath. Don't ruin the price structure by buying laxly, and
don't imagine it will be easy reselling in Europe! Look for
necklaces, pendants of silver, glass, coral, and stones; necklaces
of rutraksha seeds, amulet necklaces, bone rings, bracelets.
**Statues of Buddha:** And other gods are available in all sizes and
styles.
**Prayer Wheels**
**Diamond Scepters**
**Bells**
**Brass Lamps:** And other brass work.
**Wood Carvings:** All kinds, from cloth-printing blocks to wooden
window frames are to order at the Nepal Wood Carving Centre
Patan, Ekhalakhu Thole at Durbar Square or in Bhaktapur.

**Bone Carvings:** Statuettes of gods are often offered, but are usually not of yak bone but of plastic. Hold a cigarette lighter to
it: bone won't burn!

**Posters:** Just show your passport at the Department of Tourism
next to the stadium 11:00–16:00 h. Also in the Tourist Office in
the New Road after 13:00 h, the same in Pokhara.

**Woven Belts:** 4.-Rs to 10.-Rs.

**Lace Lamps:** In all sizes and in the most varied qualities and
colors, 20.- to 150.-.

**Kukhiri Knives:** In all sizes and at all prices.

**Cloth:** Cheaper in India, since it usually comes from there, so
don't buy in Nepal if you'll be in India.

**Where To Shop:** Kathmandu Bazaar, Freakstreet, New Road and
environs; Patna and Jawalakhel (often cheaper); Bodnath and
Badgaon (normal to good buys); Pashupatinath (too expensive);
Swayambhu (if you bargain well, normal to cheap). In Pokhara,
all souvenirs are substantially more expensive than in Kathmandu
Valley. In the villages, especially off the beaten track, you'll
often be offered wares at exceptionally low prices; don't forget to
bargain, but don't be shameless!

**Tip:** Quality has often sunk in recent years due to increasing
tourism. You'll have to look longer!

**Antiques:** Objects older than 100 years are not allowed to be
exported. Before you get into difficulties with your departure,
have the Department of Archaeology prepare an export permit.


# Folklore Shows

Nepal is a folklore happening, especially at temples and cloi-
sters. You'll enjoy plenty of music and dance performances, free,
at festivals. Commercial performances offer acceptable prices. We
attended a performance at the Royal Nepal Academy, Kamaladi, a
street north of Bagh Bazaar, where authentic singing and dancing
from ethnic groups were shown.

**Kathmandu**
  **Hotel Shanker:** In Lazimpat. Performances every evening.
  **Everest Cultural Society:** Costs 50.-Rs.
  **National Theatre:** Kanti Path, corner of Asan Thole on Ratna
  Lake in Kathmandu, occasional performances, and in season
  daily. Admission 45.-Rs.

**Pokhara**
  **Dafne Club:** Midway between the airport and the city, folklore
  performances daily 19:00–21:00 h.
  **Hotel Dragon:** Daily performances 19:30–21:30 h, costs 20.-Rs,
  reserve in the morning.
  **Fish Trail Lodge:** Daily performances 18:00–19:00 h, costs
  35.-Rs.

Look at the signs, brochures in hotels and restaurants, and in
the ads in **Rising Nepal.**

# Photo Equipment

Nepal is the best country on the Indian subcontinent for stocking up on film. Equipment and cameras are availabe in the stores on the New Road. I got the best prices in the camera shop behind the big Newspaper Tree. But compare from time to time! I got Fuji film for 90.-Rs, a Kodak cassette film for 75.-Rs, and color slide film for 150.-Rs, not including developing. Be sure to check the expiration date.

**Developing:** You can have black-&-white film developed here for 5.-. If you're staying longer, it's best to have returning tourists take your color film back to Europe for you. Take the mailing envelopes with you, stamped and addressed, for this purpose. When you come home, all your photos and slides will be finished!

**Accessories:** Bring UV-filters and sunshades to cope with the intense light at high altitudes. If necessary, stock lenses and extra batteries for your automatic light meter.

# Drugs

Many people come here just to get stoned, smoking themselves into a stupor cheap, even if the dope shops, quite unique establishments, with corresponding signs, have vanished. The sale of drugs is officially banned since July 17, 1973. Hashish is still for sale everywhere, under the name Ganja. The natives smoke the same as ever. After all, the drug is a part of traditional religious life. But prices have gone up. A tola (11 g) of best quality costs about 50.-Rs, on the Jomosom Trek 20.- to 25.-Rs. Stay Healthy, Stay Sober!

**Enforcement:** Growing has been illegal since the end of 1976, but is tolerated, like small-scale trade, in deference to the small farmers who depend on it. Enforcing the ban would be like American prohibition. Occasionally a timid package-tourist is caught with a pipe.

**Freak Street:** Trading center for drugs of all sorts is Freak Street in Kathmandu, where you will see plenty of sorry figures hanging around. They are into hard drugs, certainly a nightmare. The police make occasional sweeps "to clean things up".

**Pokhara:** A second freak haven, where, around the lake, it's even worse than Freak Street.

**Common Sense:** If you are caught trying to smuggle drugs out of Nepal, count on a steep fine or jail sentence. And they do check you. Smoking dope and buying it are illegal. The police are stricter than they used to be. Be careful of dealers in Freak Street or elsewhere! They sell, denounce, and collect the offered reward, thus earning doubly. Smoking is expressly forbidden in all cafes and restaurants!

# ARRIVING

## Flights

From Europe cheapest flights include, one-year return, Amsterdam
- Dacca - Kathmandu,    US$650.- on Bangladesh Biman Airlines.
Cheap frequently means unreliable,  which shouldn't deter a true
globetrotter. Your plane ticket provides an opportunity to practise
the Asian art of imperturbability.

A second possibility is to fly via Bangkok,  and from there,
get a direct flight for US$190.- to Kathmandu or better,  for
US$220.- via Rangoon, Burma, where you can stay for up to seven
days (advance visa required for Burma!).

Also cheap is Aeroflot via Moscow to Delhi or Calcutta. Flights
from Delhi (US$142.-) and Calcutta (US$96.-).

When planning your trip,  check the travel pages of your
newspapers and magazines. See Passage to India.

**From India:**   Passengers under 30 years old get a 25 % discount.
Delhi US$142.-(RNAC,  IA),  70 minutes,  change planes in Patna
US$118.-.  Agra US$108.- (IA),  1 h.  Patna US$41.- (RNAC,  IA),
1 h,  twice weekly.  Khajuraho US$71.- (IA), via Varanasi daily.
Varanasi US$71.- (RNAC,  IA),  50 minutes,  daily. Calcutta US$96.-
(RNAC,  IA) 1 h,  daily, via Patna just US$92.-. The Indian air-
port tax for flights to Nepal is 50.-Rs.

One interesting ticket is the IA (Indian Airlines) from Delhi
via Agra,  Khajuraho,  Varanasi,  to Kathmandu and then on via
Calcutta to Bangkok,  costs US$400.-, at Student Travels, Janpath,
Delhi, stops permitted everywhere!

**From Sri Lanka:**   Nepal's airline,  RNAC,  flies Wednesdays and
Saturdays between Kathmandu and Colombo,  costs US$200.- one
way or US$380.- return. The RNAC office in Colombo-Kollupitiya is
at 434 Galle Road,  tel.24045,  open 08:30-16:30 h.  Flights to the
Maldives, with a stopover in Colombo, are planned.

**From Pakistan:**   Several flights weekly from Karachi US$130.-,
takes 3 h.   The RNAC office is in Hotel Mehran,  Sharea Faisal,
Karachi, tel.525683.

**From Bangladesh:**   RNAC,  Biman,  and BAC offer several flights
daily from Dacca,  costs US$100.-,  takes 3 h. The airline offices
are near the new stadium and Purbani Hotel in Dacca.

**From South-East Asia:** Flights from Bangkok with Bangladesh Biman via Rangoon Burma and Dacca Bangladesh, costs US$190.-. A flight with BAC or Thai Airways just via Rangoon costs US$200.-. Flights from Singapore cost US$300.-, from Hong Kong US$280.-; both via Bangkok or Dacca.

**Burma:** Travellers to Burma require a seven-day visa, which is available only if you present a ticket out of the country. Visa extensions are not possible. Because your day of arrival and departure are counted as just one day, you can actually spend eight days in Burma. The sale of your tax-free whiskey and cigarettes can finance a couple of days' travel in Burma; but don't sell to the first taxi driver you meet! Buy tickets for domestic flights within Burma direct from BAC (Burma Airways Corp.), it is cheaper!

### KATHMANDU AIRPORT

Upon arrival, change money, get your visa and stamp if you don't already have one, and go through customs. A taxi into town costs 15.-Rs, collective taxis to Thamel cost 10.-Rs, don't pay more, except a small night surcharge!

RNAC runs buses (7.-Rs), but only for arriving and departing RNAC flights; or get one of the modern, blue-white, local buses to Rani Pokhari / Ratna Park.

Occasionally you'll be offered free transport by a hotel tout. You might accept the ride, and spend just one night before looking for something better. If you know your way around town, get a ride into town, then find a rickshaw to your favorite hotel.

# Overland From India

There are six major routes, all running via **Narayangarh** in Terai, and **Mugling** to Kathmandu or Pokhara.

1) Direct bus Delhi to Kathmandu
2) Lucknow - Gorakhpur - Sonauli / Bhairawa - Narayangarh
3) Varanasi - Sonauli / Bhairawa - Narayangarh
4) Patna - Raxaul / Birgunj - Narayangarh
5) Calcutta - Muzaffapur - Raxaul / Birgunj - Narayangarh
6) Darjeeling - Siliguri - Naxalbari / Kakarvitta - Narayangarh

**1) Direct from Delhi:** Two Freak Buses weekly provide the only regular overland connection between Delhi and Kathmandu. The buses, equipped with stereo, cooking facilities, and group dynamics in clouds of ganja smoke, cost 300.-Rs (Indian). Your route runs via Agra, Varanasi or via Lucknow, Gorakhpur and on to Bhairawa and Kathmandu. Signs in the cheap hotels announce departure times, or visit Tourist Camp, where the buses await departure. In Mugling, you can change buses to Pokhara. Tourist cars, seeking passengers to share petrol expenses, can be found in Tourist Camp between Old and New Delhi (Nehru Marg), tel.222801.

**2) Lucknow – Bhairawa:** Several trains daily from Lucknow (5-7 h, 28.-Rs) to Gorakhpur; one originates in Cochin / Kerala, others in Delhi, Ahmedabad, and Amritsar, if you're in a hurry. The 4 h bus ride to the Indian border town, **Sonauli** cost 12.-Rs. Cross the border and get a direct bus to Narayangarh and Kathmandu, see next route.

**3) Varanasi – Bhairawa:** From Varanasi, direct buses at 04:00 h, 09:00 h, 10:00 h, 11:30 h, and 12:30 h, costs 40.-Rs in 7 h to **Sonauli**, the Indian border town. Or get a deluxe from Varanasi at 09:00 h to Gorakhpur, a major station on the wide-gauge rail line between Lucknow and Chapra / Sonpur by Patna. The bus from Gorakhpur to Sonauli takes 4 h, costs 12.-Rs.

At Sonauli, walk across the border and do the formalities, exit stamp and Indian customs, entrance stamp and Nepalese customs, takes at least an hour. Just beyond the Nepalese border post, on the right side of the street, are a number of lodges **(D)**30.-Rs (Nepalese), and restaurants.

Buses direct from the border to Pokhara and Kathmandu. The people in the lodges are happy to make bus reservations for you. The ride via Narayangarh and Mugling to Kathmandu takes 10 h, costs 50.-Rs. The night bus costs 60.-Rs. If you can't find a direct bus to Pokhara, get a bus toward Kathmandu and change in Mugling.

**Tip:** From Bhairawa, visit **Lumbini**, birthplace of Buddha.

**Tip:** At Narayangarh, make a sidetrip to **Chitwan National Park**, before heading on to Kathmandu, see Terai.

**Tip:** Or fly from Bhairawa to Kathmandu, takes 40 minutes, outstanding view of the Himalayas if you get a seat on the left.

**4) Patna – Birgunj:** Since the 4 km long river bridge at Patna was completed in 1982, direct buses run from Patna to the Indian border at Raxaul. Cheap lodgings on both sides of the border, but best in Nepal. In Raxaul try RRR in the railway station **(D)**25.-. National Lodge **(S)**20.-, **(D)**30.-. Tourist Lodge **(S)**20.-, **(D)**30.-. Paris Lodge **(S)**20.-, **(D)**30.-. In Asia Lodge even cheaper. Tourist Guest House, **(S)**25.-, **(D)**40.-, very clean.

In Birgunj, by the bus stand, try Hotel De Luxe **(D)**30.-, **(Dm)**10.-. Kailas **(D)**30.-, **(Dm)**10.-. Koseli **(D)**30.-, **(Dm)**10.-. Sagar **(D)**30.-, **(Dm)**10.-. Star **(D)**30.-, **(Dm)**10.-. Demand a mosquito net, you'll need it! There is even a Chinese restaurant.

The border towns are 4 km apart, cross in a tonga (horse cart), costs 15.-Rs (Nepal) or 8.-Rs (Indian). The tonga drivers point out the various offices: passport, customs, and again passport and customs check. The crossing takes 1-2 h; baggage is rarely searched. Set your watch ahead 15 minutes for Nepal.

From the border to Kathmandu you can get a bus, truck, or plane. Cheapest riding in a truck, 30.-Rs inside, or 15.-Rs on the back, more expensive in a crowd, takes 12 h.

Buses depart Birgunj hourly 05:30-12:00 h. The earlier you depart, the better your chance of getting a room in Kathmandu, takes 10 h, costs 50.-Rs! Faster minibuses charge 60.-Rs. Don't put any luggage on the roof of the bus: professional thieves!

Buses and trucks frequently stop at cheaper restaurants. It is an enchanting ride winding through the central mountains.

**Tip:** Along the way at Hitaura in Terai, change buses and take Nepal's first highway via Daman to Kathmandu. Just after **Simbhanjyang Pass** (2548 m), get off in Daman and spend the night. At sunrise you've a lovely view of the Himalayas from Mount Everest in the east to Dhaulagiri in the west. There is an observation tower with a telescope, unique in Nepal! From here it's 4-5 h by bus to Kathmandu, where a noon arrival makes finding a room pleasant.

**Tip:** To **Chitwan National Park**, turn off the route to Narayangarh at Tari (Tandi) Bazar. No trekking permit is required in the national park, see under Terai.

**Tip:** A cheap flight offers a wonderful opportunity in good weather to see the Himalayas: Get the airport bus in the morning to Simra Field, 20 km from Birgunj for the 30 minute Twin Otter flight to Kathmandu.

You can book the entire bus ride from Varanasi, including lodgings **(Dm)** and breakfast for 150.-Rs (Indian), but it isn't worth it. You still ride the same, uncomfortable public transport buses. The same deal offered for the return trip from Kathmandu, 220.-Rs (Nepalese), is also not worthwhile.

**5) Calcutta – Muzaffarpur – Birgunj:** From Calcutta you've two trains, the 19 Gorakhpur Express, Calcutta-Howrah (22:00 h), arrives Muzaffarpur 11:15 h, or the 21 Mitkila Express, Calcutta-Howrah 16:05 h, arrives Muzaffarpur 07:15 h. Even the Tourist Quota is frequently booked out for days in advance, while regular tickets are gone more than a week ahead. Costs 51.-Rs 2nd class. In Muzaffarpur, hourly buses to Raxaul (3 h, 20.-Rs) and four Deluxe buses daily (2.5 h, 25.-Rs). Border crossing, lodgings as under route 4.

**6) Darjeeling – Siliguri – Kakarvitta:** Entering Nepal from the east is convenient for those coming from Darjeeling and Sikkim, or perhaps from northeastern India, particularly Assam. The Indian border town is Naxalbari. On the Nepal side the town is Kakarvitta.

The simplest method, reasonably priced, is a package tour offered by the Tourist Service Agency across from the GPO in Darjeeling, costs 130.-Rs (Indian) including lodging in Kakarvitta; departs at 09:00 h, arrives 24 h later in Kathmandu. Other similar offers available, shop around and bargain!

If you make it to Siliguri (by the 4 h bus ride 12.-Rs or the Toy Train from Darjeeling, or from Bangladesh, Assam, and Calcutta) there are buses from Hillcart Road Bus Station (2.-Rs) to Naxalbari (by jeep 6.-Rs), then cross the border by rickshaw, 1.-Rs including formalities. Several buses daily from Kakarvitta to Kathmandu. The Rajdoot Express Bus charges 80.-Rs (Indian), takes 12 h including stops for food and tea. Lodgings available in Kakarvitta.

Nights buses from Kakarvitta to Kathmandu 110.-Rs (Indian), bookings by Kanka Yatayat Sewa Pvt. Ltd, and others.

**Note:** You need a permit for Silguri, independent of whether you plan to visit Darjeeling or not! You may not cross the border here without a Darjeeling Permit, so apply in Calcutta or Kathmandu.

**Warning:** Don't put your baggage on the roof of the bus, professional thieves at work!

# Overland From Tibet

The opening of Tibet to foreign tourists, including the opening of the Tibet-Nepal border, provides an interesting new route into the Indian subcontinent.

**Flights:** CAAC flies daily between Chengdu and Lhasa, takes 2-3 h depending upon aircraft. Make reservations at least two days ahead, earlier during summer, costs US$120.- one way. You've a good view of the Himalayas from the left side of the plane. From Xian, there are two flights weekly via Golmud to Gonggar, Lhasa's airport. From Golmud, takes 2 h, costs US$90.- one way. Baggage travels separately the 90 km from Gonggar to Lhasa, arriving several hours later than the passengers. The bus ride takes 90 minutes. We advise carrying everything for one night in your hand luggage.

**From Golmud:** Buses and trucks traverse the 1155 km to Lhasa, buses charge Rmb 120.-, takes 30 h to 55 h, food, drink, and warm clothes are a must.

**From Gilgit, Pakistan:** You can cross the Karakorum Mountains to Kashgar in China's autonomous region of Sinkiang, and from there on to Tibet.

**Exit Permit:** In Lhasa you have to apply for an exit permit for Nepal, a simple formality. You are permitted to visit villages along the way to the border including Gyangtse and Shigatse.

## THE MOUNTAIN DRIVE
Your transport possibilities consist of trucks, chartered minibuses (six to ten seats), or buses (20 to 30 seats). Try to get a group together from among your fellow hotel guests. It is usually quite simple. The ride to the border takes three days. Many travellers, however, prefer to take their time and charter a bus for five days. For such a trip think 100 Yaun per person. Each additional day costs 200 Yaun for the entire bus.

Most of the 900 km to the border is unpaved. Over the last 300 km, the road climbs up to 4000 m for the high plains and at Jia Tsuo La Pass reaches its highest altitude at 5242 m. Another 200 km further you cross Lalung Leh Pass at 5124 m. Then it is downhill to just 2000 m at Zhangmu (Kasa), for your last night.
**To China:** The return trip overland from Nepal to China is not as much fun. You have too little time to adjust to the high altitude coming from low-lying Kathmandu Valley; expect health problems.
**Border:** After crossing the border to Kodari in Nepal, you might go on by truck to Barabise. At the end of the working day at local construction sites, there are occasional buses to and from the border. Tatopani, 1 km beyond Kodari, boasts several lodges.
**Tour:** Rover Trek in Kathmandu offers a 12-day tour to Lhasa. Runs every 14 days, costs US$385.-.
**Flights:** There is talk of starting flights between Lhasa and Kathmandu. And discussions continue on opening the border between Gyangtse in Tibet and Gangtok in Sikkim, India.
The border crossing from Nepal to Tibet is not without its difficulties, but possible, at least for groups. Things are becoming easier, so ask about the latest information.

# MOVING ON

## Flights

The following airlines maintain offices in Kathmandu: Indian
Airlines tel.411907, Thai Airways International tel.213565, Union
of Burma Airways tel.214839, Bangladesh Biman tel.212544,
Lufthansa tel.213052, British Airways tel.212266, Air France
tel.213339, Pan Am tel.411824, Pakistan International Airlines
tel.212102, Japan Airlines tel.213854, KLM tel.214896, Swiss Air
tel.412455, Air Canada. All the above airlines have offices on
Durbar Marg between Ratna Park and the palace.

Several airlines have offices on Kanti Path including: Air
India tel.212335, TWA tel.212397, Aeroflot tel.212397, and Cathay
Pacific. RNAC (Royal Nepal Airlines Corp.) tel.214511 is on Kanti
Path at New Road. Other RNAC offices at the Kathmandu airport
and at smaller domestic airstrips.

Flights to India should be booked by RNAC or Indian Airlines.
The airport tax in Kathmandu is 100.-Rs. Sale of your duty-free
cigarettes and liquor can serve as an indirect flight discount.

**To South-East Asia:** Direct flights to Bangkok with Bangladesh
Biman via Rangoon, Burma and Dacca, Bangladesh, costs
US$190.-. A flight with BAC (Burma) or Thai Airways just stop-
ping in Rangoon costs US$200.-. Flights via Calcutta to Rangoon
with BAC cost US$180.-, or US$240.- with an extended stopover.
The same flight continuing on to Bangkok runs at US$200.- or
US$300.- respectively. A return flight to Rangoon with BAC costs
US$350.-; for Burma visa see Arriving.

Flights to Singapore cost US$300.-, to Hong Kong US$280.-;
both via Bangkok or Dacca.

Apply for a China visa in Hong Kong (e.g. in Travellers'
Friendship Hostel, Chungking Mansion, B-Block, 6th Floor). Cost
depends upon waiting period, one day to one week, HK$45.-
(US$7.-), to HK$100.- (US$15.-). A visa is issued for up to three
months and can be extended five times for up to a month.

Flights via Bangkok to Sydney with Thai Airways, costs
US$700.-.

**To Europe:** The cheapest flights include a weekly flight with
Bangladesh Biman via Dacca and Bombay to Amsterdam (US$500.-).
Aeroflot offers weekly flights via Calcutta to Frankfurt (US$500.-)
and Munich (US$520.-). Air India has flights via Delhi to
Frankfurt (US$600.-). All the above are cheaper than first flying
to India and then looking for a flight there.

# Overland

**To India:** From the GPO in Kathmandu, buses to Birgunj, departs at 07:00 h, takes 8 h, costs 40.-Rs, book one or two days ahead at the two stands by the GPO. The night bus is more expensive.

**Birgunj:** Get a rickshaw for 8.-Rs (Nepalese) across the border to Raxaul. The rickshaw drivers will point out the various offices you need to visit. Be sure you get an entry stamp for India, otherwise you'll have difficulties upon departure! For lodgings by the border see arriving route above.

**Raxaul:** It is fastest and cheapest by express bus to Patna, takes 8 h, costs 25.-Rs (Indian). From Patna you've rail connections to Varanasi and Calcutta.

**Bhairawa / Sonauli:** If you choose to cross the border here, get the direct bus from Kathmandu, then change to an Indian bus (departs hourly 05:00-11:00 h) to Varanasi or Gorakhpur and continue on by rail. See arriving routes above, and the local sections at Varanasi and perhaps Agra.

**To Darjeeling:** Get the Radjoot bus from Kathmandu at 05:00 h for 100.-Rs or evenings (more comfortable) at 18:00 h for 125.-Rs, takes 13 h including stops for meals and tea to the border at Kakarvitta / Naxalbari. Then continue on to Siliguri (1 h, 1.50 Rs).
 **Darjeeling Permit:** Even if you are just travelling via Siliguri to Calcutta or elsewhere, you still have to apply in Kathmandu for a Darjeeling Permit! Costs 34.-Rs (Nepalese) for one week. They will send you back at the border if you don't have a Darjeeling Permit, so be sure you have one before heading this way. Siliguri to Darjeeling takes 4 h, costs 12.-Rs by bus.

**To Calcutta:** First as above to Bhairawa. Then continue on by bus to Gorakhpur, and from there by rail in 24 h to Calcutta-Howrah.

**Tours:** All over Kathmandu, you'll see offers from travel agencies for package tours to spots in India. No matter how you go, you'll still have to cross the border on foot. In India you change to an Indian bus. Only to Delhi can you get a direct bus for 500.-Rs, bookings by Swiss Bus near Bhimsen Pillar and DAS photography shop. Occasionally, direct buses to Goa are offered. Look for signs in restaurants.

**From Pokhara:** Direct bus connections to the border crossings at Bhairawa, Birgunj, and Kakarvitta.

# KATHMANDU

## COMING - GOING

**By Air:** Taxis from the airport, 15.-Rs. A group taxi costs 10.-Rs per person. But taxis aren't easy to find at the airport. If you arrive on an RNAC flight, rides are provided to the RNAC office (Kanti Path at New Road), costs 7.-Rs. Occasionally hotel touts offer free transport from the airport. If you know your way around, just get a rickshaw to your favorite hotel. Note: The hotel reservation desk at the airport is a waste of time; nobody there has any idea what rooms are available!

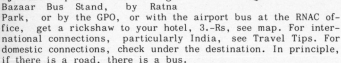

**By Bus:** Upon arrival at Bagh Bazaar Bus Stand, by Ratna Park, or by the GPO, or with the airport bus at the RNAC office, get a rickshaw to your hotel, 3.-Rs, see map. For international connections, particularly India, see Travel Tips. For domestic connections, check under the destination. In principle, if there is a road, there is a bus.

**Around Town:** Bicycle rentals, costs 8.-Rs per day, depending upon quality, return by 18:00 h. Ask about overnight rates, deposit perhaps required. Check the brakes, bell, and tire pressure. Motorcycle rentals (Honda) for 50.-Rs per hour, 350.-Rs per day, petrol not included; check it once over!

Rickshaws charge at least 3.-Rs, but that will get you way across town. Bargain the price congenially in advance. Taxis charge about 6.-Rs per mile, bargain before you start, few have meters!

Blue-White buses run in the newer sections of town, east of Kantipath. A major stop is Ratna Patk by Durbar Marg, south of Bagh Bazaar.

Minibuses to Badgaon depart from the yard near the petrol station, Bagh Bazaar at Durbar Marg.

Trolley buses (O-bus) to Badgaon (the stop there is outside town!), departs from National Stadium, at the southern end of Kanti Path.

KATHMANDU

| | | | |
|---|---|---|---|
| 1 | Kumari Mahal | 19 | Money Exchange |
| 2 | Ganesh Temple | 20 | Rastra Bank |
| 3 | Palace Entrance | 21 | Books & Magazines |
| 4 | Taleju Bell | 22 | Nepal Press |
| 5 | Taleju Temple | 23 | Foreign Post Office |
| 6 | Memorial | 24 | Photo Shop |
| 7 | Vishnu Tree | 25 | Akash Bhairab Temple |
| 8 | Dairy | 26 | KMT Guest House |
| 9 | Hotel Crystal | | Disco |
| 10 | Mona Lisa Restaurant | | Sherpa Lodge |
| 11 | Yin & Yang Restaurant | | Star Hotel |
| 12 | Restaurant | 27 | Utse |
| 13 | Fresh Stores | | Tibetan Restaurant |
| 14 | Goethe Institute | 28 | KC's, Kantipur |
| 15 | American Library | | Pie Shops, Books |
| 16 | National Theatre | 29 | Kaiser Library |
| 17 | Market Entrance | | |
| 18 | RNAC Booking Office | | |

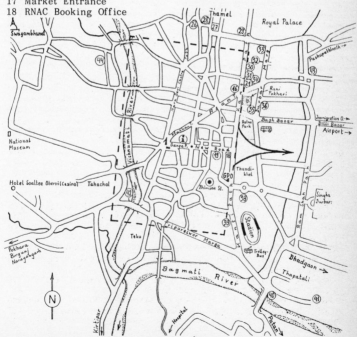

## A NIGHT'S REST

Cheapest on Freak Street (Jhochen Tole) and in Pig Alley (Maruhity) around Basanthpur Square. Since the clean-up program
(in every sense of the word) there are less freaks and much
fewer pigs.

Think **(S)**10.- to **(S)**50.- for nice rooms with bath; **(D)**20.-,
30.- to **(D)**50.- with bath; and **(Dm)**6.-, 8.-Rs. We don't make
any recommendations for this section of town; it would be
counter productive for a number of reasons. Lodgings are constantly changing both names and owners. The quality fluctuates
quickly and radically. But hotels are packed so close together
that by the second day, you should have found the spot right
for you. This is the center of town. Every morning you pass
freak shops and tourists. But this is not Nepal; just the European influences on Nepal.

In the same range of prices, you can find a room anywhere
in Kathmandu; particularly between Basanthpur Square and
northern Thamel in the bazar. This area typifies Nepalese city
life. Unlike Freak Street and Thamel, it isn't as touristy. And
within the price range, lodgings are nicer.

Thamel is a district catering exclusively to tourism these
days. Just ten minutes walk from downtown, it is cleaner and
brighter than on Freak Street or in the bazar, but more expensive too. Under **(D)**35.-Rs, you'll scarcely find a room. A few
addresses:

**Kathmandu Guest House**, tel.13628, **(D)**65.-, most 100.-, to
200.-, cold and damp cellar, lovely garden, quiet, clean, lots
of service, bike rentals, roof-top terrace. Tibetan Restaurant
Ashta Mangal is adjoining. In season, KTM Guest House is
always booked up. For stays of seven days, 10 % discount, one
month 30 %.

**Hotel Star**, tel.11004, **(S)**25.-, **(D)**30.-, 70.-, **(Tr)**45.-, quiet,
clean, roof terrace, restaurant. **Paradise Hotel**, next to KTM
Guest House, **(D)**35.-,50.-, very modern. **Everest Guest House**,
**(D)**50.-, **(Tr)**60.-, ask for a room facing the garden. **Cosy
Corner**, next to Star Hotel, **(D)**35.-. **Eleve Lodge**, next door,
**(D)**35.-. **Om Guest House**, **(D)**70.-. **Himal Cottage**, very quiet
and clean, own garden, **(D)**35.-, bike rentals 8.-Rs per day,
nice owners. **Yeti Cottage**, **(D)**45.-, pleasant garden restaurant,
camper parking 15.-Rs, **(Tr)**60.-. **Kantipur Hotel** on the Thamel
main street, **(D)**35.-. **Geeta Lodge**, new building, clean, well
kept, friendly manager, **(S)**40.-, **(D)**50.-, 70.-, **(Tr)**85.-Rs.

The best-known establishments are frequently booked. There
are a dozen other lodgings in the area. By not mentioning a
name, the open-secret syndrome is avoided. Try your luck!
Everywhere, expect a 10 % Government Tax, which you avoid by
staying for over seven days. Ask to see the room in advance!
Ask about student discounts, and try to bargain for a longer
stay! Discounts of 5-10 % in addition to the tax avoidance are
the norm, at least in the off season. During the monsoon, many

## KATHMANDU CITY

31  British Council
32  Hotel Annapurna
33  Bangladesh Biman
    Burma Airways
34  American Express
35  Park Restaurant
36  Clocktower
37  Geeta Cottage
38  War Memorial
39  Central Telegraph Office
40  Thailand Embassy
41  Burmese Embassy
42  Cremations
43  Krishna Loaf Bakery
44  Vajra Hotel & Restaurant

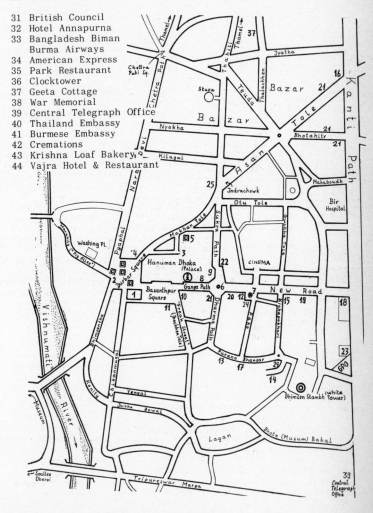

hotels charge just half price. In season, March - April and October - November, bargaining will get you little; it's hard enough finding a room. Head out early: 10:00-12:00 h is checkout time. Some hotels and lodges maintain waiting lists, but you are best off being there in person.

While you are off on a trek, many hotels will let you check your unneeded baggage, and leave your valuables in the safe. If you know the date of your return, make a reservation for this date. But it still isn't certain you will actually get the room.

**Staying A While:** Ask about rooms, or sharing a house in the outer districts of town, e.g. in Swayambhu Village, below the temple, starting at 35.-Rs per week, but without furnishings, and just well water. Somewhat better rooms cost double or triple. Similar accommodations in Bodnath and other sections of Kathmandu Valley: seek and you will find.

**Camping:** Camping is permitted everywhere in Nepal, except in National Parks. Campers can also set up their tents in the yards of many hotels, e.g. Yeti Cottage or Sherpa Lodge. Car parking costs 10.-Rs to 15.-Rs per night. There are several spots in Tahachal district.

Please ask permission in advance, and don't trample rice fields or cultural artifacts which you might just consider to be weeds (happens repeatedly). Don't cut wood for fires. Burn or bury your trash. Cans, glass bottles, and other containers are of use to the locals.

Swayambhu: **Hotel Vajra, (S)**150.-Rs, behind the northern Vish-numati River Bridge, uphill to the left; the place for comfort freaks, great. **Trekker's House, (S)**100.-Rs, once you've seen the building you'll understand the prices, and why it must be recommended; the woman manager is German, roof-top garden, restaurant, events, mail address: P.O. Box 1084, GPO, KTM, tel.14545.

## REFRESHMENT

Kathmandu is an Asian food paradise, particularly for those unaccustomed to spicy Indian food. Almost every restaurant offers a wide variety of reasonably priced food, both western and eastern. The best, including a few of the cheaper, can be found in the north of town in Thamel. Several spots around Basanthpur Square are quite good; even if those on Freak Street are often dingy.

Thamel: **Jamaly**, western and Chinese food, cakes and pudding. **Utse**, Tibetan, Chinese, Nepalese food. **Ashta Mangal**, in Kathmandu Guest House, lovely Tibetan wall painting, tasteful furnishings, western music, Tibetan, Nepalese, European and American cooking. **Kantipur Restaurant** good, clean, reasonably priced, including pies and breakfast. **K.C.'s Restaurant and Bambooze Bar**, mostly western food, but also pies and cheese or meat fondue; expensive, but with a unique Nepalese owner. Across the street, his brother runs **Govinda's**, mostly a pie shop, nothing special, expensive, but very "in". **Yeti Cottage**, pleasant garden restaurant. **Sunny Garden**, a pleasant place to sit outside. **Lhasa**, Tibetan restaurant, good, reasonable, the speciality: chung pipe (= Tibetan beer). **Narayan's Restaurant**, daily fresh pies, along with solid food, and pizza. **Restaurant Plaza** in Hotel Mona Lisa, next to K.C.'s, Austrian food, not cheap, but classic from Mozart to Strauß. **Helena's**, near Mona Lisa, pleasant, cheap, European, Indian and Chinese food, the friendly staff speaks English, French, German. **Bistro**, between Star Hotel and KTM Guest House, good meat dishes, e.g. Chateaubriand (35.-Rs), elegant, expensive. Readers recommend in Thamel, **Kingsland**, Chinese food. And **Tudor**.

Basanthpur Square: A few restaurants have maintained high standards over the years. **Yin + Yang** on Basanthpur Square at Freak Street has good music, comfortable seats, nice furnishings, great food, but high prices. **Mona Lisa**, nearby, much the same, but dirtier, good breakfast. Both the above can be quite smoky.

**Cosmopolitan**, simple food. **Paradise**, vegetarian food. **Unique**, great noodle dishes. **Lunchbox**, Italian specialities, müsli, good pies. **Lost Horizon**, off Freak Street to the right, good momos

for 10.-Rs. **Mandarin,** a Tibetan restaurant, is similar to Utse in Thamel. **Indira Restaurant,** between Rastra Bank and the Newspaper Tree on New Road, up an outside stairs, good international fare, mostly Indian, affordable prices. **Crystal Hotel,** nice view from the roof-garden restaurant, among others in the palace district.

Also worth mentioning is the tiny restaurant on the left in Maruhity, before the curve to the right, with lasagne, pizza, and pies. Readers praise **Cafe de Cabin Restaurant** upstairs in a house in Indrachowk; classical eastern instrumental music is played, nice atmosphere, Tibetan and Indian food.

**Disco:** Across from KTM Guesthouse in Thamel, till 24:00 h, closed Fridays, free admission, hot spot.

**Tipping:** Usually not included in your bill, give about 10 % of your bill, if you are satisfied with service. On the counter in the smaller restaurants is a Tip Box; the proceeds are divided among the crew.

**Pie Shops:** A speciality of the Indian subcontinent, pies and puddings to delight cost 5.-Rs and up. Our favorites include **New Style Pie Shop,** down on the left in Maruhity (Pig Alley) and **Mellow Pie Shop,** on the left at the end of Freak Street. Excellent, but expensive in **Govinda's Pie Shop** or at **Jamaly** in Thamel. Enjoy tremendous servings of great pie in **Himalayan Coffee Shop** on Basanthpur Square. Numerous other shops, perhaps just as good, are spread about town, particularly Basanthpur Square; see the restaurant list above.

**Fresh Stores:** Almost every type of European food is available, meat, sausage, cheese, chocolate, peanut butter, chicken, honey, pickled foods, jelly, red wine, etc. Canned foods are expensive. From New Road, heading toward Basanthpur Square, go left on Dharma Path; there are two Fresh Shops at the end. You'll find more shops north of the royal palace in the diplomatic quarter.

**Dairy Sale Centres:** Feature milk and cheese. One is next to the Tourist Office on Basanthpur Square. A liter of milk costs 4.-Rs, 100 g cheese is 7.-Rs. Other dairies are in Lainchaur and on Kanti Path, diagonally across from the West German embassy. A number of other shops cater to tourist and diplomatic clientele. Black bread and whole grain bread (which keeps forever) are available in **Nepal Dairy** and in the trekking shops. For large orders, go right to the bakery in the yard of Bir Restaurant, near the Bodnath Stupa. In **Bakers,** by the royal palace, good French bread and croissants are oven fresh at 16:00 h.

**Trekking Shops:** In Thamel and Freak Street. Here too you can
pick up such pseudo–Nepalese necessities as peanut butter,
jam, or trekking snacks: i.e. instant soup, cookies, cans,
etc., open 08:00–21:00 h, some open Saturdays.

Bottled cooking gas, in the industrial district, 6 kg costs
100.-Rs.

**TIPS**

**Tourist Information Centre:** Ganga Path, tel.215818, December–
February 09:00–17:00 h, otherwise until 18:00 h, between Basanthpur Square and Memorial Circle, an extension of New Road.
Occasionally they have a city map of Kathmandu including maps
of Patan and Bhadgoan, plus a map of Kathmandu Valley, along
with information brochures.

**Information Window:** At Tribhuvan Airport, opens to greet
incoming international flights.

**Tourist Office:** At the top of Pokhara.

**Bookshops:** You'll find valuable books, brochures, and photo
books about Nepal, plus city maps and trekking maps. The
managers of the hotels and lodges are happy to offer advice.

## SIGHTS

It's an endless task writing about Kathmandu's sights;  the city
is one tremendous museum! Every street,  every corner,  every
building is worthy of immortality. And the people themselves are
a treat for the eye! Still, there are a few spots nobody wants to
miss.

**Durbar Square** (Durbar = palace):  In the palace and temple district, the centre of Kathmandu, and focal point of Nepal. It is no
coincidence that Nepalese frequently call Kathmandu simply "Nepal", with its ancient, no longer inhabited royal palace.

**Hanuman Dhoka:** A rarity in pagoda architecture. The nine-storey
apartment tower, and the only round pagoda in Nepal, are richly
decorated with wood carvings and paintings. Don't let yourself be
deterred from a closer look by the ugly wing on Basanthpur
Place, costs 5.-Rs. The entrance is at Hanuman Gate (Hanuman is
the Monkey God).  In front is the terrible,  lovely shape of the
Goddess of Destruction (and Creation!), Kali.

**Taleju Temple:** With three roofs, in the center of Durbar Square,
completed in 1549 under King Mahendra Malla.  The atmosphere of
Durbar Square is best enjoyed by relaxing here at sunset and in
the early twilight.

**Kumari Mahal:** A temple dedicated to Kumari,  a living virgin
goddess. You may enter the courtyard, but photography is prohibited! Give the temple servants a tip if the Kumari presents herself.  The girl is considered a pure reincarnation of Parvati,
Shiva's wife,  and is selected from among the goldsmith daughters
by a series of tests. She relinquishes her position upon her first
bleeding,  be it from injury,  or menstrual flow. As a symbol of
respect,  each year she presents the King with a tika,  recon-
firming his rule. During this festival, she is accompanied by two
boys representing the reincarnation of Shiva as Destructor (Bhai-
rab),  and the Elephant God, Ganesh (son of Shiva and Parvati).
The Kumari is permitted to leave her palace just twice each year
to attend this,  and one other festival. After completion of her
term as Kumari,  the girl retires to a lonely life at home;  it is
bad luck to marry her.

**Kastha Mandap:** A pagoda next to Kumari Palace,  built in 1596
with wood from a single tree;  it's the root of the name
"Kathmandu".

**Ganesh Temple:** At the beginning of Pig Alley at Durbar Square,
visit in the evening. Music is played; the atmosphere is great.

**Machendra Nath Temple:** In Asan Tole (Bazaar), certainly worth a
look.  In the evening, attend Puja (prayers) with music, singing,
and a pipe of hashish is passed.  The museums,  in comparison,
are bland, and hardly worth a visit.

**Bhimsen Stambh:** Also called Bhimsen Pillar or tower,  55 m tall,
it is visible from anywhere in Kathmandu.  Nepal's tallest building was built in 1832 under Rana Prime Minister Bhimsen Thapa.

**Nayanhity Durbar:** The present royal palace, worth a look, at the
end of Durbar Marg.  Here too is the **Clock Tower**,  Nepal's first
public clock.

**The Casino:**   In Hotel Soaltee Oberoy,   near Kathmandu, your only
opportunity on the subcontinent to try your luck.   Many globetrotters see it as a chance to increase their travel budget. I
know one traveller who put US$3000.- on red with the idea of
letting fate decide how long he could travel:   he boarded a depressing flight home.   Visitors to Nepal are eligible once,   within
seven days of arrival,   upon presentation of a plane ticket at the
casino reception,   to receive a coupon worth five dollars of free
play.   Buses depart half-hourly every evening from 20:00 h on,
from Hotel Crystal (that ugly blue thing), near Durbar Square, to
the Casino,   and return every half hour until 03:00 h or 04:00 h.
If you are staying in KTM Guesthouse,   or another middle-class
hotel,   you can have yourself picked up there.   Games include
roulette,   bingo,   and slot machines. For one evening, the casino
can be interesting.

The casino is divided into a gaming area for Europeans and a
gaming area for Indians,   primarily Sikhs. Europeans, naturally,
are permitted to play where they choose.   The non-European area
is more relaxed,   and more fun.   Nepalese are prohibited from
play! Try your luck, but don't be foolish!

# KATHMANDU VALLEY

## Pashupathinath

This is a pleasant spot, where sadhus gather to wash their clothes
and utensils in the Bagmati River.
Cremations are performed on the
ghats (docks). Life and death seem
closely intertwined.

**The Golden Temple:** Dedicated to
Shiva as guardian of animals. Set
on the bank of the sacred Bagmati
River, a tributary of the Ganges.
The temple is one of the seven most
sacred Hindu sites, and the most
important place of pilgrimage in Nepal.

    Legend tells that Shiva, in-
carnated as Pashupati, came to the
Bagmati River, accompanied by Par-
vati. Shiva felt deeply moved by the beautiful countryside. He
transformed himself into a gazelle, and frolicked with a female
gazelle, Parvati. The gods, Indra, Vishnu, and Brahma, found
great pleasure in the sight of the wonderful gazelles. Shiva,
however, didn't want to stop. When they tried to subdue him,
Shiva lost a horn. He swam to the opposite bank where the temple
stands today. Shiva named it Pashupathi (= King of Animals).
Shiva proclaimed that anyone who set eyes upon Pashupati's
horn, the Shiva Lingam, would never again be reincarnated as
an animal.

    The temple is on a hill overlooking the river. Steep stairs
lead down to the water. Its origins date from the 3rd century AD. But the facilities have been expanded and altered repeatedly over the centuries.

    Non-Hindus are prohibited from entering the inner sanctuaries
of the temple district. But you can get a look inside from the
opposite bank of the river. A small stone bridge leads over the
Bagmati, to where you have a good view of cremations being
performed on the ghats. The hill on the left side of the river can
be climbed via a stair lined with hundreds of lingams. Left of
the stairs, a row of benches invites you to spend a while quietly
observing religious activities along the river and in the temple
district. You are best off coming by bicycle (5 km).

KATHMANDU VALLEY

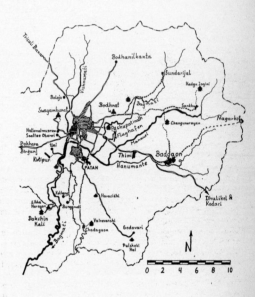

# Bodnath

Also spelled Bouddhanath, this is one of the world's greatest
stupas. It was the most important Buddhist religious site in Nepal even before the influx of lamas from Tibet. More than 2000
years old, today it is residence of the Chai Lama, a
representative of the Dalai Lama. The eyes of Buddha symbolize
his presence, guarding over the region.
**Stupa:** A place of prayer and meditation for Buddhist lamas. In
early times the semicircular structure was little more than piled
earth. "Stupa" or "chaitya" are derivatives of the Sanskrit for
"pile of ashes". Later

brick or broken stone
were used. The stupa, as
a whole, symbolizes the
human body, along with
all the major symbols at-
tached to Buddhism: the
circle, triangle, rectan-
gle, and the seven chak-
ras of meditation and en-
lightenment. Its founda-
tions resemble the man-
dala, four sides, stairs,
and eyes peering in all
four directions. Unusu-
ally, the stupa is spread
over three terraces. And
the five Dhyani Buddhas,
which every stupa has,
are missing (see Maha-
yana Buddhism). Bodnath
is revered by Tibetan
Buddhists, but not by Ne-
war Buddhists; unlike
Swayambu which is holy
to both Buddhists and
Hindus. One legend tells
that the stupa contains
relics of the Buddha Kashyapa. Another legend maintains that the
stupa was built above the ashes of a high Tibetan lama.

Bodnath is 8 km east of Kathmandu, surrounded by a circular
Tibetan village full of shops. It is a must see, easily accessible
by bicycle in conjunction with a visit to Pashupatinath. Schedule
an entire day to visit both. Around the stupa are numerous restaurants, chai shops, and souvenir stands.

**Bodhanilkanta:** A 7th-century statue of Vishnu sleeping in a bed
of snakes is cut from a single piece of rock. It is set in the
center of an artificial lake. Legend says that the King, himself a
reincarnation of Vishnu, may not view this statue, or he will
die.

BODNATH

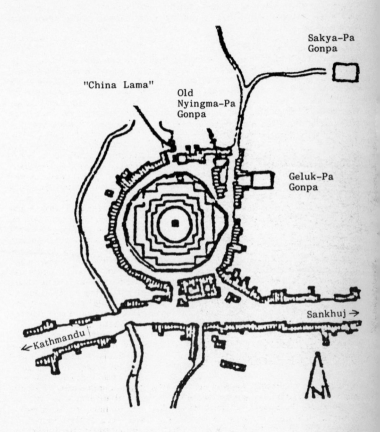

You can get a bus here from the royal palace via Lazim Path.
By bicycle, it's a 10 km ride through fields of rice along a
winding road. Here too, you can take a lovely walk along a
clear mountain stream; just follow the road past the modern
building complex (a TB sanitarium) and keep going after the
road ends.

## BALAJU

Here you'll find a public swimming pool; Thursday mornings it's
open only to women. However, tourists are rare; so you are best
off coming in a group. Located north of Kathmandu, Balaju is
easy to reach by bicycle, or by bus from the National Theater or
Kanti Path.

**The Balaju Water Garden:** Built in the 18th century. In one pool,
Vishnu sleeps on a bed of snakes. In an enclosure you can observe deer and birds.

# Swayambunath

Swayambu Temple is on a hill visible from Kathmandu. At the foot
of the hill is a village where you might find a room. It is separated from Kathmandu by the Vishnumati River, and accessible
via three bridges, from Durbar Square, Pig Alley, or from Thamel
(the prettiest route). A taxi costs 12.-Rs.

**Swayambunath Temple:** The stupa is one of the most ancient Buddhist temples. Swayambunath (= of its own creation) is a central
concept of both Buddhism and Hinduism. In Buddhism this concept
is conceived as the original Buddha who appeared here over the
then-present lake as a flame sparked by spontaneous combustion.
In Hinduism the concept is depicted by the original lingam,
which always existed, and is pictured in an egg shape. The
stupa is 2000 years old and surrounded by 211 prayer wheels
which you circle clockwise (and turn clockwise).

**The Monkey Temple:** The popular name for Swayambu is an under-
statement. You can't be certain if any of the somewhat vicious
monkeys are infected with rabies. It is a mistake to carry anything edible with you! The monkeys are sure to seize the offensive. And don't make the mistake of feeding just one or two
apes, a crowd will appear in no time. And they are quick to
anger when your supplies diminish. Besides, the monkeys are fed
by priests and local inhabitants.

Around the stupa are a number of other buildings, monasteries,
and a temple also visited by Hindus.

**International Buddhist Library:** And the Chai Shop Tantra. From
the roof of the buildings, you've a lovely view of the entire
Kathmandu Valley.

Pashupatinath

On a second hill is a Tibetan settlement and another temple. Budget enough time to see more than just the temple; the entire region is of interest. After all, you did climb 75 m (231 stairs) to get here. The best times to be here are 09:00 h, and around sunset, when monks pray to the accompaniment of horns and drums.

Swayambu Village has lots of chai shops and restaurants; try the Cave, or the Tibetan restaurant diagonally across. Food is cheaper here than in Kathmandu.

Swayambu consists of two parts. To get to the upper part mentioned above, coming from Kathmandu, enter the lower part of the village, climb the stairs leading to the temple, then follow the road along the hill.

**Prayers:**  On the road around the hill, Tibetans walk in a circle three times at sunrise and sunset to pray and meditate. Too bad there is nothing like this back home.

**Staying A While:**  You can find a nice place to stay in one of the lodges, in the camping area, or in a private home. I really enjoyed participating in local family life. Our room cost 35.-Rs per week, which buys just one night in Kathmandu. But this is only recommended for hardened travellers who've long lost their western expectations. This is a place where Nepalese, Tibetans, and westerners live in peace and harmony.

## DAKSHINKALI

This is a pilgrim town, 20 km south of Kathmandu. On Tuesday and Sunday mornings, chickens and goats are sacrificed to honor the goddess Kali. Both days are considered inauspicious. In order to placate her, only male animals are sacrificed. It is a very bloody affair, not for everyone. Minibuses here depart on Tuesdays and Sundays, from Ratna Park at 06:00 h, costs 10.-Rs return, or 7.-Rs one way. Because the bus waits only an hour, we recommend getting a one way ticket. Be sure to get here early, the most interesting part takes place between 08:00-10:00 h.

The road to Dakshinkali passes Tribhuvan University, heading
south past Kirtipur and the village of Pharping. At the end of
the road is Dakshinkali Temple. Returning, it is a half-hour
walk to Pharping and its lovely temple. From there it is 2.-Rs
by bus to Chobar Gorge. The bus stops at the large cement
factory just before Kathmandu. Walk up the hill to the suspension
bridge across the river. All the water flowing out of Kathmandu
Valley passes through this gorge. From the temple on the opposite
bank, there is a bus back to Kathmandu.

## KIRTIPUR
Six km southwest of Kathmandu, the road to Dakshinkali bypasses
Kirtipur. There is no road into the village, so you walk the last
few meters. Notice the old houses and temple, not all in the best
condition. Once upon a time, Kirtipur held a strategic position in
the Kathmandu Valley. In a long 16th-century struggle against
the Gurkhas, a Gurkha victory cost every man in the village his
nose and ears. The Gurkhas wanted to make an example for all
to see.

# Patan

Patan, 5 km south of Kathmandu, is the most ancient town in
Kathmandu Valley, even if the scholars can't agree on the exact
date of its founding. Folk legend tells that the town was founded
by India's famous Buddhist, King Ashoka during his visit to
Nepal about 250 BC. It is likely, however, that Patan was built
or expanded during the reign of King Vara Dava around 298 AD,
serving as a royal seat. The royal court sat here until the 15th
century. Its ancient name is Lalitpur (= town of beauty). As the
capital of Buddhism in Nepal, the town of 60,000 harbors a
wealth of arts and crafts. Its richly decorated temples are well
worth a visit.
    The ride by bicycle is nicest via Kathmandu's southwestern
Teku district, and via the pedestrian suspension bridge across
the Bagmati River. Then head straight on to Pulchowki Hill, Ashoka Stupa (ask the way), and to Durbar Square.

## SIGHTS
**Durbar Square:** The **Royal Palace** was completed in 1640, the royal bath, **Sundari Chowk**, somewhat later. Plus there are several
small temples, and a Museum of little interest.
**Hiranja Varna Mahavihar:** The Golden Temple, a three-storey,
gold-plated pagoda, was built in honor of Buddha by King Bhas-
kar Verma in the 13th century. Upstairs is a Buddha statue and
a large prayer wheel. Remove your shoes before entering the
Golden Temple!

**Mahabuddha:** The Temple of 1000 Buddhas was built in the 14th century. Destroyed in a 1935 earthquake, it was exactly rebuilt. Every single brick shows a depiction of Buddha. Ask the way, it is too difficult to describe here.
**Krishna Madir:** Built in the 16th century by King Siddi Narasingh Malla in honor of Krishna. The frieze features relief depictions from the Hindu epics, **RAMAYANA** and **MAHABHARATA**. The columns in front show Garuda, the Messenger God, an incarnation of Vishnu, the 8th incarnation of Krishna.
**Jawalakhel:** This village, a ten-minute walk from Patan, features a Tibetan refugee camp in the form of a traditional round village. You can support the refugees by making direct purchases of handicrafts, including handmade carpets. But don't let misplaced sympathy motivate you into paying an outrageous price!

PATAN

Durbar Square

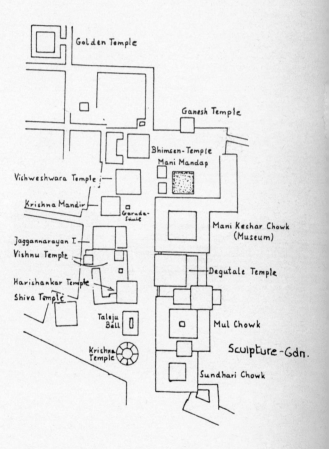

# Bhadgaon

The third largest of the ancient royal seats in Kathmandu Valley
is on a hill,  15 km east of Kathmandu.  40,000 people make their
homes in the town founded by King Ananda Malla in 889 AD.  Its
ancient name was Bhaktapur (= town of the boys).   The decayed
town has been completely restored since 1971 in an exemplary
development project financed by the West German Government.
Several million dollars,   and 15 workers from Germany were
allocated.   Local residents familiar with traditional crafts were
employed restoring their very own homes and temples,   and
installing a complete sewage system.  Rows of buildings shine in
age-old splendor.   For more information,   visit the exhibit and
information centre at Dattatreya Square.

## COMING – GOING

Come by bicycle or minibus from Kathmandu Bagh Bazaar (by
the Watch Tower),   costs 2.-Rs. The buses stop in Bhadgaon by
a large  artificial  reservoir  (Siddha Pokhari).   Occasionally
you've a lovely view of the Himalayas.   The electric bus from
Kathmandu National Stadium (1.-Rs) stops just outside town.

BHADGAON

Durbar Square

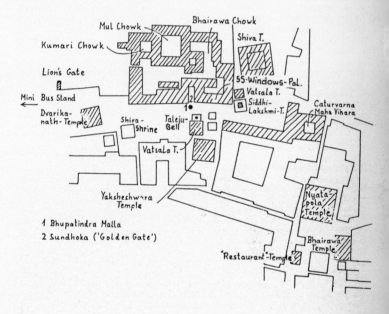

Mul Chowk

Bhairawa Chowk

Kumari Chowk

Shiva T.

Lion's Gate

55-Windows-Pal.

Mini Bus Stand

Vatsala T.

Dvarika-nath-Temple

Siddhi-Lakshmi-T.

Caturvarna Maha Vihara

Shira-Shrine

Taleju-Bell

Vatsala T.

Yaksheshwara Temple

Nyata pola Temple

1 Bhupalindra Malla
2 Sundhoka ('Golden Gate')

Bhairawa Temple

"Restaurant"-Temple

## SIGHTS

Bhadgaon is quieter than Kathmandu, but with almost as much to see.

**Durbar Square:** Features the **55-Window Palace** (1427), the **Lion's Gate**, **Golden Gate**, **Teleju Bell** (18th century). One look is worth a thousand words.

**Nyatapola Temple** (1708): The largest pagoda in Nepal, featuring five pedestals tapering toward the roof. The entrance is lined by, respectively, two wrestlers, elephants, lions, dragons, the Lion Goddess Singhini, and the Tiger Goddess Byaghini. Each of the statues is considered ten times more powerful than the previous statue. A small temple nearby on the same square (Taumadhi Thole) is now a restaurant.

**Tattreya Temple:** Built under Yaksha Malla in 1447 with wood from a single tree. The vaulted roof is richly decorated with erotic depictions; located just 1 km east of Durbar Square.

**The Peacock Window:** Considered the crowning piece of Nepalese woodcarving. It can be seen in the monastery behind the temple (Pujahari Math).

**Bhairavanath Temple:** Built originally as a one-storey temple designed to placate Bhairav, the Goddess of Terror (Kali). The upstairs was completed by 1718. As Bhairav was still unimpressed, construction of Nyatapola Temple (see above) was also begun. Restoration is complete! So pay a visit!

## AROUND KATHMANDU

**Changu Narayan:** North of Bhaktapur, 24 km from Kathmandu, on a hill visible far and wide. The most ancient temple in Kathmandu Valley. Dating from the 7th century, it is dedicated to the God Narayan (Vishnu). The temple is accessible only by foot, 2 h from Bhadgaon. On a column in front of Changu Narayan Temple is the most ancient inscription in Nepal, praising the deeds of King Manadeva (464-503 AD).

**Nagarkot:** At 2168 m, you have a great view of the Himalayas. Get a bus to Bhadgaon (from Bhag Bazaar), from the last bus stand, a minibus will take you on to Nagarkot. Or you can walk in 3-4 h from Bhadgaon. Nagarkot has several lodges, e.g. Everest Cottage, **(S)**10.-Rs. Or just ask at any house. Nagarkot Lodge is not recommended. The road up is paved, and an easy drive.

**Dhulikel:** Situated at 1650 m, on the Chinese Road, 32 km east of Kathmandu; there are a number of good reasons to visit. On clear days from October to March, you've a lovely view of the Himalayas. Buses depart hourly (4.50 Rs) from Bagh Bazaar, takes 90 minutes. Stay a couple days to enjoy a few quick treks! Dhulikel Lodge charges 20.-Rs per person. Everyone sits together for the evening meal, costs 10.-Rs.

**Bhagabati Temple:** To see the mountains by morning light, get up at 05:00 h and walk 30 minutes uphill. If you make it to the top, it is a rewarding experience, even when the mountains can't be seen.

**Treks:**  In a small brochure in Dhulikel Lodge,  exact details are provided for several treks. One heads for Panauti,  a village with an interesting temple.  Another trek visits Namobuddha, a monastery and meditation centre.  If you're interested in staying a while to study meditation,  just ask.  And,  of course,  you can enjoy shorter walks through the rice fields and hills.

**Panauti:**  Just a couple hours from Dhulikel,  Panauti is a Newar village featuring old ornamented buildings,  woodwork,  and temples.  They have seen better days.  One temple dates from the 15th century.  In January,  help celebrate **Makar Sankarati Festival.** Those joining the throng for a river swim have all their sins washed away.

**Namo Buddha:**  Equally accessible as an easy day trip from Dhulikel.  En route, take a break at some of the chai shops.  A small, white stupa is just below the peak of the tallest hill.  At the top is a Meditation Centre.  Just a few meters from the Meditation Centre,  an outcropping of rock is shrouded in legend.  Buddha is said to have been here when a tigress was killed by a hunter. Buddha discovered the tigress on this rock,  surrounded by her hungry litter. He felt such sympathy for the baby tigers that the Buddha divided his body into small pieces,  which he fed to the tiger kittens.  The litter survived. Another version of this legend is that a young prince performed this deed,  and was then killed by the wounded tigress.  As a reward for his good deed,  the prince was reincarnated as the Buddha.

**Kodari / Barabise:**  A bus trip to the border of the autonomous region of Tibet in the People's Republic of China is not always possible,  at least not all the way to the border.  Monsoon rains frequently wash out sections of road,  if not the last bridge before the Bridge of Friendship. In that case, the bus runs only as far as Barabise,  where a hydroelectric plant was built with Chinese aid.  The entire road was built with development aid from China. Surface mail between Nepal and China is transported along the road. Buses connect Kathmandu to Kodari (115 km), when running,  departing from Kathmandu GPO, reservations there are possible,  costs 30.-Rs.  The bus runs via Dhulikel.  At the border, photography is prohibited.

**Kakani:**  30 km north-west of Kathmandu,  near the paved road to Trisuli, also served by buses to Lainchaur. Have the driver show you where to get off,  then walk up to the observation point where you can see Ganesh (7409 m) and Langtang Himal (7246 m). To the west are Himalchuli (7892 m), Manaslu (8156 m) and Annapurna Massif (over 8000 m).

**Daman:**  On the road to the Indian Border at Raxaul / Birgunj, 80 km south of Kathmandu, at 2400 m, you've an exceptional view of the Himalayas.  An observation tower has been built.  The bus ride from Kathmandu takes 3 h.  Of interest as a stopover en route to the border,  or to Chitwan National Park (see Terai). Since completion of the road from Mugling to Narayangarh,  bus traffic has thinned out here.  A night's rest in the observation tower costs 15.-Rs per person.

# POKHARA

The second largest major valley in the central mountains of Nepal is Pokhara Valley (Kaski). At 900 m above sea level, it is 500 m lower than Kathmandu. And Pokhara is warmer; the lowest temperature ever measured was 8° C. Outside of monsoon season, it rains occasionally; but considering the temperature, it's pleasant.

The main attraction in Pokhara is Phewa Tal (Fewa Lake), with good swimming, and lots of lodges and restaurants. Next to Goa, it's the second largest freak colony on the subcontinent. And Pokhara is the drug capital of Nepal (marijuana and magic mushrooms). A few junkies, unfortunately, make the scene.

For trekkers, this your departure point for treks to Jomosom, Manang, Annapurna, plus countless one and two day treks. Certainly, Pokhara is the perfect vacation spot in Nepal for any type of holiday, lazing, swimming, mountain climbing, canoeing, and horseback riding.

Plus there is the unforgettable beauty of subtropical nature, combined with a view across just 30 km to Macchapuchare (6997 m), a mountain which has never been climbed! From some parts of Pokhara, you can see Annapurna I (8078 m), in the center of Annapurna Massif. It was the first 8000 m mountain ever surmounted, 3 June, 1950, by a French team, Herzog & Lachenal.

## COMING - GOING

Pokhara Valley can be visited without a trekking permit.

**By Air:**   Daily flights to Kathmandu and Jomosom. The RNAC Booking Office is at the airport.

**By Bus:**   From Kathmandu, get a minibus (40.-Rs) or Swiss bus (50.-Rs) at 07:00 h, 200 km, takes 6 h; by regular bus 8 h. Book one or two days ahead! Prithvi Highway was completed in 1972, with Chinese aid. Buses to Kathmandu drive along Phewa (also Fewa) Lake.

POKHARA

1   Money Exchange
    Hotels
    Trekking Shops
2   Cheap Hotels
    Restaurants
3   Island
    Vahari Temple
4   Royal Bungalow
5   Immigration Office
    Money Exchange
6   Pony Rentals
7   Tibetan Handicrafts Centre
8   Bus Station
9   Shining Hospital

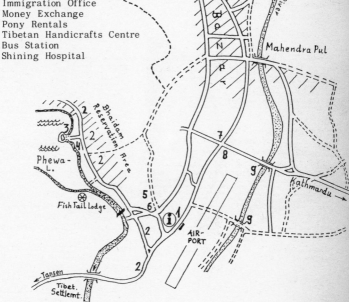

To Bhairawa or Birgunj on the Indian border, via Narayangarh (departure point for visits to Chitwan National Park), you
might have to change in Mugling to the bus from Kathmandu.
  Most lodges in Pokhara sell bus tickets to Kathmandu.  The
bus then stops in front of your door, at no extra charge.
**Around Town:** Use bus, bicycle, taxi, or taxibus.

## SIGHTS
Historic sights are lacking, but monuments of nature compensate:
  **Mahendra Gupha:** Stalactite caverns, near Batulechaur.
  **Seti Gorge:** 5 m wide, 50 m deep, below the first bridge on the
road to Kathmandu.

**Devin's Fall:** Also called Fadke.
**Sunrise:** Be sure to witness at least one sunrise (06:00–06:30 h)
over the panoramic mountains, Macchapuchara and the Annapurna Massif. Annapurna I (8091 m) becomes rose colored first.
Then other peaks according to their height.

Pokhara consists of three parts:
  **Mahendra Pul**: The northern bazar quarter.
  **Nagdunga**: The settlement by the airport, with Tourist Information, Immigration Office, trekking equipment shops, expensive
  hotels.
  **Baidam Reservation Area** (Lakeside): Where it's prettiest. Lodgings are spread along the large, warm lake.

**Hydroelectric Dam**: Has increased the size of Phewa Lake. Although the dam was briefly in service after completion in 1974,
needed repairs took it out of action until 11 August, 1982, when
a second dedication ceremony was held.
**Vahari Temple**: On the small island in the lake, by the royal
bungalow, dedicated to the goddess Vahari.
**Tibetan Handicrafts**: Available at the Tibetan settlements, Hyenja
in the north, Tashling in the south, in the Tibetan Handicrafts
Centre between the bazar and the airport, or from hawkers
around town.
**Doongas**: Dugout canoes, for rent, with a paddler 10.-Rs, without
just 6.-Rs.
**Pony Riding**: Costs 170.-Rs per day.

**A NIGHT'S REST**
  There are lodgings of every type with prices around 15.-Rs per
  person, but also with **(D)**20.-Rs. Huts and houses outside town,
  and across the lake, run at 200.- to 300.-Rs per month. A new
  area of cheap hotels has sprung up between the airport and
  the dam, south of the Immigration Office and the Money Exchange Booths. The classical cheap hotel district is further
  back, along the lakeside road. Again any hotel we'd name
  would be ruined by the time you got there.
  By the lake are restaurants, chai shops, stores, and bicycle
  rental offices.

**TIPS**
**Tourist Information Centre**: Between Hotel Mount Annapurna and
New Hotel Crystal, near the airport. Pick up the info brochure,
**Walker's Guide to Pokhara.** Nearby are:
  **RNAC Booking Office**
  **Trekking Equipment Shops**

**Post Office**: In the bazar.
**Immigration Office**: In Pardi, coming from the lake, head left at
the crossroads with the large tree, Sun-Fri 10:00–16:00 h, visa
extensions and trekking permits (see Kathmandu). No trekking
permit is required in Pokhara Valley.
**Exchange Counter**: At the Immigration Office, 10:00–18:00 h.
**Snowland**: Restaurant, also gives the bank exchange rate.

# TERAI

The Terai is a fertile flatland strip, running parallel to the Indian·border, 25-80 km wide, just 100 m above sea level, backed by Nepal's central mountains. The Terai's climatic and population structures are typical of northern India: tropical to subtropical, monsoon climate; with agriculture-oriented Indian tribes. But favorable infrastructure has attracted some industry to the region.

Traditionally, large sections of the Terai were only thinly populated due to malaria. Mosquitoes thrive in the meandering rivers flowing down from the Himalayas, through thick elephant grass and rain forest. With the exception of the Tharus, a people who over the centuries have developed a certain immunity to malaria, few immigrants stayed long to test their stamina against the fearsome illness. In the 1950s, economic conditions deteriorated in the mountains (partly due to topsoil erosion), and Nepal launched a major program to combat malaria. Quickly the population began to increase. As a result, large sections of grassland and rain forest were cut down to make room for settling farmers. Today, the Terai's population is increasing at 4 % annually!

## Chitwan National Park

Economic development jeopardizes the natural habitats of regional wildlife so severely that the extinction of several rare species, native to the region, is feared. The population of one-horned Indian rhinoceros declined from 800 in 1950 to just 100 in 1960. The rhino's natural habitat has been reduced to just one-fourth its original area. But hunting has also been spurred on in the popular Chinese belief in the aphrodisiac value of rhinoceros horn. The tiger too was considered fair game, because of its reputed danger to local inhabitants, and the popularity of its skin. In just a few years, modern hunters have participated in a feat of killing unequalled by centuries of hunting parties organized for Rana prime ministers and their guests.

In 1962, the Nepalese Government prohibited hunting in the Chitwan region, and created a nature reserve, protected by the armed and watchful eye of the Rhino Patrol. But the untrained, and ill-equipped guard faced a variety of problems. Finally the World Wildlife Fund and the United Nations Development Projects provided needed support to convert this region into a viable National Park. The region was fenced, and personnel trained. Chitwan was declared a closed region for local inhabitants. Occasionally someone will try to convince you not to visit Chitwan, claiming it is a closed military testing ground. Public relations, by park authorities, are evidently less than perfect.

Only at certain times are settlers permitted to enter the park for a controlled harvest of elephant grass, used to maintain their huts. Heavy logging in the region has led, even here, to sinking water levels. Erosion has been destructive.

The park grounds (500 km$^2$), at 120 m above sea level, on the Narayani River, are covered largely by rain forest and elephant grass 5 m tall. Three hundred of the world-wide population of 900 Indian rhinoceros make their homes here. Seventy of the last 2000 Bengali King Tigers find habitats here; 50 years ago, there were 40,000 on the subcontinent! Leopards, deer, bears, jackals, martens (cat), monkeys, and 300 species of bird abound. Two species of crocodile, for which there is a breeding station, live in the river branches.

**COMING – GOING**
  **By Air:** The expensive alternative, flights from Kathmandu to
Bharatpur.
  **By Bus:** Tandi Bazar is quicker and easier to reach from Kath-
mandu since completion of the new road from Mugling (on the
Kathmandu – Pokhara road) to Narayanghat, near the park.
Direct buses depart from Ratna Park in Kathmandu, takes 4 h
to Narayanghar(t).
  If you have the time, you might take a one-week swing
through Terai, we had fun!
  Buses run from Birgunj (2 h), direct to Tandi Bazar, near the
eastern park entrance. Lodgings are available should you ar-
rive late. Ask at the pub in the centre of town. Kathmandu to
Tandi (5 h, 30.-Rs).
  All buses between Bhairawa and Kathmandu or Pokhara run
via Narayangharh (25.-Rs), from where you've direct buses to
Hitaura and Birgunj, stopping in Tandi Bazar (3.-Rs).
  **From Tandi Bazar to the Park:** At the west end of the village,
a large wooden sign proclaims "Royal Chitwan National Park".
From here you've a 7 km walk to Sauhara at the east end of
the park. Along the way, you have to cross a river bed; a
difficulty which increases with the water level. It is a good
idea not to go alone. There are no regular connections.
  **Moving On:** Get an early start from Sauhara to Tandi, a 1.5 h
walk. From Tandi, buses at least half hourly to Narayanghar,
from where you've direct buses to Kathmandu, takes 4 h. From
Tandi, buses also to Hitaura, Birgunj and Bhairawa. If you
are heading to Pokhara, and can't get a direct bus, get a bus
toward Kathmandu and change in Mugling.


**A NIGHT'S REST**
  **Tiger Tops Jungle Lodge,** American owned, **(S)**US$90.-, including
all meals and transfers inside and outside the park, if money
is no object. Somewhat cheaper is **Tent Camp,** run by the same
company, just **(S)**US$36.-. At the east end of the park, **Hotel
Elephant Park,** **(S)**US$50.-, not including park admission and
drinks.
  In the village of Sauhara are a number of tea shops and
lodges, where you can enjoy a variety of food and **(S)**10.-Rs.
Several huts rent for 20.-Rs per night. Food is expensive.
  We had a great time celebrating Devali with a local family.
We really enjoyed ourselves here. In fact, Peter began the
first drafts of this book during his stay!


**TIPS**
**Museum:** Small, near the Sauhara park entrance, info on the
park's wildlife, creation, development, and problems, admission
free.
**Park Admission:** 65.-Rs per day.
**Elephant Rides:** 2 h and two passengers, costs 400.-Rs. Elephant
riding, outside the park, costs 100.-Rs per person for 2 h.

**Canoe Ride:** For two passengers to a spot where the crocodiles are sunning, costs 50.-Rs. Additionally, you'll have to pay a guide: costs 15.-Rs per person for a three-hour tour.

**Guides:** You are prohibited from entering the park without a guide. The lodges also provide guides for hikes both inside or outside the park. For a 4 h tour, think 30.-Rs.

**Observation Points:** At dawn and dusk, it's wonderful to observe the wildlife from the pile huts. Before heading out, check in the Museum, mentioned above, for info on how to behave when confronting animals, particularly in dangerous situations.

**Bicycle Rentals:** In Tandi Bazar (10.-Rs per day).

# Lumbini

Lumbini is the birthplace of the historical Buddha, who was born a prince, in southwestern Nepal, near Bhairawa, around 550 BC. There isn't a lot to see, but for 300 million Buddhists, this spot has the same importance as Jerusalem for Jews, Bethlehem for Christians, or Mecca for Muslims.

UN-sponsored excavations are underway. Plans call for new lodging construction, opening Lumbini to pilgrims and tourism.

## COMING - GOING

**By Air:** Flights from Kathmandu to Bhairawa, takes 40 minutes.

**By Bus:** From Kathmandu or Narayangarh, change in Bhairawa, see Chitwan Coming - Going. From Bhairawa, it's 22 km by bus to Lumbini. Taxis charge 300.-Rs per vehicle, round trip, including a long stay in Lumbini. Or hitch a ride with a truck.

If you cross the border from India for a brief stay of up to 48 h, no Nepalese visa is required, but you must return to India via the same border crossing.

## SIGHTS

**Ashoka Pillar:** Built in 250 BC on the orders of the Indian King Ashoka, himself a Buddhist, to honor the founder of his faith. The inscription is in Sanskrit. The broken pillar was unearthed in 1895 by a German archaeologist, Dr. Alois Anton Fürer.

**The Temple of Maya Devi:** A Buddhist temple and monastery, built in honor of Buddha's mother. Originally dedicated 1500 years ago, episodes from the Buddha's life are depicted in colorful wall paintings.

# TREKKING

Even if you are out of shape, and
sport never was your game, trekking is for you.   trek is one of
the most wonderful experiences you
can enjoy in Nepal.

When planning our first visit to
Nepal, we almost decided not to
trek. It seemed so complicated, all
those things to take with you. And
even after arriving in Nepal, we
still weren't sure what trekking
was all about. Strenuous work, ill-
fitting mountain boots, and ungodly
pounds of provisions to carry? Or
is it merely a pleasant walk:
bring your bath shoes?

We finally just took off with as
little as possible; too lazy to carry many provisions.   On the two
treks we did that year, to Jomosom and Helambu, you don't need
much more than a sleeping bag, which can be rented in Thamel
in Kathmandu, or in Pokhara for 5.-Rs per day. There is no need
to carry one around the subcontinent.  Other necessities include a
change of clothes, backpack, first aid kit, a pair of sneakers
with good traction (also available in Kathmandu or Pokhara),
thick socks, and a pair of thongs for evening wear. Some people
like to hike in thongs, which are okay along some routes. Most
Nepalese walk barefoot, but my feet wouldn't make it! More about
equipment below!

Before you head out, be sure you have a trekking permit,
available at any immigration office, see Nepal - Travel Tips.

The Jomosom trek is great for beginners, with good route infrastructure.  Once upon a time, a trading route (salt, silk,
scarves, and fur) ran north from Pokhara to Tibet.  The last
section before the border, in Mustang, is closed today for political reasons.

This is a trek for which you won't need porters, provisions,
nor a tent. You will need two to three weeks, and you're best off
in a small group.  The route meanders through rice fields, tropical forest, tropical mountain forest, steppe, and desert. You
cross meadows and rocky ground, through and over rivers.

We did this trek in a group of four, which minimized most problems. Some people like to walk fast, others want to look at the scenery. Everyone has their bad day with leeches or blisters. The more people you have, the better the likelihood that at least someone is in a good mood. At least on the first trek. Later you are better trained, and know how to pick yourself up when the hill has no end. Don't worry if everyone is passing you. You can sprawl in the grass every half hour. Everyone has those days.

Along the Jomosom trek route, food is excellent. Just the thought of a hearty meal was enough to keep me going. It is a wonderful feeling to be exhausted at the end of a day, in full contact with every part of your body.

**Equipment:** Backpack, sleeping bag, sturdy sneakers, bath shoes, thick socks (against blisters), salt against leeches (sprinkle on / rub into your legs), bandages, disinfectant or iodine (blisters and wounds), painkillers, something for a restless stomach, antibiotics, suntan lotion, sun protectors (scarf, hat), sunglasses, sweater and windbreaker or parka, change of clothes, wash kit. For a week of trekking expect to spend 400.-Rs. Check your excess baggage in a hotel and your valuables in a safe. Don't carry more than 6 kg per person!

**Trekking Season:** The best time to trek is October-November (warm, good visibility) or March-April (warm, rhododendrons in bloom). Your daily rhythm will follow the sun: up at 06:00 h when you've the best visibility, and early in bed. It is extremely dangerous to trek during monsoon season, and just afterward in September.

# Acute Mountain Sickness

On the treks described below, you can expect little real danger. But this is a disease which hits suddenly with dire consequences. No book about Nepal dares ignore the threat.

**Symptoms:** At 3000 m altitude, keep close watch for long-lasting headache, nausea, loss of appetite, insomnia. If you suspect AMS, don't climb any higher. If the symptoms persist after a long rest at the same altitude, then head downhill. If the symptoms go away you might continue climbing, but at a slower rate.

**Pace:** If you arrive at 3600 m and wish to continue climbing, spend at least two consecutive nights at this altitude. Afterward, don't climb more than 500 m per day. If such a climb can't be avoided, then climb to a maximum of 4200 m and then on the same day return to your base camp. On the second day you can try the entire route! But watch out for the above-mentioned symptoms! If you are careless, you can suddenly find yourself in big trouble!

**Danger Signals:** Further symptoms include loss of breath, even after rest; constant coughing with purging of watery or bloody slime; wheezing, with the sensation that you have a bubble in your lungs. These are symptoms of a pulmonary edema (water in the lungs). Equally dangerous are tremendous exhaustion, vomiting, unbearable headache, staggering walk, irrational behavior (e.g. depression or euphoria), fainting or temporary loss of consciousness. These are symptoms of a cerebral edema (water on the brain)! In either case descend immediately (at least 600 m), even at night, and even if someone must carry you. The quicker you get to a lower altitude, the better your chance of survival!

**Never Too Fast Too High!**
This is the title of a brochure published by the Himalaya Rescue Association, Durbar Marg, POB 283, Kathmandu, with detailed information on acute mountain sickness. The Association provides timely information to trekkers and climbers. Be sure to visit the Association if the trek you plan will exceed 4200 m! Nobody is completely safe from AMS; it has little to do with fitness and health. But those suffering from heart or lung ailments are twice as likely to succumb! Now don't panic; just keep close watch on yourself and you'll be okay. And have fun trekking!

**Conservation**: With all the talk about conservation these days, you'd think little need be said about the subject and Nepal. But Nepal's delicate ecological balance does make a few tips necessary. The following thoughts are courtesy of the Nepal Nature Conservation Society, which has its office in Kathmandu Guest House, Thamel.
1) If you buy eggs, chicken, fruit, vegetables, or handicrafts from villagers, you support the village economy, helping to preserve its independence from the central tourist industry.
2) Never buy animal skins, fresh game, or live animals. You would motivate people to maintain large herds which devastate the countryside and drive up prices.
3) Don't buy antiques or cult objects from temples or monasteries. The export of objects over 100 years old is prohibited, and you'd be plundering Nepal's cultural heritage. Things which you just consider pretty have great importance to Nepal!
4) Burn kerosene or other fuel you carry with you. Wood is in extremely short supply. Every tree cut for firewood intensifies Nepal's catastrophic environmental problem, erosion. Never buy wood!
5) If nothing else is available, burn only dead leaves and twigs lying on the ground!
6) Recheck the fire to be sure it is out before leaving the site.
7) Bury all trash, even that from your sloppy predecessor, and be sure your porters and guides do the same. Nepalese only know biologically degradable (clean) trash. Our civilization carries its own environmental problems with it. So we have a special responsibility.
8) Pitch camp only in designated spots, or on open ground not covered by vegetation, in order to preserve wildlife.

9) Don't cut your initials in trees or rock. They are prettier without your artwork.
10) Please obey national and local conservation laws, and National Park rules. Camping in National Parks is prohibited.
    **We Have Only Borrowed The Earth From Our Children!**

# Jomosom Trek

**Pokhara - Naudanda** (Day 1, 16 km, 6 h): Get an early-morning taxi to **Shining Hospital** in northern Pokhara. Jeep taxis depart from here to Suikhet (30.- to 40.-Rs) as soon as enough passengers are ready. This shortens the following walk by 2 h, giving you another 4 h to Naudanda.

From Shining Hospital it's 1.5 h to the Tibetan settlement, **Hyengja** (other spellings include Hengza). You have to cross an unbelievably small bridge. I get goose pimples just thinking back. But afterward there was no going back. From Hyengja (1070 m) it is 2 h either through a muddy rice field, or better, keep your feet dry with a slight curve to the right, to the small settlement **Suikhet** (1100 m), where you have to traverse your first stream. Then you head uphill to **Naudanda** (1460 m).

Just 200 m before the village, one member of our party collapsed under his backpack. But word of the chai shops and lodges ahead would invigorate the dead. When Peter removed his shoes and socks, he was shocked to discover five blood-sucking leeches. The first trekking permit check is in Naudanda.

**Naudanda - Birethanti** (Day 2, 10 km, 5 h): Get up early to enjoy the wonderful mountain panorama, breakfast well, get some tea in your flasks, and head out (3 h) over a small pass (1700 m) to **Khare** (1646 m) and **Lumle**. From Lumle you've 2 h, via **Chandrakot** (lodges, chai shops, 1563 m), and then down to **Birethanti** (1040 m) on the Modi Khola River. From Chandrakot it is all downhill, frequently with steps. Sometimes it is more tiring going downhill than uphill. Be sure to keep your knees bent (never stiffen up!), and don't try to brake at every step. Relax, go with the flow, find your natural rhythm, and let your knees bend to absorb the shock! At the bottom, after a few meters, you cross your first suspension bridge. See how quick you are into the very first lodge, fortunately a good one.

**Birethanti - Ulleri** (Day 3, 15 km, 6 h): In Birethanti at the end of the village, your trekking permit will be checked again. Follow the Bhurungi Khola uphill and down (3 h) to **Tirkhe** (1440 m). Refresh yourselves in the chai shops. This is where we separated the women from the girls. In fact it is so difficult that we let laziness have its way, and hired a porter to help us up the next hill. Actually he didn't carry us, just our bags, ahhh, part of the way. It is possible to find willing porters on a day

or half-day basis. An important point to keep in mind if you
worry about the weight of your pack and the shape of your
spine.

Leaving Tirkhe, you cross two suspension bridges, then it's
straight up, via stairs to **Ulleri** (2075 m). Again there are two
excellent lodges. While we were visiting, a festival was celebrated to which we were enthusiastically invited. We were given seats
of honor at a table with the village elders. Dances were performed, and our teacups never idled. Ulleri is a prosperous Magar village with stone-roofed buildings.

**Ulleri – Ghorepani** (Day 4, 8 km, 4 h): Other than the steady
climb, this is a pleasant day. Within 4 h you arrive in **Ghorepani** (2835 m), the village below the pass of the same name. The
entire way is through tropical mountain forest, occasionally
alongside a raging stream. Just inhale the nature! About half
way, in a clearing, is a house where you can get some tea if
you ask. Don't make too much noise, and you'll be able to see
families of monkeys playing along the last stretch before
Ghorepani.

Ghorepani is a tiny village. Stop at the very first building
on the right. Here you can get something to eat, and a fire
burns in the center of the room; very pleasant at this altitude.
It is a wonderful cottage atmosphere, great for settling down
with a good book until the light fails. Come evening, everyone
gathers around the fire and talks about leeches, acute mountain
sickness, and other pleasantries.

Between the top of the pass and Pun Hill, a five-minute walk,
is a second popular lodge. Another lodge is one hour before
Ghorepani.

Before sunrise, climb up **Pun Hill**, from where, if the weather's clear, you've a tremendous view of the Himalayas. Just follow the signs; takes at most an hour. At the top, there is a
wooden observation tower. If the weather doesn't co-operate, my
luck, then at least you are warmed up for the day's trek, and
breakfast is sure to taste better. Try again on the way back.

**Ghorepani – Tatopani** (Day 5, 16 km, 6 h): First a couple of
minutes up to **Ghorepani Pass** (2895 m), your greatest obstacle,
as high as most mountains in the Alps! It forms the watershed
for the Kali Gandaki River System, which you now follow. Then
downhill, through the rhododendron forest, and along the lightly
rolling trail through **Chitre** and **Phalata** to **Sikha** (2010 m), where
you'll find three lodges and a bite to eat. Then on to **Ghara**.
Just before the small pass in front of you, head steeply downhill
to **Tatopani** (1190 m), which again can be pretty strenuous. After
the suspension bridge, walk past the first few buildings, including a large empty building with a big yard. Kamalas Lodge
is the most popular here. Tatopani (= hot water) boasts a number
of springs. One is down by the river, but so low that during
high water, it lies submerged under the rushing stream. A second

JOMOSOM TREK

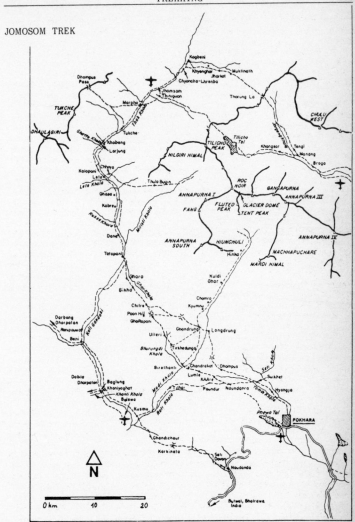

spring is behind the abandoned house. The water flows into a
basin; but not everyone finds a dip inviting. We survived. There
is another lovely spring downstream toward Beni; ask the way.

Tatopani is your last chance to stock up on delicacies. There
is a First Aid Station in case of emergency.

**Tatopani – Ghasa** (Day 6,   20 km,  7 h): The distance may seem a
lot,   but the going is generally easy;   you can make good time.
Follow the Kali Gandaki to **Dana** (3 h).   Keep by the river! Don't
let yourself be sidetracked by signs or other invitations to detour.  We made the mistake of following some idiotic scribble, and
it cost us a good hour. Your permit is again checked in Dana.

Further along (2 km) on your left is a lovely waterfall, **Ruk-
se Khola**,   and a small settlement with a watermill and a chai
shop.   Rest up,   a somewhat difficult,   but lovely stretch lies
ahead.   Follow the left side of the river (3 h) to **Ghasa**.   The
path,  hewn into rock,  has been washed away in spots.  Even
worse,  at the narrowest part of the gorge,  monkeys threw stones
at us.  But we made it, even without training as mountain climbers or animal tamers.   Beyond this narrow section of gorge is
Ghasa (2010 m),   a settlement of Thakali,   who are related to the
Tibetans,   and mercantile by tradition. This explains the relative
affluence of their village.   You might like to continue on to
Kalopani.

**Ghasa – Tukche** (Day 7,  20 km,  6 h): From Ghasa, head via **Lete**
to **Kalopani** (2400 m,   2 h).   Enjoy the tremendous mountain view.
There are two lodges.   On the next stretch you walk between
Dhaulagiri (8172 m) to the west and Annapurna Massif to the east
(Annapurna I is 8091 m).   The two peaks are just 35 km apart,
as the crow flies, making this the deepest gap in the world.

After Kalopani,   cross the bridge to the opposite bank.   After
an hour,   another bridge brings you back over to the west bank.
Then cross the deep cutting Kali Gandaki to Lujung (also spelled
Larjung,   2560 m).   Along the way you might have to ford a
branch of the river,   or detour to find a small bridge.   On the
return trip,   we met a herd of yaks being driven somewhere. A
group of Hindus, sharing the trail, actually persuaded us to ford
with them through the ice-cold water. If you get more than your
toes wet,   then warm up over tea in a Bhatti after crossing the
river.

From here on the country changes,   becoming drier and more
barren. Clouds rarely make it over the world's tallest mountains.
Follow the lightly rolling path through the meadows left of the
river to **Tukche** (2590 m).   You can see immediately that this was
a caravanserai,   with lovely buildings and monasteries. "Tuk"
means grain and "che" means flat place (a reference to the flat-
roofed buildings).   There are a number of lodges.   In November a
Masked Dance Festival is held.   Try to imagine this place as it

was when the caravans passed through, stopping to pick up fresh animals. This is part of the trade route connecting Tibet with India! You might continue on to Marpha (2 h).

**Tukche – Jomosom** (Day 8,  12 km,  4 h): If you haven't arrived already,  then today you head for **Marpha** (2600 m,  2 h). Get up early,  because a horrid wind picks up around 10:00–11:00 h, continuing until about 17:00 h.  Marpha is a place where you could stay a while.  Plan at least one day.  On the return trip, we stopped in Marpha,  bought some apples at the state–run model farm,  and had apple pancakes made for us in the lodge.  We spent the afternoon on the roof in a niche protected from the wind.  We even let ourselves be again talked into drinking butter tea. I might even get used to it.

But on to **Jomosom**:  Beyond Marpha,  try to keep by the river, plodding through the damp meadows left of the river,  until you get back on the main trail.  This way you save a half hour. Right by the STOL (Short Take Off & **Landing**), at the entrance to town,  are a number of lodges.  Jomosom (2713 m) is ugly,  and there is little to do here.  A good reason to continue right on to **Kagbeni** (2 h). You can get here an entire day earlier if you are in good shape,  or already have trekking experience.  But why hurry?  This is a holiday.  We did meet one Japanese,  or rather saw him passing by,  briefly;  he made it to Muktinath in four days!

**Jomosom – Muktinath** (Day 9, 20 km, 6 h): On the hill right of the river, and along the riverbed, head for the lonely tea shop (2 h) beyond the large gravel river bed, jutting out from the right. Now step up your pace, or you'll get caught in the wind before you make it uphill. Two villages along the way are **Khingar** and **Jharkot**; both offer lodgings for the night.

Polyandry (having more than one husband) is still practised here. The village belongs traditionally, as does this entire valley, to Mustang, a region you are prohibited from entering further. The architecture here is unusual, reminiscent of a castle. The people have an appearance all their own.

After another 2 h, you arrive in **Muktinath** (3820 m), where you sleep in the large building below the temple, called the King's House, though certainly less than royal: wooden beds, no blankets. In the evening, walk up to the Temple and Monastery to see the **Flaming Water**: from a gash in the earth, both water and natural gas pour forth, creating a unity of the four sacred elements earth, air, water, fire, symbolizing the Almighty.

From Kagbeni, you can make a day trip up to Muktinath and return; it is 4 h up and 2.5 h back down.

Or you might make the return trip via Kagbeni, lodgings available. Careful that you don't meet a sandstorm down in the valley, horrid in the early afternoon. The gusts of wind are powerful, filling your clothes, nose, eyes, and ears with sand. Every step is difficult. We know from experience. Our friend Klaus experienced the first symptoms of acute mountain sickness on this stretch! Be sure to read the AMS section above. The disease is a danger above 3000 m, and here it's almost 4000 m. The trek to **Manang** and on to **Pokhara** is now open to tourists. But for that trek you'll need better equipment, depending on snow conditions, and extra provisions to get you over a 5000 m pass beyond Muktinath.


### HEADING BACK

**Muktinath – Jomosom** (20 km, 5 h, via **Kagbeni** 6-7 h): The route back from Jomosom is child's play, now that you're experienced trekkers. Besides, you are familiar with the route, know where to turn, and what to expect. At **Tatopani**, you have a variety of choices for your return route, e.g. south via **Beni**, **Baglung** (STOL – Short Take Off & Landing) and **Kusma**, **Naudanda**. Or north via **Ghandrung**, see below.

For your orientation, we list below the travel times you should calculate for the return trip. You decide where to allocate additional time for rest. These times, however, are certainly not possible for anyone who against all advice, flies to Jomosom with the intention of trekking back. You'd be out of trekking condition, and need much longer! The numbers between the village names indicate march time:

**Muktinath** – 7 h – **Jomosom** – 1.5 h – **Marpha** (1st day). Marpha – 1.5 h – **Tuchke** – 1 h – **Lujung** – 4 h – **Lete** (2nd day). Lete – 2 h – **Ghasa** – 3 h – **Dana** – 1.5 h – **Tatopani**

(3rd day). Tatopani – 2 h – **Ghara** – 1 h – **Sikha** – 3 h – **Gorepani** (4th day). Gorepani – 2.5 h – **Ulleri** – 4 h – **Birethanti** (5th day). Birethanti – 2.5 h – **Lumle** – 3 h – **Naudanda** (6th day). Naudanda – 3.5 h – **Sarankhot** – 3.5 h – **Phewa Valley** – 1 h – airport. If you're in a big hurry, you can make it in five days. Lodgings available in all the above villages. Let's go!

# Alternative Routes

**Ghorepani – Ghandrung** (20 km, 7 h): A guide is recommended when there is snow on the trail. And you are best off in a group, since there have been robberies. 30 m from Poon Hill Lodge, a sign points the way to Ghandrung. From here, take a right, uphill to 3200 m (great view, as from Poon Hill, of Annapurna). Now constantly downhill, following the small beaten path, to a chai shop. Here take the path to the right, into the virgin forest. After a few minutes you will see a stream off to the right, which you can follow downstream to a sudden clearing with two lodges. This settlement is called **Barthante.** Get a bite to eat. From here, keep going downhill (great view of Ulleri), until, at the bottom, you run into a small river. Cross it, and go uphill, steep, 20 minutes. In **Tadapani** (2650 m) are four lodges. From here it is downhill. The small well-trodden path is easy to follow. It leads through lovely jungle to **Ghandrung.** Almost at the end of Ghandrung are several lodges, including Fish Tail Lodge with a unique view of Landrung, and Machhapuchare. Also good, Annapurna and Himalayan Trekkers Lodge.

**Ghandrung – Dhampus** (8 h): From Ghandrung, continue downhill to **Modi Kola** (1370 m). Then it's uphill to **Landrung** (1645 m), **Tolka** (six lodges), and over **Pothana Pass** (2165 m, four lodges) where you can eat and sleep. Great, view of Machhapuchare and Phewa Lake.

**Dhampus – Pokhara** (6 h):   From Dhampus follow the path via **Suikhet** (1100 m), which is half way along the trail. Then on to **Pokhara**.

The alternative route from Ghandrung to Pokhara runs via **Seule Bhati** to **Chanderkot**, back on the old route. The path leads diagonally across the slope, downhill (roughly toward Birethanti) to **Seule-Bhati**. Then along the river, don't cross the metal bridge, but cross the second wooden bridge and head through the big rocks to the first village. Now take a right on the well-maintained stepped path to **Chanderkot**, where you are back on the old trail, takes 5 h.

From **Ghandrung**, you can also walk to **Dumphus** and back.

**Tatopani – Beni** (Day 1, 7 h): For the return trip, you might try the southern variation via **Beni** and **Kusma**. From **Tatopani**, head first to **Beni** (7 h). At first it is up and downhill. After 3 h, there is a small lodge next to a suspension bridge. Beni is quite large, with several lodges.

**Beni – Kusma** (Day 2, 8 h): At first the trail has few hills, and the scenery is lovely. Just before **Kusma**, you climb a steep hill, perhaps 30 minutes. Kusma, like Beni, is large, with a doctor, and lots of lodges.

**Kusma – Naudanda** (Day 3, 9 h): Beyond Kusma you head down to the riverbed, then again uphill, takes 1 h, great view of the mountains. After another hour, you have a 2 h climb, to **Karkineta** (doctor, lodges). From Karkineta it is 1 h down to the river. Then 4 h along the river to **Naudanda**. Just before Naudanda, you've a steep hill to climb, takes 30 minutes. The scenery is lovely; lots of fields, everything in green. Buses from Naudanda until 20:00 h. To avoid darkness on the trail, be sure to get here before 18:00 h. This Naudanda is on the road from Terai to Pokhara.

# Helambu Trek

This trek through the Helambu region, north of Kathmandu, is the perfect trek for short timers. It is a quick trek you can do in seven days, starting right from the capital, but you don't have to hurry. Unlike the Jomosom route, there are few lodges, but you can find lodgings with a family in almost any house. What better way to sample Nepalese life?

You meet two new peoples:
**The Tamang**: Live in clay houses, not very affluent.
**The Sherpas**: Never cease to amaze you. Fantastically carved cabinets; old, shiny bowls which mirror the floor; open fireplaces in the rooms; and carved beds. Keep in mind that the Sherpas are a merchant people. They frequently charge double the going rate for food and lodgings, and sell expensive souvenirs, which are easy to find and cheaper in Kathmandu.

The route described below is the simplest through Helambu. The scenery is prettier, but the trail is harder, from Pati Bhanjyang via Kutumsang, Tare, and Tati, in three days to Tarke Ghyang. This variation is detailed at the end. Okay, let's go!

**Sundarijal – Pati Bhanjyang** (Day 1, 17 km, 6 h): From Kathmandu a minibus departs several times daily, from the Ratna Park Bus Stand to Sundarijal. Get as early a start as possible, so that after the good hour's ride (15 km), you can cover the first stretch to **Sundarijal**. By taxi, think 50.-Rs, takes 40 minutes. If you can't get out of Kathmandu before noon, you are best off spending a night in Sundarijal (1600 m), where you can stay in a chai shop.
   From Sundarijal, climb the water pipeline stairs to **Mulkhara** (1768 m, 1 h). Another 2 h climb brings you up to **Buslang Bhanjyang** (2438 m). Then head downhill to **Chisapani**, before a steep drop down to the Tamang village, **Pati Bhanjyang** (also Bhayang, 1850 m). Here is a small shop where you can spend the night and pick up provisions.

**Pati Bhanjyang – Taramanang** (Day 2, 12 km, 6 h): First a short stretch uphill, then at the fork, head right (east), steeply uphill, then along the slope. At the Tamang village, **Thakani**, head down to the river, toward **Kabre** (1670 m). The scenery is fantastic along the entire route. Cross the river by the watermill, and follow the slope to **Taramanang** where your permit is checked. Keep asking the way! You can stay the night at a chai shop, sleeping on mats out on a balcony.
   Notice the large suspension bridge. Take a dip in the river, preferably at the spot where the locals swim. But since only men frequent the spot, women should wait for a convenient moment.

**Taramanang – Thimbu** (Day 3, 18 km, 6 h): Follow the Malemchi River along the wide path, slightly downhill to the second suspension bridge. Cross the river. In **Keul** (1460 m), you can have a meal, and if you're in no hurry, spend a night.
   From Keul, the route runs up and downhill to **Thimbu** (1540 m), a Sherpa and Tamang village. The Sherpa houses are easy to recognize with their white prayer flags. We rented an entire house here.

**Thimbu – Tarke Ghyang** (Day 4,   16 km,   6 h): It's a steep hill
up to the lovely Sherpa village,   **Kakani** (2060 m,   7 km),   but a
tremendous view is your reward. If you don't feel like continuing
on,   spend a night here.   You can stay with a Sherpa family. If
you're lucky, you'll be offered the family bed.

Should you want to continue on,   it is 10 km up a wooded
slope,   then across a flat stretch to **Tarke Ghyang** (2560 m).   As
there is no lodge,   stay with a family in the lovely Sherpa village, with a monastery. This is a spot to spend several days.

Tarke Ghyang is a typical village of affluent traders,   living
in two-storey buildings, pressed close together, with prayer flags
waving in front.   On the lower floor are the storerooms and
stalls.   The small families live upstairs. The rooms center around
a fireplace.   Since there is no chimney, the rooms can get smoky,
which keeps vermin away,   and impregnates the roof.   There is
usually an altar at the end of the bed.   Sherpas traditionally
enjoy bargaining,   and you can buy or trade for cheap turquoise
and coral.

Along this trek,   you'll quickly notice the difference between
the relatively affluent Sherpas,   often with splendidly decorated
houses, and the Tamang with their impoverished dwellings.

If you plan to stay a while,   get up early one morning and
make the 4 h climb up to the observation point on **Yangri Danda**
(4050 m),   where,   if the weather is good,   you have a breath-
taking view of the Himalayas.

During our visit to Tarke Ghyang,   a Mani Rimdu (masked-
dance) Festival was held.   We were heartily invited to join the
festivities.   Organized by the monastery,   the festival began with
lots of food,   tremendous amounts of Rakshi were drunk,   and a
masked dance performed.   Then everyone paraded through town to
chase away the evil spirits.

If you have the time,   try to spend a couple of days. This is
a convenient   departure   point   for   the   Gosainkund or Langtang
treks. But from Tarke Ghyang, you have to cross **Thare Pati Pass**
(5123 m),   requiring ample provisions.   Along those treks,   it is
advisable to take a porter who knows the region well.   And there
have been a number of robberies where trekkers were held up.
One person we talked with was badly mistreated.   So never go
alone!

**Tarke Ghyang – Sermathang** (Day 5, 10 km, 4 h): This is a pleasant day!   Along the easy trail,   traversing the slope,   you are
soon in **Sermathang** (2500 m).   Here you'll find a monastery and
apple orchard. Stay with a family, and relax, enjoy the view.

**Sermathang – Malemchi Phul** (25 km,   7 h): Today it is all downhill, so you make good time to **Kakani** (1900 m) and then on down
to **Malemchi** (800 m).   In just one day you have descended from
the highest point of the trek (2500 m),   losing 1700 m in altitude.
Imagine what the opposite direction would be like. But descending
can be strenuous too.   Just before the river in Malemchi is the

HELAMBU
LANGTANG

clean Malemchi Lodge, the only lodge far and wide. Other possibilities for food and lodgings in the village include the three-
storey building. Here too, you can inquire about the quickest
connection to Kathmandu. A minibus departs from **Sipagat** (10.-Rs,
3 h) to **Banepa**, where you change minibuses (4.-Rs, 1.5 h) to
**Kathmandu**. Otherwise, continue trekking to **Panchkal**.

Food along the trekking route is less than varied: rice with
porridge made of shelled linseed (dhal). Occasionally the Sherpas
provide some meat. Although we ate the same thing every day,
the food tasted different each time. You can live on dhal bhat
for a week!

**Malemchi (Phul) - Panchkhal** (Day 7, 28 km, 7 h): No big hills
along the dirt road to **Bahunepati**, several chai shops invite
rest. Then a long walk along the river, great for a swim, and a
small hill up to **Rowapati**. Then another 2 h to the bus stand in
**Panchkal**, where you climb your last hill (950 m). Congratula-
tions, you made it! The last 400 m altitude, and 55 km to **Kathmandu**, can be left to the bus, several daily, takes 2 h. If you
miss the bus, you might hitch a ride with a truck to Kathmandu.

The village, above the bus stand, is easy to recognize with
its many chai shops.

The last stretch of the trek, at 800 m to 900 m, is at an
altitude much lower than Kathmandu. Temperatures, even in February, can be quite warm. We did the trek in April, and sweated
considerably.

**Trekking On:** An inviting stop on the road to Kathmandu, for
those not yet ready for city bustle, is the pass village, **Dhulikhel** (see there). So disembark and get a room in Dhulikhel Lodge.
Why not try a few day treks in the area? You've a tremendous
view of the Himalayan mountains from the lookout point.

On the return trip, you might try this variation: from **Rowapati**, don't head for Panchkhal rather go to **Nagarkot** (2168 m).
Due to the great difference in altitude, and the steep climb,
spend a night in Rowapati. Then, when you're well rested, continue on to Nagarkot and its lovely sunrise view (see Nagarkot).
From Nagarkot, you've a 2 h descent to **Bhadgaon**, and from
there minibuses to Kathmandu. The entire trek is extended by at
least a day!

## VARIATIONS ON THE HELAMBU TREK
**Sundarijal - Pati Bhanjyang** (Day 1, 17 km, 6 h): Same as
above.

**Pati Bhanjyang - Kutumsang** (Day 2, 6 h): From Pati Bhanjyang,
instead of taking the fork to the right, go left. The trail winds
uphill, 2 h, to **Chipling** (2165 m), where, unfortunately, no tea
or other service is provided. After another 2 h, you reach **Gul
Bhanjyang** (2142 m), where food is available. The path rolls up
and downhill. From here it is 2 h to **Kutumsang**, where three

buildings are home to several rather poor Sherpas. You can stay
the night in the house to the right of the trail. Bargain,   4.-Rs
was demanded,   we paid 2.-Rs.  Five minutes further is a single
building, a lodge, **(S)**5.-Rs.

**Kutumsang – Thare Pati** or **Kutumsang – Malemchigaon** (Day 3,
18 km or 20 km,   8 h): Go left at the lodge. This is a hard day,
steep uphill,   and not a single village or house before evening!
So carry plenty of provisions. About halfway, you reach a hilltop
clearing where you have a tremendous view of the snow-covered
peaks.   There is a fireplace, and enough dead wood lying around
for a small campfire.  After a total of 5-6 h (calculated from
Kutumsang),   you'll see a couple of abandoned houses in a small
valley around a spring.   And again after another hour.   Here
you'll find a pole with a white flag,   and painted sign above a
rock saying "Thare Pati Hotel - Good Food".   This is referring to
the trail to the left.  Otherwise,   no villages nor anything.   The
Thare Pati Hotel is an isolated wooden hut where accommodations
are provided,   2.-Rs for a night around a warm fire.  Food is a
bit expensive,   as you'd expect in such an isolated spot at this
altitude.   It is a great place to spend a night at 3600 m,   and
enjoy a tremendous sunrise above the mountains and clouds. From
the fork in the trail mentioned above,   it is an hour's walk.  If
you don't feel like going there, take the path to the right at the
fork.  In a good 2 h,  downhill, you reach the lovely, and affluent Sherpa village, Malemchigaon (2560 m).

**Thare Pati – Tarke Ghyang** (Day 4, 10 km, 8 h): From Thare Pati
it is steeply downhill,   through lovely virgin forest,   with ferns
and knotted trees,   to **Malemchigaon.** Cross the bridge just before
the village.  From here,   carry on to **Tarke Ghyang.** On the map,
the route seems like a frolic.  And Tarke Ghyand is at the same
altitude as Malemchigaon (256 m).   The map doesn't show a steep
descent (600 m) in between,   across a suspension bridge,   and a
steep climb of 600 m. A very strenuous trek.

# Alternative Routes

**Gosainkund Trek:** Eight days from Trisuli Bazar to Sundarijal.
**Langtang Trek:** Seven days from Trisuli Bazar round trip.
**Everest Trek:**  Thirteen days,  from Jiri to Tengboche, then on to
Lukla, for a return flight to Kathmandu.
**Rolwalking Tal:** An eight-day trek from Barabise to Beding.

# Collapsed

During a bicycle tour to Patan,   on the hill,   after the big
bridge,   a couple of workmen asked us to help them push their
three-wheeled cart, laden with teakwood, up the steep incline. At

first I didn't want to, but then the idea hit me: why not do
some work? So Barbara pushed our bikes while I lent the three
Nepalese a hand. Great, doing something productive! Light of
foot, full of energy, up the hill. After a while my strength began to wane, my legs grew heavy, my breath was short, sweat
flowed. How had the three made it this far without me? It seemed
that even the four of us weren't going to get that cart up the
hill. I was completely exhausted, sweat flowed into my eyes, and
I couldn't hold on any more; my arms were killing me. I fought
the urge to give up. And the mountain kept getting higher and
higher. Suddenly a road off to the left appeared as my savior. I
had a valid reason to stop. I just had to say we turn off here.
The last hundred meters were pure torture. I've never
experienced anything like it, and I am a workman by trade. Was
I pushing the cart by myself, or were they pulling back
downhill? And they kept talking among themselves! Absolutely
crazy! And this for 10.-Rs per day. When we reached that lovely
crossroads, I've never been so happy to see a street in my life.
I walked with my most determined gait over to my bicycle and
declined even the nicest request to help with the last stretch.
They should find another idiot!

When I got off my bike at Durbar Square in Patan, a queer
sensation consumed me: dizziness, upset stomach. This is when I
really began to sweat. I felt as if my shirt was made of rubber.
I had to sit down: anywhere. Should I throw up, sit on the toilet, get a drink? I didn't know what to do. Lie down: that's
better. Where is a toilet? Immediately! Barbara ran off to find a
spot. She never returned. An eternity passed. I can't drop my
pants in the square. Finally I went through the nearest door,
through a courtyard, another door, everything goes black... A
wall, unbuckle... bowels empty... Slowly I regained consciousness. Lie down, lie down. And I couldn't believe my eyes: a
bench. The first bench I'd seen since Greece. I fell on top. I'm
safe. My breath pants irregularly, ever faster, can't breathe...
Everything black again... Death could never be worse... Headache, completely wet, wet? Why wet? I fell asleep, and was wok-
en by a soft rain. Barbara has found me. I got up, she helped
me, swaying. That's better. At least until the next teahouse. And
they do that for under a dollar a day!

# SRI LANKA

# COUNTRY & CULTURE

## GEOGRAPHY

Like a drop in the Indian Ocean,
the island of Sri Lanka (= the
glow) is 36 km off the southern tip
of India. Across the Palk Strait, a
series of sandbanks, islands and
reefs, known as Adam's Bridge,
marks a now sunken land connection. Most of the island is lowland, particularly in the north.
There are three levels of mountains: in the north ranging from
500 m to 1000 m; the interior
mountains rise up to 2000 m; while
the high mountains include Adam's
Peak (2240 m) and the tallest,
Pidurutalagala (2528 m).

**Wet Region:** Consists of the south-west where seven months of rain
keep the evergreen tropical rain forest luscious. The central
mountains provide some of the world's greatest tea, from plantations spread throughout the tropical mountain forests.

**Dry Region:** Areas of varied precipitation, in the north and east
of the island.

**Position:** The island lies between 80° and 82° longitude and between 5.6° to 10° northern latitude. The island runs 450 km north
to south and 230 km east to west. Total area is 66,000 km$^2$.

## Climate & Travel Seasons

The Sri Lanka Tourist Office advertises that any season is the
right season to visit Sri Lanka, and it's true! But there are
seasonal variations to keep in mind. In temperate regions, e.g.
northern Europe or North America, temperature swings determine
seasons; in the tropics it is rainfall. No wonder monsoon (from
Arabic "mausim") means season.

**Southwest Monsoon** (Great Monsoon): Beginning around the end of
April, steady winds from the south-west bring water from the Indian Ocean to southern Asia. Moisture gathered over thousands of
miles of ocean is dumped when warm ocean air is pushed upward

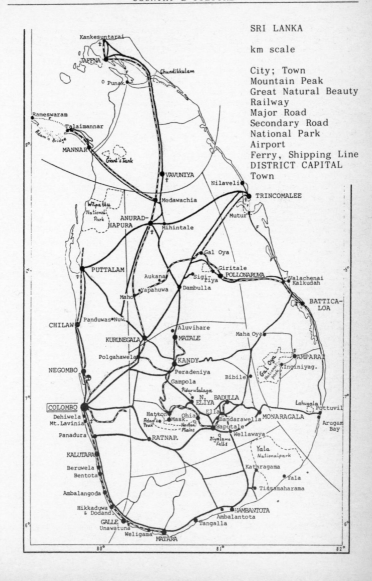

SRI LANKA

km scale

City; Town
Mountain Peak
Great Natural Beauty
Railway
Major Road
Secondary Road
National Park
Airport
Ferry, Shipping Line
DISTRICT CAPITAL
Town

to cooler altitudes by a land mass. In the western mountains, drenching rains, sometimes lasting days, can drown the spirits of even the hardiest traveller. But the heaviest rains end by mid-June, well before tourism picks up. Off-season prices are the rule along the southwest coast and in the mountains. But high seas require caution. Swim only behind protective reefs, at least until September. High humidity makes this season less than optimal.

**North-East Monsoon:** Along the east coast and in the eastern mountains, the smaller North-East Monsoon drops precipitation from November to January. Only the southeast coast remains unaffected. The best time to visit the east is from March to September. Seasonal prices reach their peak from the end of May to early September.

**Tourist Season:** Along the western and southern coasts, in the mountains, and in the historic central region, the main tourist season runs from November to March. Precipitation is low; thousands of European tourists come to escape winter in the tropics. But demand pushes up prices, reaching a peak during Christmas.

**Travel Weather:** From the end of February to early April, you've ideal travel weather everywhere on the island. However, 75 % of all hotel bookings are made in the south-west where tourism is most apparent.

**Climate:** Sri Lanka, as an island near the equator, enjoys a tropical monsoon climate, with average temperatures ranging from 30° C (86° F) during winter to 35° C in summer. In the mountains, daytime temperatures of 22° C can creep as low as 10° to 16° C at night, with occasional frost.

The warmest months are March and April when the sun is directly above Sri Lanka. Thereafter the southwest monsoon brings rain from May to August, particularly in the south-west. In the north and east of the island, the major rains come with the northeast monsoon in December and January. In the mountains you can expect rain, about 450 cm annually. Other regions, e.g. the northern flatlands and the south-east, are dry, almost desert.

# PEOPLE

Sri Lanka's almost 15 million are 72 % Singhalese,  11 % Ceylon-
Tamils,  9 % Indian Tamils,  6 % Moor (descendants of immigrated
Arabs),  and 4 % other ethnic groups including Burgher of Dutch
origin,  Portuguese,  Eurasians,  Malays,  various ethnic groups
found in India (e.g.  Parsee, Bohra, and Sindhi), and the Vedda
(a 500-strong community of ancient inhabitants living a simple
life in isolated mountain regions).  23 % of the population are
city dwellers,  68 % live off the land,  and 9 % on plantation
settlements.

**The Singhalese:** A farming people. Unlike lowland Singhalese, who
have been exposed to western influence for centuries,  the
highland Singhalese maintain much of their ethnic tradition.

**The Tamils:** The Sri Lankan Tamil population has immigrated here
over the centuries from southern India,  settling primarily in the
north and east of the island.  The "Indian Tamils" were imported
by the British during colonial rule as plantation workers.

**The Moors:** Descendants of Arab merchants,  who,  true to their
heritage,  are largely engaged in trade (precious stones) and in
service industries.

**Castes:** Despite the preponderance of casteless Buddhism as the
main religion,  a Hindu-oriented caste system determines social
structure.  The highest caste is the nobleman farmer,  to which
most Singhalese belong.

# A Few Words of Singhalese & Tamil

Since 1963 Singhalese has been the national language. Tamil is used as the official language in the north, and Tamils have the right to use their minority language in all dealings with government officials anywhere in the country. English serves as the language of commerce and education, and is spoken by the upper classes. English is taught in the schools, and most signs are in English. Generally you'll have no trouble getting by with English. Only off the beaten path will you have a problem being understood. That's why it is important to know a few words of local language.

Sometimes, gestures can be even more important than words: instead of "thank you", Singhalese often just smile. With the word of greeting "Ayubowan" (or instead of speaking) place your hands on your breast below the chin, bow slightly and smile. A wagging of the head from side to side means a definite "Yes"; don't let yourself be confused! A slight nodding of the head means "No"! Many modern words are taken from English with an added "ekak" suffix, or "kenek" referring to people. Best known is "Draiver-kenek" for "Bus Driver".

|               | Singhalese     | Tamil            |
|---------------|----------------|------------------|
| greetings     | ayubowan       | vanakkam         |
| please        | Karunakara     | Tajavu sai du    |
| thank you     | Estuti         | Nandri           |
| pardon        | samavenna      | mannijungal      |
| yes           | ou             | ahm              |
| no            | nä, naa        | illai            |
| room          | kaamare        |                  |
| bed           | anda           |                  |
| food          | kaama          | sappidu          |
| tee           | tea            | chai             |
| how much?     | kijada?        | vilai enna       |
| bus           | bas-eka        |                  |
| train station | stanaja        |                  |
| hotel         | hootale        |                  |
| toilet        | wäsikiliye     |                  |
| line, number  | ankeye         |                  |
| 1             | eka            | on dru           |
| 2             | deka           | irandu           |
| 3             | tuna           | moondru          |
| 4             | hathara        | naangu           |
| 5             | paha           | ejendu           |
| 6             | haja           | aaru             |
| 7             | hatha          | eilu             |
| 8             | ata            | ettu             |
| 9             | namaja         | onbadu           |
| 10            | dahaja         | pattu            |
| 100           | sija           | nooru            |
| 1000          | daaha          | aajiram          |

# RELIGION

According to a 1978 study, 69 % of the population practise Buddhism, 18 % Hinduism, 8 % Christianity, and 7 % Islam. These statistics follow closely the ethnic make-up (72 % Singhalese, 20 % Tamil, 6 % Moor, and 4 % others). However, studies differ by several percentage point as to the exact division. Sri Lanka's Buddhist heritage is seen as a special governmental responsibility. But other religions are tolerated. All across the country you'll find churches, temples, mosques, and dagobas. Occasionally these are revered by several religious communities. For an interesting look at Buddhism, browse through the Buddhist Publication Society in Kandy, lots of English-language books.

**Buddhism:** Founded in northern India, and brought to Sri Lanka around 250 BC by Emperor Ashoka. The meeting between Mahinda, son of Ashoka, and his accompanying Buddhist monks, with King Tissa took place at Mihintale.

**Hinayana Buddhism:** There are two major branches of Buddhist teaching: Hinayana Buddhism (small vehicle) and Mahayana Buddhism (great vehicle), See India & Nepal, Country & Culture. Singhalese practise Hinayana Buddhism, but call their faith Theravada Buddhism.

**Monks:** Today many young monks are returning to the original teachings, and choosing to live in a forest monastery. This movement finds approval among many Buddhists. There have been complaints about monks not taking their role as monks seriously, being too concerned about priestly privilege, too interested in worldly matters. It is not forgotten that the Singhalese President Bandaranaika was shot by a Buddhist monk. Buddha distanced himself from politics, which he considered bad for karma.

**Chosen People:** Singhalese newspapers are full of articles hailing the Singhalese as a chosen people with a mission to save Buddhism. Any concessions to the Tamils would mean the eradication of the Singhalese race and the end of Buddhism. Such ideas are far from Buddha's original teaching.

**Arabs:** Most members of Sri Lanka's Muslim congregation are descendants of Arab merchants who settled here centuries ago.


FESTIVALS AND HOLIDAYS

Most of Sri Lanka's festivals have religious origins: Buddhism,
Hinduism, Islam, and Christianity. The traditional Buddhist calendar is based on phases of the moon, making every full moon
day a holiday. Dates of these holidays vary from year to year,
check with the Tourist Office for exact days during your visit.
**JANUARY**
   **Duruthu Perahera:** A Buddhist festival, at Kelani Temple, 10 km
   from Colombo, during Duruthu Perahera full moon. The festival
   is second in importance only to Esala Perahera Festival in
   Kandy. Celebrating Buddha's visit and meeting with the Na-
   garaja King in the 5th century BC.
   **Thai Pongal:** A Hindu Festival in honor of the Sun God, on the
   14th of January; also thanksgiving.
   **Adam's Peak:** Traditional pilgrimages by people of all faiths.
**FEBRUARY**
   **Independence Day:** 4th of February, celebrated with parades
   and processions.
   **Adam's Peak:** Crowds of pilgrims hike on the brightly-lit hill.
   **Navam Perahera:** A procession with elephants, dancers, and
   Buddhist monks, lasting two nights through Colombo's streets,
   organized by Gangarama Temple, Hunupitiya Road, Colombo 3

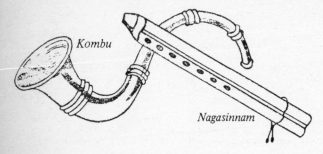

*Kombu*

*Nagasinnam*

**FEBRUARY / MARCH**
   **Maha-Shivarathri:** A Hindu Festival, at the new moon, in honor
   of Shiva and his wife Parvati.
   **Easter Passion Play:** On Duwa Island, near Negombo.
**APRIL**
   **New Year:** On the 13th / 14th of April both the Singhalese and
   the Tamils celebrate the end of the harvesting.
   **Adam's Peak:** Pilgrimages.

## MAY
**Labor Day:** 1st May, marked by holiday speeches.
**Vesak Full Moon:** Lord Buddha's birth, enlightenment, and entrance into Nirvana are celebrated.
**Republic Day:** 22 May, a National Holiday.
**Mohammed's Birthday**

## JUNE / JULY
**Poson Festival:** During full moon, the coming of Buddhism to Sri Lanka is celebrated. The major festivities are celebrated in Anauradhapura and Mihintale. In Mihintale, King Tissa converted to Buddhism.

## JULY / AUGUST
**Pilgrimages:** From Batticaloa to Kataragama.
**Esala Festival:** A nine-day Hindu festival is celebrated in Kataragama: sadhus stick rods through their cheeks and tongue without spilling blood. On the last day, other sadhus walk across glowing coals.

**Esala Perahera:** Sri Lanka's most important festival, held during the next full moon in Kandy. In a ceremonial procession, the Sacred Tooth is carried by a temple elephant through town, accompanied by torch bearers, Kandy dancers, Buddhist officials, and lots of richly decorated elephants, see p. 611.
**Vel Festival:** In Colombo, celebrated by Hindus in honor of Skanda, the God of War.
**Dondra Festival:** At the southern tip of the island, features colorful processions and a bazar.

## SEPTEMBER
**Bandaranaike Commemoration Day:** 26 September.

## OCTOBER / NOVEMBER
**Deepavali:** A Hindu festival dedicated to Lakshmi, the Goddess of Wealth.

## DECEMBER
**Sangamitta:** On full moon day, in memory of the nun who brought to Sri Lanka an offshoot of the sacred Bo tree, under which Buddha found enlightenment, considered the oldest tree in the world.
**Christmas:** Celebrated much as in the west.

# HISTORY

Only legend provides an inkling into the early history of Sri
Lanka. It is told that the island's ancient inhabitants were descended from demons and spirits. Three groups lived on the island: the Yaksha, the Naga, and the Raksha.
**Sinhabahu:** Verifiable history of Sri Lanka begins with the arrival of the northern Indian prince Vijaya and 700 companions, in
543 BC. Vijaya's history, however, begins with one of his ancestors, a Bengali king, whose daughter, according to legend,
had a love affair with the King of Animals. She named her son
Sinhabahu, because of his lion claws. Sinhabahu killed his father
and seized the throne. His favorite son was Vijaya, the father of
the Singhalese, who was banned from India due to rowdy behaviour. No wonder the Singhalese call themselves the lion sons, and
display lion symbols proudly throughout the island.
**Vijaya:** Upon arrival, he and his men were met in Sri Lanka,
which they called Tambapanni (= copper-colored hand), by the
Yaksha. These aboriginal inhabitants were easily pushed back
into the interior. Descendents of the Yaksha are the Vedda, who
have scarcely developed during centuries of isolation. Vijaya
married a southern Indian princess, who was accompanied to the
island by her ladies in waiting. Since then, 180 generations of
Singhalese kings have ruled the island in a straight line of
succession. Their legacy includes lovely palaces and colossal
architecture.
**King Tissa:** The focal point, and capital of the kingdom from
400 BC until 1000 AD was Anuradhapura. During this period, King
Tissa converted to Buddhism, beginning the spread of the faith
throughout Sri Lanka. The most ancient description of this period
is found in the **DIPAVAMSA**, a chronic written in the 4th century
BC. Its story is continued in the **MAHAVAMSA**, the Great
Chronicle, bringing us up to the 5th century AD, and later by
the **CULAVAMSA**. During this golden age of Buddhism, art and
architecture reached a peak. Many of the dagobas and ruins date
from this period. Anuradhapura had to be abandoned after
repeated Tamil attacks. The capital was moved further inland to
Polonnaruwa (1000 AD to 1235 AD).
**Attacks:** Internal differences, and continued Tamil raids, led to
the disintegration of the ancient Singhalese kingdom. In 1505 the
Portuguese were the first European visitors to the island, not
counting a couple ancient Greek and Roman seafarers. The Portuguese found three kingdoms on the island, in Kotte, Kandy, and
Jaffna. A Portuguese settlement was established on the southwestern coast. Arab merchants settled there were forced to give up
trade in cinnamon and precious jewels. An at first peaceful alli-

ance with the three kingdoms allowed the Portuguese to seize control of a section of the coast. At the heels of the Portuguese were Christian missionaries.

**Colonialism:** Portuguese rule lasted until 1658. Then the Dutch seized control from 1658 to 1796. The Vereenigde Indische Companie secured a trade monopoly, and established control of the coast, to profit from the lucrative cinnamon trade.

**The English East India Company:** Taking advantage of a crisis in Europe, the English occupied the Dutch ports on Sri Lanka. England's takeover of Sri Lanka in 1796 was relatively peaceful. In 1802, Sri Lanka became a British crown colony, though the cinnamon trade remained in company hands. The English aim was to control all of Sri Lanka, not just the coast. This required the conquest of the mountain regions and the primary resistance in Kandy. On the third try in 1815, the British flag was raised in Kandy. The last Singhalese king, Wikrama Rajasingha, was taken prisoner and sent to exile in India.

**Plantations:** By ending the traditional feudal system, the British freed the labor it needed for a plantation economy. Coffee was planted in the highlands, but this crop was abandoned after the coffee blight of 1870 to 1880. The English began experimenting with tea cultivation, for which Sri Lanka is famous today. And the coffee blight freed land for a new crop: the first caoutchouc (rubber) plants were imported, breaking a Brazilian monopoly.

**Infrastructure:** The English built roads and a railway system; European schools were established. As in India, the educated middle class sought participation in government. In 1931 universal suffrage was established. British rule lasted until the end of WW II, whereby the colonial power permitted increasing liberalization. In 1947 the British gave way to the waxing independence movement; first parliamentary elections were held.

**Independence:** On February 4, 1948, Sri Lanka was granted Dominion Status and became an independent member of the Commonwealth of Nations, under the former colonial name of Ceylon. On 22 May, 1972, a republic was declared under the historical name, Sri Lanka.

**Constitution:** Since 4 February, 1978, Sri Lanka has had a presidential constitution based on the American model. Members of Parliament are elected by a proportional system, replacing the former winner-take-all system. Since 29 April, 1982, the seat of government and parliament is the newly-built town of Jayewardenepura, near Colombo. Elections scheduled for 1983 and 1984 have been postponed.

# Independence

Colonialism and its successor - tourism, along with the first stages of industrialization and flight to the cities, have brought numerous psychological, sociological, and economic problems, i.e. unemployment, poverty, unequal distribution of land and income,

and a chronic lack of foreign exchange. The country is falling
increasingly into debt, both domestically and in the international
markets. Prices have doubled in the last five years, even more
so in tourism. Inflation is running at 25 % to 30 % annually. The
reason for this miserable development is seen in the nationali-
zation of key industries, plantations, and transportation, which
has slowed foreign investment. And there is the never-ending
political crisis.

**Education:** Tremendous efforts have been put into education since
1944, including free education from kindergarten to a university
degree. Children are required to attend school until the age of
15. Just 10 % of men and 15 % of women are illiterate.

**Health:** Widespread education, teamed with good, free, medical
attention has reduced child mortality while raising life expectancy. Even the birthrate has been reduced, keeping population
growth at 1.5 %. Hygiene, too, has reached a high standard,
compared to other Asian countries. In Sri Lanka epidemics, such
as malaria, are largely forgotten.

**Unemployment:** Young people with high school and college
education have the greatest difficulty finding work. While
universities have been churning out graduates in the humanities,
Sri Lanka desperately needs experts in the natural sciences. The
good education system has its roots in the colonial era. The well
educated inhabitants were taken into government service, where
they helped maintain the colonial status quo. Today, the
bureaucracy is no longer hiring. Agriculture too has little need
for educated workers. Total unemployment is estimated at two
million.

The Jayewardene administration is considering the creation of
a free-trade zone, à la Singapore, to attract foreign investment,
and create thousands of jobs. The first phase has gone into effect with the establishment of a Free Trade Zone around Katunayake Airport between Colombo and Negombo; numerous firms have
opened for business. Many new jobs have gone to catastrophically
paid women, who use up a third of their paychecks just getting
to and from work.

Local industry is still in the teething stages, earning just
10 % of GNP. Tourism is the number two earner of foreign
exchange.

The unstable political situation has led to a reduction of
foreign investment, even foreign aid. There is no improvement in
sight.

| | |
|---|---|
| **Country Name:** | Democratic Republic of Sri Lanka |
| **Capital:** | Jayewardenepura, in Kotte, near Colombo (seat of government & parliament) |
| **Flag:** | A saffron-yellow background, a green and a yellow vertical stripe. A yellow sword-bearing lion in a red background. |
| **National Holiday:** | 22 May, the day a Republic was proclaimed in 1972. |

# TRAVEL TIPS

## Visa

Citizens of most western countries need only a valid passport. A stamp, given at the border, is valid for 30 days. Later you can extend your visa by two weeks, occasionally four weeks.

**90 Days:** Should you want to stay longer, apply at a Sri Lankan consulate for a visa valid up to 3 months. This will spare you the exertion of acquiring an extension in Colombo, where you might be required to change US$15.- per day.

**Landing Card:** All travellers arriving by air are required to fill out an Immigration Landing Card. The first part is taken by officials upon entry. The second part you turn in upon departure.

No immunizations are required to enter Sri Lanka, except if you come from a region with yellow fever. Should you consider entering an endangered region, common sense does dictate you take precautions, see Health.

**D-Form:** Also upon arrival, you'll have to fill out a D-Form noting all currency you bring into Sri Lanka. Indian and Pakistani rupees may not be imported. Only 250.-Rs may be imported or exported at one time.

You can import or export all your material needs, but be sure anything of value is declared in your D-Form or you'll have difficulties when leaving the country. You can bring in at most two cameras with 24 rolls of film, or one camera with 10 rolls of film. Importation of drugs and pornographic material is forbidden. Baggage you don't want to bring through customs can be deposited at the customs office for pick-up upon departure for a fee of 0.25 Rs per day.

**Export:** Any souvenirs, even precious metals, can be exported almost without restriction so long as you can show you have exchanged a corresponding amount of money, and have valid sales receipts. For any gifts of value you may acquire, you'll need an export permit from the Controller of Exchange, Central

Bank, Colombo Fort, or the Controller of Imports and Exports,
National Mutual Building, Chatham Street, Colombo Fort, or the
State Gem Corporation, Colombo Fort.
**Antiques:** Prohibited is the export of antiques over 50 years old,
particularly palm-leaf manuscripts, along with animal skins,
ivory, and certain species of orchid. For an exemption, consult
the Director of Archives and the Archaeological Commissioner. You
may need a permit to import such items into your home country.
**Tea:** The export of tea is duty free up to 3 kg. Greater amounts
are taxed at 15.-Rs, up to a maximum of 7 kg. You can purchase
tea at the airport upon departure.
**Airport:** Outside the airport departure lounge only Sri Lankan
money is accepted, so spend any rupees you won't need for the
disembarkation tax (100.-Rs). Within the transit and departure
hall only foreign currency is accepted in the duty-free shop.
**Motor Vehicles:** To bring a car or motorboat temporarily onto the
island, you'll need a carnet permitting duty-free import for up to
six months. Upon presentation of an international driver's
license, you'll be issued a temporary Sri Lankan license valid
for 3 months (not extendable). Insurance is not expensive, but
required. For the latest requirements consult the Automobile
Association of Sri Lanka, 40 Sir Macan Markar Mawatha, Galle
Face, Colombo 3, tel.21528. Sri Lanka is not a place to sell your
car. Vehicles over six years old may not be imported.

# Visa Extension

Most visa extensions are valid only for 2 weeks. To get a longer
extension, you'll have to ask for the office supervisor. Before
dealing with that trauma, apply at a Sri Lankan consulate for a
three-month visa before you visit the island.
**Procedure:** The extension procedure will take all morning. Bring
a valid passport, money (150.- to 740.-Rs depending on nationality), your D-Form, and a ticket out of the country or enough
cash reserves to buy one. Usually you'll be required to show
your D-Form or exchange receipts to prove you've exchanged
US$15.- per day for the time spent on the island. Apply at the
Department of Immigration and Emigration, Galle Buck, Unit 6,
Colombo Fort, located below the lighthouse. Head down the extension of Chatham Street toward the sea, bear right. Open 08:45-
14:15 h, you'll receive a form to fill out, which you present with
your fee, payable also in stamps, then wait an hour. Check the
stamp in your passport to be sure your visa is extended for the
full duration you request!
**Alien Registration:** Should you arrive with a visa and plan to
stay for more than 30 days, you'll have to register at the Aliens' Building, 4th floor, New Secretariat Building, Colombo Fort,
in the back courtyard of the police station, left of the GPO. Be
sure to stop by within a month. You can have difficulties upon
departure if you overstay your visa by more than 3 days!

**SRI LANKA EMBASSIES**
**India:** High Commission, 21 Kautilya Marg, Chanakyapuri, Delhi 110021, tel.371226.
**Maldives:** Embassy, M/Muraka 4/44, Orchid Magu, Male, tel.2845.

**FOREIGN MISSIONS IN SRI LANKA**
**Bangladesh:** High Commission, 207/1, Dharmapala Mawatha, Colombo 7, tel.595963.
**India:** High Commission, 18, 3/1, Sir Baron Jaytilleke Mawatha, State Bank of India Building, 3rd Floor, Colombo 1, tel.21604.
**Nepal:** Honorary Consulate General, 290, R.A. de Mel Mawatha, Colombo 3, tel.575510, no sign on the street.

**Australia:** High Commission, 3, Cambridge Place, Colombo 7, tel.598767.
**Canada:** High Commission, 6, Gregory's Road, Colombo 7, tel.595841.
**United Kingdom:** 190, Galle Road, Colombo 3, tel.27611.
**United States:** 210, Galle Road, Colombo 3, tel.548007.

**Burma:** Embassy, 23, Havelock Road, Colombo 5, tel.587607.
**People's Republic of China:** Embassy, 191, Dharmapala Mawatha, Colombo 7, tel.596459.
**Indonesia:** Embassy, 1, Police Park Terrace, Colombo 5, tel.580113.
**Iran:** Embassy, 6, Sir Ernest De Silva Mawatha, Colombo 3, tel.29071.
**Japan:** Embassy, 20, Gregory's Road, Colombo 7, tel.93831.
**Malaysia:** High Commission, 63, A, Ward Place, Colombo 7, tel.94837.
**Maldives:** Embassy, 25, Melbourne Avenue, Colombo 4, tel.586762.
**Pakistan:** Embassy, 211, De Saram Place, Colombo 10, tel.596301.
**The Philippines:** Embassy, 10, Gregory's Road, Colombo 7, tel.596861.
**Thailand:** Embassy, 43, Dr. C.W.W. Kannangara Mawatha, Colombo 7, tel.597406.

# Calendar & Time Differences

Sri Lanka uses the western Gregorian calendar. Clocks are set five hours and 30 minutes ahead of Greenwich Mean Time (GMT), 13 hours 30 minutes ahead of Eastern Standard Time (EST). Sri Lanka and India are both on Indian Standard Time.

**BUSINESS HOURS**
Shops are generally open from 08:00–17:00 h. Government offices frequently close at noon. In bazars and small shops, particularly in villages, shopkeepers like to do business until dark. Colombo

is completely dead on Saturday afternoons, Sundays, and holidays, so don't wait until the last minute before you change money.

## BANKS
Open Mondays 09:00–13:00 h, Tues–Fri 09:00–13:30 h, throughout the country.
**Bank of Ceylon:** York Street, Colombo Fort, Colombo, Money Exchange Window, open daily 08:00–20:00 h.
**Airport Exchange Window:** Open at arrival and departure times.
**People's Bank:** Night Service Unit, Headquarters Branch, Sir Chittampalam A. Gardiner Mawatha, Colombo 2, tel.36948, Tues–Fri 15:30–19:00 h, Sat 09:00–13:30 h.
**American Express:** C/O McKinnons Travel Service, 7 York Street, Fort, Colombo 1, regular banking hours; clients' mail service, 09:00–12:30 h, 13:30–16:30 h.

# Money

| | |
|---|---|
| **USA:** | $1.– = 28.93Rs |
| **UK:** | £1.– = 47.43Rs |
| **AUS:** | $1.– = 20.74Rs |
| **India:** | 1.–Rs = 2.07Rs |
| **Nepal:** | 1.–Rs = 1.21Rs |

The monetary unit is the Sri Lankan rupee (Rs). One rupee contains 100 cents (= cts). Notes are denominated at 2.–Rs, 5.–Rs, 10.–Rs, 20.–Rs, 50.–Rs, 100.–Rs, 500.–Rs, and 1000.–Rs. Coins are minted in denominations of 1 ct, 2 cts, 5 cts, 10 cts, 25 cts, 50 cts, 1.–Rs, and 2.–Rs.

Exchange rates are ever changing. Traveller's checks get slightly better rates than cash. But exchange fees can be high. Most reasonable seems to be Hatton National Bank at 2.–Rs per unit. The People's Bank charges 10.–Rs per transaction. The Bank of Ceylon charges 15.–Rs per transaction no matter how many checks you cash.

Besides the banks, you can change money at numerous hotels, shops, travel agencies and airlines. No matter where you change, you'll have to present the D-Form you received from customs upon arrival. Sometimes you'll receive only a receipt instead of the exchange being noted on your D-Form. Be sure to save the receipt, along with the D-Form, for presentation upon departure.

If you want to export money not listed on your D-Form, you'll need approval from the Controller of Exchange, Central Bank, Colombo Fort.

Money not listed on your D-Form can't be officially exchanged. For safety, and the better exchange rate, bring traveller's
checks. 20-30 % of your travel budget should be in US$ cash.

Telegraphic transfers of money are faster and more reliable
than to India or Nepal. Often it takes just three days, otherwise
a week. Check at the Bank of Ceylon, Foreign Department,
27 M.I.C.H. Building, York Street, Colombo Fort, tel.20771. A
telex to Europe costs 200.-Rs. Any money received should be noted
on your D-Form!

# Information Offices

For the latest information, pick up a copy of the brochure, **Sri
Lanka Tourist Information**, at any Tourist Office.

**Ceylon Tourist Board:** 70 R.A. de Mel Mawatha (Duplication
Road), Colombo 3, Mon-Fri 08:30-16:45 h, Sat-Sun 08:30-12:30 h,
friendly answers to any tourist questions, books available,
reliable reference to other governmental or information offices.
**Katunayake International Airport:** Information Window, open at
arrival and departure times, tel.030 - 2411.
**Tourist Information:** Transwork House, Lower Chatham Street,
Colombo Fort, tel.28376.
**Tourist Information Counter:** Arts and Crafts Centre, Sangaraja
Mawatha, Kandy, Mon-Fri 08:30-16:45 h.
**Information Counter:** Lobby of the Queen's Hotel, Kandy.

# ARRIVING

## Air Travel

Book a cheap flight at one of the tiny travel agencies in Colombo
Fort. Ask your innkeeper, perhaps, for a recommendation, but be
sure he splits the commission with you. Bargain! A reduction of
500.-Rs might be built into a long-distance ticket price.
**Travel Agency:** We've heard good reports about the small  agency
just left of Aeroflot on York St. in Colombo.
**Travel Agency:** Or ask for George,  whose unusual office is at
68 Bristol St., Colombo 1, across from the YMCA.
**Expolanka Tours:** Cheap flights,  across from the duty-free shop
on Galle Rd.
**Ceylon Express:** Cheap prices (and individual arrangements for
island tours etc.),  Jim Wannigatunga,  Y.M.B.A. Building,  Sir
Baron Jayatillaka Mawatha Rd. / Lotus Rd., Colombo 1, tel.20020;
Jim's motto, "People to People".

The travel agencies mentioned above certainly offer cheaper rates
than the airlines themselves, but to check departure times, a few
important addresses:
   **Indian Airlines:**  95 Sir Baron Jayatillka Mawatha,  Colombo 1,
   tel. 34146, 29338, 23136, and 29838.
   **Maldives International Airlines:**  C/O Ceylinco Travels, Colombo
   Fort, tel. 20914 and 548130.
   **Royal Nepal Airlines:** 434 Galle Rd. Colombo 3, tel. 140445.
   **Air Lanka:**  Sir Baron Jayatillaka Mawatha,  around the corner
   from the GPO,  diagonally across from the Aliens' Building, tel.
   28331-4.
Sample prices:  Madras 1300.-Rs (officially US$80.-),  Trichy
930.-Rs (US$55.-),  Trivandrum 890.-Rs (US$53.-), Bombay 2840.-Rs
(US$170.-).
Indian Airlines offers a discount of 30 % on all southern India
routes if you originate your trip with IA in Sri Lanka or Male,
Maldives. But the Discover India Ticket (21 days unlimited travel
in India - US$375.-) is overpriced.
   Confirm your flights at least by phone (better in person)
about three days in advance,  otherwise there's no guarantee
(even with an okay on the ticket).  The airport tax on international flights at Colombo-Katunayake Airport is 100.-Rs (keep in
mind!).  Be at the airport at least two hours before your flight.
Check-in often ends an hour before departure time!

## BY SHIP TO SRI LANKA

The ferry from Talaimannar (Sri Lanka) to Rameswaram (India)
runs Tues,  Thurs,  and Sat (no service in November,  December,

and the beginning of January). Rail connection: Colombo-Fort (18:50 h) via Anuradhapura (01:03 h) arrives Talaimannar (04:45 h). The train runs only Mon, Wed, and Fri, carries 1st, 2nd, 3rd class, plus sleeping cars: 2nd class costs 110.-Rs.

Before ferry departure the small restaurant and Money Exchange Office in Talaimannar Railway Station are open. Don't believe those who'd have you believe there is no place to change money in Talaimannar, and offer their own very expensive rates. The ferry departs at 10:00 h, arrives at 14:00 h. Aboard ship, only Indian rupees and American dollars are accepted for food!

**Postponement:** Sometimes the ferry doesn't run, or no tickets are available for foreign tourists, sometimes just upper-deck tickets. Ferry tickets can be booked five days in advance at the earliest, available at Colombo-Fort Railway Station, ticket windows 4-5. A passport with an India visa is required for purchase, open Mon, Wed, Fri 08:00-18:30 h, otherwise till 14:00 h. Lower-deck tickets (if available) 250.-Rs. If you bought a return ticket in India, be sure to confirm your return booking in Colombo.
**No tickets available in Talaimannar!** Even if you arrive on time in Talaimannar, it's possible that overbooking will force you to wait 2-3 days for the next ship. You're better off flying and selling your duty-free whisky upon arrival in India (one liter brings 200.-Rs).

# COLOMBO

The island's capital is home to
1 million people. Before the arrival
of the Portuguese, Colombo (= harbor) was a small fishing and trading town, frequented by Arabs in
search of precious stones and
spices.

    The Portuguese began construc-
tion of the Fort in the early 16th
century. The Fort, today a city
district, still retains signs of its
European colonial past. The Dutch
assumed control of Colombo in 1656,
creating the districts of Wolfendahl
and Hulfsdorp, along with Cinnamon Gardens. The English arrived
in the 18th century, molding the
city in its own style. The British
built the harbor, and the first rail
line to Kandy. The two central districts of Colombo are the Fort
(everything for the European taste), and Pettah (the bazar)
where Muslim traders still have their say (bargain!). Cinnamon
Gardens is an affluent residential neighborhood, while nearby
Slave Island remains impoverished, even today.

    Most travellers find this a hectic city, lacking flair, a city
you can't avoid (bureaucracy, airport, shops), but that you do
try to get through fast.

## COMING - GOING

Colombo is the primary junction for rail and bus lines. It has
the best transport system, and the only international airport
on the island. The harbour is of only minor importance for
passengers.

**By Air:** For international flights and connections to the airport, see Sri Lanka Country & Culture. To the domestic airport,
Ratmalana (located at the southern end of Mt. Lavinia, on the
inland side of Galle Road), get any bus or minibus toward
Panadura.

**By Rail:** The main station is Colombo-Fort Railway Station,
almost every train on the island begins or ends here. Outside
the station is Railway Tourist Information, tel.35838, friendly
service, perhaps even a schedule. Baggage check is in the

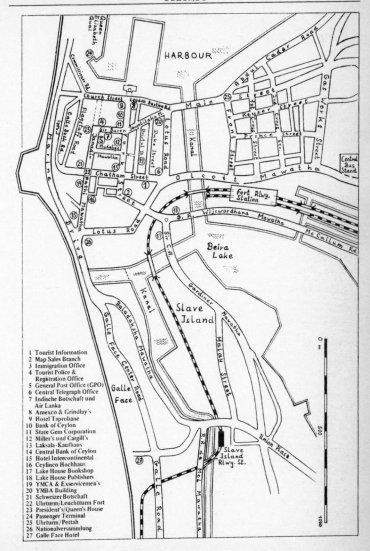

1 Tourist Information
2 Map Sales Branch
3 Immigration Office
4 Tourist Police &
   Registration Office
5 General Post Office (GPO)
6 Central Telegraph Office
7 Indische Botschaft und
   Air Lanka
8 Amexco & Grindlay's
9 Hotel Taprobane
10 Bank of Ceylon
11 State Gem Corporation
12 Miller's und Cargill's
13 Laksala-Kaufhaus
14 Central Bank of Ceylon
15 Hotel Intercontinental
16 Ceylinco Hochhaus
17 Lake House Bookshop
18 Lake House Publishers
19 YMCA & Exservicemen's
20 YMBA Building
21 Schweizer Botschaft
22 Uhrturm/Leuchtturm Fort
23 President's/Queen's House
24 Passenger Terminal
25 Uhrturm/Pettah
26 Nationalversammlung
27 Galle Face Hotel

station, 1.-Rs per day per piece, lockers (5.-Rs).
**By Bus:**   Most overland buses depart from Central Bus Station
Pettah, 200 m east of Fort Railway Station on the opposite side
of the street.   Information by the Ceylon Tourist Board, Central
Bus Station, Olcott Mawatha, Colombo, tel.28081. The important
connections are listed in the local sections.
**By Minibus:**   Minibuses depart unscheduled (when they are
full), perhaps hourly, except in the early morning, from Fort
Railway Station.
**Around Town:**   Colombo has a good and extensive local bus
system.   Only after 22:00 h is it difficult to get around.   Then
you have to take a taxi.   Be sure the taxi-meter is switched
on.   Cheaper are the three-wheeled, yellow-black scooters. You
are best off negotiating the complete price in advance, the
taxi-meter is often set too fast.
**Pickpockets:**   Light fingers have it easy in city crowds – watch
out!


## A NIGHT'S REST

It's hard to find cheap lodgings in Colombo.   Newcomers get a
shock.   But be assured that prices here reflect little on prices
throughout the island!   Most globetrotters head out to Dehiwala
or Mt. Lavinia;   that means calculating 1 h each day for a
visit to the bank or government offices.   A few suggestions
according to locations:
  Around the Fort district try:   **YMCA**,   39 Bristol Street,
tel.25252, **(S)**120.-, **(D)**190.-, 250.- depending on furnishings
(bath), reasonable self-service restaurant. **Exservicemen's Institute**, 29 Bristol Street, tel.22650, next to the YMCA, **(S)**80.-,
**(D)**180.-, **(Dm)**50.- (10 beds per room), good restaurant. **Globe
Hotel**, Mudalige Mawatha, between Nectar Cafe and the GPO,
**(D)**130.-.   **British India Hotel**, Mudalige Mawatha, between Nectar Cafe and the GPO, **(D)**130.-.   Other hotels in the district
offer the same price range.
  In Pettah, try:   **Lodgings**, Mahavidyala Mawatha (formerly
Barber Street), Colombo 13, get Bus 101 and Bus 165 toward
Kochikade, 1 km from the Fort, friendly owner, clean, poorly-
lit rooms, **(Dm)**30.-;   baggage check without worry 5.-Rs per
week. **Paul VI**, on the street leading directly away from the
railway station, in a 10-storey house, where rooms are rented
on the 8th floor.
  In the Kollupitiya, Bambalapitiya, and Wellawatta districts,
try:   **Perpetual Tourist Lodge**,   8A Bethesda Place,   tel.82419,
**(S)**130.-, **(D)**200.-, breakfast 25.-Rs, bus connections to Dickman's Road, get off at St. Paul's Church. **Tourist Guest House**,
8/1 Elibank Road, Colombo 5, **(D)**80.-, get off at Dickman's
Road Post Office.   **Hotel Nippon**, 123 Kumaran Ratnam Road,
(2 km south-east of the Fort), Colombo 2, tel.31887, **(D)**140.-,
large terrace, old furnishings, somewhat morbid, Japanese and
Chinese food in the restaurant. **Ottery Tourist Inn**, 29 Melbourne Avenue, Colombo 4, tel.83727, quiet, 8 rooms, **(S)**120.-.

**YWCA**, National Headquarters, 7 Rotunda Gardens, Colombo 3, tel.23498, **(S)**100.-, **(Dm)**80.- including breakfast, near Oberoi Hotel. **Horton Youth Hostel**, Station Road, Wellawatta. **Youth Council Hostel**, 50 Haig Road, Colombo 4, tel.81028, **(Dm)**30.-, association members **(Dm)**25.-. The following buses, from the Fort, run south along Galle Road through all three districts: Buses 100, 101, 102, 105, 106, 106, 112, 132, 134, 137, 139, 155, and 165. Minibuses between the Fort and Mt. Lavinia also use Galle Road.

Dehiwala is officially a town of its own, but is in fact a southern Colombo suburb. Between Dehiwala and the Fort, choose among CTB Buses (3.-Rs): 100, 101, 102, 105, 106, 134, 154, 155, 167, and 197, plus minibuses between the Fort and Mt. Lavinia. Most accommodations are on the lakeside of Galle Road, near St. Mary's Church, where you should disembark (ask the driver to throw you off). **The Samaritan, Big John**, 47 Albert Place, tel.715027, **(S)**45.-, **(D)**80.-, **(Dm)**30.-, Big John (the former owner) is no longer with us, but his son has inherited the great competence and connections necessary to find you a room with a family in one of the surrounding buildings if the guest house is full. **Ralph Fernando**, 34 Albert Place, a bit more expensive than Big John. **Seabreeze**, 37 Campbell Place, tel.717996, **(S)**30.-, **(D)**80.- with a shower. **Page House**, 8 Ebenezer Place (near Trio Cinema), tel.712941, **(S)**80.-. **Tourist Rest**, 7 Park Avenue, off Waidya Road, tel.714521, near the Zoo, **(D)**100.-. **Tourist Guest House**, 8/1 Elibank Road, tel.84005, **(D)**50.-. **Clement Fernando**, 13 Muhandiram Lane, tel.713401, near Holy Family Convent. Other accommodations in Mount Lavinia.

## REFRESHMENT
Around the Fort are several Chinese restaurants. Several spots on Chatham Street including **Pagoda Tea Rooms**, which receives great praise, and the less than friendly **Hotel Nanking**. Breakfast and dinner are cheap in the **YMCA Restaurant**, or next door in the **Servicemen's Institute**. There is a cheap self-service restaurant on York Street at the corner between Laksala and Miller's (Nektar). At midday, the coffee shop in **Hotel Taprobane** converts into a luxury self-service restaurant; no charge for refills, as much as you can eat. A meal ticket for rice and curry, at the hotel entrance, costs 45.-Rs. From the roof-top restaurant at the same hotel, you've a lovely view of the entire harbour, but it's expensive; the cheapest meals run to 40.-Rs. If you are willing to spend money (at least 40.-Rs), try the roof terrace of the **Ceylinco** highrise, or in **Hotel Intercontinental**, both with a view of Colombo and the sea.

On Chatham Street, across from the above-mentioned Chinese restaurant, two cafes, **Peony** and **Salsabil**, offer wonderful pies, along with traditional Chinese food and fish cakes.

Outside the Fort, you'll find lots of cheap little spots on Union Place, near the Town Hall, making a visit to the embassy district quite pleasant. Along Galle Street are countless good, if not cheap, restaurants of every type: local, Chinese, European, seafood, meat, vegetarian... Good are **Green Cabin** in Bambalpitiya, and **Ceyfish Restaurant** on Sir Chittampalam Gardiner Mawatha. **Perera & Sons**, on Galle Road at Kollupitiya Junction, near the market, is a good bakery offering dark bread, pies, pastries, in a sit-down atmosphere.

The cheap hotels, mentioned above, generally offer meals, frequently not cheap, sometimes just to order.

In Pettah are several cheap rice and curry restaurants, e.g. right across from Fort Railway Station.

Special offers, for the hefty wallet, in luxury hotels include sweets, disco, dancing, bar, folklore, etc. Sometimes a combo plays softly to aid digestion.

**Groceries:** Shopping is easy, see Tips.

## ACTIVITIES

Outside the usual big-city activities, Colombo has little special to offer; a good reason to head right out to the more interesting parts of the island.

**Water Sports:** Try the flat section of beach north and south of Mt. Lavinia Hotel, see Mount Lavinia.

**Movies, Theatre, Dance Performances:** For the current schedule, check the English-language newspapers. Theatre performances are generally in Singhalese language, e.g. in Lionel Wendt Art Centre, and in the YMBA Building.

**Casino:** In Hotel Golden Topaz, 502/1 Galle Road, Kollupitiya, tel.547605, 20:00-01:00 h.

**Golf:** Visit the 18-hole course at the Royal Colombo Golf Club, 185 Model Farm Road, Colombo 8, tel.595431, cost depends upon sex: men (300.-Rs), women (225.-Rs) per day.

## SIGHTS

**The Fort:** European roots are deep and the colonial heritage most visible. This is a district of souvenir shops, and the state-owned department store, **Laksala**. Before investing in souvenirs, see Tips. Most airlines and government ministries have offices here.

**The Lighthouse:** Also serves as a clock tower, on Chatham Street, in the Fort; this is the only lighthouse in the entire world located on a downtown street. But it is no longer in service.

**Hotel Taprobane:** In the Fort, the city's oldest hotel. This is where the captains and high-ranking officers made their billings until the ship siren or clock chimes announced departure time. Little remains of the past glamour, beyond a tremendous view from the restaurant of the entire harbour.

**YMBA Building:** A lovely Buddhist shrine.

**President's House:** Near the clock tower, across from the GPO, guarded by soldiers, the palace was built by the last Dutch governor in the late 18th century; originally called the King's House or Queen's House. The statue in front depicts the former British governor Sir Edward Barnes, under whom, in the 1830s, the road to Kandy was built. The kilometer numbers, on all major roads in the country, are measured from this statue.

**Pettah:**  This large square is frequently mentioned as a popular sight. We can't figure out why.

**Parliament Building** and **Secretariat:**  Much more interesting,   at the north end of Pettah.

**Galle Face Hotel:** At the southern end of Pettah, also claims to be the oldest hotel in the city.   Certainly it does have wonderful colonial charm.

**Churches:**  Every epoch has left its church in Colombo: the Portuguese built Roman Catholic **St. Anthony's Church** in Kochikade; the Dutch made their mark in 1757 with **Wolvendaal Kerk** in Kotahena;  British Anglicans in 1842 added **St. Andrew's Scots Kirk** in Kollupitiya.   More churches dating from the British colonial era can be seen along Galle Road.

**Hindu Temple:**  The most important Kovils are in Pettah,   **Sri New Kathiresan** and adjoining,  **Old Kathiresan Temple.** They mark the departure point for processions during the Val Festival,   when tremendous wooden wagons are pulled by the people,   6 km to Bambalapitiya.

**Kelani Temple:**  10 km from Colombo,  get Bus 235 from near the Pettah Bus Stand.  This is where the Buddha is said to have met with the Nagaraja king in the 5th century BC.  Set between a small,  white Dagoba and a tremendous Bo tree,  the outer walls are decorated with Buddhist and Hindu motifs.  Paintings inside depict the history of Buddha and Buddhism in Sri Lanka.  Plus a tremendous resting Buddha and a Buddha sitting in meditation.

**Zoo:**  Get the local bus to Dehiwala,  open 08:00-18:00 h.  One of the prettiest zoos in Asia,  an attempt is made to cage as few animals as possible,  like a botanical garden with animals. Every evening at 17:15 h,  the elephant circus is worth a look.  It is easy to spend an entire day here. Restaurant. Admission 30.-Rs.

**Mt. Lavinia:**  Accessible by rail or bus.  Left and right of the Mt. Lavinia Hotel is a long sandy beach.  You can walk way out into the water, when it isn't too stormy or dirty.

**Museums:** First mention goes to the **National Museum,** Albert Crescent,  Kollupitiya, featuring an exhibit on Ceylonese history from prehistoric times until today.  Special mention is reserved for a collection of metal statues in the first room,  depicting dancing goddesses from Polonnaruwa;  get Bus 114 or 138,  open Sun-Thurs 09:00-17:00 h,  admission 20.-Rs. Another exhibit worth visiting is in the **Dutch Period Museum,**  Prince Street at 1st Cross Street, Pettah, open Mon-Fri 09:00-17:00 h.

**Colombo Planetarium:**  Colombo 7,  entrance between Reid Avenue and Bauddhaloka,  tel.86499; on the last Saturday each month the presentation is in English, costs 4.-Rs.

**Bandaranaike Memorial International Conference Hall:** Bauddhaloka Mawatha, Colombo 7, open 09:00-16:00 h, closed Mondays, features an extensive collection of photographs,  documents,  and soundtracks of speeches by former Premier S.W.Bandaranaike.

# WEST COAST

## Ambalangoda

Tourism is king, 84 km (2 h by
bus) south of Colombo, where outstanding masks are made, while you
watch. For those interested in
masks, this is a must; J.W. Ariya-
paka lives and works here using
traditional methods of his craft.
There are lots of shops at the north
end of town.

Local sights include a lovely
temple, also in the north of town.
The entrance gate is richly decorated; the temple centre features a
number of interesting paintings.

### COMING - GOING
Situated on the main route along
the west coast, Ambalangoda is
easy to reach.
**By Rail:** Most trains between Colombo Fort and Galle stop here,
although a few express trains just stop in Bentota or Hikkaduwa, costs 15.-Rs, takes 2 h.
**By Bus:** Both CTB buses and minibuses cruise the main road
along the sea, stopping upon request. For longer distances, be
sure to get a CTB express or one of the many minibuses. On
short hops a CTB local is okay.

### A NIGHT'S REST
This is not a place where many people stop long; Hikkaduwa,
just south, is too great a magnet. This keeps prices within
reason: **Resthouse**, **(D)**275.-, lovely situation by the sea, near
the center of town. **Suyama Guest House**, 10 Goodshed Road,
Vilegoda, **(D)**50.-Rs. **Shangrela Beach Inn**, Sea Beach Road,
**(D)**160.-, a lovely privately-run hotel, tel.097 / 342. **Blue
Horizon Tour Inn**, 129 Devale Road, **(S)**60.-, **(D)**100.-,
tel.097 / 475, good food upon request. Devale Road is also
called Main Street or High Beach Road!
Private accommodations offer **(D)**20.-Rs.

Excellent lodgings 4 km south in Akurala, try **Ocean Beach Hotel**, **(D)**80.-, nice people, good food, right on the beach. **Hotel Beauty Coral**, **(S)**25.-, **(D)**50.-, beach. A lovely sandy beach, tremendous coral, and lots of fish. The artist Nayanananda exhibits his works in a gallery.

## SHOPPING
**Masks:** Souvenir-crazy tourists come primarily to buy the famous colourful masks. There are three different types: comedy masks, devil masks (yakshas), and masks designed to drive away the demons which cause disease. Prices have been driven up by naive tourists. Be sure to visit the shops alone, without a tout, or your price will be adjusted upward to pay your "guide's" commission. He'll pick his share up later, after you've gone.
**Puppets:** Small descendants of the once popular puppet theatre, which was rekindled to please tourist demand.

# Hikkaduwa

This is a spot where globetrotters and freaks traditionally gather for the winter. Tourists too now make the scene; it's scary how many hotels have gone up since 1979. While the building boom has declined, the entire coastline has grown as large hotels go up, accompanied by small shops, restaurants, and lodgings. There are no private beaches where you can wander undisturbed.
During the rainy season from June to August there is little happening. Most restaurants and shops are closed. In the hotels it is easy to bargain down the price.
In season from October to March, Galle Road transforms into a shopping street, discos open, 600 people loll on the beach. But to the south, in Narigama, there is still lots of room. Plus there is absolutely nothing happening at the beach 3 km north of the railway station, and it's lovely.
The press frequently reports from Hikkaduwa about tourists and globetrotters, in local jargon: "hippies". But Hikkaduwans have always mobilized to fight plans to drive the hippies away. Most chai shops, small restaurants, and stores cater almost exclusively to travellers, who have few inhibitions about establishing contact with local Singhalese. Hikkaduwans also emphasize that young people want to participate in local life, rather than tourist consumption; many even wear local dress, the sarong. This is a discussion which continues up to the highest levels of society.
**Nakedness:** Certainly there are problems with skinny dipping on the beach. The Singhalese police has submitted to the inevitable and tolerates topless swimsuits. The remainder may well be covered with only a loincloth, a tiny piece of cloth similar to a minitanga. Rarely, but occasionally, the police will arrest someone just to prohibit too great a relaxation of morals. Please don't put it to the test. Remember, your nakedness does offend local morals.

**Guides:** A warning is necessary about the many "guides", mostly unemployed youths, out to earn some quick money. Look for a hotel on your own, bargain the price, and remember always to bargain in the shops. With time you'll get a feeling for calculating the proper price; don't make a habit of bargaining the already thin profit down to zero. It is difficult for Singhalese to understand why tourists think nothing of chugging beer for 30.-Rs, but then are unwilling to pay the same price for several days' work producing handicrafts!

**Swimming:** Hikkaduwa's lovely beach is complemented with a coral reef. The beach behind Hotel Coral Sands is patronized mostly by package tourists.

**Freak Beach:** More relaxed, 2 km toward Galle in Narigama.

**Deserted Beach:** A third, almost unused beach, is 3 km north of the railway station on the road to Colombo. But here you'll find no lodgings or restaurants; just a chai shop in a nearby village.

**Glass-Bottom Boats:** Run by the hotels Coral Sands and Blue Coral, will take you out to the reef. Some coral is accessible by foot with beach shoes.

## COMING – GOING

Situated on the main west coast road and rail line providing easy access from north or south.

**By Rail:** Seven trains daily from Colombo Fort, takes 3 h, costs 15.-Rs (3rd class). The fastest train takes 2 h, costs 35.-Rs (2nd class). To Galle, takes 30 minutes, costs 2.-Rs.

**By Bus:** Bus 2 (Express) runs continuously the route Colombo – Galle – Matara and return. Stops also in Kalutara, Beruwela, Bentota, Ambalangoda, etc., costs 15.-Rs, takes 2.5 h. Hourly night buses take 3.5 h.

**By Minibus:** Same stops along the west cost as the express bus, Colombo – Hikkaduwa 2 h, be sure to have the 18.-Rs in exact change or you'll experience the "sorry no change" trick!

From Hikkaduwa, daily minibuses to Katunayake International Airport, by Colombo, takes 4 h, costs 100.-Rs. Drivers on these minibombers are out to make time; risky passing tactics may give you grey hair before your destination.

**Around Town:** Along Galle Road, the main street through town, you can use the CTB local bus as local transport, costs 1.-Rs from the railway station to Narigama.

You can rent a bike on almost any corner or in many lodgings, costs 2-3.-Rs per hour, 10-20.-Rs per day, depending upon duration and demand. Cars & motorbikes are also for rent, costs 150-175.-Rs per day.

## A NIGHT'S REST

No worry about finding a place here; you've the best selection on the island from cheap private houses to expensive hotels.

We always stay at **Gamini Holiday Home**, way at the north end of the village, **(D)**30.-, 40.-Rs, **(Dm)**8.-, good Singhalese food in the evening 20.-Rs; you can check your bags and valuables with the owner, Mr. Gamini, without concern; though far from the southern beach, we always gravitate here.

Other cheap lodgings further south in Narigama offer the same price range; think **(D)**40.- to 80.-Rs. Just wander about and ask. The further you get from the beach, the cheaper it is. Right on the beach costs 50.- to 150.-Rs, or even 200.-Rs. But a room which costs 200.-Rs in season can be had for just 50.-Rs out of season, just to make the difference clear. If you'd like to stay with a local family, no problem, usually further from the beach.

Camper parking at **Richard's Sons Beach Inn**, 20.-Rs.

We intentionally don't want to mention any lodgings in Hikkaduwa or Narigama. Recommendations lead to crowds, driving prices up and quality down. This is a spot where almost every traveller passes through. If you are staying a while, it is easy to find lodgings fitting your taste and wallet.

## REFRESHMENT

For restaurants, the same policy applies as for hotels: recommendations destroy a nice place. Several spots which have maintained their standards over the years:

**Chinese Dragon Restaurant**, Galle Road, near the bus stand by the petrol station. **Hotel Francis** is always popular, great food, pleasant atmosphere under the palms, at the south of town toward Narigama.

Also good nearby: **Casalanka**, **Brother's Spot**, **Curry Bowl** (vegetable curry 15.-Rs), **Silta's**, and **La Noix de Coco**.

Worth recommending are **Nanking Restaurant**, **Cool Hut**, and **Cool Spot**. In **Blue Fox** there is great fruit juice and ice cream.

More restaurants, smaller, some cheaper, and chai shops along the beach on Galle Road or by the beach in Narigama.

Try a few of the restaurants and listen to recommendations from the longer residents (with the deepest tan!). A tremendous breakfast costs 18.-Rs, a normal meal also 18.-Rs. Beer at 30.-Rs is the most expensive, soda water at 3.-Rs is the cheapest drink. We enjoy breakfast at **Goldspot**. Fun snacks and drinks in **Mama's Beach Restaurant**, both by the coral beach.

**Groceries:** Sold in northern Hikkaduwa, in the old town by the railway station where you'll find the fish and vegetable market, plus various small shops.

## SHOPPING

**Clothes:** Hikkaduwa is a good spot to buy; be sure to bargain. Your clothes will be custom tailored within a day should your size not be available off the rack. Pay close attention to the quality of the stitching, the cloth should not be cut too short. Pay a little bit more for good workmanship.

**Handicrafts:** Besides clothes, you can find good lace, batik, and jewelry, along with other Singhalese handicrafts including: bast, pottery, leather bags, dance masks.
**Used Books:** Sold in a small shop by the police station.
**Consumer Goods:** Available in the shops around the railway station and bus stand.

**Don't Buy Coral:** Please don't participate in the destruction of the reef.

# Devil Dance

If you are lucky you might experience the Devil Dance during your stay in Hikkaduwa. These are not special performances for tourists, rather ceremonies performed to heal the sick. The Singhalese understand that spirits and demons can take possession of the body with very negative effect. Hour-long ceremonies with music and dancing are necessary to exorcize the demons and spirits. Horrifying masks are worn, magic words spoken, and sacrifices made, all aimed at driving out the spirits and pacifying the devil. The patient frequently falls into a deep trance.

Of course, there are shows performed for tourists, costs 40.-Rs for two hours.

## ACTIVITIES

**Swimming:** Best at the southern beach where the waves are great, and no rocks and coral to worry about. Don't swim during monsoon season when dangerous currents will pull you out to sea!

**Snorkeling:** Only recommended from October to April. Outside this season, there are life-threatening waves, undertow, and currents. Even in safe weather, don't let yourself be washed onto or scraped along sharp coral. Wear beach (bath) shoes. Diving masks and flippers are sold everywhere, or rented (15.-Rs). You might like to learn scuba diving. Complete equipment costs 250.-Rs per day. Underwater cameras can be rented. Breaking coral and undersea hunting are strictly prohibited!

**Surfing:** Best on Narigama Beach where a board rents for 50.-Rs.

**Body Surfing:** Quite safe south of Surfer's Spot, where the beach is flattest, without rocks, and the waves are good.

**Glass-Bottom Boats:** A comfortable way to keep your toes dry and observe the colourful coral garden and fish through a window in the bottom of a motorboat. The ride is only offered in season, takes 50 minutes, costs 40.-Rs. These rides are also offered by the Coral Sands and Blue Coral hotels.

## AROUND HIKKADUWA

**Yala National Park:** Several hotels offer organized tours.

**Yala:** Reef's End Tours, 357 Galle Road, runs tours, costs 300.-Rs, an expensive alternative for people with lots of cash and little time.

**Ambalangoda:** Accessible in 30 minutes by minibus.

**Galle:** See Galle, just 30 minutes by rail or bus.

## TIPS

**Post Office:** Between the railway station and the bus stand by the petrol station is a track crossing. Follow this road 500 m uphill; the small Post Office is on the right.

**Banks:** People's Bank, across from the fish market, 100 m north of the railway station on the same side of the street. Two other banks are available for comparison. No longer is it necessary to go to Colombo just to change money!

**Behaviour:** We agree heartily with the following reader's letter! "Many women sit in restaurants clad only in a tanga. How can you make them understand that it is better not to, without seeming prudish? And many travellers brandish joints much too publicly. The owner of a newly-opened beach hotel lost his license when the police found tourist dope in a raid."

**Prostitution:** A negative side effect of tourism, practised by local, and western, boys and girls. One doesn't need much intelligence to perceive the effects of this exploitation.

# SOUTH COAST

## Galle

Galle may have been the Biblical
Tarshish (I Kings 10:22), where
King Solomon procured his jewels
and spices. The Portuguese conquered the town in 1505. Because
the Dutch confused the Ceylonese
word "gala" (= rocks) for the Latin word "gallus" (= rooster), the
Dutch East India Company put a
cock in its coat of arms. You can
still see the proud bird on the inside of the Fort gateway. The most
interesting section of town is within the confines of the Dutch Fort,
built in 1663 upon the ruins of a
Portuguese Fort. The Dutch ousted
the Portuguese in 1640, creating an

important port at Galle. You can still recognize the Dutch style
of architecture. Living today inside the Fort are the Burghers,
descendants of the Dutch; and the Moors, descendants of Arabs,
who were here before the Dutch. Take a walk through the narrow
streets and along the fortress walls. Since expansion of the Port
of Colombo, Galle's harbor has lost importance. Home of Mahinda
College, Galle is a major bastion of Buddhism. Three-fourths of
the population are Buddhist. Muslims are a major minority.

### COMING - GOING

Galle is a major junction in the south-west.
**By Rail:** All trains along the coast between Colombo and Matara, on the southern coast, put into Galle's drive-in-back-out
railway station. Eight trains daily along the coast to Colombo,
takes 2-3.5 h. the fastest trains to Colombo depart at 06:44 h
(arrives 09:25 h) and 07:50 h (09:50 h) stopping only in Hikkaduwa, Ambalangoda, and Bentota, costs 15.-Rs 3rd class to
Colombo, to Hikkaduwa (2.-Rs, 30 minutes). Four trains daily
to Matara, takes an hour.
**By Bus:** The bus stand is by the railway station. Minibuses to
Hikkaduwa, Ambalangoda, Bentota, Kalutara, Mt. Lavinia, Colombo Fort. Depart when a full load of passengers is ready,
costs 20.-Rs to Colombo Fort.

Lots of minibuses heading southeast. To Matara, takes 45 min-
utes, costs 7.-Rs. Direct minibuses to Hambantota, Wellawaya,
and Haputale.
Direct CTB-Express buses from Central Bus Stand at 05:20 h to
Badulla. To Kataragama at 06:20 h (5 h, 20.-Rs).
**Around Town:** Everything is accessible by foot. Or take a
scooter, but make him turn on the meter!
To Unawatuna, get the local CTB bus toward Matara.

## A NIGHT'S REST

Most accommodations are inside the Fort: **YMCA,** Pedlar Street
at Rampart Street, **(S)**55.-, **(Dm)**25.-, just men, cafeteria.
**Aquamarine Hotel,** next door to the YMCA, **(D)**70.-, 100.-, only
a few with showers, otherwise common showers, **(S)**40.- (no
shower), good food. **Faika's Tourist Rest,** 40 Middle Street,
right of People's Bank, **(S)**80.-, 90.-, **(D)**150.- in season,
lovely courtyard. **New Oriental,** 10 Church Street, **(S)**150.-,
**(D)**250.-, furnished with lovely antiques; the swimming pool is
sometimes dry. **Orchard Holiday Home,** 61 Lighthouse Street,
tel.(09) 2370, very popular, the seven rooms range from
**(S)**100.- to **(D)**200.-. **Beatrice House,** privately-owned by
R.K. Kodikara, 29 Rampart Street, **(S)**20.-, **(D)**50.- with fan
and mosquito net, meals 18.-Rs.
Private lodgings in the Fort, **(S)**30.-, **(D)**50.- and up. Touts
find you along Lighthouse Street, don't take the first offer.
Outside the Fort: **Sydney Hotel,** by the bus stand, **(D)**30.-.
**Rosary,** near Sacred Heart Convent, the large church behind
the railway station, Kaluwella, **(D)**30.-. **RRR,** in the railway
station for rail passengers, nothing is cheaper. During off
season, everything is half price.
Cheap lodgings 6 km from town in Unawatuna.
If you've cash for an expensive flash, try **Old Dutch Inn,**
Atapattu Walawwa, 35 Dickson Road, in the north. **Closenberg,**
on a peninsula with a view of the Bay of Galle. **Harbour Inn
Rest House Inn,** by Unawatuna on Rumassala Hill, tel.(09) 2822,
a rest house run by the Ceylon Hotels Corporation.

## REFRESHMENT

**South Ceylon Snack Bar,** across from the railway station, a great
place to enjoy a milkshake or a bite to eat after a stroll through
town. Next door, **South Ceylon Restaurant** serves Chinese and
European food. Or try **Chinese Globe Restaurant** toward the train
tracks and canal. For good seafood, in a Victorian atmosphere,
visit the **Oriental Hotel** in the Fort on Church Street. Also worth
a look is **Aquamarine Hotel.**

In **Sydney Hotel** is a pub serving Guinness, lager, stout, and
other types of beer.

## SHOPPING

**Jewelry:** Jewels, shells, lace, carved ebony. Don't buy anything
made of dark wood.

**Guides:** Never visit a shop with a "guide".
**Handicrafts:** Good quality, traditional, Sri Lankan handicrafts in
SCIA Shopping Centre, 72 A Kandewatte Road, tel.(09) 2304, by
scooter from the bus stand or railway station (5.-Rs). Prices
aren't the lowest, but you can watch things being produced and
ask questions without touts jumping all over you. The following
handicrafts are produced: tortoiseshell (please don't buy tortoiseshell - an endangered species!); batik, ebony, and carved
masks. Cutting of precious stones, jewelry making, basket making, and lacework. In 1981 the SCIA won the International Prize
for Tourist Production. Despite claims made by the owners, the
SCIA is not state-owned, and prices are not "fixed".

It is possible to get the best deal in Sri Lanka in Galle. But
you do have to be careful, and know what you are buying, or
you will get cheated.

## SIGHTS

The main attraction are the well preserved Dutch fortifications
dating from 1663, built upon the ruins of a Portuguese Fort,
covering 35 ha. The Dutch largely followed the Portuguese foundations.

Coming from the railway station or bus stand, you cross a
large field where cricket is frequently played. It once served as
a free-fire range for cannon practice. Hence the war memorial.
**The Fort:** Now walk between **Moon Bastion** with a clock tower and
**Sun Bastion** and on through the Main Gate, added by the British
in 1873, into the fortress enclosure. At the circle, follow the
street off to the left. On the right is the **New Oriental Hotel** and
the **Dutch Reformed Church**. Diagonally across on the corner is
the former **Dutch Governor's Residence**. Then down the street to
the left, you'll find the **Old Gate**, above which you can see the
Dutch East India Company's coat of arms. Between **Zwarte Bastion**, today housing the police, and **Akersloot Bastion** is the **High
Court**.

Take Hospital Street, or follow the fortress walls south to the
18 m tall **Lighthouse** on Point Utrecht Bastion. You can climb the
lighthouse for a view of the entire town, a 5.-Rs tip is expected.
Diagonally across is the Moor district (Arab people who were
settled here before the Portuguese), and a **Mosque**.

The next section of wall ends at **Flag Rock** from where ships
passing through the dangerous harbour entrance received direction. This necessity is underlined by the fact that in 1980 a rice
freighter steamed into a rock and sank. It was later dynamited.

On **Triton Bastion**, leading off to the west, a windmill once
stood (across from Aquamarine Hotel), pumping sea water into
carts which sprayed the streets to keep dust down.

Further north are **Neptune Bastion**, **Clippenberg Bastion**, and
**Aeolus Bastion**. Facing the sea, at the west end of the well fortified northern wall, is the **Star Bastion**. At the end of this tour
you arrive back at the Moon Bastion and its clock tower.

Aside from the ruined cities to the north, Galle is the most
historic of all Ceylonese towns, and it still thrives.

# Unawatuna

A lovely inlet on the southern coast featuring 2 km of sandy
beach and gentle surf, thanks to an offshore reef. Weather is
good even during the southwest monsoon. Great snorkeling. A few
years ago Unawatuna was an open secret among globetrotters. But
that has changed in recent years. Numerous guest houses, rest
houses, chai shops, and small restaurants have opened. And
construction of a 100-bed, package tourist complex (Aldiana Club
Village) got under way, before being put on hold: tourist numbers proved less than hoped.

## COMING - GOING
**By Rail:** Unawatuna does have a railway station, but not all
trains stop here. The beach is a 2 km walk from the station.
So coming from the north, get a bus in Galle.
**By Bus:** From Galle Bus Stand, by Galle Railway Station, a CTB
bus departs from Bus Platform 22, takes 15 minutes, costs
2.50 Rs. Get off at the 2nd or 3rd bus stop in Unawatuna, and
at the chai shop, head right 300 m down to the beach. From
Unawatuna, frequent buses to Galle and Matara.

## A NIGHT'S REST
**Unawatuna Beach Resort Ltd.**, Parangiyawatta, tel.(09) 2065, a
large hotel complex, right by the beach, mostly package tourists, too expensive for service rendered **(S)**200.-, **(D)**300.-, off
season half price. **The Green Lodge**, left of the main road,
tel.(09) 2910, **(S)**100.-, **(D)**150.-, off season cheaper, breakfast
25.-Rs. Nice camper parking in the yard of **Pension Strand**,
**(D)**100.-, 250.-.
Private accommodations charge 25.-Rs per person, you'll certainly be asked.
Outside Unawatuna in the district of Dalawella is **Sunshine
Inn**, B.C.D. Abey Sorriya, **(S)**70.-, 130.-Rs.

## REFRESHMENT
Meals in private accommodations costs 30.-Rs for breakfast and
dinner, generally quite good. Plus there are lots of small chai
shops and stores serving curd, fruit, and drinks. Sit outside and
enjoy a meal near the beach, moderate prices.
And there are several Chinese restaurants. **Zorba the Buddha
Rajneesh Restaurant** offers brown bread, zaziki, and expensive
prices.
Do your shopping in Galle, where the market and selection are
larger, prices cheaper.

# KANDY

This city of 120,000 is 115 km
north-east of Colombo, at an elevation of 500 m, on a bend in the
Mahaweli Ganga. The major business and tourist center in the
mountain region, Kandy is also the
heart of Buddhism on Sri Lanka. In
Kandy (kanda = hill), Ceylonese
tradition held out longest against
European influence. Not until 1815
were the British able to capture the
royal capital of that time.

Kandy is most fun during Esala
Perahera, a festival celebrated at
full moon between the end of July
and the middle of August. But at
any time of year, a visit to this
city, with its pleasant climate, is
a must.

## COMING - GOING

Kandy's infrastructure is second only to Colombo's. Connections
to any part of the island are simple. The railway station and
bus stand are close together, 500 m from town.

**By Rail:** Kandy is on a secondary line, forking off the Colombo
- Badulla line at Peradeniya Junction. Direct connections to
Colombo, Nanu Oya (Nuwara Eliya), Hatton, Haputale, Badulla.
The fastest connection with Colombo, 2.5 h, 45.-Rs (2nd class),
departs Colombo Fort at 07:00 h, departs Kandy at 15:00 h.

The day train to Badulla departs at 09:16 h, arrives in Nanu
Oya (15:28 h), Badulla (17:00 h), but expect delays. Return,
departs Badulla 08:50 h, Nanu Oya (12:44 h), and Kandy
(17:00 h).

**By Bus:** Direct CTB buses to Colombo, express buses depart half
hourly, take 3.5 h. Three luxury AC buses daily from Colombo
Pettah (08:30 h, 12:30 h, 16:30 h).

Direct connections to Anuradhapura, Polonnaruwa, Dambulla,
Sigiriya, Trincomalee, Batticaloa, Amparai, Monaragala, Nuwara
Eliya, Hatton, Haputale, Badulla, Tissamaharama, Kataragama,
and when it's running to Talaimannar.

Minibuses head, of course, all over, including to Anuradhapura (20.-Rs) and Polonnaruwa (10.-Rs).

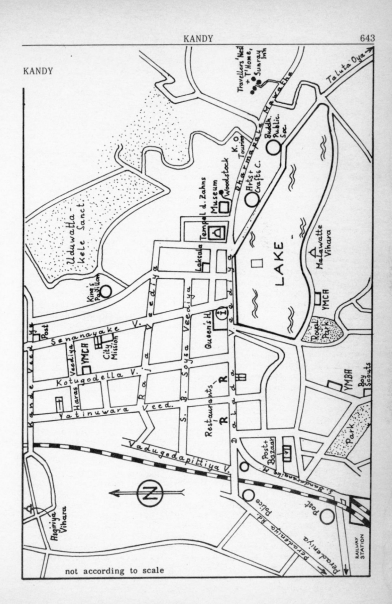

KANDY

not according to scale

All buses, public and private, depart from the bus stand by
the railway station and the clock tower. For bus information
tel.7226.

There is a daily Government Bus from Kandy to the airport,
departs Queen's Hotel at 17:00 h, arrives at 20:15 h, costs
20.-Rs.

**Around Town:** The local and regional buses stop by the clock
tower and in the near vicinity. To the cheap hotel district, get
Buses 654 or 655.

## A NIGHT'S REST

Breathe deep, the touts attack as soon as you arrive at the
railway station or bus stand. You'll never see it worse! The
best protection we can offer against the dirty tricks is an
extensive hotel list. If, as for many visitors to Sri Lanka,
this is your first stop, then beware; you are an easy mark.
Should you decide to follow one of the boys, be sure to get
confirmation in the hotel that the price you negotiated with the
boy is the actual price you pay. The touts get such a high
commission that your price for the room can be doubled! The
hotel owners don't like the situation either, and are happy if
you come on your own and they don't have to charge you for
the tout's commission. But still remember to bargain!

During the Perahera Festival in July/August, hotels are generally booked out, prices jump 2-5 times the regular rates!

A few good, clean, safe addresses:

**Travellers' Nest,** Mrs. S.W. Herath, 117/4 A. Dharmapala Mawatha, tel.22633, **(S)**50.-, **(D)**100.-, 150.-, hot water showers,
30 rooms. **Travellers' Home,** 117/3 A. Dharmapala Mawatha,
tel.22800, **(S)**40.-, 60.-, **(D)**75.-, 150.-, 200.-, depending upon
furnishings, **(Dm)**30.-, very clean, and light! **Sunray Inn
Tourist Guest House,** Alfred P. Talwatte, 117/5 A. Dharmapala
Mawatha, tel.23322, expensive lately, **(S)**75.-, 150.-, **(D)**300.-,
with bath, fan, cheaper with less comfort, 20 rooms. These are
the three best known lodgings, all 1500 m southeast of town.
On the road running up the hill from the lake, take a left at
the filling station. Or get Bus 654 or 655 from the filling station. All are peaceful (outside town).

**Prasanna Tourist Inn,** 53/29 Hewaheta Road, Talwatte,
tel.24365, beyond the filling station 500 m, off the street to the
left, **(S)**60.-, phone and the owner will pick you up at the
railway station.

On Anagarika Dharmapala Mawatha (A.D.Maw., formerly Malabar Street) are several private lodgings: **Gem Inn,** 39 A.D.
Maw., tel.24239, **(S)**20.-, **(D)**50.-, 100.-. **Nali,** 66 A.D.Maw.,
tel.22473, **(D)**20.-, 75.-, depending on furnishings and view,
before Travellers' Nest on the right. **Mrs. S. Somasundaram,**
164/1 Dharmapala Mawatha, near Travellers' Nest, **(D)**50.-,
good food, 25.-Rs.

Also in the area, accessible by Bus 655: **Mrs. Dissayanake,**
18 1st Lane Dharmaraja Road, **(D)**60.-, glance through the book

with tips, written by herself and the travellers. **Bank House**,
68/25 Lewella Road, **(S)**20.-, quiet. **Red Brick Tourist Rest**,
**(D)**50.-, get Bus 655 to Bangalawatta. **Charm Inn**, 30/34 Bangalawatta, **(S)**40.-, **(D)**125.-.
From Travellers' Nest, follow the road a bit further, then left
up the winding road.
And now back into the center of town. Right behind the Temple of the Tooth, diagonally on the left: **Constellation Hotel**,
**(D)**60.-. Follow the small path with steps up to **Woodstock**, a
lovely country home with a view of the lake, **(D)**80.-, 150.-,
**(Dm)**20.-.
On the square between the Queen's Hotel and the Temple of
the Tooth: **Old Empire**, a hotel dating from colonial times,
**(S)**80.-, 100.-, common showers, restaurant with R & C for
12.-Rs, clean.
Downtown: **Hotel Dehigama**, Raja Veediya, **(D)**200.- plus 10 %
tip, very clean, relatively new.
From Queen's Hotel, follow Senanayake Street - formerly Trin-
co(malle) Street - north to: **Burmese Rest**, 270 Senanayake
Street, run by Buddhist monks, costs 15.-Rs per person, no
matter if a lovely **(D)**30.-, or a 4-bed room, very clean,
friendly, peaceful courtyard, breakfast 8.-Rs, with egg 10.-Rs.
**Madugalle's**, 291 Senanayake Street, tel.23446, **(S)**100.-, clean
rooms, showers, good breakfast.
Kandy's youth hostels: **Y.M.B.A. Youth Hostel**, 5 Rajapihilla
Mawatha, **(Dm)**20.-. **Boy Scout Headquarters**, Keppitipola Road,
**(D)**60.-, **(Dm)**20.-. **YMCA**, Kotugodella Veediya, tel.23529,
**(Dm)**10.-, just males. **YMCA**, 4 Sangaraja Mawatha, **(Dm)**20.-,
just males, very simple.
Across from the Temple of the Tooth on the southern bank of
the lake: **Lake Cottage**, 28 Sangaraja Mawatha, picturesquely
set on the lake, **(D)**140.- with breakfast, great food.
At the east end of the lake in Ampitiya: **Sunshine**,
Mrs. P. Uduwela, 119 Ampitiya Road, **(D)**120.-, great food, a
bit above the lake. **Shangri La Guest House**, **(D)**200.-, peaceful, up the street from the east end of the lake (not toward
Taluta Oya!), good food. **Moon Valley Guesthouse**, across from
Frangipani Hotel, very quiet, safe, friendly, **(D)**75.-, with
showers, breakfast 25.- to 30.-Rs, camper parking in the yard.
In another peaceful area southwest of town is **Windy Cot** (Riverdale Road), and the comfortable and reasonably priced **Riverdale Hotel**, 32 Anniewata Road, tel.23020, behind the tunnel to
the right, **(S)**290.-, **(D)**330.-, very quiet and clean, full board
possible. Other similar lodgings in the area and on the road to
Peradeniya, also cheaper.
**The Haven**, Mrs. Padmini Uduwawala, 52 Bahirwakanda Path,
tel.22326, 15 minutes walk from town, quiet, **(S)**75.-, **(D)**100.-,
breakfast 25.-Rs.
Northwest of town in Asgiriya are several reasonable lodgings.
Get Buses 121, 122, or 221, takes 10 minutes from the bus
stand by the market, 20 minutes walk: **Rosewood Tourist Lodge**,

Mrs. Premaratne, 27/5 Sumangala Maw., by Asgiriya Vihara,
**(D)**50.-, 80.-. **T.B. Damunupola Principal** (owner), 122/7 Sumangala Mawatha, tel.22510, **(D)**50.-, dinner 25.-Rs, breakfast
15.- and 20.-Rs. **Blue Heaven Guest House**, 30/2 Poorna Lane,
near Cemetery Road.

A few more tips: **Irene Wijesinghe**, 34 Sangamitha Maw.,
**(D)**50.-, full board double. **Jingle Bells**, family operation,
royal cooking, **(D)**110.- with breakfast, dinner 45.-Rs, 10 min-
utes walk from Queen's Hotel, by Kandy Club. **Ganga Tourist
Guest House**, 27 Dutugemunu Mawatha, Lewella, 2 km from town,
**(S)**100.-, **(D)**200.-. **Resthouse Peradeniya**, **(D)**300.-, with
breakfast. **Fam. B. Abeysiri**, 15 Sarananhara Road, **(D)**40.-.
**Hillway Tourist Inn**, 15 minutes walk from the Temple of the
Tooth, **(D)**100.-, very clean, lovely view. **Regina Guest House**,
Nathtarampotha, 5 km east of Kandy toward Teldeniya, **(S)**30.-,
**(D)**45.-, nice location. **Fam. S. Dimbulana**, 1/3 Mosque Road,
**(S)**40.-, 50.-, family atmosphere, Buddhists, quiet, nice,
breakfast 25.-Rs.

## REFRESHMENT

A number of reasonable spots are on the main road, Dalada Veediya, between the clocktower and Queen's Hotel. Cheapest of the
lot is **Impala**, featuring curry and rice (8.-Rs). Further up is a
moderately priced Chinese restaurant. On the same side of the
street, **Bake House** offers wonderful cakes, curry & rice, and
crispy short eats. Across the street, **Ceylon Cold Stores** has
snacks and drinks for a quick daytime bite, closed evenings.
Next door is **Devon Restaurant** where you can eat better and
cheaper than by the Chinese.

**Old Empire**, between Queen's Hotel and the Temple of the
Tooth, in a lovely, old hotel dating from the colonial era, try
the rice dishes, and wash it down with a choice of beers: stout,
Guinness, lager... In **Lakeside Cafe**, between Old Empire and the
Buddhist Publication Society, a good breakfast costs 25.-Rs, or
you can rent a motorbike (145.- to 245.-Rs per day), and you
can have your clothes washed in real European washing machines; in addition to the 5-day service, you can pay three times
the price for 2 h service.

Dinner in **Queen's Hotel** is outstanding, but expensive, think
100.-Rs. **Lyon Cafe** offers good Chinese food, and rice & curry for
10.-Rs. The **Railway Station Restaurant** has good, cheap food in
an artificial light atmosphere. **Paivas Restaurant**, Yatinuwara
Veediya is also good and cheap.

In the lodgings, food is generally good, and in the respective
price range.
**Groceries:** Shop for fruit, vegetables, and spices in Central Market. The supermarket on Dalada Veediya has a European food
section. Did you come to Sri Lanka to eat canned pineapple?

## SHOPPING
**Central Market:** fruit, vegetables, household goods, tools, cloth,

etc. Prices are reasonable for batik (shirt 50.-Rs). First do the
grand tour, bargaining everywhere. Then head back to the
cheapest stands and bargain further. Take your time. Each time
you leave and return later, the price drops. The wares are the
same in the bazar.

**Arts & Crafts Association:** By the lake, see craftsmen at work.

## HISTORY OF KANDY & THE SACRED TOOTH

Kandy gained its importance as a religious center in the
13th century after the fall of Polonnaruwas. It became capital in 1590 when Portuguese inroads in the lowlands forced
the Ceylonese ruler to withdraw from his capital of Kotte.
The Dutch and the Portuguese never succeeded in capturing
Kandy, the royal seat, which became the bastion of resistance. Not until 1815 were the British able to capture the
Ceylonese King Wikrama Rajasinha (a tyrant) and occupy
Kandy.

Kandy is the religious center of Sri Lanka and site where
the Sacred Tooth is preserved. A Buddhist nun named Hema-
mala hid one of Buddha's teeth in her hair and smuggled
the tooth to Sri Lanka where it was presented to the King of
Anuradhapura in the 4th century AD. In the 10th century,
Anuradhapura lost importance due to internal unrest and
Tamil attacks. Buddhist monks saved the tooth by bringing it
to Ruhuna, a secure town in the south. King Parakrama
Bahu I declared war to regain the relic, captured Ruhuna
and brought the tooth back to Polonnaruwa, which succeeded
Anuradhapura as the capital of the north. From this day on,
the legitimate power of the king became bound to possession
of the tooth. When Tamil attacks continued, the relic was
moved to a safer spot further inland. Even so, the tooth was
captured and taken to India in the 13th century. After negotiations, the tooth was returned to Sri Lanka. A short time
later it was captured by the Chinese. In the early 15th
century, the tooth reappeared on the island. In the late 16th
century the tooth was seized by the Portuguese and brought
to Goa where the Archbishop ceremonially destroyed the tooth
as an object of devil worship. Buddhists claim, however,
that the Portuguese only captured a replica of the tooth, and
that Buddha's actual tooth resides today in Kandy.

Each year, the Sacred Tooth is the center of a great
procession, Esala Perahera, usually held in August.
Accompanying the tooth are torch bearers, Kandy dancers,
and Buddhist dignitaries, who steal the show on the final
day. If you want a good view, you'll have to come early.
Seats in the stands are expensive, costing 300.-Rs. The aura
radiated by the tooth can be witnessed during the
procession, but also seen in Kandy's everyday life. Take a
bus past Dalda Maligawa, Temple of the Tooth, and you'll
see your fellow passengers rise from their seats and bend in
the namasté greeting to the temple.

## SIGHTS
**Dalada Maligawa:** The primary attraction, the Temple of the Tooth, set on a rise in the old royal palace district, surrounded by a water moat. You must remove your shoes before entering the temple. The tooth is preserved in an ornamented temple shrine. Puja is held from 09:30-10:30 h and 18:30-19:30 h. Prayers are accompanied by drummers in traditional Kandy costume. In November 1979, our Singhalese guide smuggled us through the temple interior. The tooth is preserved below several gold stupas, in a splendid room upstairs. Beside the tooth were smiling monks who expected a donation for the temple. The most terrifying moment was when we were led out of the sacred presence and saw a group of Buddhists meditating. I felt like a cheat... But now anyone can enter the temple during Puja. Just look for the queue.
**Library:** In the eight-sided building by the temple, containing valuable palm-leaf manuscripts bound with carved wood. Admission is 7.-Rs, a photo permit costs 15.-Rs.
**Museum:** The royal palace features wood carvings and stonework, open Sun-Thurs 09:00-17:00 h, admission 20.-Rs.
**Kandy Lake:** You can take a boat ride, lasts 10 minutes, costs 10.-Rs per person, and at least 25.-Rs per boat. Begin a walk around the lake at **Queen's Hotel** with a private Tourist Information Counter in the foyer. Heading eastward you pass the Temple of the Tooth (Dalada Maligawa), the Museum and Library, both on the grounds of the former royal palace. After the temple, follow the road along the lake.
**Arts & Crafts Centre:** On your left, you see weavers, jewelry makers, wood turning (lathe) and other typical Singhalese craftsmen at work. They are happy to show you their tools, and sell you their wares for reasonable prices. The government **Tourist Office** is in the same building. Continue your walk along the lake...
**The Buddhist Publication Society:** Produces and sells books on southern Theravada Buddhism. Some of the books are by foreign authors, including a humorous look at Vipassana Meditation, translated by Barbara into German. You can get advice on establishing contact with Buddhists, and where you can take a meditation class.
**Wace Park** (Castle Hill Park): At the end of the lake you take the upper road back, located on the opposite bank, lovely view of the lake and town.
**Udawattakele Sanctuary:** A small jungle crisscrossed with walking paths. Worth a walk through, admission is 5.-Rs, very peaceful, see map for exact location.
**Elephants' Bathing Place:** 4 km from town in Katugastoda on the banks of the Mahaweli Ganga. The beasts are bathed between 14:00-16:00 h. The mahouts (elephant trainers) play to tourists and earn good money, 30.- to 50.-Rs per animal for elephant rides, etc. They even expect a fee for photos. Get a bus from behind the clock tower. From the suspension bridge at the last

stop of Bus 655, you can see another elephant bathing spot.
**Riverside Elephant Park:** Several readers complain that the mahouts are too aggressive, and suggest you are best off going to
Deveni, Rajasinghe Mawatha, open from 07:30-17:00 h. The park
is located several kilometers north of town, and run as a tourist
elephant zoo. You pay 35.-Rs admission, and can observe the
elephants at your leisure, touch them and ride them. Get a bus,
then it's 1 km by foot or taxi.
**Elephant Orphanage:** Another reader recommendation, in Puinawa-
la; takes 30 minutes by bus. The elephants are bathed at 12:00 h
and fed at 13:00 h.
**Kandy Dance Show:** Performances of traditional dance, in Roche-
dale Hall, by the bazar. Other performances are held in the
Buddhist Centre, Cultural Hall, Red Cross Hall, in Hotel Thai
Lanka, and in Queen's Hotel. The show by the bazar is the
cheapest. Performances last 1 h, and cost 100.-Rs including **Fire
Walking.**

## AROUND KANDY
**The Botanical Garden in Peradeniya:** Get Bus 1, 2, 652, or 654
from the clock tower by the bazar. The gardens, 6 km from Kandy, were originally constructed in 1371 as a garden of pleasure.
The grounds are laid on a horseshoe-shaped island, through
which the Mahaweli Ganga, Sri Lanka's largest river, flows.
Tropical plants, trees, and flowers, including various palms,
orchids and spice plants, are spread over 600,000 $km^2$. Hundreds
of flying lemurs make their home here. Look for them hanging
from trees upside down during the day. In the center of the park
is a lovely, but expensive restaurant, admission 15.-Rs, students
with ID half price, open 08:00-18:00 h. You can hike from Gadaladeniya Temple to Lankatilaka Temple and to the temple in Embekke. These are the treks which Herman Hesse enjoyed during
his stay on Sri Lanka.
**Gadaladeniya Temple:** 6 km from Peradeniya, accessible by bus.
But why not just walk over from the Botanical Gardens? The
600-year-old temple shows strong Hindu influences. Inside is a
bronze statue of Buddha.
**Lankatilaka Temple:** Another 3 km along the road through the
villages, completed in 1344, the Singhalese style of architecture
is much more pronounced. It is suspected, however, that the
Kandy-style roof was not added until later. The monks are
friendly and happy to open the temple for you, revealing a
lovely old statue of Buddha. Get a bus from Kandy toward
Pilimatalawa.
**Embekke:** Continuing your trek, the temple, dating from the 14th
century, is primarily known for its wood carvings. It served
originally as an entrance hall for the King of Gampola. Wood
carving is still alive in the village, carvings available for sale.
**Matale** and **Alu Vihare:** Buses to the important monastery and
caves, featuring Brahman inscriptions. Along the way, visit the

**Spice Gardens:** By late 1983, two-thirds of the spice gardens were no longer inhabited. The Tamil population was driven away in the summer unrest of 1983.

**TIPS**
**Tourist Information:** In the Arts & Craft Centre by the lake. Private tourist information in Queen's Hotel.
**Indian High Commission:** Issues visas for India.
**The British Council Library:** By the clock tower in Kandy centre, offers English books and magazines.
**Buddhist Publication Society:** By the lake.
**Banks:** Mostly on the main street, Dalada Veediya. The Money Exchange Booth in Queen's Hotel is officially just for guests, but with enough patience and a friendly word, non-guests can change a few dollars.
**Money Exchange Booth:** Bank of Ceylon, near Queen's Hotel, open daily 09:00-14:00 h.
**General Hospital:** On Hospital Road tel.22261 or tel.22170.
**Post Office:** Upstairs in Central Market, inside the main entrance, including telephone and telegraph service.
**GPO**, and **Poste Restante:** Across from the railway station.
**Meditation**
> **The Rockhill Hermitage Meditation Centre:** By Wegirikanda on the road to Gampola. Get Bus 643 from the clock tower to Ganhata Government Hospital. In the chai shop, ask directions for the path into the forest. Classes are offered between the 1st and 10th of every month.
> **Meditation Centre:** Run by Dhammiko, an Australian, in Nilambe, by Galaha. Courses are offered between the 1st and 10th of every month. Get the bus toward Galaha, 23 km to Nilambe Bungalow Junction. Get off and follow the white arrows. The path leads 1 km through tea plantations surrounding the lovely meditation centre. Classes cost 400.-Rs.

The Daily Routine (in both Meditation Centres)

| | |
|---|---|
| 04:30 h | Wake Up |
| 05:00-06:00 h | Meditation |
| 06:00-08:30 h | Breakfast |
| 08:30-11:00 h | Meditation |
| 11:00-13:00 h | Lunch Break |
| 13:00-17:00 h | Meditation |
| 17:00-18:00 h | Dinner |
| 18:00-19:00 h | Meditation |
| 19:00-... | Dharma Lesson and Questions |
| 20:30 | Bed |

Reading, writing and speaking should be repressed during the entire stay. But individual conversations with your meditation teacher are part of daily meditation. Lodgings are simple; the food is excellent. For more information, contact the Buddhist Publication Society.

# INDEX